AMERICAN NAVAL HISTORY

AMERICAN NAVAL HISTORY

An Illustrated Chronology of the U.S. Navy and Marine Corps,
1775–Present

THIRD EDITION

Jack Sweetman

NAVAL INSTITUTE PRESS
Annapolis, Maryland

Naval Institute Press
291 Wood Road
Annapolis, MD 21402

Library of Congress Cataloging-in-Publication Data
  Sweetman, Jack, 1940–
    American naval history : an illustrated chronology of the U.S.
  Navy and Marine Corps, 1775–present / Jack Sweetman, —3rd ed.
        p. cm.
    Includes bibliographical references and index.
    ISBN 1-55750-430-X (alk. paper)
    1. United States—History, Naval—Chronology. 2. United States—
    History, Naval—Pictoral works. 3. United States. Navy—History—
    Chronology. 4. United States. Marine Corps—History—
    Chronology. 5. United States. Navy—History—Pictoral works.
    6. United States. Marine Corps—History—Pictoral works. I. Title.
  E182.599.2001
  359′.00973—dc21   2001044870

Printed in the United States of America on acid-free paper ∞
09 08 07 06 05 04 03 02   9 8 7 6 5 4 3 2
First printing

To Gee

Contents

Maps

Preface

This book is a chronology of significant events in the history of the United States Navy and Marine Corps from their foundation to the present day. "Significant" is the key word; obviously, every event cannot be so classified. Upon learning that I had undertaken such a chronology, friends often asked what basis I was using to determine which events to include. My answer was the basis of ten years' teaching American naval history. That remains a fair summation, but the user of the book may benefit from a more substantial explanation of the ideas that guided it.

In the first place, it seemed to me that the work should do more than simply catalogue events. Contrary to the old saying, "the facts" do not necessarily speak for themselves. The significance of the fact that a ship has been commissioned, assuming there is nothing distinctive about said vessel, it is to an extent self-evident; but the fact that the Battle of the Sunda Strait took place on the night of February 28, 1942, is not in itself particularly enlightening. Wherever it appeared appropriate, therefore, I have given a brief description of the event and a summary of its effect on those that followed.

I have also attempted, when dealing with events of great importance, to provide earlier entries that give the background to and highlight the stages of development of these events. A chronology is by its nature strongly oriented towards the specific event, but history does not happen in freeze-frames. I hope that these background entries will help to supply a sense of context and continuity.

Overall, the entries can be divided into two broad categories. The first consists of events of obvious, intrinsic significance. Those in this category include:

- battles, landings, and campaigns
- the capture or destruction of major enemy warships
- the loss of important American naval vessels in war and peace, particularly the former
- explorations and expeditions
- the introduction of new ship types
- technological firsts
- the commissioning of all modern capital ships
- significant administrative innovations
- the appointment of all secretaries of the navy, commandants of the marine corps, superintendents of the naval academy, chiefs of naval operations, and secretaries of defense
- and a number of events, external to the sea services—the Roosevelt Corollary to the Monroe Doctrine, for instance—that influenced their activities as instruments of national policy

In the second category are events, relatively minor in themselves, chosen as examples of operations typical of their period.

To facilitate ease of reference, key entries have been given titles set in bold-faced type.

Especially up to around 1825, there is often considerable disagreement between authorities as to the exact date and details of lesser naval engagements and the characteristics of the ships involved. The number of guns credited to units of the sailing navy should be regarded as nominal, in any case, since enterprising captains often crowded on more than their ships had been designed to carry. To cite a single example, the frigate *Constellation* was officially a 36, but when she fought the *Vengeance* she actually had 50 pieces of ordnance on board.

Every effort has been made, in sometimes perplexing circumstances, to ensure the accuracy of the data given here. Much as I would like to believe that this effort has achieved 100 percent success, that is probably too much to expect. I will, therefore, be grateful to readers who suspect that they have identified errors if they would notify me, *citing the source of their information,* c/o the Naval Institute Press, so that these can be corrected in any future editions.

Acknowledgments

FIRST EDITION

One of the pleasures of completing a book is the opportunity it affords to record the thanks due to the people who helped along the way.

For their assistance in pinning down elusive dates, I am indebted to: Ms. Cathie Hall and Ms. Barbara A. Parker and their colleagues in the reference section of the Nimitz Library at the U.S. Naval Academy; Ms. Alice Creighton, head of the library's Special Collections, and to Ms. Pamela J. Sherbert and Ms. Mary Rose Catalfamo of her department; Dr. Dean Allard of the Naval History Division and Mr. Jack Shulimson of the U.S. Marine Corps History and Museums Division, and the members of their staffs; and Dr. Robert L. Scheina, the Historian of the U.S. Coast Guard. Mr. Fred H. Rainbow, managing editor of the Naval Institute *Proceedings,* also contributed useful information. Of course, the responsibility for any errors of fact or interpretation is mine, not theirs.

The selection of illustrations was aided by the friendly cooperation and expert counsel of Ms. Patty Maddocks, director of the Naval Institute Library and Photographic Service, ably seconded by Ms. Mary Sprawls; Mr. James W. Cheevers, curator of the Naval Academy Museum; Ms. Sigrid Trumpy, curator of the museum's Beverley R. Robinson Collection of naval prints; and Colonel John Miller and Mr. Benis Frank of the U.S. Marine Corps History and Museums Division.

Ms. Carol Swartz of the Naval Institute Press greatly improved the quality of the manuscript by her meticulous copy editing, and Ms. Beverly Baum met the challenge of producing a design that would be both attractive and accessible with what appears to me to be great success. Ms. Marjorie Whittington typed many long years overnight, and Mr. W. M. Shannon transformed my rough sketches into handsome maps.

I am especially grateful to Mr. Thomas F. Epley, director of the Naval Institute Press, who suggested the work and encouraged its progress with his customary editorial acumen.

And I am most grateful to Gisela, *eine wahre Wunderfrau,* whose support could not have been excelled, and to my parents, whose interest is an inspiration.

SECOND EDITION

My thanks go to those readers who, responding to the appeal in the preface of the first edition, took the initiative to suggest new entries and to call my attention to errors in previous printings, thereby helping to make this a better book—especially Chief Petty Officer Marian Heideman, USN; Lieutenant Commander B. R. Kirk, USN; Captain E. James Kohl, USNR;

Mr. Benton E. Reams; Colonel John W. Ripley, USMC; Mr. Michael St. Aubrey; Captain Oscar E. Sanden, USN (Ret.); Mr. Jack Schoch; Rear Admiral Scott Whitehouse, USNR (Ret.); and Captain Akihiko Yoshida, JMSDF (Ret.).

I am also indebted to Ms. Barbara Manvell of the Reference Section of the Naval Academy's Nimitz Library for assistance above and beyond the call of duty; Mr. Danny J. Crawford, History and Museums Division, Headquarters, U.S. Marine Corps; Ms. Karen White of the Naval Institute's design department; Ms. Mary Lou Kenney, managing editor of the Naval Institute Press, for her astute editing; Mr. William J. Clipson; and most of all (as always), to Gisela.

THIRD EDITION

For their advice and assistance in the preparation of this edition, I am indebted to Lieutenant Commander M. C. Agretti, SC, USN; Master Chief Petty Officer James C. Bunch, USCG (Ret.); Lieutenant Colonel Jon T. Hoffman, USMCR, Mr. Charles Melson, and Ms. Anne A. Ferrante of the History and Museums Division, Headquarters, U.S. Marine Corps; Lieutenant Arthur L. Northrup, USN (Ret.); Mr. Fred H. Rainbow and Colonel Gordon W. Keiser, USMC (Ret.) of the U.S. Naval Institute *Proceedings;* Mr. Fred L. Schultz of *Naval History,* another Naval Institute publication; Mr. Paul Stillwell and Ms. Dawn Stitzel of the Institute's History, Reference, and Preservation Division; and Dr. Gary Weir, Mr. Mark L. Evans, and Mr. Mike Walker of the Naval Historical Center. The selection of illustrations depended upon the cheerful collaboration of Ms. Jennifer Till, *Proceedings's* photo editor, and the handsome dustjacket reflects the talents of Ms. Karen White Doody.

Of course, any errors are my own.

AMERICAN NAVAL HISTORY

1775

April 19. **Beginning of the American Revolution.** The first shots of the war are fired in Massachusetts at the Battle of Lexington and Concord.

June 12. **First naval action of the revolution.** Citizens of Machias, Maine, led by Jeremiah O'Brien, board and capture the British armed schooner *Margaretta*, Midshipman James Moore, in Machias Bay.

June 15. **First "official" naval action.** Two armed vessels chartered by the government of Rhode Island, sailing under the command of Captain Abraham Whipple, capture a tender belonging to the British frigate *Rose* in Narragansett Bay.

August 26. The Rhode Island legislature instructs its delegates to the Continental Congress to propose the foundation of a continental navy. They do so on October 3.

September 2. **Birth of "Washington's Navy."** General George Washington, commanding the American forces at Boston, charters the *Hannah,* a schooner of 78 tons, to attack British transports and supply ships. In the following months other ships are similarly engaged. Before the squadron is disbanded in 1777, it has included 11 vessels and taken 55 prizes, many containing provisions much needed by Washington's army.

October 13. **Foundation of the Continental Navy.** Acting on the Rhode Island proposal, Congress authorizes the outfitting of two vessels "of ten carriage guns . . . for a cruise of three months" against British supply ships. A Naval Committee of three members—Silas Deane, Christopher Gadsden, and John Langdon—is appointed to supervise the work.

October 16. **Attack on Falmouth.** A British squadron of five vessels under Lieutenant Henry Mouatt shells Falmouth (present-day Portland), Maine. A landing party is repulsed, but much of the town is destroyed. American opinion is outraged.

October 30. Congress approves the outfitting of another two vessels and adds four members to the Naval Committee: John Adams, Joseph Hewes, Stephen Hopkins, and Richard Henry Lee.

November 2. **First Continental Fleet.** The Naval Committee is voted $100,000 to obtain and equip ships of war. It purchases and renames eight merchant vessels: the *Alfred,* 24 guns; *Columbus,* 18–20; *Andrew Doria,* 14; *Cabot,* 14; *Providence,* 12; *Hornet,* 10; *Wasp,* 8; and *Fly,* 8.

November 10. **Foundation of the Continental Marines.** A resolution providing for the organization of two battalions of "American Marines" is passed by Congress. The senior officer is Captain Samuel Nicholas, now considered first commandant of the U.S. Marine Corps.

November 25. **Privateering.** Congress authorizes privateering against all vessels in British government service and urges the individual colonies to establish prize courts. In the course of the conflict, Congress will issue letters of marque to 1,697 vessels, which take 600 prizes—triple the captures made by ships of the Continental Navy.

November 28. Off Cape Anne, Massachusetts, Washington's Navy makes its most valuable capture when the schooner *Lee,* 4, Captain John Manly, takes the brig *Nancy,* whose cargo includes 2,000 stands of arms, a number of artillery pieces, and 30 tons of shot.

November 28. **First naval regulations.** Congress issues "Rules for the Regulation of the Navy of the United Colonies." They were written by John Adams.

December 3. At Philadelphia, Lieutenant John Paul Jones raises the Grand Union flag (having 13 stripes, with the British jack in the field) aboard the *Alfred.* This is the first time an American flag has been unfurled over a Continental warship.

December 11–14.   A permanent Marine Committee, consisting of one member from each of the 13 colonies, is established by Congress "to devise ways and means for furnishing these colonies with a naval armament."

December 22.   **First naval construction.** The Marine Committee submits a report, approved by Congress, calling for the construction of 13 frigates: five of 32 guns, five of 28, and three of 24. It is specified that four of these vessels will be built in Pennsylvania, two each in Massachusetts, New York, and Rhode Island, and one each in Connecticut, Maryland, and New Hampshire. Only seven will ever get to sea, and all will be lost during the war.

December 22.   **First officers are commissioned.** Congress appoints the first eighteen officers of the Continental Navy. The senior is Commodore Esek Hopkins, "commander in chief of the fleet." Below him are four captains: Dudley Saltonstall *(Alfred);* Abraham Whipple *(Columbus);* Nicholas Biddle *(Andrew Doria);* and the commodore's son John Burroughs Hopkins *(Cabot).* The list of five first lieutenants is headed by a 28-year-old Scotsman, John Paul Jones.

1776

January 5.   Commodore Hopkins is ordered by Congress to take the fleet to sea to clear the Chesapeake Bay and the coasts of Virginia and the Carolinas of British raiders.

February 17.   **First operation of the Continental Navy.** In accordance with the above orders, Hopkins sails from the Delaware with a squadron consisting of the eight vessels purchased in November 1775. On the evening of February 19, the *Hornet* and the *Fly* lose contact with the squadron and go their separate ways. Hopkins takes advantage of a discretionary clause in his orders and instead of operating off the American coast, sets course for the Bahamas.

March 3.   **Capture of New Providence Island.** Hopkins lands a force of 300 men under Captain Samuel Nicholas, Continental Marines, which, covered by the guns of the *Providence* and the *Wasp,* storms Forts Nassau and Montagu and occupies New Providence Island in the Bahamas. Some 73 cannons and mortars and a large quantity of munitions are captured and loaded aboard ship to be carried back to the Continental Army. This is the first amphibious operation involving American marines.

March 17.   Hopkins's squadron sails from New Providence, bound for home.

March 17.   The British evacuate Boston.

March 23.   Congress authorizes privateering against all ships "belonging to any inhabitant or inhabitants of Great Britain," whether or not in government service.

April 4.   **First engagement with an enemy warship.** On the voyage from the Bahamas, one of Hopkins's ships, the *Columbus,* 20, Captain Abraham Whipple, captures the British schooner *Hawk,* 6, Lieutenant Wallace, off Block Island, Rhode Island.

April 5.   Hopkins's flagship, the *Alfred,* 24, captures the British brig *Bolton,* 8, Lieutenant Edward Sneyd.

April 6.   **Action with HMS Glasgow.** Shortly past midnight, Hopkins's fleet encounters the British sloop-of-war *Glasgow,* 20, Captain Tryingham Howe, and her tender, which crowd on sail for Newport. The pursuit is not well managed. Her tender is taken, but the *Glasgow* escapes after disabling the *Cabot.* American losses are 10 men killed and 14 wounded; British, 1 killed and 3 wounded.

April 7.   The Continental brig *Lexington,* 16, Captain John Barry, captures the British sloop *Edward,* 6, Lieutenant Boucher, after an hour's action off the Virginia Capes.

April 8.   Hopkins's squadron arrives at New London, Connecticut. It never again sails as a unit, for the profits of privateering lure seamen from the navy, and Hopkins is unable to keep his crews up to strength. All that he can do is send out single ships to attack enemy commerce.

May 10.   John Paul Jones receives his first independent command, the sloop *Providence,* 12.

May 16.   **Cruise of the Andrew Doria.** The Continental brig *Andrew Doria,* 14, Captain Nicholas Biddle, is ordered to sea. During a cruise of four months between the Delaware Capes and Maine, she takes 10 prizes, including two British transports with 400 men embarked.

June 28.   **Unsuccessful attack on Charleston.** A British fleet of 10 ships commanded by Admiral Sir Peter Parker with 30 transports carrying 2,500 troops under General Sir Henry Clinton is driven off by the earthwork fortifications on Sullivan's Island, defending Charleston, South Carolina. Parker's flagship, HMS *Bristol,* is hulled 70 times. Two years will pass before the British undertake another operation in the South.

June 29.   **Beginning of the campaign for New York.** Following the British evacuation of Boston, Washington

The British attack on Charleston, South Carolina (aquatint, London: 1815). *Courtesy Beverley R. Robinson Collection, U.S. Naval Academy Museum.*

began concentrating his forces at New York, where he arrived in April, correctly anticipating that the city was the most likely site for a British landing. On this day a fleet commanded by Admiral Richard Howe and the transports of an invasion force under his brother, Major General Sir William Howe, more than 100 sail altogether, anchor in New York harbor. They are soon joined by the expedition that has been repulsed at Charleston. The strategic problem Washington faces is insoluble: how to defend Long Island and Manhattan Island when the British can use their command of the sea to land troops wherever they please.

July 4.   **Congress issues the Declaration of Independence.** Henceforth the colonies are fighting, not to improve their status within the British Empire, but to withdraw from it.

July 27.   **Reprisal vs. Shark.** The Continental brig *Reprisal*, 18, Captain Lambert Wickes, is detailed to carry a colonial commercial and naval agent, William Bingham, to Martinique. En route, three prizes are captured and manned. At the entrance to the harbor of St. Pierre, the *Reprisal* is challenged by the British sloop-of-war *Shark*, 16, Captain Chapman. Although short-handed, the *Reprisal* shows such fight the *Shark* soon withdraws.

August 8.   John Paul Jones is promoted to the rank of captain in the Continental Navy.

August 21–October 8.   **Cruise of the Providence.** On her first war cruise under the command of John Paul Jones, the Continental sloop *Providence*, 12, captures 16 prizes between the Delaware Capes and Nova Scotia, narrowly escaping the British frigate *Solebay*, 28, by Jones's superb shiphandling.

August 27.   **Battle of Long Island.** At New York, General Howe lands 20,000 men who turn the flank of the American defenders.

August 29–30.   Washington evacuates Long Island.

September 5.   The first uniforms are prescribed for the navy and marine corps.

September 7.   **First submarine operation.** At New York a 34-year-old Yale graduate, David Bushnell, has built a one-man submarine, the *American Turtle*. Propulsion is by means of a screw on a hand-crank. On this evening Sergeant Ezra Lee of the Continental Army takes the *Turtle* out to attack HMS *Eagle*, 64, off Staten Island. His plan is to bore a hold in her hull and attach a time-bomb. Unfortunately, his drill is unable to penetrate the ship's copper sheathing.

September 12.   Washington concludes that he must evacuate New York.

September 16.   **Battle of Harlem Heights.** Washington checks Howe's pursuit, but is forced to fall back when the British advance up the East River.

October 3.   Congress authorizes a frigate and two cutters to be procured in Europe.

October 11–13.   **Battle of Valcour Island.** In 1775 American forces under General Philip Schuyler and (later) Richard Montgomery invaded Canada via the avenue through the wilderness formed by almost uninterrupted waterway (the Hudson River, Lake George, Lake Champlain, the Richelieu River) from New York to Montreal. Defeated before the gates of Quebec on December 31, 1775, they held Montreal until the summer of 1776, when the arrival of 8,000 British reinforcements enabled the Governor General of Canada, Major General Sir Guy Carleton, to launch a coun-

The Battle of Valcour Island: an engraving published in London in December 1776. *Official U.S. Navy photograph.*

teroffensive south along the same route. At Lake Champlain, Brigadier General Benedict Arnold (not yet turned traitor) began a furious ship-building program to dispute command of the lake. Carleton, dependent on water-borne supplies, was compelled to halt and build a fleet of his own. This consumed the remainder of the summer and most of the fall. By the time the British are ready to fight they have achieved a marked superiority, and Arnold's force, consisting of the sloop *Enterprise,* 12; the schooners *Royal Savage,* 12, *Liberty,* 8, *Revenge,* 8; eight gundalows; and five galleys, is destroyed in a running battle on October 11–13. The season is so far advanced, however, that Carleton falls back to Canada to go into winter quarters, postponing the continuation of the offensive until the following spring. The delay is decisive. When a British army under Major General John Burgoyne pushes south in 1777, it is captured at the Battle of Saratoga, prompting France to enter the war on the American side. Although tactically a defeat, strategically Valcour Island is by far the greatest victory won by American naval forces during the War of the Revolution.

October 16.   Commodore Hopkins is censured by Congress for having departed from his instructions in failing to clear the American coast of raiders during his cruise earlier in the year.

November 1–December 18. **Cruise of the Alfred and the Providence.** The Continental sloop-of-war *Alfred,* 24, Captain John Paul Jones, and *Providence,* 12, Captain Hoysted Hacker, sail from Providence, Rhode Island, with orders from Commodore Hopkins to raid British shipping off Cape Breton, Nova Scotia. The *Providence* develops leaks and turns back on November 13. Jones continues the cruise in the *Alfred,* taking or destroying nine ships. One of his prizes, the *John,* 10, is recaptured during a brush with the British frigate *Milford,* 28, Captain John Burr, on December 8–9.

November 15.   Congress establishes a new pay scale for naval officers and relative ranks for officers of the army and navy.

November 16.   **First salute to the flag.** Entering port at St. Eustatius, Dutch West Indies, to purchase supplies for the Continental Army, the brig *Andrew Doria,* 14, Captain Isaiah Robinson, exchanges salutes with the shore fortifications. Subsequently, the British government protests so strongly that the Dutch dismiss the governor of the port and disavow the salute.

November 20.   Congress authorizes the construction of three 74-gun ships of the line, five frigates of 36 guns, and two smaller vessels. Of the ships of the line only the *America,* and of the frigates, only the *Alliance* will be completed.

November 29.   **First Continental ship in European waters.** The brig *Reprisal,* 18, Captain Lambert Wickes, enters Quiberon Bay, France, carrying three diplomatic commissioners—Benjamin Franklin, Silas Deane, and Arthur Lee—sent by the Continental Congress to treat with the French government.

December (late).   **Andrew Doria vs. Racehorse.** Returning from St. Eustatius, the Continental brig *Andrew*

Doria, 14, Captain Isaiah Robinson, captures the British sloop *Racehorse*, 12, Lieutenant James Jones, in a hard-fought action lasting two hours off the west coast of Puerto Rico.

December 20.　**Adventures of the Lexington.** The Continental brig *Lexington*, 16, Captain William Hallock, is captured by the frigate *Pearle*, 32, while returning from the West Indies with a cargo of military stores. That evening the *Lexington*'s company overpower the British prize crew and sail on to Baltimore. Among the leaders in the recapture of the vessel is Master's Mate Richard Dale, later John Paul Jones's executive officer in the *Bonhomme Richard*.

1777

January 15(?)–February 14.　**Cruise of the Reprisal.** The Continental brig *Reprisal*, 18, Captain Lambert Wickes, takes five prizes off the Atlantic coasts of France and Spain.

January 23.　Congress approves the construction of two more frigates, one of 36 guns and one of 28.

February 7.　The British government authorizes privateering against the United States.

March 3.　**Loss of the Cabot.** The Continental brig *Cabot*, 14, Captain Joseph Olney, runs aground and is captured by the British frigate *Milford*, 28, Captain John Burr, during an engagement off the coast of Nova Scotia. The *Cabot*'s crew escape ashore, seize a schooner and sail home.

April 19.　Congress establishes a Navy Board of the Eastern Department at Boston to supervise "all naval and maritime affairs" in Massachusetts, Connecticut, New Hampshire, and Rhode Island under the direction of the Marine Committee. The activities and initiative of this board, composed of James Warren, William Vernon, and James Deshon, make a major contribution to the Continental war effort.

April 19.　Two British transports are captured by the frigate *Trumbull*, 28, Captain Dudley Saltonstall, off New York.

May 1.　**Cruise of the Surprize.** The lugger *Surprize*, 10, Captain Gustavus Connyngham, sails from Dunkirk, France, to attack enemy commerce in European waters. She captures the mail packet *Prince of Orange* in the English Channel (May 3) and the brig *Joseph* off the Dutch coast (May 4). The British reaction is so strong that when the *Surprize* returns to port, the French, still officially neutral and undecided whether to enter the war, seize the ship and arrest Connyngham. For a time it appears they may hand him over to the British, but in the end the American commissioners arrange his release.

May 21.　The Continental frigates *Boston*, 24, Captain Hector McNeill, and *Hancock*, 32, Captain John Manley, sail from Boston for a North Atlantic Cruise.

May 28.　**First squadron in European waters.** The brig *Reprisal*, 18, Captain Lambert Wickes, brig *Lexington*, 16, Captain Henry Johnson, and cutter *Dolphin*, 10, Lieutenant Samuel Nicholson, sail from Nantes, France, under the overall command of Wickes to attack shipping in British waters. They return to France late in June, having taken 18 prizes and narrowly escaped the British ship-of-the-line *Burford*, 74.

June 7.　In the North Atlantic, the British frigate *Fox*, 28, Captain Patrick Fotheringham, is captured by the frigates *Boston*, 24, Captain Hector McNeill, and *Hancock*, 32, Captain John Manley, which have previously taken two British merchantmen.

June 14.　**Adoption of the American flag.** Congress approves the design of a national flag to consist of 13 red-and-white stripes, representing the 13 states, with a blue field containing one star for each state.

June 14.　John Paul Jones is appointed to command the ship sloop *Ranger*, 18.

July 4.　The first Stars-and-Stripes flag to fly over an American warship is hoisted by John Paul Jones in the *Ranger* in Portsmouth, New Hampshire.

July 7.　**Loss of the Hancock.** The Continental frigate *Hancock*, 32, Captain John Manley, is captured and the prize frigate *Fox* retaken by HMS *Rainbow*, 44, Captain Sir George Collier, *Flora*, 32, and *Victor*, 18, off Halifax, Nova Scotia. The *Boston* makes away, for which Captain McNeill is dismissed from the navy.

July 17.　**Cruises of the Revenge.** The Continental cutter *Revenge*, 14, Captain Gustavus Connyngham, sails from Dunkirk, France, on a raid in British coastal waters, during which she will take at least 20 prizes. During the following months Connyngham operates out of Spanish ports. Eventually British diplomatic pressure on Spain wears out Connyngham's welcome, and he sails for America. By the time he reaches Martinique, on September 1, 1778, he has captured a total of 60 British merchantmen.

September 2–4.　**Action in the North Atlantic.** The new Continental frigate *Raleigh*, 32, Captain Thomas Thompson, and ship *Alfred*, 24, Captain Elisha Hinman, capture the *Nancy,* a straggler from a British convoy of 60 ships homeward bound from the West Indies. The next morning the *Raleigh* infiltrates the convoy, and the following day disables the sloop-of-war *Druid,* 14, Commander Peter Cartaret, before the approach of other British escorts forces her to break off the action. The two Continental ships shadow the convoy for several days.

September 14. **Loss of the Reprisal.** The brig *Reprisal,* 18, Captain Lambert Wickes, sails for home from France. Off the coast of Newfoundland she goes down in a gale, with the loss of all hands except the ship's cook. Wickes's death deprives the Continental Navy of one of its most aggressive officers.

September 20. **Lexington vs. Alert.** The Continental brig *Lexington,* 16, Captain Henry Johnson, is captured off Ushant, France, by the British cutter *Alert,* 10, Lieutenant John Bazely, after a sharp action during which she runs out of ammunition.

September 26. **Fall of Philadelphia.** A British army of 18,500 men under Major General Sir William Howe, embarking at New York on July 23, lands at the head of the Chesapeake Bay on August 25, defeats Washington's 10,500 men at the Battle of Brandywine on September 11, and proceeds to occupy the Continental capital. For Howe to hold Philadelphia, however, it will be necessary for him to gain control of the Delaware River, which is defended by a system of forts and obstructions and a sizable force of Continental and Pennsylvania state vessels, all under the command of Commodore J. Hazlewood of the Pennsylvania State Marine.

September 27. **Loss of the Delaware.** The new Continental frigate *Delaware,* 24, Captain Charles Alexander, the most powerful of the American vessels in the Delaware, runs aground and surrenders while engaging British shore batteries.

October 1–November 22. **Defense of the Delaware River.** To open river communications between Howe's army at Philadelphia and the sea, a British task force commanded by Admiral Richard Howe, consisting of the ships-of-the-line *Augusta,* 64, and *Somerset,* 64, the 44-gun ship *Roebuck,* the frigates *Liverpool,* 32, and *Pearl,* 32, the sloop-of-war *Merlin,* 18, and several smaller vessels, begins to push up the Delaware against obstinate American resistance. The *Augusta,* Captain Francis Reynolds, and *Merlin,* Commander Samuel Reeve, ground on obstructions, where they are attacked and burned on October 22. Eventually, however, the British

break through, overcoming Forts Mifflin and Mercer and forcing the Americans to destroy their ships to keep them from being captured. Lost on November 21 are the Continental brig *Andrew Doria,* 14, the sloops-of-war *Hornet,* 10, *Racehorse,* 10, *Wasp,* 8, and *Fly,* 8, and the entire Pennsylvania state navy.

October 6. **Loss of the Congress and the Montgomery.** On the Hudson River, the *Congress,* 28, and the *Montgomery,* 24, 2 of the 13 frigates authorized by Congress in December 1775, are burned to prevent their capture.

October 17. **Saratoga: turning point of the Revolution.** A British army under Major General John Burgoyne, initially of 7,200 men, attempts to renew the offensive down the Hudson Valley invasion highway that has been blocked by Arnold's defense of Lake Champlain in 1776. After many misadventures, Burgoyne is compelled to surrender to the Continental army of Major General Horatio Gates at Saratoga, in upper New York state. This victory gives Benjamin Franklin the leverage necessary to persuade the French government to intervene in the conflict.

November 1. John Paul Jones sails from Portsmouth, New Hampshire, for France in command of the ship sloop *Ranger,* 18. He anchors at Nantes on December 2, having taken two prizes en route, the brigs *George* and *Mary.*

December 31. In the course of the year, American ships have captured a total of 464 British vessels.

1778

January 2. Commodore Hopkins is dismissed from the Continental Navy. No other naval commander-in-chief is appointed.

January 27. **Second capture of New Providence Island.** The brig *Providence,* 12, Captain John P. Rathbun, repeats Hopkins's exploit by landing a party that captures the seat of British government in the Bahamas. An attack by the British sloop-of-war *Grayton* is beaten off; a privateer, five other vessels, and a quantity of munitions are captured, and 20 American prisoners are released.

February 6. **Treaties of commerce and alliance are signed with France.** The secret treaty of alliance is to enter into effect should Great Britain go to war with France, an event that now becomes inevitable. When this occurs, the War of the Revolution expands into a worldwide conflict.

February 14.   First official salute to the American flag. In Quiberon Bay, on the Atlantic coast of France, the Continental sloop-of-war *Ranger*, 18, Captain John Paul Jones, exchanges salutes with the *Robuste*, flagship of the French Admiral Lamotte-Picquet.

February 26.   At Fort Penn, on the Delaware River, an American boat party of 27 men under Captain John Barry board and capture four transports and the schooner *Alert*, 10, whose crew of 116 is locked below deck.

March 7.   Randolph vs. Yarmouth. While escorting a merchant convoy, the Continental frigate *Randolph*, 32, Captain Nicholas Biddle, engages the British ship-of-the-line *Yarmouth*, 64, Captain Nicholas Vincent. After a sharp action of 15 minutes, the *Randolph* blows up. Of her crew of 315, there are only 4 survivors. This is the greatest loss of life suffered by an American vessel in action prior to the sinking of the battleship *Arizona* at Pearl Harbor. Biddle is among those lost. He was the Continental Navy's only professionally trained officer, having served as a midshipman in the Royal Navy.

March 9.   Loss of the Alfred. Returning from France, the Continental ship *Alfred*, 24, Captain Elisha Hinman, is captured by the British sloop-of-war *Ariadne*, 24, Captain Thomas Pringle, and *Ceres*, 18, Commander James R. Dacres.

March 27.   Loss of the Columbus. The Continental ship *Columbus*, 20, Captain Abraham Whipple, is driven ashore and burned by a British squadron at Point Judith, Rhode Island.

March 31.   Loss of the Virginia. The Continental frigate *Virginia*, 28, Captain James Nicholson, runs aground in the Chesapeake Bay and surrenders to HMS *Emerald*, 32, and *Conqueror*.

April 10.   John Paul Jones's first cruise in British waters. Jones sails from Brest, France, in the ship sloop *Ranger*, 18, to attack enemy commerce.

April 13.   In anticipation of the outbreak of war with Britain, the French Toulon squadron, 12 ships of the line commanded by Vice Admiral Charles Henri Comte d'Estaing, sails for North America.

April 22–23.   Whitehaven Raid. Around midnight, John Paul Jones leads a boat expedition of 40 men from the *Ranger* ashore at Whitehaven, on the west coast of England, to burn ships in harbor. One of the men deserts and alarms the inhabitants, who extinguish the fire, but the news of the raid causes a sensation. It is the first time since 1667 that an enemy landing party has set foot on English soil.

John Paul Jones, as depicted on the obverse of his congressional gold medal. The engraver, Augustin Dupré, modeled the profile on the bust for which Jones posed for the sculptor Jean-Antoine Houdon. *Courtesy U.S. Naval Academy Museum.*

April 23.   Raid on St. Mary's Isle. Jones lands a party on St. Mary's Isle, off Kirkcudbright in the Irish Sea, with the aim of seizing the Earl of Selkirk, whom he believes would be valuable as a political prisoner. The earl is absent, but greatly to Jones's chagrin, his men insist on seizing the Selkirk family silver. He later buys it from them and restores it to the Selkirks at his own expense.

April 24.   Ranger vs. Drake. Jones captures the British sloop-of-war *Drake*, 20, Commander George Burdon, in an hour's action off Carrickfergus, Ireland. The *Drake* loses 4 men killed (including her captain) and 19 wounded; the *Ranger*, 3 killed (including Lieutenant Samuel Wallingford, Continental Marines) and 5 wounded.

April 24.   Loss of the Independence. The Continental sloop *Independence*, 10, Captain John Young, runs aground while attempting to enter Ocracoke Inlet, North Carolina.

April 27.   Congress authorizes the acquisition of another 12 vessels.

May 7.   Loss of the Effingham and Washington. The Continental frigates *Effingham*, 28, and *Washington*, 32, are burned in the Delaware River by a British raiding party without ever having gotten to sea.

June 17.   **France officially enters the war.** In the English Channel four French naval vessels are pursued by a British fleet under Admiral Augustus Lord Keppel. The frigate *Licorne,* 32, Lieutenant de Belizal, and the lugger *Coureur,* 10, are captured.

July 6.   **First French fleet.** For France, North America is only one theater of an almost-global war with Britain. The movements of the fleets she sends to the Western Hemisphere follow a seasonal rhythm. These forces spend much of the year in the West Indies, fighting for control of the "sugar islands," whose exports are more valuable than those of all the Thirteen Colonies combined. Only during the Caribbean hurricane season, from July through October, are they available for operations in North America. The first French fleet, sailing from Toulon under the command of Vice Admiral Charles Henri Comte d'Estaing, reaches the Delaware Capes on July 6. The hopes raised by its arrival are soon disappointed. A concerted land-sea attack on New York, where Admiral Richard Howe has only 4 ships of the line to d'Estaing's 12, must be abandoned when, on July 16, it is learned that the French ships draw too much water to cross the bar into the harbor. D'Estaing then proposes to act against the British position at Newport, Rhode Island. Washington concurs, and the fleet proceeds to Narragansett Bay. Preparations are being made for the land attack when Admiral Howe, who has been reinforced, appears off Newport on August 9 with 8 ships of the line. D'Estaing sails to meet him. Before an engagement can take place, however, both fleets are badly damaged in a storm. D'Estaing withdraws to Boston to refit and sails for the West Indies in November.

September 24–27.   **Loss of the Raleigh.** The Continental frigate *Raleigh,* 32, Captain John Barry, is pursued by the British ships *Experiment,* 50, Captain Sir James Wallace, and *Unicorn,* 28, Commander Matthew Squire. After losing part of her masts in action with the *Unicorn,* the *Raleigh* is run aground on an island off the coast of Maine. Barry and about half his men escape.

1779

January 5.   Stephen Decatur is born at Spinepuxent on the Eastern Shore of Maryland.

January 14.   The Continental frigate *Alliance,* 36, Captain Pierre Landais, sails from Boston to carry the 20-year-old Marquis de Lafayette, who has been serving as a volunteer on Washington's staff, back to France to concert arrangements for the dispatch of a French expeditionary force.

February 7.   **The Bonhomme Richard.** The French government purchases an old East Indiaman, *Le Duc de Duras,* of 850 to 900 tons burthen and places her at the disposal of John Paul Jones. Jones renames the ship *Bonhomme Richard,* in honor of Benjamin Franklin, the French translation of whose famous *Poor Richard's Almanac* is entitled *Les Maxims du Bonhomme Richard.* It will take Jones six months to arm and outfit his new command.

March 13.   The Continental frigates *Warren,* 32, Captain John B. Hopkins, and *Queen of France,* 28, Captain Joseph Olney, and ship sloop *Ranger,* 18, Captain Thomas Simpson, sail from Boston for a month's cruise along the eastern seaboard, during which they capture the privateer *Hibernia,* 8, and 7 of 9 vessels in a British merchant convoy, including the ship *Jason,* 20.

May 7.   **Providence vs. Diligent.** The Continental sloop *Providence,* 12, Captain Hoysted Hacker, captures the British brig *Diligent,* 12, Lieutenant Thomas Walbeoff, in the Atlantic.

June 6.   On a cruise from the Delaware the Continental frigates *Confederacy,* 32, Captain Seth Harding, and *Boston,* 24, Captain Samuel Tucker, capture the privateer *Pole,* 24, Captain J. Maddock, and two other vessels.

June 21.   **Spanish intervention.** Spain declares war on Great Britain. Unlike France, however, she does not recognize the independence of the United States.

July 15.   A Continental squadron consisting of the frigates *Providence,* 28, Captain Abraham Whipple, and *Queen of France,* 28, Captain J. P. Rathbun, and ship sloop *Ranger,* 18, Captain Thomas Simpson, encounter a homeward-bound British West Indian convoy of some 60 sail off Newfoundland. Operating under cover of a dense fog, they succeed in cutting out 11 vessels in one of the most successful attacks of the war.

July 19–August 17.   **Disaster at Penobscot.** The largest American amphibious operation of the war is undertaken to eliminate a British force that has fortified a base at Castine on the Penobscot River in Maine. The naval component, under the command of Captain Dudley Saltonstall, consists of the Continental frigate *Warrant,* 32, brig *Diligent,* 12, and sloop *Providence,* 12; three vessels from the Massachusetts and New Hampshire state navies; and 13 privateers temporarily in Massachusetts state service. The landing force, commanded by Brigadier General Solomon Lovell, is made up of 3,000 Massachusetts militia embarked on 20 transports. Siege operations begin on July 25, but the British are still holding out on August 14, on which day the Continental forces have scheduled a concerted attack by land and sea. Just before it is to begin, a British squadron arrives on the scene from New York. Commanded by Commodore Sir George Collier, it consists of the ship-of-the-line *Raisonable,* 64, frigates *Blonde,* 32, and *Virginia,* 32, and sloops *Greyhound,* 20, *Camilla,* 20, *Galatea,* 20, and *Otter,* 14. Saltonstall has little choice but to order his ships to scatter. Not one escapes. Most flee up the river, where they are either captured or burned by their crews, who take to the woods. British casualties number 14; American, 474. Saltonstall is court-martialed and dismissed from the service.

August 2–24.   The French-built Continental frigate *Deane,* 32, Captain Samuel Nicholson, and *Boston,* 24, Captain Samuel Tucker, capture 8 prizes, including the sloop-of-war *Thorn,* 16, Lieutenant William Wardlaw, in a cruise from the Chesapeake Bay.

August 14.   **Cruise of the Bonhomme Richard.** A squadron of seven ships sails under the command of John Paul Jones from the Ile de Groix, France, to raid British coastal waters. It consists of Jones's own ship, the frigate *Bonhomme Richard,* 40, the Continental frigate *Alliance,* 36, Captain Pierre Landais, the French frigate *Pallas,* 32, Captain Denis-Nicolas Cottineau, the French corvette *La Vengeance,* 12, Captain Philippe-Nicolas Ricot, the French cutter *Cerf,* 18, Captain Joseph Varage, and two French privateers, the *Monsieur,* 38, and *Granville,* 10. The latter three vessels soon leave the squadron.

August 31–October 9.   **Second French fleet.** At the end of the Caribbean campaigning season, a French fleet commanded by Vice Admiral Charles Henri Comte d'Estaing appears to answer an appeal, received on July 31, to assist American forces in the recapture of Savannah, Georgia. Washington, who would have much preferred a combined operation against New York, does not learn of d'Estaing's arrival until mid-September. As d'Estaing had already disregarded orders to return to Toulon, however, there could be no question of prolonging his stay in American waters. At Savannah the troops landed from the French squadron and patriot forces led by Brigadier General Benjamin Lincoln are stoutly opposed by a British garrison of 3,500 under General Augustine Prevost. Anxious to bring the operation to a conclusion, d'Estaing insists on an assault in which the storming columns are repulsed with heavy losses and he himself is wounded. On October 18 the siege is lifted and the French fleet sails for home.

September.   **Action on Lake Pontchartrain.** The Spanish colonial government of Louisiana provides an armed schooner, renamed the *Morris,* with which Captain William Pickles captures the British sloop-of-war *West Florida,* 14, Lieutenant John W. Payne.

September 23.   **Battle off Flamborough Head: Bonhomme Richard vs. Serapis.** Sailing south along the east coast of England, John Paul Jones's squadron (see August 14), now consisting of the frigates *Bonhomme Richard,* 40, and *Alliance,* 36, Captain Pierre Landais, and *Pallas,* 32, Captain Denis-Nicolas Cottineau, encounter a British convoy of 41 sail homeward-bound from the Baltic off Flamborough Head, Yorkshire. Escorting the convoy are two British warships, the frigate *Serapis,* 50, Captain Richard Pearson, and the sloop-of-war *Countess of Scarborough,* 20, Commander Thomas Piercy, which place themselves between the merchantmen and Jones's squadron. Jones engages the *Serapis,* a faster ship with a much heavier broadside, in the *Bonhomme Richard,* while the *Pallas* takes on the *Countess of Scarborough.* The *Alliance,* whose captain was probably mentally deranged, keeps clear of both actions at first, eventually intervenes to pour three destructive broadsides into the *Bonhomme Richard,* and then withdraws. Realizing that his only hope of victory is to close, Jones succeeds in making his ship fast to the *Serapis.* It is at this early stage of the action that he replies to Captain Pearson's demand to surrender with the defiant promise, "I have not yet begun to fight!" After a grueling combat of around three hours, during which both ships are reduced to little more than wrecks, the *Serapis* strikes her colors. The *Countess of Scarborough* has already surrendered to the *Pallas.* The *Bonhomme Richard* has lost 150 men killed and wounded out of a crew of 322; the *Serapis,* 170 of 325 (both figures approximate). Pearson's action has, however, allowed his convoy to escape. The battered *Bonhomme Richard* sinks on September 25 and Jones transfers his captives and crew to the *Serapis,* in which he enters the

The *Bonhomme Richard* vs. the *Serapis*. This contemporary painting by a British naval officer, Lieutenant William Elliot, is among the most accurate representations of the engagement. *Courtesy U.S. Naval Academy Museum.*

Texel on October 3. Both captains receive heroes' welcomes. Jones is made a Chevalier of the French Order of Military Merit and presented with a magnificent court-sword by Louis XVI; Pearson is knighted by George III.

October 28.   The Continental Marine Committee is replaced by a Board of Admiralty consisting of two members of Congress and three commissioners.

November 20.   In anticipation of a British attack on Charleston, South Carolina, a Continental squadron consisting of the frigates *Boston,* 24, *Providence,* 28, and *Queen of France,* 28, and the ship sloop *Ranger,* 18, is formed under the command of Captain Abraham Whipple and sent to assist in the defense of the port.

1780

February 11.   **Second Attack on Charleston.** The British have adopted a "southern strategy" designed to roll the revolution up from the south. As the Americans had expected, the blow falls on Charleston, South

Carolina, where a British army of 14,000 men under Major General Sir Henry Clinton is supported by a powerful naval squadron commanded by Vice Admiral Marriot Arbuthnot. Despite an energetic defense conducted by Brigadier General Benjamin Lincoln, the investment of the city is completed on April 11. The four vessels of Whipple's squadron (see November 20, 1779) serve as floating batteries.

March 14.   **Capture of Mobile.** the prize sloop *West Florida,* Captain William Pickles, cooperates with Spanish colonial forces in the campaign leading to the capture of Mobile, then capital of British West Florida.

May 4.   Congress adopts the first official Navy seal.

May 12.   **Fall of Charleston.** The greatest American defeat of the war occurs when the city's 5,400 defenders are compelled to surrender to the British forces. Of the Continental ships present, the frigates *Boston,* 24, and *Providence,* 28, and ship sloop *Ranger,* 18, are captured and the *Queen of France* is scuttled. Their loss reduces the strength of the Continental Navy to seven vessels (two on loan from France): the frigates *Alliance, Confederacy, Deane, Pallas,* and *Trumbull,* and the sloops *Ariel* and *Saratoga.* Following the occupation of the city, a

British army under General Charles Lord Cornwallis moves north in an attempt to pacify the Carolinas.

June 1.   **Trumbull vs. Watt.** On a cruise along the American coast the Continental frigate *Trumbull*, 28, Captain James Nicholson, encounters the British privateer *Watt*, 32, Captain John Coulthard. After an exceptionally fierce engagement of two-and-one-half hours, the *Trumbull* loses her main and mizzen masts and the badly battered privateer breaks off the action.

July 11.   **The French arrive.** An expeditionary force of 6,000 troops led by Lieutenant General Jean Baptiste Comte de Rochambeau lands at Newport, Rhode Island. It has crossed the Atlantic in 30 transports escorted by a squadron of seven ships of the line and two frigates commanded by the Chevalier de Ternay. The French fortify Newport, where the squadron is blockaded and de Ternay dies on December 15.

December 18.   John Paul Jones sails from France for America in command of the sloop-of-war *Ariel*, 14. Near the West Indies he engages the British privateer *Triumph*, 20, Captain John Pindar, which strikes her colors, but then escapes. This is the last action Jones fights in the Continental Navy.

1781

February 7.   Congress creates the office of Secretary of Marine to take over the management of naval affairs from the Board of Admiralty, but cannot agree on a man to fill it.

March 1.   Congress adopts the Articles of Confederation, by which the country will be governed until the adoption of the Constitution in 1788.

March 14.   John Paul Jones and his men receive a congressional vote of thanks.

March 18.   **Loss of the Saratoga.** The Continental ship sloop *Saratoga*, 18, Captain John Young, goes down with all hands in a sudden gale three days after sailing from Cap Français, Hispaniola, as part of the escort force of a Franco-American merchant convoy. Her loss is witnessed by the prize crew of an English merchantman she had left the convoy to capture.

April 2.   Off the coast of France, the Continental frigate *Alliance*, 36, Captain John Barry, captures the British privateer sloops *Mars*, 26, Captain J. Privo, and *Minerva*, 10, Captain J. Lecoster.

April 14.   **Loss of the Confederacy.** The Continental frigate *Confederacy*, 32, Captain Seth Harding, is cap-

tured by the British two-decker *Roebuck*, 44, Captain John Orde, and frigate *Orpheus*, 32, Captain John Colpoys, off the Virginia Capes.

May 21.   **Origins of the Yorktown Campaign.** Washington and de Rochambeau meet at Wethersfield, Connecticut, to plan strategy for the coming year. De Rochambeau has been informed that a French fleet commanded by Vice Admiral François Comte de Grasse is to arrive late in the summer to free the squadron blockaded at Newport, but is under orders not to reveal this to Washington. In the discussion Washington revives the idea of a concerted land-sea offensive against the British forces at New York. De Rochambeau is not enthusiastic about attacking New York, and in writing de Grasse, suggests that the Chesapeake Bay might be a more promising theater for joint operations. The decision is left to de Grasse.

May 29.   **Alliance vs. Trepassy and Atalanta.** The Continental frigate *Alliance*, 36, Captain John Barry, is attacked by the British brigs *Atalanta*, 16, Commander Sampson Edwards, and *Trepassy*, 14, Commander James Smyth. Both enemy ships are compelled to strike after a spirited action in which Barry is seriously wounded.

June 13.   The American privateers *Pilgrim* and *Rambler* capture the British sloop *Snake*, 12, Lieutenant William Jackson, in the Atlantic.

August 4.   **Cornwallis reaches Yorktown.** The British army of Lord Cornwallis, some 7,000 strong, establishes itself at Yorktown, Virginia, where it can maintain sea communications with Clinton in New York. Lafayette, following at a distance with a force of 4,500, informs Washington.

August 5.   **De Grasse starts north.** De Grasse sails from Cap Français, Hispaniola, sending a fast frigate ahead to America with the information that he is bound for the Chesapeake Bay.

August 9.   **Trumbull vs. Iris and General Monk.** The Continental frigate *Trumbull*, 28, Captain James Nicholson, strikes her colors after an hour's action off the Delaware Capes with the British frigate *Iris*, 32, (formerly the Continental frigate *Hancock*), and brig *General Monk*, 18.

August 14.   Washington receives de Grasse's communication (see August 5).

August 21.   Washington marches south, having prepared an elaborate and successful deception that convinces the British that he is preparing to attack Staten Island, New York.

A contemporary French map of the Yorktown campaign. *Official U.S. Navy photograph of an engraving in the Library of Congress.*

August 29.   Unable to find a Secretary of Marine, as a temporary expedient Congress establishes the office of Agent of Marine.

August 30.   **De Grasse reaches Yorktown.** There he begins to land 3,000 French troops under the Marquis de Saint-Simon to strengthen Lafayette's little army.

September 5.   **Battle of the Virginia Capes.** A British fleet of 19 ships of the line, one 50-gun ship and six frigates commanded by Admiral Thomas Lord Graves appears at the mouth of the Chesapeake, having hurried from New York to evacuate Cornwallis's army. De Grasse, who has detached four ships of the line to blockade the York and James rivers, goes out to fight with his other 24 ships, fearing that to remain in the bay would allow the British to intercept the French squadron that has been ordered down from Newport. The French fleet mounts considerably more guns than the British,

1,794 to 1,410, but many of them cannot be manned as almost 2,000 of its crewmen have been caught ashore, unloading provisions and troops. The opposing lines meet at an angle and only their van and center divisions become engaged. The fighting dies out at dusk. No ships are sunk on either side, but the British suffer much more damage than the French. Casualties are 336 for Graves and 240 for de Grasse. The two fleets maneuver in close proximity for several days, but the action is not renewed.

September 5.   The armies of Washington and de Rochambeau unite at Chesterfield, Pennsylvania, the same day on which Washington learns that de Grasse's fleet has entered the Chesapeake.

September 6.   Off Charleston, South Carolina, the privateer *Congress,* 24, captures the British sloop *Savage,* 16, Commander Charles Stirling.

September 7.   Congress appoints Robert Morris Agent of Marine.

September 10.   The French Newport squadron, eight ships, now commanded by Admiral Comte de Barras de Saint Laurent, slips past the British fleet and enters the Chesapeake Bay. Under its escort are 18 transports carrying munitions and de Rochambeau's siege artillery. The squadron's arrival raises de Grasse's strength to 36 ships of the line against Graves's 19.

September 11.   De Grasse reenters the Chesapeake Bay.

September 13.   Finding the French forces united inside the bay, Graves sails to New York to gather reinforcements.

September 14–26.   **Washington's and Rochambeau's forces reach Yorktown.** Most of the troops are transported down the bay from Head of Elk (Elkton), Baltimore, and Annapolis, Maryland, in French ships.

September 28.   **The siege of Yorktown begins.** Cornwallis's 8,000 men are faced by 9,500 Americans and 7,000 French regulars.

October 19.   **Cornwallis surrenders.** For practical purposes, the War of the Revolution is over. Independence has been won.

October 24.   Admiral Graves returns to the Chesapeake with a stronger fleet and 7,000 troops under Major General Sir Henry Clinton, to discover that he is too late.

December 31.   At year's end, the Continental Navy retains only two vessels in commission, the frigates *Alliance* and *Deane,* plus two others, the *Ariel* and *Pallas,* on loan from France.

1782

April 8.   **Hyder Ally vs. General Monk.** The Pennsylvania state sloop-of-war *Hyder Ally,* 16, Captain Joshua Barney, captures the British brig *General Monk,* 18, Commander Josiah Rogers, after a fierce, 30-minute action in Delaware Bay.

September 2.   The only Continental ship of the line to be completed, the *America,* 74, is presented to France in compensation for the loss of the *Magnifique,* which had grounded in Boston harbor on August 9. She was to have been commanded by John Paul Jones.

November 30.   A preliminary peace treaty is signed by representatives for the United States and Great Britain. It is to become effective upon the conclusion of peace between Great Britain and France, the terms of the Franco-American Treaty of Alliance having stipulated that neither nation would make a separate peace.

1783

January 30.   France and Spain sign preliminary peace treaties with Britain, clearing the way for a final settlement.

March 10.   **Last naval action of the American Revolution.** The frigate *Alliance,* 36, Captain John Barry, one of the two Continental ships still in commission, engages the British frigate *Sybil,* 28, Captain James Vashon, off the Atlantic coast of Florida. The *Sybil* is heavily damaged, but the *Alliance* is forced to break off the action upon the appearance of two other British warships.

March 24.   Congress orders all Continental naval vessels and privateers home.

April 11.   The cessation of hostilities with Great Britain is proclaimed by Congress.

September 3.   **Official end of the War of the Revolution.** In Paris, the American and British commissioners sign the definitive treaty of peace.

November 1.   Robert Morris resigns the office of Agent of Marine. No successor is appointed.

1785

June 3.   **End of the Continental Navy.** Congress authorizes the sale of the one remaining American naval vessel, the frigate *Alliance.* For the next nine years, the nation will have no navy.

1787

September 17.   The Constitutional Convention, called to organize a stronger federal government for the United States, approves the Constitution, which is then submitted to the individual states for ratification. Among the powers to be specifically vested in the new government is "to provide and maintain a Navy." The process of ratification is completed in the summer of 1788, but years will pass before a navy is actually established.

October 16.   Congress votes unanimously to award a gold medal to John Paul Jones.

1788

April 15.   **John Paul Jones in Russia.** The Empress Catherine the Great decides to offer Jones a commission as rear admiral in the Imperial Russian Navy. He accepts.

June 17.   **First Battle of the Liman.** Jones commands one of the two Russian squadrons engaged against the Turks in an action in the estuary (Liman) of the Dnieper on the Black Sea coast. His dispositions are responsible for the repulse of the Turkish fleet.

June 28–29.   **Second Battle of the Liman.** The Turkish fleet is badly defeated, losing 15 vessels, in a battle planned and dominated by Jones. Another foreign officer in Russian service, the German Prince Nassau-Siegen, manages to steal most of the credit, and Jones leaves Russia in August 1789 without having obtained another command.

1789

August 7.   The War Department is established. Its responsibilities include naval affairs, of which there are none.

1790

August 4.   **Foundation of the U.S. Coast Guard.** Congress creates the Revenue Marine, which evolves into the U.S. Coast Guard.

1791

January 6.   **The Barbary pirates.** For centuries the four Barbary powers on the coast of North Africa—from west to east, Morocco, Algiers, Tunis, and Tripoli—have operated a maritime protection racket, demanding tribute from foreign nations not to attack their ships. As long as the thirteen states were British colonies, they could rely on the protection of the Royal Navy, but after the revolution they are on their own, and ships begin to be seized as early as October 1783. The United States concludes a treaty involving the payment of tribute with Morocco in 1787, but Algiers, in particular, continues to prey on American vessels. On this date the Senate Committee on Mediterranean Trade reports that only a naval force can assure the safety of American shipping in that area.

1792

April 20.   **Beginning of the wars of the French Revolution and Empire.** The French Legislative Assembly declares war on Austria, initiating a titanic struggle that will keep Europe in turmoil for the next 23 years. When in 1793 Great Britain enters the conflict, President George Washington proclaims American neutrality and calls upon his countrymen to display a "friendly and impartial" attitude towards the warring powers. But it is not that easy. At sea, the efforts of each antagonist to prevent trade with the other will result in a consistent disregard of neutral ships and grave injury to the American merchant marine. Before a lasting peace is concluded in 1815, the United States will have been drawn into wars with both Britain and France.

July 18.   **John Paul Jones dies in Paris at the age of 45.** Upon its discovery in 1905 his body is so well preserved that it is possible to perform an autopsy, revealing the cause of death to be a combination of jaundice, nephritis, and bronchial pneumonia.

1793

April 22.   President George Washington recommends the construction of six frigates to protect American commerce from Algerine corsairs.

July 8–25.   During this period, no fewer than eight American merchantmen are captured by the Algerines.

1794

January 2.   A Congressional resolution calls for the establishment of a navy to protect American shipping from the Algerines. Supported by Alexander Hamilton's Federalist Party, which speaks for the northeastern mercantile and maritime community, the bill is bitterly opposed by Thomas Jefferson's Republicans, who represent the agrarian South and inland areas. The latter fear that a navy will be a ruinously expensive, aristocratic institution, subversive of democratic ideals, whose glory-hungry officers will drag the country into unwanted adventures overseas.

March 27.   **Foundation of the U.S. Navy.** A compromise is achieved. Congress authorizes the construction or purchase of six frigates, three of 44 guns and three of 36, but it is stipulated that they will be canceled in the event peace is made with Algiers prior to their completion.

June 28.   **Humphreys's frigates.** Joshua Humphreys, a prominent Philadelphia shipbuilder, is engaged to design the two classes of frigates authorized by the Navy Act of March 27, 1794. His plans, developed in collaboration with William Doughty, a draftsman in his employ, and Josiah Fox, an English emigrant, produce the largest and most powerful frigates afloat, at no sacrifice of speed. These well-nigh revolutionary vessels will prove their worth in the Quasi-War with France and even more in the War of 1812.

June 28.   The first officers of the new navy are appointed. There are six captains: Joshua Barney, John Barry, Richard Dale, Samuel Nicholson, Silas Talbot, and Thomas Truxtun.

1795

February 23.   **Foundation of the Supply Corps.** Congress establishes the Office of Purveyor of Supplies.

September 5.   **Peace with Algiers.** A treaty is negotiated with the Dey of Algiers, according to which attacks on American merchantmen will cease in exchange for the payment of a $525,000 ransom for the seamen already captured, the gift of a 36-gun frigate, and an annual tribute of $21,000 in naval stores.

1796

March 2.   Congress ratifies the treaty with Algiers. According to the provisions of the Navy Act of March 27, 1794, construction of the six frigates is to cease.

March 15.   President Washington urges Congress to complete the frigates.

April 20.   **Three frigates instead.** Once again, a compromise is reached. Despite the conclusion of peace with Algiers, Congress authorizes the completion of the *Constitution,* 44, the *United States,* 44, and the *Constellation,* 36. The three unfinished frigates will be put "in ordinary" (mothballed).

November 4.   **Peace with Tripoli.** A treaty of peace is concluded between the United States and the Pasha of Tripoli.

December 6.   In a message to Congress, President Washington recommends that the strength of the navy should be increased.

1797

February 27.   Secretary of State Timothy Pickering presents a report detailing French attacks upon, and injuries to, the American merchant marine.

May 10.   The frigate *United States,* 44, is launched at Philadelphia.

May 16.   The new president, John Adams, repeats Washington's recommendation to Congress to increase the strength of the navy.

July 1.   The first "Navy Regulations" are approved by Congress.

August 14.   **Peace with Tunis.** In Paris, U.S. commissioner David Humphreys approves a treaty of peace his agents have negotiated with Tunis. By the terms of this treaty, confirmed by the Senate in 1799, the United States agrees to pay the Barbary power $107,000 not to attack its shipping.

September 7.   The frigate *Constellation,* 36, is launched at Baltimore.

October 4.   **XYZ Affair.** An American delegation consisting of Charles C. Pickney, John Marshall, and Elbridge Gerry is sent to France in an attempt to repair relations between the two countries and bring an end to French harassment of American merchant shipping. In Paris they are met by three French agents—"X, Y, and Z"—who inform them that they must pay a substantial bribe to so much as see the foreign minister. The Americans indignantly refuse. News of the incident provokes a storm of outrage in the United States and sets the stage for the Quasi-War with France.

October 21.   The frigate *Constitution,* 44, is launched at Boston, Massachusetts.

The frigate *Constitution:* a contemporary engraving (undated) published in Boston. *Courtesy Beverley R. Robinson Collection, U.S. Naval Academy Museum.*

1798

January 27.   France declares that all vessels trading with Britain will be liable to seizure and sale.

March 27.   Congress directs that the three frigates launched in 1797 are to be equipped for active operations.

April 27.   Congress authorizes President Adams to procure another 12 ships mounting up to 22 guns each.

April 30.   Foundation of the Navy Department. An Act of Congress creates the new department and the office of secretary of the navy.

May 4.   President Adams is authorized by Congress to build or purchase 10 small vessels for the defense of the American coast.

May 18.   Benjamin Stoddert is nominated by President Adams to be the first secretary of the navy. The Senate confirms his appointment three days later.

May 24.   First naval vessel to sail. The ship *Ganges,* 26, Captain Richard Dale, leaves Philadelphia to become the first ship in America's new navy to actually get underway.

May 28.   Quasi-War with France. An undeclared naval war begins when Congress instructs U.S. warships "to capture any French vessel found near the coast preying upon American commerce." In the course of the conflict the number of American fighting ships in service, including revenue cutters, will reach a total of 54.

June 25.   American merchant vessels are authorized to resist interference by French ships.

June 28.   Congress approves the sale of lawful captures, part of the proceeds from which are to be used to pay prize money to American crews.

July 7.   The United States abrogates all existing treaties with France.

July 7.   First capture of the Quasi-War. The sloop-of-war *Delaware,* 20, Captain Stephen Decatur (Sr.), captures the French privateer *Le Croyable,* 14, off the Delaware. She is taken into U.S. service under the name *Retaliation.*

July 9.   Privateering against French vessels is authorized by Congress. Some 365 letters of marque and reprisal are issued in the next nine months.

July 11.   Birthday of the U.S. Marine Corps. President John Adams approves an act "for Establishing and Organizing a Marine Corps." The bill had been introduced by Samuel Sewall, chairman of the House Naval Committee. William Ward Burrows is ap-

pointed major commandant. The strength of the corps is set at 33 officers and 848 men.

July 16.   Congress authorizes the completion of the three unfinished frigates (*Congress,* 36, *Chesapeake,* 36, and *President,* 44).

November 16.   Escorting a convoy from Charleston to Havana, the ship sloop *Baltimore,* 20, Captain Isaac Philips, meets a British squadron, including three ships of the line, which impresses five of his seamen. Upon his return the unfortunate Philips is dismissed from the service.

November 20.   Loss of the Retaliation. The schooner *Retaliation,* 44, Lieutenant William Bainbridge, is overtaken by two French frigates, surrendering to *L'Insurgente,* 40, Captain M. P. Barreaut.

December 31.   Progress of the Quasi-War. Including *Le Croyable,* to date three French privateers have been captured.

1799

February 9.   First victory over an enemy warship: Constellation vs. L'Insurgente. Between the Caribbean islands of Nevis and St. Kitts, the frigate *Constellation,* 48, Captain Thomas Truxtun, overtakes the French frigate *L'Insurgente,* 40, Captain M. P. Barreaut. The *Constellation* enjoys a slight superiority in the weight of her broadside, but *L'Insurgente* has the larger crew, more than 400 to the *Constellation's* 309 men. Skillfully avoiding the enemy's attempt to close, Truxtun

The *Constellation* vs. *L'Insurgente:* an engraving published in Philadelphia in 1799. *Courtesy Beverley R. Robinson Collection, U.S. Naval Academy Museum.*

crosses her bow twice to deliver a deadly raking fire. When he is in position to rake a third time, *L'Insurgente* hauls down her colors. French losses are 29 men killed and 41 wounded; American, 2 killed and 3 wounded. The captured vessel is commissioned into the U.S. Navy as the *Insurgent*.

February 25.   Congress authorizes the construction of six ships of the line and six sloops of war, but they are never built.

March 2.   Congress approves the establishment of naval pensions and an increase in the strength of the Marine Corps.

August 15.   The *Congress*, 36, fourth of the six frigates authorized by the Navy Act of 1794, is launched in Portsmouth, New Hampshire.

October 2.   The Washington Navy Yard is established.

December 2.   The frigate *Chesapeake*, 36, fifth of the original six, is launched in Norfolk, Virginia.

1800

February 1.   **Constellation vs. Vengeance.** After a full day's chase, the frigate *Constellation*, 50, Captain Thomas Truxtun, overtakes the French frigate *Vengeance*, 56, Captain A. M. Pitot, southwest of Guadeloupe. The ensuing night action lasts five hours. Although the *Vengeance* is considerably superior in weight of broadside, she receives much of the worst of the action and strikes her colors twice, but resumes resistance when her surrender is unobserved. Eventually the *Constellation* loses her mainmast and the *Vengeance* sheers away, limping into Curaçao to report that she has been attacked by a ship of the line. French casualties are approximately 50 killed and 110 wounded of a crew of 330; American, 14 killed and 25 wounded of a crew of 310.

February 7.   **First across the equator.** En route to the East Indies, the frigate *Essex*, 32, Captain Edward Preble, becomes the first U.S. naval vessel to cross the equator.

April 1.   The *President*, 44, last of the original six frigates, is launched at New York.

July 1.   **First convoy.** The frigate *Essex*, 32, Captain Edward Preble, sails from the Sunda Strait, escorting 14 American merchantmen home from the Dutch East Indies.

August 8.   **Loss of the Insurgent.** The U.S. (late French) frigate *Insurgent,* Captain Patrick Fletcher, sails from Norfolk, Virginia, bound for the West Indies. Somewhere en route she is lost with her entire company (340 men).

August 20.   **Loss of the Pickering.** The revenue cutter *Pickering,* 14, Lieutenant B. Hillar, sails from New Castle, Delaware, for the West Indies, and disappears at sea.

September 30.   **Preliminary peace.** In Paris, American and French representatives sign the Convention of 1800, winding down the Quasi-War. France agrees to the abrogation of the treaties of 1778, in return for which the United States government assumes the liability for the losses to American citizens caused by French actions since 1793. President Adams regarded the settlement of this conflict as his greatest achievement.

October 12.   **Boston vs. Le Berceau.** The frigate *Boston*, 28, Captain George Little, captures the French frigate *Le Berceau*, 24, Captain André Senez, after a severe engagement 600 miles northwest of Guadeloupe. *Le Berceau* loses 34 men killed and 18 wounded.

October 20.   **Seizure of the George Washington.** The frigate *George Washington*, 32, Captain William Bainbridge, is ordered to carry American tribute to the Dey of Algiers. Upon her arrival, the Dey demands that the ship be placed in his service to transport an Algerine embassy and tribute to the Sultan of Turkey. Bainbridge and American consul Richard O'Brien protest strongly, but finally conclude that if they refuse to humor him the Dey will resume attacks on American merchantmen. On this day, the chagrined Bainbridge sets sail for Constantinople, Algerines aboard. His frustration is partially allayed by the respectful welcome he receives from the Turks.

December 31.   In the course of the year the navy has captured 49 French privateers or merchantmen and the frigate *Le Berceau* and recaptured numerous prizes without losing a ship to enemy action.

1801

February 3.   **End of the Quasi-War with France.** The Senate ratifies the convention of 1800 without serious debate. During the conflict, in which the *Retaliation* was the only American warship lost, the navy has taken 85 French ships, including two frigates.

March 3.   Congress passes the Peace Establishment Act, reducing the strength of the navy from 33 to 13 ships.

March 4.   **Thomas Jefferson assumes the presidency.** The new chief executive's attitude towards the navy has not changed much since the days when he opposed its foundation. Apprehensive that ocean-going warships may involve the young republic in foreign wars, he sponsors the creation of a "gunboat navy" of small vessels of one or two guns meant to complement the army's coastal fortifications in defending the country against invasion.

May 14.   **War with Tripoli.** Declaring that the amount of tribute being paid him by the United States is insufficient, the Pasha of Tripoli, Yusuf Karamanli, declares war.

May 20.   **The first American squadron is sent to the Mediterranean.** Although the news of the Tripolitan declaration of war has not yet been received, prior reports of the pasha's discontent have led President Jefferson to the decision to dispatch a naval force to protect the American commerce in the Mediterranean. Commanded by Commodore Richard Dale, the squadron consists of the frigates *President,* 44 (flag), Captain James Barron, *Philadelphia,* 36, Captain Samuel Barron, and *Essex,* 32, Captain William Bainbridge, and the schooner *Enterprise,* 12, Lieutenant Andrew Sterrett.

July 5.   Future admiral David Glasgow Farragut is born in Knoxville, Tennessee.

July 27.   Robert Smith is appointed second secretary of the navy.

August 1.   **First action of the War with Tripoli.** The *Enterprise,* 12, Lieutenant Andrew Sterrett, captures the Tripolitan polacre *Tripoli,* 14, off Malta after a three-hour fight during which the enemy feigns surrender twice. The Tripolitan losses are 20 killed and 30 wounded; the *Enterprise* suffers not a single casualty. As the American squadron's orders exclude the taking of prizes, Sterrett jettisons the *Tripoli*'s cannons and leaves her with one mast to limp back home. Congress awards Sterrett a sword of honor.

1802

March 3.   **Truxtun resigns.** Commodore Thomas Truxtun, the leading American naval officer in the Quasi-War with France, is offered command of the second squadron to be sent to the Mediterranean. Angered by Secretary of the Navy Smith's refusal to authorize him to have a flag captain, he resigns his commission.

March 10.   **Second Mediterranean Squadron.** Commodore Dale sails from Gibraltar for home on this date. He has been unable to accomplish a great deal during his nine months in the Mediterranean, his squadron being too weak to enforce an effective blockade of Tripoli or to attack its fortifications. His replacement is Commodore Richard V. Morris, who arrives in the Mediterranean in the frigate *Chesapeake,* 36, in May. The ships of his squadron, which reach their station between March and November, are the frigates *Constellation,* 36, *New York,* 36, *Adams,* 28, and *John Adams,* 28, and the schooner *Enterprise,* 12. The frigate *Boston,* 28, is nominally assigned to this force, but leaves for home.

July 22.   The frigate *Constellation,* 36, Captain Alexander Murray, engages a Tripolitan galley and eight gunboats, sinking two.

1803

May 12.   Blockading off Tripoli, the frigate *John Adams,* 28, Captain John Rodgers, captures the Tripolitan ship *Meshuda,* 20, without resistance as she attempts to slip into port under the Moroccan flag.

May 23.   Lieutenant David Porter leads a party of 50 men from the frigate *New York,* 36, ashore to destroy a dozen Tripolitan feluccas drawn up on the beach 35 miles west of the city. A sharp action is fought with the feluccas' crews, who manage to extinguish the fires set in half of their vessels, and Porter retires, having suffered 15 casualties.

June 22.   The frigate *John Adams,* 28, engages a Tripolitan polacre of 22 guns anchored near shore several miles west of Tripoli. After an action of 45 minutes the Tripolitans abandon their ship, which blows up before Rodgers's men reach her.

June 26.   Apprehensive of trouble with Morocco, Commodore Morris lifts the blockade of Tripoli.

August 26.   Only two days after entering the Mediterranean, the frigate *Philadelphia,* 36, Captain William Bainbridge, captures the Moroccan ship *Mirboha,* 22, Ibrahim Lubarez, with an American prize (the brig *Celia*) in tow near Cape de Gata, Spain.

September 13.   **Preble reaches the Mediterranean.** Commodore Edward Preble, a flinty, 42-year-old native of Maine, reaches Tangiers in the frigate *Constitution,* 44, to command the third American Mediterranean Squadron. Orders directing Commodore Morris to return home had been written on June 21. In the spring of 1804 he will be censured by a court of inquiry for "inactive and dilatory conduct" while in command in the Mediterranean and, shortly thereafter, dismissed from the navy. Preble's squadron, the last of which ar-

Commodore Edward Preble, from the obverse of his congressional gold medal, engraved by John Reich from a drawing by Rembrandt Peale. *Courtesy U.S. Naval Academy Museum.*

rives in November, consists of the frigates *Constitution* (flag) and *Philadelphia,* 36, Captain William Bainbridge; the brigs *Argus,* 16, Lieutenant Stephen Decatur, and *Syren,* 16, Lieutenant Charles Stewart; and the schooners *Enterprise,* 12, Lieutenant Isaac Hull, *Nautilus,* 12, Lieutenant Richard Somers, and *Vixen,* 12, Lieutenant John Smith. These officers, none of whom is over 30 years old, will become known to history as "Preble's Boys."

October 12. **Peace with Morocco.** In a meeting with Commodore Preble and James Simpson, U.S. consul at Tangiers, the Sultan of Morocco, Mulai Suleiman, ratifies the treaty of peace originally concluded in 1787.

October 31. **Capture of the Philadelphia.** On patrol off Tripoli the frigate *Philadelphia,* 36, Captain William Bainbridge, sights a ship trying to slip into harbor. Having earlier dispatched the schooner *Vixen,* 12, on an independent search, Bainbridge pursues the enemy into shallow water with his frigate and runs hard aground on an uncharted reef. Every means of refloating the ship, including cutting away her foremast and jettisoning most of her cannon, is tried, without success. Soon Tripolitan gunboats appear and open fire, which the *Philadelphia* cannot return. After consulting his officers, Bainbridge surrenders to avoid use-

less loss of life; 307 officers and men enter captivity. A few days later a storm frees the ship and the Tripolitans bring her into the harbor.

November 25. A British warship informs Commodore Preble of the capture of the *Philadelphia.* Once the shock has passed, he begins to consider how she can be destroyed.

December 23. The schooner *Enterprise,* 12, Lieutenant Stephen Decatur, captures the Tripolitan ketch *Mastico.* The ship is taken into the U.S. Navy under the name *Intrepid.*

1804

February 16. **Decatur destroys the Philadelphia.** At nightfall, Lieutenant Stephen Decatur sails into Tripoli harbor with 80 volunteers in the *Intrepid* (ex-*Mastico*) to burn the frigate *Philadelphia.* The *Intrepid*'s Mediterranean rig leads the Tripolitans to assume that she is a local trader, a misimpression reinforced by the fact that the men on her deck—Decatur, Italian pilot Salvador Catalano, and a few others—are dressed in Maltese costume. The seven or eight guards in the *Philadelphia* see through the ruse at the last moment,

Captain Stephen Decatur: a portrait painted by Olivio Sozzi in 1805. *Courtesy U.S. Naval Academy Museum.*

but it is too late. Decatur's boarding party overcomes them and sets the frigate ablaze. Only one of his men is wounded. Britain's Lord Nelson calls the exploit "the most daring act of the age." Decatur is promoted to captain, aged twenty-five. To this day he remains the youngest man ever to hold that rank.

March 7.   Lieutenant Colonel Franklin Wharton is appointed third commandant of the marine corps.

May 13.   After months of negotiation with the kingdom of Naples, Preble is informed that six gunboats and two bomb ketches will be placed at his disposal for use against Tripoli. A lack of ships has hampered Preble ever since his arrival in the Mediterranean, and he has repeatedly requested reinforcements, in vain. By summer 1804, the effects of the blockade he has maintained are beginning to be felt in Tripoli, but he is anxious to take more forceful action.

July 25.   The eight Neapolitan ships join Preble's squadron.

August 3.   **First bombardment of Tripoli.** Covered by the frigate *Constitution*, Preble's borrowed gunboats and bomb ketches (with American captains and crews) stand in towards Tripoli. The two ketches deliver a desultory bombardment of the city while the six gunboats engage a flotilla of 19 Tripolitan gunboats. Three

of the latter are captured in savage, hand-to-hand fighting by boarding parties, two led by Lieutenant Stephen Decatur, the other by Sailing Master John Trippe, and the remainder are driven into the harbor.

August 7.   **Second bombardment of Tripoli.** Preble renews the attack on Tripoli from a new location, the bay east of the city. The prizes taken on August 3 raise the number of his gunboats to nine. In the midst of the action, one of these prizes, *Gunboat No. 9,* blows up. Her commander, Lieutenant James R. Caldwell, and 9 of the 28 men aboard are killed; 6 others are wounded.

August 7.   A few hours after breaking off the bombardment of Tripoli, Preble is joined by the frigate *John Adams,* 28, Master Commandant Isaac Chauncey, from the United States. She carries dispatches informing Preble that, galvanized by the loss of the *Philadelphia,* the government is sending four more frigates to the Mediterranean, one under Captain Samuel Barron, who, as Preble's senior, will assume command of the squadron.

August 11–24.   Determined to do everything in his power to end the war before his relief arrives, Preble makes six attempts to bombard Tripoli by night. Wind and

The destruction of the *Philadelphia* in Tripoli harbor: an engraving by J. B. Guerazzi sold in Leghorn, Italy, in 1805. *Courtesy Beverley R. Robinson Collection, U.S. Naval Academy Museum.*

The Bombardment of Tripoli: a painting for Commodore Preble by Michel F. Corné. From left to right, foreground: the *Enterprise, Nautilus, Argus, Syren, Vixen,* and *Constitution. Courtesy U.S. Naval Academy Museum.*

currents foil the first five and the sixth, delivered in the night of August 23–24, is ineffective.

August 27.   **Fourth bombardment of Tripoli.** Preble tries again. Beginning around 3:00 A.M., the frigate *Constitution* and the gunboats shell Tripoli for four hours. Afterwards, the French consul, Bonaventure Beaussier, who is acting as Preble's diplomatic intermediary to the Tripolitans, informs him that Pasha Yusuf Karamanli has not been impressed.

September 2.   **Fifth bombardment of Tripoli.** Preble shells the city for the last time, but no serious damage is done.

September 3.   **The Intrepid.** Meanwhile, realizing that the bombardments of Tripoli have not moved the Pasha closer to peace, Preble has reverted to an idea that occurred to him in March. It is to destroy the Tripolitan flotilla by sailing a ship filled with explosives into the harbor under cover of darkness. Once the vessel comes within range of the flotilla, a fire will be set some ways from the powder, giving the crew time to escape in small boats and deterring the Tripolitans from boarding her. The vessel chosen is the ketch *Intrepid.* Volunteers for the mission are numerous. Preble selects those who have missed an opportunity to distinguish themselves in previous actions: Lieutenant Richard Somers, Midshipmen Henry Wadsworth and Joseph Israel, and 10 seamen. The first attempt to enter the harbor on September 1 is defeated when the wind fails. On September 3, the *Intrepid* gets under way at 8:00 P.M. At 9:47 P.M., there is a terrific explosion. Later it is learned that the *Intrepid* blew up at the entrance to the harbor, well short of any target, with the loss of everyone aboard. The reason for her premature detonation remains a mystery, but her officers had declared that they would never allow the five tons of powder she carried to fall into enemy hands.

September 9.   Commodore Samuel Barron, flying his pennant in the frigate *President,* 44, relieves Commodore Preble as commander of the Mediterranean Squadron. In the following months he maintains the blockade of Tripoli.

1805

February 25.   Commodore Edward Preble reaches the United States and discovers that his energetic prosecution of the War with Tripoli has made him a national hero. On March 3, he is awarded a congressional gold medal.

March 2.   Congress authorizes the construction of 25 gunboats for coast defense.

March 8.   **March on Tripoli.** Since 1801, William Eaton, then U.S. consul at Tunis, has advocated putting pressure on Tripolitan Pasha Yusuf Karamanli by supporting the pretensions of his elder brother, Hamet, from whom Yusuf had seized the throne in 1795.

The explosion of the *Intrepid:* an unsigned contemporary engraving. *Courtesy Beverley R. Robinson Collection, U.S. Naval Academy Museum.*

Commodore Preble had seriously considered the idea, but finally decided against it. In the meanwhile, Eaton has been to the United States and returned with the title of "Navy Agent to the Barbary States" and authority to put his project into execution. On this date he and Hamet begin a march from Alexandria, Egypt, Hamet's home in exile, with an army of 400 Arabs and seven marines commanded by First Lieutenant Presley O'Bannon.

April 27.   **Capture of Derna.** After an almost 600-mile desert march during which Hamet Karamanli often indicates his readiness to forget the whole thing, Eaton's forces arrive outside Derna, on the Tripolitan frontier, on April 26. Supported by fire from the brig *Argus,* 16, Master Commandant Isaac Hull, the schooner *Nautilus,* 12, Master Commandant J. H. Dent, and the sloop *Hornet,* 10, Lieutenant S. Evans, the little army captures the city the next day. The American flag raised by Lieutenant O'Bannon is the first to fly over an enemy fortress outside the Western Hemisphere.

May 26.   **Negotiations with Tripoli.** Colonel Tobias Lear, U.S. counsel general at Algiers, arrives off Tripoli in the frigate *Essex* and opens negotiations with Pasha Yusuf Karamanli, who has tired of the war.

June 3.   **Peace with Tripoli.** The preliminary treaty is signed. The United States agrees to pay $60,000 for the release of the American prisoners and to evacuate Derna; Tripoli waives all claims to future tribute.

June 4.   Tripoli releases Captain Bainbridge and the crew of the *Philadelphia.*

June 10.   The final treaty of peace between the United Stats and Tripoli is signed.

June 12.   A British squadron impresses three sailors from *Gunboat No. 6,* Lieutenant James Lawrence, off Cadiz, Spain.

1806

April 23.   **Nonimportation Act.** Congress declares that unless Britain agrees to abandon maritime policies injurious to American interests—most especially, the impressment of American seamen—a ban on specified British imports will go into effect on November 15, 1806. President Jefferson later extends the deadline in hopes that negotiations will be successful, but no agreement is reached.

May 16.   **Fox's Blockade.** The British government imposes a blockade, named after Foreign Secretary Charles James Fox, on the coast of Europe from Brest to the mouth of the Elbe. By the end of 1807 the blockade will have been extended to every port under French control.

November 21.   **Berlin Decree.** Napoleon counters the British blockade by a decree prohibiting all trade with the British Isles. This marks the birth of Napoleon's "Continental System" of economic warfare against England.

1807

June 22.   **Chesapeake-Leopard Affair.** The frigate *Chesapeake, 36,* Captain Charles Gordon, sails from Hampton Roads, Virginia, carrying Commodore James Barron to assume command in the Mediterranean. Just outside the mouth of the Chesapeake Bay she is intercepted by the British frigate *Leopard, 56,* Captain S. P. Humphreys, who demands to search the ship for British deserters presumed aboard. When Barron refuses to allow this, the *Leopard* opens fire. The *Chesapeake* is completely unprepared for action; after 15 minutes of confusion, Lieutenant William Henry Allen saves the ship's honor by carrying a burning coal from the galley to fire a single gun in her defense. Barron then strikes his colors. Four of the *Chesapeake's* company have been killed or mortally wounded and twenty, including the commodore, wounded. A British boarding party seizes four crewmen, one of whom is really a British deserter. He is taken to Halifax, Nova Scotia, and hanged. After four years of diplomatic protests, the United States secures the release of the two surviving sailors, the third having died in British service. Commodore Barron is court-martialed, found guilty of negligence in not clearing for action before the attack, and suspended from the navy for five years.

News of the incident provokes a furious outcry throughout the United States.

July 2.   President Jefferson expresses his indignation over the *Chesapeake-Leopard* affair by ordering all British naval vessels to leave American ports.

August 11.   **First steamship.** Robert Fulton's *Clermont* makes her maiden voyage up the Hudson from New York to Albany.

August 25.   Commodore Edward Preble dies of a stomach ailment in Portland, Maine.

November 11.   **British Orders in Council.** Beginning to feel the pinch of the Berlin Decree, Britain responds by declaring that all neutral ships trading with the Continent must obtain a license in a British port; those which do not will be subject to lawful capture.

December 11.   **Milan Decree.** Napoleon counters the British Orders in Council by decreeing that neutral ships that submit to them will be treated as enemy vessels. The United States, being the largest neutral carrier, is caught squarely in the middle of the rival systems of economic warfare.

December 14.   The Nonimportation Act goes into force.

December 18.   **More gunboats.** Congress approves the construction of another 188 gunboats for coast defense.

December 22.   **Embargo Act.** Hoping to persuade Britain to mend her maritime ways by economic coercion, President Jefferson sponsors an act that prohibits American ships from trading with any foreign country. This does not work. The British economy is scarcely affected, but the American economy is nearly ruined.

1808

April 17.   **Bayonne Decree.** Napoleon responds to the Embargo Act by declaring that the claim to American nationality of any vessels entering French-controlled ports will be considered fraudulent and the ships and their cargoes seized. His Rambouillet Decree of March 23, 1810, orders these vessels sold. Nearly 140 American merchantmen with cargoes valued at $10,000,000 are victimized by these rulings.

1809

March 1.   **Non-intercourse Act.** Three days before President James Madison enters office the highly unpopular Embargo Act is repealed and, with his blessing, replaced by the Non-intercourse Act, which reopens American commerce with all nations except Great Britain and France and stipulates that trade with either or both of them will resume as soon as they abandon policies inimical to the American merchant marine.

May 15.   Paul Hamilton enters office as third secretary of the navy.

1810

February.   In the course of the month, the ketch *Vesuvius,* 11, Lieutenant Benjamin F. Reed, and a boat party under Midshipman Francis H. Gregory capture the pirate ships *Duke of Montebello,* 5, *Diomede,* 1, and *Alexandria,* 4, off the mouth of the Mississippi.

May 1.   **Macon's Bill Number 2.** Following the expiration of the Non-intercourse Act, Congress passes a bill that authorizes the resumption of trade with both Great Britain and France, but states that should one revoke policies injurious to American shipping, a prohibition will be placed on trade with the other.

1811

January 9.   The schooner *Revenge,* 12, Lieutenant Oliver Hazard Perry, grounds and is lost off Newport, Rhode Island. Her crew is saved.

May 1.   HMS *Guerrière* stops the American merchant ship *Spitfire* and impresses several seamen off Sandy Hook, New Jersey.

May 6.   The U.S. frigate *President,* 44, Commodore John Rodgers, is sent to patrol off Sandy Hook.

May 16.   **President and Little Belt.** Around 12:30 P.M., the *President* encounters the British sloop-of-war *Little Belt,* 20, Captain Arthur B. Bingham, approximately 45 miles northeast of Cape Henry, Virginia. After a long chase, during which Rodgers is unable to identify the other vessel as anything more than a man-of-war, the *President* overtakes the *Little Belt* at about 8:30 P.M., and firing breaks out. Later, both sides accuse the other of having fired the first shot. The *Little Belt* is heavily damaged, losing 13 killed and 19 wounded; the *President* has 1 boy wounded. At daybreak Rodgers sends a boat to the *Little Belt* to express his regrets and offer

The *President* attacks the *Little Belt:* an aquatint published in London in October 1811. *Courtesy Beverley R. Robinson Collection, U.S. Naval Academy Museum.*

to help her with repairs. Rodgers is commended by President Madison and Secretary Hamilton.

August 7.   Off Pensacola, Florida, *Gunboat No. 162*, 5, Midshipman F. H. Gregory, attacks and cripples the pirate schooner *La Franchise*, 5.

August 10.   *Gunboat No. 162* captures the pirate schooner *Santa Maria*, 4, off Mobile, Alabama.

September 11.   *Gunboat No. 162*, still commanded by the redoubtable Midshipman Gregory, captures the pirate ship *La Divina Pastora*, 14, and the schooners *La Sophie*, 6, and *Le Vengeance*, 4, between Brassa and Barataria, Louisiana.

1812

June 1.   President James Madison asks Congress to declare war on Great Britain.

June 17.   Hoping to head off war with the United States, the British cabinet revokes the Orders in Council to which Americans so object.

June 18.   **War of 1812.** It is too late. Congress votes for war with Britain. As of this date, the U.S. fleet (excluding gunboats) consists of 17 seaworthy ships: 9 frigates and 8 smaller vessels. The Royal Navy numbers more than 1,048, including approximately 120 ships of the line and 116 frigates. These odds ensure that American ships will be used, as they had in the Revolution, for coast defense and commerce raiding. (In the course of the conflict, naval vessels and privateers will capture approximately 1,800 British merchantmen.) On land, the United States appears to enjoy an immense advantage, with a regular army of 6,700 men and state militias numbering, in the aggregate, several hundred thousands to oppose the British garrison of Canada—4,500 regular troops, and a modest Canadian militia. But many American militia units exist only on paper; most of those that take the field are undisciplined and ill-trained, and the caliber of American military leadership at the beginning of the war leaves much to be desired.

June 21–August 29.   **Cruise of Rodgers's squadron.** Commodore John Rodgers, the senior-ranking American naval officer, sails from Boston with a squadron consisting of the frigates *President*, 44 (flag), *United States*, 44, *Congress*, 36, sloop *Hornet*, 18, and brig *Argus*, 16, to raid British commerce in the North Atlantic. On June 23, the squadron encounters, but cannot overtake, the British frigate *Belvidera*, 36. Altogether, it captures only

seven merchantmen, a meager showing. Hereafter, the strategy of squadron operations is abandoned, and American warships cruise singly or, infrequently, in groups of two or three.

July 3–September 7.   **First Cruise of the Essex.** Master Commandant David Porter sails from New York in the small frigate *Essex*, 32, on a cruise in which he captures seven merchantmen, a transport, and the first British warship taken in the War of 1812 (See August 13).

July 17.   **Loss of the Nautilus.** The brig *Nautilus*, 12, Lieutenant William M. Crane, is captured off New York by the ship-of-the-line *Africa*, 64, and the frigates *Aeolus*, 32, and *Shannon*, 38. She is the first U.S. naval vessel lost in the War of 1812.

July 17–20.   **Escape of the Constitution.** Off the coast of New Jersey the frigate *Constitution*, 44, Captain Isaac Hull, is becalmed in the presence of seven British ships. She escapes through brilliant seamanship after an epic chase lasting 66 hours.

July–August.   **Defeats on land.** American plans for an invasion of Canada quickly come to grief. The British capture Fort Mackinac, on Lake Huron, on July 17. Fort Dearborn (modern-day Chicago) falls on August 15, and the next day, at Detroit, General William Hull surrenders his 2,500 men to a force of 1,300 Canadians and Indians under Brigadier General Sir Isaac Brock.

August 9.   A British squadron bombards Stonington, Connecticut.

August 13.   **Essex vs. Alert.** The frigate *Essex*, 32, Master Commandant David Porter, captures the sloop *Alert*, 20, Captain Thomas L. P. Laugharne, after an eight-minute action in the Atlantic. The *Alert* is the first British warship taken in the War of 1812.

August 19.   **Constitution vs. Guerrière.** The war's first battle between frigates results in an American victory when the *Constitution*, 44, Captain Isaac Hull, dismasts and captures the *Guerrière*, 38, Captain James R. Dacres, in a 40-minute action 700 miles east of Boston. The *Guerrière*, which is so badly damaged that she must be sunk, loses 23 men killed and 56 wounded; the *Constitution*, 7 and 7, respectively. The news of this victory, following the dreary succession of defeats on land, sends a wave of jubilation throughout the country.

September 3.   **War on the Great Lakes.** Commodore Isaac Chauncey, commandant of the New York Navy Yard, is ordered to take command on Lake Erie and Lake Ontario. British control of the lakes had played a

The *Constitution* vs. the *Guerrière: Dropping Astern,* the third of a series of four paintings of the action done for Captain Hull by Michel F. Corné. *Courtesy U.S. Naval Academy Museum.*

crucial role in General Brock's victories in July and August. Establishing his headquarters at Sacket's Harbor, New York, on the eastern shore of Lake Ontario, Chauncey begins a building race that will continue throughout the war.

October 8.   **Action on Lake Erie.** Before daybreak, the British brigs *Detroit,* 6, and *Caledonia,* 2, are captured off Fort Erie by two boat parties under the command of Lieutenant Jesse D. Elliott.

October 8.   On Lake Ontario, the brig *Oneida,* 16, and four schooners under Commodore Chauncey pursue the British sloop *Royal George,* 22, into Kingston Harbor, where she runs aground under cover of the shore batteries.

October 18.   **Wasp vs. Frolic.** Five days out of Philadelphia, the sloop *Wasp,* 18, Master Commandant Jacob Jones, encounters a British merchant convoy of six ships escorted by the sloop *Frolic,* 18, Captain T. Whinyates, which she attacks. The *Frolic* surrenders to a boarding party led by Lieutenant James Biddle after a spirited action of 43 minutes. American losses are 5 men killed and the same number wounded out of a crew of 135; British losses, approximately 30 killed and 45 wounded of a crew of 110. A few hours later the *Wasp* and her prize, both more-or-less crippled, are captured by the British 74-gun ship-of-the-line *Poictiers,* Captain John Poer Beresford.

October 25.   **United States vs. Macedonian.** The British frigate *Macedonian,* 38, Captain John S. Carden, surrenders to the frigate *United States,* 44, Captain Stephen Decatur, after an action lasting one hour and 50 minutes in the central Atlantic. British casualties are 36 killed and 48 wounded; American, 5 killed and 7

wounded. A prize crew sails the *Macedonian* to Newport, Rhode Island, where she is repaired and taken into the U.S. Navy.

October 28–March 28, 1814.   **Second cruise of the Essex.** The frigate *Essex,* 32, Captain David Porter, sails from Chester, Pennsylvania, to join the frigate *Constitution* and sloop *Hornet* on a raid on British commerce extending as far as the Indian Ocean. Failing to make contact with these vessels at the prearranged rendezvous in the South Atlantic, Porter decides to proceed into the Pacific on a voyage in which the *Essex* will become the first American warship to round Cape Horn, destroy the British whaling industry, and annex America's first overseas territory.

November 9.   On Lake Ontario, a squadron of seven American ships under Commodore Isaac Chauncey shells the forts guarding Kingston, on the Canadian shore, but withdraws when the weather becomes threatening.

November 19.   An attempted invasion of Canada along the Lake Champlain route by an army of 5,000 men under Major General Henry Dearborn is stymied when his militia units refuse to leave American soil.

November 22.   The schooner *Vixen,* 12, Lieutenant George W. Read, is captured by the British frigate *Southampton,* 32, Captain Sir James L. Yeo, in the West Indies.

November 29.   **Constitution vs. Java.** The U.S. Navy wins its third consecutive frigate action when the *Constitution,* 44, Captain William Bainbridge, meets the *Java,* 44, Captain Henry Lambert, 30 miles off the coast of Brazil. The two vessels are relatively well matched and the engagement, which lasts almost two hours, is the

The *Constitution* vs. the *Java:* a preliminary study by Michel F. Corné. *Official U.S. Navy photograph.*

hardest fought of the frigate actions to date. In the end, the Americans' superior gunnery and slightly heavier broadside are decisive. British casualties number 122 of the crew of 426; American, 34 of 475.

December 26.   **British blockade.** Britain proclaims a blockade of the Chesapeake and Delaware Bays. Leaving New York and the New England states open to trade is intended to divide American opinion and strengthen antiwar sentiment in New England.

1813

January 2.   **Naval build-up.** Congress authorizes the construction of two 74-gun ships of the line (the navy's first) and six 44-gun frigates.

January 13.   The British blockade of the Chesapeake and Delaware Bays, announced in December, is made real by the arrival on the American coast of a squadron commanded by Rear Admiral Sir George Cockburn.

January 17.   The brig *Viper*, 10, Lieutenant John D. Henley, is captured by the British frigate *Narcissus*, 38, Captain John Richard Lumley, off Belize, British Honduras.

January 19.   William Jones becomes the fourth secretary of the navy.

February 14.   **The Essex in the Pacific.** The frigate *Essex*, 32, Captain David Porter, rounds Cape Horn into the Pacific, where she will virtually destroy the British whaling fleet, taking 12 prizes around the Galápagos Islands from April through July. She also recaptures the American whaler *Barclay* and disarms the Peruvian privateer *Nereyda*.

February 17.   Master Commandant Oliver Hazard Perry is ordered to assume command of American naval forces on Lake Erie.

February 24.   **Hornet vs. Peacock.** The sloop *Hornet*, 18, Master Commandant James Lawrence, defeats the British brig *Peacock*, 18, Captain William Peake, in a brief action off British Guiana. The *Hornet* has four men killed and four wounded; the *Peacock*, which sinks immediately after the action, has five killed and thirty-three wounded.

March 4.   **British on the Chesapeake.** Rear Admiral Sir George Cockburn enters the bay with the ship-of-the-line *Marlborough*, 74, several frigates, and a number of smaller vessels. Joined later by Vice Admiral Sir John B. Warren, commander of the North American Station, with additional ships of all classes, Cockburn remains on the Chesapeake until the end of June, send-

Commodore Oliver Hazard Perry, by an unknown artist. *Courtesy U.S. Naval Academy Museum.*

ing expeditions up the navigable rivers of tidewater Maryland and Virginia to destroy shipping, supplies, and stores. Personal property is generally respected, but where resistance is offered (as it is at Havre-de-Grace, Fredericktown, and Georgetown) unoccupied dwellings are put to the torch.

April 9.   The British privateer *Caledonia*, 8, is captured by the schooner *Nonsuch*, 14, Sailing Master James Mork, off the southern Atlantic coast.

April 27–May 8.   **Capture of York.** On Lake Ontario, Commodore Isaac Chauncey's squadron, now grown to number 12 vessels, lands an expedition of 1,700 men under Major General Henry Dearborn, which briefly occupies York (now Toronto), the capital of Upper Canada. The British schooner *Duke of Gloucester*, 10, is captured, and the nearly completed 24-gun sloop *Sir Isaac Brock* is destroyed on the stocks. Contrary to orders, the troops burn the government buildings at York.

May 27.   Nine of Commodore Chauncey's ships cooperate with 4,000 troops under Colonel Winfield Scott in an amphibious operation that captures Fort George at the mouth of the Niagara River.

May 28–29.   A British amphibious assault on Sacket's Harbor, the American naval base on Lake Ontario, is repulsed by New York militia.

The *Chesapeake* vs. the *Shannon:* a contemporary engraving (undated) published in London under the supervision of a British officer who had served in the *Shannon. Courtesy Beverley R. Robinson Collection, U.S. Naval Academy Museum.*

June 1.   **Chesapeake vs. Shannon.** The succession of American frigate victories comes to an end when Captain James Lawrence, newly appointed to command the *Chesapeake,* 36, at Boston, takes his ship out with an untrained and disaffected crew to engage the *Shannon,* 38, Captain Philip B. V. Broke, probably the best-drilled frigate in the Royal Navy. Lawrence is mortally wounded at the opening of the action and carried below, calling, "Don't give up the ship!" The *Shannon's* raking broadsides quickly clear the *Chesapeake's* spardeck, and Broke leads a boarding party that secures the ship after a short, sharp fight, during which he is badly wounded by a cutlass blow to the skull. From start to finish, the engagement lasts only 15 minutes. American casualties are 148 men killed and wounded; British, 83. Captain Broke is made a knight baronet.

June 3.   The sloops *Growler* and *Eagle* are captured by British gunboats in the Sorel river, at the northern end of Lake Champlain.

June 13.   Future admiral David Dixon Porter is born in Chester, Pennsylvania.

June 18–August 14.   **Cruise of the Argus.** The brig *Argus,* 16, Lieutenant William Henry Allen, carries U.S. Min-ister W. H. Crawford to France and then captures 20 British merchant ships in a daring raid in the English Channel.

July 14.   **Gamble of the Greenwich.** In the South Pacific the armed whaler *Greenwich,* 10, a prize of the frigate *Essex,* engages and captures the British privateer *Seringapatam,* 22. What makes this event unusual is that the *Greenwich's* captain is Lieutenant James Marshall Gamble, USMC, who remains today the only marine officer ever to have commanded a ship. He was given the *Greenwich* when the *Essex* ran out of naval officers to use as prize captains.

July 30.   York, the capital of Upper Canada, is captured for a second time by an amphibious expedition consisting of 12 ships of Commodore Chauncey's squadron and 300 regulars under Colonel Winfield Scott. The landing is unopposed and the expedition withdraws the next day, having captured various military material.

August 7–11.   On Lake Ontario, Commodore Chauncey's squadron of 13 vessels (128 guns) spars with Captain Sir James L. Yeo's British squadron of 6 vessels (99 guns) without ever coming to close quarters. Two American ships, the schooners *Scourge,* 12, and *Hamil-*

Lieutenant James Marshall Gamble, USMC, shown as a brevet lieutenant colonel in a painting by A. de Rose, circa 1830. *Defense Department photograph (Marine Corps).*

ton, 9, sink in a storm on August 8, and the gunboats *Growler,* 2, and *Julia,* 2, are captured on August 10.

August 14.   **Argus vs. Pelican.** The brig *Argus,* 16, Lieutenant William Henry Allen, is captured by the British brig *Pelican,* 18, Captain John F. Maples, off the coast of Ireland. American casualties are 10 killed, including Allen, and 14 wounded; British, 2 killed and 5 wounded.

September 5.   **Enterprise vs. Boxer.** The *Enterprise,* 16, Lieutenant William Burrows, captures the British brig *Boxer,* 14, Lieutenant Samuel Blythe, in an action fought off Portland, Maine. Burrows is the only man killed on the American side.

September 10.   **Battle of Lake Erie.** The most important naval action of the war to date is fought hundreds of miles from the sea, when a squadron of nine ships mounting 54 guns under 28-year-old Commodore Oliver Hazard Perry meets a British squadron of six ships mounting 64 guns under Commodore Robert H. Barclay, a one-armed veteran of the Battle of Trafalgar. Closing the British line in his flagship, the brig *Lawrence,* 20, behind the schooners *Ariel,* 4, and *Scorpion,* 2, Perry is left to fight alone for two hours, the remainder of his squadron inexplicably failing to come to his support. When the *Lawrence* is completely disabled, he rows back to the brig *Niagara,* 20, and returns

The Battle of Lake Erie: a contemporary engraving (undated) published in Philadelphia. *Courtesy Beverley R. Robinson Collection, U.S. Naval Academy Museum.*

to break the British line. Every ship in the enemy squadron is taken. This victory gives the Americans control of Lake Erie and enables General William Henry Harrison, who has assembled an army of 7,000 men on its southern shore, to launch an offensive to recover Detroit.

September 11.   Commodore Chauncey's squadron engages in another inconclusive, long-range action with the British on Lake Ontario.

September 22.   The British schooner *High Flyer,* 5, Lieutenant William Hutchinson, a tender to the ship-of-the-line *St. Domingo,* is captured in the Atlantic by the frigate *President,* 44, Commodore John Rodgers.

September 28.   Still another indecisive action is fought on Lake Ontario by Commodore Chauncey's squadron against a smaller British force under Captain Sir James L. Yeo.

September 29.   The American army of General William Henry Harrison, most of which is transported across Lake Erie in Perry's ships, recaptures Detroit and pursues the British up the Thames River.

October 4.   The British privateer *Dart,* 6, Captain Ross, is boarded and captured by the revenue cutter *Vigilant,* Captain John Cahoone, off Newport, Rhode Island.

October 5.   **Battle of the Thames.** With 3,500 men, General Harrison overtakes and effectively destroys Brigadier General Henry A. Proctor's army of 1,800 British regulars and Indian warriors. This action leaves the Americans in lasting control of the northwestern theater.

October 5.   On Lake Ontario, the small British schooners *Drummond, Lady Gore, Mary, Hamilton* (ex-USS *Growler*), and *Confiance* (ex-USS *Julia*) are captured by the corvette *General Pike,* 24, Lieutenant Arthur Sinclair, schooners *Sylph,* 16, *Governor Tomkins,* 6, and *Lady of the Lake,* 5.

October 25.   **Battle of Chateauguay.** Another American advance on Canada up Lake Champlain, this time by an army of 4,000 men under Brigadier General Wade Hampton, is repulsed by 1,000 Canadians and Indians.

November 19.   In the South Pacific, Captain David Porter of the frigate *Essex* annexes Nukahiva Island, in the Marquesas, to the United States. Informed months later, the U.S. Government ignores his initiative.

December 18–31.   **Defeats on the Niagara frontier.** Following the surrender of Fort Niagara, at the mouth of the Niagara River on the southern shore of Lake Ontario, British and Indian forces advance into New York, capturing and burning Buffalo, Black Rock, and several villages. The American schooners *Chippewa,* 3,

and *Little Belt,* 3, and sloop *Trippe,* 1, are destroyed in Buffalo Creek.

December 25.   The brig *Vixen* (II), 14, Captain Thomas Hall, is captured by the British frigate *Belvidera,* 36, Captain Richard Byron, off the middle Atlantic seaboard.

1814

February 2.   The schooner *Ferret,* 8, Lieutenant Lawrence Kearny, wrecks without loss of life at Stono Inlet, North Carolina.

February 28.   **Capture of the Essex.** The frigate *Essex,* 32, Captain David Porter, is forced to strike her colors after a grueling action of two-and-a-half hours off Valparaiso, Chile, with the frigate *Phoebe,* 36, Captain James Hillyar, and sloop *Cherub,* 28, Captain Thomas J. Tucker. All except 6 of the 46 guns the *Essex* actually carried are short-range carronades. The two British ships keep out of range of the carronades, skillfully avoiding Porter's attempts to close, and pound the *Essex* to pieces. By the time of the surrender, the *Essex* has lost 58 men killed, 65 wounded, and 31 missing— 60 percent of her crew. British losses are 5 dead and 10 wounded.

April.   **British offensive.** With the defeat of Napoleon, whose first abdication is signed on April 6, the British government is able to apply more of its resources to the war in North America. Its plans include a series of raids on the eastern seaboard, principally in the Chesapeake Bay area; a major invasion of the northeastern United States down the Lake Champlain corridor; and the capture of New Orleans.

April 7.   A British landing party raids Pettipaug, Connecticut, destroying 20 boats.

April 20.   **Loss of the Frolic.** The ship sloop *Frolic,* 18, Master Commandent Joseph Bainbridge, is captured by the British frigate *Orpheus,* 36, Captain Hugh Pigot, in the Florida Straits.

April 23.   The British blockade is extended to cover the entire coastline of the United States.

April 29.   **Peacock vs. Epervier.** The British brig *Epervier,* 18, Captain Richard W. Wales, is captured by the ship sloop *Peacock,* 18, Master Commandent Lewis Warrington, after an action lasting 45 minutes off Cape Canaveral, Florida.

May 6.   A British amphibious expedition commanded by Captain Sir James L. Yeo captures Fort Oswego, on the southern shore of Lake Ontario, and the schooner *Growler*, 2. This is the third time that vessel has changed hands.

May–December.   **British return to the Chesapeake.** Establishing an advanced base at Tangier Island, at the mouth of the bay, powerful British amphibious forces under Rear Admiral Sir George Cockburn appear in the Chesapeake for the second consecutive summer. Once again, they will sweep the Tidewater, but this time they will also attack Washington and Baltimore.

June 8–10.   In St. Leonard's Creek off the Patuxent River, Maryland, the 13 gunboats off Commodore Joshua Barney's Chesapeake Bay Flotilla repulse repeated attacks by British boat parties.

June 19.   On Lake Ontario, three boats commanded by Lieutenant Francis H. Gregory capture and scuttle the British gunboat *Blacksnake*, 1, Lieutenant H. Landon.

June 22.   The brig *Rattlesnake*, 14, Lieutenant James Renshaw, is captured by the British frigate *Leander*, 50, Captain Sir George R. Collier, off Cape Sable, Nova Scotia.

June 26.   The British frigates *Loire*, Captain T. Brown, and *Narcissus*, Captain John R. Lumley, retire down the Patuxent River, Maryland, after being shelled by Commodore Joshua Barney's Chesapeake Bay Flotilla.

June 28.   **Wasp vs. Reindeer.** The new sloop *Wasp*, 18, Master Commandant Johnston Blakeley, captures the British brig *Reindeer*, 18, Captain William Manners, after a 29-minute action in the North Atlantic. Captain Manners is killed leading a gallant attempt to board the *Wasp*. American losses are 11 dead and 15 wounded from a crew of 173; the British, 33 dead and 34 wounded from a crew of 118.

July 1.   At Presqu'ile, Lake Ontario, a boat party commanded by Lieutenant Francis H. Gregory burns a 10-gun British schooner on the stocks ready for launching.

July 14.   Off the coast of New England, *Gunboat No. 88*, Sailing Master G. Clement, captures the British schooner *Chebacque*, Lieutenant C. L. Baker.

July 20.   **Operations on Lake Huron.** Captain Arthur Sinclair enters Lake Huron in command of an amphibious expedition composed of the brigs *Niagara*, 20, *Lawrence*, 20, and *Caledonia*, 3, and the schooners *Scorpion*, 2, and *Tigress*, 1, with 750 troops embarked. His mission is to disrupt the British fur trade and recapture Fort Mackinac. Operations begin on this date with the destruction of the trading post and fort at St. Joseph's. The post at Sault-St.-Marie suffers the same fate, but an attack on Fort Mackinac on August 4 is repulsed.

Sinclair then destroys the blockhouse at the mouth of the Nautawassaga River, through which Mackinac is supplied, and leaves the *Scorpion* and *Tigress* to blockade the river mouth.

July 25.   An American invasion of Canada across the Niagara River is checked at the Battle of Lundy's Lane, near Niagara Falls.

July 31.   On Lake Ontario, the British brig *Magnet*, 14, is chased ashore and burned by the schooner *Sylph*, 16, Master Commandant Jesse D. Elliott.

August 12.   British parties led by Captain Alexander Dobbs of the brig *Charwell* carry six boats 28 miles overland from Lake Ontario to Lake Erie to surprise and capture the American schooners *Somers*, 2, and *Ohio*, 1, Lieutenant Augustus Conkling.

August 14–17.   The British forces already operating in the Chesapeake Bay are joined by a squadron under Vice Admiral Sir Alexander Cochrane with transports carrying 5,400 veteran troops under Major General Robert Ross for the attack on Washington.

August 19.   **March on Washington.** General Ross's army lands unopposed at Benedict, on the Patuxent River, Maryland, to begin its advance on the U.S. capital.

August 22.   Commodore Joshua Barney burns the boats of his Chesapeake flotilla on the upper Patuxent and takes his crews—approximately 400 seamen and marines— to join the land forces assembling to defend Washington.

August 24.   **Battle of Bladensburg.** An American force of 6,500 men, mostly militia, is routed by the advance guard of General Ross's army in a brief action east of the capital. Only Commodore Barney's naval brigade and a handful of U.S. regulars stand by their guns. Barney and marine Captain Samuel Miller are wounded and captured covering the retreat.

August 24–25.   **Burning of Washington.** The British army occupies Washington, setting fire to the White House and other public buildings in retaliation for the burning of York (see April 27, 1813). At the Navy Yard, the old frigates *Boston*, *General Greene*, and *New York* and two ships under construction, the frigate *Columbia* and sloop *Argus* (II), are destroyed to prevent their capture.

August 28.   A second British force, advancing up the Potomac, occupies Alexandria, Virginia.

August 30.   General Ross's British army reembarks at Benedict on the Patuxent and proceeds up the Chesapeake Bay to Baltimore.

September 1.   Castine and Belfast, Maine, are captured by a British amphibious expedition under Captain Hyde Parker.

September 1.   Wasp vs. Avon. The sloop *Wasp,* 18, Master Commandant Johnston Blakeley, sinks the British brig *Avon,* 18, Captain the Honourable James Arbuthnot, in a night action in the eastern Atlantic.

September 1, 4. On Lake Huron, the schooners *Tigress,* 1, Sailing Master Champlin, and *Scorpion,* 2, Midshipman Henry B. Turner, are captured in boarding actions led by Lieutenant A. H. Bulger, Royal Newfoundland Regiment, and Lieutenant Worseley, RN.

September 3. The frigate *Adams,* 28, Captain Charles Morris, is burned to prevent her capture at Hampden, Maine.

September 11.   Battle of Lake Champlain. The major British military effort of the war begins in August, when an army of 11,000 men under Major General Sir George Prevost, Governor General of Canada, moves down the Richelieu River towards Lake Champlain and the Hudson River Valley—the same route taken by Carleton in 1777 and Burgoyne in 1778. To oppose him on land, the Americans muster only 1,500 regulars and perhaps 3,000 militia, with which Brigadier General Alexander Macomb fortifies a position below Plattsburg, on the western shore of Lake Champlain; but Prevost believes, as had Carleton, that to continue his advance he must hold command of the lake, which is contested by Commodore Thomas Macdonough's American squadron, com-

Commodore Thomas Macdonough, by Gilbert Stuart. *Courtesy National Gallery of Art, Mellon Collection.*

posed of the corvette *Saratoga,* 26 (flag), brig *Eagle,* 20, schooner *Ticonderoga,* 17, sloop *Preble,* 7, and 10 gunboats. On this date Macdonough's ships, anchored bow to stern in Plattsburg Bay, await the attack of a British squadron consisting of the frigate *Confiance,* 37 (flag), brig *Linnet,* 16, sloop *Chub,* 11, and *Finch,* 11, and 13 gunboats under Commodore George Downie. In an action of two hours and 20 minutes, all four of the principal British vessels are forced to surrender, 3 gunboats are sunk, and the others are put to flight. General Prevost begins a precipitate retreat to Canada that evening. This event, more than any other, convinces the British government to seek peace.

September 11–October 1.   Action against Lafitte. The pirate stronghold of Jean Lafitte on Barataria Island, near the mouth of the Mississippi, is attacked by an expedition under Commodore Daniel T. Patterson, consisting of the schooners *Carolina,* 14, and *Seahorse,* 1, and six gunboats, supported by 70 men of the 44th Infantry. The settlement is burned, and 11 vessels, mounting up to 20 guns, are captured.

September 12–14.   Attack on Baltimore. The British army of Major General Robert Ross, fresh from the scorching of Washington, lands at North Point, on the Patapsco River, while Vice Admiral Sir Alexander Cochrane's ships continue upstream and begin to bombard Fort McHenry, commanding Baltimore harbor. Ross is mortally wounded in action with militia who do not run away, and Fort McHenry, the defense of which eyewitness Francis Scott Key immortalizes in "The Star-Spangled Banner," is not silenced. The British reembark.

September 24. *Gunboat No. 23,* 5, Lieutenant Isaac McKeever, captures a pirate craft off Southwest Pass, Mississippi.

September 26–27.   Defense of the General Armstrong. The American privateer *General Armstrong,* 8, Captain Samuel C. Reid, is attacked after nightfall in the neutral port of Fayal, in the Azores, by boat parties from the ship-of-the-line *Plantagenet,* 74, frigate *Rota,* 38, and brig *Carnation,* 18. The boats are beaten off with heavy losses, those of the *Rota* alone having 34 men killed and 85 wounded, against American casualties of 2 dead and 7 wounded. At dawn the *Carnation* stands in to engage, whereupon Reid sets fire to his ship and leads his men ashore.

October 9. The sloop *Wasp,* Master Commandant, Johnston Blakeley, vanishes at sea, being last sighted on this date.

October 29.   **The Demologos (Fulton I).** The world's first steam-powered warship is launched in New York. Designed by Robert Fulton for harbor defense, it is propelled by a central paddle wheel and carries 32 cannon.

December 8.   **Beginning of the campaign for New Orleans.** The leading elements of a major British amphibious expedition that includes 7,500 battle-hardened Peninsula veterans under Major General Sir Edward M. Pakenham anchor at Chandeleur Island off the mouth of the Mississippi. Vice Admiral Sir Alexander Cochrane decides that in view of the difficulty of contending with the Mississippi currents, the advance on New Orleans will be made by way of Lake Borgne.

December 13.   The British passage through Lake Borgne is barred by a tiny American squadron of five gunboats and two tenders under Lieutenant Thomas ap Catesby Jones. On this date one of the tenders, the schooner *Seahorse,* 1, Sailing Master William Johnson, is burned to prevent her capture, after first repelling an attack by seven British launches.

December 14.   Jones's other tender, the sloop *Alligator,* 1, Sailing Master Richard S. Shepperd, is captured while attempting to join his gunboats.

December 14.   **Battle of Lake Borgne.** Lieutenant Thomas ap Catesby Jones's five gunboats, anchored in the line of battle, are overwhelmed by 42 British barges commanded by Captain Nicholas Lockyer, RN, after an action lasting an hour and 40 minutes. American casualties are 6 men killed and 35 wounded, including Lieutenant Jones; British, 17 killed and 77 wounded, including Captain Lockyer.

December 23.   The schooner *Carolina,* 14, Master Commandant John D. Henley, drops down the Mississippi from New Orleans and shells the British forces encamped at Villeré's plantation.

December 24.   **Treaty of Ghent.** At Ghent, Belgium, where peace negotiations began in August, American and British commissioners agree on a simple return to the prewar *status quo.* Britain refuses to relinquish the right of impressment, but having vanquished Napoleon, no longer needs to practice it. The treaty does not reach the United States until February 15, 1815, and hostilities continue for some months.

December 27.   On the Mississippi River below New Orleans, the schooner *Carolina,* 14, Master Commandant John D. Henley, is destroyed by red-hot shot from British land batteries.

December 29–31.   **Naval battery at New Orleans.** Commodore Daniel T. Patterson lands guns from his remaining vessel, the sloop *Louisiana,* 16, to establish a naval battery on the west bank of the Mississippi, where its fire can cover the front of the fortifications General Andrew Jackson has built on the opposite bank.

The Battle of Lake Borgne: a painting by T. L. Hornbrook. *Courtesy U.S. Naval Academy Museum.*

1815

January 6. On Lake Borgne, Louisiana, the British brig *Cyprus*, 4, carrying clothing for Pakenham's army, is boarded and captured by a boat party of 38 men under Sailing Master William Johnson.

January 8. **Battle of New Orleans.** General Pakenham launches his troops against the American lines on both sides of the Mississippi. The naval battery on the west bank is overrun, but not before its flanking fire has contributed to the bloody repulse of the main attack on Jackson's position on the east bank. By midafternoon, when the fighting ends, the British have lost 2,036 men killed, wounded, and missing, including General Pakenham, who is picked off while leading an assault; the American losses are only 71. The attack is not renewed.

January 13–15. **Capture of the President.** Attempting to run the blockade out of New York, the frigate *President*, 44, Captain Stephen Decatur, encounters the British frigates *Majestic*, 54, *Endymion*, 24, *Pomone*, and *Tenedos*. After a long chase, Decatur turns and disables the *Endymion*, but this allows the *Pomone* and *Tenedos* to overtake him. With almost 20 percent of his crew already dead or wounded, Decatur deems the situation hopeless and strikes his flag.

January 16. Benjamin Crowninshield becomes the fifth secretary of the navy.

January 19–21. Six boats carrying 50 men under the command of Purser Thomas Shields capture two British schooners, a launch, and six boats on Lake Borgne, Louisiana.

January 29. Off North Edisto, South Carolina, Lieutenant Lawrence Kearny leads 25 men in three barges to board and capture the tender and launch of the British frigate *Hebrus*.

February 7. **Board of Navy Commissioners.** A permanent board of three senior captains is established to supervise all matters relating to naval construction, equipment, and repair. Its first members are Commodores John Rodgers, David Porter, and Isaac Hull (soon replaced by Stephen Decatur).

February 17. **Official end of the War of 1812.** Congress ratifies the Treaty of Ghent.

February 20. **Constitution vs. Levant and Cyane.** Some 180 miles east of Madeira, the frigate *Constitution*, 44, Captain Charles Stewart, encounters the British frigate *Cyane*, 34, Captain Thomas G. Falcon, and sloop *Levant*, 18, Captain the Honourable George Douglas. Although the two British ships together are superior to his own, by skillful seamanship Stewart engages and captures each in turn.

The *Constitution* captures the *Levant* and *Cyane:* a contemporary lithograph from *U.S. Military Magazine. Courtesy Beverley R. Robinson Collection, U.S. Naval Academy Museum.*

March 2.   **War with Algiers.** The Dey of Algiers, dissatisfied with the tribute being paid him, has expelled the U.S. consul and renewed the attack on American merchant shipping, capturing the brig *Edwin* of Salem and enslaving her crew. Eight days after the conclusion of peace with Great Britain, President Madison urges Congress to declare war on Algiers. It does so on this date.

March 23.   **Hornet vs. Penguin.** The sloop *Hornet,* 18, Master Commandant James Biddle, takes the British sloop *Penguin,* 19, Commander James Dickenson, off the island of Tristan de Cunha in the South Atlantic.

May 20.   **Decatur sails for the Mediterranean.** An American squadron of three frigates—the *Guerrière,* 44, *Constellation,* 36, and *Macedonian,* 38—and seven smaller vessels leaves New York under the command of Commodore Stephen Decatur to prosecute the war with Algiers.

June 17.   The Algerine flagship *Mashouda,* 46, Rais Hamida, is captured by the *Guerrière,* 44, *Constellation,* 36, *Ontario,* 18, and *Epervier,* 18. Thirty of her crewmen are killed and 406 made prisoner.

June 19.   A second Algerine vessel, the brig *Estedio,* 22, is run aground by four of Decatur's smaller ships off Cape de Gata.

June 30.   **Peace with Algiers.** The Dey of Algiers accepts a treaty of peace, dictated in Decatur's words, "at the mouths of our cannons." According to its terms, Algiers releases the American prisoners, pays a $10,000 indemnity for the attack on the *Edwin,* and relinquishes her claim to tribute from the United States.

June 30.   **Peacock vs. Nautilus.** The final naval action of the War of 1812 is fought in the Sunda Strait by the sloop *Peacock,* 18, Master Commandant Lewis Warrington, and the East India Company brig *Nautilus,* 14, Lieutenant Charles Boyce. Boyce first hailed the *Peacock,* reporting that the war was over, but Warrington would not take his word for it. The *Nautilus* surrenders after a brief action in which she has six men killed and eight wounded.

July 3.   A second American squadron of nine ships under Commodore William Bainbridge sails for the Mediterranean to reinforce Decatur.

July 14.   **Loss of the Epervier.** The sloop-of-war *Epervier,* 18, Lieutenant John T. Shubrick, sails from Gibraltar for the United States and disappears en route.

July 26.   **Settling with Tunis.** Proceeding from Algiers to Tunis, Decatur learns that during the War of 1812 the Bey violated the terms of his treaty with the United States by allowing the British to repossess prizes an American privateer had sent into port. As compensation for this misbehavior, Decatur demands $46,000. It is duly, albeit reluctantly, paid.

August 5.   Continuing to Tripoli, whose Pasha also has turned American prizes over to the British, Decatur demands and collects a $25,000 indemnity.

1816

April 29.   **Naval build-up.** Taking the lessons of the War of 1812 to heart, Congress appropriates $8,000,000 to be spent over an eight-year period to complete or begin construction of nine 74-gun ships of the line and twelve frigates of 44 guns.

December 23.   **End of the Barbary Wars.** A final treaty of peace is signed by the United States and Algiers.

1818

August 19.   The Oregon Territory is claimed for the United States by Captain James Biddle of the sloop *Ontario,* who lands at Cape Disappointment on the Columbia River. According to the terms of the Anglo-American Convention of 1818, the territory will be jointly occupied by the United States and Great Britain.

1819

January 1.   Smith Thompson enters office as sixth secretary of the navy.

February 26.   **War against pirates.** The Caribbean swarms with pirates, many outfitted with meaningless letters of marque issued by the governments of Spain and her rebellious South American colonies. Hundreds of merchantmen are plundered annually. On this date, Congress passes an act, signed by President James Monroe on March 3, "to protect the commerce of the United States, and to punish the crime of piracy." Navy vessels are authorized to convoy American merchant ships and to recapture those unlawfully seized at sea.

March 3.   **Slave patrol.** Congress passes an act authorizing the president to use the navy to suppress American participation in the West African slave trade. To carry out the prerequisite patrols and also to support the colonization of Liberia by American blacks, an African Squadron is established in 1820. Deactivated three years later, after which only individual ships are intermittently on station, it is reestablished following the conclusion of the Webster-Ashburton Treaty with Britain in 1842.

March 3.   Major Anthony Gale becomes fourth commandant of the marine corps.

August 13.   Commodore Oliver Hazard Perry dies of yellow fever aboard the schooner *Nonsuch* at Trinidad after a diplomatic mission to Venezuela. He was thirty-four.

1820

March 22.   **Decatur-Barron duel.** Commodore Stephen Decatur is mortally wounded in a duel with Commodore James Barron at Bladensburg, Maryland, a short distance outside the District of Columbia. Once close friends, they had become estranged when Decatur, despite his request to be excused, was ordered to sit on the court-martial that found Barron guilty of negligence in the *Chesapeake-Leopard* affair. During his suspension from duty Barron entered the merchant marine. Caught in Europe at the outbreak of the War of 1812, he did not return home to reenter the service until the conclusion of peace. Although Barron claimed that it had been impossible for him to arrange passage during the conflict, many officers ascribed his absence to cowardice. Hearing that Decatur was among this number, Barron challenged him, hoping in this manner to demonstrate his courage. There is something very close to a reconciliation between the two men on the dueling field, and had their seconds (Commodore William Bainbridge for Decatur and Captain Jesse D. Elliot for Barron) shown proper initiative, the quarrel could probably have been resolved without bloodshed. As it is, neither of them shoots to kill. Barron is hit in the thigh. Decatur is struck in the hip by a ball that ricochets up into his groin. He dies, aged forty, after 12 hours of extreme agony. Barron recovers and lives on eventually to become the most senior officer in the navy, but he is never given command at sea.

April 5–12.   Five slave ships are captured by the frigate *Cyane,* 34, Captain Edward Trenchard, between Cape Mount and the mouth of the River Gallinas (now the Moa) off present-day Liberia.

May 16.   The frigate *Congress,* 36, Captain J. D. Henley, sails from Hampton Roads, Virginia, to become the first U.S. naval vessel to visit China. She arrives there in December.

October 17.   Brevet Major Archibald Henderson is appointed fifth commandant of the marine corps, which post he will hold for almost 40 years.

1821

January 21.   The schooner *Lynx,* 6, Lieutenant J.R. Madison, sails from St. Mary's, Georgia, for the West Indies and disappears en route. She probably wrecked on Carysfort Reef, Florida.

May 17–25.   Four French slavers are captured off the mouth of the River Gallinas (now the Moa) on the west coast of Africa by the schooner *Alligator,* 12, Lieutenant Robert F. Stockton.

October 16.   The brig *Enterprise,* 16, Lieutenant Lawrence Kearny, discovers four pirate schooners and a sloop in the act of plundering three American merchantmen off Cape San Antonio, Cuba. The pirates set fire to two of their vessels and attempt to escape in the others, but all are captured.

October 29.   The pirate schooner *Moscow* is captured off the coast of Santo Domingo by the sloop *Hornet,* 18, Captain Robert Henley.

November 5.   **Alligator vs. Marianno Flora.** The schooner *Alligator,* 12, Lieutenant Robert F. Stockton, is fired on by the Portuguese warship *Marianno Flora,* 12, in the central Atlantic. The latter is then captured after an action of one hour and twenty minutes.

November 8.   The schooner *Porpoise,* Lieutenant James Ramage, destroys a pirate vessel off Cape San Antonio, Cuba.

December 21.   A pirate schooner is burned by the brig *Enterprise,* 16, Lieutenant Lawrence Kearny, near Cape San Antonio, Cuba. The *Enterprise* also lands a party that destroys the pirate base ashore.

1822

January 7.   In the West Indies, the brig *Spark,* 12, Lieutenant John H. Elton, recaptures a Dutch merchantman taken by pirates and lands a party that destroys a pirate base.

January 7.   A boat expedition from the schooner *Porpoise,* 12, Lieutenant James Ramage, destroys a pirate base and six vessels near Bahia Honda, Cuba.

March 7.   The schooner *Revenge* (formerly *Gunboat No. 158*), 1, Lieutenant G.W. Hamersley, captures a pirate barge in the West Indies.

March 8.   Seven small pirate vessels are destroyed off Cape San Antonio, Cuba, by the brig *Enterprise,* 16, Lieutenant Lawrence Kearny.

March 26.   **Foundation of the West India Squadron.** Commodore James Biddle is given command and charged with protecting American shipping and suppressing piracy off the coasts of Cuba, Puerto Rico, and Central America. The force assigned him consists of the frigates *Congress,* 36, *John Adams,* 28, *Macedonian,* 38, and *Cyane,* 34; the sloops *Hornet,* 18, and *Peacock,* 18; the brigs *Enterprise,* 16, and *Spark,* 12; the schooners *Alligator,* 12, *Grampus,* 12, *Porpoise,* 12, *Shark,* 12, *Revenge,* 1; and *Gunboat No. 168.*

April 30.   The Columbian privateer *Cienega,* 5, is taken near the Windward Islands by the schooner *Alligator,* 12, Lieutenant W. W. McKean.

May 1.   Near Sugar Key, Cuba, boat parties from the *Alligator,* 12, *Grampus,* 12, and the chartered ship *Jane* commanded by Sailing Master Barney capture four pirate schooners and release a pirate prize.

June.   The schooners *Shark,* 12, Lieutenant Matthew C. Perry, and *Grampus,* 12, Lieutenant Francis H. Gregory, capture the pirate schooner *Bandera de Sangre* ("Bloody Banner") off the northern coast of Cuba.

August 16.   The privateer *Palmyra* (ex-*Pancheta*), 9, surrenders to the schooner *Grampus,* 12, Lieutenant Francis H. Gregory, after a brief action off Puerto Rico.

September 28–30.   Five pirate ships are captured, and the pirate settlement at Bahia Honda, Cuba, is destroyed by the sloop *Peacock,* 18, Captain Stephen Cassin, and revenue cutter *Louisiana,* 8.

November 9.   Three pirate schooners in possession of five American merchantmen are attacked in shoal water 45 miles east of Matanzas, Cuba, by boat parties led by Lieutenant William Howard Allen of the schooner *Alligator.* The merchant ships are freed, and one of the pirate schooners is captured. Allen is mortally wounded. The bodies of 14 pirates are counted.

November 19.   The *Alligator,* Lieutenant W. W. McKean, wrecks without loss of life on Carysfort Reef, Florida.

December 21.   Commodore David Porter is appointed commander of the West India Squadron.

1823

February 14.   **First steamer to see action.** Commodore Porter sails from New York to assume command of the West India Squadron. For inshore operations in the shallow waters of the Cuban and Puerto Rican coasts, he has ordered the construction of five 20-oared barges, the *Gallinipper, Gnat, Midge, Mosquito,* and *Sandfly,* and purchased eight small schooners (Chesapeake "bay boats"), each mounting three guns, the *Beagle, Ferret, Fox, Greyhound, Jackall, Terrier, Weasel,* and *Wild Cat;* the schooner *Decoy,* 6; and the former Hudson River ferryboat, *Sea Gull,* 3, a paddle-wheeler that becomes the first steamship in the world to enter combat.

March 6.   Lieutenant William H. Cocke, commanding the schooner *Fox,* is mortally wounded when his ship is fired on while entering San Juan, Puerto Rico. The Spanish governor apologizes for the error.

April 8.   Supported by the sloop *Peacock,* 18, Captain Stephen Cassin, the 20-oar barges *Gallinipper,* Lieu-

Commodore David Porter, by an unknown artist. *Courtesy U.S. Naval Academy Museum.*

tenant William H. Watson, and *Mosquito*, Lieutenant Cornelius K. Stribling, capture the pirate schooner *Pilot* near Havana, Cuba, and land marines to pursue the pirates ashore.

April 16.   The *Peacock* captures two pirate ships off Colorados, Cuba.

May 22.   Off Campeche, Mexico, two pirate vessels are captured by the schooner *Grampus*, 12, Lieutenant Francis H. Gregory.

July.   The pirate schooner *Catalina* and a launch under the pirate leader Diaboleto are captured near Sigaumpa Bay, Cuba, by the barges *Gallinipper*, Lieutenant William H. Watson, and *Mosquito*, Lieutenant W. T. Inman. Approximately 75 pirates are killed or captured. Diaboleto is among the former.

July 9.   The brig *Enterprise*, 16, Lieutenant Lawrence Kearny, is wrecked without loss of life on Little Curaçao Island in the West Indies.

July 22.   **Action at Cape Cruz, Cuba.** The schooners *Beagle*, 3, Lieutenant J. T. Newton, and *Greyhound*, 3, Lieutenant Lawrence Kearny, shell the pirate stronghold at Cape Cruz from the sea while a landing party of sailors and marines under Lieutenant David Glasgow Farragut circles around to attack from the rear. Eight armed boats are captured with the village.

August 3.   The Spanish schooner *Gallago Segunda*, 1, fires on and then surrenders to the schooner *Weasel*, 3, Lieutenant Beverley Kennon, off Colorados, Cuba. After adjudication, the vessel is returned to her owners.

September 16.   Samuel Southard enters office as seventh secretary of the navy.

December 2.   **Monroe Doctrine.** In his seventh annual message to Congress, President Monroe declares that the Americas "are henceforth not to be considered as subjects for the future colonization by any European powers . . . [and] that we should consider any attempt on their part to extend their system to any portion of this hemisphere as dangerous to our peace and safety." At this time the doctrine is supported principally by the ships of the Royal Navy, for Britain does not want to see Spanish authority and exclusionary trade policies reasserted in that country's former colonies in South and Central America.

1824

August 17.   A pirate launch is captured off Havana, Cuba, by the schooner *Terrier*, 3, Lieutenant Thomas Paine, Jr.

August 26.   The *Terrier* captures a pirate schooner in Bahia Honda, Cuba.

October 20.   Near Matanzas, Cuba, the schooner *Porpoise*, 12, Lieutenant Charles W. Skinner, supported by five boats under Lieutenant William M. Hunter, captures a pirate schooner and three boats.

October 27.   Accompanied by Midshipman Robert Ritchie, Lieutenant Charles Platt, commanding officer of the schooner *Beagle*, 3, lands at Fajardo, on the east coast of Puerto Rico, to confer with Spanish officials regarding the rumored presence in the town of property stolen from the American consul on St. Thomas. The local authorities pretend to disbelieve that he is an American officer, and he and Ritchie are detained most of the day.

October 28.   The schooner *Wild Cat*, 3, Midshipman L. M. Booth, is lost with all hands between Cuba and Thompson's Island, West Indies.

November 14.   **"Foxhardo" Affair.** Outraged by the treatment Lieutenant Platt received at Fajardo (see October 27), Commodore David Porter goes ashore with 200 seamen and marines from the frigate *John Adams* and sends a message to the town demanding an apology to the lieutenant. "If any resistance is made," he warns, "the total destruction of Foxhardo will be the certain and immediate consequence." The apology is promptly tendered. Upon returning to the United States in the spring of 1825, Porter is court-martialed for exceeding his instructions and suspended from duty for six months, albeit at full pay. Outraged again, he begins to investigate the possibility of obtaining a commission in the Mexican Navy.

December 27.   Captain Lewis Warrington succeeds David Porter as commodore of the West India Squadron.

1825

February 4.   The schooner *Ferret*, 3, Lieutenant C. H. Bell, capsizes in a storm off the Cuban coast with the loss of nine lives.

March 4.   The schooner *Grampus*, 12, Lieutenant John D. Sloat, captures a pirate sloop after an action of 45 minutes off Ponce, Puerto Rico. Sloat receives the thanks of the governor of Puerto Rico.

March 4.   A prize sloop with a crew of 26 men under Lieutenant G. Pendergast captures a pirate sloop near Boca del Inferno, West Indies, after a sharp action lasting 40 minutes.

March 25.   An Anglo-American expedition under Lieutenant Isaac McKeever of the barge *Gallinipper*, supported by boat parties from HMS *Dartmouth, Lion,* and *Union,* destroys a pirate lair at Rio Sagua la Grande, east of Matanzas, Cuba.

September 7.   The Marquis de Lafayette, "Hero of Two Worlds," ends a triumphant American tour by boarding the frigate *Brandywine* to return to France.

1826

July 1.   **Porter resigns.** Smarting under the censure he received for the "Foxhardo" Affair, Commodore David Porter resigns his commission after 28 years' service to accept the appointment of commander-in-chief of the Mexican Navy.

September 3.   **First U.S. Navy circumnavigation.** The new ship sloop *Vincennes*, 18, Captain W. B. Finch, sails for the Pacific to become the first U.S. naval vessel to sail around the world. She returns home in June 1830.

1827

October 4.   **Anti-pirate operations in the Mediterranean.** During the Greek war of independence from Turkey, now nearing its conclusion, the revolutionary government has licensed many privateers. Especially after the destruction of the Turkish fleet by an allied British, French, and Russian force at the Battle of Navarino in April 1827, these privateers swarm throughout the eastern Mediterranean, often crossing the line into piracy. On this date the sloop *Warren*, 18, Master Commandant Lawrence J. Kearny, captures a pirate brig of 16 guns and a pirate boat off the village of Carabusa in the Greek Cyclades Islands.

October 16.   The schooner *Porpoise*, 12, Lieutenant Benjamin Cooper, is convoying merchant ships from Smyrna, Turkey, to Port Mahon, Minorca. After nightfall one of her charges, an English brig, is attacked and captured by several Greek caiques in Doro Passage. Cooper lowers four boats carrying 40 men under Lieutenants Louis M. Goldsborough, John A. Carr, and Thomas J. Manning and Midshipman Alexander W. Wilson, who drive off the pirates, killing around 40, and recapture the brig. There are no American casualties.

October 25.   The sloop *Warren*, 18, Master Commandant Lawrence Kearny, pursues a Carabusan pirate brig of 10 guns, which grounds herself and sinks off Argenteira Island. The crew escapes ashore.

October 28.   The *Warren* recovers the captured American brig *Cherub* at Syra, Greece.

October 30–31.   Cruising off Miconi (Mikonos) in the Cyclades Islands, the *Warren* captures a pirate galley of 40 oars.

November 1.   The *Warren* sends a party ashore at Mikonos. The detachment recovers equipment and stores from three captured merchant vessels and burns a pirate boat.

November 7.   A boat party from the *Warren* under Lieutenant William L. Hudson captures a pirate boat and burns another during a cruise around Andros Island in the Aegean Sea.

1829

March 9.   John Branch enters office as eighth secretary of the navy.

June 4.   **Loss of the Fulton (Demologos).** The navy's first steamship, built during the War of 1812, blows up at Brooklyn, killing 24 persons and injuring 9.

August 16.   **Loss of the Hornet.** The ship sloop *Hornet*, 18 (another veteran of the War of 1812), Lieutenant O. Norris, sails from Pensacola, Florida, and disappears. She probably went down in a storm off Tampico, Mexico, on September 10.

1830

December 6.   **Naval Observatory.** The depot of Charts and Instruments, later named the Naval Observatory, is established at Washington, D.C., under the command of Lieutenant Louis M. Goldsborough.

1831

May 23.   Levi Woodbury assumes office as ninth secretary of the navy.

August 28.   The frigate *Potomac*, 44, Captain John Downes, sails from Sandy Hook for the East Indies to protect American commerce from the Sumatran pirates.

1832

January 1.   **Landing in the Falklands.** The sloop *Lexington,* 18, Master Commandant Silas Duncan, lands a party of sailors and marines to obtain redress for the seizure of two American whalers in the Falklands Islands, then nominally under Argentine administration.

February 6.   **Battle of Kuala Batu (Quallah Battoo).** The frigate *Potomac,* 44, Captain John Downes, has been sent to chastise Kuala Batu, a town on the western coast of Sumatra, whose inhabitants had plundered the American trader *Friendship* and killed three of her crew. Disguised as a Danish merchantman, the *Potomac* anchors off Kuala Batu at dawn and lands a detachment of 286 sailors and marines divided into four parties commanded by First Lieutenant Alvin Edson, USMC, and Lieutenants Irvine Shubrick, Henry Hoff, and Jonathan Ingersoll, USN. Four forts defending the town are taken after two hours' hard fighting, and Kuala Batu is captured and burned. Some 150 Sumatrans are killed, including their leader, Rajah Po Mahomet. American casualties are two dead and eleven wounded.

1833

March 20.   **First Far Eastern Treaty.** A treaty of commerce between the United States and Siam is concluded by Captain David Geisinger of the sloop *Peacock.*

June 17.   **First dry dock.** The navy's first dry dock opens to receive the ship-of-the-line *Delaware,* at the Charleston Navy Yard at Boston, Massachusetts.

October 31.   A detachment of 43 seamen and marines lands from the sloop *Lexington,* 18, to protect foreign interests at Buenos Aires, Argentina.

1834

June 30.   Congress appropriates the sum of $5,000 for research on shipboard steam engines, and passes an Act "For the Better Organization of the United States Marine Corps." Commandant Archibald Henderson is promoted to the rank of colonel; the authorized strength of the corps is increased to 63 officers and 1,224 NCOs and men; and it is clearly established that the marine corps is part of the naval service.

July 1.   Mahlon Dickerson assumes office as tenth secretary of the navy.

1835

November 19.   **First U.S. naval vessel visits Guam.** The sloop *Vincennes,* 18, Commander John A. Aulick, anchors at Apra.

December 17.   The marine detachment of the frigate *Brandywine,* 44, is landed to protect the U.S. consulate at Lima, Peru. The marines are withdrawn on January 24, 1836.

December 28.   **Dade Massacre: outbreak of the Second Seminole War.** Plans to move them west of the Mississippi have aroused the ire of the Florida Seminoles. Two companies of U.S. regulars under Major Francis L. Dade are ordered from Fort Brooke, inland of Tampa Bay, to reinforce the garrison of Fort King, near Silver Springs, where increasingly acrimonious negotiations are being held. En route, the column is ambushed by a considerably larger force of Seminoles incited by Osceola; 3 of its 110 men escape. The ensuing conflict is the largest Indian War fought by the United States east of the Mississippi and the only one in which the navy will play a significant role.

1836

January 21.   **Blockade of Florida.** Commodore Alexander J. Dallas, commander of the West India Squadron, is directed to institute a blockade of southern Florida, whose settlers are certain that the Seminoles are receiving arms from Cuba and the Bahamas. Although not a single gunrunner is ever apprehended, state and military authorities remain convinced that the arms traffic exists, and the blockade is maintained throughout the war.

January 21.   **Marines reinforce Fort Brooke.** A detachment of 57 marines under First Lieutenant Nathaniel S. Waldron arrive on a chartered brig to bolster the garrison of Fort Brooke, Florida. They were sent from Key West by Commodore Dallas.

March 16–30.   The revenue cutter *Washington,* Captain Ezekiel Jones, U.S. Revenue Marine, reinforced by 15 seamen under Lieutenant William Smith, explores the shores of Charlotte Harbor for signs of the Indians and lands parties that push inland as far as 10 miles.

March 17–28.   A boat expedition from the sloop *Vandalia,* 18, under Lieutenant Levin M. Powell makes a similar reconnaissance of the Manatee River and the keys around Tampa Bay.

April 1. **Action with the Seminoles.** On a second expedition from the *Vandalia,* Powell sends a detachment under Lieutenant Stephen C. Rowan to intercept a band of Seminoles who have plundered a fishing village on Josefa (probably present-day Useppa) Island. Rowan surprises the Indian encampment, killing two and capturing two others.

May 23. **Creek War.** President Andrew Jackson orders marine corps commandant Colonel Archibald Henderson to send all available men to aid the army in suppressing the Creek Indian uprising in Georgia and Alabama. Henderson personally leads two battalions—more than half the corps—into the field. On the conclusion of the campaign, late in the summer, the marines continue south to fight the Seminoles.

July 12. **First engineering officer.** Charles H. Haswell, who designed the engines for the second steamship built for the navy, the side-wheeler *Fulton* (II), is the first engineer to be commissioned in the U.S. Navy. He later becomes engineer-in-chief.

October 6–November 20. A force of 50 seamen and 95 marines under Lieutenant Levin M. Powell, with two chartered schooners and six boats, searches the coast of Florida from Charlotte Harbor to the St. Lucie River for Seminoles, without success.

November 21. **Battle of the Wahoo Swamp.** One of the relatively few pitched battles of the Seminole War is fought in eastern Central Florida between the hostiles and a mixed force of regulars, volunteers, and friendly Creeks led by marine officers.

1837

January 27. **Battle of the Hatchee-Lustee.** Colonel Archibald Henderson, USMC, who has been given command of one of the two brigades of the army in Florida, fights a sharp action with the Seminoles at Hatchee-Lustee Creek, on the edge of the Great Cypress Swamp near Lake Tohopekaliga. In 1843, Henderson is brevetted brigadier general for his services against the Creeks and the Seminoles, thus becoming the corps's first general officer.

December 13. The sidewheel steamer *Fulton* (II), 4, the first seagoing steamship built for the navy, is commissioned at New York.

December 26. Future admiral George Dewey is born in Montpelier, Vermont.

1838

January 15. **Battle on the Jupiter River.** In December, Lieutenant Levin M. Powell leads a fourth expedition against the Seminoles. His aim is to penetrate the Everglades, where no troops have yet ventured, with a force of approximately 200 seamen, soldiers, and marines in flat-bottomed boats. Prior to reaching the Everglades, however, he discovers a trail near Jupiter Inlet and follows it to attack a Seminole encampment in a cypress swamp five miles from the coast. After an initial advance, his 75 men are driven back to their boats in some disorder. Four are killed and 22 wounded.

March 22. A combined expedition of regulars and Tennessee volunteers under Colonel James Bankhead and a detachment of soldiers and sailors under Lieutenant Powell drive the Seminoles from an island encampment in the Everglades. This is one of the first times U.S. forces have penetrated the great swamp.

July 1. James K. Paulding becomes the 11th secretary of the navy.

August 19–July 6, 1842. **Wilkes Expedition.** An expedition consisting of the sloops *Vincennes,* 18, and *Peacock,* 18, brig *Porpoise,* 12, converted pilot boats *Sea Gull* and *Flying Fish,* and storeship *Relief,* under the command of Lieutenant Charles Wilkes, sails from Norfolk, Virginia, with orders to survey various parts of the Pacific and to explore the south polar regions. Officially designated the U.S. Exploring Expedition, it is the first large operation of its kind conducted by the navy. In voyages lasting nearly four years, the expedition sails approximately 85,000 miles, charts 280 islands, collects thousands of scientific specimens, and discovers the Antarctic continent.

August 19. A boat part of 24 men under Second Lieutenant John Faunce, U.S. Revenue Marine (now Coast Guard), from the revenue cutter *Campbell* surprises a band of Seminoles near Cape Florida, killing three and putting a dozen to flight. A few days earlier the Indians had massacred the crews of three New England fishing sloops and also the crew of a merchant brig that grounded in a gale.

1839

January 1–2. **Second Battle of Kuala Batu (Quallah Battoo).** Commodore George C. Read, commander of the East India Squadron, launches an attack on the

The attack on the Sumatran village of Muckee, near Kuala Batu: a contemporary print (undated). *Courtesy Mystic Seaport, Inc.*

Sumatran villages of Muckee and Kuala Batu, which had undergone a similar experience in 1832, in retaliation for the murder of the captain of the merchantman *Eclipse.* Supported by the ships' fire, a landing party of 360 men under Commander T. W. Wyman from the frigate *Columbia,* 44, and sloop *John Adams,* 18, captures and destroys five forts and most of the two villages. An indemnity is collected and the inhabitants promise to mend their ways.

April 5.   **The Florida Expedition.** Convinced that the navy's blockade is not preventing a flow of arms to the Seminoles from Cuba and the Bahamas, in 1838 the War Department purchased two schooners, the *Wave* and the *Otsego,* and a number of barges to support the revenue cutters already under its orders in maintaining an inshore blockade of the southern tip of Florida. These vessels are manned by navy crews. Command of this force, commonly referred to as the Florida Expedition and strengthened by the acquisition of the side-wheel steamer *Poinsett,* is now unified under Commander Isaac Mayo.

April 26.   The converted pilot boat *Sea Gull,* Midshipman J. W. E. Reid, a tender to the Wilkes Expedition, becomes separated from the *Flying Fish* en route from Tierra del Fuego to Valparaiso and disappears at sea. She carried a crew of 16.

May 18.   General Alexander Macomb concludes a treaty of peace with the Seminoles.

July 23.   **Harney Massacre.** The Seminole War resumes when a trading post on the Caloosahatchee River, established in accordance with Macomb's treaty by a 26-man detachment under Colonel William S. Harney, USA, is attacked by warriors led by Hospetarke and Chakaika. Harney and 13 men escape.

August 26.   Off New London, Connecticut, the brig *Washington,* 10, Lieutenant T. R. Gedney, seizes the Cuban schooner Amistad, of which embarked slaves have gained control. After lengthy legal proceedings, the 35 surviving Africans are allowed to return to their homelands.

December 2.   **Genesis of the Mosquito Fleet.** Lieutenant John T. McLaughlin, whose ideas of carrying the war to the Seminoles in the Everglades are similar to those advanced earlier by Lieutenant L. M. Powell, succeeds Commander Isaac Mayo in command of the Florida Expedition. His force soon becomes known as the Mosquito Fleet.

1840

January 19.   **Discovery of Antarctica.** Lieutenant Charles Wilkes, in the sloop *Vincennes,* flagship of the U.S. Exploring Expedition, discovers Antarctica, one day before d'Urville's French expedition sights the continent 400 miles to the west. Wilkes's observations, long contested, were confirmed by Sir Ernest Shackleton in 1908–9.

April 10.   In Florida 24 sailors and marines from the Mosquito Fleet schooner *Otsego,* landed to examine the shoreline at Cape Sable, is attacked by a party of 50 to 80 Seminoles. The Indians withdraw upon the approach of boats bringing reinforcements from the schooners *Wave* and *Flirt.*

July 26.   At Malolo, in the Fiji Islands, Lieutenant Charles Wilkes leads a landing party that destroys the towns of Sualib and Arro in retribution for the murder of two of the exploring expedition's officers.

August 6–7. **Indian Key Massacre.** Chief Chakaika makes the only Indian amphibious assault in history, leading a war party of about 135 Seminoles who paddle across 30 miles of open water after nightfall to attack the 70 settlers on Indian Key, Florida, only few miles from the Mosquito Fleet's hospital on Tea Table Key. Most of the settlers manage to flee to a schooner anchored off the island and reach Tea Table Key, but 13 are killed. At the navy base, there are only five able-bodied men, commanded by Midshipman Francis K. Murray. This detail and seven patients load a pair of four-pounders on two barges and row to Indian Key, where Murray opens fire on the canoes drawn up on the beach, hoping to strand the Seminoles until the squadron's return. Both his guns recoil overboard on the third shot; the Indians return fire with the settlement's six-pounder, and Murray retires.

September.   The pirate brig *Malek Adhel,* 4, is captured by the schooner *Enterprise,* 10, Lieutenant Louis M. Goldsborough, off Bahia, Brazil.

September 27.   Alfred Thayer Mahan is born in West Point, New York.

December.   **Harney's revenge.** Colonel W. S. Harney borrows 16 canoes from the Mosquito Fleet and, guided by a black slave who has recently escaped from the Seminoles, enters the Everglades with a detachment of 90 men to attack Chakaika's village. This time the troops, disguised as Seminoles, achieve surprise. Chakaika is killed and his band dispersed.

December 31–January 19, 1841.   **First crossing of the Everglades.** A combined force of 240 sailors, marines, and soldiers under Colonel Harney and Lieutenant John T. McLaughlin enter the Everglades from Fort Dallas, on the Atlantic. Harney returns to the coast after several days, but leaves his guides with McLaughlin, who pushes on with 90 sailors and 60 marines to emerge on the Gulf on January 19. These men are the first whites to cross the Everglades.

The U.S. Exploring Expedition: Lieutenant Wilkes's flagship, the sloop *Vincennes,* in Disappointment Bay, January 25, 1840. Wilkes gave the bay that name because the ice shelf barred his approach to the newly discovered Antarctic continent. A lithograph of this painting, based on a sketch by Wilkes, appeared in his official *Narrative of the United States Exploring Expedition* (1845). *Courtesy Peabody Museum of Salem.*

1841

February 25.   The sloop *Peacock,* 18, a vessel of the Wilkes Expedition, lands 70 sailors and marines who burn three native villages on Upolu, in the Samoan Islands, in retaliation for the murder of an American merchant seaman.

March 6.   George E. Badger becomes the 12th secretary of the navy.

April 9.   A detachment of 80 men from the *Peacock* disperse 800 native warriors and burn two villages on Drummond Island in the Gilberts in an unsuccessful attempt to rescue a seaman who had been kidnapped from one of the ship's shore parties.

July 18.   The *Peacock,* Lieutenant William L. Hudson, wrecks without loss of life on a bar off the Columbia River, Oregon.

October 10–27.   A force of 200 sailors and marines of Lieutenant John T. McLaughlin's Mosquito Fleet enters the Everglades by Shark River to cooperate with an army detachment in an unsuccessful sweep for the band of Seminoles led by Chief Sam Jones.

October 11.   Abel P. Upshur enters office as the 13th secretary of the navy.

November 3–December 23.   Lieutenant McLaughlin leads two more expeditions into the Everglades to harry the Seminoles. At the close of the operations almost 25 percent of McLaughlin's men are incapacitated by exhaustion or disease.

1842

February 11.   **Final operations in the Everglades.** Elements of Lieutenant McLaughlin's Mosquito Fleet execute a pincers movement through the Everglades. One party, under Lieutenant John Rodgers, enters the swamp from the east coast; the other, under Lieutenant John B. Marchand, from the west. The operation continues for 60 days, during which the men live in dug-out canoes and endure appalling hardships. Few Seminoles are encountered, but many fields and dwellings are destroyed.

May 10.   **End of the Seminole War.** Secretary of War John C. Spencer notifies Colonel William J. Worth, the army commander in Florida, that he may cease operations. It is estimated that there are at most 300 Seminoles left in the territory. A treaty of peace is never signed.

Lieutenant Matthew Fontaine Maury, from a photograph. *Courtesy U.S. Naval Academy Museum.*

June 20.   The Florida Expedition (Mosquito Fleet) is disestablished.

June 29.   **Pathfinder of the Seas.** Lieutenant Matthew Fontaine Maury, disqualified for sea duty by a leg injury, is appointed superintendent of the Depot of Charts and Instruments. In this post, he will promote the research and collect the data that lay the foundations for the science of oceanography.

August 9.   **Webster-Ashburton Treaty.** A treaty between the United States and Great Britain settles the long-standing controversy over disputed territories on the Canadian-American frontier and provides that each country will maintain a naval squadron off the west coast of Africa to prevent the slave trade from being carried on under its flag.

August 11.   The campaign against the Seminoles is officially concluded.

August 31.   **Bureau System.** The administrative organization under which the navy will operate for more than a century is established when Congress abolishes the Board of Navy Commissioners and creates five bureaus: Yards and Docks; Construction and Repair; Provisions and Clothing; Ordnance and Hydrography; and Medicine and Surgery.

October 2.   The sloop *Concord*, 24, Commander William Boerum, wrecks with the loss of three lives in the Mozambique Channel.

October 21–23.   **Occupation of Monterey.** Mistakenly believing that the United States has gone to war with Mexico, Commodore Thomas ap Catesby Jones, commander of the Pacific Squadron, seizes Monterey, in the Mexican province of Upper California, with landing parties from the frigate *United States*, 44, and sloop *Cyane*, 20. He is relieved of command for this excess of zeal in 1843, but reappointed to the same post in 1848.

December 1.   **Somers Mutiny.** Commander Alexander Slidell Mackenzie hangs three men for conspiring to mutiny on the brig *Somers*: Seaman Elisha Small, Boatswain's Mate Samuel Cromwell, and 19-year-old Midshipman Philip Spencer, the son of Secretary of War John C. Spencer. Mackenzie learned of the plans for the mutiny when Purser's Steward James Wales reported that Spencer had asked him to join in it. A search of Spencer's possessions produced incriminating papers, and Mackenzie had Spencer, Cromwell, and Small put in irons on the quarterdeck. The attitude of the crew, composed mostly of impressionable, teenaged apprentice boys, grew threatening, however, and Mackenzie convened a court-martial composed of the *Somer*'s officers and midshipmen, who unanimously recommended that for the safety of the vessel the three men should be put to death. Mackenzie's decision to follow that council remains controversial to this day, even though Spencer confessed his intentions. The prominence of Spencer's father makes the incident the subject of national attention and generates debate on methods of officer selection and training. This is the only mutiny in the history of the U.S. Navy.

1843

March 11.   The schooner *Grampus*, 12, Lieutenant A. E. Downes, sails from Charleston, South Carolina, for Norfolk, Virginia, and is lost en route with all hands.

July 24.   David Henshaw assumes office as 14th secretary of the navy.

August 25.   The side-wheel frigate *Missouri*, 10, Captain John T. Newton, arrives at Gibraltar to become the first steam-powered U.S. naval vessel to cross the Atlantic. The next night fire breaks out in one of her storerooms, and the ship is destroyed.

September 9.   The navy's first screw steamer, the *Princeton*, 14, is commissioned at Philadelphia, Pennsylvania, Captain Robert F. Stockton, commanding. All of the navy's previous steamers were side-wheelers.

December 5.   **First iron ship.** The steamer *Michigan*, the navy's first iron-hulled vessel, is launched at Erie, Pennsylvania, to patrol the Great Lakes. She is also the navy's first prefabricated ship, having been built in Pittsburgh and transported to Erie for assembly.

December 15.   Commodore Matthew C. Perry, commander of the newly reconstituted Africa Squadron, lands with a party of 200 sailors and marines at the village of Little Berebee on the Ivory Coast, where two years earlier the crew of the American trader *Mary Carver* had been massacred. A palaver with the native leader, King Ben Krako, ends in a scuffle in which the king is mortally wounded and made prisoner. The landing party then captures and burns Little Berebee.

1844

February 19.   Thomas W. Gilmer enters office as 15th secretary of the navy.

February 28.   **"Peacemaker" disaster.** Captain Robert F. Stockton invites President John Tyler and other dignitaries for a cruise down the Potomac on the *Princeton*, the navy's first screw steamer. During the voyage Stockton demonstrates the "Peacemaker," a 12-inch wrought-iron gun of his design. Unfortunately, his knowledge of metallurgy is not extensive. After several successful firings the gun bursts, cutting a swath through the bystanders. Eight persons are killed and nine wounded. Among the dead are Secretary of State (and former secretary of the navy) Abel P. Upshur, Secretary of the Navy Thomas W. Gilmer, Senator David Gardner, and Captain Beverley Kennon, Chief of the Bureau of Construction, Equipment and Repair. Stockton is slightly wounded.

March 26.   John Y. Mason becomes the 16th secretary of the navy.

March 29.   Uriah P. Levy, who had entered the navy during the War of 1812, is the first Jewish officer promoted to the rank of captain. In 1859 he attains flag rank as commander of the Mediterranean Squadron.

June 19–July 20.   A detachment of marines from the sloop *St. Louis*, 20, is landed at Whampoa Island, off Canton, China, where a mob has surrounded the American trading compound.

1845

March 1.   **Origin of the Mexican War.** President John Tyler signs a congressional resolution calling for the annexation of the Republic of Texas, which Mexico claims still belongs to her.

March 11.   **Genesis of the Naval Academy.** George Bancroft, the distinguished historian, becomes the 17th secretary of the navy. Soon after he enters office William Chauvenet, a brilliant young mathematician in charge of the navy school at Philadelphia, sends him a plan, previously rejected by Secretary Mason, for transforming the existing cram course into a formal, two-year program. Bancroft likes the idea, but decides that the school should be located at Annapolis, Maryland, where an obsolete army post, Fort Severn, can be converted into a campus.

March 31.   Mexico breaks diplomatic relations with the United States.

July 25.   In anticipation of troubles with Mexico, an American army under General Zachary Taylor lands near Corpus Christi, Texas.

August 15.   At Annapolis, Fort Severn is transferred to the navy. Commander Franklin Buchanan, whom Secretary Bancroft had earlier asked to prepare a plan of organization for the naval school, is appointed superintendent on the same day.

October 10.   The U.S. Naval School, as it is originally known, commences classes at Annapolis, Maryland, with a student body of 56 and a staff of 8: Commander Buchanan, Lieutenant James H. Ward, Passed Midshipman Samuel L. Marcy, Surgeon John A. Lockwood, Chaplain George Jones, and Professors William Chauvenet, Arsène N. Girault, and Henry H. Lockwood. Henceforward, all midshipmen entering the navy will attend the school for two years, between which, however, they will serve a three-year apprenticeship at sea.

October 30.   **Gillespie mission.** President Polk personally directs First Lieutenant Archibald H. Gillespie, USMC, to carry a secret message to Thomas O. Larkin, U.S. consul at Monterey, California, instructing him to encourage the Californians to revolt against Mexico and to urge them not to accept assistance from any power except the United States.

December 29.   Texas is admitted to the Union.

1846

April 23.   **Beginning of the Mexican War.** Mexico declares war on the United States.

May 8.   A Mexican army that has crossed the Rio Grande into Texas is defeated by General Zachary Taylor's forces at the Battle of Palo Alto, the first major clash of the Mexican War.

May 13.   The United States declares war on Mexico.

May 14.   **Blockade of Mexico.** Commodore David Conner, commanding the U.S. Home Squadron, proclaims a blockade of the Mexican Gulf ports of Matamoros, Tampico, Alvarado, and Veracruz. Not a single Mexican naval vessel will put to sea during the war.

May 16.   Eleven Revenue Marine (Coast Guard) cutters are detailed to support the army and navy during the Mexican War.

May 24.   The Mexican schooners *Criolla* and *Amada* are captured by the sloop *Falmouth*, Commander Joseph R. Jarvis, and the brig *Somers*, Commander Duncan N. Ingraham, respectively. Although Commodore Conner releases both ships upon learning that Mexico allowed four American vessels caught in Veracruz by the outbreak of the war to depart, they are the first of numerous Mexican merchantmen taken by the U.S. Navy in the course of the conflict.

June 8.   The sloop *St. Mary's*, 20, Commander John L. Saunders, shells Tampico, Mexico.

June 14.   Boat parties from the *St. Mary's* make an unsuccessful attempt to cut out three Mexican gunboats at Tampico, Mexico.

July 4.   In California, American settlers proclaim the independence of the Bear Flag Republic.

July 7.   Commodore John D. Sloat, commander of the Pacific Squadron, lands a party of 140 seamen and 85 marines under Captain William Mervine of the sloop *Cyane*, 20, to occupy Monterey, in the Mexican province of California. The landing is unopposed.

July 9.   Seventy seamen and marines landed from the sloop *Portsmouth*, 20, Commander John B. Montgomery, take possession of the villages of San Francisco and Yerba Buena, California, also without encountering opposition.

July 10.   John Y. Mason becomes the 18th secretary of the navy. He had held the same position in 1844–45.

July 20.   Commodore James Biddle anchors in Edo (Tokyo) Bay with the *Columbus*, 74, and the sloop *Vincennes*, 18, in an unsuccessful attempt to open diplomatic relations with Japan. His vessels are the first American warships to visit that country.

July 29.   Commodore Robert F. Stockton relieves Commodore Sloat in command of the Pacific Squadron. His energetic leadership will make him the man most responsible for the conquest of California.

July 29.   The sloop *Cyane,* 20, Captain William Mervine, arrives off San Diego, California, having sailed from Monterey on July 25 with a battalion of California volunteers under Captain John C. Frémont, USA. A naval detachment commanded by Lieutenant Stephen C. Rowan lands unopposed and takes possession of the town, after which Frémont's men go ashore.

August 4.   A landing party from the frigate *Congress,* 54, Commander Samuel F. Du Pont, flagship of the Pacific Squadron, takes possession of Santa Barbara, California. No resistance is encountered.

August 6.   San Pedro, California, is peacefully occupied by a marine detachment under First Lieutenant Jacob Zeilin from the frigate *Congress.*

August 7.   **First attack on Alvarado.** On the Gulf coast of Mexico nine ships of Commodore Conner's Home Squadron, including the screw steamer *Princeton,* 13, Commander Frederick Engle, and the paddle-wheeler *Mississippi,* 10, Captain Andrew Fitzhugh, bombard the forts and gunboats guarding the mouth of the Alvarado River. Conner breaks off the attack when the weather turns threatening.

August 13.   A naval brigade of 360 men advancing from San Pedro under Commodore Robert F. Stockton occupies Los Angeles, California. Captain Frémont's California Battalion, which had taken another route, arrives an hour later.

August 14.   Mexican forces in California surrender.

August 14.   The brig *Truxtun,* 10, Commander Edward W. Carpenter, grounds without loss of life on Tuxpan Reef, off the east coast of Mexico, and surrenders to enemy forces ashore the next day. On August 22, a boat party from the steamer *Princeton* burns the empty ship.

September 2.   Lieutenant Stephen C. Rowan leads a landing party from the sloop *Cyane,* 20, which spikes 24 enemy cannons at San Blas, Mexico.

September 7.   A boat party of 69 men under Lieutenant William Radford from the sloop *Warren,* 20, cuts out the Mexican merchant brig *Malek Adhel* in the harbor of Mazatlán, Mexico. The prize is taken into U.S. service.

September 10.   The schooner *Shark,* 12, Lieutenant Neil M. Howison, wrecks without loss of life at the mouth of the Columbia River, Oregon.

September 23.   **Californian revolt.** Mexican army Captain José Maria Flores becomes the leader of an uprising by native Californians against the small and scattered American occupation forces. The first fighting occurs at Los Angeles, where Lieutenant Archibald H. Gillespie, USMC, commands a 48-man garrison from Frémont's California Battalion. He is compelled to surrender, but allowed to withdraw on September 29. Santa Barbara is evacuated soon afterward.

October 7.   The sloop *Cyane,* 20, Commander Samuel F. Du Pont, shells Guaymas, Sonora, destroying the Mexican gunboats *Anahuac* and *Sonorense,* and sends a boat expedition under Lieutenant George W. Harrison, which cuts out the merchant brig *Condor.*

October 7–8.   Captain William Mervin advances from San Pedro with 225 men from the frigate *Savannah* and Lieutenant Gillespie's Californians to recapture Los Angeles. His column is forced back by California cavalry equipped with a cannon, of which he has none.

October 15.   **Second attack on Alvarado.** Seven vessels of the Home Squadron make another attempt to enter the Alvarado River. Commodore Conner orders them to withdraw when the side-wheel steamer *McLane,* 6, which is to tow three sailing ships into the river, proves unable to cross the bar.

October 23.   **First Tabasco Expedition.** A squadron of seven vessels under Commodore Matthew C. Perry enters the Tabasco River, capturing the coastal town of Frontera, and pushes 72 miles upstream to reach and briefly occupy the city of Tabasco (present-day Villahermosa) on October 25. Seven Mexican vessels are taken during these operations. No resistance is encountered until the next day, when Mexican troops reoccupy Tabasco and open fire on the ships. Perry shells the city until their firing ceases and returns to the coast.

November 14.   **Pánuco Expedition.** Commodore David Conner leads a force of six ships and boat parties from five others into the Pánuco River, on the Mexican Gulf coast. The port of Tampico is occupied without resistance that afternoon. Five vessels, four of which become U.S. gunboats, are also taken. On November 19, Commander Josiah Tattnall pushes 25 miles upstream with the side-wheel steamer *Spitfire* and schooner *Petrel* to capture the town of Pánuco, where he destroys a number of Mexican cannons. Tampico will be held by U.S. forces for the remainder of the war.

November 15.   The sloop *Boston,* 18, Commander George F. Pearson, wrecks without loss of life on Eleuthera Island in the Bahamas.

November 26.   After nightfall, the Mexican brig *Criolla,* which had slipped through the American blockade into Veracruz, is burned beneath the guns of Fortress San Juan de Ulloa by a boat party from the brig *Somers* consisting of Lieutenant James L. Parker, Passed Midshipmen John R. Hynson and R. Clay Rogers, and five men. Unfortunately, the *Criolla* was a spy ship that Commodore Conner had deliberately let pass.

December 8.   **Loss of the Somers.** Blockading off Veracruz, the brig *Somers,* 10, Lieutenant Raphael Semmes, is capsized by a sudden squall. Of her 76 crewmen, 32 are lost.

December 21.   A squadron of four ships commanded by Commodore Matthew C. Perry occupies Carmen, a Mexican port on the Bay of Campeche, without opposition.

1847

January 2.   **Action near the Mission Santa Clara.** A detachment of 101 marines and volunteers with one gun under Captain Ward Marston, USMC, defeats a Californian uprising led by Francisco Sanchez, former military commandant of San Francisco. Sanchez surrenders four days later.

January 8.   **Battle of San Gabriel.** Commodore Robert F. Stockton has planned a two-pronged offensive to recapture Los Angeles. While Captain J. C. Frémont, USA, moves south from Santa Barbara with his California Battalion, Stockton will advance north from San Diego with a naval brigade and a detachment of U.S. dragoons who have marched overland from Kansas under Colonel Steven W. Kearny. His force consists of 607 men and four guns. On this date it defeats the Californian army of 450 men and two guns under Captain José M. Flores, which had attempted to prevent it from crossing the San Gabriel River.

January 9.   **Battle of La Mesa.** Commodore Stockton's column defeats and disperses the remainder of Captain Flores's Californian army—perhaps 300 men—in an action of two-and-a-half hours south of the Los Angeles River.

January 10.   American forces reoccupy Los Angeles. Three days later the Californians sign the Treaty of Cahuenga, ending the war in California.

March 9.   **Landing at Veracruz.** Despite General Taylor's victories in northern Mexico, culminating in the occupation of Monterrey, the Mexican government refuses to make peace. Plans are then developed to land another American army under General Winfield Scott at Veracruz for an advance on Mexico City. Commodore Conner's Home Squadron lands 8,600 of Scott's men on Collado Beach, two-and-a-half miles south of the city, in less than five hours without the loss of a single life. This is the first major amphibious operation conducted by the U.S. Navy and a model of its kind.

The landing of General Scott's army near Veracruz, a lithograph published in Philadelphia in 1847 from a drawing by eyewitness Lieutenant Charles C. Barton, USN. *Courtesy Beverley R. Robinson Collection, U.S. Naval Academy Museum.*

March 10.   The paddle-wheel steamer *Spitfire, 3*, Commander Josiah Tattnall, shells Castle San Juan de Ulloa while Scott's army encircles Veracruz.

March 15.   Commander George P. Upshur becomes the second superintendent of the Naval Academy.

March 21.   Commodore Matthew C. Perry relieves Commodore Conner as commander of the Home Squadron.

March 22.   General Scott's three siege batteries, supported by fire from seven ships of the Home Squadron, begin to bombard Veracruz.

March 22.   **The Naval Battery at Veracruz.** Three 32-pounders and three 8-inch-shell guns are landed from ships of the Home Squadron to augment the army's heavy artillery in the bombardment of Veracruz. Commanded by Captain John H. Aulick of the frigate *Potomac,* the naval battery opens fire on the morning of March 24. Two of its men are killed and three wounded in the course of the siege.

March 23.   **Tattnall and the Spitfire.** Directed to renew the bombardment of Veracruz, Commander Josiah Tattnall leads a flotilla consisting of the steamers *Spitfire, 3*, and *Vixen, 3*, towing the schooners *Petrel,* 1, *Tampico*, 1, *Bonita,* 1, and *Reefer,* 1, to a position only 600 yards from the Mexican fortifications. Perry orders him to open the range after an hour, during which Tattnall's ships suffer remarkably little damage, probably because they were too close for the Mexican guns to depress on them.

March 27.   Veracruz surrenders.

March 30.   In Baja California, the port of San José del Cabo is briefly occupied by a landing party of 140 men under Lieutenant Benjamin F. B. Hunter from the sloop *Portsmouth.*

March 31.   **Capture of Alvarado.** Following the surrender of Veracruz, General Scott lays plans for the capture of Alvarado, off which the Home Squadron had been repulsed in August and October 1846. On March 30, a brigade commanded by Brigadier General John A. Quitman marches south along the coast for Alvarado, where it is to be met and supported by twelve vessels under Commodore Perry. The steamer *Scourge, 3*, Lieutenant Charles G. Hunter, is sent ahead of the expedition. Arriving off Alvarado on March 30, Hunter shells the fort guarding the river mouth. It surrenders the next morning and Hunter crosses the bar, takes the city of Alvarado and three Mexican vessels, and pushes upstream to capture the village of Tlacotalpán on April 1. Perry is outraged. Averring that the *Scourge's* actions allowed the Mexicans to destroy or withdraw supplies that could have been captured, he has Hunter court-martialed and dismissed from the Home Squadron.

April 3.   The marine detachment from the sloop *Portsmouth* briefly occupies the village of San Lucas in Baja California.

April 13.   A landing party from the *Portsmouth* under Lieutenant John S. Missroon occupies La Paz, the capital of Baja California.

The naval battery at Veracruz. This lithograph, published by Sarony and Major in New York in 1848, was based on a watercolor by eyewitness Lieutenant Henry Walke, USN. *Courtesy Library of Congress.*

The capture of the Mexican forts during the Tuxpan expedition, April 19, 1847. Another lithograph by Sarony and Major after an eyewitness painting by Lieutenant Walke. *Courtesy U.S. Naval Academy Museum.*

April 18.   **Tuxpan expedition.** Commodore Matthew C. Perry enters the Tuxpan River with a force consisting of the steamers *Scourge,* 3, *Spitfire,* 3, and *Vixen,* 3, schooners *Bonita,* 1, *Petrel,* 1, and *Reefer,* 1, and 30 barges carrying a landing force of 1,519 men under Captain Samuel L. Breese. The forts of La Peña and La Palmasola, which oppose the flotilla's advance, are captured, and the city of Tuxpan is occupied. Perry withdraws from the river, having destroyed its fortifications, on April 22.

May 12.   **Coatzacoalcos expedition.** A flotilla of Commodore Perry's Home Squadron enters the Coatzacoalcos River, on the Gulf of Campeche. Two ships under Commander Abraham Bigelow push on to the village of Minatitlán, 24 miles upstream, to gather intelligence.

May 16.   Continuing south from Coatzoacoalcos, Commodore Perry occupies the town and island of Carmen.

June 14.   **Second Tabasco expedition.** Commodore Perry leads an expedition into the Tabasco River to capture the city of the same name (present-day Villahermosa). His force consists of the steamers *Scourge,* 3, *Scorpion,* 4, *Spitfire,* 3, and *Vixen,* 3, the schooner *Bonita,* 1, the brigs *Etna,* 1, *Stromboli,* 1, *Vesuvius,* 1, and *Washington,* 1, and 47 boats carrying a landing force of 1,173 men and seven guns. The river defenses, considerably strengthened since Perry's expedition of October 1846, consist of four earthworks mounting eight guns and garrisoned by 900 Mexican troops. Perry lands the naval brigade which, with himself at its head, supports the ships in the capture of all four works and occupies Tabasco on June 16. An outbreak of yellow fever causes him to evacuate the town on July 22.

June 30.   Mexican troops occupying the village of Tamulté, four miles upstream from Tabasco, are scattered by an expedition consisting of the steamers *Scourge* and *Vixen* and a land force of 200 men. The operation was mounted by Commander Abraham Bigelow, the military governor of Tabasco.

July 16.   **To the halls of Montezuma.** A marine battalion of 357 officers and men under Brevet Lieutenant

Commodore Matthew C. Perry leads the landing party at Seven Palms during the second Tabasco expedition, June 16, 1847. A lithograph by Sarony and Major after a painting by Lieutenant Walke, published in 1849. *Courtesy U.S. Naval Academy Museum.*

Colonel Samuel F. Watson arrives at Veracruz to participate in General Scott's advance on Mexico City.

August 4.   Secretary of the Navy Mason instructs Commodore Perry not to occupy any more Mexican ports.

September 13.   **Storming of Chapultepec.** The marine battalion plays a leading part in the capture of Chapultepec Castle, the key to Mexico City. Lieutenant Colonel Watson having been given command of an army brigade, the marines go into action under Major Levi Twiggs, who is killed beneath the walls of the castle. Captain George H. Terrett's company, 67 officers and men, diverge from the battalion's advance and, joining forces with 24 men of the 4th Infantry under Lieutenant U.S. Grant, become the first American troops to enter Mexico City. Thirty-nine marines are killed or wounded in the day's fighting, and 14 of the 23 officers present receive brevet promotions for gallantry.

October 1.   A Mexican garrison is driven from the village of Mulejé in Baja California by a party of 50 men under Lieutenant T. A. M. Craven landed from Commander Thomas O. Selfridge's sloop *Dale,* 16.

October 5.   A landing party from the *Dale,* again led by Lieutenant Craven, seizes three cannons and other arms at the village of Loreto, Baja California.

October 20.   The frigate *Congress,* 54, Captain Elie A. F. La Vallette, and sloop *Portsmouth,* 22, Commander John B. Montgomery, bombard Mexican forces defending Guaymas, Sonora. The Mexicans withdraw after an hour, and the town is briefly occupied by a naval landing party.

November 11.   **Capture of Mazatlán.** Mexico's most important Pacific port is occupied and garrisoned by a landing party of 730 men from the frigates *Congress* and *Independence* and the sloop *Cyane* under Captain Elie A. F. La Vallette of the *Congress.*

November 11.   **Revolt in Baja California.** Anti-American sentiment in Lower California results in an uprising headed by Captain Manuel Pineda. It begins on this date with an unsuccessful surprise attack on the garrison of La Paz. Another assault is beaten off on November 17.

November 17.   Informed of Mexican activity around Guaymas, Sonora, Commander Thomas O. Selfridge, commanding the sloop *Dale*, 16, lands with a party of 67 seamen and marines as a show of force. They are attacked by 250 troops. Selfridge is badly wounded, and his men are pinned down until the *Dale* disperses the Mexicans with her fire.

November 19–22.   After the two attempts to recapture La Paz, Mexican forces in Baja California attack San José del Cabo, where a marine garrison of 24 men under Lieutenant Charles Heywood had been stationed on November 8. The marines hold out in a mission compound until the Mexicans, seeing the sails of two whaling vessels on the horizon, suppose that they are warships and withdraw.

November 20.   A Mexican company at Urias, 10 miles south of Mazatlán, is routed in a dawn attack by landing parties under Lieutenants George L. Selden and Stephen C. Rowan.

December 12.   After nightfall, a naval detachment of 43 men under Lieutenant Montgomery Lewis surprises and scatters a band of Mexicans 10 miles from Mazatlán.

December 13.   A patrol of 20 marines under Lieutenant William W. Russell disperses a group of Mexicans at Palos Prietos, near Mazatlán. This is the last skirmish in that area.

1848

January 12.   The guns defending the port of San Blas, on the west coast of Mexico, are removed by a landing party of 47 men from the bark *Whiton* and storeship *Lexington*, 6, under Lieutenant Frederick Chatard, the *Whiton*'s commanding officer.

January 17.   Lieutenant Chatard lands a party from the *Whiton* that spikes the guns at Manzanillo, Mexico. This leaves Acapulco the only defended Mexican port on the Pacific.

January 22–February 14.   In Baja California, the Mexicans again attack San José del Cabo, where Lieutenant Heywood's original garrison has been increased to 62 men. The siege is lifted by the arrival of the sloop *Cyane*, Commander S. F. Du Pont, who lands a detachment of 102 men. Before it can reach him, Heywood leads a sortie that drives the discouraged Mexicans from town.

January 30.   A Mexican detachment at Cochori, eight miles east of Guaymas, Sonora, is routed in a dawn attack by a landing party under Lieutenant T.A.M. Craven from the sloop *Dale*.

February 2.   **Treaty of Guadalupe Hidalgo.** A treaty of peace between Mexico and the United States, ratified by the U.S. Senate, on March 10, is signed at a village outside Mexico City. According to its terms, Mexico recognizes the American claim to Texas and cedes the United States an additional 500,000 square miles: all of present-day Arizona, California, Nevada, and Utah, most of New Mexico, and part of Colorado and Wyoming. The United States pays Mexico $15,000,000 and assumes all claims of American citizens against the Mexican government.

February 13.   A Mexican force at Bocachicacampo, four miles north of Guaymas, Sonora, is attacked and dispersed by a party of 60 of the *Dale*'s seamen and marines led by Lieutenant Fabius Stanly.

April 8–May 10.   **Dead Sea Expedition.** Lieutenant William F. Lynch leads a small party that surveys the Sea of Galilee (Lake Tiberias) and proceeds from there via the River Jordan to the Dead Sea.

April 9.   A landing party from the *Dale*, again commanded by Lieutenant Fabius Stanly, marches 12 miles inland to spike three Mexican guns near Guaymas, Sonora. On its return march, the detachment fights a short skirmish with Mexican forces. These are the last shots fired by the U.S. Navy in the war with Mexico.

1849

March 3.   The Nautical Almanac Office is established at Harvard University under the superintendency of 42-year-old Lieutenant Charles H. Davis, under whose able leadership it becomes America's first real scientific institute.

March 8.   William B. Preston becomes the 19th secretary of the navy.

August 16.   **U.S. Astronomical Expedition to the Southern Hemisphere.** Lieutenant James M. Gilliss, formerly chief of the Depot of Charts and Instruments, sails from New York to conduct astronomical observations that will aid navigators in determining the exact position of ships at sea. His work, performed in an observatory he builds near Santiago, Chile, is completed in the summer of 1852.

1850

May 26.   **First Grinnell Expedition.** Two brigs especially outfitted for the Arctic, the *Advance* and the *Rescue,* sail from New York to search for the British Arctic expedition of Captain Sir John Franklin, RN, which has not been heard from since 1847. Loaned to the government by Henry Grinnell, the ships are manned by navy volunteer crews under Lieutenant Edward J. De Haven. The site of Franklin's first winter quarters (and the graves of three of his men) are located on August 27, but little progress can be made thereafter, and on September 14 both vessels are frozen in. The expedition winters over, suffering considerable hardship, and renews the search, without success, in the summer of 1851 before returning to New York.

July 1.   Commander Cornelius K. Stribling becomes the third superintendent of the Naval Academy. On this same date the curriculum is extended to four years—still broken in the middle by three years at sea—and the institution is officially renamed the U.S. Naval Academy.

August 2.   William A. Graham becomes the 20th secretary of the navy.

September 2.   Congress abolishes flogging as a disciplinary action in the U.S. Navy.

September 6.   The ship sloop *Yorktown,* 16, Commander John Marston, wrecks without loss of life on Isla de Mayo in the Cape Verde Islands.

1851

May 21.   **Herndon Expedition.** Lieutenant William L. Herndon, Passed Midshipman Lardner Gibbon, and Master's Mate Henry J. Richards leave Lima, Peru, to explore the Amazon basin. Herndon reaches the city of Para (now Bélem), Brazil, after a journey of 4,366 miles on April 11, 1852; Gibbon and Richards, who follow a different route, arrive there in November. The primary purpose of the expedition, conceived by Lieutenant Matthew Fontaine Maury, was to determine the navigability of the Amazon River.

August 6.   The sloop *Dale,* 16, Commander William C. Pearson, anchors off Johanna (now Grande Comore) Island in the Indian Ocean to demand an indemnity from King Selim for the temporary imprisonment of a New England merchant skipper. When the king refuses to comply, the *Dale* shells his town. The indemnity is paid the next day.

November 15.   The four-year curriculum at the Naval Academy is made continuous, the sea training for which it had been interrupted being provided by annual summer cruises.

1852

February 3.   Marines are landed from the Brazil Squadron, Commodore Isaac McKeever, to protect American citizens at Buenos Aires, Argentina.

July 26.   John P. Kennedy becomes the 21st secretary of the navy.

September 17.   The sloop *Jamestown* lands her marines to protect Americans at Buenos Aires, Argentina.

September 30–November 12, 1853.   The brig *Dolphin,* 10, Lieutenant S. P. Lee, sails from New York to verify the theories advanced by Lieutenant Matthew Fontaine Maury, the founder of oceanography, regarding the winds and currents of the Atlantic.

1853

January 19.   The paddle-wheel steamer *Water Witch,* Lieutenant Thomas J. Page, sails from Baltimore to explore and survey the River Plate and its tributaries. She returns home on February 3, 1856.

March 8.   James C. Dobbin enters office as 22nd secretary of the navy.

March 11.   The sloop *Cyane,* 20, lands her marine detachment to protect American citizens and property at San Juan del Norte, Nicaragua.

May 30.   **Second Grinnell Expedition.** An unofficial Arctic expedition privately financed by Henry Grinnell sails from New York in the steamer *Advance.* It is led by Dr. Elisha Kent Kane, a navy surgeon who had served under Lieutenant De Haven in the expedition of 1850–51. Trapped in pack ice later in 1853, the *Advance* remains imprisoned at the height of the Arctic summer in April 1855. Kane then abandons the vessel and leads his men on an 83-day sledge journey across the ice to Upernavik, Greenland, arriving there on July 24, 1855.

June 11–October 19, 1855.   **North Pacific Surveying and Exploring Expedition.** The coasts and islands of the Pacific are charted from the Aleutians to Japan and Hawaii by an expedition headed by Commanders Cadwallader Ringgold (1852–54) and John Rodgers

(1854–55), the son of Commodore John Rodgers of the War of 1812.

June 21.   **Koszta incident.** At Smyrna, Turkey, Martin Koszta, a naturalized American citizen who had participated in the Hungarian revolution of 1848, is seized by the Austrian consul and confined aboard the Austrian brig *Hussar.* The sloop *St. Louis,* 20, Commander Duncan N. Ingraham, is also at Smyrna. Upon learning what has happened, Ingraham clears his ship for action and sets a deadline for Koszta's release. The *Hussar* and another Austrian warship in harbor clear for action, too, but in the end Koszta is freed. Congress awards Commander Ingraham a gold medal for his determination in upholding the rights of American citizenship.

July 8.   **Perry Expedition.** A squadron consisting of the side-wheel steamers *Mississippi,* 10 (flag), and *Susquehanna,* 9, and the 20-gun sloops *Plymouth* and *Saratoga* under the command of Commodore Matthew C. Perry enters Edo (Tokyo) Bay to establish relations with Japan. Perry had sailed from Norfolk, Virginia, on November 24, 1852. The Japanese have traditionally shunned contact with the outside world, but they are impressed by Perry's firm and dignified manner—as well as by the technological marvel of his steamships. Staunchly refusing to deal with subordinate officials, on July 14 he lands to meet the joint governors of Uraga, to whom he presents a letter from President Fillmore to the emperor of Japan. Three days later he sails for China, informing the Japanese that he will return to resume negotiations the following spring.

November 1.   Commander Louis M. Goldsborough becomes the fourth superintendent of the Naval Academy.

1854

January 19.   **Cyane expedition.** Lieutenant Isaac G. Strain leads a detachment of 12 officers and 13 seamen from the sloop *Cyane,* 20, on an expedition across the Isthmus of Panama from Caledonia on

The *St. Louis (left)* and the *Hussar* at Smyrna during the Koszta incident: a lithograph published in New York in 1853. *Courtesy Beverley R. Robinson Collection, U.S. Naval Academy Museum.*

the Atlantic coast to Darien on the Pacific to reconnoiter a route for an interoceanic canal. The expedition undergoes extreme hardship, from which nine of its members perish. Lieutenant Strain pushes on alone to reach the coast by March 12 and leads a party back to rescue the others.

February 13.   Commodore Perry returns to Japan, anchoring off Yokohama with a squadron consisting of the side-wheel steamers *Mississippi* (flag), *Susquehanna*, and *Powhatan*, the sloops *Macedonian*, *Saratoga*, *Lexington*, and *Vandalia*, and the storeship *Southampton*.

March 8–31.   **Treaty of Kanagawa.** After three weeks' negotiations, Commodore Perry concludes a treaty of peace and amity with Japan. Although the Japanese still refuse to enter into commercial relations with the United States, these will soon be established. Japan has been opened to the western world.

April 4–5.   **Action at Shanghai.** The foreign concessions at Shanghai are threatened by the fighting between Chinese government troops and Taiping rebels. A landing party of 90 men under Commander John Kelly from the sloop *Portsmouth*, 20, joins with a British naval detachment to avert the danger by driving both Chinese forces out of the city. One American is killed and three wounded.

Commodore Perry lands to meet the Japanese commissioners at Yokohama, March 8, 1854. This lithograph, by Sarony and Major, was one of the illustrations in the official *Narrative of the Expedition of an American Squadron to the China Seas and Japan* (1856). *Courtesy Beverley R. Robinson Collection, U.S. Naval Academy Museum.*

July 11.   **Treaty of Naha.** Commodore Perry concludes a treaty of peace and amity with the regency of the Loo Choo (Ryukyu) Islands.

July 13.   **Bombardment of Greytown.** The sloop *Cyane*, 20, Commander George N. Hollins, arrives at Greytown, Nicaragua, where the American ambassador had been arrested and held overnight, to demand an apology and an indemnity. When neither is forthcoming, Hollins gives the town a day's notice that he will bombard it and duly does so. Most of Greytown is consumed in the consequent fires. His robust initiative is subsequently approved by the State Department.

September 21.   The brig *Porpoise*, 12, Lieutenant William K. Bridge, disappears at sea after being sighted in the vicinity of Formosa on this date.

September 29.   The sloop *Albany*, 22, Commander James T. Gerry, with a crew of 193, sails from Aspinwall, Panama, for New York and is never seen again.

November 17.   The sloop *Vincennes*, 18, lands sailors and marines at Okinawa to enforce the provisions of the Treaty of Naha.

1855

May 19.   The side-wheel steamer *Powhatan*, Captain William J. McCluney, lands her marine detachment to protect American interests in Shanghai, China.

August 4.   Parties from the *Powhatan* and the British sloop *Rattler* destroy 17 pirate junks in Ty-Ho Bay, near Hong Kong, China.

August 28.   The sloop *Germantown*, 22, Commander William F. Lynch, lands her marines to safeguard Americans at Montevideo, Uruguay.

September 12.   The sloop *John Adams*, 18, Commander E. B. Boutwell, sends a party ashore at Nukulau in the Fiji Islands to obtain redress for damages to American citizens.

September 22.   A landing party from the *John Adams* seizes the native king of Viti Levu, Fiji Islands, and carries him back to the ship, where he is compelled to sign a treaty promising to compensate American citizens for the damage or destruction of their property.

October 28–31.   Returning to Viti Levu, Commander Boutwell finds that the Fijian king has not honored the treaty made the preceding month. The *John Adams* then lands a party of sailors and marines under Lieutenant Louis C. Sartori that burns three native villages at a cost of one man killed and three wounded.

November 27.   A detachment of 100 seamen and marines under Lieutenant Augustus S. Nicholson from the sloop *Germantown* joins landing parties from three other navies to guard the foreign consulates and customs house during an insurrection at Montevideo, Uruguay.

1856

January 26.   Fire support and a small landing party from the sloop *Decatur,* 14, Commander Guert Gansevoort, help the settlers of Seattle, Washington, repel an attack by 1,000 hostile Indians.

September 20.   The frigate *Independence,* 54, and sloop *St. Mary's,* 20, land a party of 160 sailors and marines under Captain Addison Garland, USMC, to protect American citizens during a period of disturbances at Panama City, in the Colombian province of Panama.

October 23.   A landing party of 150 men from the sloops *Portsmouth,* 20, and *Levant,* 22, goes ashore to protect American lives and property at Canton, China.

November 15–16.   The Chinese Barrier Forts commanding the Pearl River below Canton fire on U.S. vessels that have come to withdraw the detachment landed in October.

November 20–22.   **The Barrier Forts.** Following orders from Commodore James Armstrong, the ailing commander of the East India Squadron, Commander Andrew H. Foote lands with 287 seamen and marines to storm the Barrier forts. In three days' fighting the landing party, supported by fire from the sloops *Levant* and *Portsmouth,* captures four modern forts mounting 170 guns, plus a six-gun battery, and repulses counterattacks from two Chinese columns, the first with an estimated strength of 2,000, the second of 4,000. All of the captured fortifications and cannons are destroyed. American casualties number 42; approximately 400 Chinese are killed.

1857

March 7.   Isaac Toucey enters office as 23rd secretary of the navy.

September 15.   Captain George S. Blake becomes the fifth superintendent of the Naval Academy.

1858

January 2.   The marine detachment of the frigate *St. Lawrence* is landed to safeguard Americans during disturbances at Montevideo, Uruguay.

July 29.   **First Atlantic cable.** The steam frigate *Niagara,* Captain William L. Hudson, and HMS *Agamemnon* cooperate to lay a telegraph cable across the Atlantic. The work is completed on August 5 and the first message, from Queen Victoria to President James Buchanan, is sent on August 16. The cable fails weeks later, but the practicality of the project has been established, and a permanent cable will be laid by the giant British steamer *Great Eastern* in 1866.

The *Portsmouth* begins the bombardment of the Barrier Forts near Canton: a contemporary lithograph (undated). *Courtesy Beverley R. Robinson Collection, U.S. Naval Academy Museum.*

Commodore Josiah Tattnall: a woodcut from *Harper's Weekly*, October 22, 1859. *Courtesy U.S. Naval Academy Museum.*

October 6.   A punitive expedition of 44 men under Lieutenant C. H. B. Caldwell from the ship sloop *Vandalia*, 18, destroys a village on the island of Waya in the Fijis in retribution for the murder of two American traders.

October 17.   The largest U.S. naval squadron ever assembled, 19 ships under Flag Officer William B. Shubrick, commander of the Brazil Squadron, sails to obtain satisfaction from Paraguay for firing on the survey vessel *Water Witch* in the Paraguay River in February 1855. Schubrick performs his mission with great success. Entering the La Plata on January 25, 1859, he quickly secures an indemnity for the attack on the *Water Witch* and concludes a new commercial treaty with Paraguay.

1859

January 6.   Colonel Archibald Henderson dies after 39 years as commandant of the marine corps. He is succeeded by 68-year-old Lieutenant Colonel John Harris, a veteran of the War of 1812.

April 21.   At the mouth of the Congo, the ship sloop *Marion*, 16, Commander F. W. Blunt, captures the first of the five slavers that will be taken by U.S. naval vessels in the course of the year.

June 25.   **"Blood is thicker than water."** Britain and France are engaged in the Second Opium War with China. Commodore Josiah Tattnall, commander of the U.S. East India Squadron, is aboard the chartered steamer *Toey-Wan* when gunboats of the Royal Navy begin to remove obstructions the Chinese have placed at the mouth of the Pei-Ho River. Seeing the British come under heavy fire from the Taku forts, Tattnall takes a boat party to the British flagship to help out, remarking, "Blood is thicker than water." One American seaman is killed, and an officer is wounded in the action. Later Tattnall uses the *Toey-Wan* to tow British reinforcements forward. The U.S. government subsequently approves his initiative.

July 31.   At the request of the U.S. consul, Captain William C. Nicholson lands a party from the side-wheel steamer *Mississippi*, 10, to protect American lives and property at Shanghai, China.

October 16–18.   **John Brown's Raid.** The fanatical abolitionist John Brown seizes the U.S. arsenal at Harpers Ferry, West Virginia, in hopes of igniting a slave uprising. The uprising does not occur, but several hostages are taken, and eight of Brown's men and a

U.S. Marines storming the engine house held by John Brown's raiders at Harpers Ferry, West Virginia, a contemporary woodcut from *Harper's Weekly. Defense Department photograph (U.S. Marine Corps).*

number of townsfolk are killed or mortally wounded in exchanges of fire. The first U.S. troops to reach the scene are a company of 86 marines sent from Washington under Lieutenant Israel Greene; they arrive shortly before midnight on October 17. The next morning army Colonel Robert E. Lee, to whom the suppression of the insurrection is entrusted, sends Lieutenant J. E. B. Stuart to demand the raiders' surrender. Upon Brown's refusal, a storming party of 26 marines breaks into the arsenal. Two of the raiders are bayoneted, Brown is wounded by a slash from Lieutenant Greene's saber, and five others are captured. One marine is killed and another wounded.

1860

February 6.   **Antislavery operations.** Beginning on this date, in the course of the year U.S. naval vessels capture 13 slave ships.

March 1–2, 4.   A party of 50 seamen and marines from the ship sloop *Marion*, 16, Commander Thomas W. Brent, is landed to protect American property at Kissembo, in present-day Angola.

September 25.   The ship sloop *Levant*, 22, Commander William E. Hunt, sails from Hilo, Hawaii, bound for Aspinwall, Colombia, and disappears somewhere en route.

September 27.   The sloop *St. Mary's*, 20, lands a party of marines to help quell an insurrection in Panama City, Colombia (present-day Panama). A detachment from HMS *Clio* soon follows.

November 1.   Plans are announced to convert seven of the navy's sailing ships to steam power. The cost of the conversion will be $3,064,000.

November 6.   **Abraham Lincoln is elected president.** He has been viewed as the abolitionist candidate. Many Southerners regard his election as a sign that the time has come for their states to leave the Union.

December 20.   South Carolina becomes the first state to secede from the United States. Six other states of the Deep South follow by February 1, 1861.

December 26.   Major Robert Anderson, USA, commanding the defenses at Charleston, South Carolina, evacuates Fort Moultrie and moves his forces to Fort Sumter, on an island in the harbor.

1861

January 9.   At Charleston, South Carolina, forces, including cadets from The Citadel, fire on the chartered steamer *Star of the West* as she attempts to enter the harbor carrying reinforcements and supplies for Fort Sumter. The vessel returns to New York.

January 10.   At Pensacola, Florida, Lieutenant Adam J. Slemmer, commanding Company G. 1st U.S. Artillery, transfers his men from the mainland to Fort Pickens, on Santa Rosa Island. Although the navy yard is soon occupied by Southern troops, Pickens remains in Union Hands.

January 14.   The South Carolina legislature announces that any attempt to reinforce Fort Sumter will be regarded as an act of war.

February 8.   **The Confederacy is formed.** In Montgomery, Alabama, representatives of the seceded states adopt a constitution for the Confederate States of America.

February 9.   Jefferson Davis of Mississippi is chosen to be the president of the provisional government of the Confederate States.

February 20.   The Confederate States Navy Department is established.

February 21.   Stephen R. Mallory of Florida, formerly chairman of the U.S. House Naval Affairs Committee, is appointed secretary of the navy of the Confederate States.

February 27.   Congress approves the construction of seven steam sloops.

March 7.   Gideon Welles, a newspaper editor from Hartford, Connecticut, assumes office as the 24th secretary of the navy.

April 11.   Major Robert Anderson, USA, refuses a demand by General P. G. T. Beauregard, commanding Confederate forces at Charleston, South Carolina, to evacuate Fort Sumter.

April 12.   **First shots of the Civil War.** The Confederate batteries around Charleston Harbor open fire on Fort Sumter. Later in the day an expedition consisting of the steamship *Baltic*, USS *Pawnee*, and revenue cutter *Harriet Lane* under the command of Gustavus V. Fox, a former naval officer acting under special authority from the president, arrives off the harbor to reinforce Sumter, but it is too late.

April 13.   Major Anderson surrenders Fort Sumter. His garrison is evacuated by Fox's ships.

April 15.   President Lincoln calls for 75,000 90-day volunteers.

April 17.   Virginia casts her lot with the Confederacy.

April 17.   President Davis invites all interested parties to apply for letters of marque and reprisal.

April 19.   **The Blockade.** President Lincoln proclaims a blockade of the Confederate coast from Texas to South Carolina.

April 20.   **Seizure of the Norfolk Navy Yard.** Due in part to the lack of energy of its elderly commander, Captain Charles S. McCauley, Virginia forces seize this important installation almost intact. An expedition sent from Washington under the command of Captain Hiram Paulding on April 18 manages to burn nine of the vessels in the yard, tow away the sloop *Cumberland,* 32, and set fire to the facilities, but the Southern troops who burst into the yard upon its evacuation extinguish the flames. The dry dock and ordnance workshops are major gains to the Confederacy, as are hundreds of captured cannons that will soon be mounted in fortifications up and down the Atlantic coast. The Confederates are also successful in raising the screw frigate *Merrimack,* which had been burned to the waterline and sunk.

April 24.   **The Naval Academy leaves Annapolis.** Fearing that Maryland secessionists plan to attack the academy, Captain George S. Blake embarks the faculty and midshipmen on the frigate *Constitution* and sails to New York. On May 9, the academy relocates at Newport, Rhode Island, where it will remain throughout the war. In Annapolis the academy yard is transformed into an army hospital.

April 27.   President Lincoln extends the blockade to include the coasts of North Carolina and Virginia.

May 2–3.   **The Anaconda Plan.** In letters to President Lincoln and General George B. McClellan, General Winfield Scott outlines a plan for a "complete blockade" of the Confederate coast and a "powerful movement down the Mississippi . . . so as to envelop the insurgent states." Coupled with army offensives on the Southern land frontier, this strategy—soon dubbed the Anaconda Plan—will be pursued through the fours years of war to final victory.

May 3.   President Lincoln calls for the enlistment of 18,000 seamen.

May 6.   **Confederate privateering.** The Confederate Congress authorizes the issue of letters of marque and reprisal. Few Southern privateers ever put to sea, however, as blockade running offers greater profits at lesser risks; the Confederate war on Union shipping is waged almost exclusively by government cruisers.

May 6.   Arkansas leaves the Union.

May 7.   Tennessee indirectly withdraws from the Union by making an alliance with the Confederacy.

May 9.   **Bulloch to England.** Commander James D. Bulloch, CSN, is sent to England by Secretary Mallory to purchase and outfit the warships the Confederacy cannot build for herself. Because of neutrality laws, these purchases must be disguised. For almost four years Bulloch wages a brilliant battle of wits with the U.S. Ambassador Charles Francis Adams. Although his plans to procure European-built ironclads are finally frustrated, the cruisers he commissions—the *Alabama,* the *Florida,* and the *Shenandoah*—sweep the Northern merchant marine from the seas.

May 10.   In a letter to the Committee on Naval Affairs of the Confederate Congress, Secretary Mallory calls for the construction of "an iron-armored ship as a matter of the first necessity."

May 10.   The blockade of Charleston, South Carolina, is established by the screw frigate *Niagara,* Captain William W. McKean.

May 13.   The blockade of Pensacola, Florida, is established by the frigate *Sabine,* Captain N. S. Adams.

May 20.   North Carolina secedes from the Union.

May 24.   **Capture of Alexandria.** Commander Stephen C. Rowan, captain of the screw sloop *Pawnee,* commands an expedition, embarked at the Washington Navy Yard, which occupies Alexandria, Virginia.

May 26.   The blockade of New Orleans, Louisiana, and the mouth of the Mississippi is established by the screw sloop *Brooklyn,* Commander Charles H. Poor.

May 26.   The blockade of Mobile, Alabama, is established by the side-wheel steamer *Powhatan,* Lieutenant David Dixon Porter.

May 29.   The blockade of Savannah, Georgia, is established by the steamer *Union,* Commander John R. Goldsborough.

June 10.   **Work begins on the CSS Virginia.** At Norfolk, Lieutenant John M. Brooke, CSN, is placed in charge of converting the former wooden frigate *Merrimack,* which was raised on May 30, into the ironclad ram *Virginia.*

June 27.   **First naval officer killed in the war.** Union vessels on the Potomac have been engaging Confederate batteries on the Virginia shore since April.

The CSS *Virginia,* a possibly contemporary outboard profile discovered in the files of the old Bureau of Construction and Repair, now in the National Archives. *Official U.S. Navy photograph.*

Commander James H. Ward, first commandant of midshipmen at the Naval Academy, becomes the first U.S. Navy officer killed in the Civil War when he is picked off by a Confederate sharpshooter during an engagement at Mathias Point, Virginia.

June 27. **Blockade Strategy Board.** A board is convened to consider the implementation of the blockade and the seizure of advanced bases on the Confederate coast. It consists of Captain Samuel F. Du Pont, Commander Charles H. Davis, Major John G. Barnard of the army corps of engineers, and Professor Alexander D. Bache, superintendent of the coast survey.

June 28–29. **Capture of the St. Nicholas.** Confederates, led by Captain George N. Hollins, CSN, and Colonel Richard Thomas, CSA, capture the passenger steamer *St. Nicholas,* which they have boarded disguised as passengers on her regular route from Baltimore to Georgetown, District of Columbia. They had hoped to encounter the screw sloop *Pawnee* in the Potomac, but are unable to locate her and put into the Chesapeake Bay, where they capture three merchant vessels.

June 30–January 18, 1862. **Cruise of the CSS Sumter.** Sailing from New Orleans, the screw steamer *Sumter* slips past the blockader *Brooklyn* at the mouth of the Mississippi and begins her career as a commerce destroyer under the command of the redoubtable Raphael Semmes. In six months she takes 18 prizes. Her cruise ends at Gibraltar, where Semmes is unable to obtain coal. The *Sumter* is soon blockaded by three Union vessels and in April 1862 Semmes lays her up. He and his men receive the thanks of the Confederate Congress.

July 2: The blockade of Galveston, Texas, is established by the screw steamer *South Carolina,* Commander James Alden.

July 8. **First Confederate mines.** The screw tug *Resolute* picks up two floating "torpedoes"—mines—in the Potomac. In the course of the conflict the Confederates will show great resourcefulness in the development of this new type of naval weapon. More than 40 Union warships will be sunk or damaged by Confederate mines.

July 14. The blockade of Wilmington, North Carolina, is established by the screw steamer *Daylight,* Commander Samuel Lockwood.

July 21. **Battle of Bull Run.** Northern hopes for a short war evaporate when the Union army of General Irwin McDowell is defeated in the first major battle of the war. A detachment of U.S. Marines commanded by Major John Reynolds is present; 9 are killed, 19 wounded, and 16 missing. Union and Confederate naval batteries are also engaged, the former of which loses two guns.

July 24. Congress passes an act "for the temporary increase of the navy" authorizing President Lincoln to expand the service by whatever extent appears necessary.

August 1. Gustavus V. Fox, a former naval officer who had commanded the expedition to relieve Fort Sumter, is appointed assistant secretary of the navy. The legislation creating this position had been passed on July 24.

August 3. **First "navy air."** The navy has its first experience with aeronautics when John La Mountain ascends in a captive balloon from the U.S. steamer *Fanny* to observe the Confederate batteries at Sewell's Point, Virginia, near Hampton Roads.

August 3.   **Ironclad Board.** Congress appropriates $1.5 million for the construction of iron- or steel-clad ships and appoints an Ironclad Board of three officers to evaluate designs.

August 7.   **Eads's Turtles.** James B. Eads of St. Louis is given a contract by the war department to build seven shallow-draft, ironclad gunboats for service on western waters. The vessels—the *Cairo, Carondelet, Cincinnati, Louisville, Mound City, Pittsburgh,* and *St. Louis*—form the core of the gunboat flotilla that supports the Union army in breaching the defenses of the central Confederacy. Because of their humpbacked silhouettes, they are often referred to as "Eads's Turtles" or "Pooks's Turtles," after Constructor Samuel M. Pooks, USN, who is responsible for their design.

August 28–29.   **Hatteras Expedition.** Confederate forts Hatteras and Clark defending strategic Hatteras Inlet, North Carolina, are captured by a joint army-navy expedition consisting of 8 warships commanded by Flag Officer Silas H. Stringham and 2 transports carrying 900 troops under Major General Benjamin F. Butler. In addition to depriving the blockade runners of the most convenient entrance to Pamlico Sound, the occupation of this point provides the blockading squadrons with an advanced base. This is the first amphibious operation of the Civil War.

September 6.   **Capture of Paducah and Smithland.** In Kentucky, the gunboats *Tyler,* Commander John Rodgers, and *Lexington,* Commander Roger Stembel, support General U. S. Grant in the seizure of these strategic locations at the mouths of the Tennessee and Cumberland rivers.

The gunboat *Cairo,* one of the "turtles" that penetrated the Confederacy's waterways. She was sunk by a mine on December 12, 1862. *Courtesy Library of Congress.*

September 14.   At Pensacola, Florida, a party of 100 men in four boats from the screw frigate *Colorado,* under the command of Lieutenant John H. Russell, destroy the Confederate schooner *Judah.*

September 16.   In a report to Secretary Welles, the Ironclad Board enthusiastically endorses the concept of ironclad vessels and recommends the construction of designs it has considered for the *Monitor,* the *New Ironsides,* and the *Galena.*

October 1.   In Pamlico Sound, North Carolina, three small Confederate gunboats commanded by Flag Officer William F. Lynch capture the U.S. steamer *Fanny* with a detachment of troops aboard.

October 12.   **Action at Head of Passes.** A Confederate force consisting of the lightly armored ram *Manassas* and the armed steamers *Ivy* and *James L. Day* sails from New Orleans under the command of Commodore

The second day's action at Hatteras Inlet *(from left to right):* the *Susquehanna, Cumberland, Minnesota,* and *Wabash.* A drawing by eyewitness Alfred R. Waud, a war artist for *Harper's Weekly. Courtesy Library of Congress.*

George N. Hollins, CSN, to surprise the Union blockading squadron near Head of Passes on the Mississippi. The latter consists of the steam sloop *Richmond,* sloops *Preble* and *Vincennes,* gunboat *Water Witch,* and storeship *Nightingale.* In a hot action, the *Manassas* rams the *Richmond,* which runs aground, as does the *Vincennes.* The Confederates then withdraw.

October 25.   **Work begins on the Monitor.** At Greenpoint, New York, the brilliant, Swedish-born engineer John Ericsson commences construction of his revolutionary ironclad.

November 7.   **Capture of Port Royal Sound.** The largest fleet yet assembled under the U.S. flag, 77 vessels, is put under the command of Flag Officer Samuel F. Du Pont to seize an advanced base for the Atlantic blockading squadrons at Port Royal Sound, South Carolina, midway between Charleston and Savannah. It is accompanied by an army expeditionary force of 16,000 men under Brigadier General Thomas W. Sherman. The fire from Du Pont's ships forces the Confederates to evacuate Forts Walker and Beauregard, whose garrisons are ferried to the mainland by Commodore Josiah Tattnall's little Confederate squadron. U.S. forces land unopposed.

November 8.   **Trent Affair.** The screw frigate *San Jacinto,* Captain Charles Wilkes, stops the British mail steamer *Trent* in Old Bahama Channel and seizes James Mason and John Slidell, the Confederate envoys to Great Britain and France. Wilkes's action precipitates a major international incident. On December 27, Secretary of State Seward apologizes to Her Majesty's Government for Wilkes's conduct and orders the envoys released.

November 11.   Another aerial reconnaissance is made from shipboard when "aeronaut" Professor Thaddeus Lowe ascends in a captive balloon from the "balloon boat" *G. W. Parke Custis* in the Potomac River.

December 2.   Secretary Welles advises President Lincoln that since the establishment of the blockade the navy has captured 153 vessels.

December 17.   **Stone Fleets.** Seven old vessels laden with stones and concrete are sunk by the blockading squadron at the entrance to Savannah harbor in an attempt to impede navigation. "Stone Fleets" will be sunk at various other places and times in the course of the war by both Union and Confederate forces with the aim of preventing one another from getting in or out of particular ports or rivers. They are not especially effective.

December 21.   **Medal of Honor.** Congress creates the Navy Medal of Honor to reward petty officers, seamen, and marines "as shall most distinguish themselves by their gallantry in action and other seamanlike qualities." Commissioned officers will not become eligible until 1915. A total of 375 medals are awarded for the Civil War. The Army Medal of Honor is instituted six months later, on July 12, 1862.

1862

January 9.   Flag Officer David F. Farragut is assigned to command the West Gulf Blockading Squadron. His appointment reflects the government's decision that he is the man to carry out the single most important naval operation undertaken so far in the war: an attack on New Orleans, the South's largest city and principal seaport.

January 16.   The Eads gunboats are commissioned.

February 4–6.   **Capture of Fort Henry.** The defenses of the central Confederacy extend from the Mississippi to the Appalachians. The keys to the center of this position are Forts Henry and Donelson, which command the Tennessee and Cumberland rivers, respectively. Plans for a joint, army-navy attack on the forts by forces under General U. S. Grant and Flag Officer Andrew H. Foote are frustrated when rains delay Grant's advance and Foote decides to tackle Fort Henry with his ships alone. The attack is led by the ironclads *Carondelet, Cincinnati, Essex* (which is disabled during the action), and *St. Louis,* supported by the wooden gunboats *Conestoga, Lexington,* and *Tyler.* Their fire is so effective that all but four of the fort's guns are dismounted and its commander, Brigadier General Lloyd Tilghman, CSA, surrenders the position.

February 7–8.   **Capture of Roanoke Island.** An army-navy expedition under Brigadier General Ambrose E. Burnside and Flag Officer Louis M. Goldsborough overwhelms the Confederate defenders to take Roanoke Island, on Albemarle Sound, North Carolina. This victory completes the Union hold on the Carolina sounds.

February 10.   **Battle of Elizabeth City.** Following the capture of the Roanoke Island, the small Confederate squadron on Albemarle Sound—five "cottonclad" gunboats under Flag Officer William F. Lynch—withdrew up the Pasquotank River to Elizabeth City, North

Carolina. There it is destroyed by a superior Union force under Commander Stephen C. Rowan.

February 14.   **Attack on Fort Donelson.** In Tennessee the gunboats of Flag Officer Foote's flotilla cooperate with land forces under General U. S. Grant in operations against Fort Donelson, commanding the Cumberland River. In a sharp action, the flagship *St. Louis* and the *Louisville* are disabled, and Foote receives a wound from the lingering effects of which he will die in June 1863. The continued presence of the gunboats on the river greatly restricts the Confederates' freedom of action, however, and the fort surrenders to Grant's army on February 16. The loss of Forts Henry and Donelson opens western Tennessee to invasion and compels Confederate General Albert Sidney Johnson to withdraw from Kentucky.

February 17.   At Norfolk, Virginia, the ironclad ram CSS *Virginia* is commissioned under the command of Captain Franklin Buchanan.

February 25.   At New York, the USS *Monitor* is commissioned under the command of Lieutenant John L. Worden.

March 8.   **Battle of Hampton Roads.** Accompanied by two small gunboats, the Confederate ironclad *Virginia* attacks the Union blockading squadron at Hampton Roads, Virginia. After ramming and sinking the sloop *Cumberland,* 32, Lieutenant George U. Morris, she at-tacks the frigate *Congress,* 52, Lieutenant Joseph B. Smith, which runs aground and is destroyed by the *Virginia*'s incendiary shells. Captain Buchanan is wounded in the course of the action, and the *Virginia,* which left part of her ram in the *Cumberland,* returns to Norfolk for repairs. For a few hours it appears that the South may be in possession of a means to break the blockade, but the *Monitor* reaches Hampton Roads that evening.

March 9.   **First battle between ironclads.** Returning to Hampton Roads to complete her work of destruction, the CSS *Virginia,* now commanded by Lieutenant Catesby ap R. Jones, is confronted by Lieutenant Worden's *Monitor.* The ensuing action, fought at close ranges over a period of four hours, ends in a draw. Strategically, too, the honors are even. The *Monitor* has preserved the blockade, but the *Virginia* prevents McClellan's army from using the James River in its upcoming Peninsula Campaign.

March 13.   Confederate forces evacuate New Madrid, Missouri, covered by three gunboats of Flag Officer George N. Hollins's squadron.

March 14.   **Capture of New Bern.** Thirteen warships under Commander Stephen C. Rowan provide gunfire support for a force of 12,000 men under Brigadier General Ambrose E. Burnside in the seizure of New Bern, on the Neuse River in North Carolina.

The CSS *Virginia* rams the *Cumberland,* whose crew's washing still hangs on the lines: a painting by Alexander C. Stuart. *U.S. Marine Corps photograph.*

The second day at Hampton Roads: the *Monitor* and the *Virginia* (ex-*Merrimack*) fight to a draw. This Currier and Ives lithograph was published in New York in 1862. *Courtesy Beverley R. Robinson Collection, U.S. Naval Academy Museum.*

March 16–April 7. **Struggle for Island No. 10.** Following the fall of Forts Henry and Donelson, the South sought to establish a western anchor for the defense of the central Confederacy by fortifying a large, wooded island in the Mississippi River on the northern border of Tennessee. The gunboats and mortar boats of Flag Officer Foote's flotilla engage the Confederate batteries there, but are unable to silence them. Then, on the stormy night of April 5, the ironclad *Carondelet,* Commander Henry W. Walke, runs the gauntlet past the island. The ironclad *Pittsburgh,* Commander Egbert Thompson, duplicates this feat on April 7. That same day they cover a Union army that crosses the river to the east to operate against Island No. 10. Confederate Brigadier General William W. Mackall thereupon surrenders the position and its defenders—more than 5,000 men and 20 pieces of heavy artillery.

March 22. The Confederacy's first British-built cruiser, the CSS *Florida,* sails under the command of Acting Master John Low from Liverpool for the Bahamas, where she will receive her guns. Her cover name is the *Oreto.*

March 28. **The America.** A boat party under Lieutenant Thomas F. Stevens returns to Jacksonville, Florida, after an expedition up the St. John's River, during which it had raised the famous racing yacht *America*

(CSS *Memphis*). Purchased by the Confederacy from an English sympathizer for use as a commerce raider, she had been scuttled when Union forces trapped her in the river. She is taken into the U.S. Navy under her original name.

April 6. **Battle of Shiloh.** Confederate forces led by General Albert Sidney Johnson surprise Grant's army at Pittsburgh Landing (Shiloh), Tennessee, and threaten to push it into the Tennessee River. Fire from the gunboats *Lexington,* Lieutenant James W. Shirk, and *Tyler,* Lieutenant William Gwin, is instrumental in stemming the Confederate advance.

April 14. On the upper Mississippi, Flag Officer Foote's mortar boats begin bombarding Fort Pillow, Tennessee, the next Confederate stronghold below Island No. 10.

April 18. **Beginning of the battle for New Orleans.** A flotilla of Union mortar boats under Commander David Dixon Porter begins to bombard Fort Jackson, on the Mississippi River below New Orleans.

April 20. In an effort to prevent Union forces from ascending the Mississippi, the Confederates have stretched an obstruction, consisting of hulks linked together by a huge chain, across the river under the guns of Forts Jackson and St. Philip. It is breached by the

Flag Officer and soon-to-be Rear Admiral David G. Farragut still wears a captain's uniform in this *carte de visite* photograph made in New Orleans in 1862. *Courtesy U.S. Naval Academy Museum.*

gunboats *Itasca* and *Pinola,* both under the orders of Captain Henry H. Bell.

April 24.   **The Battle of New Orleans.** Concluding that the bombardment of Fort Jackson is getting nowhere, Flag Officer Farragut resolves to lead his fleet—17 vessels, all wooden, plus Porter's mortar schooners—upstream between the Confederate fortifications. The movement begins at 2:00 A.M. Miraculously, not a single one of Farragut's ships is disabled by the forts' fire. Upriver, a fierce, confused action is fought with Commander John K. Mitchell's Confederate flotilla, consisting of the thin-skinned ironclad ram *Manassas,* the gunboats *McRae* and *Jackson,* two armed launches, the Louisiana State gunboats *General Quitman* and *Governor Moore,* and six River Defense gunboats mounting 1 or 2 guns apiece. The screw sloop *Varuna,* 10, Com-

mander Charles S. Boggs, is rammed and sunk by the *Governor Moore,* 2, Lieutenant Beverley Kennon, and the *Stonewall Jackson,* 1, Captain George W. Philips, but she is the only Union ship lost. The Confederate forces are annihilated. The total number of Union casualties for the operation of April 18–26 is 39 men killed and 171 wounded.

April 25.   The city of New Orleans surrenders to Farragut. Its loss is the greatest blow the Confederacy has suffered. The unfinished ironclad *Mississippi,* the most powerful vessel ever put under construction in the Confederate States, is destroyed to prevent her capture.

April 26.   An amphibious operation under Commander Samuel Lockwood and Brigadier General John G. Parke captures Fort Macon, North Carolina.

April 28.   The defenders of Forts Jackson and St. Philip, isolated by the capture of New Orleans, surrender to Farragut's fleet. The unfinished ironclad *Louisiana* is destroyed to prevent her capture, as are the CSS *Defiance* and *McRae.*

May 10.   Union forces capture Norfolk, Virginia, and reoccupy the Norfolk Navy Yard.

May 10.   Stunned by the news of Farragut's success in passing Forts Jackson and St. Philip, the Confederates evacuate Pensacola, Florida. It is promptly occupied by Union forces.

May 10.   **Action at Plum Point Bend.** Captain James E. Montgomery leads his Confederate River Defense Fleet of eight cottonclad gunboats in a spirited attack on the Union gunboats and mortar schooners bombarding Fort Pillow on the Mississippi River. The CSS *General Bragg* rams and sinks the gunboat *Cincinnati,* Commander R. N. Stembel, and the *Mound City,* Commander A. H. Kilty, is rammed by the CSS *General Earl Van Dorn,* Captain Isaac D. Fulkerson, and runs aground to keep from sinking. The Confederates then return to Fort Pillow.

May 11.   **Destruction of the CSS Virginia.** The fall of Norfolk seals the fate of the Confederate ironclad. Finding that the vessel draws too much water to retire up the James River, Flag Officer Josiah Tattnall, who has replaced the wounded Buchanan, reluctantly orders her to be blown up.

May 15.   On the James River, Virginia, a Union squadron consisting of the *Monitor,* the ironclads *Galena* and *Naugatuck,* and the wooden gunboats *Aroostook* and *Port Royal* under the command of Commander John Rodgers pushes upstream to within eight miles of

Richmond before being halted by Confederate batteries at Drewry's Bluff.

June 4–5.   Hammered by the fire of Union vessels on the Mississippi, Confederate forces evacuate Fort Pillow, the last fortification above Memphis, Tennessee.

June 6.   **Battle of Memphis.** Captain J. E. Montgomery's Confederate River Defense Fleet is destroyed in a sharp, close action with the ironclad gunboats *Benton, Cairo, Carondelet, Louisville,* and *St. Louis,* Captain Charles H. Davis, and the rams *Monarch* and *Queen of the West,* Colonel Charles Ellet, Jr. The Confederate ships *General Beauregard, General Bragg, General M. Jeff Thompson, General Sterling Price, General Sumter,* and *Little Rebel* are captured, grounded, or sunk; only the *General Earl Van Dorn* escapes. Colonel Ellet is mortally wounded. Memphis surrenders to Davis, opening the Mississippi all the way to Vicksburg.

June 28.   Flag Officer Farragut's fleet runs past the batteries at Vicksburg, the last great Confederate bastion on the Mississippi.

July 1.   Farragut's fleet meets the Western Gunboat Flotilla of newly promoted Flag Officer Charles H. Davis above Vicksburg.

July 1.   **Malvern Hill.** In April General George B. McClellan exploited Union command of the sea to land the Army of the Potomac on the tip of the peninsula between the James and York rivers and launched an advance on Richmond from the rear. Defeated in a series of battles on the outskirts of Richmond by General Robert E. Lee, who had just assumed command of the Army of Northern Virginia, late in June McClellan begins to withdraw towards the James. Lee makes several unsuccessful attempts to intercept his retreat, the last at Malvern Hill on the bank of the river. Here the ironclad *Galena* and the gunboats *Aroostook* and *Jacob Bell* are able to enfilade the right flank of the Confederate line, materially contributing to the repulse of Lee's attack.

July 4.   The Confederate minelayer and balloon ship *Teaser,* Lieutenant Hunter Davidson, is captured by the gunboat *Maratanza,* Lieutenant T. H. Stevens, at Haxall's on the James River, Virginia. Her crew escapes ashore.

July 5.   **Bureau system reorganized.** The number of the Navy Department's bureaus is increased to eight by the creation of the bureaus of Equipment and Recruiting, Navigation, and Steam Engineering.

July 14.   Congress abolishes the navy's daily spirit ration to enlisted men.

July 15.   **The Arkansas.** On a reconnaissance up the Yazoo River, Mississippi, the gunboats *Carondelet,* Commander Henry W. Walke, and *Tyler,* Lieutenant William Gwin, and the ram *Queen of the West* are met by the new Confederate ironclad ram *Arkansas,* Lieutenant Isaac N. Brown. The *Arkansas* pursues the three ships into the Mississippi, heavily damaging the *Carondelet* and *Tyler,* and proceeds to run through Farragut's fleet to take refuge beneath the guns of Vicksburg.

July 16.   **First rear admiral.** Congress creates the rank of rear admiral and first confers it on David Glasgow Far-

The Battle of Memphis: a contemporary lithograph by Currier and Ives. *Official U.S. Navy photograph.*

ragut as a reward for the capture of New Orleans. The act also establishes the ranks of commodore and lieutenant commander.

July 19. **Pension bill.** Congress provides that all naval personnel disabled in the line of duty will be granted lifetime pensions.

July 22. Anchored beneath the guns of Vicksburg, the Confederate ironclad ram *Arkansas,* Commander Isaac N. Brown, fights off an attack by the ironclad *Essex,* Commander William B. ("Dirty Bill") Porter, and the ram *Queen of the West,* Lieutenant Colonel Alfred W. Ellet.

July 24. Falling water forces Farragut's fleet to pull back downstream to Baton Rouge and New Orleans.

August 6. **Destruction of the Arkansas.** Confederate Major General Earl Van Dorn orders Lieutenant Henry Stevens, temporarily commanding the ironclad ram *Arkansas* while Commander Brown is on sick leave, to support an attack on Baton Rouge, Louisiana. The ram's engines break down during an engagement with Commander W. B. Porter's ironclad *Essex,* and Lieutenant Stevens sets his ship afire to prevent her from being captured.

August 10. At a secret rendezvous at Green Cay in the Bahamas, the cruiser *Florida* is armed and commissioned into Confederate service by Lieutenant John N. Maffit. She is the first of the Confederate cruisers Commander Bulloch has had built in England.

August 24–June 19, 1864. **Cruise of the Alabama.** CSS *Alabama,* another of Commander Bulloch's British-built cruisers, is commissioned off Terciera, Azores, by Captain Raphael Semmes. She will become the most successful commerce raider of all time, capturing 68 merchantmen valued at more than $15,500,000 and sinking 1 warship on a cruise that lasts for 22 months and extends from the Gulf of Mexico to the China Sea.

August 26. Captain Franklin Buchanan is promoted to become the first rear admiral in the Confederate States Navy.

September 4. The CSS *Florida,* Lieutenant John N. Maffit, runs the blockade into Mobile Bay after yellow fever breaks out on board.

October 1. The army's Western Gunboat Fleet is transferred to the Navy Department and renamed the Mississippi Squadron. Upon the recommendation of Farragut, who found Rear Admiral Charles H. Davis deficient in energy, Acting Rear Admiral David Dixon Porter is placed in command.

October 3–9. The defenses and city of Galveston, Texas, are bombarded and captured by naval forces under Commander William B. Renshaw, consisting of the wooden gunboats *Clifton, Harriet Lane, Owasco,* and *Westfield* and the mortar schooner *Henry James.*

October 28. In the Chesapeake Bay, the ship *Alleghanian* is captured and burned off the mouth of the Rappahannock by a Confederate boat party led by Lieutenant John Taylor Wood, CSN.

October 31. **Mine warfare.** In the course of the month, Confederates establish a Torpedo Bureau under Brigadier General Gabriel J. Rains and a Naval Submarine Battery Service under Lieutenant Hunter

The Confederate cruiser *Alabama* leaving Port Royal, Jamaica: a woodcut from the *Illustrated London News,* April 11, 1863. *U.S. Naval Institute Collection.*

Davidson. Both the "torpedoes" and the "submarine batteries" are what are now called mines. Several Confederate naval officers, most notably Commander Matthew Fontaine Maury, had experimented with mines. Davidson took charge after Maury was sent to Britain to second Commander Bulloch's efforts to buy warships abroad. The Confederates will make extensive use of mines in harbor and river defense.

December 12.   **First ship mined.** The ironclad *Cairo*, Lieutenant Commander Thomas O. Selfridge, Jr., is sunk by a mine in the Yazoo River, Mississippi. She is the first of more than 40 Union vessels that will be destroyed or damaged by mines during the war.

December 20–27.   **Beginning of the Vicksburg campaign.** With Memphis and New Orleans in Northern hands, Vicksburg is the principal Southern stronghold on the Mississippi. To capture it would fulfill one of the objectives of the Anaconda Plan, cutting the Confederacy in two and reopening the Northwest's outlet to the sea. The first advance on the city is made by two Union armies, one moving overland under Major General U. S. Grant and the other down the Mississippi under Major General William T. Sherman. It ends in failure when Confederate cavalry destroy the railways and supply depots in Grant's rear (December 20), compelling him to retire, and Vicksburg's defenders repulse Sherman's landing at Chickasaw Bluffs, a few miles north of the city (December 27).

1863

January 1.   **Recapture of Galveston.** A Confederate surprise attack by land and sea recaptures Galveston, Texas. The Union naval force anchored off the town consists of the wooden gunboats *Harriet Lane, Westfield, Clifton, Corypheus, Owasco,* and *Sachem,* and is under Commander William B. Renshaw. It is engaged by a Confederate flotilla commanded by Major Leon Smith, CSA, composed of the cottonclad gunboats *Bayou City* and *Neptune* and the tenders *John F. Carr* and *Lady Gwin.* The *Harriet Lane,* Commander Jonathan M. Wainwright, sinks the *Neptune,* but is captured by the *Bayou City* in a hard-fought boarding action in which Wainwright is killed. The *Westfield* runs aground. Commander Renshaw sets her afire to keep her from being captured and is killed when she blows up before his boat party can get clear. The other four Union ships hurriedly put to sea.

January 4–11.   **Arkansas Post.** A joint army-navy expedition, 30,000 men under Major General John A. McClernand and six gunboats under Rear Admiral David Dixon Porter, succeeds in the capture of Fort Hindman, at Arkansas Post. The Confederate garrison, 4,700 men commanded by Brigadier General Thomas J. Churchill, CSA, surrenders after a two-day bombardment in which Porter's ships disable every one of the fort's guns.

January 11.   The Confederate cruiser *Alabama,* Captain Raphael Semmes, surprises and sinks the side-wheel gunboat *Hatteras,* Lieutenant Commander Homer C. Blake, in a sharp night action 30 miles off Galveston, Texas.

January 16–August 23.   **First cruise of the Florida.** The Confederate cruiser *Florida,* Lieutenant John N. Maffit, runs the blockade out of Mobile, Alabama, to begin her career as a commerce raider. Operating primarily in the South Atlantic, she takes 22 prizes before entering port at Brest, France, to refit. It will be six months before she returns to sea.

January 21.   At Sabine Pass, Texas, the small blockaders *Morning Light,* Acting Master John Dillingham, and *Velocity,* Acting Master Nathan W. Drummond, are captured by the Confederate cottonclads *Josiah Bell* and *Uncle Ben,* under Major Oscar M. Watkins, CSA.

January 30.   The gunboat *Isaac Smith,* Acting Lieutenant Francis S. Conover, is captured by Confederate land forces while on a reconnaissance up the Stono River, South Carolina.

January 31.   **Charleston sortie.** Flag Officer Duncan N. Ingraham, CSN, leads the ironclad rams *Chicora,* Commander John R. ("Handsome Jack") Tucker, and *Palmetto State,* Lieutenant John Rutledge, on a dawn attack on the blockading fleet off Charleston, South Carolina. The gunboat *Mercedita,* Commander H. S. Stellwagen, is rammed by and surrenders to the *Palmetto State,* while the *Keystone State,* Commander William E. Le Roy, is heavily damaged by the *Chicora.* The blockading squadron retires to the open sea, and Confederate authorities at Charleston try unsuccessfully to persuade the foreign consuls that the blockade has been broken.

February 3–March 17.   **Yazoo Pass expedition.** Following the failure of his overland advance on Vicksburg (see December 20–27, 1862), Grant moves his army down the Mississippi to Milliken's Bend, barely 10 miles above the city. Unusually high water adds to the difficulties of campaigning in the marshy lowlands around Vicks-

The Confederate cruiser *Florida* at Brest, France: a woodcut from *L'Illustration*, 1863. *U.S. Naval Institute Collection.*

burg, but Grant is determined to retain the initiative. He has already decided that the only way to take the city is from the high ground to its east. His problem is how to get there. First he undertakes to cut a canal across the peninsula opposite the city, which would allow Porter's fleet to move south without having to run past the Vicksburg batteries. This project is finally abandoned on March 29. Simultaneously, two other attempts are made to open a passage south through the bayous west of the Mississippi, and two essentially naval operations are conducted east of the river with the aim of approaching Vicksburg from the north. The first, to which Porter commits eight light-draft gunboats under Lieutenant Commander William Smith, is to move down the Tallahatchie and Yazoo rivers from the Yazoo Pass, 325 miles upstream. To counter this threat, the Confederates hurriedly construct Fort Pemberton, just above the junction of the two rivers. There Smith's gunboats are halted on March 11. They are unable to silence the fort with their fire, and there is no place in the flooded countryside for the troops accompanying them to land. On March 17 the gunboats begin to fall back. By then the Steele's Bayou expedition is under way (See March 14–24).

February 3.   A Confederate attack on Fort Donelson, Tennessee, is repulsed with the help of a squadron of gunboats—the *Brilliant, Fairplay, Lexington, Robb, St. Clair,* and *Silver Lake*—under Lieutenant Commander Le Roy Fitch.

February 14.   The ironclad ram *Queen of the West,* Colonel C. R. Ellet, grounds under the fire of three enemy batteries while on a patrol up the Red River, Louisiana. Ellet abandons the ship, which is taken into Confederate service.

February 24.   Major Joseph L. Brent, CSA, leads a squadron consisting of the recently captured ironclad ram *Queen of the West,* the ram *Webb,* and the cottonclad *Beatty* to attack the ironclad *Indianola,* Lieutenant Commander George Brown, near Warrenton, Mississippi. Rammed by the *Queen of the West,* the *Indianola* fills with water, grounds herself, and surrenders. The Confederates immediately begin efforts to refloat her.

February 25.   **Porter's ruse.** The Confederates give up the attempt to salvage the *Indianola* and burn her to the waterline upon the approach of a large Union gunboat. This "gunboat" turns out to be a barge, rigged with dummy stacks, superstructure, and guns, which Admiral Porter sent floating downstream in hopes that it would produce the result it did.

February 28.   The Confederate blockade runner *Rattlesnake* (ex-CSS *Nashville*) is shelled and destroyed under the guns of Fort McAllister, on the Ogeechee River, Georgia, by the monitor *Montauk,* Commander John L. Worden.

March 13–14.   A Confederate night attack on Fort Anderson, on the Neuse River, North Carolina, is beaten off with the help of the gunboats *Ceres, Hetzel, Hunchback,*

Rear Admiral David Dixon Porter appears as a lieutenant commander in this *carte de visite* photograph made early in 1862. *U.S. Naval Academy Museum.*

and *Shawsheen* and two small craft under Commander Henry K. Davenport.

March 14.   **Farragut at Port Hudson.** Rear Admiral David G. Farragut leads a squadron of seven ships up the Mississippi to establish a blockade at the mouth of the Red River. This force must pass the powerful batteries the Confederates have emplaced at Port Hudson, Louisiana. The veteran side-wheeler *Mississippi*, Captain Melancton Smith, runs aground and is destroyed in the attempt, and several other vessels are damaged. Only Farragut's flagship, the *Hartford,* and the gunboat *Albatross,* which is lashed alongside, succeed in fighting their way through. Continuing upstream to Warrenton, Mississippi (just south of Vicksburg), Farragut establishes communications with Porter on the 20th and then begins to blockade the Red River, from which Confederate trade is entering the Mississippi.

March 14–24.   **Steele's Bayou expedition.** When the Yazoo Pass expedition is halted at Fort Pemberton (see February 3–March 17), Grant asks Porter to make another attempt to reach Vicksburg by the waterways east of the Mississippi, this time by pushing north from Milliken's Bend up Steele's Bayou to enter the Yazoo via Deer Creek, Rolling Fork, and the Sunflower River. Porter himself takes command of the expedition, which consists of the gunboats

Carondelet, Cincinnati, Louisville, Mound City, and *Pittsburgh,* four mortar schooners, and four tugs. Pushing through the tortuous river channels in the face of a resourceful defense, Porter reaches Rolling Fork on March 19. Obstructions in the channel stop the gunboats here, and when the Confederates begin felling trees across the river behind them it appears that they may be trapped. Union infantry, following the ships along the marshy river banks, press forward in a fatiguing night march to reach them on March 21. The expedition then retires.

March 25.   The ironclad ram *Lancaster,* Lieutenant Colonel John A. Ellet, is sunk and her sistership, the *Switzerland,* Colonel C. R. Ellet, is heavily damaged in an attempt to pass the Vicksburg batteries to reinforce Farragut at the Red River.

April 2.   **Final campaign against Vicksburg.** Meeting with Admiral Porter, Grant proposes a new plan of operations against the city. While Sherman distracts the defense by a feint at Haynes's Bluff, north of Vicksburg, Grant's army will march south along the western bank of the Mississippi. At the same time, Porter's fleet and the army's empty transports will run south past the Vicksburg batteries. The two forces will meet at Hard Times, 30 miles below the city, where the transports will carry Grant's men across the river to its eastern shore. This plan will bring victory.

April 7.   **First attack on Charleston.** Rear Admiral Samuel F. Du Pont, commanding the South Atlantic Blockading Squadron, attacks the fortifications of Charleston harbor with an ironclad squadron of nine ships: the *New Ironsides* (flag) and the monitors *Catskill, Keokuk, Montauk, Nahant, Nantucket, Passaic, Patapsco,* and *Weehawken.* The defenses of Charleston are by far the strongest of any Confederate port, some of masonry construction, bolstered by underwater obstacles and large numbers of both contact and electrical mines. Du Pont's ships slug it out with the forts at point-blank range for 50 minutes. Little damage is done to the Confederate works, but the monitors take a hammering. The *Catskill* is hit 20 times; the *Passaic,* 35; the *Nahant,* 36, the *Patapsco,* 47, the *Nantucket,* 51, the *Weehawken,* 53, and the *Keokuk,* which sinks the next morning, 90. Du Pont plans to renew the attack the following day, but his captains convince him that no good would come of it. Charleston cannot be captured by ships alone.

April 9–October 28.   **Cruise of the Georgia.** At a secret rendezvous off the coast of France, Commander

William L. Maury commissions the former merchantman *Japan* into Southern service as the CSS *Georgia*. The vessel had been purchased in Scotland by Maury's father, Commander Matthew Fontaine Maury. The *Georgia* takes nine prizes on a cruise to the Cape of Good Hope and is sold upon her return to Europe, her sailing characteristics having proven unsuitable for commerce raiding.

April 16–17.   On the Mississippi, Admiral Porter's gunboats and the army's empty transports run south past the Vicksburg batteries under cover of darkness. Despite heavy fire from the bluffs, only one vessel—a transport—is sunk.

April 20.   Land and sea forces cooperate to capture a Confederate redoubt mounting five guns at Hill's Point, on the Nansemond River, Virginia.

April 20.   Confederate defenders of Fort Burton, at Butte à la Rose, Louisiana, surrender after being bombarded by a small naval force headed by the side-wheel *Estrella*, Lieutenant Commander A. P. Cooke.

April 29.   Porter's gunboats engage the Confederate batteries at Grand Gulf, Mississippi, enabling the empty army transports to pass safely in the night.

April 30–May 1.   **Grant crosses the Mississippi.** The transports that Porter has shepherded south ferry Grant's army across the Mississippi from Hard Times to Bruinsburg, 10 miles below Grand Gulf. This movement solves the strategic problem with which Grant has been contending since February. His army is on the east bank of the Mississippi, in position to advance on Vicksburg from the rear.

May 3.   Returning to engage the Confederate positions at Grand Gulf, Porter finds that the garrison, outflanked by Grant's advance, has withdrawn.

May 4.   Admiral Porter pushes up the Red River, Louisiana, with a force consisting of the ironclads *Arizona, Benton, Estrella, Lafayette, Pittsburgh,* and *Switzerland* and the wooden gunboat *General Sterling Price.* Upon his arrival Admiral Farragut, who had been blockading the mouth of the Red River since late March, returns to New Orleans.

May 5.   Porter's squadron reaches Fort De Russy, Louisiana, which the Confederates have evacuated in the face of the Union advance.

May 6.   **"Savez" Read.** Off the coast of Brazil the CSS *Florida* captures the brig *Clarence,* which is commissioned into Confederate service under Lieutenant Charles W. ("Savez") Read, the "anchor man" of the Naval Academy Class of 1860. Commencing his op-

Lieutenant Charles W. Read, CSN. This "class picture" was made upon his graduation from the U.S. Naval Academy in 1860. He stood last in his class. *Nimitz Library Special Collection.*

erations off the mid-Atlantic seaboard, between June 6–12 Read takes six prizes, to one of which, the bark *Tacony,* he transfers his crew, destroying the *Clarence.* Between June 12–24 he makes another 15 captures and again transfers his crew, this time to the schooner *Archer,* in which he sails into Portland, Maine, with the idea of cutting out the revenue cutter *Caleb Cushing.* The raiders succeed in getting the *Cushing* out of the harbor on the night of June 26–27 but are overtaken by five pursuing steamers the next morning. Read orders his men into the lifeboats and sets fire to the *Cushing,* which blows up just after their capture.

May 7.   Alexandria, Louisiana, is occupied by Porter's squadron.

May 16, 18.   **Grant's advance.** Having brushed away Confederate forces to the east of Vicksburg, Grant turns back towards the city. Lieutenant General John C. Pemberton, commanding the city's defenders, moves to block his advance and is defeated at the battles of Champion's Hill and Big Black River.

May 18.   Admiral Porter sends six gunboats under Lieutenant Commander John Grimes Walker up the Yazoo River to support Grant's army in the operations east of Vicksburg. The force reaches Yazoo City on May 21, compelling the Confederates to destroy three unfinished rams and a well-equipped navy yard.

May 19–July 3.   **Siege of Vicksburg.** After unsuccessful attempts to take Vicksburg by storm on May 19 and 22, Grant settles down to a regular siege. The vessels of Porter's squadron are active throughout the ensuing operations, firing a weekly average of almost 2,000 shells into the city. The gunboat *Cincinnati*, Lieutenant George M. Bache, is sunk in action with the Vicksburg batteries on May 27.

May 27–July 8.   **Siege of Port Hudson.** To the south of Vicksburg, a Union army under Major General Nathaniel P. Banks closes around Port Hudson, Louisiana, the other Confederate strongpoint on the Mississippi. Farragut's ships support the siege, bombarding the city for three to five hours each night.

June 7.   A Confederate attack on Union forces at Milliken's Bend on the Mississippi is repelled with the help of fire support from the ironclad ram *Choctaw*, Lieutenant Commander Francis M. Ramsay, and gunboat *Lexington*, Lieutenant George M. Bache.

June 8.   The steam tug *Boston* is captured at Pass à l'Outre on the Mississippi by a boat party led by Master James Duke, CSN. Putting to sea in their prize, the Confederates capture and burn the barks *Lenox* and *Texana* before running the blockade into Mobile on June 11.

June 17.   The Confederate ironclad ram *Atlanta,* Commander William A. Webb, runs aground and is captured while engaging the monitors *Weehawken*, Captain John Rodgers, and *Nahant,* Commander John Downes, in Wassaw Sound, Georgia.

July 4.   **Vicksburg surrenders.** Port Hudson follows on July 9. The Confederacy has been cut in two along the line of the Mississippi. These events, occurring almost simultaneously with Lee's defeat at Gettysburg (July 1–3), signal the beginning of the end of the Confederacy.

July 4.   Fire support from the gunboat *Tyler,* Lieutenant Commander James M. Prichett, aids the Union garrison in repelling a Confederate attack on Helena, Arkansas.

July 10.   **Beginning of the siege of Charleston.** The failure of the naval attack of April 7 to overcome the harbor defenses of Charleston, South Carolina, leads to the initiation of combined operations against the city. To conduct them, Brigadier General Quincy A. Gillmore is put in command of the Department of the South (June 12), and Admiral Du Pont is replaced as commander of South Atlantic Blockading Squadron by Rear Admiral John A. Dahlgren (July 6). Gillmore believes that if the army can neutralize Fort Sumter, squarely in the mouth of the harbor, the fleet can enter and reduce the remaining fortifications. The first step must be the capture of Battery Wagner, on the northern end of Morris Island, from which the army's guns can reach Sumter. On this date one of Gillmore's brigades, covered by the fire of Dahlgren's ships, crosses the inlet from Folly Island, already in Union possession, to land on the southern shore of Morris Island.

July 11.   A Union attempt to storm Battery Wagner is repulsed with heavy losses.

July 13.   On the Yazoo River, Mississippi, Lieutenant Commander J. G. Walkers's gunboats land troops who capture Yazoo City.

July 14.   A squadron of eight gunboats under Rear Admiral Samuel P. Lee captures Fort Powhatan on the James River, Virginia.

July 16.   Commander James Bulloch, the Confederate purchasing officer in Europe, contracts with the Bordeaux firm of Lucien Arman for the construction of two double-turreted ironclad rams, one of which will eventually be commissioned as the CSS *Stonewall.*

July 16.   **Shimonoseki incident.** On June 25, the American merchant steamer *Pembroke* was fired on while passing through the Shimonoseki Strait, between the Japanese islands of Kyushu and Honshu, by ships belonging to a feudal lord, Prince Nagata. In retribution, the screw sloop *Wyoming,* Captain David McDougal, enters the straits and although outgunned, sinks all three of the prince's warships present and shells the forts ashore.

July 18.   At Charleston, South Carolina, a second assault on Battery Wagner, again supported by the ships of Admiral Dahlgren's fleet, is repulsed.

July 19.   **Morgan's raid.** On July 9, with a command of 2,400 cavalry, Confederate Brigadier General John Hunt Morgan crossed the Ohio River into Indiana and proceeded east into Ohio on his most audacious raid. Among the Union forces that begin to pursue Morgan's column is a squadron of gunboats under Lieutenant Commander Le Roy Fitch. Ten days later the Confederates attempt to recross the Ohio River into West Virginia at Buffington Island, only to find their way blocked by a Union entrenchment supported by the gunboats *Allegheny Belle* and *Moose.*

Most of the raiders are then captured by land forces coming up behind them.

July 21.   On the Mississippi, the transport *Sallie Ward,* disabled by Confederate artillery fire, drifts aground on Island No. 82 and is destroyed.

August 23.   A Confederate boat party led by Lieutenant John Taylor Wood captures the gunboats *Reliance,* Acting Ensign Henry Walter, and *Satellite,* Acting Master Robinson, at anchor off Windmill Point on the Rappahannock River, Virginia.

August 25.   Lieutenant Wood uses the *Satellite* to capture the schooners *Golden Rod, Coquette,* and *Two Brothers* at the mouth of the Rappahannock, after which he strips and burns all five of his prizes.

September 6.   At Charleston, South Carolina, the Confederate garrison of Battery Wagner on Morris Island is evacuated under cover of darkness in barges manned by the crews of the rams *Chicora* and *Palmetto State.* Union picket boats, unaware of the movement until it is nearly completed, succeed in capturing the last three barges.

September 8.   **Battle of Sabine Pass.** Ordered to establish a Union presence in Texas, Major General Nathaniel P. Banks, commander of the Department of the Gulf, organizes an amphibious operation to capture Sabine Pass. The expedition consists of 4,000 men under Major General William B. Franklin, in transports accompanied by four light-draft gunboats—the *Arizona, Clifton, Granite City,* and *Sachem*—under Acting Volunteer Lieutenant Frederick Crocker. To defend Sabine Pass the Confederates have erected Fort Griffin, an earthwork mounting five guns, for one of which there is no ammunition, garrisoned by 42 men of the Davis Guards commanded by 20-year-old Lieutenant Richard Dowling. Holding fire until the gunboats are well within range, the defenders open a well-aimed cannonade that soon disables the *Clifton* and *Sachem.* Both ships and their crews, approximately 315 officers and men, are captured. The expedition returns to New Orleans.

September 8–9.   **Assault on Fort Sumter.** At Charleston, Admiral Dahlgren and General Gillmore plan to follow up the occupation of Morris Island with an amphibious assault on Fort Sumter, most of whose guns have been disabled to repeated bombardments by Dahlgren's monitors and Gillmore's artillery. Each service organizes its own separate landing party. The approach to the fort is made in small boats under cover of darkness. The navy's 500 sailors and marines

under Commander Thomas H. Stevens have the misfortune to reach Sumter first. There they discover that, despite the damage done to the fort, the garrison is full of fight and the walls cannot be scaled. The guns of the other harbor fortifications and the CSS *Chicora* open up, and the landing forces draw off, leaving approximately 100 prisoners in Confederate hands.

September 19–23.   In the Chesapeake Bay, a Confederate boat expedition commanded by Acting Masters John Y. Beall and Edward McGuire captures and destroys the schooners *Alliance, J. J. Houseman, Samuel Pearsall,* and *Alexandria.*

October 5.   **The Davids.** In Charleston harbor the ironclad screw steamer *New Ironsides,* Captain Stephen C. Rowan, is damaged by a spar torpedo rammed into her side by the *David,* Lieutenant William T. Glassell, CSN. The *David,* which gives her name to a type of Confederate warship, is a small, cylindrical steamer with a very low silhouette, built specifically for delivering torpedo attacks. A number of such craft are subsequently constructed at Charleston and elsewhere.

October 9.   **Seizure of the Laird rams.** Ceaselessly prodded by American Ambassador Charles Francis Adams and increasingly doubtful that the Confederacy will be able to sustain its independence, the British government seizes two nearly completed ironclad rams being built for Commander Bulloch by Lairds of Birkenhead. This action, though not entirely unexpected, is a great blow to Southern hopes of breaking the blockade. Unlike the primitive, casemated, strictly coastal rams that could be cobbled together in the Confederacy, the Lairds were sea-going, double-turreted, state-of-the-art ships.

October 26–December 4.   **Bombardment of Fort Sumter.** At Charleston, Union batteries on Morris Island and Admiral Dahlgren's monitors begin an intensive, 40-day bombardment of Fort Sumter, which is reduced to little more than rubble.

October.   **Confederate States Naval Academy.** The Confederate Congress had authorized the establishment of a naval academy on April 21, 1862. This month classes commence, with 52 of the Confederacy's 106 midshipmen in attendance, aboard the school ship *Patrick Henry* at Drewry's Bluff on the James River below Richmond. The superintendent is Lieutenant William Harwar Parker, formerly head of the Department of Seamanship at the U.S. Naval Academy.

December 6. The monitor *Weehawken,* Commander James M. Duncan, sinks with the loss of more than 20 lives while tied to a buoy outside Charleston harbor.

December 7. A party of 15 Confederate sympathizers led by John C. Braine seize the steamer *Chesapeake,* which they had boarded as passengers, during her regular run between New York and Portland, Maine. The plot was organized by "John Parker" (real name: Vernon G. Locke, formerly captain of the Confederate privateer *Retribution*), who boards the ship from a pilot boat in the Bay of Fundy. The conspirators intend to run the blockade into Wilmington, North Carolina, but the *Chesapeake* is recovered by the U.S. gunboats *Annie* and *Ella,* Acting Lieutenant J. Frederick Nickels, while coaling near Halifax, Nova Scotia, on December 17. Braine, "Parker," and most of their followers escape ashore. Although Braine claims to be a lieutenant in the Confederate States Navy, in fact none of the men involved hold Confederate commissions, and the Confederate government disavows their actions.

The Confederate submarine *Hunley:* an engraving of a painting made at Charleston in December 1863. *Official U.S. Navy photograph.*

1864

February 2. Confederate boat parties led by Commander John Taylor Wood capture and destroy the Union gunboat *Underwriter,* Acting Master Jacob Westerveldt, in the Neuse River, near New Bern, North Carolina. Westerveldt is killed in hand-to-hand fighting on the deck of his ship, which was taken by surprise. For this and previous exploits, Wood receives the thanks of the Confederate Congress.

February 12. **Second cruise of the Florida.** The Confederate cruiser *Florida,* Lieutenant Charles M. Morris, slips out of Brest, France, past the blockading screw sloop *Kearsarge,* Captain John B. Winslow. She takes 15 prizes between this date and her capture on October 7.

February 17. **Sinking of the Housatonic.** The screw sloop *Housatonic,* Captain Charles W. Pickering, is sunk by the Confederate submarine *H. L. Hunley,* Lieutenant George E. Dixon, CSA, while at anchor on blockade duty off Charleston, South Carolina. The *Hunley,* operating on the surface, strikes the *Housatonic* with a spar torpedo and is herself lost with all hands, probably as a result of the explosion.

March 5. Commander John Taylor Wood, CSN, leads 15 men who cross the Chesapeake Bay at night in barges to seize and destroy the Union telegraph station at Cherrystone Point, Virginia. Wood also captures the small army steamers *Aeolus,* which he disables, and *Titan,* which he sails back across the bay into the Piankatank River and destroys.

March 6. In the North Edisto River, near Charleston, South Carolina, the gunboat *Memphis,* Acting Master Robert O. Patterson, is struck twice by a spar torpedo mounted on a Confederate David commanded by First Assistant Engineer C. S. Tombs, but the torpedo fails to detonate.

March 12. **Red River expedition.** Rear Admiral David Dixon Porter leads 13 ironclads, 4 tinclads, and 5 wooden gunboats of the Mississippi Squadron up the Red River to cooperate with land forces commanded by Major General Nathaniel P. Banks. The immediate object of the expedition is to capture Shreveport, Louisiana, after which it is to advance into Texas, thereby cutting the trickle of supplies that continues to reach the eastern Confederacy via the Red River and, by strengthening Union presence west of the Mississippi, to discourage French Emperor Napoleon III from meddling in Mexico.

March 16. A landing party from the monitor *Osage,* Lieutenant Commander Thomas O. Selfridge, Jr., occupies Alexandria, Louisiana, on the Red River. Nine of Porter's vessels reach the town that morning.

March 25. A Confederate attack on Union forces at Paducah, Kentucky, is repulsed with the help of fire support from the gunboats *Paw Paw,* Acting Lieutenant A. Frank O'Neil, and Peosta, Acting Lieutenant Thomas E. Smith.

April 1.   The army transport *Maple Leaf* is destroyed by a Confederate mine near Mandarin Point on the St. John's River, Florida.

April 3.   Nine of Admiral Porter's ironclads and three wooden steamers convoy transports carrying an army corps commanded by Major General A. J. Smith up the Red River from Alexandria to Grand Ecore, Louisiana. From Grand Ecore the troops are to march to Natchitoches to join Banks's army for the advance on Shreveport.

April 9.   Blockading off Newport News, Virginia, the steam frigate *Minnesota,* Lieutenant Commander John H. Upshur, is damaged by a spar torpedo in a night attack by the Confederate David craft *Squib,* Lieutenant Hunter Davidson.

April 10.   Withdrawal from the Red River. At Springfield Landing, only 30 miles below Shreveport, Louisiana, Admiral Porter finds that the Confederates have blocked the river by sinking a huge steamer, the *New Falls City,* across the stream. Before the obstruction can be removed, word is received that General Banks's army has been defeated at the Battle of Sabine Crossroads and is in retreat. Porter has no choice but to withdraw downstream. Falling water and the opposition of Confederate land forces makes this a perilous operation.

April 12.   Action at Blair's Landing. Retiring down the Red River, Porter's fleet fights its way past Confederate batteries supported by dismounted cavalry under Brigadier General Thomas Green, CSA, who is killed in the action.

April 15.   The ironclad *Eastport,* Lieutenant Commander S. Ledyard Phelps, is crippled by a mine in the Red River near Grand Ecore, Louisiana. Her crew keeps her going for some days, but on April 26 Admiral Porter orders her destroyed.

April 16.   The army transport *General Hunter* is destroyed by a mine near Mandarin Point in the St. John's River, Florida.

April 17.   A Confederate attack on Plymouth, North Carolina, is repulsed with the help of fire support from the gunboats *Miami* and *Southfield.* The army steamer *Bombshell* is sunk during the action.

April 19.   The Albemarle. The new Confederate ironclad ram *Albemarle,* Commander James W. Cooke, attacks the wooden gunboats *Miami* and *Southfield* off Plymouth, North Carolina. Lieutenant Commander Charles W. Flusser, the senior Union officer, has lashed the two gunboats together in anticipation of the ram's appearance and boldly advances to meet her. The *Albemarle* rams and sinks the *Southfield* and drives away the *Miami,* the tinclad *Whitehead,* and the little steamer *Ceres.* Flusser is killed early in the action.

April 20.   Supported by the *Albemarle,* Confederate land forces recapture Plymouth, North Carolina.

April 21.   The tinclad gunboat *Petrel,* Acting Master T. McElroy, is disabled and captured by Confederate land forces near Yazoo City, on the Yazoo River, Mississippi.

April 26–27.   On the Red River, Admiral Porter's vessels reach Alexandria, Louisiana, after heavy engagements with Confederate land forces, during which the small steamer *Champion No. 3* is disabled, *Champion No. 5* is destroyed, and several other ships are damaged.

May 2–13.   Passing the Red River rapids. At Alexandria, Louisiana, Admiral Porter's squadron is trapped by falling water above the Red River rapids, and it appears as though he may have to destroy his ships to keep them from being captured and then withdraw overland. Fortunately, Lieutenant Colonel Joseph Bailey, an army officer in the brigade that has remained with the squadron, conceives the idea of building a dam across the river until the water reaches the necessary seven-foot minimum depth. The dam would then be opened, and the ships could ride the torrent to safety. Bailey's first dam gives way on May 9, but four ships take advantage of the rush of water to pass through the rapids. A second dam is then constructed, and the remainder of the squadron makes its escape.

May 4–7.   A successful amphibious assault on Tampa, Florida, is supported by the steamers *Sunflower,* Acting Master Edward Van Sice, and *Honduras,* Acting Master John H. Platt, and the sailing bark *J. L. Davis,* Acting Master William Fales.

May 5.   The Confederate ironclad *Albemarle,* Commander James W. Cooke, enters Albemarle Sound in company with the gunboats *Bombshell* and *Cotton Plant* to engage the Union forces at the mouth of the Roanoke River. The *Bombshell* is soon captured, and the *Cotton Plant* retires upriver, but the *Albemarle* disables the wooden side-wheel gunboat *Sassacus,* Lieutenant Commander Francis A. Roe, and continues to engage the side-wheelers *Mattabesett,* Captain Melancton Smith, and *Wyalusing,* Lieutenant Commander Walter W. Queen, until nightfall brings an end to the action.

May 5.   In a sharp action near Dunn's Bayou on the Red River, Louisiana, Confederate forces ashore capture or

Admiral Porter's ironclads passing the dam at Alexandria, Louisiana, during the withdrawal from the Red River: a woodcut from *Harper's Pictorial History of the Civil War*, May 1864. *U.S. Naval Institute Collection.*

destroy the wooden steamers *Covington,* Acting Lieutenant George P. Lord, and *Signal,* Acting Lieutenant Edward Morgan, and the transport *Warner.*

May 6.   The side-wheel steamer *Commodore Jones,* Acting Lieutenant Thomas Wade, is blown up by an electric mine while sweeping mines in the James River, Virginia. Forty of her crewmen are killed.

May 6.   The Confederate ironclad ram *Raleigh,* Flag Officer William F. Lynch, sorties from the Cape Fear River, North Carolina, and drives off the blockaders *Britannia* and *Nansemond,* allowing a blockade runner to slip out. After exchanging fire with other blockaders the next morning, the *Raleigh* grounds while attempting to enter the river and is destroyed to keep her from falling into enemy hands.

May 6.   The wooden steamer *Granite City,* Acting Master C. W. Lamson, and the tinclad *Wave,* Acting Lieutenant Benjamin A. Loring, are captured by Confederate land forces during an engagement at Calasieu Pass, Louisiana.

May 7.   Confederate land forces surprise and capture the side-wheel steamer *Shawsheen,* Acting Ensign Charles Ringot, near Chaffin's Bluff, on the James River, Virginia.

May 10.   The army transport *Harriet A. Ward* is sunk by a mine in the St. John's River, Florida.

May 23.   The gunboat *Columbine,* Acting Ensign Sanborn, is attacked and captured at Horse's Landing on the St.

John's River, near Palatka, Florida, by a party of 16 sharpshooters and two guns under the command of Captain J. J. Dickison, 2nd Florida Cavalry.

May 25.   A boat party from the side-wheeler *Mattabesett,* Captain Melancton Smith, makes an unsuccessful attempt to destroy the Confederate ironclad ram *Albemarle* at her anchorage in the Roanoke River, near Plymouth, North Carolina.

June 3.   Around 2:00 A.M., a Confederate boat expedition of 130 men led by Lieutenant Thomas P. Pelot surprises and captures the blockader *Water Witch,* Lieutenant Commander Austin Pendergast, at anchor off Ossabaw Island, Georgia. Pelot is killed in the boarding action.

June 10.   Colonel Jacob Zeilin becomes the seventh commandant of the marine corps.

June 19.   **Kearsarge vs. the Alabama.** The Confederate cruiser *Alabama,* Captain Raphael Semmes, which put into Cherbourg, France, on June 13, stands out to engage the screw sloop *Kearsarge,* Captain John B. Winslow, which appeared off the port the next day. Some of the *Alabama*'s shells fail to explode, and Semmes gives the order to abandon his sinking ship after a one-sided action of 70 minutes. Semmes and 40 of his officers and men escape captivity when they are rescued by boats from the English yacht *Deerhound.*

June 24.   The paddle-wheel steamer *Queen City,* Acting Master Michael Hickey, is surprised and captured by

The *Kearsarge* vs. the *Alabama:* a lithograph published in Berlin in 1864. *Courtesy Beverley R. Robinson Collection, U.S. Naval Academy Museum.*

Confederate cavalry with artillery on the White River off Clarendon, Arkansas.

August 5. **Battle of Mobile Bay.** Rear Admiral David G. Farragut advances to attack the defenses of Mobile Bay, Alabama, with a squadron consisting of the monitors *Chickasaw, Manhattan, Tecumseh,* and *Winnebago* and 14 wooden ships, including his flagship, the screw sloop *Hartford.* To enter the bay his ships must pass through a narrow channel, the western side of which is mined, between Fort Gaines on Dauphin Island to the west and Fort Morgan on Mobile Point to the east. Inside the bay is a Confederate squadron under Rear Admiral Franklin Buchanan composed of the ironclad ram *Tennessee* (flag) and the small wooden gunboats *Gaines, Morgan,* and *Selma.* The column of the monitors is headed by the *Tecumseh,* Commander T. A. M. Craven. Upon sighting the *Tennessee,* Craven makes straight for her, skirting the edge of the minefield, where the *Tecumseh* strikes a mine and sinks in a matter of seconds, taking 90 of her 114 crewmen, including Craven, with her. The screw sloop *Brooklyn,* Captain James Alden, heading the wooden ships, then begins to back water, threatening to throw the entire column into confusion directly below the guns of Fort Morgan. At this critical moment, Farragut shouts to Flag Captain Percival Drayton: "Damn the torpedoes! Full speed ahead, Drayton!" and the *Hartford* surges past the *Brooklyn* to lead the wooden ships into the bay. Not a single vessel is disabled by the forts' fire. The

Rear Admiral Franklin Buchanan CSN. *Official U.S. Navy photograph.*

CSS *Selma,* Lieutenant Peter U. Murphey, strikes her colors after a sharp action with the *Metacomet,* Lieutenant James Jouett; the CSS *Gaines,* Lieutenant John W. Bennett, is severely damaged and runs aground near Fort Morgan; and the CSS *Morgan,* Commander George W. Harrison, escapes up the bay to Mobile. Admiral Buchanan singlehandedly engages the Union

An August Morning with Farragut at the Battle of Mobile Bay: the famous late-nineteenth-century painting by W. H. Overender. *Official U.S. Navy photograph.*

fleet with the *Tennessee* for an hour before his battered flagship is compelled to surrender. This action effectively closes the last major port on the Confederacy's Gulf coast.

August 6–23.   **Cruise of the Tallahassee.** Commander John Taylor Wood, CSN, slips out of Wilmington, North Carolina, in the steamer *Tallahassee* to attack Northern shipping off the eastern seaboard. In a cruise of a little more than two weeks, he takes 31 prizes and, eluding a dragnet of Union warships, runs the blockade back into Wilmington.

August 9.   City Point, on the James River, Virginia, General Grant's headquarters and base of supply, is rocked by explosions that result when two members of the Confederate Secret Service, John Maxwell, and R. K. Dillard, place a time-bomb aboard a Union army transport.

September 19.   **Confederates on the Great Lakes.** On Lake Erie, 28 men led by Acting Master John Yates Beall, CSN, seize and burn the steamers *Philo Parsons* and *Island Queen* before retiring into Canada. The seizure of the ships was the only successful part of a

daring plan to free the Confederate prisoners of war confined on Johnson's Island, near Sandusky, Ohio. Beall is later captured and hanged as a spy.

September 29.   The steamer *Roanoke* is captured off the coast of Cuba by John C. Braine and a party of Confederate sympathizers who had boarded her as passengers in Havana. Braine sails the ship to Bermuda with the aim of running the blockade back into the Confederacy, but in the end decides to burn her.

September 29–October 1.   Confederate Flag Officer John K. Mitchell's James River Squadron provides fire support for southern forces ashore during the fighting around Fort Harrison, Virginia.

October 7.   **Capture of the Florida.** Commander Napoleon Collins, commanding the screw sloop *Wachusett*, attacks and captures the Confederate cruiser *Florida*, Lieutenant Charles M. Morris, in the neutral harbor of Bahia, Brazil. His action precipitates an international incident. Commander Collins is court-martialed and sentenced to be dismissed from the navy, but Secretary Welles quashes the verdict. The *Florida* is ordered to be returned to the Brazilian government, but mysteriously sinks at her mooring at Hampton Roads, Virginia.

October 19.   **The Shenandoah.** In the Madeiras the English steamer *Sea King,* secretly purchased by Commander James D. Bulloch, CSN, is commissioned as the Confederate cruiser *Shenandoah.* Under the command of Lieutenant James I. Waddell, she will take 38 prizes and virtually destroy the New England whaling fleet.

October 27.   **Destruction of the Albemarle.** Lieutenant William B. Cushing sinks the Confederate ironclad ram *Albemarle* at her mooring in the Roanoke River near Plymouth, North Carolina. Approaching in a steam launch under cover of darkness, Cushing rams a spar torpedo into the ironclad's side. Thirteen of his fourteen men are captured or killed, but Cushing and one other swim safely away.

October 28–November 19.   **Cruise of the Chickamauga.** The Confederate cruiser *Chickamauga,* Lieutenant John Wilkinson, runs the blockade out of Wilmington, North Carolina. Three weeks later she returns to Wilmington under cover of a dense fog, having taken seven prizes.

October 29–November 7.   **Cruise of the Olustee.** The CSS *Olustee* (ex-*Tallahassee*), Lieutenant William H. Ward, slips out of and back into Wilmington, North Carolina, on a brief cruise in which she takes seven prizes.

October 29–November 1.   Exploiting the advantage gained by Cushing's destruction of the *Albemarle,* Union naval forces under Commander W. H. Macomb recapture Plymouth, North Carolina. The Carolina sounds are again closed to the South.

October 30.   The gunboat *Undine,* Acting Master Bryant, and the transports *Cheeseman* and *Venus* are captured by Confederate land forces on the Tennessee River near Johnsonville, Tennessee.

November 4.   The paddle-wheelers *Key West,* Acting Volunteer Lieutenant E. M. King, and *Tawah,* Acting Volunteer Lieutenant J. Goudy, and the steamer *Elfin,* Acting Master A. F. Thompson, support Union land forces in defending the supply depot at Johnsonville, on the Tennessee River, Tennessee, against an attack by Confederates under Major General Nathan Bedford Forrest. The enemy batteries are overwhelming, and at the end of the engagement both ships and stores are fired to prevent them from being captured.

November 27.   The *Greyhound,* headquarters steamer of Major General Benjamin F. Butler, is destroyed by an unexplained explosion and fire in the James River, Virginia. Admiral Porter and Major General R. C. Schenk are also aboard at the time. Porter suspects that the ex-

The Confederate cruiser *Tallahassee:* a woodcut from the *Illustrated London News,* April 29, 1865. *U.S. Naval Institute Collection.*

plosion was caused by a Confederate "coal torpedo"—a bomb in a big lump of coal.

November 30.   A naval brigade of 500 seamen and marines from the ships of the South Atlantic Blockading Squadron under Commander George H. Preble supports Union land forces in an action at Honey Hill, near Grahamville, South Carolina.

December 5–9.   Commander Preble's naval brigade continues to support army units in a series of actions near Tulifinny Crossroads, Georgia, the objective of which is to reach and cut the Savannah-Charleston Railroad, thereby facilitating Sherman's March to the Sea. Confederate forces succeed in halting the advance just short of the railway.

December 7.   The steam tug *Narcissus,* Acting Ensign William G. Jones, is sunk by a Confederate mine in Mobile Bay, Alabama.

December 9.   The gunboat *Otsego,* Lieutenant Commander H. N. T. Arnold, and the tug *Bazely* are sunk by Confederate mines in the Roanoke River near Jamesville, North Carolina.

December 15–16.   **Battle of Nashville.** Seven gunboats of the Mississippi River Squadron under Lieutenant Commander Le Roy Fitch provide fire support for forces ashore in this decisive battle, which virtually destroys the Confederate Army of Tennessee.

December 21.   At Savannah, Georgia, Confederate naval forces destroy the *Savannah, Isondiga, Firefly,* and *Georgia* to prevent their capture by Sherman's army, then approaching the city.

December 23.   The rank of vice admiral is created and conferred on David Glasgow Farragut.

December 23–27.   **First Fort Fisher expedition.** Wilmington, North Carolina, is the last major port open in the eastern Confederacy. It is guarded by Fort Fisher, a large earthwork fortification commanding the entrance to the Cape Fear River. To capture the fort, the Union mounts a joint expedition consisting of the largest American fleet yet assembled—55 warships, including the ironclad screw steamer *New Ironsides* and the monitors *Canonicus, Mahopac, Monadnock,* and *Saugus,* and nearly 45 auxiliaries and transports, under Rear Admiral David Dixon Porter—and 6,500 troops poorly led by Major General Benjamin F. Butler. A ship loaded with explosives with which Butler expected to level the fortifications is blown up without effect on the evening of December 23–24. The fleet smothers the fort with shell fire on the 24th, and approximately 2,000 troops land under cover of the ships' guns on Christmas Day. Butler then decides that the bombardment has not damaged the fort enough to make an assault practical and has them reembarked.

1865

January 1.   The screw frigate *San Jacinto,* Captain R. W. Meade, wrecks on No Name Cay in the Bahamas.

January 13–15.   **Capture of Fort Fisher.** A joint expedition composed of 60 warships under Rear Admiral David Dixon Porter and 8,500 troops under Brigadier General Alfred H. Terry makes a second attempt to capture Fort Fisher, guarding the mouth

Admiral Porter's fleet bombarding Fort Fisher, January 15, 1865: a lithograph published in New York in 1865. *Courtesy Library of Congress.*

of the Cape Fear River, North Carolina. The troops land on January 13 under intense covering fire from the fleet. A naval brigade of 1,600 seamen and 400 marines under Lieutenant Commander K. R. Breese is put ashore on January 15 to deliver a diversionary attack. Their charge is repulsed with heavy losses—309 casualties—but absorbs the defenders' attention so that Terry's troops can storm into the fort from the rear. Some 500 Confederates are killed or wounded and 2,083 taken prisoner; total Union losses are 691.

January 15.   The monitor *Patapsco*, Lieutenant Commander S. P. Quackenbush, is sunk by a mine outside Charleston, South Carolina, with the loss of nearly half her crew.

January 23–24.   **Action at Trent's Reach.** The Confederate James River Squadron, Commodore John K. Mitchell, makes a desperate attempt to fight its way through the Union obstructions at Trent's Reach and destroy Grant's supply depot at City Point. Mitchell's force consists of the ironclads *Virginia II*, *Fredericksburg*, and *Richmond*, the gunboats *Drewry* and *Torpedo*, and the torpedo boats *Hornet*, *Scorpion*, and *Wasp*. The *Virginia II* and the *Richmond* run aground on January 23, and the next day, while refloating the *Virginia*, the *Drewry* is destroyed by a hit that detonates her magazines. The *Scorpion*, severely damaged by this explosion, is abandoned. Fire from the monitors *Massasoit* and *Onondaga* then compels the squadron to retire.

January 28.   The steam gunboat *Valley City*, Acting Master J. A. J. Brooks, provides fire support for a force of Union troops during a night attack on their encampment at Colerain, North Carolina.

January 28.   Blockading off Mobile, Alabama, the side-wheel steamer *Octorara*, Lieutenant Commander William W. Low, is hit by a spar torpedo carried by the CSS *St. Patrick*, Lieutenant J. T. Walker. The torpedo fails to fire, and neither vessel is damaged.

February 17–18.   **Fall of Charleston.** Confederate forces withdraw from Charleston, South Carolina, upon the approach of Sherman's army, first destroying the ironclads *Charleston*, *Chicora*, and *Palmetto State*. The city had withstood a siege of 567 days.

February 17–18.   Fort Anderson, North Carolina, is shelled and captured by a Union squadron commanded by Rear Admiral David Dixon Porter.

February 25.   The armed tug *Catalpa*, Ensign Allen K. Noyes, lands a party that drives off a force of Confederate cavalry and captures Georgetown, on the Peedee River, South Carolina.

February 29.   The side-wheel steamer *Harvest Moon*, flagship of Rear Admiral John A. Dahlgren, commander of the South Atlantic Blockading Squadron, is sunk by a mine in Winyah Bay, South Carolina.

March 4.   The side-wheel gunboats *General Burnside*, Lieutenant Moreau Forrest, and *General Thomas*, Acting Master Gilbert Morton, attack and capture the encampment of a Confederate force commanded by Brigadier General Philip D. Roddey at Mussel Shoals, on the Tennessee River, Alabama.

March 24.   The French-built, Confederate ironclad ram *Stonewall Jackson*, Commander Thomas J. Page, sails from El Ferrol, Spain, for America. Two Union warships, the steam frigate *Niagara* and screw sloop *Sacramento*, present under the command of Commodore Thomas T. Craven, make no attempt to interfere with her departure. Craven is later court-martialed for failing to engage the enemy. Despite his plea that the ram constituted a clearly superior force, he is convicted, but Secretary Welles sets the verdict aside.

March 28.   The ironclad gunboat *Milwaukee*, Lieutenant Commander J. H. Gillis, is sunk by a mine in the Blakely River, Alabama.

March 29.   The monitor *Osage*, Lieutenant Commander W. M. Gamble, is sunk by a mine in the Blakely River, Alabama.

April 1.   The tinclad *Rodolph*, Master N. M. Dyer, is sunk by a mine in the Blakely River, Alabama.

April 2.   **Fall of Richmond.** Following the disastrous Battle of Five Forks, General Lee informs President Davis that his army can no longer defend the Confederate capital. The ships of the James River Squadron—the ironclads *Virginia II*, *Fredericksburg*, and *Richmond*, wooden gunboats *Hampton*, *Nansemond*, *Roanoke* (formerly *Raleigh*), and *Torpedo*, picket boat *Shrapnel*, and the school-ship *Patrick Henry* are burned and their crews formed into a naval brigade under the squadron commander, Rear Admiral Raphael Semmes, who is given the twin commission of brigadier general, CSA. The brigade joins the Confederate army in North Carolina and lays down its arms at Greensboro on May 1. The midshipmen from the *Patrick Henry* are chosen to guard the train containing the Confederacy's gold reserves during the disintegrating government's flight to the south.

April 9.   **Appomattox.** General Lee surrenders the Army of Northern Virginia to vastly superior Union forces at Appomattox Court House. Although President Davis still has hopes of fighting on and the Confederate forces in the Trans-Mississippi will not surrender until May, the Civil War is effectively over.

April 13.   The armed tug *Ida,* Acting Ensign F. Ellms, is sunk by a mine near Chocktaw Pass in Mobile Bay, Alabama.

April 14.   The gunboat *Sciota,* Volunteer Lieutenant J. W. Magune, is sunk by a mine in Mobile Bay, Alabama.

April 22.   The side-wheel steamer *Black Hawk,* Lieutenant Commander James A. Greer, burns and sinks at Mound City, Illinois.

April 25.   **The Webb.** The Confederate side-wheel ram *Webb,* Lieutenant Charles W. Read, is destroyed in a daring attempt to reach the sea. Running the Union blockade of the mouth of the Red River, through sheer bluff the *Webb* made her way down the Mississippi to New Orleans before being recognized. Below the city she came upon the steam sloop *Richmond.* Incorrectly assuming that the more powerful Union vessel is ready to contest his passage, Read runs the *Webb* ashore and sets her afire to keep her from being captured.

May 19.   Discovering that the war has ended by the time his ship reaches the Western Hemisphere, Commander Thomas J. Page turns the Confederate ironclad ram *Stonewall Jackson* over to the Spanish authorities in Havana, Cuba.

June 3.   The European (formerly the Mediterranean) Squadron is reestablished.

June 28.   **Last shots of the Civil War.** Using the time-honored technique of a shot across the bow, the Confederate cruiser *Shenandoah* halts and burns ten Union whaling ships in the Bering Sea. Some of their captains protest that the war is over, but Lieutenant Waddell does not believe them. On August 2, he learns from a British ship that the war is indeed over. Apprehensive that the victorious North will regard the *Shenandoah's* operations as acts of piracy, Waddell decides to sail her to England for internment there.

September 9.   Rear Admiral David Dixon Porter becomes the sixth superintendent of the U.S. Naval Academy.

October.   The U.S. Naval Academy returns to Annapolis, Maryland, from Newport, Rhode Island, where it had been located during the Civil War.

November 5.   **Farewell to the Stars and Bars.** Lieutenant James I. Waddell brings the Confederate cruiser *Shenandoah* into Liverpool, England, after a voyage of 122 days entirely out of sight of land. The following day he hauls down the last Confederate flag still flying anywhere in the world.

1866

January 4.   The armed tug *Narcissus,* Acting Ensign Isaac S. Bradbury, is wrecked on Egmont Key, Florida, with the loss of her entire company of 32 men.

June 20.   A party of 100 seamen and marines under Lieutenant John W. Philip from the screw sloop *Wachusett* is landed at New Chwang, China, to seize a bandit leader whose followers had assaulted the American consul. Local authorities were unwilling to arrest the man.

June 21.   Congress approves the establishment of a Hydrographic Office to take over the work previously performed by M. F. Maury's Hydrographical Office. The new bureau, the brainchild of Rear Admiral C. H. Davis, is given space in the Nautical Almanac Office, which had been moved to the capital earlier in the year.

July 25.   Congress creates the unique, new rank of admiral and confers it on David Glasgow Farragut in recognition of his great services in the late war. David Dixon Porter is promoted to become the navy's second vice admiral.

1867

March 2.   **Civil Engineering Corps.** Congress establishes the Civil Engineering Corps. On March 3, 1871, it directs that at the discretion of the president members of the corps will be given relative rank to line officers.

June 13.   **Formosan expedition.** The screw sloops *Hartford* and *Wyoming* land a naval brigade of 181 men under Commander George C. Belknap who attack the aborigines on Formosa in retaliation for the massacre of the crew of the American merchant bark *Rover.* Lieutenant Alexander S. Mackenzie is mortally wounded in the action.

June 19.   **Loss of the Sacramento.** The screw sloop *Sacramento,* Captain Napoleon Collins, wrecks without loss of life off the coast of Madras, India.

December 28.   **Annexation of Midway.** The United States claims the central Pacific island of Midway, over which

Captain William Reynolds of the screw sloop *Lackawanna* has raised the U.S. flag on August 28. The island is America's first overseas territory.

1868

February 4.   The screw sloop *Oneida* sends a party of seamen and marines ashore to protect American citizens and property at Hiogo, Japan.

February 7–26.   Detachments from five ships of the South Atlantic Squadron, Rear Admiral Charles H. Davis, are landed to protect foreign nationals during an insurrection at Montevideo, Uruguay.

February 8.   A party from the screw sloop *Shenandoah* lands to safeguard Americans at Nagasaki, Japan.

April 4.   The steam sloop *Iroquois* and side-wheel gunboat *Monocacy* land 25 marines to protect American interests at Yokohama, Japan.

July 9.   **Loss of the Suwanee.** The side-wheel gunboat *Suwanee*, Commander Richard S. Law, strikes an uncharted rock and sinks without loss of life in Queen Victoria Sound off Vancouver Island, British Columbia.

July 27.   **Japanese midshipmen.** In response to a request from the government of Japan, Congress passes an act allowing Japanese nationals to attend the U.S. Naval Academy, providing their country pays the cost. The first Japanese midshipman, Jiunzo Matsumura, graduates in the Class of 1873. He will rise to the rank of vice admiral in the Imperial Japanese Navy. A total of 16 Japanese midshipmen attend the academy between 1869 and 1906.

August 13.   **Arica hurricane.** The side-wheel gunboat *Wateree*, Commander James H. Gillis, and storeship *Fredonia*, Captain G. W. Doty, are among the vessels driven ashore by a tidal wave at Arica, Peru. Twenty-seven of their crewmen are lost.

November 19.   **Globe and anchor.** The marine corps's emblem is approved by the secretary of the navy. The design was by a board consisting of Major G. R. Graham and Captains R. W. Huntington and C. F. Williams.

1869

March 9.   Adolf E. Borie succeeds Gideon Welles to become 25th secretary of the navy.

April 26.   **Good Conduct Medal.** Congress authorizes the Navy Good Conduct Medal to reward enlisted per-

Midshipman Jiunzo Matsumura, Class of 1873, the Naval Academy's first Japanese graduate. *Nimitz Library Special Collections.*

sonnel for blameless service. The award was originally a nickel Maltese cross. Its design was changed to the present bronze medal in 1892.

June 9.   The Navy Department issues orders for the construction of a torpedo station—the navy's first—on Goat Island, at Newport, Rhode Island.

June 26.   George M. Robeson enters office as the 26th secretary of the navy.

June 28.   William M. Wood is named the navy's first surgeon-general.

December 1.   Commodore John L. Worden, the hero of the *Monitor*, relieves Vice Admiral David D. Porter to become the seventh superintendent of the U.S. Naval Academy.

1870

January 22.   Commander Thomas O. Selfridge, Jr., sails the gunboat *Nipsic* on an expedition to ascertain the best location for an interoceanic canal across the Isthmus of Darien. His report, based on a survey of four possible routes, is completed in 1874.

January 24. **Loss of the Oneida.** The screw sloop *Oneida*, Commander Edward P. Williams, sinks off Yokohama, Japan, with the loss of 117 lives after being struck by the British P. & O. Steamer *City of Bombay*, which continues on her way.

June 17. Lieutenant Willard H. Brownson leads a party of six boats from the screw sloop *Mohican* to attack a band of pirates in the Teacapan River on the Pacific coast of Mexico. The pirates are dispersed and their ship, the former British gunboat *Forward*, is burned.

August 14. Admiral David Glasgow Farragut dies, aged 69, in Portsmouth, New Hampshire.

October 29. **Loss of the Saginaw.** The side-wheel steamer *Saginaw*, Commander Montgomery Sicard, strikes a reef and breaks up off remote Ocean Island, in the mid-Pacific. The ship's company gets safely ashore, but the prospects of rescue are slight. On November 18 Lieutenant John G. Talbot, the *Saginaw*'s executive officer, sets out in the ship's gig with five volunteers to sail 1,500 miles to Hawaii for help. Approaching Kauai 31 days later the boat swamps in the surf. Talbot and four of his men are drowned, but Coxswain William Halford survives to bring aid to his stranded shipmates.

1871

March 3. The Pay Corps is established by an act of Congress. In 1919 it is renamed the Supply Corps.

May 30. **Korean expedition.** A squadron of five ships under Rear Admiral John Rodgers carries Frederick Low, U.S. minister to China, to negotiate a treaty of amity and commerce with the "Hermit Kingdom" of Korea, where the crew of the American merchantman *General Sherman* was massacred in 1866. The vessels are the screw frigate *Colorado* (flag), screw gunboat *Alaska*, screw sloop *Benicia*, side-wheel gunboat *Monocacy*, and screw tug *Palos*. They anchor at the mouth of the channel (then known as the Salee River) leading to the Han River, near Chemulpo (now Inchon) on May 30. The next day the *Palos* is fired on by one of the five forts along the river. The ships reply, and two men are wounded before the fort ceases firing. Admiral Rodgers demands an apology. It is not forthcoming, and on June 10 he lands a naval brigade under Commander L. A. Kimberly consisting of 575 bluejackets led by Lieutenant Commander Silas Casey, Jr., and 109 marines under Captain McLane Tilton, Asiatic Squadron Marine Officer, with seven guns. The brigade's advance is sup-

ported by fire from the *Monocacy* and the *Palos*, and the defenders of the first two forts withdraw without offering serious resistance. The next day the brigade pushes on towards the principal fort, "The Citadel," and its two secondary works. Here the Koreans await the assault. The first man inside The Citadel, navy Lieutenant Hugh W. McKee, is speared, and there is fierce fighting before the position is won. Only 20 Koreans, some wounded, surrender; 243 are killed. The storming party has three men killed and seven wounded. Captured are 481 cannon of various calibers, hundreds of matchlock muskets, and 50 flags and standards. The expedition sails, without resuming negotiations, on July 3. Six of Captain Tilton's marines are awarded the Medal of Honor.

1873

May 7–12. A landing party of 200 men goes ashore from the screw sloop *Tuscarora* to protect Americans during one of the recurrent revolutions in the Colombian province of Panama.

September 23–October 9. Another revolutionary disturbance in Panama leads to the landing of 190 men from the screw steamer *Pensacola* and screw sloop *Benicia*.

October 9. **U.S. Naval Institute.** At Annapolis, fifteen officers assigned to the Naval Academy meet to establish a society "for the purpose of discussing matters of professional interest." The first issue of the Naval Institute *Proceedings* appears a little more than a year later, in 1875. In time this private organization, dedicated to "the advancement of professional, literary and scientific knowledge in the Navy," becomes the open forum of the American naval service and one of the foremost societies of its kind in the world.

October 31. **Virginius affair.** The steamer *Virginius*, a Cuban-owned vessel falsely registered under the American flag, is captured by the Spanish cruiser *Tornado* while carrying men and guns to support a rebellion in Cuba. The prisoners, including a number of Americans, are tried before a Spanish court-martial in Havana, and 50 are shot before American and British protests bring the executions to a halt. Among those killed is the *Virginius*'s captain, Joseph Fry, a Naval Academy graduate who had been an officer in the United States and Confederate navies. News of the incident provokes a storm of indignation in the United States, and for a time war with Spain appears distinctly possible.

Bluejackets and marines inside Fort DeConde (as they named it), one of the Korean positions captured on June 10, 1871. *Courtesy Naval Historical Foundation.*

1874

February 12.   Landing parties totaling 150 officers and men are put ashore at Honolulu, Hawaii, from the sloop *Portsmouth,* Commander Joseph S. Skerrett, and screw sloop *Tuscarora,* Commander George E. Belknap, to protect Americans during the disturbances following the coronation of King Kalakaua.

July 31.   The first U.S. naval vessel armed with torpedoes, the 438-ton screw steamer *Intrepid,* is commissioned at Boston. She is not a success.

September 22.   Rear Admiral C. R. P. Rodgers becomes the eighth superintendent of the U.S. Naval Academy.

1875

May 6.   Future Fleet Admiral William D. Leahy is born in Hampton, Iowa.

June 18.   The 1,463-ton side-wheel sloop-of-war *Saranac,* Captain Walter W. Queen, strikes a rock and sinks in the Seymour Narrows, off Vancouver Island, British Columbia. No lives are lost.

1876

November 1.   Colonel Charles G. McCawley becomes eight commandant of the marine corps.

1877

March 13.   Richard W. Thompson assumes office as 27th secretary of the navy.

November 24.   The sloop-rigged iron steamer *Huron,* Commander George P. Ryan, is wrecked in a storm off Nags Head, North Carolina. Of her company of 132 men, 98 are lost.

1878

June 18.   The U.S. Life-Saving Service is established by Act of Congress. In 1915 it will be combined with the Revenue Cutter Service to form the U.S. Coast Guard.

July 1.   Commodore Foxhall A. Parker becomes ninth superintendent of the U.S. Naval Academy.

November 23.   Future Fleet Admiral Ernest J. King is born at Lorain, Ohio.

December 7.   The screw sloop *Ticonderoga,* Commodore Robert W. Shufeldt, sails from Hampton Roads, Virginia, to become the first steam-powered American naval vessel to circumnavigate the globe. During the voyage Shufeldt lays the foundation for the first American treaty of commerce with Korea.

1879

August 2.   Rear Admiral George P. Balch becomes the 10th superintendent of the U.S. Naval Academy.

August 7–March 23, 1882.   **Jeannette Expedition.** The steam bark *Jeannette,* presented to the navy by *New York Herald* publisher James Gordon Bennett, sails from San Francisco under the command of Lieutenant George Washington DeLong with the goal of reaching the North Pole through the Bering Strait. Her all-volunteer crew consists of 28 navy officers and men and 3 civilians. Reaching the Arctic early in September, the *Jeannette* is almost immediately trapped in pack ice and remains imprisoned for 21 months. Throughout this trying period the members of the expedition carefully record scientific observations that will prove of value to later explorers. Finally, on June 13, 1881, the *Jeannette*'s specially reinforced hull is crushed by the tremendous pressure of shifting ice, and the expedition begins an agonizing journey over the ice to the west, toward Siberia. Arriving at the edge of the ice pack on September 12, they sail for the mainland in three boats they had hauled from the *Jeannette.* One broaches and goes down with all hands; the other two, commanded by Lieutenant DeLong and Chief Engineer George W. Melville, are separated. Melville's party lands on the western side of the Lena delta, where they are found and cared for by natives. DeLong's party lands on the uninhabited eastern bank of the Lena and attempts to push on overland. As his men's physical condition deteriorates, DeLong makes camp and sends two of the strongest ahead for help. They encounter a caravan, but are unable to communicate that there are others in need. Eventually the two are united with Melville's party, but by then it is too late. Melville finds the frozen bodies of DeLong and his 14 companions, together with the expedition's records, on March 23, 1882.

1880

November 9.   The screw sloop *Ticonderoga,* Commodore Robert W. Shufeldt, returns to Hampton Roads, Virginia, completing the first circumnavigation of the globe by a steam-powered vessel of the U.S. Navy.

1881

January 7.   Nathan Goff, Jr., becomes the 28th secretary of the navy.

March 7.   William H. Hunt becomes the 29th secretary of the navy.

June 13.   Rear Admiral C. R. P. Rodgers is appointed 11th superintendent of the Naval Academy, thus becoming the first man to hold that post twice.

November 14.   Captain Francis M. Ramsay becomes the 12th superintendent of the Naval Academy.

Lieutenant G. W. DeLong, commander of the ill-fated *Jeannette* expedition, left this photograph "For my wife to look at when she is wondering where I am." *Courtesy U.S. Naval Academy Museum.*

1882

March 23.   **ONI.** The Office of Naval Intelligence is established.

April 17.   William E. Chandler becomes 30th secretary of the navy.

May 22.   Commodore Robert W. Shufeldt completes the negotiation of a commercial treaty between the United States and the kingdom of Korea.

July 14.   **Maintaining order in Alexandria.** On July 11, the British Mediterranean Fleet bombards Alexandria, Egypt, where a nationalist revolution headed by Colonel Arabi Pasha has seized power. Three days later the U.S. gunboat *Nipsic,* screw sloop *Lancaster,* and screw steamer *Quinnebaug* land a detachment of 73 marines and 60 seamen under Captain H. C. Cochrane, USMC, to guard the American consulate and assist British landing parties to maintain order in the seething city. The conduct of this force is later commended by British authorities.

October 30.   Future Fleet Admiral William F. ("Bull") Halsey is born in Elizabeth, New Jersey.

November 15.   **First naval attaché.** Lieutenant French Ensor Chadwick is accredited to the London embassy to report on technological developments in European navies.

1883

February 18.   The side-wheel gunboat *Ashuelot,* Commander Horace E. Mullan, grounds near Swatow, China, with the loss of 11 lives.

March 3.   **ABCDs.** Congress authorizes the construction of four steel warships—the protected cruisers *Atlanta, Boston,* and *Chicago* and the dispatch-vessel *Dolphin.* The cruisers are "protected" by armored decks to prevent plunging fire from penetrating to their engine spaces. Later known as the White Squadron, they are the first really modern ships to enter the fleet since the Civil War. The decision to build them is generally regarded as the beginning of the American naval renaissance.

1884

April 25–May 10.   **Greely Relief Expedition.** A rescue expedition consisting of the steamers *Thetis, Bear,* Lieutenant William H. Emory, and *Alert,* Commander George W. Coffin, sails from New York for the Arctic under the command of Commander W. S. Schley to search for the 25-man Lady Franklin Bay

The protected cruiser *Atlanta,* one of the ABCDs, an engraving from a drawing by J. O. Davidson in *Harper's Weekly,* May 21, 1887. *Courtesy U.S. Naval Academy Museum.*

Commander W. S. Schley *(fourth from left),* and the officers of the Greely Relief Expedition in cold-weather gear aboard the *Thetis. Courtesy U.S. Naval Academy Museum.*

expedition under First Lieutenant Adolphus W. Greely, USA, which had set out for the North Pole in 1881.

June 22.   Schley rescues Lieutenant Greely and his six surviving companions, all near death from starvation, at Cape Sabine, Grinnell Land (Ellesmere Island).

July 7.   Congress authorizes the organization of the Office of Naval Records (originally called the Naval War Records Office). The work is carried out by former Naval Academy Professor James Russell Soley, who had taken charge of the Navy Library in 1882.

Rear Admiral Stephen B. Luce. *Courtesy U.S. Naval Academy Museum.*

October 6.   **Naval War College.** Secretary of the Navy Chandler establishes the Naval War College at Newport, Rhode Island. Commodore Stephen B. Luce, who had long advocated the foundation of such an institution, is appointed its first president.

1885

January 18.   The gunboat *Alliance* lands her marines at Aspinwall (now Colón), on the Atlantic coast of the Colombian province of Panama, where a revolution has broken out. They are to guard the terminal of the trans-isthmian railroad and protect American interests.

February 24.   Future Fleet Admiral Chester W. Nimitz is born in Fredericksburg, Texas.

March 7.   William C. Whitney becomes the 31st secretary of the navy.

March 16–May 25.   **Panamanian intervention.** The progress of the Panamanian revolution has blocked free transit of the isthmus, to which the United States is entitled to by treaty with Colombia. On March 26, the screw sloop *Galena* puts her landing party ashore at Aspinwall (Colón), where it is soon joined by detachments from the *Iroquois, Shenandoah,* and *Swatara.* On April 12, a battalion of 232 marines under Lieutenant Colonel Charles Heywood, rushed from the United States, lands at Aspinwall and reopens the railway to Panama City, on the Pacific. Three days later Heywood's men are reinforced by a battalion each of bluejackets and marines under Commander Bowman H. McCalla, who is given command of U.S. forces ashore. McCalla concentrates his brigade at Panama City and maintains order until Colombian troops suppress the insurrection.

September 3.   The Naval War College holds its first formal classes.

1886

July 3.   Future Admiral Raymond A. Spruance, victor of the battles of Midway and the Philippine Sea, is born at Baltimore, Maryland.

August 6.   **First American battleships.** Congress authorizes the construction of the *Maine,* originally designated an armored cruiser, and the *Texas,* which is referred to as an "armored battleship" from the beginning. The two vessels are similar in displacement (6,682 and 6,315 tons, respectively) and design, having their two main turrets placed diagonally on the starboard bow and port quarter, but the *Maine* carries four 10-inch guns in contrast to the *Texas*'s two 12-inchers. The immediate impetus to the appropriation was Brazil's acquisition of the British-built armored cruiser *Riachuelo,* which was considered capable of defeating the entire U.S. fleet.

September 9.   Commander William T. Sampson becomes the 13th superintendent of the Naval Academy.

1887

March 3.   The protected cruisers *Philadelphia* (C 4) and *San Francisco* (C 5) and two gunboats are authorized by Congress.

1888

May 17.   **Origin of the naval reserve.** Massachusetts becomes the first state to organize a naval militia. Others follow, and eventually these units are transformed into the naval reserve.

June 19.   Twenty-five men from the screw steamer *Essex* land at Chemulpo (Inchon), Korea, under First Lieutenant Robert D. Wainwright and proceed to Seoul to protect American citizens.

September 7.   The first American armored cruiser, the *New York* (ACR 2), and six smaller cruisers, including the *Olympia* (C 6), are authorized by Congress.

November 14.   The gunboat *Nipsic* lands her marines at Apia, Upolu Island, Samoa, to protect American traders during a civil war.

December 20.   An American steamer seized by Haiti is released following the appearance of the screw sloop *Galena* and gunboat *Yantic* at Port-au-Prince.

1889

March 6.   Benjamin F. Tracy becomes the 32nd secretary of the navy.

March 15–16.   **Samoan hurricane.** Because of their strategic location on the trade route to Australia, the 14 islands of the Samoan archipelago have long been of interest to the American shipping community as well as to the navy. In 1878 the United States executed a treaty with a native chieftain whereby it obtained the right to establish a coaling station at Pago Pago in return for a pledge to use its good offices should Samoa become involved in a dispute with a third power. Eight years later the newborn German Empire began to show a strong interest in the area, actively intervening in tribal politics. Great Britain also entered the controversy, supporting Germany's demand for a partition of the islands. An international conference sponsored by the United States failed to relieve the mounting tension, and Germany sent three warships to Apia harbor on Upolu Island in an exercise of gunboat diplomacy. President Grover Cleveland responded by ordering three American vessels to Apia, and Germany adopted a more conciliatory attitude. On March 15–16, the rivalry is abruptly defused by an act of nature when a hurricane strikes Apia, where one British, three American, and three German warships and six merchantmen are anchored. HMS *Calliope* is the only vessel that succeeds in getting out of the harbor. The captain of the U.S. gunboat *Nipsic,* Commander D. W. Mullin, is able to beach his ship. The screw steamer *Trenton,* Captain Norman H. Farquhar (flagship of Rear Admiral Lewis A. Kimberly, commanding the Pacific

Station), and screw sloop *Vandalia,* Captain Cornelius M. Schoonmaker, are sunk, together with the German warships *Adler, Eber,* and *Olga* and all six merchantmen. Approximately 150 seamen, including 49 Americans, lose their lives. The following month a conference meets at Berlin, where the three powers agree to a tripartite protectorate over Samoa. This arrangement endures until 1899, when the islands are partitioned between, and annexed by, Germany and the United States.

July 30.   Marines from the screw gunboat *Adams* are landed to protect the U.S. legation during disturbances at Honolulu in the kingdom of Hawaii.

1890

April 23.   **First torpedo boat.** The *Cushing* (TB 1) is commissioned at Bristol, Rhode Island. One hundred and four feet in length and only 15 feet 1 inch abeam, she carries a crew of 22 and has a top speed of 23 knots.

May.   **Command of the sea.** Captain Alfred Thayer Mahan's *The Influence of Sea Power Upon History, 1660–1783* is published by Little, Brown and Company of Boston. The most important strategic study ever written by an American, the work is an extension of Mahan's lectures as a professor at the new Naval War College. Using the long maritime struggle between Britain and France as a historical test case, Mahan argues that the traditional French (and American) strategy of commerce raiding is a recipe for defeat. Victory comes only when a navy concentrates its operations, as had the British, on vanquishing the

The torpedo boat *Cushing. U.S. Naval Institute Collection.*

Captain Alfred Thayer Mahan. *U.S. Naval Institute Collection.*

opposing fleet to win command of the sea. Quickly recognized as a classic, the work provides renewed impetus and a strategic direction to the American naval renaissance.

June 13.   Captain Robert L. Phythian becomes the 14th superintendent of the U.S. Naval Academy.

June 30.   **More battleships.** Congress authorizes the construction of the three *Indiana*-class battleships: the *Indiana,* the *Massachusetts* and the *Oregon.* These 10,000-ton ships are a third again as large as the *Maine* and the *Texas* and carry their four 13-inch guns in what becomes the standard arrangement of centerline turrets. When hull numbers are retroactively assigned to battleships in 1920, they are respectively designated BB 1, BB 2, and BB 3.

July 30.   A detachment of marines is landed at Buenos Aires, Argentina, from the side-wheel steamer *Tallapoosa* to guard the U.S. legation during a period of unrest.

November 29.   **First Army-Navy game.** The Naval Academy football team travels to West Point to win the first athletic contest ever held between the service academies, 24–0.

1891

January 30.   Lieutenant Colonel Charles Heywood succeeds Colonel Charles G. McCawley to become ninth commandant of the marine corps.

February 13.   Vice Admiral David Dixon Porter dies, aged 77.

March 3.   The office of assistant secretary of the navy, held during the Civil War by Gustavus V. Fox, is revived. Its first occupant is former Naval Academy professor James Russell Soley.

May 1.   **First marine school.** The "School of Application" is established for newly commissioned marine officers at the Marine Barracks, Washington, D.C.

June 2.   The screw sloop *Kearsarge* lands her marines to preserve order on Navassa Island, Hawaii.

August 28.   The cruisers *Baltimore* (C 3) and *San Francisco* (C 5) land a party commanded by Captain William S. Muse, USMC, to guard the U.S. Consulate at Valparaiso during the Chilean civil war.

October 16.   **Incident at the True Blue Saloon.** Two sailors are killed and sixteen injured when a liberty party from the cruiser *Baltimore* becomes embroiled with a mob of Chileans at the True Blue Saloon in Valparaiso. Offensive remarks by the Chilean foreign minister aggravate the ensuing crisis so that by December war between the United States and Chile appears quite possible. Americans are chagrined to note that materially the Chilean fleet is superior to their own.

1892

January 21.   **Chilean crisis.** President Benjamin Harrison sends an ultimatum threatening to break diplomatic relations unless an apology is made for her foreign minister's remarks (see October 16, 1891).

January 27.   The crisis is resolved when Chile apologizes and pays an indemnity of $75,000 to the families of the two dead sailors.

July 19.   Congress authorizes the construction of a sixth battleship, the *Iowa* (BB 4).

1893

January 16.   **Hawaiian intervention.** American settlers in Hawaii revolt against Queen Liliukalani, who has proclaimed a new constitution designed to reduce their influence in the islands' government. The success of the uprising is assured when U.S. Minister John L. Stevens has the cruiser *Boston,* then at Honolulu, land 150 sailors and marines, ostensibly to protect the American legation. The settlers want the United States to annex the islands, but the incoming, Democratic administration of President Grover Cleveland disappoints them, and in 1894 Hawaii becomes an independent republic.

March 7.   Hilary A. Herbert becomes the 33rd secretary of the navy.

August 1.   The navy's first armored cruiser, the 8,150-ton *New York* (ACR 2), is commissioned at Philadelphia.

1894

February 2.   The old screw sloop *Kearsarge,* Commander Oscar F. Heyerman, wrecks without loss of life on Roncador Reef, off Central America.

July 6.   The cruiser *Columbia* (C 12) lands a detachment of sailors and marines to safeguard American lives and property at Bluefields, Nicaragua.

July 24.   A party of 50 sailors and marines under Captain George Fielding Elliott, USMC, is sent from the cruiser *Baltimore* (C 3) to guard the American legation at Seoul, Korea, during the Sino-Japanese War. The Japanese had landed troops in Korea.

September 17.   **Philo McGiffen at the Yalu.** A graduate of the USNA Class of 1882 serving in the Imperial Chinese Navy, McGiffen becomes the first American to command a modern battleship in action when he takes over from the captain of the *Chen Yuen* at the Battle of the Yalu during the Sino-Japanese War.

November 15.   Captain Philip H. Cooper becomes 15th superintendent of the Naval Academy.

1895

February 25.   **Cuban insurrection.** Another of the recurrent revolts against Spanish rule breaks out in Cuba. This one will eventually lead to American intervention.

March 2.   Congress authorizes the construction of the battleships *Kearsarge* (BB 5) and *Kentucky* (BB 6).

March 8.   The cruiser *Atlanta* lands a party to protect American interests at Boca del Toro, Colombia.

August 15.   The *Texas* is the first American battleship to be commissioned.

September 17.   The battleship *Maine* is commissioned.

November 20.   The battleship *Indiana* (BB 1) is commissioned.

The armored cruiser *New York. Official U.S. Navy photograph.*

1896

May 2–4.   The gunboat *Alert* sends her landing party ashore to safeguard American citizens and interests at Corinto, Nicaragua.

June 10.   The battleship *Massachusetts* (BB 2) is commissioned.

July 15.   The battleship *Oregon* (BB 3) is commissioned.

July 20.   An act of Congress establishes the Marine Corps Good Conduct Medal to reward enlisted men for blameless service. It was personally designed by the corps's commandant, Brigadier General Charles F. Heywood.

1897

March 6.   John D. Long becomes the 34th secretary of the navy.

June 16.   The battleship *Iowa* (BB 4) is commissioned.

1898

February 7.   The gunboat *Alert,* Commander Eugene H. C. Leutze, lands a detachment of bluejackets and marines to protect the U.S. Consulate during revolutionary disturbances at San Juan del Sur, Nicaragua.

February 9.   **De Lôme Letter.** The American public is angered when the *New York Journal* publishes an intercepted private letter in which the Spanish ambassador to the United States, Dupuy de Lôme, makes a number of highly uncomplimentary references to President McKinley.

February 15.   **"Remember the Maine!"** The battleship *Maine,* Captain Charles D. Sigsbee, which entered Havana harbor for a good-will visit on January 25, is destroyed by an explosion of undetermined origin. More than half her complement—253 of 358 officers and men—are killed. After examining the wreck, a naval court of inquiry headed by Captain William T. Sampson finds that the effects of the blast "could have been produced only by . . . a mine situated under the bottom of the ship." A furious country concludes that the Spanish are to blame. (Recent research indicates that the explosion was caused by a fire in a coal bunker, which ignited an adjacent magazine.)

March 8.   Congress unanimously appropriates $50,000,000 for national defense, to be spent at the discretion of the president.

March 17.   Senator Redfield Proctor, a Republican moderate who has just returned from a visit to Cuba, delivers a powerful speech condemning the brutality of the methods by which the Spanish are attempting to suppress the insurrection there. Many persons who had opposed American intervention become convinced that it is a humanitarian duty.

The battleship *Maine. Courtesy National Archives.*

The wreck of the *Maine. Courtesy Nimitz Library.*

The battleship *Oregon* immediately after the Battle of Santiago. *U.S. Naval Institute Collection.*

March 18.   In view of the possibility of war with Spain, a Flying Squadron is formed for the defense of the eastern seaboard. Commanded by Acting Commodore Winfield Scott Schley, it consists of the armored cruiser *Brooklyn* (ACR 3) (flag), the battleships *Massachusetts* (BB 2) and *Texas,* and the cruisers *Columbia* (C 12) and *Minneapolis* (C 13).

March 19–24.   **Voyage of the Oregon.** The battleship *Oregon* (BB 3), Captain Charles E. Clark, sails from San Francisco, California, to join the forces in the Caribbean. She arrivers at Jupiter Inlet, Florida, after an unprecedented 67-day voyage of 14,700 miles at an average speed of almost 12 knots. No other warship had ever approached this achievement.

March 24.   Captain William T. Sampson relieves ailing Rear Admiral Montgomery B. Sicard in command of the North Atlantic Squadron.

March 26.   Under great pressure from public opinion eager for war with Spain, President McKinley sends an ultimatum to the Spanish government demanding, among other things, independence for Cuba. The Spanish reply, received March 31, is conciliatory, but ignores the question of Cuban independence.

April 9.   The Spanish government agrees to enter an armistice with the Cuban rebels, one of the demands of McKinley's ultimatum of March 26, but the concession comes too late.

April 11.   **War message.** President McKinley asks Congress for authority to intervene in Cuba.

April 19.   Congress authorizes the president to use force to expel the Spanish from Cuba. The Teller Amendment to the war resolution pledges the United States not to annex the island. McKinley signs the act on April 20.

April 22.   **Blockade of Cuba.** President McKinley proclaims a blockade of the coast of Cuba from Havana to Cienfuegos. Acting Rear Admiral William T. Sampson's North Atlantic Squadron, concentrated at Key West, Florida, sails for Cuba early this morning.

April 22.   **First shots of the war.** En route to Cuba with the North Atlantic Squadron, the gunboat *Nashville* (PG 7), Commander Washburn Maynard, captures the Spanish freighter *Buenaventura.* The two shots fired across her bow are the first of the Spanish-American War. Dozens of other Spanish merchantmen will be taken in the brief course of the conflict.

April 23.   The North Atlantic Squadron establishes a blockade of the Cuban ports of Havana, Mariel, Matanzas, Cárdenas, and Cienfuegos.

April 25.   **War with Spain.** Congress declares that a state of war has existed with Spain since April 21. Secretary of the Navy Long cables Commodore George Dewey, commanding the Asiatic Squadron at Hong Kong, "Proceed at once to Philippine Islands. Commence operations . . . against Spanish fleet. You must capture vessels or destroy."

April 27.   The U.S. Asiatic Squadron, four cruisers, two gunboats, and a revenue cutter under Commodore George Dewey, sails from Mirs Bay, near Hong Kong, for Manila, seat of the Spanish government in the Philippines.

April 27.   **First action.** The armored cruiser *New York* (ACR 2), flagship of Admiral Sampson, cruiser

The protected cruiser *Olympia,* flagship of the Asiatic Squadron at the Battle of Manila Bay. *U.S. Naval Institute Collection.*

Cincinnati (C 7), and monitor *Puritan* (BM 1) engage and silence two Spanish batteries at Matanzas, Cuba, without damage to themselves. The batteries had previously fired on the torpedo boat *Foote* (TB 3).

April 30.   Arriving off the Philippine island of Luzon, the Asiatic Squadron searches Subic Bay for the Spanish fleet, which is not there.

May 1.   **Battle of Manila Bay.** Certain that the enemy fleet is off Manila, Commodore Dewey leads the Asiatic Squadron past the shore batteries into the bay under cover of darkness, accepting the risk that the channel may be mined. Most of the ships have passed the batteries before the Spanish open fire, and no damage is done. At dawn the fleet of Rear Admiral Patricio Montojo y Parasón is found lying at anchor off the Cavite Navy Yard. The odds are distinctly in Dewey's favor. His squadron consists of the protected cruisers *Olympia* (C 6) (flag), Captain Charles V. Gridley, *Baltimore* (C 3), Captain Nehemiah M. Dyer, *Boston,* Captain Frank Wildes, and *Raleigh* (C 8), Captain Joseph B. Coghlan, the gunboats *Concord* (PG 3), Commander Asa Walker, and *Petrel* (PG 2), Commander Edward P. Wood, and the revenue cutter *Hugh McCulloch,* Captain Daniel B. Hodgson, U.S. Revenue Cutter Service, plus the transports *Nanshan* and *Zafiro.* The combined broadsides of these ships is 3,700 pounds. The Spanish fleet is formed of one modern but unseaworthy steel cruiser, the *Reina Maria Cristina* (flag); an old wooden cruiser, the *Castillo;* and five small cruisers and gunboats, the *Don Antonio de Ulloa, Don Juan de Austria, Isla de Cuba, Isla de Luzon,* and *Marqués de Duero.* Its combined broadside is only 1,273 pounds. In view of this disparity, Admiral

Montojo has elected to fight at anchor, where his vessels can be supported by the Spanish shore fortifications. His tactic is reasonable but unavailing. The *Maria Cristina, Castillo,* and *Ulloa* are sunk, the other vessels disabled, and the forts silenced. Three small Spanish gunboats that did not take part in the action—the *Elcano, General Lezo,* and *Velasco*—and the transport *Isla de Mindanao* are destroyed by shell fire in the navy yard. Spanish losses, afloat and ashore, are 91 men killed and 280 wounded. American casualties are two officers and six men slightly wounded. Informing the Navy Department of the victory, Dewey explains that he can take Manila at any time, but lacks enough men to hold it. Plans are then set in motion to dispatch an army expeditionary force from the West Coast.

May 1.   **Cervera's squadron.** In the United States it is learned that a Spanish squadron of four cruisers and three destroyers commanded by Rear Admiral Pascual Cervera y Topete sailed from the Cape Verde Islands on April 29. Admiral Sampson is confident that it is bound for the Caribbean.

May 2.   The Spanish naval arsenal at Cavite, near Manila, is occupied by a detachment from the gunboat *Petrel* (PG 2).

May 3.   A party under Lieutenant Dion Williams, USMC, from the cruisers *Baltimore* (C 3) and *Raleigh* (C 8)

Commodore George Dewey aboard the *Olympia,* after his promotion to rear admiral, with his dog, Bob. *Courtesy U.S. Naval Academy Museum.*

lands on Corregidor in Manila Bay, captures the Spanish garrison, and spikes the island's guns.

May 11. **Cable cutting at Cienfuegos.** To sever communications between the Spanish colonial administration in Cuba and the government in Madrid, the decision is made to cut the three underwater cables leading from Cienfuegos to Santiago and thence to Jamaica. (The cable running from Havana to Key West, Florida, had already been cut.) On this date, volunteer boat parties from the cruiser *Marblehead* (C 11) and gunboat *Nashville* (PG 7) commanded by Lieutenant C. M. Winslow and E. A. Anderson row to within 100 feet of the beach to dredge up the cables at Cienfuegos. Soon taken under small-arms fire by Spanish soldiers ashore, they persist in their work for two-and-a-half hours, during which they cut two cables at a cost of four men killed or mortally wounded and seven others hit. Some 54 Medals of Honor are awarded for this operation.

May 11. **Action at Cárdenas.** Backed by the gunboats *Machias* (PG 5) and *Wilmington* (PG 8) and the revenue cutter *Hudson,* the torpedo boat *Winslow* (TB 5), Lieutenant John B. Bernadou, runs into the harbor at Cárdenas, Cuba, with the aim of cutting out one of three small Spanish gunboats tied up at the pier. During her approach the *Winslow* is struck three times by Spanish shore batteries, and her steering gear is disabled. The *Hudson,* Lieutenant F. H. Newcomb, U.S. Revenue Cutter Service, tows her to safety. Lieutenant Bernadou and two other men are wounded and four are killed. Among the dead is Ensign Worth Bagley, the only naval officer killed in the Spanish-American War.

May 12. **The search for Cervera.** Assuming that the Spanish Cape Verde squadron will make for Puerto Rico, Admiral Sampson proceeds there with the armored cruiser *New York* (ACR 2) (flag), battleships *Indiana* (BB 1) and *Iowa* (BB 4), the monitors *Amphitrite* (BM 2) and *Terror* (BM 4), the cruisers *Detroit* (C 10) and *Montgomery* (C 9), and two auxiliaries, arriving off San Juan before dawn. The Spanish squadron is not present. After bombarding the harbor fortifications for two hours, during which one seaman is killed and six wounded, Sampson shapes course for Key West, which he reaches on May 18. Here he learns that Cervera's ships coaled at Curaçao, Netherlands West Indies, on May 14–15 and departed in the direction of Cuba.

May 19. **The search for Cervera continues.** Upon the news that the Spanish squadron has appeared in the Caribbean, the Navy Department ordered Com-

Ensign Worth Bagley, the only naval officer killed in the Spanish-American War. *Nimitz Library Special Collections.*

modore Schley's Flying Squadron to Key West. Sampson finds that it has just arrived when he returns from Puerto Rico and directs Schley to establish a blockade of the southern Cuban port of Cienfuegos, certain that Cervera will appear at either Cienfuegos or Havana. Schley sails early on the morning of the 19th—the day Cervera slips into Santiago—with the armored cruiser *Brooklyn* (ACR 3) (flag), the battleships *Massachusetts* (BB 2) and *Texas,* and the armed yacht *Scorpion.* Sampson promises to send the battleship *Iowa* (BB 4) to reinforce the Flying Squadron as soon as she can coal.

May 21. Sampson sails from Key West to patrol the Nicholas Channel, off the northern coast of Cuba, in position to intercept Cervera should he attempt to reach Havana.

May 21–24. **Schley off Cienfuegos.** Approaching Cienfuegos, whose harbor cannot be seen from the sea, Schley hears the sound of cannon fire, which he as-

Rear Admiral William T. Sampson. *Courtesy U.S. Naval Academy Museum.*

sumes to be a salute fired in honor of the arrival of Cervera's squadron. On May 23 he receives a dispatch from Sampson, reporting "Spanish squadron probably at Santiago" and instructing him to proceed there "if you are satisfied that they are not at Cienfuegos." Since Schley believes they are indeed at Cienfuegos, he stays where he is. The next day the cruiser *Marblehead* (C 11) arrives and informs him that a secret signal system, of which he was previously unaware, has been devised for communicating with Cuban insurgents ashore. Through these signals, Schley learns that the Spanish squadron is definitely not at Cienfuegos.

May 24–26.   **Schley's advance to Santiago.** Departing Cienfuegos around 6:00 P.M. on the 24th, Schley steams slowly down the coast towards Santiago. Twenty miles from the city he decides that his ships' need of coal and the difficulty of coaling at sea necessitate his return to Key West, and he reverses course. His decision is influenced by the fact that Captain Charles D. Sigsbee of the auxiliary cruiser *St. Paul,* which had been on patrol off Santiago for several days, reports having seen "absolutely nothing of the Spanish fleet."

May 27.   Around 9:30 A.M. the auxiliary *Harvard* reaches the Flying Squadron carrying a dispatch from the Navy Department, dated May 25, ordering Commodore Schley to Santiago to ascertain if the Spanish squadron is there. He replies, "Much to be regretted, can not obey orders of the department; forced to proceed for coal to Key West. . . ." That night, however, the sea abates. The battleship *Texas* succeeds in taking on some coal from the *Merrimac,* and Schley turns back towards Santiago.

May 28.   **Cervera is found.** Reaching Santiago this afternoon, Schley sends the cruiser *Marblehead* (C 11), Commander Bowman H. McCalla, to scout the mouth of the channel leading to the harbor. The ships of the Spanish squadron are clearly visible at anchor off the city. The next morning Schley makes an inshore sweep with his entire squadron, confirming the sighting, and institutes a blockage of the port. Admiral Sampson later terms Schley's conduct of the search for Cervera "reprehensible."

May 29.   Informed by dispatch boat that Schley has located the Spanish squadron, Sampson hastens to Key West to advise the Navy Department and starts for Santiago with the *New York* (ACR 2), collecting the battleship *Oregon* (BB 3), the torpedo boat *Porter* (TB 6), and auxiliary destroyer *Mayflower* en route.

May 31.   Commodore Schley conducts a long-range bombardment of the coastal fortifications at Santiago with the battleships *Massachusetts* (BB 2) (flag) and *Iowa* (BB 4), and the cruiser *New Orleans.*

June 1.   **Sampson reaches Santiago.** Admiral Sampson arrives to assume command of U.S. naval forces off Santiago. For the moment, the strategic situation is stalemated. Sampson cannot enter the harbor, which is located at the end of a narrow, twisting channel commanded by powerful shore fortifications and presumably defended by minefields; and Cervera cannot leave without encountering Sampson's greatly superior fleet.

June 3.   **Dewey Medal.** Congress authorizes the award of a medal for the officers and men who participated in the Battle of Manila Bay. This is the first official American campaign medal.

June 3.   **Hobson and the Merrimac.** With no way of getting into Santiago harbor to attack Cervera's squadron, Sampson tries to bottle it up there. After nightfall a volunteer crew of seven bluejackets headed by Lieutenant Richmond P. Hobson sets out to sink the collier *Merrimac* across the channel. A hail of fire from the Spanish batteries disables the ship's steering

Lieutenant Richmond P. Hobson, the hero of the *Merrimac.*
Courtesy U.S. Naval Academy Museum.

before she reaches a blocking position, and she settles along the edge of the channel. Miraculously, all of her crew members survive and are rescued by a Spanish launch in which Hobson is surprised to find Admiral Cervera. The seven enlisted men are awarded the Medal of Honor in 1899; as an officer, Hobson is ineligible for the honor at that date, but receives it through a special Act of Congress in 1933.

June 6. The fortifications covering the channel into Santiago are shelled by Sampson's squadron, consisting of the battleships *Iowa* (BB 4), *Massachusetts* (BB 2), *Oregon* (BB 3), and *Texas,* the armored cruisers *Brooklyn* (ACR 3) and *New York* (ACR 2), the cruisers *Marblehead* (C 11) and *New Orleans,* the auxiliary cruisers *Suwanee, Vixen,* and *Yankee,* and the dispatch boat *Dolphin.* The Spanish cruiser *Reina Mercedes,* lying at the mouth of the harbor, is also engaged.

June 7. The cruiser *Marblehead* (C 11), Commander Bowman H. McCalla, and auxiliary cruiser *Yankee,* Captain Willard A. Brownson, test the defenses of Guantánamo Bay, 40 miles east of Santiago, silencing a

The bombardment of Santiago, June 6, 1898. This previously unpublished drawing was made by R. W. Bennett, a crewman on the cruiser *New Orleans,* on the back of a leaf from her log. *Courtesy U.S. Naval Academy Museum.*

Spanish battery and driving the gunboat *Sandoval* into the inner harbor. Admiral Sampson has decided to seize the bay for use as a coaling station and advanced base.

June 10.   Marines at Guantánamo. Supported by fire from the battleship *Oregon* (BB 3), a marine battalion under Lieutenant Colonel R. W. Huntington lands at Guantánamo. Its members are the first American troops to set foot on Cuban soil.

June 11–14.   Beginning late in the afternoon of the 11th, the Spanish harass the marine encampment at Guantánamo with sniper fire. Three days later Lieutenant Colonel Huntington learns from Cuban guerillas that Spanish forces in the area are dependent on a water supply point in the Cuzco Valley, two miles from his camp. Upon receiving this information, he sends two companies and 75 Cubans under his youngest company officer, 52-year-old Captain George Fielding Elliott, to destroy the enemy installation. The operation is supported by fire from the dispatch boat *Dolphin*. Elliott accomplishes his mission, defeating a Spanish detachment of 500 men and wrecking the windmill and well at a cost of 6 men killed and 16 wounded. The sniping ceases.

June 14.   The army embarks. The V Corps, a 17,000-man expeditionary force commanded by corpulent Major General William T. Shafter, sails under naval escort from Tampa, Florida, to begin operations around Santiago. Sampson hopes that its appearance will force Cervera to leave the harbor.

June 15.   The Spanish fort at Ciamanera, on Guantánamo Bay, is destroyed by fire from the battleship *Texas*, Captain John W. Philip, the cruiser *Marblehead* (C 11), Commander Bowman H. McCalla, and the auxiliary cruiser *Suwanee*, Commander Daniel Delehanty.

June 20.   Admiral Sampson and General Shafter meet to plan the strategy of the Santiago campaign. Sampson leaves the conference convinced that Shafter has agreed that the army's objective is the capture of the batteries commanding the channel into the harbor; Shafter believes that Sampson agrees its objective is the capture of the city itself.

June 21.   Seizure of Guam. In the Pacific, the cruiser *Charleston* (C 2), Captain Henry Glass, captures the island of Guam. The Spanish colonial authorities were unaware that there was a war under way.

June 22–25.   Landing at Daiquirí. The V Corps goes ashore in an unopposed landing at the village of Daiquirí, 16 miles east of Santiago.

June 22.   Arriving to establish a blockade of San Juan, Puerto Rico, the auxiliary cruiser *St. Paul*, Captain Charles D. Sigsbee, disables the Spanish destroyer *Terror* when she advances to attack her with the support of the light cruiser *Isabel II* and the guns of the shore batteries.

June 28.   President McKinley proclaims a blockade of the southern coast of Cuba.

June 28.   Off San Juan, Puerto Rico, the auxiliary cruiser *Yosemite*, Commander William H. Emory, manned by the Michigan Naval Militia, intercepts the transport *Antonio Lopez*, nearing port with supplies for the garrison. Despite efforts by the Spanish cruisers *Isabel II* and *Alfonso XIII* and a torpedo boat to cover the *Lopez's* approach, the *Yosemite* drives her on a reef and wrecks her with gunfire.

June 30.   The auxiliary cruisers *Hist*, Lieutenant Lucien Young, and *Hornet*, Lieutenant J. M. Helm, and the armed tug *Wompatuck*, Commander Charles W. Jungen, sink two small Spanish warships in separate engagements off Manzanillo, Cuba.

July 1.   Escorted by the cruiser *Charleston* (C 2), transports carrying the first 2,500 men of the expeditionary force to the Philippines reach Manila Bay.

July 1.   El Caney and San Juan Hill. Advancing on Santiago, General Shafter's troops carry two strong Spanish positions by frontal assaults in which 1,572 of them—almost 10 percent of the entire expeditionary force—are killed or wounded.

July 2.   Alarmed by his casualties in the previous day's battles, Shafter sends Sampson a message urging him to force the entrance to Santiago harbor "to avoid losses among my men." Sampson is appalled. Instead of helping the navy by capturing the batteries, the army is asking the navy to help it capture the city. Sampson makes arrangements to confer with Shafter at Siboney, east of Santiago, the next day.

July 3.   Battle of Santiago. Shortly after his flagship, the armored cruiser *New York* (ACR 2), leaves the blockade line to carry Sampson down the coast to Siboney, the Spanish squadron solves his problem by a desperate attempt to escape. The orders for the sortie had been issued, over Admiral Cervera's objections, by the governor general of Cuba. The bow of the cruiser *Infanta María Teresa*, Cervera's flagship, is sighted in the channel, leading the squadron out, at 9:31 A.M. On her approach Commodore Schley's flagship, the *Brooklyn* (ACR 3), turns to port, away from the Spanish vessel, a maneuver for which Schley later receives consider-

The smoldering wreck of the Spanish cruiser *Vizcaya* at the conclusion of the Battle of Santiago. *U.S. Naval Institute Collection.*

able criticism. Upon reaching deep water the *Maria Teresa* turns west on a course paralleling the Cuban coast. Cervera's other three cruisers follow. Smothered by fire from the battleships *Indiana* (BB 1), Captain Henry C. Taylor, *Iowa* (BB 4), Captain Robley D. Evans, *Oregon* (BB 3), Captain Charles Clark, and *Texas,* Captain John W. Philip, and the *Brooklyn,* Captain Francis A. Cook, the Spanish flagship beaches herself six-and-a-half miles down the coast at 10:15. The *Almirante Oquendo,* the last cruiser in the Spanish line, is driven ashore at 10:35. The *Vizcaya* and *Cristóbal Colón* continue their flight to the west, pursued by the *Oregon*—the only battleship to have all her boilers lit when the Spanish sortied—the *Brooklyn,* the *Texas,* and the *Iowa,* in that order. Around 11:00 the *Vizcaya* turns towards the coast with the evident intention of beaching herself, and Admiral Sampson, whose flagship has gradually overtaken the action, signals the *Iowa* to follow and finish her. The action then settles into a stern chase in which the *Colón* draws away from all her pursuers except the *Oregon,* "the bulldog of the fleet," and the *Brooklyn.* At 1:10 P.M. a 13-inch shell fired at maximum elevation from the *Oregon's* fore turret strikes beside the *Colón,* whose speed has begun to slacken, and the cruiser runs aground off the mouth of Rio Tarquino. The two destroyers that followed the cruisers out of Santiago have already been destroyed: the *Plutón* by a direct hit from a battleship, probably the *Indiana;* and the *Furor* in a close action with Lieutenant Comman-

der Richard Wainwright's auxiliary gunboat *Gloucester* formerly J. P. Morgan's yacht *Corsair).* Spanish losses are 323 dead and 151 wounded; the latter and most of the other 1,800 survivors, including Admiral Cervera, are rescued by Sampson's ships. American casualties are one man killed and one seriously wounded. Sampson opens his report of the action with the words, "The fleet under my command offers the nation as a Fourth of July present the whole of Cervera's fleet."

July 4.   After nightfall, the Spanish attempt to block the channel to Santiago by scuttling the cruiser *Reina Mercedes* across it. The movement is detected, and the Spanish ship is quickly sunk by fire from the *Massachusetts* (BB 2) and the *Texas.*

July 7.   The United States annexes Hawaii.

July 10.   The battleships *Indiana* (BB 1) and *Texas* and the armored cruisers *Brooklyn* (ACR 3) and *New York* (ACR 2) bombard Santiago.

July 15.   Rear Admiral Frederick V. McNair becomes the 16th superintendent of the Naval Academy.

July 17.   **Fall of Santiago.** General José Toral, commanding the Spanish forces around Santiago, surrenders the city to General Shafter. Eight Spanish vessels, including the gunboat *Alvarado,* are captured in the harbor.

July 18.   A squadron consisting of the gunboats *Wilmington* (PG 8), Commander C. C. Todd, and *Helena,* Commander W. T. Swinburne, the auxiliary cruisers *Hist,* Lieutenant Lucien Young, and *Scorpion,* Lieutenant Commander Adolph Marix, and the armed tugs *Osceola,* Lieutenant J. L. Purcell, and *Wompatuck,* Commander Charles M. Jungen, enters Manzanillo harbor, where it destroys the Spanish gunboats *Cuba Española, Delgado Perado, Estrella de Guantánamo, Guardián, José Garcia, María Pontón,* and *Sentinel Delgado,* and the blockade runner *El Purísima Concepción.*

July 19.   A second contingent of American troops reaches Manila.

July 21.   The fortifications of Nipe, on the northern coast of Cuba, are shelled by the gunboats *Annapolis* (PG 10), Commander J. J. Hunker, and *Topeka,* Lieutenant Commander W. S. Cowles, the auxiliary cruiser *Wasp,* Lieutenant A. Ward, and the armed tug *Leydon,* Ensign W. S. Crosley. The Spanish light cruiser *Jorge Juan* sorties to engage this force and is quickly sunk.

July 21.   **Expedition to Puerto Rico.** Major General A. Miles sails from Guantánamo for the invasion of Puerto Rico with 3,400 troops in eight transports escorted by the battleship *Massachusetts* (BB 2), Captain F. J. Higginson, the cruiser *Columbia* (C 12), Captain

J. H. Sands, and the auxiliary cruisers *Dixie,* Commander C. H. Davis, *Gloucester,* Lieutenant Commander Richard Wainwright, and *Yale,* Commander W. C. Wise.

July 25.   Guánica, Puerto Rico, is seized by a landing party under Lieutenant Henry P. Huse from the *Gloucester.*

July 25.   Major General Wesley Merritt reaches Manila with a third contingent of troops, raising the strength of the American expeditionary force to 10,000 men, and begins operations against the Philippine capital.

July 26.   General Miles's expeditionary force lands at Guánica, Puerto Rico.

July 28.   Ponce, the largest city on the southern coast of Puerto Rico, surrenders to Commander C. H. Davis of the auxiliary cruiser *Dixie.*

August 12.   In Washington, D.C., representatives of the United States and Spain sign an armistice ending the Spanish-American War. Spain agrees to free Cuba and to cede Puerto Rico and Guam to the United States. The negotiation of the definitive treaty of peace is scheduled to begin in Paris in October.

August 12–13.   The port of Manzanillo, Cuba, is shelled and captured by a squadron consisting of the cruiser *Newark* (C 1), Captain Caspar F. Goodrich, the auxiliary cruisers *Hist,* Lieutenant Lucien Young, and *Suwanee,* Commander Daniel Delehanty, the captured gunboat *Alvarado,* Lieutenant Victor Blue, and the armed tug *Osceola* (AT 47), Lieutenant J. L. Purcell. Only afterwards is it learned that the war is over.

August 13.   **Capture of Manila.** Spanish authorities at Manila are anxious to surrender the city to American forces rather than to the insurrectionary Filipino army of General Emilio Aguinaldo. The Belgian consul acts as an intermediary for secret negotiations between the Spanish and Commodore Dewey, through which it is arranged that the city will surrender following token resistance to a naval bombardment and land attack. Accordingly, on this date the cruiser *Olympia* (C 6) and the gunboat *Petrel* (PG 2) shell Fort San Antonio, which does not return their fire, for an hour and a quarter. The Spanish then strike their colors and Dewey's Flag Lieutenant Thomas N. Brumby lands to raise the American flag over Manila. Six hundred troops go ashore from the transport *Zafiro* to begin the occupation later that afternoon.

August 14.   The last shots of the Spanish-American War are fired when the armed lighthouse supply ship *Mangrove,* Lieutenant Commander D. D. V. Stuart, engages two Spanish gunboats off Caibarién, Cuba. The Spaniards raise a flag of truce and explain that an armistice has been signed.

November 4.   A detachment of 15 marines under First Lieutenant Robert McM. Dutton from the cruisers *Baltimore* (C 3), *Boston,* and *Raleigh* (C 8), establish a U.S. Legation Guard at Peking, China.

December 10.   **Peace with Spain.** The definitive treaty is signed in Paris. It presents the United States with an instant empire consisting of the islands of Guam, Puerto Rico, and the Philippines, for all of which Spain is paid $20,000,000. President McKinley had not intended to keep the Philippines, but during the negotiations American opinion came out strongly in favor of annexation. These far-distant territories can be defended only by a battle fleet dedicated to the Mahanian concept of command of the sea. America's commitment to sea power is clenched.

December 23.   The Navy Department is assigned the responsibility of administering the island of Guam.

1899

January 17.   Commander E. D. Taussig, captain of the gunboat *Bennington* (PG 4), claims Wake Island for the United States.

February 4.   **Outbreak of the Philippine insurrection.** Disgruntled by the United States' annexation of the Philippines, the insurrectionary army of General Emilio Aguinaldo attacks the American lines around Manila. In the ensuing conflict, which will last for more than two years, the navy plays an active role as a transport, patrol, bombardment, and landing force.

February 5.   The cruiser *Charleston* (C 2), monitor *Monadnock* (BM 3), and gunboats *Callao* and *Concord* (PG 3) provide fire support for the advance of American ground forces outside Manila.

February 11.   **Action at Ilo-Ilo.** The gunboat *Petrel* (PG 2) shells an insurgent fort on Panay, which is then occupied by a naval landing party.

February 22.   A landing party from the *Petrel* takes possession of the Philippine island of Cebu.

February 24.   The gunboat *Marietta* (PG 15) lands a detachment to protect American interests at Bluefields, Nicaragua.

March 2.   Admiral George Dewey is elevated to the rank of Admiral of the Navy. He remains today the only officer to have held that rank.

March 3.   President McKinley signs the Naval Personnel Act of 1899, which amalgamates the navy's engineers with its line officers and thereby eliminates the friction that had existed between the two groups since the advent of steam power.

April 1.   **Samoan uprising.** Late in 1898 intertribal warfare broke out in the Samoan Islands, which are jointly administered by the United States, Great Britain, and Germany. American and British landing parties, the former from the protected cruiser *Philadelphia* (C 4), are put ashore to guard their consulates. On April 1, an Anglo-American patrol is ambushed in the jungle near Apia, on Upolu Island. Four Americans and three British are killed and seven wounded. The dead include the American landing force commander, Lieutenant Philip Van Horn Lansdale, USN. The uprising is suppressed by April 25 by a combination of shore bombardments and punitive expeditions into the interior.

April 27.   The transport *Resolute* lands a party of 80 marines to preserve order in Havana, Cuba.

May 23.   **Marines to the Philippines.** Colonel Percival C. Pope's 1st Battalion of Marines, 275 strong, is landed to provide security for the naval base at Cavite, on the Philippine island of Luzon.

June 10.   A squadron consisting of the monitors *Monadnock* (BM 3) and *Monterey* (BM 6) and four gunboats gives fire support for a major army offensive south from Manila into Cavite Province.

June 13.   The six ships engaged on June 10 plus three additional vessels provide fire support for a successful army assault on the insurgent position along the Zapote River in Cavite Province.

September 18–23.   A squadron consisting of the monitor *Monterey* (BM 6), cruisers *Baltimore* (C 3) and *Charleston* (C 2), gunboat *Concord* (PG 3), and transport *Zafiro* shell and seize the insurgent positions at Olongapo, securing control of Subic Bay on the west coast of Luzon.

September 21.   The 2nd Battalion of Marines, 364 officers and men under future commandant Lieutenant Colonel George Fielding Elliott, arrives at Cavite.

September 25.   The armed patrol boat *Urdaneta*, Naval Cadet Welborn C. Wood (USNA 1899), is ambushed by insurgents in the delta of the Pampanga River near Orani on the island of Luzon. Cadet Wood and four

Marines guard the residence of the U.S. consul at Matautu Point, Apia, Upolu Island, during the Samoan uprising. *U.S. Naval Institute Collection.*

of his eight men are killed in the ensuing fire fight; the others are captured in an attempt to escape ashore. The *Urdaneta* is the only naval vessel lost in the Philippine Insurrection.

October 8.   **Action at Novaleta.** Lieutenant Colonel G. F. Elliott's 2nd Marine Battalion cooperates in the capture of this insurgent stronghold between Manila and Cavite. The operation, in which the marines lose 11 men killed and wounded, is supported by fire from the gunboats *Callao* and *Petrel* (PG 2).

November 2.   The protected cruiser *Charleston* (C 2), Captain C. W. Pigman, wrecks without loss of life on an uncharted reef near Camiguin Island in the Philippines.

November 7.   A squadron of six ships under Commander Harry Knox supports the landing of 2,500 troops at San Fabian, on the Lingayen Gulf coast of Luzon.

November 26.   The battleship *Oregon*'s marine detachment, 49 men commanded by Captain Dion Williams, occupies Vigan, north of Lingayen Gulf, without opposition. It is relieved by army troops two days later.

December 10.   Landing parties from the *Oregon* (BB 3) and the cruiser *Baltimore* (C 3) take possession of the navy yard at Olongapo on Subic Bay. A company of marines arrives to garrison the town 10 days later.

December 15.   A third marine battalion, 340 men commanded by Major L. W. T. Waller, reaches the Philippines.

1900

Course of the Philippine Insurrection.

Throughout the year the navy continues to participate in the suppression of the insurrection. Most of its operations are carried out by gunboats, which frequently shell enemy positions, land detachments of sailors and marines to occupy coastal villages, and intercept insurgent vessels. Marine units also play an active role in the fighting ashore.

January 11.   The gunboat *Princeton,* Commander Harry Knox, takes possession of the Batan Islands in the northern Philippines.

February 10.   **American Samoa.** Commander Seaton Schroeder becomes the first naval governor of the American portion of the Samoan Islands, which were divided between the United States and Germany in 1899.

February 19.   President McKinley places the administration of American Samoa under the Navy Department.

A marine patrol near Olongapo on Luzon during the Philippine Insurrection. *Defense Department photo (Marine Corps).*

February 20.   The battleship *Kearsarge* (BB 5) is commissioned.

March 13.   **General Board of the Navy.** A permanent board of senior officers is established under the presidency of Admiral Dewey to provide the secretary of the navy with professional advice on naval operations and policy.

March 15.   Commander Richard Wainwright becomes 17th superintendent of the Naval Academy.

May 15.   The battleship *Kentucky* (BB 6) is commissioned.

May 18.   **The Boxer Rebellion.** The Western penetration of China has provoked a violently xenophobic mass movement, the Righteous Society of Heavenly Fists, whose adherents foreigners refer to as Boxers. With the tacit approval of the Imperial Chinese government, in two years the movement spreads from outlying areas to the vicinity of Peking, seat of the foreign embassies to the Manchu Court. On this date, U.S. Minister Edwin Conger telegraphs a request to the Asiatic Squadron to send a force to guard the American legation. On May 28 his colleagues of the Corps Diplomatique send similar appeals to their navies.

May 31.   **Reinforcements reach Peking.** The foreign warships assembled off Taku Bar at the mouth of the Pei-Ho River send an international force of 337 American,

Heroes of the Boxer Rebellion: *second from left,* Captain Newt Hall, USMC; *third from left,* Captain Bowman H. Mc-Calla, USN; *far right,* Captain John T. Myers. *Defense Department photo (Marine Corps).*

British, French, Italian, Japanese, and Russian seamen and marines to guard the legations at Peking. The American contingent, landed from Captain Bowman H. McCalla's cruiser *Newark* (C 1), consists of 48 marines and 5 bluejackets under Captains John T. ("Handsome Jack") Myers and Newt H. Hall, USMC. A detachment of 89 Austrian and German sailors follow on June 3.

June 8.   The Boxers cut the telegraph line from Peking to Tientsin, isolating the legations.

June 10.   **Seymour Expedition.** Vice Admiral Sir Edward Seymour, KCG, the senior foreign officer in northern China, leads a force of 2,129 men representing eight nationalities from Tientsin to reopen communications with Peking. The expedition includes 112 American seamen and marines from the cruiser *Newark* (C 1) under Captain Bowman H. McCalla. First attacked by Boxers on June 13, the column is forced to retire four days later after pushing to within 25 miles of Peking.

June 15.   The Boxers besiege the international settlement at Tientsin, which is defended by 2,400 troops, mostly Russian.

June 19–20.   A detachment of 140 U.S. marines, rushed from the Philippines under Major L. W. T. Waller, and 440 Russian infantry are beaten back in an attempt to relieve Tientsin.

June 21–August 14.   **Defense of the Legations.** The three-quarters-square-mile Legation Quarter of Peking has been put in a state of defense in anticipation of the attacks that begin on this date. For 55 days, the 409 legation guards and 125 civilian volunteers defend the quarter against attacks by thousands of Boxers, intermittently aided by Chinese regular troops. Before their relief, 66 of the defenders are killed and 150 wounded. The conduct of Captain Myers's marines, who hold a key sector of the compound walls, is highly praised by all present.

June 22.   Retreating toward Tientsin, the Seymour Expedition captures Hsiku Arsenal, six miles from the city and, burdened by 250 wounded, prepares to defend itself there.

June 23.   **Relief of Tientsin.** An allied force of 2,000 men, including Major Waller's marines, fight their way through Tientsin.

June 25.   **Relief of the Seymour Expedition.** Following the relief of Tientsin, the allies send out a strong column that escorts Seymour's battered expedition back to the city.

July 10.   The remainder of the First Marine Regiment, 318 men under Colonel Robert W. Meade (a Civil War veteran), reach Tientsin.

July 13–14.   **Capture of Tientsin.** The walled, native city of Tientsin, held by at least 20,000 Boxers, is stormed by 5,650 allied troops under British Brigadier General A. R. F. Dorward, DSO. The American contingent, commanded by marine Colonel R. W. Meade, consists of 1,021 men of the First Marines and Ninth Infantry. It is during this operation that the U.S. Marine Corps develops its friendship with the Royal Welsh Fusiliers.

August 3–14.   **Relief of the Legations.** An International Relief Expedition of 18,600 men commanded by Brigadier General Sir Alfred Gaselee, KCB, advancing from Tientsin, relieves the legations at Peking. This force includes 482 U.S. Marines and 2,000 soldiers under Major General Adna R. Chaffee.

October 11.   U.S. Marines are withdrawn from China.

October 12.   **The Holland.** The U.S. Navy's first submarine, the *Holland* (SS 1), is put in commission, Lieutenant Harry H. Caldwell, commanding. Privately built by John P. Holland, an Irish emigrant who devoted his life to submarine construction, she is 53 feet 10 inches in length, displaces 64 tons, has four torpedo tubes, and carries a crew of seven.

October 16.   The battleship *Alabama* (BB 8) is commissioned.

The *Holland,* the navy's first submarine. *Official U.S. Navy photograph.*

1901

January 2–3. Four boat parties under Lieutenant F. R. Payne capture 18 insurgent boats on the Imus River, near Cavite, in the Philippines.

January 17. The gunboat *Don Juan of Austria,* Commander T. C. McLean, shells insurgent positions and lands an army detachment at Donsol on the island of Luzon.

January 28. The *Don Juan of Austria* provides fire support for an army attack on Maringondon, Luzon.

January 31–February 3. Parties from the *Don Juan of Austria* capture the villages of Jamaruan, Calveria, and San Pascual on Luzon.

February 4. The battleship *Wisconsin* (BB 9) is commissioned.

February 23–March 3. The gunboat *Villalobos,* Lieutenant Henry P. Huse, supports army operations at Loorg Bay and Lubang Island in the Philippines.

March 18–28. The gunboat *Vicksburg* (PG 11), Commander E. B. Barry, supports the army in operations on the Philippine island of Palawan.

March 23. **End of the Philippine Insurrection; Moro Insurrection.** General Emilio Aguinaldo, the Filipino insurgent leader, is captured by American forces. Though operations continue on a diminishing scale for some months, for practical purposes the revolt has been extinguished. In the meantime, however, a new insurrection has broken out among the proud, Moslem Moros inhabiting the southern Philippine islands of Samar, Mindanao, and Jolo.

July 3–17. The armed patrol vessel *Basco,* Naval Cadet J. H. Comfort, fights a series of actions with insurgents on the Gandara River on the island of Samar.

July 4. The military government of the Philippines is replaced by a civil government headed by future president William Howard Taft.

September 16. The battleship *Illinois* (BB 7) is commissioned.

October 24. Four companies of marines under Major Littleton Waller Tazewell ("Tony") Waller are placed under the command of Brigadier General Jacob M. ("Hell-Roaring Jake") Smith, USA, to suppress Moro insurgents on the Philippine island of Samar, where a company of the Ninth Infantry was massacred on September 28. By November 12, Waller's columns have killed 39 and captured 18 insurgents and burned 255 huts at a cost of only two dead.

November 15. **Battle of the Sohoton River.** Major Waller's marines assault and capture a supposedly impregnable insurgent stronghold deep in the mountains of Samar.

November 16. **Sims writes the president.** Around 1890 a small number of progressive-minded naval officers, most notably the inventive Bradley A. Fiske, began to consider techniques and devices through which the quality of American naval gunnery could be improved. The record of the battles of Manila Bay and Santiago, after which it was found that only about 3 percent of the shells fired hit their targets, showed that improvement was needed. The results achieved by the Royal Navy's gunnery expert, Captain Percy Scott, proved that it was possible. Conservative senior officers in the Bureau of Ordnance were, however, slow to respond to the reformers' inventions and prescriptions. Finally, Lieutenant William S. Sims, to whom Scott has personally explained his system, takes the daring step of writing directly to President Theodore Roosevelt to condemn the navy's gunnery. His presentation converts the president to his cause. Sims is made inspector of target practice, and with the support of Fiske, Lieutenant Commander Albert P. Niblack, and the chief executive, sets out to revolutionize American gunnery methods. By the beginning of 1907 the navy has developed the elements of modern fire control.

November 16.   Three boat parties from the gunboat *Vicksburg* (PG 11), Lieutenant Commander J. H. Glennan, support a marine expedition against Philippine insurgents up the Basey River on the island of Samar.

November 24–December 4.   **Panamanian intervention.** Marines are landed in Panama at Panama City and Colón from the ships *Concord* (PG 3), *Iowa* (BB 4), *Machias* (PG 5), and *Marietta* (PG 15) to protect American interests—most particularly the transisthmian railway—during one of the recurrent revolts against Colombian rule. They are withdrawn after the *Iowa's* Captain Thomas Perry negotiates an agreement between the opposing forces to respect American property.

November 28.   **Hay-Pauncefort Treaty.** A new agreement with Great Britain abrogates the Clayton-Bulwer Treaty of 1850 and provides that the United States may singly build, fortify, and control a canal across Central America. Diplomatically, the way is clear to the construction of the Panama Canal.

December 13.   **Sampson-Schley controversy.** During the Spanish-American War, Admiral Sampson and other officers thought that Commodore Schley's conduct of the search for Cervera was woefully lacking in energy and enterprise. Secretary of the Navy Long's agreement with this view was reflected in his postwar promotion list, which proposed raising both Sampson and Schley to the permanent rank of rear admiral, but moving Sampson ahead of Schley, to whom he had been junior. After lengthy hearings, Congress voted to advance the two men the same number of places, thus preserving Schley's prewar seniority. This question was settled in April 1899. Controversy erupts again in the spring of 1901, when an updated edition of Edgar S. Maclay's *History of the Navy,* a book used as a text at the Naval Academy, presents Schley's actions at the Battle of Santiago as well as during the search for Cervera in a most unflattering light. Schley thereupon requests a court of inquiry into his conduct throughout the war. The court, of which Admiral Dewey is president, submits its opinion on this date—but its opinion is divided. The majority report condemns Schley's performance; a minority report, prepared by Dewey himself, commends it. Schley wants to continue the contest, but President Theodore Roosevelt, apprehensive of the disruptive effect of the quarrel on the service as a whole, declares the case closed. The spectacle of this unseemly squabble may be responsible for the almost obsessive discretion a new generation of naval leaders will observe in discussing the command decisions of World War II.

December 28.   **The ordeal of Samar.** With 54 marines, 2 Filipino guides, and 33 native bearers, Major L. W. T. Waller sets out to cross the interior of southern Samar. The march becomes a disaster as wrong turns multiply and rations dwindle. Eleven marines die of starvation and fatigue. Waller reaches his destination, the coastal town of Basey, on January 17, 1902. Three days later, certain that his Filipinos betrayed him, he holds a drum-head court-martial and executes 11 of them. Greatly to his surprise, he himself is then court-martialed on charges of murder. He is acquitted and eventually rises to the rank of major general.

1902

April 16–22.   The gunboat *Machias* (PG 5) lands a detachment of sailors and marines at Boca del Toro in the Colombian province of Panama. This is the first of several landings that will be made in the course of the year to protect American lives and property during the revolution in Panama.

May 1.   William H. Moody becomes 35th secretary of the navy.

September 17.   A detachment of seamen and marines is landed from the cruiser *Cincinnati* (C 7) to protect American property at Colón, Panama.

September 18.   The survey ship *Ranger* lands seamen and marines to safeguard American interests at Panama City, Panama.

September 23–November 18.   A battalion of marines under Lieutenant Colonel B. R. Russell, landed from the transport *Panther,* occupies Colón, Panama. The commander of American naval forces off the Panamanian coast, Rear Admiral Silas Casey, refuses to permit Colombian troops to cross the isthmus to attack the rebels and arranges a compromise peace.

November 6.   Captain Willard H. Brownson becomes the 18th superintendent of the U.S. Naval Academy.

November 24.   **First U.S. destroyer.** The torpedo boat destroyer *Bainbridge* (DD 1) is commissioned. Of 420

The destroyer *Decatur,* a sister ship of the *Bainbridge. Courtesy Library of Congress.*

tons displacement, she is 250 feet in length, carries a crew of 75, and has a speed of 29 knots.

December 22.   The battleship *Maine* (BB 10) is commissioned.

December–January 1903.   **Venezuelan crisis.** Germany, Great Britain, and Italy initiate a naval blockade of Venezuela, whose government has defaulted on the payment of debts owed to European investors, and the Germans go so far as to shell several Venezuelan forts. Determined to prevent European powers from intervening in the Western Hemisphere, President Theodore Roosevelt sends a naval force into the Caribbean and takes a leading role in negotiations that persuade the creditor nations to submit their case to the International Court of Justice at The Hague. In February 1904 the court rules that Venezuela must pay.

1903

January 22.   **Hay-Herrán Treaty.** U.S. Secretary of State John Hay and Colombian chargé d'affaires Tomás Herrán conclude a treaty whereby Colombia is to grant the United States a 100-year lease to build and control a canal across the province of Panama in return for a payment of $10,000,000 and an annual subsidy of $250,000. The U.S. Senate approves the treaty in March, but in August the Colombian Senate rejects it.

February 23.   **Gitmo.** The United States leases Guantánamo Bay, Cuba, where it will establish a major naval base.

March 21–April 16.   **Honduras Expeditionary Service.** A peace-keeping force consisting of the cruisers *Olympia* (C 6), *Raleigh* (C 8), and *San Francisco* (C 5), gunboat *Marietta* (PG 15), and the transport *Panther* operates off the coast of Honduras during a revolution there. Marines are landed to protect the U.S. Embassy at Puerto Cortez.

April 1–19.   A detachment of marines from the cruiser *Atlanta* is landed to guard the U.S. Consulate at Santo Domingo during an insurrection in the Dominican Republic.

May 22.   A Cuban-American treaty is concluded, granting the United States the right to intervene in Cuba to maintain order or to preserve the island's independence.

September 7–13.   The cruiser *Brooklyn* (ACR 3) lands a party of sailors and marines at Beirut, in the Turkish province of Syria (present-day Lebanon), to protect U.S. citizens and the American University during a period of political disturbances.

October 3.   Colonel George F. Elliott becomes 10th commandant of the marine corps.

October 10–17.   Seamen and marines go ashore from the cruiser *San Francisco* (C 5) to safeguard American interests amid renewed disorders in Beirut.

November 3.   **Revolution in Panama.** According to the terms of the Hay-Herrán Treaty, the United States was to pay the stockholders of the French company that had tried to build a canal across Panama the sum of $40,000,000. The Colombian Senate's rejection of the treaty confronts these investors with the prospect of losing everything. At this point, the company's chief lobbyist (and a major stockholder), Philippe Bunau-Varilla, goes into action. Justly confident that the Roosevelt administration will support his initiative, from a suite in the Waldorf-Astoria Hotel in New York Bunau-Varilla arranges for the Panama City fire department to stage a revolution against Colombia.

November 4.   Enter the Nashville. At Panama City, the rebels proclaim Panamanian independence. Simultaneously, the gunboat *Nashville* (PG 7) reaches Colón, on the Atlantic coast, where a force of 474 Colombian soldiers has landed and is preparing to cross the isthmus and crush the rebellion. The *Nashville*'s Commander John Hubbard sends a small party ashore and, with the support of the American superintendent of the Panama Railroad, keeps the Colombians from taking the train to Panama City.

November 5.   The transport *Dixie* arrives at Colón carrying a marine battalion commanded by Major John A. Lejeune, who immediately puts two companies ashore. The Colombian troops concede the point and board a ship for home.

November 6.   The United States recognizes the independence of Panama.

November 18.   Hay–Bunau-Varilla Treaty. Secretary of State John Hay and Philippe Bunau-Varilla, who has promptly been appointed Panamanian ambassador to the United States, conclude a treaty for the construction of a canal in Panama. The United States is granted sovereign rights in perpetuity to a 10-mile-wide canal zone across the country, in return for which it agrees to pay a lump sum of $10,000,000, an annuity of $250,000, and to maintain the independence of Panama. (Another $25,000,000 will be paid to Colombia upon approval of a Treaty of Bogotá in February 1921.)

December 1.   The battleship *Missouri* (BB 11) is commissioned.

December 18–January 15, 1904.   **Journey to Addis Ababa.** A detachment of 19 marines under Captain George C. Thorpe, USMC, and Lieutenant Charles L. Hussey, USN, escorts a U.S. diplomatic mission hundreds of miles overland on an arduous journey to the capital of Emperor Menelik II of Ethiopia.

1904

January 3.   The cruiser *Detroit* (C 10) lands her marine detachment at Puerto Plata, Dominican Republic, to protect American interests during an insurrection.

January 3.   **Marines in Panama.** In view of the unsettled relations with Panama, three marine battalions are sent to reinforce Major Lejeune, whose battalion has been in garrison there since December. They land on this date, and a provisional marine brigade is organized under Brigadier General Commandant George F. Elliott. This is the last time a commandant of the marine corps will take personal command in the field. It soon becomes evident that Colombia does not want war, and the brigade is disbanded on February 16.

January 5–April 23.   The transport *Zafiro* sends a party of 103 seamen and marines to guard the U.S. Legation at Seoul, Korea. Most of the party is withdrawn on the latter date, but 25 remain on duty until November 11, 1905.

January 7.   The cruiser *Detroit* (C 10) lands a detachment at Sosúa, in the Dominican Republic, to safeguard Americans during a revolution in that country.

January 17.   Seamen and marines from the *Detroit* and the old screw sloop *Hartford* land to protect American citizens at Puerto Plata, Dominican Republic.

February 11.   Insurgent forces in Santo Domingo, Dominican Republic, fire on the steamer *New York*. A force of 300 bluejackets and marines from the cruisers *Columbia* (C 12) and *Newark* (C 1) commanded by Lieutenant Commander James P. Parker lands under covering fire from the *Newark* to expel the rebels from the city. It returns aboard ship, mission accomplished, that evening.

February 22.   The United States Senate ratifies the Hay–Bunau-Varilla Treaty by a vote of 66–14.

February 25–27.   The training ship *Yankee* lands her marine detachment to guard the U.S. Consulate at Santo Domingo, Dominican Republic.

March 12.   The marine detachment of the cruiser *Cincinnati* (C 7) conducts the evacuation of American citizens, caught up in the Russo-Japanese War, from Seoul and Chemulpo (Inchon), Korea.

May 4.   **Beginning the Panama Canal.** Lieutenant Mark Brooke, Corps of Engineers, formally takes possession of the canal works at Panama for the United States. Construction of the canal commences almost immediately, at first using the French equipment already present, in accordance with President Theodore Roosevelt's announced intention "to make the dirt fly." The work will take 10 years to complete.

May 30.   **Landing at Tangier.** In Morocco, a naturalized American citizen, Ion Perdicaris, has been kidnapped by the bandit chieftain Raisouli. President Theodore Roosevelt informs the Moroccan government that he wants "Perdicaris alive or Raisouli dead" and lands Captain J. T. ("Handsome Jack") Myers's marine detachment from the cruiser *Brooklyn* (ACR 3) at Tangier. Raisouli releases Perdicaris.

July 1.   Paul Morton becomes the 36th secretary of the navy.

October 4.   The battleship *Ohio* (BB 12) is commissioned.

December 6.   **Roosevelt Corollary.** Determined to deprive European powers, especially the rambunctious German Empire, of a pretext for intervention in the Americas, President Theodore Roosevelt proclaims that "Chronic wrongdoing . . . in the Western Hemisphere . . . may force the United States . . . to the exercise of an international police power." Considered to be a corollary to the Monroe Doctrine, this proposition will lead to American occupation of Haiti, the Dominican Republic, and Nicaragua and the employment of the U.S. Marines as colonial infantry in a series of so-called banana wars in Central America and the Caribbean.

1905

January 20.   **Dominican customs agreement.** U.S. Navy and Marine Corps officers assume control of the customs service of the debt-ridden Dominican Republic. A treaty, negotiated on the initiative of the Dominican president, is finally approved by the U.S. and Dominican senates in February and May 1907, respectively. By this time Dominican customs revenues, efficiently collected by American officers, had been used to reduce the country's public debt from $30,000,000 to $17,000,000.

April 7.   After a search lasting six years, General Horace Porter, U.S. Ambassador to France, finds the body of John Paul Jones in Paris. The old Protestant cemetery in which Jones was buried had been abandoned and a Parisian suburb built on the site.

July 1.   Rear Admiral James H. Sands becomes the 19th superintendent of the Naval Academy. He is the last Civil War veteran to hold that post.

July 7.   Charles J. Bonaparte becomes the 37th secretary of the navy.

July 21.   Sixty men are killed by a boiler explosion aboard the gunboat *Bennington* (PG 4) at San Diego, California.

July 23.   **The return of John Paul Jones.** The body of John Paul Jones is brought ashore at Annapolis, Maryland, where, upon the urging of President Theodore Roosevelt, Congress has decided that it will be interred in the crypt of the Naval Academy Chapel. Jones's remains were escorted across the Atlantic by an honor squadron, commanded by Rear Admiral Charles D. Sigsbee, of four cruisers—the *Brooklyn* (ACR 3), *Chattanooga* (C 16), *Galveston* (C 17), and *Tacoma* (C 18)—and the French cruiser *Jurien de la Gravière*. This squadron was joined off the Nantucket Shoals by the seven battleships of Rear Admiral Robley D. Evans's North Atlantic Fleet.

September 12.   **Legation guard.** By direction of President Theodore Roosevelt, the marine corps relieves the army in providing a guard for the U.S. Legation in Peking, China. A marine detachment will remain at the legation until 1941.

1906

February 19.   The battleship *Rhode Island* (BB 17) is commissioned.

March 8.   A naval landing under Ensign H. D. Cooke, Jr., joins an army detachment in storming a Moro position at Mount Dajo on the Philippine island of Jolo.

April 18.   **San Francisco earthquake.** Bluejackets and marines from the Mare Island Navy Yard assist in fighting fires and doing relief work following the disastrous earthquake that all but levels San Francisco, California.

April 21.   On his seventh Arctic expedition 49-year-old Commander Robert Peary, Civil Engineer Corps, reaches latitude 87° 6' North, the nearest anyone has yet to come to the Pole.

May 7.   The battleship *Virginia* (BB 13) is commissioned.

May 12.   The battleship *New Jersey* (BB 16) is commissioned.

June 2.   The battleship *Louisiana* (BB 19) is commissioned.

September 13.   **Cuban Pacification.** When a widespread revolution breaks out in Cuba following the elections of August 1906, President Theodore Roosevelt decides that the United States must intervene. A detachment of 120 bluejackets and marines from the cruiser *Denver* (C 14) lands at the request of the Cuban governor to maintain order in Havana on September 13–14; a battalion of marines under Major Albertus W. Catlin goes ashore from the transport *Dixie* to protect American interests at Cienfuegos on September 18; and five more marine battalions are rushed to Cuba.

September 24. The battleship *Georgia* (BB 15) is commissioned.

September 29. The battleship *Connecticut* (BB 18) is commissioned.

October 1. Colonel L. W. T. Waller, USMC, arrives at Havana and organizes the two marine regiments in Cuba into a provisional brigade with a strength of 2,900 officers and men. This force, whose equipment comes to include an armored train, occupies 24 strategic posts throughout the island and begins to disarm the insurgent forces. The first units of an Army of Cuban Pacification land on October 10 and, with the situation well in hand, the marine brigade is soon disbanded. The First Marine Regiment is, however, retained in Cuba until the withdrawal of the army on January 23, 1909.

December 17. Victor H. Metcalf becomes 38th secretary of the navy.

1907

March 4. The battleship *Vermont* (BB 20) is commissioned.

March 9. The battleship *Minnesota* (BB 22) is commissioned.

April 18. The battleship *Kansas* (BB 21) is commissioned.

April 28–May 23. The 12-man marine detachment of the gunboat *Paducah* (PG 18) is landed under the command of Ensign Lawrence P. Treadwell to safeguard American interests at Laguna, Honduras, during a war between Honduras and Nicaragua.

May 24–June 8. The *Paducah*'s marines move inland to protect Americans at Choloma, Honduras.

July 1. The battleship *Nebraska* (BB 14) is commissioned.

July 15. Captain Charles J. Badger becomes the 29th superintendent of the Naval Academy.

December 16–February 22, 1909. **Voyage of the Great White Fleet.** Sixteen American battleships—the *Connecticut* (BB 18), *Georgia* (BB 15), *Illinois* (BB 7), *Kansas* (BB 21), *Kearsarge* (BB 5), *Kentucky* (BB 6), *Louisiana* (BB 19), *Minnesota* (BB 22), *Missouri* (BB 11), *Nebraska* (BB 14), *New Jersey* (BB 16), *Ohio* (BB 12), *Rhode Island* (BB 17), *Vermont* (BB 20), *Virginia* (BB 13), and *Wisconsin* (BB 9)—with colliers and auxiliaries, sail from Hampton Roads, Virginia, under the command of Rear Admiral Robert D. ("Fighting Bob") Evans on an unprecedented round-the-world cruise. Conceived by President Theodore Roosevelt, the voyage is undertaken as a dramatic demonstration of America's newly established naval power. No cruise approaching this length has ever been attempted by steam-powered, steel battleships, and it is freely predicted that it will prove technologically impractical. These forebodings are unfounded. Proceeding around Cape Horn to the West Coast of the United States, the fleet crosses the Pacific to visit Australia and New Zealand, steams

The Great White Fleet entering San Francisco Bay. *Official U.S. Navy photograph.*

north to the Philippines and Japan, turns south through the China Sea to enter the Indian Ocean, and returns to Hampton Roads via the Red Sea, the Suez Canal, the Mediterranean, and the North Atlantic to complete a voyage of 46,000 miles without a single serious breakdown. Admiral Evans falls ill before the fleet leaves the West Coast, and the major part of the voyage is made under the command of Rear Admiral Charles S. Sperry. The fleet takes its name from the battleships' dazzling white hulls.

1908

February 1.   The battleship *Mississippi* (BB 23) is commissioned.

March 19.   The battleship *New Hampshire* (BB 25) is commissioned.

April 1.   The battleship *Idaho* (BB 24) is commissioned. She is the last American pre-dreadnought to enter service.

May 13.   The Navy Nurse Corps is established.

August 15.   The navy's first shipboard post offices are opened.

September 3–17.   Two official navy observers—Lieutenant George C. Sweet and Naval Constructor William McEntee—witnesses the first military trials of the Wright brothers' aircraft. The tests are conducted by the U.S. Army at Fort Myer, Virginia.

November 12.   **TR tries to remove the marines.** Influenced by the views of Commander William H. Fullam, who devotes much of his career to a crusade to remove marine detachments from the navy's ships, President Theodore Roosevelt signs Executive Order No. 969, "defining the duties of the United States Marine Corps." Shipboard service is conspicuous by its absence. The president had already directed Secretary of the Navy Metcalf to begin withdrawing the marines from ships on October 23.

December 1.   Truman H. Newberry becomes 39th secretary of the navy.

1909

February 22.   The Great White Fleet returns to Hampton Roads, Virginia.

March 3.   **Congress upholds the marines.** President Theodore Roosevelt's plan to remove the marines from shipboard duty (see November 12, 1908) is

Commander Robert E. Peary. *U.S. Naval Institute Collection.*

thwarted when Congress attaches a rider to the naval appropriations bill stipulating that none of the funds allocated the marine corps are to be expended "unless officers and men shall serve as heretofore" on ships.

March 6.   George von Lengerke Myer becomes 40th secretary of the navy.

April 6.   **Peary at the Pole.** Commander Robert E. Peary, Civil Engineer Crops, is the first man to reach the North Pole, where he raises the American flag. With him are his faithful companion, Matthew Henson, a black, and four Eskimos. This is Peary's seventh Arctic expedition, and at the age of 52, previously having lost all but two toes to frostbite, he knows that it must be his last. Peary's distinction is immediately contested by Dr. Frederick H. Cook, who claims to have discovered the Pole several months earlier, but the National Geographic Society and other leading geographical and scientific organizations reject Cook's contentions.

June 10.   Captain John M. Bowyers becomes the 21st superintendent of the Naval Academy.

November 11.   Plans are undertaken to build a naval base at Pearl Harbor, on the Hawaiian island of Oahu.

December 1.   **The aide system.** Since 1900 Congress has rebuffed several attempts to establish a naval general staff. Through an initiative intended to rationalize naval administration in the absence of such a staff, Secretary of the Navy Myer divides his department into four divisions—fleet operations, materiel, inspections, and personnel—each headed by an "aide" who reports directly to him. The post of aide for operations foreshadows that of chief of naval operations, which will be created six years later.

December 18.   **Revolution in Nicaragua.** A provisional marine battalion under Colonel E. J. Mahoney is embarked on the transport *Buffalo* for Corinto, on the Atlantic coast of Nicaragua, where it is joined by the Panama Battalion under Major Smedley B. Butler. The dispatch of these forces is occasioned by the outbreak of a revolution against Nicaraguan President José S. Zelaya, an ambitious dictator whose grandiose dreams of a Central American empire have kept the area in turmoil for 16 years. President William Howard Taft's predictable preference for Zelaya's opponents increased after two American citizens serving in the rebel forces were captured and executed by government troops. In December, while the marines remain aboard ship off Corinto, the United States formally withdraws recognition of the Zelaya regime and dismisses the Nicaraguan ambassador. American pressure persuades Zelaya to resign the presidency on December 20. The fighting gradually dies down, and in March 1910 the marines are withdrawn.

1910

January 4.   **The American dreadnought.** The battleship *Michigan* (BB 27) is commissioned. She is the first American dreadnought, the "all big gun" battleship that makes every earlier battleship obsolete overnight. The type is named for the first such ship to enter service, the British *Dreadnought,* which was commissioned in 1906. The plans, though not the construction, of the *Michigan* and her sistership, the *South Carolina* (BB 26), actually predate those of the *Dreadnought,* having been drawn in 1904. The American design is also the first to employ superimposed turrets, so that all eight of the ships' 12-inch guns can be trained to either side.

March 1.   The battleship *South Carolina* (BB 26) is commissioned.

April 4.   The battleship *Delaware* (BB 28) is commissioned.

The battleship *Michigan,* the first American dreadnought. *Courtesy National Archives.*

April 11.   The battleship *North Dakota* (BB 29) is commissioned.

May 19.   Seamen and marines from the gunboats *Dubuque* (PG 17) and *Paducah* (PG 18) land at Bluefields, Nicaragua, to protect American lives and property when fighting flares up between government forces and rebel troops defending the city. Commander William W. Gilmer of the *Paducah* forbids the Nicaraguan gunboat *Venus* to shell Bluefields, declaring that the vessel is not a man-of-war and that there are no military targets for her to engage.

May 30.   Major Smedley D. Butler's marine battalion, which had just returned to Panama in March after three months aboard ship off Corinto, is rushed back to Nicaragua to establish a neutral zone around Bluefields. Butler and two of his companies land from the gunboat *Dubuque* (PG 17) on this date. Two other companies join them early in June. The battalion remains at Bluefields until September 4, by which time the rebel forces favored by the United States have gained control of the government.

October 13.   Secretary of the Navy Myer approves a recommendation that two officers should be detailed to examine and report on the progress of aviation.

October 22–30.   **Aviation advocate.** Captain Washington Irving Chambers, who as assistant aide for materiel has been assigned the duty of monitoring the progress of aviation, is an official observer at the International Air Meet at Belmont Park, New York. What he sees there makes him an enthusiastic advocate of the creation of a naval air service, the development of which he guides until his relief by Captain Mark L. Bristol in 1914.

November 14.   **First shipboard take-off.** Twenty-four-year-old Eugene B. Ely, a civilian barnstormer, becomes the first pilot to fly off a ship. He nurses his Curtiss pusher biplane into the air from a wooden platform erected over the bow of the cruiser *Birmingham* (CL 2) at Hampton Roads, Virginia.

November 29.   Aviation pioneer Glenn Curtiss offers to instruct a naval officer "in the operation and construction" of his aircraft.

December 23.   **First flight training.** In response to Curtiss's offer, the navy details Lieutenant T. Gordon ("Spuds") Ellyson to attend the course of instruction at the Glenn Curtiss Aviation Center at San Diego, California.

1911

January 18.   **First shipboard landing.** Civilian Eugene B. Ely, the first man to fly an airplane off a ship, becomes the first man to land on one when he brings his Curtiss pusher down on a wooden platform jury-rigged on the cruiser *Pennsylvania* (ACR 4) in San Francisco Bay. Killed in a crash ashore later in the year, Ely is posthumously awarded the Distinguished Flying Cross in 1933.

February 1.   The cruiser *Tacoma* (C 18) lands a party to protect American interests at Puerto Cortez, Honduras.

February 3.   Colonel William P. Biddle becomes the 11th commandant of the marine corps.

March 4.   The first Naval Appropriations Act including funds for naval aviation ($25,000) is approved by Congress.

March 13.   A provisional marine battalion under Major George C. Thorpe is landed at Guantánamo Bay, Cuba, to defend American interests during a period of political tension.

April 12.   **Naval Aviator Number One.** Upon the completion of his training at the Curtiss Aviation Center, Lieutenant T. Gordon Ellyson becomes the navy's first pilot.

April 26.   **Marine Corps Association.** Alarmed by the consistent hostility of the Roosevelt and Taft administrations to the marine corps, Colonel F. J. Moses calls a meeting of the offices of the 1st Provisional Marine Brigade at Guantánamo, Cuba, "to discuss defenses against being abolished by the navy." This is the genesis of the Marine Corps Association, which adopts a written charter on April 25, 1913.

May 8.   **Beginning of navy air.** Captain Washington Irving Chambers completes the contract specifications for the first two naval aircraft. Although invitations to bid are not sent to plane builders until three weeks later, this date is officially considered to be the birthday of naval aviation. The contracts are awarded to Glenn Curtiss.

May 15.   Captain John H. Gibbons becomes the 22nd superintendent of the Naval Academy.

June 6.   The United States concludes a treaty with Nicaragua, whereby the latter is granted a large loan from American bankers to begin the repayment of the public debt and American officers are to collect Nicaraguan customs revenues to pay off the remainder.

Ely lands on the *Pennsylvania*. The sandbags on either side of the landing platform are connected by ropes meant to snag a hook on the bottom of the aircraft. They brought Ely to a halt a few feet short of a wooden barricade at the end of the little runway. *Official U.S. Navy photograph.*

July 1.   Glenn Curtiss successfully demonstrates his 80 h.p. A-1 Triad "hydroaeroplane," the first aircraft built for the navy, taking off and landing on Lake Keuka at Hammondsport, New York.

August 31.   The battleship *Utah* (BB 31) is commissioned.

September 15.   The battleship *Florida* (BB 30) is commissioned.

September.   **First naval air station.** An "aviation encampment" is established at the Navy Engineering Experiment Station at Annapolis, Maryland, across the Severn River from the Naval Academy.

October 10–January 19, 1914.   A battalion of marines under Major Philip M. Bannon is rushed from the Philippines to reinforce the legation guard at Peking during the Chinese revolution.

November 4–14.   Twenty-four marines are landed from the cruiser *Albany* (CL 23) and transport *Rainbow* to guard the cable station at Shanghai, China.

November 24.   The armored cruiser *Saratoga* (ex-*New York*) (ACR 2) carries a company of marines from Shanghai to protect American missionaries at Taku, China.

December 14.   The fleet base at Pearl Harbor, Hawaii, is ceremonially opened when the armed cruiser *California* (ACR 6) steams through the new channel.

1912

May 19.   The cruiser *Birmingham* (CL 2) begins the first American ice patrol in the North Atlantic. That such a patrol was needed had been made tragically evident by the sinking of the White Star liner *Titanic* the previous month. An International Ice Patrol is established in 1914, and the responsibility of the United States is assumed by the coast guard.

May 22.   **Beginning of marine aviation.** Marine Second Lieutenant Alfred A. Cunningham reports to the aviation camp at Annapolis, Maryland, for flight training and soon qualifies as the first marine aviator.

May 28.   **Peace-keeping in Cuba.** A black revolution in Cuba leads to the hurried organization of the First Provisional Marine Regiment, which lands at Guantánamo from the transport *Prairie* on this date. A second regiment goes ashore on June 5, and a provisional marine brigade is formed under the command of Colonel Lincoln Karmany. The marines garrison 26 towns in the vicinity of Guantánamo and Santiago and also serve as railway guards. Order is restored by the end of July, and the brigade is withdrawn the following month.

July 16.   Rear Admiral Bradley A. Fiske patents the first aerial torpedo.

July 27.   The first radio communication between an aircraft and a ship is established over the Chesapeake Bay near Annapolis, Maryland, when Lieutenant John Rodgers (Naval Aviator No. 2) and Midshipman Charles Maddox flying the Wright B-1 hydroaeroplane transmit the letter D in Morse code to the torpedo boat *Bailey* (TB 21) more than a mile away.

July 31.   The navy's first attempt to launch an aircraft by a compressed-air catapult is made by Lieutenant T. Gordon Ellyson in the Curtiss A-1 hydroaeroplane at the Santee Wharf at the U.S. Naval Academy. The plane, which is not secured to the track, cartwheels into the Severn River. Ellyson is unhurt.

August 3.   A permanent marine garrison of 250 men is established to provide security for the naval base at Guantánamo Bay, Cuba.

August 4.   **Intervention in Nicaragua.** In Nicaragua revolution has broken out against President Adolfo Díaz, who enjoys the support of the United States. On this date, a detachment of 100 bluejackets and marines from the gunboat *Annapolis* (PG 10) lands at Corinto and proceeds inland to guard the American legation in Managua. Major Smedley D. Butler's battalion is also ordered to Nicaragua—for the third time since 1909.

August 14.   Major Butler's Panama Battalion—354 officers and men—lands at Corinto, Nicaragua, and reaches Managua the next day.

August 17.   The cruiser *Tacoma* (C 18) lands a party of bluejackets and marines to maintain order at Bluefields, on the Atlantic coast of Nicaragua.

August 24 and 26.   A company of marines from the transport *Rainbow* is put ashore near Shanghai, China, to protect American lives and property during a period of revolutionary disturbances.

August 28.   A battalion of 364 bluejackets and marines from the armored cruiser *California* (ACR 6) lands at Corinto, Nicaragua.

August 30.   The cruiser *Denver* (C 14) lands a party of bluejackets and marines at San Juan del Sur, Nicaragua.

September 4.   The First Provisional Marine Regiment, 790 men under Colonel Joseph H. ("Uncle Joe") Pendleton, reaches Corinto from Philadelphia in the transport *Buffalo*. Pendleton assumes command of all U.S. forces ashore in Nicaragua.

September 5.   A battalion of 323 seamen and marines lands at Corinto from the armored cruiser *Colorado* (ACR 7), raising the strength of the forces available to Colonel Pendleton in western Nicaragua to approximately 2,000 men. He deploys them to take control of the railway from Corinto through Managua to Granada, which is, in effect, the artery of the revolution.

September 17.   The battleship *Arkansas* (BB 33) is commissioned.

September 22.   **Relief of Granada.** A column composed of two marine battalions and an artillery battery under Major Smedley D. Butler relieves the government garrison of Granada, Nicaragua, and disarms the rebel army of General Mena, by which the town had been besieged.

September 25.   The battleship *Wyoming* (BB 32) is commissioned.

October 2–4.   **Action at Coyotope.** A Nicaraguan rebel force of 1,000 men under General Benjamin Zeledón is entrenched on two hills overlooking the railway near Masaya, roughly midway between Managua and Granada. It refuses to surrender when Major Butler's battalion, with which it had skirmished on September 19, returns from Granada. Butler shells the rebel position on Coyotope Hill on October 3, during which Colonel Pendleton arrives with a third marine battalion and the *California*'s landing battalion. Coyotope is stormed at dawn on October 4. Afterwards marines count the bodies of more than 60 rebels, including that of General Zeledón, who is shot by his own men. The marines suffer 18 casualties.

October 6.   **Capture of León.** A force of 1,200 seamen and marines under Lieutenant Colonel C. G. ("Squeegee") Long captures the rebel-held city of León, between Corinto and Managua, at the cost of 6 casualties. Although mopping-up operations continue until November 2, the Nicaraguan revolution has been crushed.

November 12.   **First catapult launching.** Undeterred by his dunking on July 31, Lieutenant T. Gordon Ellyson succeeds in getting his new Curtiss A-1 hydroaeroplane into the air after a catapult launch from a barge anchored in the Anacostia River off the Washington Navy Yard.

November 21.   **Wind-down in Nicaragua.** The revolution over, Colonel Pendleton's provisional regiment embarks on the transport *Buffalo* at Bluefields. A battalion under Lieutenant Colonel C. G. Long garrisons León until January 17, 1913, and a legation guard of 100 men at Managua remains until August 1925.

November 30.   **First flying boat.** Lieutenant T. Gordon Ellyson tests the navy's first flying boat, the Curtiss C-1, at Lake Keuka in Hammondsport, New York.

1913

January 6. The navy's Aviation Detachment arrives at Guantánamo, Cuba, aboard the collier *Sterling* to take part in the annual fleet maneuvers in the Caribbean. This will be the first time airplanes have participated in these exercises.

February 1. PG School. The Naval Postgraduate School opens at Annapolis in the Naval Academy's former Marine Barracks (later named Halligan Hall). After World War II, the school will be transferred to Monterey, California.

March 5. North Carolina newspaper editor Josephus Daniels becomes the 41st and perhaps the most controversial secretary of the navy.

June 20. First aviation casualty. Ensign W. D. Billingsley (Naval Aviator No. 9) falls to his death when he is thrown from the Wright B-2 hydroaeroplane by a violent down-draft while flying at an altitude of 1,600 feet over the Chesapeake Bay near St. Michael's, Maryland. Lieutenant John H. Towers clings to the plane and survives, with serious injuries, when it crashes into the bay. Neither man was wearing a safety belt.

July 7. The protected cruiser *Albany* (CL 23) lands her marine detachment to protect American interests during disorders at Shanghai, China.

August 30. The General Board of the Navy, still headed by Civil War veteran George Dewey, recommends the immediate establishment of "an efficient Naval Air Service."

September 5–7. A detachment of marines from the transport *Buffalo* conducts the evacuation of American citizens from Ciaris Estero, Mexico, during a period of revolutionary disturbances.

October 7. Secretary of the Navy Daniels appoints an Aeronautic Board to consider the future of naval aviation. Its recommendations include the establishment of an Aeronautic Center at Pensacola, Florida, and the attachment of an aircraft to every major battleship and cruiser.

December 19. By act of Congress, the tenure of the commandant of the marine corps is limited to four years, with the possibility of reappointment for a second term.

December 23. Advanced Base Force. A marine brigade of two regiments is organized under Colonel George Barnett to participate in the 1914 fleet maneuvers. The professionalism with which this Advanced Base Force "defends" the Caribbean island of Culebra impresses naval observers and points the way to the amphibious mission the corps will adopt in the 1920s and `30s.

December 27. Birth of marine corps aviation. The Aviation Detachment, Advanced Base Force, is established with a strength of two officers, seven enlisted men, and two navy flying boats.

1914

January 20. Pensacola. Upon the recommendation of Captain W. I. Chambers, the navy's aviation detachment—9 officers and 23 men—is transferred from Annapolis, Maryland, to the unused navy base at Pensacola, Florida, where it is to develop a complete "aeronautical center." Lieutenant John H. Towers, the detachment commander, has a flight school in operation by the beginning of February.

January 28–February 9. The marine detachment of the battleship *South Carolina* (BB 26) joins British, French, and German landing parties to maintain order in Port-au-Prince during one of Haiti's recurrent revolutions.

February 7. Captain William F. Fullam becomes the 23rd superintendent of the Naval Academy.

February 25. Colonel George Barnett becomes 12th commandant of the marine corps. He is the first Naval Academy graduate to hold this post.

March 12. The battleship *Texas* (BB 35) is commissioned.

Early days at Pensacola: Lieutenant P. N. L. Bellinger at the controls of a Curtiss hydroaeroplane. *Official U.S. Navy photograph.*

April 9. **Tampico incident.** Since October 1913, U.S. naval forces have been stationed off the Gulf Coast of Mexico to protect American lives and investments from the revolution raging in that country. On this date a boat party of eight seamen under Assistant Paymaster Charles W. Copp is seized and detained for approximately half an hour by Mexican government forces when it inadvertently enters a military zone on the Pánuco River. Although the local Mexican commander, General Ignacio Morelos Zaragoza, expresses regrets for the incident, Rear Admiral Henry T. Mayo, commanding the Fourth Division of the Atlantic Fleet, sends him an ultimatum demanding that he proffer a formal apology and fire a 21-gun salute to the American flag. Zaragoza obtains an extension of the 24-hour time limit originally set for a reply and forwards the admiral's message to Mexican President Victoriano Huerta. President Woodrow Wilson strongly endorses Mayo's action. Wilson has been trying to force Huerta, a military dictator for whom he feels a profound repugnance, to relinquish his office since August 1913.

April 11.   Huerta apologizes for the arrest of Paymaster Copp's party, but declines to hoist and salute the American flag.

April 13.   In Washington, President Wilson promises reporters "The salute will be fired."

April 14.   The Mexican government agrees to fire the salute providing U.S. forces promise to return it round for round. Admiral Mayo had stated in his ultimatum of April 10 that the salute would be returned, but President Wilson rejects the condition. Huerta's compliance must be unqualified. The Atlantic Fleet is ordered to concentrate off the east coast of Mexico.

April 15.   The battleship *New York* (BB 34) is commissioned.

April 18.   **Enter the Ypiranga.** William W. Canada, U.S. consul at Veracruz, Mexico, notifies the State Department that a German steamer, the *Ypiranga,* is scheduled to arrive at the city on April 21 with an enormous cargo of arms and ammunition for the Mexican government. President Wilson determines that these arms must not be allowed to reach Huerta.

April 20.   A final deadline set by the president for the salute having expired on April 18, Wilson goes before a joint session of Congress to request authority to employ armed force against Mexico. The measure passes the House of Representatives, but is delayed by debate in the Senate, which adjourns without taking action,

placing it at the head of the agenda for April 22.

April 20.   Secretary of the Navy Daniels sends a message to Rear Admiral Frank F. Fletcher, commanding the First Division of the Atlantic Fleet off Veracruz, Mexico, that the *Ypiranga* must not be permitted to land her munitions.

April 21.   At 2:30 A.M. President Wilson is awakened and informed that the State Department has received a cable from the U.S. consul in Veracruz, reporting that the *Ypiranga* is to reach the city that morning and that three trains are in readiness to rush her cargo into the interior. Wilson directs Secretary of the Navy Daniels to order Admiral Fletcher to seize the customs house at Veracruz. This action will enable U.S. forces to intercept the *Ypiranga's* arms as they come ashore, thereby avoiding diplomatic complications with Germany.

April 21.   **The landing at Veracruz.** Admiral Fletcher receives Secretary Daniel's message at 8:00 A.M. The landing is made two-and-a-half hours later by a force of 787 men—502 marines from the transport *Prairie* under Lieutenant Colonel Wendell C. Neville and 285 bluejackets and marines from the battleship *Florida* (BB 30), all under the command of the *Florida's* Captain William R. ("Wild Bill") Rush. In the meantime, Fletcher has sent officers ashore to advise Mexican authorities of the landing and to express the hope that no resistance will be offered. This hope proves to be in vain. Although the Mexican government orders the garrison to withdraw from the city, its commander, General Gustavo Maas, has already sent 100 men to the waterfront "to repel the invasion" and freed and

The landing at Veracruz: a bluejacket stands amid Mexican bodies at the corner of Calle Miguel Lerdo and Calle Morelos, where the firing broke out. *U.S. Naval Institute Collection.*

armed the prisoners in the city jail. The cadets of the Mexican Naval Academy, members of the home guard, and assorted private citizens also take arms. Firing begins shortly after the landing is made. Ensign George M. Lowry's *Florida* company pushes on to take the customs house and by 3:00 P.M. American forces, reinforced by a battalion of seamen and marines from the battleship *Utah* (BB 31), are in control of the waterfront. Admiral Fletcher then makes an effort to arrange a cease-fire and when it fails, decides to await the arrival of the ships converging on Veracruz before resuming the advance. Meanwhile, the *Ypiranga* enters the harbor, where she will remain, without unloading her arms, until May 3. The cruisers *San Francisco* (C 5) and *Chester* (CS 1) and the battleships *Arkansas* (BB 33), *New Hampshire* (BB 25), *New Jersey* (BB 16), *South Carolina* (BB 26), and *Vermont* (BB 20) arrive after nightfall and land detachments that are organized into the Second Seamen Regiment, commanded by Captain E. A. Anderson of the *New Hampshire,* and into the Third Provisional Marine Regiment under Major Albertus W. Catlin.

April 22.   At 7:45 A.M. the naval brigade, now nearly 4,000 strong, pushes into Veracruz. The strongest resistance comes from the cadets at the Mexican Naval Academy, who repel the initial advance of the Second Seaman Regiment, but are overcome by accurate fire from Commander William A. Moffett's cruiser *Chester* (CS 1). The occupation of the city is completed by noon. American casualties are 17 dead and 63 wounded. At least 126 Mexicans have been killed and 195 wounded. A total of 55 Medals of Honor are awarded for Veracruz, the greatest number ever granted for a single engagement. The recipients include 37 navy and marine corps officers, who are made eligible for the medal by an act of March 3, 1915.

April 23.   At 2:25 A.M., after hours of debate, the Senate passes the resolution authorizing President Wilson to use force against Mexico.

April 24.   President Wilson accepts the offer of the ABC Powers—Argentina, Brazil, and Chile—to mediate the dispute between Mexico and the United Stats. U.S. forces at Veracruz are ordered not to undertake offensive operations.

April 24.   The 1st and 2nd Aero Sections (of two aircraft each), commanded by Lieutenants John H. Towers and P. N. L. Bellinger, reach Veracruz aboard the cruiser *Birmingham* (CL 2) and battleship *Mississippi* (BB 23).

April 25.   The first navy flight in a combat environment is made at Veracruz when Lieutenant P. N. L. Bellinger takes the Curtiss AB-3 flying boat from the *Mississippi* over the harbor to look for mines.

April 30.   The naval forces occupying Veracruz are relieved by an army brigade commanded by Brigadier General Frederick Funston. The marines and the navy's Aero Sections stay on.

May 3.   The *Ypiranga* sails from Veracruz. Later in the month she lands her arms at Puerto Mexico (now Coatzacoalcos).

May 6.   The Curtiss AH-3 hydroplane, Lieutenant P. N. L. Bellinger, pilot, and Lieutenant (jg) Richard C. Saufley, observer, is hit by rifle fire while on a reconnaissance flight inland from Veracruz. It is the first naval aircraft to be damaged by hostile fire.

July 1.   **The navy goes dry.** Secretary of the Navy Josephus Daniels abolishes the traditional officers' wine mess aboard naval vessels. U.S. warships have been dry ever since.

July 1.   The Office of Naval Aeronautics is established under the command of Captain Mark L. Bristol, who has replaced Captain W. I. Chambers as officer in charge of the navy's aviation program.

July 15.   The object of President Wilson's Mexican policy is attained when General Huerta resigns as provisional president of Mexico.

July 28.   **Outbreak of World War I.** Austria declares war on Serbia, beginning a chain reaction that will lead the world to war. Germany declares war on Russia on August 1 and on France on August 3, the same day she invades Belgium. Great Britain declares war on Germany on August 4.

August 5.   **Bryan-Chamorro Treaty.** U.S. Secretary of State William Jennings Bryan and Nicaraguan ambassador Emiliano Chamorro conclude a treaty whereby, in exchange for a payment of $3,000,000 and the promise to preserve Nicaraguan independence, the United States is granted the right to construct a canal across the country and to build naval bases on both coasts. The administration of the country's chaotic finances also passes under American control.

October 1.   **The Panama Canal is opened.** The collier *Jupiter* (AC 3) becomes the first U.S. naval vessel to transit the canal, October 10–12.

November 23.   Captain Mark L. Bristol is officially designated director of naval aeronautics.

November 23.   American forces withdraw from Veracruz, Mexico, after an occupation of seven months.

December 1.   Rear Admiral Alfred Thayer Mahan, dies, aged 74, in Washington, D.C.

December 17.   **Haitian gold.** Rumors arise that the revolutionary government that took power in Haiti on November 20 plans to refill the country's empty treasury by seizing the gold reserves of the Banque Nationale d'Haiti, which is backed by the National City Bank of New York. Both banks and the U.S. State Department take a dim view of this prospect. To prevent its occurrence, the gunboat *Machias* (PG 5) is ordered to reclaim part of the reserve. Landing at Port-au-Prince on this date, the *Machias's* marine detachment, 65 men under Major C. B. Hatch, secretly transfer $500,000 in gold to their ship, which then sails for New York.

1915

January 21.   The Bureau of Navigation issues the first seven "Navy Air Pilot" certificates.

January 28.   The German auxiliary cruiser *Prinz Eitel Friedrich* sinks the American schooner *William P. Frye,* whose cargo of wheat is consigned to an English firm. This ship is the first American merchantman to be lost in World War I.

January 28.   The Revenue Cutter Service and the U.S. Life-Saving Service merge to create the U.S. Coast Guard.

March 3.   **First CNO.** The office of chief of naval operations is established. The creation of such a post, long advocated by navy reformers such as Admiral Bradley A. Fiske, had been fiercely resisted by Secretary of the Navy Josephus Daniels, who saw in it a threat to the primacy of civilian authority. As its first holder, on May 11 Daniels appoints Rear Admiral William S. Benson, a conventional officer who has never been identified with the cause of naval reform.

March 3.   **Naval Reserve.** The Navy Act of 1915, which creates the post of chief of naval operations, also establishes the U.S. Navy Reserve Force.

March 23.   The British passenger steamer *Falaba* is sunk by a German U-boat in St. George's Channel between Wales and Ireland. Although the U-boat surfaces and gives the liner's passengers and crew a few minutes to abandon ship, more than 50 lives are lost. Among the dead is Leon C. Thrasher, the first American citizen to die as a result of German naval action.

March 25.   The *F-4* (SS 23) becomes the first American submarine casualty, sinking with the loss of 21 lives off Honolulu, Hawaii.

May 1.   The American oil tanker *Gulflight* is torpedoed without warning by a German U-boat near the Scilly Isles, off the southwestern coast of England.

May 7.   **The Lusitania.** The British Cunard liner *Lusitania* is torpedoed without warning by the *U-20,* Kapitänleutnant Walther Schwieger, off Old Head of Kinsdale, 10 miles from the Irish coast, and sinks in 20 minutes; 1,198 of 1,959 passengers and crew are lost, 124 Americans among them.

May 13.   **Wilson protests.** President Woodrow Wilson responds to the sinking of the *Lusitania* with a stiff note to the Imperial German government. In it, he demands that Germany disavow the action, pay reparations for the American lives lost, and pledge that its submarines will conform to the rules of cruiser warfare, giving passengers and crew time to abandon a ship before sinking it. The president also asserts the right of American citizens to travel safely on merchant ships of belligerent nations. In the ensuing exchange of notes, which continues through the summer, the German government eventually expresses regret over the destruction of the *Lusitania* and admits liability for the incident.

July 1.   **Revolution in Haiti.** In March 1915 General Vilbrun Guillaume Sam, having led a successful revolution, was "elected" president of Haiti. Shortly thereafter, Dr. Rosalvo Bobo started a revolt against President Sam. On this date Rear Admiral William B. Caperton arrives at Cap-Haitien in the armored cruiser *Washington* (ACR 11) with orders from Secretary of the Navy Daniels to keep the peace. Caperton informs the government forces holding Cap-Haitien and the rebel troops outside it that there must be no fighting in or near the city. He also lands a detachment of marines to establish radio communication between the American consulate and his flagship.

July 27.   **Massacre at Port-au-Prince.** Hearing an outbreak of firing near the Presidential Palace, General Oscar Etienne, military governor of Port-au-Prince, elects to execute 167 prominent political hostages being held in the National Penitentiary. Upon the news of this massacre the capital goes wild. President Sam seeks refuge in the French embassy, General Etienne in the Dominican; both are dragged out and hacked to pieces. The Haitian government also ceases to exist.

July 28.   **Intervention in Haiti.** Learning of the events in Port-au-Prince, Admiral Caperton hurries to the scene, where he receives a message from Secretary Daniels to land troops and restore order. Two companies of marines and three of bluejackets under Captain George Van Orden, USMC, go ashore at the Haitian navy yard at Bizoton, three miles west of Port-au-Prince, and quickly take control of the capital. While this operation is under way, Caperton requests reinforcements. Back at Cap-Haitien, the gunboat *Eagle* lands a party of 20 men to protect the French consulate.

July 29.   The 24th Company of marines reaches Port-au-Prince from Guantánamo in the collier *Jason* (AC 12).

August 1.   The marine detachment from the gunboat *Nashville* (PG 7) occupies Cap-Haitien, Haiti's second-largest city, without opposition.

August 4.   Five companies of the Second Marine Regiment under Colonel E. K. Cole arrive at Port-au-Prince aboard the battleship *Connecticut* (BB 18) after a full-speed run from Philadelphia.

August 6.   Revolutionary elements are expelled from Port-au-Prince.

August 12.   Prompted by Admiral Caperton, the Haitian Congress elects Sudre Dartiguenave president—Haiti's seventh in seven years. On this same date, Caperton installs a military government at Cap-Haitien, where the locals' fear of Dr. Bobo prevents the formation of a civilian administration.

August 15.   Colonel L. W. T. Waller reaches Haiti aboard the armored cruiser *Tennessee* (ACR 10) with eight companies of the First Marine Regiment and the headquarters of the 1st Marine Brigade, of which he assumes command. Once ashore, Waller launches a vigorous campaign to suppress the *cacos*—bandit banks—which, by selling their services to would-be presidents, have effectively dominated Haitian politics for years. At the end of August, Waller's force numbers 2,209 officers and men.

September 1.   **Arabic Pledge.** Following the torpedoing of the British liner *Arabic,* in which two American citizens lose their lives, the German government promises President Wilson that no more passenger liners will be sunk without warning.

September 18.   The first shots of the Haitian intervention are fired when a marine patrol from Gonaïves skirmishes with a band of about 75 cacos.

September 20.   The 1st Battalion, First Marine Regiment, commanded by Colonel E. K. Cole, defeats the cacos in a sharp action outside Cap-Haitien.

September 20.   Captain Edward W. Eberle becomes the 24th superintendent of the Naval Academy.

September 27.   Five companies of marines under Colonel

Major Smedley Darlington Butler, USMC. *Defense Department photo (Marine Corps).*

Cole capture Quartier Morin, Haiti, a bandit hangout a few miles from Cap-Haitien.

October 19.   **New London.** A submarine base is established at New London, Connecticut.

October 24–25.   **Butler's patrol.** A 40-man marine patrol under Major Smedley D. Butler is ambushed in the dark after locating the caco stronghold at Fort Capois in northern Haiti. In this action Gunnery Sergeant Dan Daly, who had won his first Medal of Honor during the Boxer Rebellion, wins his second by slipping through the caco lines to retrieve a machine gun packed on a horse that had been killed at the beginning of the action. At dawn Butler counterattacks. The bandits break and the marines assault and destroy nearby Fort Dipité. By November 8, columns under Butler and Captain Chandler Campbell have captured three more forts, including Fort Capois.

October 28.   **Parris Island.** The marine corps establishes a recruit training depot, named Parris Island in 1917, at the former naval station at Port Royal, South Carolina.

November 5.   The first catapult launching from a ship under way is made by Lieutenant Commander Henry C. Mustin in the Curtiss AB-2 flying boat from the armored cruiser *North Carolina* (ACR 12) in Pensacola Bay, Florida.

November 11.   **Treaty with Haiti.** Under pressure from Admiral Caperton, the Haitian Senate reluctantly ratifies a treaty, signed by President Dartiguenave on September 16, formalizing the American occupation of Haiti. According to its terms, American officials will take charge of the Haitian customs service, collecting revenues and allocating them to reduce the public debt, which cannot be increased without the approval of the United States; American officials will also administer the public works and sanitary services; and the Haitian government promises to raise an "efficient constabulary" commanded by Americans. This latter stipulation is the charter of the marine-led *Gendarmerie d'Haiti,* by which the existing Haitian army is speedily replaced. Ratified by the U.S. Senate on February 23, 1916, the treaty is to remain in force for 10 years and to be renewable for the same period at the desire of either country.

November 17.   **The storming of Fort Rivière, Haiti.** Major Smedley D. Butler is given three marine companies, the marine detachment from the battleship *Connecticut* (BB 18), and a company of bluejackets from the same ship to assault the last caco bastion, Fort Rivière, an old, French-built masonry work on the crest of Montagne Noire about eight miles south of the town of Grande Rivière du Nord. At dawn, covered by his men's fire, Butler leads a storming party of 26 marines up the bare slope to capture the fort and win his second Medal of Honor. The two marines who precede him into the fort, Sergeant Ross L. Iams and Private Samuel Gross, are also awarded the coveted medal. More than 50 cacos are killed, and the fort is dynamited. This action brings the caco rebellion temporarily to an end.

1916

January 8.   A permanent West Coast marine base (later named Camp Pendleton) is established at San Diego, California.

March 11.   The battleship *Nevada* (BB 36) is commissioned.

March 24.   **Renewed friction with Germany.** Several American citizens are injured when the *UB-29* torpedoes the French cross-channel steamer *Sussex.* This attack on an unarmed passenger ship clearly violates the Germany government's *Arabic* pledge of September 1, 1915.

April 16.   Outraged by the sinking of the *Sussex,* President Wilson hands German Ambassador Count Johann von Bernstorff a stiff note, warning that the United States will sever relations with his country unless it changes its way of conducting submarine warfare.

May 2.   The battleship *Oklahoma* (BB 37) is commissioned.

May 4.   **Sussex pledge.** The Imperial German government replies to Wilson's protest by promising that it will not sink merchant vessels without warning and due consideration for the safety of the noncombatants aboard.

May 5.   **Dominican intervention.** In April civil war breaks out in the Dominican Republic when General Desiderio Arias, the minister of war, launches a revolt against President Juan Isidro Jiménez. After attempting unsuccessfully to negotiate a settlement between the two factions, the U.S. minister asks for marines to be landed. Two companies under Captain Frederick M. ("Dopey") Wise go ashore from the transport *Prairie* at Santo Domingo on this date. Besides protecting the American legation and consulate, he is to support President Jiménez, but that intention is frustrated by the president's resignation on May 6. Disorder persists, however, as government forces refuse to recognize Arias. Reinforced by 130 bluejackets and the marine detachment from the gunboat *Castine* (PG 6), Wise arranges a temporary truce.

May 12.   Rear Admiral William B. Caperton, commander of the Cruiser Squadron of the Atlantic Fleet, arrives at Santo Domingo in the dispatch vessel *Dolphin* (PG 24), and three marine companies land from the store ship *Culgoa.*

May 14.   Admiral Caperton meets with General Arias and demands that he disband his forces. Arias refuses to do so, but agrees to withdraw them from Santo Domingo. The marines complete the occupation of the city on May 15.

May 28.   By this date 11 companies of marines have been landed in the Dominican Republic. General Arias has withdrawn to Santiago, in the interior of the country, and it is obvious that the government forces are incapable of crushing the rebellion. That task is assigned to the marines.

June 1.   The port of Monte Cristi, on the northern coast of the Dominican Republic, is peacefully occupied by marines landed from the repair ship *Panther* (AD 6) and the destroyer *Lamson* (DD 18) under the command of Captain Frederick M. Wise.

June 1.   On the same day, two companies of marines and a small bluejacket battalion from the gunboat *Sacra-*

mento (PG 19) seize Puerto Plata, 60 miles east of Monte Cristi, after a skirmish with rebel irregulars in which Captain Herbert J. Hirshinger becomes the first marine killed in action in the Dominican campaign.

June 12.   The battleship *Pennsylvania* (BB 38) is commissioned.

June 21.   Colonel Joseph H. Pendleton's Fourth Marine Regiment lands at Monte Cristi from the transport *Hancock* (AP 3). Pendleton assumes command of marine forces in the Dominican Republic, which become the 2nd Provisional Marine Brigade.

June 26.   **Advance on Santiago.** The marines move on General Arias's stronghold in two columns: Colonel Pendleton's Fourth Regiment, with artillery—837 men in all—from Monte Cristi; and four companies, of which Major Hiram I. ("Hike 'em") Bearss takes command on June 28, from Puerto Plata.

June 27.   **Action at Las Trencheras.** Rebel forces entrenched on two hilltops barring the road to Santiago are driven away by Colonel Pendleton's column, leaving five dead.

June 29.   Major Bearss's Puerto Plata column breaks through 200 rebels entrenched across the railroad at Alta Mira at a cost of two men wounded.

July 3.   **Action at Guayacanas.** The major engagement of the Dominican campaign is fought when Colonel Pendleton's column disperses a sizeable rebel force entrenched in heavy underbrush. The marines lose 1 man killed and 10 wounded; the bodies of 27 rebels are found on the field.

July 4.   As planned, the two marine columns advancing on Santiago unite at Navarette.

July 5.   **Occupation of Santiago.** As the marine column nears Santiago, General Arias sends a message to Colonel Pendleton that he is disbanding his army. The marines occupy the city without opposition the next day.

August 19.   The U.S. Navy Reserve Force is formally organized.

August 24.   **Gendarmerie agreement.** The United States and Haiti conclude an agreement detailing the organization and responsibilities of the *Gendarmerie d'Haiti*. Authorized strength of the force is set at 115 officers and 2,533 NCOs and men.

August 29.   **A navy second to none.** Made apprehensive by the spectacle of the war in Europe, Congress approves President Wilson's request to build a navy equal to any other in the world. By the Naval Act of 1916, passed on this date, it authorizes almost $500 million

Gendarmarie d'Haiti: inspection arms. *U.S. Naval Institute Collection.*

for a three-year building program to produce 10 battleships, 6 battlecruisers, 10 scout cruisers, 50 destroyers, 9 fleet submarines, 58 coastal submarines, and 16 auxiliary vessels. Incomparably the greatest naval appropriation yet passed, the act also signifies the adoption of a new goal for American naval policy, one which has been adhered to ever since.

August 29.   The cruiser *Memphis* (ACR 10), Captain Edward L. Beach, is wrecked by a tidal wave at Santo Domingo, in the Dominican Republic. Forty of her crewmen are killed and 204 injured.

September 7.   **Shipping Board.** Congress establishes the Shipping Board, with powers to buy, build, and charter merchant ships for naval and military purposes. In 1917–18 this board will be instrumental in assembling shipping to supply American forces in Europe.

October 17.   The battleship *Arizona* (BB 39) is commissioned.

November 29.   Captain Harry S. Knapp is appointed military governor of the Dominican Republic, which is declared to be under the military jurisdiction of the United States.

November 29.   Juan Perez, the governor of the Dominican province of San Francisco de Macoris and an adherent of General Arias, has refused orders to have his followers surrender their arms to American authorities. After nightfall two marine companies surround the fortress at San Francisco and First Lieutenant Ernest C. Williams leads 12 picked men to rush the gateway before it can be closed. Eight of the party are wounded in the performance of this mission, but the fort is quickly captured. Williams is awarded the Medal of Honor.

1917

January 13. The cruiser *Milwaukee* (CL 21) strands off Eureka, California, while attempting to refloat the submarine *H-3* (SS 30). No lives are lost, but the ship is eventually wrecked.

January 16. Admiral of the Navy George Dewey dies, still on active duty at age 79.

January 17. The United States purchases the Virgin Islands from Denmark.

February 1. **Unrestricted submarine warfare.** Accepting the risk of American intervention in the world war, the Imperial German government announces the initiation of a policy of unrestricted submarine warfare around the British Isles. The German navy believes it can starve out Britain in six months, long before American belligerence could become effective. The U-boats come close, but are finally frustrated by the adoption of the convoy system in the summer of 1917.

February 3. The United States severs relations with the German Empire.

February 24. **Zimmermann telegram.** President Wilson is outraged when the British government gives him a copy of an intercepted cable in which German Foreign Secretary Alfred Zimmerman promises the Mexican government assistance in the recovery of her lost provinces—most of the American Southwest—in exchange for a military alliance in the event the United States enters the war against Germany. Wilson releases the message to the public, with predictable results.

February 25. **"Sugar Intervention."** Marines begin to land from vessels of the Atlantic Fleet when revolution breaks out in eastern Cuba; they guard American property, mainly sugar plantations, while the Cuban Army engages the rebels. Withdrawn late in May, the marines return in August and remain in regimental and, briefly, brigade strength until August 1919. Two companies continue to garrison Camaguey until February 6, 1922.

February 25. The British liner *Laconia* is torpedoed and sunk by a German submarine; three Americans lose their lives.

March 1. President Wilson requests and receives from Congress authority to arm American merchantmen.

March 9. Without consulting Congress, President Wilson assigns navy crews to man the deck guns being placed aboard American merchant ships.

March 14–21. Five American merchant vessels are sunk by German submarines.

March 17. **Yeomanettes.** The navy is authorized to enlist women to perform yeoman's (clerical) duties. Some 11,275 women will serve during World War I.

March 26. The Joint Army-Navy Airship Board is established to study the question of constructing rigid airships in the United States.

April 6. **War with Germany.** Meeting in joint session, the Congress overwhelmingly approves President Wilson's request for a declaration of war on Germany. The strength of the navy at this time is 4,376 officers and 69,680 men.

April 7. **Guardia Nacional.** Admiral Harry S. Knapp, military governor of the Dominican Republic, disbands the remnants of the Dominican Army and gives orders for the formation of a constabulary similar to the *Gendarmerie d'Haiti,* called the *Guardia Nacional Dominica* and officered by U.S. Marines.

April 8. The United States breaks diplomatic relations with Austria-Hungary.

April 9. **Sims to London.** Rear Admiral William S. Sims arrives in London to establish high-level contact with British naval authorities. In secret briefings at the Admiralty he is shocked to learn that, contrary to published information, the British are losing the war at sea; U-boats are sinking merchant ships faster than

Admiral William S. Sims. *Courtesy U.S. Naval Academy Museum.*

The Return of the Mayflower, by Bernard F. Gribble, shows British fishermen cheering the arrival of Commander Taussig's destroyers. *Courtesy U.S. Naval Academy Museum.*

they can be built. Britain stands on the threshold of starvation. Sims responds to the crisis by urging the Navy Department to rush all possible destroyers and patrol craft to European waters and to suspend the capital ship construction called for by the Naval Act of 1916 in favor of a crash program of building antisubmarine vessels and cargo ships. His recommendations encounter considerable resistance, but in the end they prevail. Sims also supports the British officers advocating the adoption of a convoy system, which is tried on an experimental basis in May and proves an immediate success. The admiral remains in London as Commander, U.S. Naval Forces Operating in European Waters, throughout the war.

May 4. **The Return of the Mayflower.** The first U.S. warships to reach the European war zone, the six vessels of Commander Joseph K. Taussig's Destroyer Squadron 8—the *Wadsworth* (DD 60) (flag), *Conyngham* (DD 58), *Davis* (DD 65), *McDougal* (DD 54), *Porter* (DD 59), and *Wainwright* (DD 62)—arrive at the British naval base at Queenstown (now Cobh), Ireland. Asked by the British commander, Vice Admiral Sir Lewis Bayly, when his squadron will be ready for service, Taussig replies, "We are ready now, sir." The arrival of Taussig's force becomes the subject of Bernard Gribble's famous painting, *The Return of the Mayflower.*

May 14. **Quantico.** The marine corps's need of its own East Coast base is filled by the establishment of the Marine Barracks at Quantico, Virginia.

May 24. The first American Atlantic convoy sails from Hampton Roads, Virginia.

May 29. **Cruiser and Transport Force.** Rear Admiral Albert Gleaves is made commander of the force, eventually numbering 45 transports and 24 cruisers, organized to carry troops of the American Expeditionary Force to Europe. It will move 911,047 soldiers— almost half the AEF—to France and England without the loss of a single life as a result of enemy action. (The other troops are carried in British transports.)

June 5–6. **Navy air.** The first naval aviation unit to reach France, Lieutenant Kenneth Whiting's 1st Aeronautical Detachment, arrives at Bordeaux and St. Nazaire aboard the colliers *Jupiter* and *Neptune* (AC 8). By the war's end the strength of navy air in Europe will have grown to 16,000 officers and men, with 500 aircraft, plus kite balloons and dirigibles, distributed between 26 naval air stations: 16 in France, 5 in Ireland, 3 in England, and 2 in Italy.

June 9. **U.S. Patrol Squadron.** Six armed yachts sail from New York for Brest, France, to form the nucleus of the U.S. Patrol Squadron. This force will relieve the escort vessels of the Cruiser-Transport Force of the responsibility for the security of American convoys upon the latter's entry into French coastal waters. Commanded after November 1, 1917, by Rear Admiral Henry B. Wilson, the patrol force will reach a strength of 38 destroyers and 16 armed yachts, plus minesweepers, tenders, and tugs.

The Cruiser-Transport Force safeguarded the passage of the American Expeditionary Force to France. Here, in November 1917, members of the 6th Marine Regiment crowd the rails of the *Von Steuben* to view the *Agamemnon,* carrying troops of the 42nd ("Rainbow") Division. *U.S. Naval Institute Collection.*

June 14.   The first ground combat units of the AEF, the 1st Infantry Division and Colonel Charles A. Doyen's newly organized Fifth Marine Regiment, sail for France.

August 14.   The first experimental launching of a torpedo from an aircraft is conducted by Lieutenant Edward O. McDonnell at Huntington Bay, New York. The test was carried out on the initiative of Rear Admiral Bradley A. Fiske, who had been trying to interest the navy in the idea of a torpedo plane since 1912.

September 16.   Gunner's Mate First Class Osmond K. Ingram becomes the first navy man to be killed in action in World War I when he is blown overboard from the destroyer *Cassin* (DD 43) by a German torpedo. Ingram saw the torpedo coming and was trying to roll a depth-charge over the side at the moment of impact. He is posthumously awarded the Medal of Honor, and the destroyer *Ingram* (DD 255) is named after him.

October 17.   The army transport *Antilles* is sunk by a U-boat while homeward bound from France.

October 23.   **The Marine Brigade.** In France, the Fifth and Sixth Marine Regiments are organized as the 4th Marine Brigade under the command of Brigadier General Charles A. Doyen. The 6th Machine Gun Battalion of Marines joins shortly afterwards.

October 28.   The homeward-bound, army transport *Finland,* to which the survivors of the *Antilles* had been transferred, is torpedoed by a U-boat, but succeeds in making her way back to Brest, France.

November 5.   The converted yacht *Alcedo* (SP 166), Lieutenant Commander William T. Conn, is torpedoed and sunk with the loss of 22 lives by the *UC-71* while patrolling off the coast of France. She is the first U.S. naval vessel lost in World War I.

November 17.   **First U-boat kill.** Two of the destroyers based at Queenstown (Cobh), Ireland—the *Fanning* (DD 37), Lieutenant Arthur S. Carpender, and *Nicholson* (DD 52), Commander Frank D. Berrien—depth-charge the *U-58.* Kapitänleutnant Gustav Amberger brings his stricken submarine to the surface, and the crew is rescued before her final plunge.

November 18.   Planes based at Le Croisic, France, at the mouth of the Loire, fly the navy's first patrols over European waters.

November 19.   The destroyer *Chauncey* (DD 3), Lieutenant Commander Walter E. Reno, sinks with the loss of 21 lives after being rammed by the SS *Rose,* a British merchantman, 110 miles west of Gibraltar.

December 6.   The destroyer *Jacob Jones* (DD 61), Lieutenant Commander David W. Bagley, is torpedoed and sunk by the *U-53,* Kapitänleutnant Hans Rose, near the Scilly Isles. Sixty-four of her crewmen go down with her. The U-boat commander surfaces, takes two prisoners, and chivalrously radios the position of the sinking to the U.S. naval base at Queenstown (Cobh), Ireland, facilitating the rescue of the other 35 survivors.

December 7.   **Battleships to Britain.** The five dreadnoughts comprising Battleship Division 9—the *Delaware* (BB 28), *Florida* (BB 30), *New York* (BB 34), *Texas* (BB 35), and *Wyoming* (BB 32)—Rear Admiral Hugh Rodman, commanding, arrive at Scapa Flow in the Orkneys to reinforce the British Grand Fleet, in which they become the Sixth Battle Squadron.

December 17.   The submarines *F-1* (SS 20) and *F-3* (SS 22) collide off San Pedro, California, and the former sinks with the loss of 19 lives.

December 18.   The battleship *Mississippi* (BB 41) is commissioned.

1918

January 3.   **NOTS.** The Naval Overseas Transportation Service is established under Commander Charles Belknap to control the shipment of supplies to American forces in Europe. Of the more than 450 cargo ships that eventually belong to the service, only 8 will be lost as a result of enemy action.

January 21. The 1st Marine Aeronautics Company, Captain Francis T. Evans, lands at Ponta Delgada on São Miguel Island in the Azores, from which it will fly antisubmarine patrols. It is the first marine aviation unit to reach the European war zone.

March 4. **Disappearance of the Cyclops.** The collier *Cyclops*, Lieutenant Commander George W. Worley, USNRF, puts out from Barbados, British West Indies, with a crew of 280 and is never seen again.

March 17. **Into the trenches.** In France, marine units enter the front line for the first time.

March 19. The destroyer *Manley* (DD 74), Commander Robert L. Berry, is severely damaged, and 56 of her crew are killed by the accidental detonation of 18 depth charges when she rolls against the British auxiliary cruiser *Motagua* off the Irish coast.

March 19. **First aerial victory.** Ensign Stephen Potter (Naval Aviator No. 130) becomes the first navy pilot to shoot down an enemy aircraft, destroying a German seaplane near the island of Heligoland in the North Sea, while on a long-range patrol with the Royal Air Force. A little over a month later, on April 25, he is killed in an air battle with seven German aircraft off Felixstowe, England.

April 11. The NOTS cargo ship *Lake Moor* is torpedoed by *UB-73* off the Corsewall Light, Scotland, and sinks with the loss of 46 lives.

May 8. In the Mediterranean, the armed yacht *Lydonia* (SP 700), Lieutenant Commander Richard P. McCullough, collaborates with the British destroyer *Basilisk* to sink the *UB-70*.

May 12. **Subchasers.** The first six of the new, 110-foot, wooden-hulled, American subchasers reach the European war zone. Before the war's end 121 of these little craft will be employed in British and French waters and in the Mediterranean.

May 20. The battleship *New Mexico* (BB 40) is commissioned.

May 21. The NOTS tanker *William Rockefeller*, Lieutenant Commander Richard E. Tull, USNRF, is torpedoed and sunk by the *UC-58* while en route from Lamlash to Rosyth, Scotland. All except 3 of her 51 crewmen are saved.

May 24. **Intervention in Russia.** The outbreak of the Russian revolution and the Bolsheviks' withdrawal from the war in March 1918 leaves huge amounts of arms and munitions, sent by the Allies to supply the czar's army, stockpiled at Archangel. To avert the possibility of these stores falling into unfriendly hands, the Allies decide to occupy Archangel, using Murmansk as a base. On this date the cruiser *Olympia* (C 6), Captain Bion B. Bierer, lands a detachment to cooperate with British forces in the unopposed seizure of Murmansk. In June, 55 of the cruiser's men participate in the advance on and occupation of Archangel.

May 25. **U-boat operations in American waters.** *U-151*, the first of six long-range German submarines that will be sent into American coastal waters during the war, begins her operations by attacking three small schooners off Cape Charles, Virginia. Relatively little damage is done by these raids.

May 31. The transport *President Lincoln*, Captain Percy W. Foote, is sunk by the *U-90* when two days out of Brest, France, bound for New York. Of the 715 men aboard, 26 are lost. The submarine surfaces after the sinking and take Lieutenant Edouard V. Izac prisoner from a lifeboat. While aboard the *U-90* Izac gathers so much information regarding German submarine operations that upon his arrival in Germany he resolves to escape in order to put this intelligence at the disposal of the Allied navies. His first breakout ends in his recapture, but on the second he succeeds in making his way through the German lines. Lieutenant Izac's heroism and initiative are rewarded by the Medal of Honor.

June 5. **Belleau Wood.** On May 27, a German offensive breaks through the French front in the Chemin des Dames, northeast of Paris. The 4th Marine Brigade, commanded by Brigadier General James G. Harbord,

The *Cyclops*, whose disappearance remains a mystery. *Official U.S. Navy photograph.*

Marines in France, riding the famous *hommes 40, cheveux 8* French railway cars. *Courtesy National Archives.*

USA, is rushed to meet the threat. On this date, the marines repel German attacks along the Paris-Metz highway. The following day they counterattack strongly fortified German positions in Belleau Wood, between the villages of Lucy-le-Bocage and Bouresches. As the marines advance towards the wood under heavy machine-gun and rifle fire, Gunnery Sergeant Dan Daly, winner of two Medals of Honor, encourages them with the shout, "Come on, you sons of bitches! Do you want to live forever?" The German resistance is tenacious. By June 26, the brigade has suffered 50 percent casualties (4,677 killed and wounded), but Major Maurice Shearer, commanding the 3rd Battalion, Fifth Marines, is able to report, "Woods now U.S. Marine Corps entirely." General Jean Degoutte, commander of the French Sixth Army, decrees that henceforth the wood will be known as the *Bois de la Brigade de Marine.*

June 8.   North Sea mine barrage. U.S. naval forces under the command of Rear Admiral Joseph Strauss begin the enormous task of laying a minefield across 240 miles of open sea from Scotland to Norway with the object of penning Germany's U-boats inside the North Sea. The British had considered undertaking such a project, but decided that it was technically infeasible. The belt is completed on September 20, and operations to increase its density and width continue until the armistice. A total of 70,263 mines are laid, including 13,652 by cooperating British forces. Many U-boats slip through the barrage, but as many as six may have been destroyed in the attempt.

June 29–August 28.   Marines in Russia. The cruiser *Brooklyn* (ACR 3), flagship of the U.S. Asiatic Fleet, lands her marine detachment to safeguard the American consulate at Vladivostok during the convulsions of the Russian Civil War. The marines remain ashore until relieved by an infantry brigade from the Philippines.

July 1. The transport *Covington,* Captain Raymond De L. Hasbrouck, is torpedoed by the *U-86* off Brest, France, and sinks while under tow the next day; 770 of the 776 men aboard are saved.

July 11. The cargo ship *Westover* is torpedoed by the *U-92* off the coast of France and sinks with the loss of 11 lives.

June 14. In France, Colonel Wendell C. ("Buck") Neville, CO of the Fifth Marines, is promoted to the rank of brigadier general and assumes command of the 4th Marine Brigade, General Harbord having been moved up to command the 2nd Infantry Division.

July 18–19.   Battle of Soissons. The 4th Marine Brigade takes part in the counterattack that throws back the last German offensive of the war, advancing six-and-

U.S. minesweepers, painted in camouflage colors, laying the North Sea mine barrage. *U.S. Naval Institute Collection.*

one-half miles and sustaining 1,972 casualties in 48 hours.

July 19.   **Loss of the San Diego.** The cruiser *San Diego* (ex-*California*) (ACR 6), Captain Harley H. Christy, hits a mine laid by *U-156,* Kapitänleutnant Richard Feldt, off Fire Island, New York, and sinks with the loss of 6 lives. She is the only major American warship lost in World War I. On her return voyage to Germany, the *U-156* will be sunk in the North Sea mine barrage.

July 21.   Four seaplanes from the Naval Air Station, Chatham, Massachusetts, attack the surfaced German *U-156* that has sunk the tug *Perth Amboy* and four barges off Cape Cod. The submarine submerges after returning the planes' fire.

July 25.   The navy is assigned the responsibility for developing rigid airships for the American armed forces.

July 28.   In France, Brigadier General John A. Lejeune is given command of the 2nd Infantry Division. The first marine officer to command a formation larger than a brigade, he will be promoted to the rank of major general on August 7.

July 30.   The 1st Marine Aviation Force, 100 officers and 657 men under Major Alfred A. Cunningham, lands in France from the transport *De Kalb.*

August 12.   **Marinettes.** The marine corps is authorized to enlist women in the marine corps reserve to perform

Marinettes (and two male marines) outside the Corps's headquarters in Washington, D.C. *Defense Department photo (Marine Corps).*

clerical duties. Mrs. Opha M. Johnson becomes the first woman marine.

August 21.   One of a flight of three seaplanes from the Naval Air Station, Porto Corsini, Italy, is shot down in a dogfight with enemy land planes near the Austrian naval base at Pola, on the Adriatic. Ensign Charles H. Hammann, USNRF, becomes the first naval aviator to win the Medal of Honor when he lands his plane on the water to pick up the downed pilot.

August 23.   **More battleships to Britain.** A battleship division consisting of the *Nevada* (BB 36), *Oklahoma* (BB 37), and *Utah* (BB 31) under the command of Rear Admiral T. S. Rodgers reaches Bantry Bay, Ireland, to serve as a force in readiness in the event a German battlecruiser should break out to attack the North Atlantic convoys.

September 6.   **Railway guns.** A naval battery of five 14-inch railway guns, commanded by Rear Admiral Charles P. Plunkett, goes into action in France, delivering a long-range bombardment of German positions north of Soissons. This unit is humorously known as the Woozlefinches.

September 12–15.   **St. Mihiel offensive.** Brigadier General Wendell C. Neville's 4th Marine Brigade, still assigned

Major General John A. Lejeune awarding decorations, a few weeks after the close of hostilities. *Courtesy National Archives.*

One of the navy's 14-inch railway guns in action on the Western Front. *Courtesy National Archives.*

to the 2nd Infantry Division, takes part in the first all-American offensive on the Western Front, the reduction of the German St. Mihiel salient. The Germans are in the process of withdrawing from the salient when the attack is launched, and American casualties are relatively light.

September 15.   The transport *Mount Vernon*, Captain Douglas E. Dismukes, is torpedoed by a U-boat while homeward bound from Brest, France. Thirty-six men are killed, but the ship succeeds in returning to Brest.

September 16.   The cargo ship *Buena Ventura*, Lieutenant Commander H. Fitzsimmons, USNRF, is torpedoed by the *U-46* two days out of Bordeaux, France, and sinks with the loss of 19 lives.

September 24.   **First navy ace.** Nineteen-year-old Lieutenant David S. Ingalls, flying a Sopwith Camel on temporary duty with No. 213 Squadron, RAF, in northern France, scores his fifth aerial victory, thereby becoming the navy's first and only ace of World War I.

September 26.   The coast guard cutter *Tampa*, carrying a crew of 115, is lost with all hands in the Bristol Channel, off the west coast of England, after being torpedoed by the *UB-91*.

September 29.   The battleship *Minnesota* (BB 22), Captain J. V. Chase, is slightly damaged by a German mine off the Delaware capes.

September 30.   **Ticonderoga vs. U-152.** The Naval Overseas Transportation Service ship *Ticonderoga*, Lieutenant Commander James J. Madison, USNRF, is sunk in mid-Atlantic after a heroic, two-hour surface action with the *U-152*. Only 25 of the 237 men aboard survive, including Madison, who is awarded the Medal of Honor.

October 2.   **Durazzo raid.** In the Adriatic, 11 American subchasers under Captain C. P. Nelson screen an Allied British, French, and Italian force that bombards the Austrian naval base at Durazzo.

October 3–10.   **Blanc Mont Ridge.** In France General Lejeune's 2nd Infantry Division, including the 4th Marine Brigade, attacks Blanc Mont Ridge, a naturally strong and heavily fortified German position on the Champagne sector. The ridge and the village of Etienne, in its rear, are taken after a week's fighting, which costs the marines 2,538 casualties.

October 4.   **First armistice note.** The Imperial German government appeals to President Wilson to arrange an armistice.

October 14.   **First air raid.** Navy and marine corps aviation in northern France is organized as the Northern Bombing Group, consisting of a Marine Day Wing and a Navy Night Wing. The group's first major raid is made on this date when a marine squadron of eight DeHavilland DH-4s led by Captain Douglas B. Robin bombs the rail yards at Thielt, Belgium. Second Lieutenant Ralph Talbot and his observer, Gunnery Sergeant Robert G. Robinson, shoot down 2 of 12 German planes by which their aircraft is attacked. Both are awarded the Medal of Honor, the first marine aviators to gain that distinction.

October 17.   **Caco uprising.** The relative peace that has prevailed in Haiti since late 1915 is shattered when a band of approximately 100 cacos under the dynamic, new leadership of French-educated Charlemagne Péralte attacks the *gendarmerie* post at Hinche, in the central part of the country. The cacos are beaten off, leaving 35 dead, but hundreds more soon flock to

The NOTS *Ticonderoga. U.S. Naval Institute Collection.*

Charlemagne's side. The second Haitian campaign has begun.

October 17. The SS *Lucia* gains the unwanted distinction of being the last ship torpedoed by a German U-boat in World War I. She sinks the next day. On October 21, the German government accedes to President Wilson's demand for the cessation of submarine operations as a prerequisite to armistice negotiations.

October 29. **The German Fleet mutinies.** Learning of plans for what they interpret as a death or glory sortie down the Belgian coast, the crews of the heavy surface units of the German High Seas Fleet mutiny. Their action sparks a spontaneous revolution among the war-weary civilian population ashore.

November 1. **Marines in the Meuse-Argonne.** In a single day's fighting the 4th Marine Brigade penetrates the Germans' Hindenburg Line, capturing the Brünhilde and Freya strongpoints, taking 1,700 prisoners and advancing more than four miles.

November 9. The Imperial German government is overthrown and a republic proclaimed. The Kaiser crosses the border into neutral Holland the next day.

November 9–10. The Fifth Marines cross the Meuse River against heavy resistance.

November 10. In Haiti, 60 cacos led by Charlemagne Péralte rout the 10-man *gendarmerie* garrison at Maissade, northwest of Hinche, and plunder the town.

November 11. **Armistice.** The cease-fire ending World War I goes into effect at 11:00 A.M.

November 21. **Surrender of the German Fleet.** In accordance with the terms of the armistice agreement, 14 German capital ships cross the North Sea to be interned at the British base at Scapa Flow in the Orkneys. The American battleships serving with the British Grand Fleet are present at the surrender.

December 1. At the Naval Air Station, Hampton Roads, Virginia, the dirigible *C-7* becomes the first American airship to be filled with helium, in place of the highly flammable hydrogen formerly used. Hereafter, all American lighter-than-air craft will use helium.

1919

February 4. The Navy Cross and the Navy Distinguished Service Medal are created by act of Congress.

February 12. Captain Archibald H. Scales becomes the 25th superintendent of the Naval Academy.

March 8. An upsurge of political banditry in the Dominican Republic leads to the reinforcement of the 2nd Marine Brigade by Colonel James C. Breckinridge's Fifteenth Marine Regiment and the 1st Air Squadron—six Curtiss JN6 "Jennies"—which land at Santo Domingo on this date. These arrivals increase the brigade's strength to 2,600 officers and men.

March 9. Lieutenant Commander E. O. McDonnell, in a Sopwith Camel, makes the first flight from a turret platform aboard the battleship *Texas* (BB 35) at Guantánamo, Cuba.

March 16. **Second Haitian Campaign.** Major General (marine colonel) Alexander S. Williams, commandant of the *Gendarmerie d'Haiti,* notifies Brigadier General Albertus W. Catlin, commanding the 1st Marine Brigade, that the assistance of marine forces is needed to crush Péralte's caco rebellion. The number of hostile contacts since the first of the year make it evident that a full-scale rebellion is under way. Four companies are transferred from Guantánamo, Cuba, to reinforce the brigade later in the month, and approximately 1,000 marines are put into the field. From April through September the marines and *gendarmerie* are engaged in no less than 131 actions, large and small.

March 21. A *gendarmerie* patrol of five men led by Lieutenant (marine sergeant) Nicolas B. Moskoff is ambushed by around 100 cacos at Dufailly, Haiti. Moskoff is mortally wounded at the first fire, and his Haitian second-in-command is later killed, but the surviving *gendarmes* fight their way back to Mirebalais, carrying Moskoff with them.

March 24. The battleship *Idaho* (BB 42) is commissioned.

March 31. Squadron E, marine corps aviation, arrives at Port-au-Prince, Haiti, for service against the cacos.

May 8–31. **First across.** Three Navy/Curtiss ("Nancy") flying boats—the NC-1, NC-3, and NC-4—set out on the first transatlantic flight, with lay-overs at Trepassy, Newfoundland, and the Azores. Two drop out before readying the latter, but the NC-4, piloted by Lieutenant Commander Albert C. ("Putty") Read, pushes on to reach Lisbon, Portugal, on May 27 and Plymouth, England, on the 31st. In 1929 Congress awards a gold medal to Read, his four crewmen, and their squadron leader, Commander John H. Towers. Today the NC-4 is on exhibit at the Smithsonian Institution in Washington, D.C.

May 28. The General Board of the Navy recommends the completion of the great construction program projected by the Naval Act of 1916.

The NC-4. *U.S. Naval Institute Collection.*

June 21.   The German fleet, interned at Scapa Flow in the Orkneys, is scuttled by its crews.

June 28.   The Treaty of Versailles is signed, officially ending World War I. Because ratification of the treaty would include acceptance of the covenant of the League of Nations, it will be rejected by the U.S. Senate.

July 11.   The navy pay corps is renamed the supply corps.

July 23.   Planes of the marine 1st Air Squadron attack a party of bandits at Meta de la Palma in the Dominican Republic.

July 30–August 1.   The marine detachment of the cruiser *New Orleans* (CL 22) lands to protect American interests at Tyutuke Bay, near Vladivostok, Russia.

August.   **Air-ground action.** In Haiti two marine aircraft—a Curtiss Jenny and a DeHavilland DH-4—support ground forces in a surprise attack on a caco encampment on a hilltop near Mirebalais. More than 200 bandits are killed. This is the first instance of the coordinated, air-ground action that will later become a marine corps specialty.

October 2.   Colonel John H. Russell assumes command of the 1st Marine Brigade in Haiti.

October 7.   **Attack on Port-au-Prince.** Charlemagne Péralte sends 300 of his followers to raid the Haitian capital. The cacos are repulsed and pursued by the marines and the *gendarmerie.*

October 31.   **The end of Charlemagne.** *Gendarmerie* Captain (marine sergeant) Herman H. Hanneken and First Lieutenant (marine corporal) William R. Button blacken their faces and lead a patrol of 16 hand-picked *gendarmes,* all disguised as cacos, through six enemy outposts to penetrate the camp of Charlemagne Péralte. Hanneken kills Péralte with two shots from his .45. The caco leader's corpse is later photographed,

and prints are distributed to convince his followers that he is indeed dead. Hanneken and Button are both awarded the U.S. Medal of Honor and the Haitian Médaille Militaire.

November 1.   Rear Admiral Robert E. Coontz becomes the second chief of naval operations.

November 2.   A detachment of *gendarmes* led by Captain Hanneken storms the caco stronghold of Fort Capois, effectively ending the insurrection in northern Haiti.

December 17.   The Eighth Marine Regiment is reconstituted and ordered to Haiti under the command of Lieutenant Colonel L. McCarty Little.

December 25.   **YangPat.** The American gunboats that have been operating on China's Yangtze River since 1903 are formally organized into the Yangtze Patrol under the command of Captain T. A. Kearney, first ComYangPat.

1920

January 1.   **Campaign against the cacos.** In Haiti Colonel John H. Russell, commanding the 1st Marine Brigade, intensifies efforts to suppress the cacos.

January 15.   **Second attack on Port-au-Prince.** Benoit Batraville, who has succeeded Charlemagne Péralte as the principal caco chieftain, sends a party of 300 men to assault the Haitian capital. The cacos penetrate the city before dawn, but are soon driven out, suffering 50 percent casualties.

April 4.   Climbing Morne Michel, near Las Cahobas, Haiti, a patrol led by *gendarmerie* Lieutenant (marine sergeant) Lawrence Muth is ambushed by cacos under

YangPat: the *Guam,* a gunboat commissioned in 1927, on patrol on the Yangtze. *Official U.S. Navy photograph.*

Benoit Batraville. Muth, wounded and left for dead, is decapitated by Batraville.

April 10.   U.S. Marines enter Guatemala City, Guatemala, to protect the American embassy during a revolution.

May 19.   **Crushing the cacos.** A marine patrol led by Captain Jesse L. Perkins surprises Benoit Batraville's camp in Petit Bois Peine, near Las Cahobas, Haiti. Batraville is killed in the action. His death marks the end of the caco rebellion. By the close of the year, the pacification of the country is complete.

June 30.   The battleship *Tennessee* (BB 43) is commissioned.

July 1.   Major General John A. Lejeune becomes the 13th commandant of the marine corps.

July 12.   Naval forces afloat are organized into the Atlantic, Pacific, and Asiatic Fleets.

July 18.   The ex-German light cruiser *Frankfurt* is sunk by navy aircraft in bombing experiments off Hampton Roads, Virginia.

July 29.   The cruiser *St. Louis* (CA 18) and six destroyers are dispatched to Turkish waters to protect American citizens during the disturbances resulting from the Graeco-Turkish War.

September 1.   The submarine *S-5* (SS 110) is lost during trials off the Delaware Capes. The crew survives.

October 14–November 1.   The obsolete battleship *Indiana* (BB 1) is sunk in Tangier Sound, in the Chesapeake Bay, after a series of air attacks and explosions designed to test the efficacy of her underwater compartmentation and double hull.

1921

February 26.   The destroyer *Woolsey* (DD 77) sinks with the loss of 16 lives after a collision with the freighter *Steel Inventor.*

March 5.   Edwin Denby becomes the 42nd secretary of the navy.

July 5.   Rear Admiral Henry B. Wilson becomes the 26th superintendent of the Naval Academy.

July 21.   The formerly German battleship *Ostfriesland* is sunk off the Virginia Capes by aerial bombing supervised by Brigadier General "Billy" Mitchell, the controversial chief of the U.S. Army Air Service. Even though the planes have to break the prearranged rules of engagement to give the stationary old ship the *coup de grâce,* Mitchell proclaims that her sinking signals the end of the surface warship.

July 21.   The battleship *Maryland* (BB 46) is commissioned.

July 23.   **Pete Ellis's plan.** Major General Commandant John A. Lejeune, USMC, approves Operation Plan 712, "Advanced Base Operations in Micronesia," prepared by Lieutenant Colonel Earl H. ("Pete") Ellis. This remarkable document, the marine corps's contribution to the Orange Plan prepared by the navy for use in the event of war with Japan, calls for the development of the amphibious capability the corps would demonstrate in World War II and accurately forecasts the general course of the Pacific campaigns. A brilliant, troubled man, Ellis will die of alcoholism while on a secret mission to reconnoiter Japan's island possessions in 1923.

August 10.   **BuAer.** Rear Admiral William A. Moffett is appointed chief of the fledgling Bureau of Aeronautics. This is the first new bureau created since the Civil War.

August 10.   The battleship *California* (BB 44) is commissioned.

August 24.   **Loss of the R-38.** The dirigible *R-38* (ZR-2), built in England for the U.S. Navy, breaks up, burns, and crashes into the Humber River while on a test flight near Hull, England. Of the 17 Americans and 27 Englishmen aboard, all except 1 of the former and 5 of the latter perish.

November 7.   **Marines guard the mails.** Two mail-train robberies spur President Warren G. Harding to detail 23 marine officers and 2,200 men to guard the U.S. mails. The robberies cease, and the marines are withdrawn in March 1922.

November 11.   **Washington Conference.** On the third anniversary of the armistice, U.S. Secretary of State Charles Evans Hughes welcomes the delegates of eight foreign nations—Great Britain, Japan, France, Italy, The Netherlands, Belgium, Portugal, and China—to the First International Conference on Limitation of Naval Armaments. The idea had been championed by Senator William E. Borah, who feared the development of a naval race between the United States, Britain, and Japan, and in June a congressional resolution urging President Harding to organize such a conference passed by a landslide.

1922

January 25.   The cruiser *Galveston* (CL 19) lands her marine detachment at Corinto, Nicaragua, to reinforce the Managua legation guard during a period of political tension.

February 6. **Washington Naval Treaty.** The United States, Great Britain, Japan, France, and Italy conclude the Five-Power Treaty of naval arms limitations, establishing a ratio of capital ships (battleships and aircraft carriers) of 5:5:3:1¾:1¾, respectively. This is the first time in recent history that Great Britain, traditional ruler of the waves, has conceded parity to any other naval power. To meet treaty limitations (which allow the United States 525,000 tons for battleships and 181,000 tons for aircraft carriers), the three principal powers agree to scrap more than 60 capital ships, completed or under construction. Other articles of the treaty provide for a 10-year moratorium ("naval holiday") on the laying down of new capital ships, which are defined as vessels of more than 10,000 tons with greater than 8-inch guns; they limit capital ships to 35,000 tons and 16-inch guns; and they compensate the Japanese for their inferiority in tonnage by a Non-Fortification Clause, whereby the United States and Great Britain pledge not to strengthen the fortifications of their Pacific possessions (Australia, New Zealand, and Singapore excepted), while the Japanese are free to increase the defenses of their Home Islands.

February 11. To centralize the administration of the U.S. occupation of Haiti, Congress creates the office of the U.S. High Commissioner, with ambassadorial rank. Brigadier General John H. Russell, commanding the 1st Marine Brigade in Haiti, is appointed to the post. He will serve in this capacity until November 12, 1930.

March 20. **First carrier.** The U.S. Navy's first aircraft carrier, the *Langley* (CV 1), is commissioned at Norfolk, Virginia, Commander Kenneth Whiting, commanding. She was converted from the collier *Jupiter.*

April 22. A spotter aircraft is assigned to every battleship and cruiser in the navy.

April 28. The cruiser *Albany* (CL 23) lands her marine detachment to reinforce the legation guard at Peking amid the disorders of the Chinese civil war.

May 5. A provisional battalion of marines, assembled from ships of the Asiatic Fleet, is landed at Taku, China, ready to advance to Peking should need arise.

July 1. The conversion of the unfinished battlecruisers *Lexington* and *Saratoga* to aircraft carriers is authorized by Congress.

September 16. **Evacuation of the Anatolian Greeks.** Following its victory in the Graeco-Turkish War, the Turkish government expels the 250,000 Greeks living in Asia Minor. On this date, Commander Halsey Powell, captain of the destroyer *Edsall* (DD 219), assumes control of the evacuation of this unfortunate population to Greece. Although most of the refugees are actually transported in Greek merchant ships, American destroyers also assist in the movement.

October 17. **First take-off from a U.S. carrier.** Lieutenant Commander Virgil C. Griffin takes off from the flight deck of the newly commissioned carrier *Langley* (CV 1) in a Vought VE-7SF.

October 26. Lieutenant Commander Godfrey DeC. ("Chevy") Chevalier becomes the first pilot to land on an American carrier while under way, setting his Aeromarine 39B down on the deck of the *Langley* off Cape Henry, Virginia.

November 18. Another landmark event in the development of naval aviation occurs aboard the *Langley* when her commanding officer, Commander Kenneth Whiting, makes the first catapult launching from a U.S. carrier.

The *Langley,* the navy's first carrier, affectionately known as "the old covered wagon." *Official U.S. Navy photograph.*

December 6.   The Atlantic and Pacific fleets are combined to form the United States Fleet.

1923

February 14.   The gunboat *Asheville* (PG 21) lands a small marine detachment to protect American citizens from bandits on Matsu Island, China.

June 2.   The Naval Research Laboratory is established.

July 31.   Admiral Edward W. Eberle becomes the third chief of naval operations.

August 30.   The battleship *Colorado* (BB 45) is commissioned.

September 4.   Under the command of Captain Frank R. McCrary, the airship *Shenandoah* (ZR-1) makes its first flight at the Naval Air Station, Lakehurst, New Jersey.

September 5.   The U.S. Asiatic Fleet anchors off Yokohama, Japan, to assist in disaster relief following the great Kondo Plain earthquake that nearly leveled both Yokohama and Tokyo.

September 8.   **Disaster at the Devil's Jaw.** Seven ships of the Destroyer Squadron (Desron) 11—the *Chauncey* (DD 296), *Delphy* (DD 261), *Fuller* (DD 297), *Nicolas* (DD 311), *S. P. Lee* (DD 310), *Woodbury* (DD 309), and *Young* (DD 312)—run ground in a heavy fog at Point Pendernales (often called the Devil's Jaw), off Santa Barbara, California. Twenty-two lives are lost, and the ships are completely wrecked.

November 15.   A detachment of marines is landed to protect a group of American missionaries at Tungsham, China.

December 1.   The battleship *West Virginia* (BB 48) is commissioned.

December 6.   Destroyers from the U.S. Asiatic Fleet are ordered to join units of other navies off Canton to assist in safeguarding foreign lives and property during the Chinese civil wars.

1924

January 16.   The cruiser *Tacoma* (CL 20) wrecks on Blanquilla Reef, off Veracruz, Mexico, with the loss of four lives.

January 23.   Marines from the gunboat *Sacramento* (PG 21) occupy Socorro, on Boca Grande Island in the Philippines, where the Moros are revolting against the local government. The insurrection is suppressed by mid-February.

February 28–March 2.   Seamen and marines from the cruiser *Denver* (C 14) land at La Ceiba, Honduras, to protect American interests during the latest revolution in that country.

March 3.   The destroyer *Billingsley* (DD 293) lands a detachment of bluejackets and marines to safeguard American property at Tela, Honduras.

March 4.   The *Denver's* landing battalion goes ashore to defend Americans at Puerto Cortez, Honduras.

The ruins of Destroyer Squadron 11 off Point Pedernales, California. *Official U.S. Navy photograph.*

March 9.   Marines from the cruiser *Denver* (C 14) land to protect Americans at La Ceiba, Honduras.

March 17–19.   A detachment of 176 officers and men goes ashore to establish a neutral zone around Tegucigalpa, Honduras.

March 19.   Curtis D. Wilbur becomes 43rd secretary of the navy.

June 12.   Three officers and 44 men are killed in a turret explosion aboard the battleship *Mississippi* (BB 41).

August 8.   The airship *Shenandoah* (ZR-1) secures to a mooring mast on the oiler *Patoka* (AO 9) while the latter is under way in Narragansett Bay. This is the first test of that maneuver.

September 10.   The cruiser *Rochester* (ex-*New York*) (ACR 2) lands 111 seamen and marines to safeguard American interests at La Ceiba, Honduras.

September 18.   **Withdrawal from the Dominican Republic.** The last elements of the 2nd Provisional Marine Brigade board ship at Santo Domingo, ending an occupation of eight years. A treaty signed on December 24 formally terminates the American protectorate over the Dominican Republic.

October 6.   As the Chinese civil war approaches Shanghai, ships of the Asiatic Fleet land detachments to cooperate with contingents from other foreign navies in protecting the International Settlement at Shanghai.

October 7–25.   **Flight of the Shenandoah.** The airship *Shenandoah* (ZR-1), Lieutenant Commander Zachary Lansdowne, makes a transcontinental good-will cruise from the Naval Air Station, Lakehurst, New Jersey, covering 9,317 miles in 258 hours aloft.

November 25.   The navy's German-built airship *Los Angeles* (ZR-3) is christened by Mrs. Calvin Coolidge at the Anacostia Naval Air Station, Washington, D.C.

1925

January 15.   The marine detachment of the gunboat *Sacramento* (PG 19) is landed to reinforce the defenders of the International Settlement at Shanghai during the tumults of the Chinese civil war. Several other marine units will land to serve briefly in the city in the course of the year.

February 17.   The five signatories of the Washington Naval Treaty report that they have scrapped all the ships necessary to comply with its terms.

February 23.   Rear Admiral Louis M. Nulton becomes the 27th superintendent of the U.S. Naval Academy.

March 2–11.   The *Langley* (CV 1) is the first aircraft carrier to participate in a fleet problem.

March 4.   **NROTC.** The Naval Reserve Officers Training Corps is established by Act of Congress. Programs open at six universities in 1926.

April 1.   The first night landing on an American carrier is made by Lieutenant Commander John D. Price on the *Langley* (CV 1) off San Diego, California.

April 20.   The cruiser *Denver* (C 14) lands marines to protect American interests at La Ceiba, Honduras.

August 1.   **Withdrawal from Nicaragua.** The 100-man marine legation guard is recalled from Managua, Nicaragua, where it had been established in January 1913.

The airship *Shenandoah* at a mooring mast. *U.S. Naval Institute Collection.*

The wreck of the *Shenandoah. Courtesy National Archives.*

September 1. A four-engined PN-9 flying boat piloted by Commander John Rodgers runs out of gas 470 miles short of its goal after covering 1,841 miles on an attempted nonstop flight from San Francisco to Honolulu. Rodgers and his crew rig a sail from the airplane's wing fabric and reach a point only 20 miles from Hawaii when they are rescued by the submarine *R-4* (SS 81).

September 3. Loss of the Shenandoah. The airship *Shenandoah* (ZR-1), Lieutenant Commander Zachary Lansdowne, breaks in two in a severe storm near Ava, Ohio, while on a second transcontinental goodwill tour. Lansdowne and 13 others of the ship's 43 crew members are killed.

September 25. Loss of the S-51. The submarine *S-51* (SS 162) sinks with the loss of 33 lives after a collision with the SS *City of Rome* off Block Island, New York.

1926

May 7–June 5. The marine detachment of the cruiser *Cleveland* (C 19) lands to protect American and other foreign interests at Bluefields, Nicaragua, when civil war breaks out between the Liberals and the Conservatives.

May 9. First over the Pole. Piloting a Fokker tri-motor monoplane, Lieutenant Commander Richard E. Byrd and Chief Aviation Pilot Floyd Bennett become the first men to fly over the North Pole. Their roundtrip flight from Spitzbergen lasts 15$^{1}/_{2}$ hours.

August 27. A flare-up of fighting in Nicaragua leads to the landing of 200 seamen and marines from the cruiser *Galveston* (C 17) to maintain a neutral zone around Bluefields. This force is subsequently relieved by detachments from the cruiser *Rochester* (ACR 2) (October 31) and *Denver* (C 14) (November 30).

October 10. A detachment of seamen and marines from the cruiser *Denver* (C 14) lands at Corinto, Nicaragua, to preserve order during a conference between warring Liberal and Conservative leaders. The meeting proves unproductive.

October 20. For the second time, a rash of robberies prompts the president to assign marine detachments to guard the U.S. mails.

October 22. The first fleet exercise involving dive-bombing is held when a squadron of planes delivers a simulated surprise attack on the Pacific fleet as it stands out from San Pedro, California. The tactic is deemed highly satisfactory.

November 12. A detachment of 125 marines is landed from the transport *Gold Star* to protect American interests at Chingwangtao, China.

1927

January 6.   A marine detachment landed from the cruiser *Galveston* (C 17) reestablishes the U.S. Legation Guard at Managua, Nicaragua.

January 10.   The 2nd Battalion, Fifth Marines, lands to preserve order at Bluefields, Nicaragua. On January 18, all except one company proceed to Managua.

February 9.   A battalion of marines is landed to protect the International Settlement at Shanghai, China, from the disturbances generated by the Chinese civil war.

February 9.   Rear Admiral Julian L. Latimer, commander of the Special Services Squadron operating off the coast of Nicaragua, orders the marines to take control of the Corinto-Managua railway to prevent it from being disrupted by the civil war. This action is accomplished by detachments from the cruisers *Galveston* (C 17), *Milwaukee* (C 21), and *Raleigh* (CL 7).

February 21.   A battalion of 200 marines from the battleships *Arkansas* (BB 33), *Florida* (BB 30), and *Texas* (BB 35) reaches Nicaragua aboard the cruiser *Trenton* (CL 11) to guard the railway towns of Chinandega and León.

March 7.   The remainder of the Fifth Marine Regiment and the headquarters of the 2nd Marine Brigade land at Corinto, Nicaragua. Marine Observation Squadron 1 arrived on February 28.

March 16.   **China marines.** The Fourth Marine Regiment lands at Shanghai, China, to reinforce the battalion garrisoning the International Settlement. The regiment will remain there until 1941.

May 2.   The Sixth Marine Regiment lands at Shanghai, China, and is combined with the forces already present to form the 3rd Marine Brigade under Brigadier General Smedley D. Butler.

May 4.   **Peace of Tipitapa.** Former secretary of state (and future secretary of war) Henry L. Stimson negotiates a peace between the Nicaraguan Liberal and Conservative parties. Under its terms, both factions are to lay down their arms, and the existing Conservative government will remain in office until American-supervised elections are held in 1928. In the meantime, U.S. marines will be responsible for maintaining order and training a national constabulary, the *Guardia Nacional*.

May 16.   More than 200 Nicaraguan bandits attack the railway town of La Paz Centro, garrisoned by a detachment of marines under Captain Richard B. Buchanan.

The raiders are driven off after an action in which 14 of them and 2 marines, including Buchanan, are killed. He is the first marine officer to die in the Second Nicaraguan Campaign.

June 30–August 4.   **Geneva Naval Conference.** The United States, Great Britain, and Japan meet in an attempt to establish limitations on types of warships—principally cruisers—not covered by the Washington Naval Treaty. No agreement can be reached.

July 16.   **Action at Ocotal.** Augusto C. Sandino, a minor Nicaraguan Liberal leader, has refused to accept the terms of the Treaty of Tipitapa. At 1:15 A.M. on this date he leads a band of 800 rebels to attack a detachment of 37 marines and 47 *guardias* under Captain Gilbert D. Hatfield garrisoning Ocotal, the capital of Nueva Segovia Province. The marines hold out until daylight, when the Sandinistas are dispersed by five DH-4s led by Major Ross E. Rowell, the commander of Marine Observation Squadron 1, in the first actual dive-bombing attack in history. Approximately 300 rebels and 1 marine are killed.

August 28.   **Kellogg-Briand Pact.** Fifteen nations, including the United States, sign the Pact of Paris, renouncing recourse to arms as an instrument of national policy. Eventually almost every nation in the world subscribes. There are no enforcement provisions.

September 19.   **Action at Telpaneca.** A garrison of 21 marines and 25 Nicaraguan *guardias* under *Guardia* Captain (marine first lieutenant) Herbert S. Keimling at the village of Telpaneca, 10 miles from Ocotal, is attacked by Sandinistas in the early morning hours. The enemy withdraws at dawn, having suffered 50 casualties to the defenders' 3.

October 10.   A marine patrol advancing from Jicaro, Nicaragua, under the command of First Lieutenant George J. O'Shea, to rescue the pilot and co-pilot of a DH-4 that had crashed the previous day, is ambushed by Sandinistas and compelled to withdraw. The fliers are captured and killed.

October 26–28.   Two marine patrols searching for the downed aircraft (which is finally found) are heavily engaged by Sandinistas near Sapotillal Ridge.

November 14.   Rear Admiral Charles Frederick Hughes becomes the fourth chief of naval operations.

November 16.   The carrier *Saratoga* (CV 3) is commissioned.

December 14.   The carrier *Lexington* (CV 2) is commissioned.

December 17.   While running submerged off Provincetown, Massachusetts, the submarine *S-4* (SS 109) sinks with the loss of 39 lives after being struck by the coast guard cutter *Paulding*.

December 30–January 8, 1928.   **Actions around Quilali.** In November, a marine reconnaissance flight locates Sandino's headquarters, a fortified mountaintop called El Chipote, near Sapotillal Ridge, Nicaragua, 26 miles from the Honduran border. On December 19, two marine columns—one of 115 men under Captain Richard Livingstone from Jinotega, the other of 65 men under First Lieutenant Merton A. Richal from Telpaneca—are sent to establish a base at Quilali and push on to take Chipote. Sandino, who is believed to have 300–500 men, actually has around 1,000. Both columns, heavily engaged on December 30–31, are besieged in Quilali on January 1, having had 8 men killed and 30 wounded, including both column commanders. Between January 6–8, 1928, Lieutenant Christian F. Schilt makes 10 flights to an emergency airfield laid out at Quilali, bringing provisions and evacuating the most seriously wounded. The combined columns then withdraw. Schilt is awarded the Medal of Honor.

1928

January 14.   In Nicaragua, Sandino's headquarters at El Chipote is bombed and strafed by a flight of four planes of Marine Observation Squadron 7 (VO-7M) led by Major Ross E. Rowell.

January 26.   **Capture of El Chipote.** Marine columns advancing from San Albino under Major Archibald Young occupy and destroy Sandino's base at El Chipote. No significant resistance is encountered.

February 27.   A packtrain escorted by 35 marines led by First Lieutenant Edward F. O'Day is ambushed by 600 Sandinistas near Bromaderos, Nicaragua. The marines fight off repeated attacks and are relieved the next day.

May 13.   A column of marines engages the Sandinistas at the Cua River, northeast of Santa Cruz, Nicaragua.

June 16.   Rear Admiral Samuel S. Robison becomes the 28th superintendent of the Naval Academy.

August 7.   **Coco River Patrol.** Late in July, Captain Merritt A. ("Red Mike") Edson, USMC, starts up the Coco River with 49 marines in native dugouts to penetrate the jungle highlands of northern Nicaragua, to which Sandino has withdrawn. On this date Edson's men defeat a body of 60 rebels who attempt to ambush them 60 miles above Bocay. Sandino's

A marine mounted patrol in Nicaragua. *U.S. Naval Institute Collection.*

base camp near Poteca is captured without opposition 10 days later.

November.   Free elections, supervised by 1,500 seamen and marines under the direction of army Brigadier General Frank R. McCoy, are held in Nicaragua. The Liberal candidate, General José M. Moncada, is elected president.

1929

January 19.   The 3rd Marine Brigade is disbanded at Tientsin, China, and all units except the Fourth Marines and the Peking legation guard are withdrawn from the country.

January 23–27.   **Fleet Problem IX.** The carriers *Lexington* (CV 2) and *Saratoga* (CV 3) participate in their first fleet problem. Rear Admiral Joseph M. ("Bull") Reeves, Commander Aircraft Squadrons, Battle Fleet, demonstrates the carrier's potential when he has the *Saratoga* make an end-run around the defending forces (which include the *Lexington*) to launch an air strike that "destroys" the Panama Canal.

March 5.   Charles F. Adams becomes the 44th secretary of the navy.

March 5.   Major General Wendell C. Neville becomes the 14th commandant of the marine corps.

May 8.   **Momsen Lung.** The first test is made of the submarine escape lung developed by Lieutenant Charles D. Momsen, Chief Gunner Clarence L. Tibbals, and Frank Hobson, a civilian engineer.

August 20.   Marine troop strength in Nicaragua is reduced to 2,000. The marine-trained *Guardia Nacional* has been fully committed to action by this time, and Sandino had fled the country in June.

November 28.   Lieutenant Commander Richard E. Byrd becomes the first man to fly over the South Pole. He had been first over the North Pole in 1926.

1930

April 22.   **London Naval Treaty.** The signatories of the Washington Naval Treaty agree to extend its terms for five years. The United States, Great Britain, and Japan also establish a 10:10:7 ratio of cruiser tonnage.

May 15.   **The Narwhal.** The navy's first streamlined submarine, the *Narwhal* (SC 1) is commissioned. She is 371 feet in length, 33 feet abeam, and displaces 2,730 tons.

June 19.   Augusto Sandino, who has returned to Nicaragua from Mexico in May, is wounded in a marine air strike led by Captain B. F. Johnson on a body of 600 rebels. This is the marines' last major action with the Sandinistas.

The *Saratoga* during fleet maneuvers off Guantánamo, Cuba, in March 1930. *Official U.S. Navy photograph.*

July 9.   Major General Ben H. Fuller becomes the 15th commandant of the marine corps.

September 17.   Admiral William V. Pratt becomes the fifth chief of naval operations.

1931

May 1.   Rear Admiral Thomas C. Hart becomes 29th superintendent of the Naval Academy.

September 18.   Following the Mukden incident, in which a Japanese railway line is very slightly damaged by a small explosion, Japan invades and conquers the Chinese portion of Manchuria. There it establishes the puppet Kingdom of Manchukuo, towards which the United States adopts a policy of nonrecognition. This is the first major international act of aggression since World War I.

1932

February 3.   The cruiser *Houston* (CA 30) lands her marine detachment to reinforce the Fourth Marines in protecting American interests at Shanghai, China, following a Japanese attack on the city.

June 30.   The dirigible *Los Angeles* (ZR-3) is decommissioned at the Naval Air Station, Lakehurst, New Jersey, after eight years in service. She was the navy's only rigid airship that did not meet a violent end.

September 20–30.   **Puller's patrol.** *Guardia* Captain (marine first lieutenant) Lewis B. ("Chesty") Puller and *Guardia* Lieutenant (gunnery sergeant) William A. Lee lead 41 men of the Nicaraguan *Guardia Nacional* on a classic patrol into the jungle northeast of Jinotega. During 10 days in the field, the force marches more than 150 miles, fights 4 actions, destroys 30 rebel camps, and kills at least 30 rebels, at a cost of 2 men killed and 4 wounded.

1933

January 2.   The last elements of the 2nd Marine Brigade leave Nicaragua.

March 4.   Claude A. Swanson becomes the 45th secretary of the navy.

April 4.   **Loss of the Akron.** The dirigible *Akron* (ZRS-4), Commander Frank McCord, crashes into the sea in a

Lieutenant Lewis B. "Chesty" Puller *(second from left)*, with Gunnery Sergeant W. A. Lee and two *Guardia* sergeants in Nicaragua in 1931. *Defense Department photo (Marine Corps).*

Rear Admiral William A. Moffett *(facing the camera)* in the control car of the airship *Akron,* with Commander C. E. Rosendahl *(right). Official U.S. Navy photograph.*

storm off Barnegat Light, New Jersey. Of the 76 men aboard, 73 are lost, including the Chief of the Bureau of Aeronautics, Rear Admiral William A. Moffett.

April 12.   **Good Neighbor Policy.** In a speech to the Governing Board of the Pan-American Union in Washington, D.C., newly elected President Franklin D. Roosevelt inaugurates the "Good Neighbor Policy" towards the Latin-American countries. Eight months later the United States formally renounces the right of intervention at the Seventh Inter-American Conference. The result is the end of the marine corps's long involvement in the Caribbean and the termination of its role as colonial infantry.

June 16.   President Franklin D. Roosevelt begins to rebuild the U.S. Navy by allocating for naval construction $238,000,000 from the National Industrial Recovery Act passed on this date. The program calls for 32 vessels to be laid down over a three-year period, including the carriers *Yorktown* (CV 5) and *Enterprise* (CV 6).

June 23.   The dirigible *Macon* (ZRS-5) is commissioned. She is the last airship of her type to be built for the U.S. Navy.

July 1.   Admiral William H. Standley becomes the sixth chief of naval operations.

October 28.   The development of the PBY Catalina flying boat, a workhorse of naval aviation in World War II, is begun by the award of a contract to the Consolidated Aircraft Company.

December 7.   The Fleet Marine Force is established.

1934

January.   **Tentative Manual for Landing Operations.** On November 14, 1933, Major General John H. Russell, acting commandant of the marine corps, suspended classes at the officers' schools and set the students to work to develop "rules and doctrines for landing operations." The *Tentative Manual,* based in part on a Joint Army-Navy Board study of *Joint Overseas Operations* and unpublished marine corps material, is completed this month. The concepts and procedures it sets forth, refined by subsequent training exercises, provide the foundation for the unparalleled amphibious capability that the corps will demonstrate in World War II.

January.   The marine detachment from the gunboat *Tulsa* (PG 22) is landed to protect the American consulate at Foochow, China, until Nationalist troops can restore order.

February 22.   In Nicaragua the marines' old adversary, Augusto Sandino, is executed by General Anastasio Somoza, commander of the *Guardia Nacional.*

March 1.   Major General John H. Russell, Jr., becomes 16th commandant of the marine corps.

March 27.   **Vinson-Trammel Act.** Representative Carl Vinson, Chairman of the House Naval Affairs Committee, co-sponsors legislation that authorizes the navy to be built up to the limits allowed by the Washington and London naval treaties over a period of eight years. Among the construction that immediately results is the carrier *Wasp* (CV 7).

June 4.   The first U.S. naval vessel built as a carrier from the keel up, the 14,500-ton *Ranger* (CV 4), is commissioned.

June 18.   Rear Admiral David F. Sellers becomes 30th superintendent of the Naval Academy.

August 15.   The last elements of the 1st Marine Brigade withdraw from Haiti, ending an occupation of 19 years.

November 18.   Development of the Dauntless dive bombers extensively used in World War II is initiated by the award of a contract to the Northrop Corporation.

1935

February 12.   **Loss of the Macon.** The dirigible *Macon* (ZRS-5), Commander Herbert V. Wiley, goes down in the sea off Point Sur, California, with the loss of two lives. This disaster ends the navy's operation of rigid airships.

July 30.   Lieutenant Frank Akers makes the first blind landing on a carrier, flying an OJ-2 observation plane aboard the *Langley* (CV 1).

The airship *Macon* over Manhattan. *Official U.S. Navy photograph.*

August 31. **Neutrality Acts.** As Japanese aggression in Asia and the rearmament of National Socialist Germany raise the specter of another great war, the U.S. Congress passes legislation intended to avert a recurrence of the circumstances that are believed to have led to America's involvement in the last one. On this date, it outlaws the export of arms and ammunition to any belligerent nation. Subsequent neutrality acts prohibit Americans from loaning money to belligerents (1936), traveling on vessels belonging to belligerents, and selling goods of any kind to them on other than a "cash and carry" basis (1937).

December 9. **Second London Conference.** A second naval disarmament conference between the United States, Great Britain, Japan, France, and Italy convenes at London to renegotiate the agreements reached at Washington in 1922 and London in 1930. It is a failure. Japan withdraws when the United States rejects her claim to parity; Italy remains, but refuses to sign the final agreement; and the treaty concluded between the United States, Great Britain, and France on March 25, 1936, contains so many contingency clauses that it is meaningless. The era of naval arms limitations has ended.

1936

March 25. The London Naval Agreement is signed. (For details, see December 9, 1935.)

September 18. A small navy squadron commanded by Rear Admiral Arthur P. Fairfield is sent to evacuate American citizens from Spain, at the time convulsed by an exceptionally ferocious civil war.

December 1. Major General Thomas Holcombe becomes 17th commandant of the marine corps.

1937

January 2. Admiral William D. Leahy becomes the seventh chief of naval operations.

July 7. **War in the Far East.** Japan invades China proper, beginning a conflict that will flow into World War II.

September 30. The carrier *Yorktown* (CV 5) is commissioned.

December 12. **Panay Incident.** The Yangtze River gunboat *Panay* (PR 5), Lieutenant Commander James J. Hughes, is attacked and sunk by low-flying Japanese aircraft near Nanking, China, despite her prominently displayed American markings. Two crewmen are killed and 43 wounded. Japan apologizes for the attack, which it calls an unfortunate error, and pays a large indemnity.

1938

February 1. Rear Admiral Wilson Brown becomes 31st superintendent of the Naval Academy.

The Yangtze River gunboat *Panay*. *U.S. Naval Institute Collection.*

April.   **Fleet Problem XIX.** In the course of this exercise, the carrier *Saratoga* (CV 3) launches a surprise attack on the fleet base at Pearl Harbor, foreshadowing the Japanese attack of December 1941.

May 12.   The carrier *Enterprise* (CV 6) is commissioned.

May 17.   The Navy Expansion Act authorizes a significant increase in the strength of the fleet and the procurement of 3,000 aircraft. Among the ships built as a result of this legislation is the carrier *Essex* (CV 9).

1939

May 23.   **The Squalus.** The submarine *Squalus* (SS 192), Lieutenant O. F. Naquin, sinks during a practice dive off Portsmouth, New Hampshire. Of her 85 crewmen, 59 are rescued by means of a diving bell. Raised in difficult salvage operations directed by Rear Admiral Ernest J. King, she is renamed the *Sailfish* and serves with distinction in World War II.

June 11–13.   Exercises conducted by the carrier *Saratoga* (CV 3) and the oiler *Kanawaha* (AO 1) off the west coast demonstrate the feasibility of underway replenishment. This technique, pioneered by the U.S. Navy, will prove to be of inestimable value during World War II.

July 7.   The Lighthouse Bureau is absorbed by the U.S. Coast Guard.

August 1.   Admiral Harold R. Stark becomes the eighth chief of naval operations.

September 1.   **Beginning of World War II.** Germany invades Poland. Two days later, Britain and France declare war on Germany.

September 5.   **Neutrality Patrol.** President Roosevelt proclaims American neutrality and directs the chief of naval operations, Admiral Harold R. Stark, to establish a Neutrality Patrol of sea and air units to prevent belligerent acts in U.S. waters.

September 8.   The existence of a "Limited National Emergency" is declared by President Roosevelt.

September 21.   The president asks Congress to repeal the neutrality laws prohibiting the sale of arms and ammunition to warring nations on a cash-and-carry basis. As a consolation for isolationist opinion, he also requests authority to prohibit American ships from entering "danger zones," to be designated according to circumstances, where they are likely to be attacked.

October 2.   **Act of Panama.** The Congress of American States, meeting at Panama, establishes a "neutral zone" extending 300 miles from the coast of the Americas, in which belligerent forces are not to conduct hostilities. The area from Maine to Trinidad will be patrolled by the U.S. Navy.

November 4.   **Neutrality Act of 1939.** Congress accedes to the president's request of September 21. He immediately declares the waters surrounding the British Isles to be a danger zone.

1940

January 2.   Charles Edison becomes the 46th secretary of the navy.

April 25.   The carrier *Wasp* (CV 7) is commissioned.

May 16.   President Roosevelt asks Congress to appropriate $1.18 billion for national defense.

May 17.   The president announces that 35 mothballed World War I destroyers are to be recommissioned.

June 14.   The Naval Expansion Act of 1940 is signed by President Roosevelt, authorizing an 11 percent increase in the strength of the fleet.

June 14.   **Fall of France.** The German Army enters Paris. The defeat of France, since 1918 regarded as the world's premier military power, probably does more than any other single event to convince American leaders that the United States must prepare to enter the war.

June 17.   **Two-ocean navy.** Admiral Harold R. Stark, the chief of naval operations, appears before Congress to request funds to build a two-ocean navy: $4 billion, which will more than double the 1,250,000 tons of the existing combat fleet, and 15,000 naval aircraft. Congress approves the appropriation, and President Roosevelt signs the new Naval Expansion Act into law on July 19.

June 20.   The Bureau of Construction and Repair and the Bureau of Engineering are combined to form the Bureau of Ships, and the office of under secretary of the navy is created.

June 25.   The Naval Construction Corps is merged into the navy line, and its members given "engineering duty only" status.

July 2.   **Export Control Act.** Congress grants the president authority to control the export of war materials and related commodities. Three days later he prohibits the sale of such goods to Japan.

July 11.   Frank Knox becomes 47th secretary of the navy.

September 2.   **Destroyers for bases deal.** President Roosevelt and Prime Minister Winston Churchill conclude an agreement whereby 50 World War I destroyers, urgently needed by Britain to fight German U-boats in the Battle of the Atlantic, will be transferred to the Royal Navy in exchange for 99-year leases to British bases in the West Indies, Bermuda, and Newfoundland.

September 16.   With the signing of the Selective Training and Service Act, the president establishes the first peacetime draft in American history.

September 27.   **Tripartite Pact.** Japan concludes an alliance with Germany and Italy.

1941

February 1.   The U.S. Fleet is divided into the Atlantic and Pacific Fleets, and the 1st and 2nd Marine Brigades are expanded into divisions.

February 1.   Rear Admiral Russell Willson becomes 32nd superintendent of the Naval Academy.

March 11.   **Lend-Lease.** Congress relaxes the provisions of the Neutrality Act of 1939 to permit the Allied Powers, which have run short of cash, to obtain war materials on credit or loan.

March 27.   **ABC-1 Staff Agreement.** In Washington, D.C., naval and military representatives of the United States and Great Britain sign an agreement establishing the basis of Anglo-American cooperation in the event the United States enters the war. Its key provisions are that: (1) both countries will concentrate their war efforts on the defeat of Germany, deemed the most dangerous of the Axis Powers; (2) the British and American chiefs of staff will work together as the combined chiefs of staff; and (3) the U.S. Atlantic Fleet will begin assisting the Royal Navy in Atlantic convoy escort as soon as it is able. The latter provision is effective immediately.

April 9.   The battleship *North Carolina* (BB 55) is commissioned. She is the first American battleship to enter service since the *West Virginia* (BB 48) in 1923.

April 10.   The destroyer *Niblack* (DD 424), Lieutenant Commander E. R. Durgin, depth-charges a German U-boat while rescuing the crew of a torpedoed Dutch freighter. This is the first hostile action taken by an American naval vessel against the Axis Powers.

May 15.   The battleship *Washington* (BB 56) is commissioned.

May 21.   The freighter *Robin Moore,* torpedoed and sunk by a German U-boat in the South Atlantic, becomes the first American merchantman lost in World War II.

May 27.   President Roosevelt proclaims a state of "Unlimited National Emergency."

May 27.   **Destruction of the Bismarck.** On May 26, an American officer, Ensign Leonard B. Smith, flying as co-pilot in a PBY Catalina on loan to the Royal Navy, sights the German battleship *Bismarck* making for the coast of France. The next day another American officer, Lieutenant Commander Joseph H. Wellings, returning to the United States as a passenger on the British battleship *Rodney,* is present at the action in which the *Bismarck* is sunk.

June 12.   The U.S. Naval Reserve is mobilized.

June 20.   The submarine *O-9* (SS 70) sinks with the loss of all hands (33 men) in a test dive off Portsmouth, New Hampshire.

The battleship *North Carolina. U.S. Naval Institute Collection.*

July 1.   **Sea Frontiers.** The American coastline is divided into six "sea frontiers" whose commanders will be responsible for convoy escort, antisubmarine warfare, and patrols in their designated areas. Two additional frontiers are established for Hawaii and the Philippines.

July 7.   Following agreement with the government of Iceland, U.S. naval forces assume responsibility for the defense of that country. Marines are landed at Reykjavik.

July 24.   Japanese troops move into French Indochina.

July 26.   **The last straw.** In response to the occupation of Indochina, President Roosevelt freezes Japanese assets in the United States and halts the sale of oil to Japan. Its utter dependence on imported oil is Japan's Achilles heel. The president's action confronts the Japanese with the necessity of either reaching an accommodation with the United States or striking out to obtain oil fields of their own by the conquest of the European colonies in Southeast Asia.

July 30.   The Yangtze River gunboat *Tutuila* (PG 44) is attacked by Japanese planes at Chungking, China. A day later, Japan apologizes for the incident.

August 9–12.   **Argentia conference.** President Roosevelt and British Prime Minister Churchill meet secretly at Placentia Bay, Argentia, Newfoundland. The president travels on the cruiser *Augusta* (CA 31), the prime minister on the battleship *Prince of Wales*. It is at this, their first meeting, that the two leaders agree on the principles set forth in the Atlantic Charter.

September 4.   **Greer incident.** Patrolling south of Iceland, the destroyer *Greer* (DD 145), Lieutenant Commander L. H. Frost, is attacked by the *U-652*. The submarine's torpedoes miss, whereupon the *Greer* drops depth charges, also without effect.

September 11.   **"Shoot on sight."** Following the *Greer* incident, President Roosevelt orders naval vessels to attack any ship that threatens American shipping or foreign shipping under American escort.

September 16.   **Beginning of convey escort.** In accordance with the provisions of the ABC-1 Staff Agreement, the U.S. Navy joins the Royal Canadian Navy in escorting North Atlantic convoys to and from a Mid-Ocean Meeting Point (MOMP) with the Royal Navy.

September 27.   **Liberty ships.** The first Liberty ship, the *Patrick Henry*, is launched. These vessels and the Victory ships that follow in 1943 are built to replace the merchantmen sunk by Axis submarines.

October 2.   After almost two months of consideration, President Roosevelt rejects Japanese Prime Minister

The destroyer *Reuben James*. *U.S. Naval Institute Collection.*

Prince Fuminaro Konoye's request for a summit conference. Konoye, who had hoped to avoid war, is then replaced by bellicose General Hideki Tojo.

October 17.   **Kearny incident.** The destroyer *Kearny* (DD 432), Lieutenant Commander A. L. Danis, is torpedoed but not sunk by a U-boat while patrolling south of Greenland. Eleven of her company are killed.

October 20.   The carrier *Hornet* (CV 8) is commissioned under the command of Captain Marc A. Mitscher.

October 30.   The oiler *Salinas* (AO 19) is torpedoed in mid-Atlantic, but reaches port safely. There are no casualties.

October 31.   **Sinking of the Reuben James.** The destroyer *Reuben James* (DD 245), Lieutenant Commander H. L. Edwards, is torpedoed and sunk with the loss of 115 lives by the *U-562* while escorting a convoy from Halifax, Nova Scotia. She is the first U.S. naval vessel destroyed by the Axis Powers.

November 1.   The coast guard is placed under naval control for the duration of the National Emergency.

November 6.   **Odenwald incident.** The German blockade runner *Odenwald* is captured by the cruiser *Omaha* (CL 4) and destroyer *Somers* (DD 381) in the central Atlantic. She was disguised as the American merchantman *Willmoto*.

November 17.   Congress authorizes the arming of U.S. merchant ships.

November 20.   Japanese Special Envoy Saburo Kurusu presents U.S. Secretary of State Cordell Hull with Japan's final negotiating program. Agreement to its terms would concede Japan a free hand in the Far East. It is rejected.

November 26.   Secretary of State Hull hands Japanese Ambassador Kichisaburo Nomura the American counterproposal for a general settlement in the Far East. Among other things, it calls for Japan to withdraw from both China and Indochina. There is little expectation that the Japanese will accept these terms, nor do they.

November 26.   A Japanese strike force consisting of six carriers, two battleships, three cruisers, nine destroyers, and three fleet submarines, plus tankers, secretly sails from the Kurile Islands under the command of Vice Admiral Chuichi Nagumo. Unless an agreement can be reached with the United States by December 5, it is to attack the Pacific Fleet at Pearl Harbor.

November 27.   The chief of naval operations, Admiral Harold R. Stark, sends a "war warning" message to the commanders of the Atlantic, Pacific, and Asiatic fleets.

November 27–28.   The Fourth Marine Regiment is withdrawn from Shanghai after 14 years' service in China.

December 7.   **Pearl Harbor.** At 7:55 A.M. Sunday morning the Pacific Fleet is attacked while at anchor at Pearl Harbor by 191 Japanese torpedo-bombers, dive-bombers, high-altitude bombers, and fighters from the carriers *Akagi, Hiryu, Kaga, Shokaku, Soryu,* and *Zuikaku* of Vice Admiral Chuichi Nagumo's strike force. The attackers withdraw at 8:25 A.M., but are followed by a second wave of 170 planes at 8:40 A.M. For-

tunately, all three of the Pacific Fleet carriers—the *Lexington* (CV 2), *Saratoga* (CV 3), and *Enterprise* (CV 6)—are elsewhere, and, overlooking the strategically vital oil tank farm, repair facilities, and submarine pens, the Japanese concentrate on the battleships anchored off Ford Island. The *Arizona* (BB 39) is destroyed by a bomb that detonates her forward magazine, killing 1,103 of 1,400 men aboard. The *Oklahoma* (BB 37) capsizes due to flooding, with the loss of 415 of her 1,354 officers and men; and the *California* (BB 44) is heavily damaged and settles to her superstructure, as do the *West Virginia* (BB 48) and the *Nevada* (BB 36)—the only battleship to get under way. The *Maryland* (BB 46), *Pennsylvania* (BB 38), and *Tennessee* (BB 43) are damaged, but can steam to the West Coast under their own power for repairs three weeks later. More than half of the army, navy, and marine planes on airfields ashore are also destroyed. All except 29 of the Japanese aircraft involved return to their carriers. Altogether, 2,403 American servicemen are killed and 1,178 wounded, with the navy suffering by far the greatest losses. This "day of infamy," as President Roosevelt describes it, unites the American people in the determination to defeat Japan.

December 8.   At Shanghai, China, the Yangtze River gunboat *Wake* (PG 43) surrenders to the Japanese after an attempt to scuttle her fails. She is the only U.S. naval vessel to strike her flag in World War II.

The beginning of the attack on Pearl Harbor, photographed from a Japanese aircraft. Moored off the far side of Ford Island are *(from left to right)* the battleship *Nevada*, the battleship *Arizona* (with the repair ship *Vestal* outboard), the battleships *Tennessee* and *West Virginia* (outboard), *Maryland* and *Oklahoma* (outboard), the fleet oiler *Neosho*, and the battleship *California*. The *Oklahoma* has just taken a torpedo hit, probably from the plane banking above the *Neosho*. *Courtesy National Archives.*

December 10.   Off the coast of Malaya, Japanese aircraft sink the British battleship *Prince of Wales* and battle-cruiser *Repulse.*

December 10.   Japanese forces occupy Guam.

December 10.   Japanese forces land on the Philippine island of Luzon.

December 10.   The marine detachments at Peking and Tientsin, China, approximately 500 strong, are taken prisoner by the Japanese.

December 11.   Germany and Italy declare war on the United States.

December 11.   **Defense of Wake Island.** The Japanese suffer their first reverse of the war when a sea-borne assault on Wake Island is repulsed by the 388 officers and men of Major James P. Devereux's 1st Defense Battalion and the pilots of Major Paul A. Putnam's Marine Fighting Squadron (VMF) 211. Two destroyers, the first significant Japanese surface ships lost in the war, are sunk: the *Hayate* by the garrison's 5-inch guns and the *Kisaragi* by air attack; a transport is also destroyed, and a light cruiser, two destroyers, and a freighter are damaged.

December 15–23.   **Wake relief force.** A task force commanded by Rear Admiral Frank Jack Fletcher is sent to reinforce the garrison of Wake Island. Built around the carrier *Saratoga* (CV 3), it includes three heavy cruisers, nine destroyers, and the 12-knot oiler *Neches* (AO 5). Unfortunately, the *Neches* is allowed to dictate the force's speed, and the day of December 22 is spent refueling on a course that brings the force no closer to the island.

December 17.   Admiral Husband E. Kimmel is relieved as commander-in-chief, Pacific Fleet.

December 20.   Admiral Ernest J. King is appointed commander-in-chief, U.S. Fleet.

December 23.   **Fall of Wake Island.** After their repulse on December 11, the Japanese bomb the island daily. The marines' last 2 aircraft are destroyed engaging 39 enemy carrier planes on December 22. Before dawn the next day two Japanese patrol craft ground themselves to land approximately 1,000 men of the Special Naval Landing Force. After several hours of increasingly hopeless fighting Commander Winfield Scott Cunningham, the island commander, authorizes Major Devereux to surrender. Admiral Fletcher's relief force, which has reached a point 425 miles from the island, is recalled.

December 31.   Admiral Chester W. Nimitz assumes command of the Pacific Fleet.

Admiral Chester W. Nimitz. *Courtesy National Archives.*

1942

January 2.   The Philippine capital of Manila and the Cavite Naval Base are occupied by the Japanese.

January 3.   **ABDA.** A unified American, British, Dutch, Australian command, formally activated on January 15, is established under General Sir Archibald P. Wavell for the defense of the southwest Pacific. Admiral Thomas C. Hart, CO of the U.S. Asiatic Fleet, is made naval commander. At this time the Allies still hope to stop the Japanese at the "Malay barrier" extending from Malaya through the Netherlands East Indies, a hope that will be cruelly disappointed.

January 9.   On Luzon, the first strong Japanese attack on the American and Filipino forces holding the Bataan Peninsula is repulsed.

January 11.   The Japanese invade the Netherlands East Indies.

January 12.   Congress increases the authorized strength of the navy to 500,000 men.

January 14.   **Arcadia.** The first Washington Conference (Arcadia), which had begun on December 23, comes to an end. During it, President Roosevelt, Prime Minister Churchill, and key members of their staffs discussed the joint conduct of the war into which the United States had just been plunged. Although affirming the "Germany first" priority established at the

ABC-1 Staff Conference (see March 27, 1941), it is agreed that Australia and the bases along its line of communications with the United States—New Caledonia, the Fijis, and American Samoa—must be held against Japan. The United States assumes the responsibility of conducting the war in the Pacific. Other important decisions reached are to mount an Anglo-American invasion of French North Africa in 1942 and to set up a combined chiefs of staff committee, anticipated in the ABC-1 accords, through which the joint chiefs of staff and the British chiefs of staff will concert the strategy of the Allied war effort.

January 20.   Off Darwin, Australia, the destroyer *Edsall* (DD 219), Lieutenant Joshua J. Nix, cooperates with three Royal Australian Navy corvettes to sink the *I-124*. The latter is the first Japanese submarine in whose destruction American surface forces play a part.

January 20.   On patrol in the poorly charted waters of the Makassar Strait, the submarine *S-36* (SS 141), Lieutenant John S. McKnight, Jr., runs aground and has to be scuttled. Dutch vessels rescue her crew.

January 24.   **Battle of Balikpapan.** In the first surface action fought by U.S. naval forces since the Spanish-American War, a division of four elderly destroyers under Commander Paul Talbot—the *John D. Ford* (DD 228) (flag), *Parrott* (DD 218), *Paul Jones* (DD 230), and *Pope* (DD 225)—surprise a Japanese invasion force off Balikpapan, Borneo, and sink 4 of 12 transports and a patrol boat in a night torpedo attack. None of the destroyers is seriously damaged. This engagement is also known as the Battle of the Makassar Strait.

January 24.   The submarine *S-26* (SS 131) is rammed and sunk by *PC-460* in the Gulf of Panama. Only three men survive.

January 27.   The submarine *Gudgeon* (SS 211), Lieutenant

Commander E. H. ("Joe") Grenfell, sinks the Japanese submarine *I-173* west of Midway Atoll. Of the 130 Japanese fleet submarines sunk by 1945, at least 23 will be destroyed by their American counterparts.

January 31.   Rear Admiral John R. Beardall becomes the 33rd superintendent of the U.S. Naval Academy.

February 1.   **Raid on the Gilberts and Marshalls.** The first American carrier strikes of the war are made under the command of Vice Admiral William F. ("Bull") Halsey. Task Group 8, formed around the *Enterprise* (CV 6), attacks Japanese bases on Kwajalein in the Marshall Islands, while Task Group 17, built around the *Yorktown* (CV 5), hits the Gilberts.

February 3.   The submarine *Trout* (SS 202), Commander Frank W. ("Mike") Fenno, evacuates from Corregidor 20 tons of gold and silver taken from Manila banks. During the opening months of the war, submarines are frequently used as transports to and from the Philippines.

February 4.   An ABDA naval force consisting of the Dutch cruisers *De Ruyter* (flag) and *Tromp*, the American cruisers *Houston* (CA 30) and *Marblehead* (CL 12), and six American and four Dutch destroyers, under the command of Rear Admiral Karel Doorman, Royal Netherlands Navy, is attacked by Japanese aircraft while attempting to intercept a Japanese invasion fleet off Borneo. The *Marblehead* is so seriously damaged that she must return to the United States; the *Houston* loses her after 8-inch turret; and the *De Ruyter* is also hard hit. Lacking air cover, the ABDA force is compelled to retire.

February 7.   The submarine *Shark* (SS 174), Lieutenant Commander Louis Shane, Jr., is lost in the vicinity of the Moluccas Passage, probably on this date.

February 14.   Dutch and British pressure results in the replacement of Admiral Thomas C. Hart as commander-

The cruiser *Houston* as she appeared in 1935. *Official U.S. Navy photograph.*

in-chief, Allied Naval Forces, Southwest Pacific, by Vice Admiral C. E. L. Helfrich, Royal Netherlands Navy.

February 15.   **Fall of Singapore.** British Lieutenant General Arthur E. Percival surrenders the island and city of Singapore, supposedly "the Gibraltar of the East," and its 64,000 British, Australian, and Indian defenders to a numerically inferior Japanese army commanded by General Tomoyuki Yamashita.

February 19.   The destroyer *Peary* (DD 226), Lieutenant Commander J. M. Bermingham, is sunk in a Japanese air raid on Darwin, Australia.

February 19–20.   **Battle of the Badung Strait.** A confused night action ensues when an ABDA force under Dutch Admiral K. W. F. Doorman—consisting of the Dutch cruisers *De Ruyter*, *Java,* and *Tromp,* one Dutch and six American destroyers, and five Dutch PT boats—attacks a Japanese invasion force that has just landed troops on the island of Bali. Three Japanese destroyers are damaged; the Dutch destroyer is sunk, and the USS *Stewart* (DD 224) is damaged.

February 20.   **Raid on Rabaul.** A task force consisting of the carriers *Lexington* (CV 2) and *Yorktown* (CV 5), seven American cruisers, and four British, one Australian, and 16 American destroyers under the command of Vice Admiral Wilson Brown, is sent to attack the Japanese air and naval base at Rabaul, on New Britain. The raid is canceled when the force is spotted by the Japanese, but the largest air battle to date in the Pacific war develops. Lieutenant Edward H. ("Butch") O'Hare accounts for 5 of the 18 enemy planes destroyed, thus becoming the navy's first ace of World War II and winning the Medal of Honor. Only two American aircraft are lost.

February 23.   The oil refinery at Ellwood, near Santa Barbara, California, is shelled by the Japanese submarine *I-17.*

February 24.   **Wake Island Raid.** Japanese occupation forces are attacked by planes from the carrier *Enterprise* (CV 6) task force under Vice Admiral W. F. Halsey.

February 27.   The *Langley,* the navy's first carrier (CV 1), now redesignated an aviation transport (AV 3), is sunk by Japanese aircraft while ferrying army planes to Tjilatiap, Java.

February 27–28.   **Battle of the Java Sea.** Admiral Karel Doorman, RNN, leads the ABDA Strike Force—five cruisers: the Dutch *De Ruyter* (flag) and *Java,* USS *Houston* (CA 30), HMS *Exeter,* and HMAS *Perth,* and four American, three British, and three Dutch destroyers—on a sortie from Surabaja, Java, in an attempt to intercept two large Japanese invasion forces approaching the island. Instead, at 4:00 P.M. he encounters Rear Admiral Takeo Takagi's support force, consisting of 4 cruisers and 13 destroyers. In the course of an intermittent action lasting more than seven hours, the superiority of the Japanese Long Lance torpedo and the ABDA squadron's lack of spotter aircraft prove decisive. Both Dutch cruisers and three of the destroyers are sunk. Only one Japanese destroyer is damaged. The Malay Barrier has been breached.

February 28.   **Battle of the Sunda Strait.** After nightfall, the cruisers *Houston* (CA 30), Captain Albert H. Rooks, and HMAS *Perth,* Captain H. M. L. Waller, RAN, survivors of the Battle of the Java Sea proceeding in company towards the Sunda Strait on the western end of the island of Java, encounter a Japanese landing in progress in Banten Bay. Three enemy transports are destroyed—two by friendly fire—and three are damaged in the melee before the cruisers are sunk by the Japanese covering force of three cruisers and nine destroyers under Rear Admiral Takeo Kurita.

February 28.   The destroyer *Jacob Jones* (DD 130), Lieutenant Commander H. D. Black, Jr., is sunk with almost all hands by a German U-boat off the Delaware Capes.

March 1.   Three other survivors of the Java Sea, the British cruiser *Exeter* and the destroyers USS *Pope* (DD 225), Lieutenant Commander W. C. Blinn, and HMS *Encounter,* are sunk by Japanese air and surface forces off Surabaja, Java. The destroyer *Edsall* (DD 219), Lieutenant J. J. Nix, is sunk in a separate action.

March 1.   The destroyer *Pillsbury* (DD 227), Lieutenant Commander H. C. Pound, gunboat *Asheville* (PG 21), and the Australian gunboat *Yarra* are destroyed off the coast of Java in a surface action with vastly superior Japanese forces.

March 1.   The German *U-656* is destroyed by aircraft of Patrol Wing 82 south of Newfoundland. She is the U.S. Navy's first U-boat kill of the war.

March 2.   The submarine *Perch* (SS 176), Lieutenant Commander David A. Hurt, is depth-charged and badly damaged by Japanese destroyers while on patrol off Surabaja, Netherlands East Indies. The next day she is forced to scuttle when a cruiser-destroyer group catches her limping along on the surface, unable to submerge. The Japanese rescue her crew.

March 4.   **Marcus Island raid.** Aircraft from Admiral Halsey's *Enterprise* (CV 6) task force strike the Japanese base at Marcus Island, in the central Pacific 800 miles northwest of Wake.

March 8.   The Japanese land forces at Lae and Salamaua on the northeastern coast of New Guinea.

March 10.   The Netherlands East Indies surrenders to the Japanese.

March 10.   **Lae and Salamaua raids.** More than 100 planes from the carriers *Lexington* (CV 2) and *Yorktown* (CV 5) of Vice Admiral Wilson Brown's task force strike Japanese positions on the northern coast of New Guinea.

March 11.   **MacArthur escapes from Corregidor.** General Douglas MacArthur, whom President Roosevelt has personally ordered to leave the Philippines, escapes from Corregidor with his family and selected staff members aboard the four boats of Lieutenant John D. Bulkeley's Motor Torpedo Boat Squadron 3. Eluding Japanese naval patrols, MacArthur reaches Mindanao on March 14 and continues his journey by air to Darwin, Australia, on March 17.

March 12.   The duties of chief of naval operations and commander-in-chief, U.S. Fleet, are combined under Admiral Ernest J. King, although he does not officially relieve Admiral Stark as CNO until March 26.

March 17.   General MacArthur is appointed Allied Supreme Commander in the Southwest Pacific.

Admiral Ernest J. King. *Official U.S. Navy photograph.*

March 20.   The battleship *South Dakota* (BB 57), is commissioned.

March 25.   **Operations in European waters.** Task Force 39 is sent to reinforce the Royal Navy in European waters, where the British are temporarily weakened by the dispatch of an expedition to Madagascar. Originally commanded by Rear Admiral John W. Wilcox, Jr., who is lost overboard in mid-Atlantic and replaced by Rear Admiral R. C. Giffen, it consists of the battleship *Washington* (BB 56), carrier *Wasp* (CV 7), heavy cruisers *Tuscaloosa* (CA 37) and *Wichita* (CA 45), and a squadron of destroyers. In April and May this force, less the *Wasp*, will join the British Home Fleet in escorting convoys to Russia.

March 30.   To clarify command relations, the Pacific theater is divided into two zones: the Pacific Ocean Area, under Admiral Chester W. Nimitz, and the Southwest Pacific Area, under General Douglas MacArthur.

April 4–9.   **Indian Ocean raid.** A Japanese task force formed around five Pearl Harbor carriers under the command of Vice Admiral Chuichi Nagumo attacks Admiral Sir James Somerville's British Far Eastern Fleet in the Bay of Bengal, sinking the light carrier *Hermes*, cruisers *Cornwall* and *Dorsetshire*, and several smaller vessels.

April 9.   American and Filipino troops defending the Bataan Peninsula surrender to the Japanese. The garrison of Corregidor, "The Rock" in Manila Bay, continues to fight on.

April 18.   **Halsey-Doolittle Raid.** At 8:24 A.M., Vice Admiral W. F. Halsey's Task Force 16 launches a very special air raid. Sixteen twin-engined B-25 bombers commanded by Lieutenant Colonel James H. Doolittle, USA, take off from the deck of Captain Marc A. Mitscher's carrier *Hornet* (CV 8) to strike the first blows against the Japanese homeland. Tokyo, Yokohama, Kobe, and Nagoya are bombed. The B-25s fly on to China, where most reach friendly lines, only two crews being captured. The psychological effect of the raid is disproportionate to the relatively minor damage it does. The American people are thrilled that, after so many disasters, their armed forces have begun to hit back; the Japanese navy is deeply chagrined that it has failed to keep the Home Islands safe from attack.

April 20.   **The Wasp in the Mediterranean.** At the request of the Royal Navy, the carrier *Wasp* (CV 7), Captain J. W. Reeves, Jr., is used to stage 58 Spitfire fighters into Malta. The island, lying athwart the supply line to

The Halsey-Doolittle raid: B-25 bombers on the deck of the *Hornet. Official U.S. Navy photograph.*

North Africa, is under siege by the German Luftwaffe. Returning to the Mediterranean with the British carrier *Eagle,* the *Wasp* launches another 47 "Spitties" on May 7. These reinforcements play a vital role in keeping the island's air defense in operation.

April 26.   The destroyer *Sturtevant* (DD 240), Lieutenant Commander C. L. Weigle, goes down in the Florida Keys after running into an American minefield of which no one aboard had been informed.

April 30.   The battleship *Indiana* (BB 58) is commissioned.

May 1.   The submarine *Drum* (SS 228), Commander Robert H. Rice, sinks the 9,000-ton seaplane carrier *Mizuho* off Honshu in the Japanese Home Islands.

May 6.   **Fall of the Philippines.** Lieutenant General Jonathan M. Wainwright surrenders the Philippines to Japanese Lieutenant General Masaharu Homma. Wainwright had intended to surrender only the fortress of Corregidor, in Manila Bay, but Homma insisted on a general capitulation before ceasing to attack on the island. Some garrisons initially ignore Wainwright's order, and it is June 9 before formal resistance ends.

May 7–8.   **Battle of the Coral Sea.** Japanese forces suffer their first strategic defeat of World War II when the Pacific Fleet code-breakers at Honolulu learn of a plan to seize Port Moresby, on the southern coast of New Guinea, through which the Australian forces fighting on that island are supplied, and the island of Tulagi in the Solomons. The Tulagi landing is unopposed, but Rear Admiral Frank Jack Fletcher's Task Force 17, formed around the carriers *Lexington* (CV 2) and *Yorktown* (CV 5), is on hand to intercept the units that enter the Coral Sea—an amphibious force of 12 transports screened by the light carrier *Shoho,* cruisers, and destroyers, and a Carrier Strike Force composed of the fleet carriers *Shokaku* and *Zuikaku* under Vice Admiral Takeo Takagi. The resulting action is the first carrier air battle ever fought. On May 7, planes of the Carrier Strike Force sink the fleet oiler *Neosho* (AO 23), Captain J. S. Phillips, and destroyer *Sims* (DD 409), Lieutenant Commander W. M. Hyman, which they mistake for a carrier and a cruiser, and TF 17s sink the light carrier *Shoho.* On May 8, the Americans damage the *Shokaku,* while a Japanese attack destroys the *Lexington,* Captain Frederick C. Sherman. The *Zuikaku* is ordered to retire, and the Port Moresby Invasion Force, now lacking air defense, is recalled.

The Japanese light carrier *Shoho,* already burning, is hit by an American torpedo bomber during the Battle of the Coral Sea. *Official U.S. Navy photograph.*

Abandon ship: the crew of the *Lexington* going over the side in the Coral Sea. *Official U.S. Navy photograph.*

May 12. The battleship *Massachusetts* (BB 59) is commissioned.

May 13. The Bureau of Navigation is renamed the Bureau of Personnel, its scientific functions having already been transferred to the office of the chief of naval personnel.

June 4–6. **Battle of Midway.** The turning point in the war with Japan comes in the Central Pacific. Admiral Yamamoto launches an operation of ill-advised complexity designed to extend the Japanese defensive perimeter by seizing Midway atoll, 1,100 miles west of Honolulu, thereby preventing a recurrence of the humiliating Halsey-Doolittle Raid. He also believes that an attack on Midway will bring the American carriers out to be destroyed, completing the job begun at Pearl Harbor. Numerically, the Japanese fleet appears to enjoy an insurmountable advantage in every class of vessel, from carriers (8 to 3) and battleships (7 to 0) to destroyers (55 to 33). Much of that advantage is dispelled, however, by the fact that at Pearl Harbor Commander Joseph J. Rochefort's basement code-breakers of the Communications Intelligence Unit have decoded the Japanese battle plans, and are aware, for instance, that the diversionary assault

The Battle of Midway: the *Yorktown* is hit by a Japanese bomber. *Official U.S. Navy photograph.*

The Japanese heavy cruiser *Mikuma* afire and soon to sink, June 6, 1942. *Official U.S. Navy photograph.*

on the Aleutians, to which Yamamoto assigns two light carriers, is indeed a diversion. Thus it is that all three of Admiral Nimitz's carriers are waiting off Midway on June 4—the *Yorktown* (CV 5) in Rear Admiral Frank Jack Fletcher's Task Force 17, the *Enterprise* (CV 6) and *Hornet* (CV 8) in Rear Admiral Raymond A. Spruance's Task Force 16. Fletcher is officer in tactical command. In the course of a day's furious fighting, American carrier planes sink all four fleet carriers of Vice Admiral Chuichi Nagumo's Carrier Strike Force—the *Akagi, Hiyru, Kaga,* and *Soryu.* Aircraft from the *Hiryu,* last of the Japanese carriers to go down, severely damage the *Yorktown,* Captain Elliott Buckmaster, after which Admiral Fletcher transfers command to Admiral Spruance. That evening Spruance declines to pursue the Japanese to the west, apprehending that they might attempt to ambush his carriers in a night surface action, which is exactly what Yamamoto has in mind. The next day Spruance's planes sink the heavy cruiser *Mikuma,* and on June 6, a Japanese submarine sinks the crippled *Yorktown* and the destroyer *Hammann* (DD 412), Commander A. E. True.

June 7.   In the North Pacific, Japanese forces land unopposed on the Aleutian islands of Attu and Kiska.

June 18.   The obsolescent submarine *S-27* (SS 132), Lieutenant Herbert L. Jukes, runs aground off Amchitka Island while on a reconnaissance mission to investigate Japanese activity in the Aleutians. Her crew reaches shore safely and is rescued by PBY flying boats.

June 19–25.   **Second Washington Conference.** Prime Minister Churchill and the British chiefs of staff return to discuss operations in the European theater in 1942. Despite the tentative agreement reached at the Arcadia Conference (see January 14) to invade North Africa in 1942, later General George C. Marshall, U.S. Army chief of staff, promoted the idea of establishing a beachhead in northern France instead. The British unenthusiastically assented in March, but by mid-summer their misgivings have increased. At Washington they advocate postponing the landing in France until 1943 and going ahead with the invasion of North Africa in 1942. No decision is reached, but on July 8, Churchill informs Roosevelt that the British War Cabinet is inflexibly opposed to invading France this year. Roosevelt then sends General Marshall and Admiral King to London to reach an agreement with the British on some joint action in the European theater in 1942. The American chiefs have no choice but to accept the British proposal for invading North Africa.

June 21.   Fort Stevens, Oregon, is shelled by a Japanese submarine.

June 26.   The German government announces the initiation of unrestricted submarine warfare off the American eastern seaboard.

July 20.   Admiral William D. Leahy, former chief of naval operations (1937–1939) and ambassador to Vichy France (1941–1942), is appointed chief of staff to President Roosevelt. He also acts as chairman of the joint chiefs of staff, in which capacity he plays an important role in the formulation of American strategy.

July 21.   **Advance on Port Moresby.** The Japanese land at Buna, on the northeastern coast of New Guinea and launch an advance across the Owen Stanley Mountains on Port Moresby, the objective of the amphibious force that had been turned back at the Battle of the Coral Sea. The Japanese offensive is halted 30 miles short of its goal by Australian and American troops on September 13.

July 30.   **WAVES.** The WAVES (Women Accepted for Volunteer Emergency Service) are established. Lieutenant Commander Mildred H. McAfee receives the first WAVE commission and becomes the new organization's director on August 2.

July 30.   The submarine *Grunion* (SS 216), Lieutenant Commander Mannert L. Abele, is lost on a North Pacific war patrol after being last heard from on this date.

August 4.   The destroyer *Tucker* (DD 374), Lieutenant Commander W. R. Terrell, is lost in an American minefield off Espiritu Santo in the New Hebrides.

August 7.   **Guadalcanal (Operation Watchtower).** Especially in view of the victory at Midway, Admiral King is determined to go over to the offensive in the Pacific. On July 2, the joint chiefs of staff approve his plan of employing Major General Alexander A. Vandegrift's 1st Marine Division, already en route to the Southwest Pacific, to seize Tulagi, where the Japanese are constructing a seaplane base, and nearby islands in the eastern Solomons. Rear Admiral Richmond Kelly Turner commands the amphibious force; Vice Admiral Frank Jack Fletcher, the attack force. Tulagi, the small adjacent islands of Gavutu and Tanambogo, and the much larger island Guadalcanal, on which the landing is unopposed, are secured by the evening of August 9. An airstrip, Henderson Field, becomes fully operational on Guadalcanal on August 17. In the meanwhile, however, the Japanese have won a stunning naval victory at the Battle of Savo Island (described below) and begun moving troops towards Guadalcanal, initiating a contest that will last for six months of the most concentrated combat in the history of the American sea services. During the hours of daylight, American land-based and carrier aircraft control the sea around Guadalcanal, but after darkness falls the Japanese Navy, which possesses a distinct advantage in night fighting at this point in the war, is able to move down "The Slot" through the Central Solomons to Guadalcanal to reinforce and resupply Japanese troops on the island

Admiral William D. Leahy. *Official U.S. Navy photograph.*

and to bombard Henderson Field with such regularity that the marines call these runs the Tokyo Express.

August 8–9.   **Battle of Savo Island.** Vice Admiral Gunichi Mikawa sorties from Rabaul under orders from Admiral Yamamoto to break up the invasion of Guadalcanal with a force consisting of the heavy cruisers *Aoba, Chokai, Furutaka, Kako,* and *Kinugasa,* light cruisers *Tenryu* and *Yubari,* and destroyer *Yunagi.* Entering Ironbottom Sound shortly after midnight unobserved by American picket destroyers, Mikawa inflicts one of the worse defeats in the history of the U.S. Navy, sinking four heavy cruisers—the *Astoria* (CA 34), Captain W. G. Greenman, HMAS *Canberra,* Captain F. E. Getting, RAN, the *Quincy* (CA 39), Captain S. N. Moore, and the *Vincennes* (CA 44), Captain F. L. Riefkohl—without suffering significant damage to a single vessel of his own. Fortunately for his enemies, he then throws away the fruits of victory, leaving the scene without molesting the American amphibious forces that he has just rendered defenseless.

August 9.   The destroyer *Jarvis* (DD 393), Lieutenant Commander W. W. Graham, Jr., damaged by an air attack on the 8th and hit again during the Battle of Savo Island, is sunk by Japanese torpedo planes with the loss of all hands.

August 10.   Off Kavieng, New Ireland, Lieutenant Commander John R. ("Dinty") Moore's antique submarine

A marine patrol on Guadalcanal. *Official U.S. Navy photograph.*

S-44 (SS 155) sinks the Japanese heavy cruiser *Kako,* which is on her way home from the Battle of Savo Island. This cruiser is the first major warship put down by a U.S. submarine.

August 14.   The submarine *S-39* (SS 144), Lieutenant Commander Francis E. Brown, runs aground near Rossel Island on a Pacific patrol. An Australian naval vessel rescues her crew.

August 16.   The battleship *Alabama* (BB 60) is commissioned.

August 17.   **Makin Raid.** Lieutenant Colonel Evans F. Carlson's marine 2nd Raider Battalion ("Carlson's Raiders"), 222 strong, is landed by submarine on the island of Makin in the Gilberts. After destroying the 83-man Japanese garrison, the raiders reembark. The operation boosts morale on the American home front, but also alerts the Japanese of the need to reinforce their garrisons in the islands.

August 20–21.   **Battle of the Tenaru River.** On Guadalcanal the marines repulse the first major Japanese counterattack, destroying an elite regiment, the Ichiki Unit, which had been landed on the night of the 18th.

August 22.   The destroyer *Blue* (DD 387), Commander H. N. Williams, is torpedoed by the Japanese destroyer *Kawakaze* in a night encounter off Guadalcanal and scuttled the next night.

August 23–25.   **Battle of the Eastern Solomons.** Admiral Yamamoto devises a characteristically complicated plan to defeat U.S. naval forces in the Solomons and reinforce Guadalcanal. The Combined Fleet moves south from Truk, in the Carolines, with the heavy carriers *Shokaku* and *Zuikaku,* three battleships, and supporting units to engage the U.S. carriers. At the same time three high-speed transports carrying 1,500 troops set out from the Shortlands, escorted by a cruiser-destroyer force commanded by Rear Admiral Raizo Tanaka and covered by a single-carrier task force formed around the *Ryujo* under Rear Admiral Chuichi Hara. These units are engaged by Vice Admiral Frank Jack Fletcher's Task Force 61, composed of the carriers *Enterprise* (CV 6), *Saratoga* (CV 3), and *Wasp* (CV 7), battleship *North Carolina* (BB 55), plus cruisers and destroyers. The result is an inconclusive American victory. Planes from the *Enterprise* sink the light carrier *Ryujo,* but the "Big E" is then damaged by a strike from the Japanese fleet carriers. U.S. aircraft also turn back the troop convoy, sinking the largest transport and the destroyer *Mutsuki.*

August 25.   A force of 1,500 Japanese troops land at Milne Bay, on the southeastern tip of New Guinea. Counterattacks by Australian infantry and Allied air strikes make the beachhead too hot to hold, however, and on September 5, the Japanese withdraw.

August 28.   The Japanese destroyer *Asagiri*, one of a three-destroyer Tokyo Express carrying reinforcements to Guadalcanal, is sunk off Santa Isabel Island by marine aircraft from Henderson Field.

August 30.   Japanese aircraft sink the fast transport (former destroyer) *Colhoun* (APD 2), Lieutenant Commander G. B. Madden, off Guadalcanal.

September 1.   **Seabees.** The 6th Naval Construction Battalion arrives at Guadalcanal, thereby becoming the first Seabee unit to enter a combat zone. The Seabees, who will perform sterling service throughout the Pacific War, had been organized by Rear Admiral Ben Moreell, Chief of the Bureau of Yards and Docks, in October 1941.

September 5.   The destroyer transports *Gregory* (APD 3), Lieutenant Commander Harry F. Bauer, and *Little* (APD 4), Lieutenant Commander G. B. Lofberg, are sunk in a night gunnery action with the Japanese destroyers *Hatsuyuki*, *Murakumo*, and *Yudachi* while patrolling off Lunga Point, Guadalcanal.

September 12–14.   **Battle of Bloody Ridge.** The second major attack on the marine positions at Guadalcanal, made by a force of approximately 3,500 men under Major General Seikin Kawaguchi, is beaten off with heavy losses to the Japanese.

September 15.   **Loss of the Wasp.** While screening a troop convoy to Guadalcanal, the carrier *Wasp* (CV 7), Captain Forrest P. Sherman, is torpedoed by the Japanese submarine *I-19*. Efforts to save her are unavailing, and the flaming wreck finally has to be sunk by an escorting destroyer. Of her 2,247 crewmen, 193 are killed and 366 wounded.

September 27.   A gallant little action occurs in the South Atlantic when the Liberty Ship *Stephen Hopkins,* merchant marine Captain Paul Buck, is attacked by the German surface raider *Stier* (Ship 23) and the blockade runner *Tannenfels*. The *Hopkins* has only one 4-inch gun, manned by a naval armed guard under Lieutenant Kenneth M. Willett, USNR, against the raider's six 5.9-inchers, but in the end both ships go down. The *Hopkins*'s 15 survivors reach Brazil after 31 days in a lifeboat.

October 12.   **Battle of Cape Esperance.** A Japanese force of three heavy cruisers and two destroyers under Rear Admiral Aritomo Goto is sent to escort a troop convoy to Guadalcanal and afterwards bombard Henderson Field. A few minutes before midnight it is intercepted by Rear Admiral Norman Scott's Task Force 64, consisting of the heavy cruisers *San Francisco* (CA 38) and

Salt Lake City (CL 25) and light cruisers *Boise* (CL 47) and *Helena* (CL 50), and five destroyers. The Japanese cruiser *Furutake* limps away from the action to sink a few hours later, as does the U.S. destroyer *Duncan* (DD 485), Lieutenant Commander E. B. Taylor.

October 15.   The destroyer *Meredith* (DD 434), Lieutenant Commander Harry E. Hubbard, is sunk by a Japanese torpedo plane off San Cristobal Island in the Solomons.

October 16.   Planes from the *Hornet* (CV 8) attack Japanese positions on Guadalcanal and San Cristobal.

October 18.   Dissatisfied with Admiral R. L. Ghormley's conduct of the Solomons campaign, Admiral Nimitz replaces him as commander of the South Pacific Area and South Pacific Force with fire-eating Vice Admiral William F. Halsey. The news of Halsey's appointment produces a wave of jubilation throughout the theater.

October 19.   The destroyer *O'Brien* (DD 415), torpedoed on September 15, sinks off Samoa while en route home for repairs.

October 22–26.   **Battle for Henderson Field.** Lieutenant General Harukichi Hyakutake, commander of the Japanese Seventeenth Army, makes what proves to be the last big push against the marines on Guadalcanal, throwing 22,000 men into a two-pronged attack on the perimeter around Henderson Field. It fails.

October 25.   Off Guadalcanal, B-17 bombers severely damage the Japanese light cruiser *Yura,* which is then sunk by the Japanese.

October 26–27.   **Battle of the Santa Cruz Islands.** Admiral Yamamoto sends the Combined Fleet—4 carriers, 4 battleships, 14 cruisers, and 44 destroyers—south in another attempt to destroy the U.S. naval forces supporting the struggle for Guadalcanal. These forces, commanded by Vice Admiral William F. Halsey, consist of the carriers *Hornet* (CV 8) and *Enterprise* (CV 6), the battleship *South Dakota* (BB 57), 6 cruisers, and 14 destroyers. In the ensuing battle, the Japanese win a tactical victory, sinking the *Hornet,* Captain Charles P. Mason, and damaging several other vessels, while the submarine *I-22* sinks the destroyer *Porter* (DD 356), Lieutenant Commander D. G. Roberts. No Japanese ships are lost, although the fleet carrier *Shokaku* and heavy cruiser *Chikuma* are heavily damaged. Yet strategically the victory belongs to the Americans. The Southwest Pacific forces remain off Guadalcanal.

November 8–11.   **Invasion of North Africa (Operation Torch).** American ground forces under Major General Dwight D. Eisenhower enter combat in the European

Admiral William F. Halsey. *Official U.S. Navy photograph.*

theater with a series of landings on the coast of French North Africa. Admiral Sir Andrew B. Cunningham, CO of the British Mediterranean Fleet, commands Allied naval forces, which are divided into three components: the Western Naval Task Force, Rear Admiral H. Kent Hewitt, which lands 35,000 American troops under Major General George S. Patton at three locations (Safi, Fedala, and Port Lyautey) around Casablanca in French Morocco; the Center Naval Force, Commodore Sir Thomas Troubridge, RN, which lands 39,000 Americans under Major General L. R. Fredenall around Oran, Algeria; and the Eastern Naval Task Force, Rear Admiral Sir H. M. Burrough, RN, which lands 10,000 American and 23,000 British troops around Algiers. Initially the French resist the landings, and a naval action is fought off Casablanca on November 8 when French destroyers and the light cruiser *Primauguet* bravely sortie to attack greatly superior American forces, including the battleship *Massachusetts* (BB 59). The *Primauguet* and the destroyers *Boulonnais, Brestois, Fougeux,* and *Frondeur* are sunk, and the unfinished battleship *Jean Bart* is damaged in port. A cease-fire is signed on November 11.

November 12–13. Naval Battle of Guadalcanal: the Cruiser Action. Admiral Yamamoto has determined to have Rear Admiral Raizo Tanaka's Tokyo Express carry the 38th Division to reinforce the defenders of Guadalcanal. First, however, he plans to soften up the American opposition by delivering a heavy bombardment of Henderson Field. This mission is assigned to Admiral Hiroaki Abe's Raiding Force, consisting of the battleships *Hiei* and *Kirishima,* light cruiser *Nagara,* and 14 destroyers. At approximately 1:50 A.M. on the 13th, this force is intercepted off Lunga Point by Rear Admiral Daniel J. Callaghan's Task Force 67.4, composed of the heavy cruisers *Portland* (CA 33) and *San Francisco* (CA 38), the light cruisers *Atlanta* (CL 51), *Helena* (CL 50), and *Juneau* (CL 52), and eight destroyers. The ensuing action lasts less than a quarter-hour, but is one of the fiercest of the war as the U.S. force, steaming line ahead, literally sails through the wedge-shaped, Japanese formation. Callaghan and the other American flag officer present, Rear Admiral Norman Scott, are killed in the opening minutes, Callaghan in the *San Francisco,* Scott in the *Atlanta.* Sunk or so battered that they must be scuttled are, on the American side, the cruiser *Atlanta* and destroyers *Barton* (DD 599), Lieutenant Commander D. H. Fox, *Cushing* (DD 376), Lieutenant Commander E. N. Parker, and *Laffey* (DD 459), Lieutenant Commander C. E. McCombs; on the Japanese side, the destroyers *Akatsuki* and *Yudachi.* The *San Francisco* is severely damaged and several other vessels, Japanese and American, more or less so. Admiral Abe retires without having shelled Guadalcanal. The battleship *Hiei,* crippled by 30 hits, is sunk by American planes the next afternoon, hours after the Japanese submarine *I-22* sinks the cruiser *Juneau,* Captain Lyman K. Swenson.

November 14. Naval Battle of Guadalcanal: the Air Action. Admiral Tanaka's Tokyo Express sets out from the Shortlands with 11 destroyers escorting an equal number of high-speed transports to carry the 38th Division to Guadalcanal. U.S. aircraft sink six transports and damage another, which turns back. Tanaka shepherds the last four to the island, where they begin unloading under cover or darkness, but are destroyed by artillery fire the next morning. Only 2,000 of the 10,000 men originally embarked reach the island. On the same day, *Enterprise* (CV 6) aircraft destroy the heavy cruiser *Kinugasa.*

November 14–15. Naval Battle of Guadalcanal: the Battleship Action. To cover the landing of Tanaka's transports, Admiral Yamamoto sends another heavy surface force to shell Henderson Field. Commanded

Bringing supplies ashore at St. Leu, near Oran, Algeria, November 8, 1942. *U.S. Army photograph.*

by Admiral Nobutake Kondo, it consists of the battleship *Kirishima,* two heavy cruisers, one light cruiser, and six destroyers. Off Savo Island it is intercepted by Rear Admiral Willis A. ("Ching") Lee's Task Force 64, formed of the new battleships *South Dakota* (BB 57) and *Washington* (BB 56) and four destroyers. In an action that begins shortly before midnight, the *Kirishima* and destroyer *Ayanami* are sunk and Kondo retires. The American destroyers *Preston* (DD 379), Commander M. C. Stormes, and *Walke* (DD 416), Commander T. E. Fraser, are sunk; the destroyer *Benham* (DD 397), Lieutenant Commander John B. Taylor, is so badly hurt that she sinks the following afternoon, and the *South Dakota* is heavily damaged.

November 30.   **Battle of Tassafaronga.** Off Guadalcanal, Rear Admiral Carleton H. Wright's Task Force 67—composed of the heavy cruisers *Minneapolis* (CA 36), *New Orleans* (CA 32), *Northampton* (CA 26), and *Pensacola* (CA 24), light cruiser *Honolulu* (CL 48), and six destroyers—encounters eight destroyers of "Tenacious" Tanaka's Tokyo Express. American gunfire obliterates the destroyer *Takanami,* but Tanaka's other ships launch a salvo of torpedoes that sink the *Northampton,* Captain W. A. Kitts, and hit every other cruiser except the *Honolulu.*

December 11.   The last Pacific surface action of 1942 takes place off Guadalcanal when a force of PT boats attack a Tokyo Express of ten destroyers. HIJMS *Teruzuki* and *PT 44* are sunk in the engagement.

December 12.   The Japanese Navy recommends abandoning the struggle for Guadalcanal.

December 15.   **"Black Cats."** Night-flying PBY Catalinas—"Black Cats"—begin to operate off Henderson Field. Although the big planes are too slow for day combat, they prove extremely useful for nighttime bombing raids, searches, and attacks upon enemy shipping.

December 18.   The Japanese light cruiser *Tenryu* is sunk by the submarine *Albacore* (SS 218), Commander Richard C. Lake, off northern New Guinea.

December 31.   The carrier *Essex* (CV 9) is commissioned. She is the name-ship of a class of ten 27,100-ton carriers, all of which will enter service during World War II.

December 31.   Japanese Imperial General Headquarters concedes defeat and orders the navy to conduct a staged evacuation of Guadalcanal.

1943

January 10.   The transport submarine *Argonaut* (APS 1), Lieutenant Commander John R. Pierce, is sunk while attacking an enemy convoy between New Britain and Bougainville.

January 14.   The carrier *Independence* (CV 22) is commissioned.

January 14–23.   **Casablanca Conference.** President Roosevelt, Prime Minister Churchill, and the combined chiefs of staff meet to formulate Allied strategy for 1943. By now it is evident that the German and Italian forces in North Africa are destined for defeat. The

Americans reluctantly defer their hopes for a cross-channel invasion of France in 1943 to the British proposal to maintain Allied momentum in the Mediterranean theater by landing in Sicily. Admiral King secures approval for opening a second line of advance against Japan, through the Central Pacific towards the Marshalls and Carolines. Other major agreements are to intensify the strategic bombing of Germany and the antisubmarine campaign in the North Atlantic. President Roosevelt surprises his confrères by announcing that the Axis powers will be required to surrender unconditionally.

January 14–February 7.   **Mush Morton and the Wahoo.** Commander Dudley W. ("Mush") Morton, new skipper of the submarine *Wahoo* (SS 238), commands the most aggressive patrol to date in the Pacific War. Ordered to reconnoiter the harbor of Wewak, on the northern coast of New Guinea, Morton not only threads his way into the enemy anchorage, but torpedoes a destroyer with a dangerous "down the throat" shot. The next day he encounters a Japanese convoy of two freighters, a large transport, and a tanker en route to Palau. In a 10-hour running battle, he sinks the first three vessels and damages the fourth. These exploits, for which he receives both the Navy Cross and the Distinguished Service Cross, serve as an example and an inspiration to the entire submarine service.

January 22.   American and Australian troops commanded by General Douglas MacArthur crush the last pockets of Japanese resistance at Buna, on the northeastern coast of New Guinea, ending the Papuan campaign.

January 29–30.   **Battle of Rennell Island.** Approaching Guadalcanal from the south, Rear Admiral Robert C. ("Ike") Giffen, commander of Task Force 18, leaves his two escort carriers because their slow speed will prevent him from making a scheduled rendezvous with another force and presses on with seven cruisers and six destroyers. At twilight he is attacked near Rennell Island by land-based Japanese planes, which torpedo the heavy cruiser *Chicago* (CA 29). The next day Giffen's ships come under the air umbrella of the *Enterprise* (CV 6), but Japanese bombers penetrate the screen to sink the crippled cruiser.

February.   Three of the five submarines that leave Brisbane, Australia, on patrol this month fail to return. They are the *Amberjack* (SS 219), Lieutenant Commander John A. Bole, Jr.; *Grampus* (SS 207), Commander John R. Craig; and *Triton* (SS 201), Lieutenant Commander George K. MacKenzie, Jr.

February 1.   The destroyer *De Haven* (DD 469), Commander C. E. Tolman, is sunk by Japanese dive bombers off Guadalcanal.

February 1–8.   **Operation KE.** Despite opposition from American aircraft, destroyers, and PT boats, the destroyers of the Tokyo Express succeed in evacuating 11,706 troops from Guadalcanal. The U.S. command never realizes that an evacuation is under way, assuming that the Japanese are continuing to reinforce the island.

February 9.   **Guadalcanal secured.** The Japanese are discovered to have withdrawn from the island. Of the 36,000 troops Japan committed to the struggle, 14,800 were killed, 9,000 died of disease, and 1,000 were captured. Casualties among the 60,000 American soldiers and marines who fought on the island were 1,600 dead and 4,200 wounded. With the completion of this grueling campaign, the tide of war in the Pacific turns in favor of the United States.

The *Wahoo* in July 1943. *U.S. Naval Institute Collection.*

February 17.   The carrier *Lexington* (CV 16) is commissioned.

February 21.   American forces land unopposed on the Russell Islands, 30 miles northwest of Guadalcanal, beginning the advance through the central Solomons.

February 22.   The battleship *Iowa* (BB 61) is commissioned.

February 25.   The carrier *Princeton* (CV 23) is commissioned.

March 1–4.   **Battle of the Bismarck Sea.** A Japanese convoy of 16 ships—8 transports and 8 destroyers—under Rear Admiral Masatomi Kimura sets out from Rabaul on February 28 to carry 6,900 men to reinforce the garrison at Lae, New Guinea. Discovered by American aerial reconnaissance in the Bismarck Sea, it is attacked by Fifth Air Force planes flying from New Guinea. The convoy's air screen is overwhelmed, and all 8 transports and 4 destroyers are sunk. More than 3,000 troops drown.

March 1–20.   **Slaughter in the Atlantic.** The wolfpacks score their greatest success, sinking 85 Allied ships at a cost of only 6 U-boats. It appears as though the Germans may finally attain their goal of severing the North Atlantic sea lanes of communication.

March 5.   The *Bogue* (CVE 9) becomes the first escort carrier assigned to antisubmarine operations. Convoy escort groups formed around these little carriers will make a major contribution in the Battle of the Atlantic.

March 6.   Three light cruisers and three destroyers under Rear Admiral A. Stanton Merrill shell Japanese installations at Vila, on Kolombangara, and sink the Japanese destroyers *Minegumo* and *Murasame.*

March 15.   The practice, still followed, of numbering U.S. fleets is introduced by Admiral King.

March 26.   **Battle of the Komandorskis.** A classic, daylight gunnery action occurs in the Aleutians when Rear Admiral Charles H. ("Soc") McMorris's Task Group 16.6—consisting of the light cruiser *Richmond* (CL 9) (flag), heavy cruiser *Salt Lake City* (CA 25), and destroyers *Bailey* (DD 492), *Coghlan* (DD 606), *Dale* (DD 353), and *Monaghan* (DD 354)—encounters a greatly superior Japanese force of two heavy cruisers, two light cruisers, and four destroyers escorting two transports to Kiska. After a bold attempt to reach the transports, McMorris is compelled to turn away. The Japanese pursue. For more than three hours the American ships evade disaster in a skillful running battle. The *Salt Lake City* is finally disabled, but Japanese Vice

Admiral Boshiro Hosogaya has had enough and breaks off the action.

March 31.   The carrier *Belleau Wood* (CV 24) is commissioned.

April 1.   A bomber base, Carney Field, becomes operational on Guadalcanal. Aircraft based here will play an important role in the conquest of the Solomons.

April 7.   **Operation "I."** In hopes of slowing the American build-up in the Solomons, Admiral Yamamoto launches an air offensive, reinforcing the land-based Eleventh Air Fleet with carrier aircraft. The destroyer *Aaron Ward* (DD 483), oiler *Kanawaha* (AO 1), and the New Zealand corvette *Moa* are sunk at Tulagi on this date, and two Dutch cargo ships go down later. Japanese pilots greatly inflate their success, however, and Yamamoto terminates the operation on April 16.

April 7.   On this date the submarine *Pickerel* (SS 177), Lieutenant Commander A. H. Alston, Jr., is lost in the vicinity of Honshu sometime after sinking a Japanese freighter.

April 9.   The rank of commodore is revived.

April 15.   The carrier *Yorktown* (CV 10) is commissioned.

April 18.   **Get Yamamoto.** Navy code-breakers learn that the Fleet Admiral Isoroku Yamamoto, commander of the Japanese Combined Fleet, has planned a tour of inspection during which he will fly into Kahili, Buin, a point within range of U.S. aircraft. This intelligence is presented to Admiral Nimitz, who directs Rear Admiral Marc A. Mitscher, Commander Air Solomons, to arrange a reception. Sixteen Lockheed P-38 Lightnings from Henderson Field, Guadalcanal, are waiting when the two bombers carrying Yamamoto and his staff approach Kahili. The admiral is killed in the crash of his plane.

April 22.   The submarine *Grenadier* (SS 210), Lieutenant Commander John Fitzgerald, is forced to scuttle after being damaged by a Japanese air attack off the coast of Malaya. Fitzgerald and his men are rescued by a Japanese freighter, and though cruelly treated, most are alive at war's end.

May.   **Climax of the Battle of the Atlantic.** The turning point in the North Atlantic comes with the passage of Convoy ONS 5, 43 merchantmen bound from the United Kingdom to Halifax, Nova Scotia. It is attacked by three wolfpacks totaling no less than 51 U-boats, almost half the number on patrol. Aided by aircraft from Greenland and Iceland, the convoy escort, a maximum of nine ships successively commanded by Commanders Peter W. Gretton, RN, and

R. E. Sherwood, RN, destroys six U-boats. Only 13 merchant ships are lost. Subsequent convoys also take a heavy toll of their attackers, and on May 24 Grand Admiral Karl Doenitz, commander-in-chief of the German Navy, recalls his boats from the North Atlantic. Never again will the wolfpacks threaten the lifeline of the Western Democracies.

May 8.   In the Solomon Islands, the Japanese destroyer *Kuroshio* is sunk and the destroyers *Kagero* and *Oyashio* damaged by American mines laid a day earlier. The cripples are sunk by an air strike from Guadalcanal.

May 11–30.   **Reconquest of Attu.** Rear Admiral Thomas C. Kinkaid's North Pacific Force lands 11,000 men of the 7th Infantry Division, Major General A. E. Brown, on the Aleutian island of Attu. The Japanese garrison of 2,500 fights almost literally to the last man. American casualties are 600 killed and 1,200 wounded.

May 13.   **Victory in North Africa.** General Jürgen von Arnim surrenders the 238,000 Axis troops crowded into the Cape Bon Peninsula, Tunisia, to the Allies.

May 17–25.   **Washington Conference (Trident).** President Roosevelt, Prime Minister Churchill, and the combined chiefs of staff meet at Washington, D.C., to frame a comprehensive strategic plan for the war against the Axis. General George C. Marshall, U.S. Army chief of staff, proposes an invasion of northern France in the fall of 1943; the British, still certain that a cross-Channel attack would be premature, advocate a landing on mainland Italy, which they believe would force that country out of the war. After earnest discussions, a compromise is reached: the Americans agree to commit limited forces to an invasion of Italy in 1943 in exchange for a British commitment to join in a landing in France on May 1, 1944. The British also accept Admiral King's arguments for intensifying the war against Japan.

May 20.   **Tenth Fleet.** The Tenth Fleet is established under the command of Admiral Ernest J. King, chief of naval operations, to direct the American antisubmarine war in the Atlantic. There is no new fleet, however; the new organization is strictly an operational headquarters.

May 22.   The *Bogue* (CVE 9), Captain Giles E. Short, is the first escort carrier to destroy a German submarine, sinking the *U-569* in the North Atlantic.

May 23.   The battleship *New Jersey* (BB 62) is commissioned.

May 25.   The carrier *Bunker Hill* (CV 17) is commissioned.

May 28.   The carrier *Cowpens* (CV 25) is commissioned.

June 12.   The submarine *R-12* (SS 89) is lost through accident off Key West, Florida. All 42 men aboard perish.

June 17.   The carrier *Monterey* (CV 26) is commissioned.

June 30.   **Offensive in New Guinea.** General MacArthur's forces begin their advance along the northern coast of New Guinea. The newly established Seventh Amphibious Force, commanded by Rear Admiral Daniel E. Barbey (who will soon become known as Uncle Dan, the Amphibious Man), lands army units at Nassau Bay on Huon Gulf slightly south of Salamaua, and in the Trobriand and Woodlark islands off the northeastern tip of New Guinea.

June 30–August 25.   **Campaign for New Georgia.** The reconquest of the Solomons continues with the invasion of New Georgia (Operation Toenail), the primary objective being the capture of the airfield at Munda Point. Rear Admiral Richmond Kelly Turner commands the amphibious force (Task Force 31); support is provided by carrier and cruiser groups and two battleship divisions organized as Task Force 36 directly under Third Fleet commander Vice Admiral William F. Halsey. The operation begins on June 30 with a landing on Rendova Island, five miles from New Georgia, and on three other nearby islands. New Georgia itself, defended by more than 5,000 Japanese troops under General Noboru Sasaki, is invaded on July 2. Three infantry divisions and Colonel H. B. ("Harry the Horse") Liversedge's First Marine Raider Regiment are eventually committed to the struggle. The Munda airfield is taken after fierce jungle fighting on August 5, and organized resistance ceases on August 25.

July 5.   In a chance encounter between American and Japanese naval forces in Kula Gulf, between New Georgia and Kolombangara, the destroyer *Strong* (DD 467), Commander J. H. Wellings, is sunk shortly after midnight with the loss of 46 lives.

July 6.   **Battle of Kula Gulf.** Around midafternoon on July 5, the Third Fleet learns that a "Tokyo Express" is en route south from Bougainville with Japanese reinforcements for the Central Solomons. Rear Admiral Walden L. ("Pug") Ainsworth's Task Group 36.1, consisting of the light cruisers *Honolulu* (CL 48) (flag), *Helena* (CL 50), and *St. Louis* (CL 49) and four destroyers, makes full speed to Kula Gulf to intercept the Japanese. It meets the enemy force—ten destroyers, seven of which are being used as transports, under Rear Admiral Teruo Akiyama—a few minutes past midnight. In a confused action that lasts almost until dawn, Admiral Akiyama's flagship, the *Niizuki,* is sunk and the

Nagatsuki driven ashore, where she is destroyed by U.S. planes during the day; but the destroyer-transports succeed in unloading their troops on Kolombangara, and the *Helena,* Captain Charles P. Cecil, is sunk by three torpedoes fired by the *Suzukaze* and *Tanikaze.*

July 10. **Invasion of Sicily (Operation Husky).** The largest amphibious assault in history, in terms of both the number of troops put ashore at one time and the extent of coastline covered, is made when eight American and British divisions are landed over a frontage of more than 100 miles on the southern and eastern coasts of Sicily. The naval forces involved—more than 1,400 ships and landing craft—are commanded by British Admiral Sir Andrew B. Cunningham, the land forces by General Sir Harold Alexander. Three American divisions of Lieutenant General George S. Patton's Seventh Army are put ashore in southern Sicily by the Western Naval Task Force, Vice Admiral H. Kent Hewitt, USN. Five British divisions of Lieutenant General Sir Bernard L. Montgomery's Eighth Army are landed on their right by the Western Naval Force, Vice Admiral Sir Bertram Ramsay, RN. A total of 470,000 men are committed to the operation. Sicily is defended by 300,000 Italian and 50,000 German troops under General Alfredo Guzzoni, but the Italians are sick of the war, and only the Germans show fight.

July 10. The destroyer *Maddox* (DD 622), Lieutenant Commander E. R. Sarsfield, is sunk with heavy loss of life by a German dive-bomber off Gela, Sicily.

July 11. **Fire support on Sicily.** Fire from the light cruisers *Boise* (CL 47) and *Savannah* (CL 42) and eight destroyers helps defeat an armored thrust by the Hermann Goering Division on the Allied beachhead at Gela, Sicily. After their attempts to repel the landing are unsuccessful, the Germans fight an expert rearguard action to the north towards the Straits of Messina.

July 13. **Battle of Kolombangara.** On his 15th patrol up The Slot, Rear Admiral W. L. Ainsworth fights another night action with the Tokyo Express. This time he has the light cruisers *Honolulu* (CL 48) (flag), *St. Louis* (CL 49), and HMNZS *Leander,* and 10 destroyers. The Japanese force, commanded by Rear Admiral Shunji Izaki, consists of the light cruiser *Jintsu* (flag), five destroyers, and five destroyer-transports. The *Jintsu* is literally blown out of the water, and the *Leander* is badly damaged by a torpedo in the opening moments of the action. Then the failure to promptly identify the destroyers of the Japanese escort force allows them to

The light cruiser *Boise* crosses the bow of the *LST 325* while providing fire support for U.S. forces ashore near Gela, Sicily, July 11, 1943. *U.S. Army photograph.*

reach a position to launch torpedoes that blow up the destroyer *Gwin* (DD 433), Lieutenant Commander John B. Fellows, and damage the cruisers *Honolulu* and *St. Louis.* The Japanese destroyer-transports succeed in landing their troops on Kolombangara.

July 19–20. The Japanese destroyers *Yugure* and *Kiyonami,* members of a 13-ship Tokyo Express, are sunk by army and navy planes in The Slot north of Kolombangara.

July 20. The submarine *Runner* (SS 275), Lieutenant Commander Joseph H. Bourland, is reported overdue and presumed lost in the Pacific.

July 22. Navy planes sink the Japanese seaplane carrier *Nisshin* in Bougainville Strait.

July 23. Patrol Squadron 63 arrives in Britain to participate in the Royal Air Force Coastal Command's offensive against German U-boats crossing the Bay of Biscay. It is the first U.S. Navy air unit to be based in Britain.

July 24. The carrier *Cabot* (CVL 28) is commissioned.

July 25. Following the Allied landings in Sicily, Benito Mussolini, *Il Duce* of Fascist Italy, is overthrown and imprisoned by a *coup d'état* organized around King Victor Emanuel III. German special forces led by Colonel Otto Skorzeny later rescue Mussolini, and he is installed as president of the German-backed Salò Republic in northern Italy.

July 28. Undetected by U.S. forces, a Japanese task force commanded by Vice Admiral Shiro Kawase evacuates the 5,183-man garrison of the Aleutian island of Kiska.

PT 109. U.S. Naval Institute Collection.

August 1–2.   **PT 109.** After nightfall 15 U.S. torpedo boats engage a four-destroyer Tokyo Express off Kolombangara. The only loss on either side occurs when the *Amagiri* rams the *PT 109,* Lieutenant (and future president) John F. Kennedy, USNR. Eleven of the boat's thirteen crewmen survive. The next day they swim to a neighboring island, Kennedy towing a badly injured man. Friendly natives carry a message Kennedy carves on a coconut shell to an Australian coastwatcher on another island, and the party is rescued on August 7. Kennedy is awarded the Navy and Marine Corps Medal.

August 3–17.   **Evacuation of Sicily.** Despite Allied air and naval superiority, a total of 39,500 Germans and 62,000 Italians succeed in crossing the Straits of Messina to reach the Italian mainland. A total of 167,000 Axis troops (37,000 German) are killed, wounded, or captured in the 39 days of the Sicilian campaign. American and British casualties amount to 25,000.

August 6–7.   **Battle of Vella Gulf.** The U.S. Navy wins its first unequivocal night-fighting victory of the Pacific war when seven destroyers under Commander Frederick Moosbrugger intercept four Japanese destroyers on a Tokyo Express run in Vella Gulf, between Vella Lavella and Kolombangara. The first spread of torpedoes launched by Moosbrugger's ships hit the *Arashi, Hagikaze,* and *Kawakaze,* all of which are soon sunk. Only the *Shigure* escapes. The American destroyers emerge from the action unscathed.

August 13.   Faced with unacceptable losses, especially of aircraft and destroyers, Japanese Imperial Headquarters decides to cease reinforcing the Solomons.

August 14–24.   **Quebec Conference (Quadrant).** The president, prime minister, and the combined chiefs of staff meet to discuss plans for the landing in France—about which the Americans suspect the British still harbor reservations—and the future conduct of the war against Japan. May 1, 1944, is confirmed as the target date for the cross-Channel invasion; General MacArthur is to continue his advance up the coast of New Guinea, by-passing Rabaul; and the U.S. Navy will launch an offensive across the Central Pacific to the Marianas.

August 15.   **Leapfrogging to Vella Lavella.** The Third Amphibious Force, Rear Admiral Theodore S. ("Ping") Wilkinson, lands 4,600 men under Brigadier General Robert B. McClure, USA, on the virtually undefended Solomon Island of Vella Lavella, bypassing and neutralizing strongly garrisoned Kolombangara.

August 15.   **Anticlimax at Kiska.** After a heavy preinvasion bombardment, Rear Admiral Thomas C. Kinkaid's North Pacific Force lands 34,400 American and Canadian troops on Kiska, in the Aleutians, which the Japanese had secretly evacuated on July 28.

August 16.   The carrier *Intrepid* (CV 11) is commissioned.

August 27.   The submarine *Grayling* (SS 209), Lieutenant Commander Robert M. Brinker, is lost in Philippine waters sometime after sinking a Japanese cargo ship on this date.

August 31.   Japanese installations on Marcus Island, 800 miles northwest of Wake, are attacked by aircraft from the carriers *Essex* (CV 9), *Independence* (CVL 22), and *Yorktown* (CV 10) of Rear Admiral C. A. Pownall's Task Force 15.

August 31.   The carrier *Langley* (CVL 27) is commissioned.

September 3.   British troops of General Sir Bernard L. Montgomery's Eighth Army cross the narrows of the Straits of Messina to land at Reggio de Calabria on the Italian mainland opposite Sicily.

September 3.   **Italian armistice.** An armistice is secretly signed with the new Italian government of Marshal Pietro Badoglio. It is to become effective on September 8. This date is chosen to coincide with the major landings to be made by American forces at Salerno.

September 4.   **Assault on Lae.** The Japanese positions at Salamaua, Lae, and Finschhafen on the northern coast of New Guinea must be eliminated before General MacArthur can continue his advance. On this date Rear Admiral Daniel E. Barbey's Seventh Amphibious Force lands the 9th Australian Division east of Lae. The next day American paratroopers capture an airfield at the village of Nadzab, west of Lae, and the 7th Australian Division is flown in. Faced by convergent attacks, the Japanese garrison withdraws on September 15.

September 8.   **The Italian armistice is announced.** Simultaneously, the Italian fleet sorties to surrender to Allied naval authorities. The German Luftwaffe attacks the ships at sea and succeeds in sinking the battleship *Roma* and damaging other vessels, but most of Italy's active fleet escapes.

September 9.   **Salerno.** Lieutenant General Mark Clark's American Fifth Army lands at Salerno, on the ankle of the Italian boot. The naval component of the operation is commanded by Vice Admiral H. Kent Hewitt. Simultaneously, the Germans react to the Italian armistice by seizing Rome (September 10) and rushing reinforcements to the south. Between September 12 and 16, Field Marshal Albert Kesselring, commanding German forces in Italy, makes repeated and dangerous attempts to repel the invasion. Naval gunfire plays an important part in halting these thrusts. The Fifth Army links up with Montgomery's Eighth Army on the 16th, and Kesselring pulls back. For the next 19 months the Germans will exploit the defensive potential of the mountainous spine of the Italian peninsula to slow the Allied push to the north.

September 11.   The destroyer *Rowan* (DD 405), Lieutenant Commander Joel C. Ford, is sunk with the loss of 202 lives by a German PT boat off Salerno, and the light cruiser *Savannah* (CL 42) is damaged by radio-controlled bombs dropped by German aircraft.

September 18.   In the Pacific, Tarawa Atoll, Gilbert Islands, is hit by carrier planes from Rear Admiral C. A. Pownall's Task Force 15.

September 19.   The submarine *Cisco* (SS 290), Commander James W. Coe, sails from Darwin, Australia, and disappears at sea. She was probably sunk by Japanese forces on September 28.

September 22.   **Finschhafen landing.** The last of the three Japanese positions on the Huon Gulf in northern New Guinea falls when Rear Admiral Barbey's Seventh Amphibious Force lands the Australian 20th Brigade at Finschhafen, taking the Japanese garrison by surprise. Despite stiff resistance by units of the Special Naval Landing Force, the village is secured on October 2.

September 25.   On this date, the submarine *Pompano* (SS 181), Commander Willis M. Thomas, is lost sometime after sinking a freighter off the Japanese coast.

October 3.   The destroyer *Henley* (DD 391), Lieutenant Commander A. R. Theobald, Jr., is sunk by a Japanese

This neat hole in the top of the number three 6-inch turret of the light cruiser *Savannah* was made by a radio-controlled glide bomb launched from a German aircraft off the Salerno beachhead. The bomb penetrated three decks to explode in the lower handling room, killing 197 men and seriously wounding 15 others. *U.S. Navy photograph.*

submarine off Finschhafen, New Guinea. Seventeen lives are lost.

October 4.   A U.S. task force consisting of the carrier *Ranger* (CV 4), heavy cruiser *Tuscaloosa* (CA 37), and a destroyer division under the command of Rear Admiral Olaf M. Hustvedt participates in a raid by the British Home Fleet on German shipping at Bodö, Norway. Six enemy freighters are sunk and four damaged by Allied air strikes.

October 5–6.   In the Central Pacific, Wake Island is attacked by carrier aircraft and shelled by cruisers of Rear Admiral A. E. Montgomery's Task Force 14.

October 6–7.   **Battle of Vella Lavella.** Another night action takes place in the Solomons when the Japanese send a force of 9 destroyers and 12 small craft under Rear Admiral Matsuji Ijuin to evacuate the 600 troops on Vella Lavella. It is intercepted by six destroyers commanded by Captain Frank R. Walker. One destroyer is sunk on each side—HIJMS *Yugumo* and the USS *Chevalier* (DD 451), Lieutenant Commander George R. Wilson—and two American destroyers are damaged. The Japanese small craft extricate the island's garrison. This is the last engagement fought in the central Solomons.

October 7.   The submarine *S-44* (SS 155), Lieutenant Commander Francis E. Brown, is sunk in a surface action with a Japanese destroyer at Paramushiro in the Kuriles.

October 9.   The destroyer *Buck* (DD 420), Lieutenant Commander Michael J. Klein, is sunk with the loss of 166 lives by the *U-616* off Salerno, Italy.

October 13.   Italy declares war on Germany.

October 13.   The destroyer *Bristol* (DD 453), Commander J. A. Glick, is sunk with the loss of 52 lives by the *U-317* off the coast of Algeria.

October 17.   The submarine *Tarpon* (SS 175), Commander Thomas L. Wogan, sinks the German raider *Michel* off Honshu, Japan.

October 19–30.   **Moscow Conference.** U.S. Secretary of State Cordell Hull, British Foreign Secretary Sir Anthony Eden, and Soviet Foreign Secretary Vyacheslav Molotov confer. Hull and Eden assure Molotov that the western Allies will land in France in May 1944, satisfying Stalin's longstanding plea for the opening of a second front in northern Europe, and promise that they will not make a separate peace with Germany. Molotov hints that the Soviet Union may enter the war against Japan.

October 24.   The submarine *Dorado* (SS 248), Lieutenant Commander Earl K. Schneider, is reported overdue and presumed lost in the Atlantic.

October 27–November 6.   **Landing in the Treasury Islands.** Mono and Stirling, the two little islands comprising the Treasury group, are seized for use as a base for the invasion of Bougainville.

October 27–November 4.   As a feint to distract the Japanese from the attack on Bougainville, the marine 2nd Parachute Battalion, Lieutenant Colonel Victor H. ("Brute") Krulak, is landed on and then withdrawn from Choiseul Island.

November 1.   **The Borie vs. U-405.** Seven hundred miles north of the Azores, the old destroyer *Borie* (DD 215), Lieutenant Commander Charles H. Hutchins, USNR, fights a night surface action with the *U-405*. After an hour's gunnery duel, the *Borie* succeeds in ramming the U-boat. The vessels are locked together for some minutes, during which the two crews exchange small-arms fire from their decks. Eventually the *U-405* wrenches away, crippled, to surrender shortly thereafter. The *Borie* sinks the following day as a result of the damage to her bow.

November 1.   **Bougainville.** Rear Admiral Theodore S. Wilkinson's Third Amphibious Force lands the 3rd Marine Division, Major General Allen H. Turnage, at Empress Augusta Bay on the west coast of Bougainville in the northern Solomons. Possession of an airfield here will put the Japanese stronghold at Rabaul, New Britain, within range of land-based planes. The beachhead is secured by nightfall. Later counterattacks by an enemy battalion brought down on the Tokyo Express from Rabaul and by Japanese forces garrisoned elsewhere on Bougainville are defeated. Marine casualties are 423 dead and 1,418 wounded.

November 2.   **Battle of Empress Augusta Bay.** Rear Admiral Sentaro Omori sorties from the Japanese fleet base at Rabaul with two heavy cruisers, two light cruisers, and six destroyers to break up the Bougainville landing. Arriving at the mouth of Empress Augusta Bay around 2:30 A.M., he is met by Rear Admiral A. Stanton ("Tip") Merrill's Task Force 39, consisting of four light cruisers and two destroyer divisions of four ships each under Captain Arleigh A. ("31-knot") Burke and Commander Bernard L. ("Count") Austin. The Japanese force, though greatly superior in firepower, is repulsed in an exemplary action, losing the light cruiser *Sendai* and destroyer *Hatsukaze*. No American ships are sunk and only one, the destroyer *Foote* (DD 511), is seriously damaged.

November 5.   Still hoping to repel the invasion of Bougainville, Admiral Mineichi Koga, Yamamoto's successor as commander of the Japanese Combined Fleet, sends seven heavy cruisers, a light cruiser, and four destroyers under Vice Admiral Takeo Kurita to reinforce the Eighth Fleet at Rabaul. Admiral Halsey responds by ordering Rear Admiral Frederick C. Sherman's carrier Task Force 38 to raid the Japanese fleet base. Aircraft from the *Saratoga* (CV 3) and *Princeton* (CVL 23) deliver a devastating attack on the ships at Rabaul, seriously damaging the heavy cruisers *Atago, Chikuma, Maya, Mogami,* and *Takao.* This strike eliminates the possibility of further action by Japanese heavy surface units against the Bougainville beachhead. Only 10 of the 97 planes involved are shot down.

November 6.   The destroyer *Beatty* (DD 640), Lieutenant Commander W. Outerson, is sunk by German aircraft off Cape Bougaroun, Algeria.

November 9.   **Loss of the Wahoo.** Captain Dudley W. ("Mush") Morton's *Wahoo* (SS 238) is reported overdue and presumed lost on her fifth war patrol. She was probably destroyed by a Japanese aircraft on October 11 while exiting La Pérouse Strait after sinking four ships in the Sea of Japan.

November 13.   Daily air strikes on Japanese installations in the Gilbert and Marshall islands are begun by American carrier and land planes in preparation for the launching of the navy's offensive through the central Pacific.

November 16.   The submarine *Corvina* (SS 226), Commander Roderick S. Rooney, is sunk by the Japanese submarine *I-176*, which sights her running on the surface south of Truk. This is the only occasion in the war in which an American submarine is destroyed by a Japanese submarine.

November 17.   A Japanese air attack on a troop convoy to Bougainville sinks the destroyer transport *McKean* (APD 5), Lieutenant Commander Ralph L. Ramey, with the loss of 116 lives.

November 17.   The carrier *Bataan* (CVL 29) is commissioned.

November 19.   In the Central Pacific, the submarine *Sculpin* (SS 191), Commander Fred Connaway, is depth-charged, forced to the surface, and sunk by the Japanese destroyer *Yamagumo*. Aboard her, ready to form a wolf pack should the Japanese fleet sail from Truk, is Captain John P. Cromwell, commander of the Submarine Division 43. Cromwell's duties ashore have made him aware of the vital role navy code-breaking

plays in the success of the American undersea war. Deciding that he knows too much to permit himself to be taken prisoner, he deliberately stays in the *Sculpin* when she does down for the last time. The testimony of the boat's survivors, who are rescued by the *Yamagumo*, will later result in the posthumous award of the Medal of Honor to Captain Cromwell.

November 20–23.   **Tarawa (Operation Galvanic).** The navy launches its Central Pacific drive, in effect reviving the prewar War Plan Orange for a conflict against Japan, with landings on Betio, Makin, and Apamama islands of the Tarawa Atoll in the Gilberts. The operation is executed by Vice Admiral Raymond A. Spruance's Fifth Fleet. Rear Admiral Richmond Kelly Turner commands the assault force, Major General Holland M. ("Howlin' Mad") Smith, commander of the newly established V Amphibious Corps, the landing force. Makin and Apamama are taken against relatively light resistance. Betio, garrisoned by 4,836 naval troops (including 2,619 men of the elite Special Naval Landing Force) under Rear Admiral Keiji Shibasaki, is the linchpin of the Japanese defense. It is assaulted by Major General Julian C. Smith's 2nd Marine Division

Tarawa: landing craft, looking like water bugs, make for the beach. *Official U.S. Navy photograph.*

and secured after 76 hours of bitter fighting in which 990 marines are killed, 2,391 wounded, and only 17 defenders are taken prisoner. The landing demonstrates the basic soundness of the amphibious doctrines that the marine corps developed between the world wars. It also reveals the need for more intensive pre-landing bombardment, improvements in communications and air support, and the increased use of amphibian tractors (Landing Vehicles, Tracked).

November 22–26. **First Cairo Conference (Sextant).** President Roosevelt, Prime Minister Churchill, and the combined chiefs of staff meet to finalize plans for 1944. Churchill's attempt to secure approval for an enlargement of the Allied war effort in the Mediterranean is rebuffed, as is the American idea of establishing a supreme Allied commander for the entire European theater. Generalissimo and Madame Chiang Kai-shek are also present and, with the Americans, urge the British to make a greater effort against the Japanese in the China-Burma-India theater.

November 24. The escort carrier *Liscombe Bay* (CVE 56), Captain I. D. Wiltsie, flagship of Task Group 52.3, is torpedoed and sunk with the loss of 644 lives by the Japanese submarine *I-175* in the Gilbert Islands. Among those killed are Captain Wiltsie and the task group commander, Rear Admiral Henry M. Mullinnix.

November 24. The carrier *Wasp* (CV 18) is commissioned.

November 25. **Battle of Cape St. George.** Captain Arleigh A. Burke fights a brilliant night action when

Marines ashore during the savage struggle for Tarawa. *Defense Department photo (Marine Corps).*

Destroyer Squadron 23 intercepts a Tokyo Express under Captain Kiyoto Kagawa transporting reinforcements to Buka, the island immediately north of Bougainville. The odds are even, five destroyers a side. Both ships of the Japanese screen, the *Onami* (flag) and *Makinawi,* are hit by Burke's opening salvo of torpedoes. The former blows up; the latter and the *Yugiri* are then sunk by gunfire. The two remaining enemies turn tail. Burke's ships do not take a single hit.

November 28–December 1. **Teheran Conference (Eureka).** Leaving Cairo, the Western leaders fly to Teheran for their first meeting with Soviet Premier Stalin. Churchill renews his arguments for additional operations in the Mediterranean, but Stalin makes plain his preference for an invasion of France and is assured that it will be made in 1944.

November 29. The destroyer *Perkins* (DD 377), Lieutenant Commander G. L. Ketchum, sinks following a collision with the Australian transport *Duntroon* off eastern New Guinea.

November 29. The carrier *Hornet* (CV 12) is commissioned.

December 2. The submarine *Capelin* (SS 289), Commander Elliott E. ("Steam") Marshall, is lost sometime after being sighted on this date by the *Bonefish* (SS 223) and *Bowfin* (SS 287) in the Makassar Strait.

December 3–7. **Second Cairo Conference.** Roosevelt, Churchill, and their staffs return to Cairo from Teheran to make plans for an invasion of southern France, Operation Anvil, which is to complement the cross-Channel assault. The number of landing craft needed for this operation necessitates the cancellation of Operation Buccaneer, a projected British assault on the coast of Burma.

December 4. The submarine *Sailfish* (SS 192, originally *Squalus*), Lieutenant Commander Robert E. Ward, sinks the Japanese carrier *Chuyo* off the coast of Japan.

December 15. **Landing at Arawe.** General MacArthur believes that to secure safe passage for naval forces through the Vitiaz and Dampier straits between New Guinea and New Britain it is necessary to occupy the western end of the latter island. The operation commences when Rear Admiral Barbey's Seventh Amphibious Force lands the 112th Cavalry Regiment (dismounted) at Arawe, on the southwestern shore of New Britain. Little resistance is encountered.

December 15. The carrier *San Jacinto* (CVL 30) is commissioned. She is the last of the eleven fleet and four light carriers to enter service this year.

Japanese shipping in harbor at Rabaul, New Britain, under attack by aircraft from the carriers *Princeton* and *Saratoga*, November 5, 1943. *Official U.S. Navy photograph.*

December 17. **Neutralizing Rabaul.** The Japanese fleet base at Rabaul, New Britain, the principal objective of the American drive through the Solomons, is taken under almost daily attack by land-based aircraft of the U.S. Army, Navy, and Marines and the Australian and New Zealand armed forces flying from nearby airfields. The usefulness of the base to the Japanese is destroyed.

December 24. Escorting a North Atlantic convoy, the destroyer *Leary* (DD 158), Commander James E. Kyes, becomes the third (and last) American destroyer to be sunk by a U-boat.

December 26. **Landing at Cape Gloucester.** Rear Admiral Barbey's Seventh Amphibious Force lands the 1st Marine Division, Major General William H. Rupertus, at Cape Gloucester on the western tip of New Britain. The airfield is taken on December 30, but it is not until January 16, 1944, that the Japanese are driven from the area.

December 26. The destroyer *Brownson* (DD 518), Lieutenant Commander J. B. Maher, is sunk by Japanese dive-bombers off Cape Gloucester.

1944

January 1. Major General Alexander A. Vandegrift becomes the 18th commandant of the marine corps.

January 2. **Landing at Saidor.** MacArthur's progress up the coast of New Guinea continues with the landing of an army regiment at Saidor, an undefended village at the western entrance of the Vitiaz Strait. This operation leapfrogs the 12,000 Japanese troops garrisoning Sio, 75 miles to the east.

January 3. The destroyer *Turner* (DD 648), Commander H. S. Wygant, Jr., sinks with the loss of 100 lives following an internal explosion in Ambrose Channel, New York.

January 22. **Anzio (Operation Shingle).** A stalwart German defense has held the Allied advance up the mountainous Italian peninsula to a snail's pace. Hoping to get the campaign moving, the Allies attempt an amphibious end-run around the German front by landing in the Anzio-Nettuno area, almost due west of Rome. From there, the assault force is to press on to occupy the Alban Hills, scarcely 20 miles inland, from which its artillery will dominate the roads carrying supplies

Troops and equipment cross the beach at Anzio, Italy, on the day of the invasion. The column of smoke in the left background is from a burning LCI (Landing Craft, Infantry). *U.S. Army photograph.*

to the German army in the south. The idea of undertaking such an operation had been indefatigably promoted by Prime Minister Churchill. The two divisions—one American, one British—comprising the VI Corps, Major General J. P. Lucas, USA, are put ashore by Rear Admiral Frank J. Lowry's Anglo-American Task Force 81 on this date. Surprise is achieved, but instead of striking for the Alban Hills, Lucas pauses to consolidate the beachhead, which may have been a blessing, since the German reaction is swifter and stronger than had been anticipated. Marshal Kesselring soon has more Germans surrounding the beachhead than there are Americans and British inside it. Naval fire support contributes to the frustration of his plans to hurl the invaders into the sea. As it is, the Germans succeed in containing the beachhead, which is finally reached by Mark Clark's Fifth Army, pushing up from the south on May 25. Some 5,000 Allied troops have been killed, 17,000 wounded and 6,800 captured in the fighting.

January 29–February 6.   **Softening up the Marshalls.** The aircraft and ships of Rear Admiral Marc A. Mitscher's Task Force 58 join land-based planes in bombarding Japanese positions on Kwajalein, Wotje, Eniwetok, and Taroa in the Marshall Islands.

January 30–February 9.   Naval aircraft from Midway repeatedly attack Wake Island, neutralizing the Japanese airfield there in preparation for the invasion of the Marshalls.

January 31.   The carrier *Franklin* (CV 13) is commissioned.

January 31–February 5.   **The Marshalls (Operation Flintlock).** The Central Pacific offensive advances with a series of landings on the coral islands of Kwajalein Atoll. The operation is conducted by Vice Admiral Raymond A. Spruance's Fifth Fleet. The assault force is commanded by Rear Admiral Richmond Kelly Turner, the landing force (V Amphibious Corps) by Major General Holland M. Smith. Undefended Majuro Atoll, some 200 miles to the southeast, is occupied for use as an advanced base. Kwajalein, at the southern end of the atoll to which it gives its name, is stormed by the 7th Infantry Division, Major General C. H. Corlett, USA. Major General Harry Schmidt's 4th Marine Division lands on the Siamese-twin islands of Roi and Namur, on the northeastern angle of the atoll on February 1. The latter, defended by 3,600 Japanese naval troops, are secured by the afternoon of February 2. Only 91 members of their garrison are taken alive. Marine casualties are 195 killed and 545 wounded. These figures reflect the improvements in amphibious techniques made as a result of the experience gained at Tarawa. Kwajalein is secured on February 5.

February 15.   **Landing in the Green Islands.** The 3rd New Zealand Division, Major General H. E. Barraclough, is landed on the Green Islands, 55 miles east of New Ireland, by Rear Admiral Theodore S. ("Ping") Wilkinson's Task Force 31. The purpose of the operation, ordered by Admiral Halsey, is to obtain another airfield for use against Rabaul.

February 17–18.   **Attack on Truk.** Carrier task groups of Admiral Spruance's Fifth Fleet strike the Japanese fleet base at Truk, the cornerstone of the enemy position in the southwest Pacific. More than 1,200 sorties are flown. The light cruiser *Naka* and three destroyers are sunk and approximately 265 aircraft damaged or destroyed. Spruance's own Task Group 50.9, a surface action force built around the fast battleships *Iowa* (BB 61) and *New Jersey* (BB 62), intercepts and sinks the fleeing light cruiser *Katori* and a destroyer. Numerous smaller vessels and cargo ships are also destroyed. The only serious damage to the U.S. fleet occurs when the carrier *Intrepid* (CV 11) is hit by a Japanese torpedo plane.

February 18–23.   **Capture of Eniwetok (Operation Catchpole).** It had not been necessary to commit the V Amphibious Corps reserve at Kwajalein. That force, composed of the Twenty-Second Marines and the One Hundred and Sixth Infantry, under Brigadier General T. E. Watson, USMC, is employed to attack Eniwetok, another Marshalls atoll some 360 miles northwest of Kwajalein. Rear Admiral Harry W. ("Handsome Harry") Hill is designated commander of the Eniwetok Expeditionary Force (Task Force 51.11). The marines capture Engebi and Parry islands—the army regiment, Eniwetok.

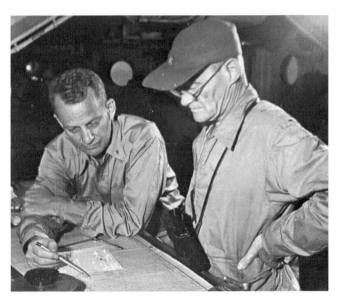

Vice Admiral Marc A. Mitscher *(right)* and Commodore Arleigh Burke, his chief of staff, at the chart table, March 1944. *U.S. Naval Institute Collection.*

February 19.   For the last time, a major air battle takes place over Rabaul. The air defense of the base, which has cost the Japanese more than 300 planes since November, is abandoned.

February 23.   **First Attack on the Marianas.** Six carriers of Rear Admiral Marc A. Mitscher's Task Groups 58.2 and 58.3 strike Japanese positions on Guam, Rota, Saipan, and Tinian in preparation for the invasion of the Marianas.

February 27.   The submarine *Grayback* (SS 208), Commander John A. Moore, is sunk by a Japanese aircraft in the East China Sea.

February 29.   The submarine *Trout* (SS 202), Lieutenant Commander Albert H. Clark, is lost sometime after successfully attacking a Japanese troop convoy en route to the Marianas, sinking one transport and damaging another. She may have been destroyed by the convoy's escort vessels.

February 29–March 9.   **Landing in the Admiralties.** The strategic ring around Rabaul is strengthened when a Seventh Fleet amphibious force commanded by Rear Admiral William M. Fechteler lands elements of the 1st Cavalry Division on Los Negros Island in the Admiralty group, west of New Britain. The beachhead is secured on March 5 and two days later LSTs ferry troops to nearby Manus Island. Meaningful enemy resistance ends on April 3.

March 6.   The submarine *Scorpion* (SS 278), Commander

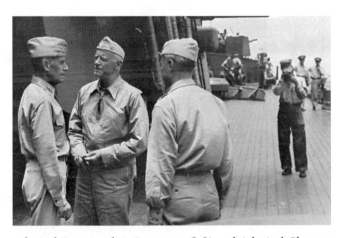

Admiral Raymond A. Spruance *(left)* and Admiral Chester W. Nimitz *(center)* aboard the battleship *New Jersey* off Majuro Atoll in the Marshalls, April 8, 1944. *Official U.S. Navy photograph.*

Maximilian G. Schmidt, is reported overdue and presumed lost. She was probably destroyed in a minefield in the East China Sea.

March 9.   The destroyer escort *Leopold* (DE 319), Lieutenant Commander K. C. Phillips, USCG, is sunk with the loss of 171 lives by the *U-255* while escorting a North Atlantic convoy.

March 13.   The Japanese light cruiser *Tatsuta* is sunk off the Home Island of Honshu by the submarine *Sand Lance* (SS 381), Lieutenant Commander Malcolm E. Garrison.

March 20.   In the Southwest Pacific, the Fourth Marine Regiment lands on unoccupied Emirau Island in the St. Matthias group, midway between New Ireland and the Admiralties, completing the encirclement of Rabaul.

March 26.   The submarine *Tullibee* (SS 284), Commander Charles F. Brindupke, is sunk while attacking a Japanese convoy near the Palaus, probably by one of her own torpedoes making a circular run.

March 30–April 1.   Japanese positions in the Palaus and the Carolines are attacked by the fast carrier forces of the Fifth Fleet.

April 15.   The carrier *Hancock* (CV 19) is commissioned.

April 16.   The battleship *Wisconsin* (BB 64) is commissioned.

April 19.   Planes from the carriers *Saratoga* (CV 3) and HMS *Illustrious* of an Allied task force commanded by Admiral Sir James Somerville, RN, strike Japanese installations at Sabang in the Netherlands East Indies.

April 20.   The destroyer *Lansdale* (DD 426), Lieutenant Commander D. M. Swift, is sunk with the loss of 49 lives by German aircraft in the eastern Mediterranean.

April 22.   **Hollandia.** Rear Admiral Daniel E. Barbey's Seventh Amphibious Force lands two divisions of the I Army Corps, Lieutenant General Robert L. Eichelberger, around Humboldt Bay, on the border of Netherlands New Guinea 300 miles behind the Japanese front line. American planners refer to the area as Hollandia, the name of tiny village on an arm of Humboldt Bay. Landings are made near it, on Tanahmerah Bay and at Aitape. This is one of MacArthur's most brilliant operations, bypassing the Japanese Eighteenth Army at Wewak, 90 miles to the east, and trapping it between the Americans at Hollandia and Australian forces advancing up the coast. Japanese resistance in the area is soon overcome and Hollandia becomes a major air and naval base for the next stage of the New Guinea campaign. Vice Admiral Mitscher's Fifth Fleet carriers are briefly loaned to MacArthur to support these landings.

April 27.   The submarine *Bluegill* (SS 242), Commander Eric L. Barr, Jr., sinks the Japanese light cruiser *Yubari* near the Caroline Islands.

April 28.   Secretary of the Navy Knox dies in Washington, D.C.

April 29–May 1.   The Fifth Fleet attacks Japanese positions in the Carolines. Aircraft from Admiral Mitscher's carriers strike the fleet base at Truk and the port facilities at Ponape, the latter of which is also shelled by a battleship force commanded by Rear Admiral Willis A. Lee, and a cruiser-destroyer force under Rear Admiral Jesse B. Oldendorf shells the airfield at Satawan.

May 8.   The carrier *Ticonderoga* (CV 14) is commissioned.

May 17.   Japanese shipping and port facilities at Surabaja, Java, are attacked by carrier planes from an Allied task force commanded by Admiral Sir James F. Somerville, RN.

May 17–18.   On the coast of New Guinea the Seventh Amphibious Force, temporarily commanded by Rear Admiral W. M. Fechteler, lands the 163rd Regimental Combat Team at the village of Toem and the offshore island of Wakde, 120 miles west of Hollandia.

May 19.   James V. Forrestal enters office as 48th secretary of the navy.

May 19–20.   Marcus Island, northwest of Wake, is attacked by planes of the carriers *Essex* (CV 9), *San Jacinto* (CVL 30), and *Wasp* (CV 18) of Rear Admiral A. E. Montgomery's Task Force 58.6. Wake itself is hit three days later.

May 19.   **The England.** In the Bismarck Archipelago, the destroyer escort *England* (DE 635), Lieutenant Commander Walton B. Pendleton, begins a phenomenal string of successes in which she sinks six Japanese submarines in twelve days: the *I-16* on the 19th, the *RO-106* on the 22nd, the *RO-104* on the 23rd, the *RO-116* on the 24th, the *RO-108* on the 26th, and the *RO-105* May 30. No other American warship ever approaches this record.

May 27.   Admiral Fechteler's Seventh Amphibious Force lands the 41st Infantry Division, Major General H. H. Fuller, on Biak, a sizable island off the northern coast of New Guinea 150 miles west of Wakde, where the previous landing had been made only 10 days before. The island is garrisoned by 11,500 well-led Japanese army and navy troops who retain control of its airfield until June 22.

The *England. Official U.S. Navy photograph.*

May 29.   **Loss of the Block Island.** Northwest of the Canary Islands the escort carrier *Block Island* (CVE 21), Captain Francis M. Hughes, is torpedoed and sunk by the *U-549*. The submarine also hits the *Barr* (DE 576), one of the four destroyer escorts screening the carrier, but is in turn sunk by another of them, the *Eugene E. Elmore* (DE 686), Lieutenant Commander G. L. Conkey. The *Block Island* is the only American carrier lost in the Battle of the Atlantic.

June 1.   The submarine *Herring* (SS 233), Lieutenant Commander David Zabriskie, Jr., is sunk while attacking Japanese shipping at Matsuwa Island in the Kuriles on her eighth war patrol.

June 4.   **Capture of the U-505.** Captain Daniel V. Gallery captures a submarine when his hunter-killer group, consisting of the escort carrier *Guadalcanal* (CVE 60) and five destroyers, encounters the *U-505* homeward bound off the Atlantic coast of North Africa. Depth-charged to the surface and abandoned by her crew, the *U-505* is boarded and saved by a party Gallery had organized in anticipation of just such an occasion. The only U-boat captured by the U.S. Navy in World War II, today she is exhibited at the Chicago Museum of Science and Industry.

June 6.   **D-Day (Operation Overlord/Neptune).** The most fateful landings of World War II are made at dawn when five Allied divisions—two American, two British, and one Canadian—storm ashore on the beaches of Normandy. A few hours earlier, two American and one British airborne divisions, and a Polish airborne brigade had been dropped behind enemy lines to create confusion and seize strategic points. The Germans are taken by surprise. Although well aware that the long-awaited cross-Channel invasion was imminent, they had expected the blow to fall to the north, in the Pas de Calais. General Dwight D. Eisenhower is Supreme Commander, Allied Expeditionary Force. The naval aspects of the assault (Operation Neptune) are commanded by Admiral Sir Bertram H. Ramsay, RN. The movement to the American beaches (Utah and Omaha) is conducted by the Western Naval Task Force, Rear Admiral Alan G. Kirk; to the British beaches (Gold, Juno, and Sword) by the Eastern Naval Task Force, Admiral Sir Philip Vian, RN. The strength of these two forces, in terms of vessels that cross the Channel on their own bottoms, is 911 and 1,796 ships, respectively. Resistance is fiercest at Omaha Beach, where fire support from destroyers running close inshore is instrumental to the success of the landing. The destroyer *Corry* (DD 463), Lieutenant Commander G. D. Hoffman, is sunk by a mine off Utah Beach. By the morning of June 7, some 66,000 Allied troops have crossed the beaches. The defeat of Germany is assured.

June 7.   **"Mulberries."** Two artificial harbors are created off the Normandy beaches by sinking concrete caissons. The coast's lack of port facilities was one of the reasons the Germans had believed landings would be made in the Pas de Calais. Mulberry A, off Omaha Beach, is destroyed by a great storm on June 18–22, but by then more than 250,000 Allied soldiers are ashore.

D-Day: LCIs head for the landing beaches in the protective presence of the cruiser *Augusta. Official U.S. Navy photograph.*

June 7.   The submarine *Gudgeon* (SS 211), Lieutenant Commander Robert A. Bonin, is reported overdue and presumed lost.

June 8.   Off the Normandy beaches, the destroyer escort *Rich* (DE 695), Lieutenant Commander E. A. Michel, is sunk with the loss of 89 lives and the destroyers *Glennon* (DD 620) and *Meredith* (DD 726) are damaged by German mines.

June 8–9.   In the Southwest Pacific, a force consisting of the cruiser HMAS *Australia,* the light cruisers *Boise* (CL 47) and *Phoenix* (CL 46), and 14 destroyers under Rear Admiral V. A. C. Crutchley, VC, DSC, RN, breaks up a Japanese attempt to reinforce Biak by sea.

June 9.   The destroyer *Meredith* (DD 726), Commander George Knuepfer, damaged by a mine off the coast of Normandy, breaks up and sinks.

June 10.   A German shore battery sinks the destroyer *Glennon* (DD 620), Commander C. A. Johnson, damaged by a mine two days earlier, off Normandy.

June 11.   The battleship *Missouri* (BB 63) is commissioned.

June 15.   **Saipan.** The navy's Central Pacific offensive takes a giant stride across more than 700 miles of open water to assault the Marianas (Operation Forager), which Admiral King has long regarded as the key to that theater. Saipan is the first island to be attacked. As in the Marshalls, Admiral Raymond A. Spruance commands the Fifth Fleet; Vice Admiral R. K. Turner, the Joint Expeditionary Force (Task Force 51); and Lieutenant General H. M. Smith, the Expeditionary Troops. The assault is made by the 2nd Marine Division, Major General T. E. Watson, and the 4th Marine

A Japanese bomber goes down in flames in the Marianas Turkey Shoot. *Official U.S. Navy photograph.*

Division, Major General Harry Schmidt. In reserve is Major General Ralph C. Smith's 27th Infantry Division, which is landed on the night of June 17–18. The island is defended by 29,662 Japanese army and navy troops under Lieutenant General Yoshitsugu Saito and Admiral Chuichi Nagumo, who had commanded the Japanese carriers that attacked Pearl Harbor; both commit hara-kiri at the end of the struggle. Resistance is stiff. Marine Lieutenant General Smith, dissatisfied with the performance of the 27th Division, provokes a bitter, interservice controversy by summarily relieving army Major General Smith of command. The fighting ends on July 12. U.S. casualties are 3,426 killed and 13,099 wounded, three-quarters of them marines. Only 1,780 Japanese surrender. Possession of Saipan places Japan within range of land-based B-29 bombers.

June 19–20. **Battle of the Philippine Sea (Marianas Turkey Shoot).** The Japanese fleet comes out in strength for the first time since October 1942 in an attempt to break up the invasion of Saipan. Commanded by Vice Admiral Jisaburo Ozawa, it includes 5 fleet carriers, 4 light carriers, and 5 battleships, plus cruisers (13) and destroyers (28). Admiral Spruance's Fifth Fleet, consisting of 7 fleet carriers, 8 light carriers, and 7 battleships, plus cruisers (21) and destroyers (69), is clearly a superior force—most notably, perhaps, in aircraft, 956 to 473 of all types. Ozawa hopes to offset the odds by exploiting his planes' greater range to remain beyond the reach of the American carriers. He also believes that his attack will be supported by land-based air in the Marianas and that it

will be possible for his fliers to shuttle-bomb the American fleet, landing to rearm on Saipan and hitting the invaders again on the way back to their carriers. Most of these calculations go wrong. Vice Admiral Marc A. Mitscher's carrier planes have destroyed Japanese air power in the Marianas and made the islands' runways unusable. Even the plan of remaining out of range of the American carriers might have misfired had Admiral Spruance steered toward Ozawa's fleet on the evening of June 18, when its approach was known to him, but he chose to remain within close supporting range of the beachhead, fearing that the Japanese might attempt to slip around his fleet to attack the amphibious forces. This conservative decision is later criticized by members of the aviation community. The air battle with the largely inexperienced Japanese pilots on June 19 is so one-sided that Mitscher's men call it "The Marianas Turkey Shoot." A total of 346 Japanese planes are shot down, against only 30 American. Meanwhile, the submarine *Albacore* (SS 218), Commander James W. Blanchard, sinks the 33,000-ton Japanese carrier and fleet flagship *Taiho,* and the *Cavalla* (SS 244), Lieutenant Commander Herbert J.

Japanese ships, including the carrier *Zuikaku (center)* maneuvering under attack from American aircraft at the Battle of the Philippine Sea. *Official U.S. Navy photograph.*

Kossler, sinks the Pearl Harbor carrier *Shokaku*. The next day Spruance pursues the retiring enemy fleet, and four torpedo bombers from the *Belleau Wood* (CVL 24) sink the carrier *Hiyo*. Another 65 of Ozawa's planes are destroyed in this action, reducing the strength of the Japanese carrier fleet to 35 aircraft. As the American pilots return to their carriers after nightfall, Admiral Mitscher orders his ships to turn on their lights and to help them land.

June 19.   **Navy ace.** Commander David McCampbell's personal score in the Marianas Turkey Shoot is seven enemy aircraft. Four months later, during the Battle of Leyte Gulf, he will shoot down nine Japanese planes on a single day. For these actions, he is awarded the Medal of Honor. At war's end he is the navy's leading ace, with 34 confirmed victories.

June 25.   German positions at Cherbourg, France, are shelled by a heavy surface force under Rear Admiral Morton L. Deyo. The battleship *Texas* (BB 35) and four destroyers are damaged by the enemy's shore batteries.

June 26.   The garrison of Cherbourg capitulates.

July 2.   **Landing at Noemfoor Island.** The next-to-last leap in MacArthur's advance along the coast of New

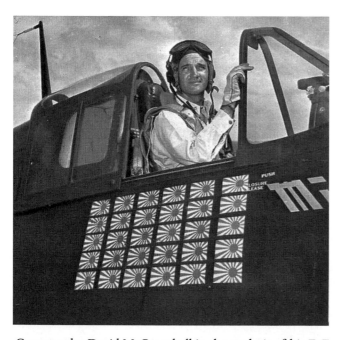

Commander David McCampbell in the cockpit of his F6F Hellcat. This picture was taken after the Battle of Leyte Gulf, when his score of enemy aircraft had reached 30. *Official U.S. Navy photograph.*

Guinea is made to Noemfoor, an island approximately 50 miles west of Biak. The island's three Japanese-built airfields will be useful in supporting the invasion of the Vogelkop Peninsula on the western end of New Guinea. Rear Admiral W. M. Fechteler's Naval Attack Force conducts the landing of the 168th Infantry (reinforced), which secures the island at a cost of 409 casualties.

July 4.   Aircraft and ships of the Fifth Fleet bombard Japanese installations on Chichi Jima, Haha Jima, and Iwo Jima in the Bonins.

July 4.   The submarine *S-28* (SS 133) disappears while on exercises off Oahu.

July 19.   The Japanese light cruiser *Oi* is sunk by the submarine *Flasher* (SS 249), Commander Reuben T. Whitaker, in the South China Sea.

July 21.   **Guam (Operation Stevedore).** The second of the Marianas is captured when Rear Admiral Richard L. Connolly's Southern Attack Force (Task Force 53) lands the 3rd Marine Division, the 1st Provisional Marine Brigade, and the 77th Infantry Division on Guam. Major General Roy S. Geiger, USMC, is the landing force commander. The largest of the Marianas, Guam is defended by 19,000 Japanese army and navy troops under Lieutenant General Takeshi Takashima. The island is secured by August 10, although some 9,000 of the enemy remain at large in the interior, and sporadic fighting continues until the end of the war. American casualties are 1,435 killed or missing and 5,648 wounded, nearly all marines.

July 24.   **Tinian.** The island of Tinian, in the Marianas only five miles southwest of Saipan, is invaded by the 2nd Marine Division, Major General T. E. Watson, and the 4th Marine Division, Major General Clifton B. Cates. Rear Admiral Harry W. Hill commands the attack force (Task Force 51); Major General Roy S. Geiger, the landing force. Defending the island are 9,162 Japanese army and navy troops under Vice Admiral Kakuji Kakuta and Colonel Keishi Ogata. They are overcome by August 1 in what Lieutenant General H. M. Smith calls the best-executed amphibious operation of the war. Neither Admiral Kakuta nor Colonel Ogata survive the struggle; no Japanese island commander will ever be taken alive. Marine casualties are 328 dead and 1,571 wounded.

July 25–28.   Japanese positions at Ulithi, Yap, Ngulu, and the Palaus are hit by carrier planes from Vice Admiral Marc A. Mitscher's Task Force 58.

A medium tank supports the advance of marine riflemen on Tinian, in the Marianas. *Defense Department photo (Marine Corps).*

July 26.   The submarine *Robalo* (SS 273), Lieutenant Commander Manning M. Kimmel, is lost, probably by striking a mine, off the Philippine island of Palawan.

July 26–29.   **The Philippines or Formosa?** President Roosevelt meets with General MacArthur and Admiral Nimitz at Honolulu to discuss the next steps in the war against Japan. Nimitz presents Admiral King's view that the Central Pacific drive should continue to Formosa, but both he and the president are convinced by MacArthur's argument that moral as well as military grounds dictate the United States must proceed at the earliest possible moment to liberate the Philippines, with successive landings on Mindanao, Leyte, and Luzon. The joint chiefs of staff take longer to make up their minds. The invasion of Mindanao and Leyte is not authorized until September, and the question of whether to go on to Luzon or Formosa remains unsettled even then.

July 28.   The submarine *Golet* (SS 361), Lieutenant James S. Clark, is reported overdue and presumed lost on her second Pacific war patrol. She was probably destroyed by Japanese surface forces on June 14.

July 30–31.   **Triumph in New Guinea.** The New Guinea campaign comes to a victorious conclusion when the 6th Infantry Division, Major General Franklin C. Sibert, is landed unopposed by Rear Admiral W. M. Fechteler's Seventh Amphibious Force at two villages near Cape Sansapor on the northern coast of the Vogelkop Peninsula. In the 14 weeks since the landing at Hollandia, MacArthur's forces have advanced 550 miles.

August 2.   In the North Atlantic, the destroyer escort *Fiske* (DE 143), Lieutenant John A. Comly, USNR, is sunk with the loss of 30 lives while attacking the *U-804*.

August 4–5.   Fifth Fleet carrier forces commanded by Vice Admirals Marc A. Mitscher and J. S. McCain attack Japanese installations on Chichi Jima and Haha Jima in the Bonin Islands.

August 6.   The carrier *Bennington* (CV 20) is commissioned.

August 7.   The Japanese light cruiser *Nagara* is sunk by the submarine *Croaker* (SS 246), Commander John E. Lee, off the Japanese Home Island of Kyushu.

August 13.   The submarine *Flier* (SS 250), Commander John D. Crowley, is lost while running on the surface of the Balabac Strait, off British North Borneo. She probably hit a mine. Eight of her crewmen survive.

August 15.   **Invasion of Southern France (Operation Dragoon).** Vice Admiral H. Kent Hewitt's Western Naval Task Force lands three American divisions between St.-Tropez and Cannes on the Mediterranean coast of France. Two French divisions follow. The beaches, lightly defended in the first place, are subjected to an intensive, daylight naval bombardment, and German resistance is weak. This landing originally had been planned to coincide with the invasion of Normandy, but had to be postponed because of a shortage of landing craft. General Eisenhower decided that it should still be made in order to gain the use of the port of Marseille for the campaign in France. Prime Minister Churchill argued unsuccessfully in favor of switching the site of the invasion to Trieste,

The Honolulu conference *(from left to right):* General Douglas MacArthur, President Franklin D. Roosevelt, Admiral Chester W. Nimitz, and Admiral William D. Leahy. *Courtesy National Archives.*

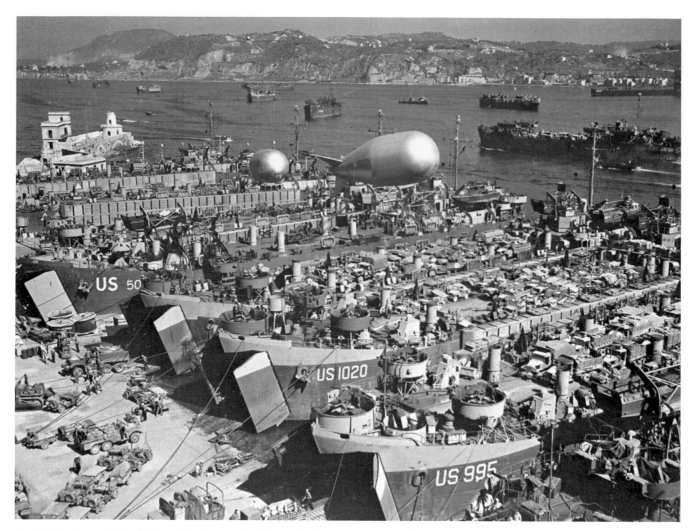

At Nisida, Italy, LSTs sheltered by barrage balloons load equipment for the invasion of southern France. *Official U.S. Navy photograph.*

at the head of the Adriatic, in hopes that an army landed there could beat the Russians into the Balkans.

August 18.   The submarine *Hardhead* (SS 365), Commander Fitzhugh McMaster, sinks the Japanese light cruiser *Natori* in San Bernardino Strait.

August 24.   Loss of the Harder. The submarine *Harder* (SS 257), Commander Samuel D. Dealey, is depthcharged and destroyed by a Japanese minesweeper off Luzon. One of the most aggressive sub commanders, in his five previous patrols Dealey had sunk 16 Japanese ships, including 4 destroyers and 2 frigates. He is posthumously awarded the Medal of Honor.

August 31–September 2.   Ships and aircraft of Rear Admiral R. E. Davison's Task Group 38.4 bombard Japanese positions on Iwo Jima in the Bonin Islands.

September 6.   Vice Admiral Marc A. Mitscher's Task Force 38, comprising 12 attack carriers, 1 light carrier, 6 battleships, 3 heavy cruisers, and numerous light cruisers and destroyers, bombs and shells Japanese positions in the Palaus and the Carolines.

September 9–10.   The planes of Task Force 38 attack Japanese airfields on the southern Philippine island of Mindanao.

September 10–16.   Task Force 38 strikes Japanese positions in the Palau Islands, the Visayas, and Mindanao in preparation for and support of the landing on Peleliu, which is made on September 15.

September 11–16.   Second Quebec Conference (Octagon). President Roosevelt, Prime Minister Churchill, and the combined chiefs of staff meet. Held at Churchill's request, the conference deals primarily with the question of British participation in the war in the Pacific. The prime minister is anxious for the Royal Navy to play a role in the closing operations against Japan. Admiral King is adamantly opposed to the appearance of the British fleet in the Central Pacific, but President Roosevelt, more sensitive to diplomatic considerations, overrules him. The combined chiefs of staff also approve a recommendation initiated by Admiral Halsey and endorsed by Admiral Nimitz and General MacArthur to advance the date of the invasion of Leyte in the Philippines from December 20 to October 20 and to cancel the previously planned, intermediate landings in the Talaud Islands and on Mindanao. The question of whether to go on from Leyte to Luzon or Formosa remains unresolved.

September 13.   The destroyer minesweeper *Perry* (DMS 17) strikes a mine and sinks off the Palau Islands.

September 13.   The destroyer *Warrington* (DD 383), Commander Frank Quarles, goes down during a storm in the Atlantic.

September 15.   **Landing on Morotai.** The Seventh Amphibious Force, back under the command of Rear Admiral Daniel E. Barbey, lands the 41st Infantry Division on the almost unoccupied island of Morotai, roughly midway between New Guinea and the Philippines. An airfield will be established there to support the invasion of Leyte.

September 15.   **Peleliu (Operation Stalemate II).** From the Marianas the Central Pacific drive leaps 600 miles southwest to the Palaus. Peleliu, an island of 12 square miles, is defended by 10,700 Japanese troops under the command of Colonel Kunio Nakagawa. The invasion is conducted by Vice Admiral T. S. Wilkinson's Third Amphibious Force and Major General Roy S. Geiger's III Amphibious Corps, composed of the 1st Marine Division, Major General W. H. Rupertus, and the 81st Infantry Division, Major General P. J. Muller, which is left in reserve. Japanese resistance, strong from the start, becomes even more deadly when the marines reach the complex of caves and tunnels along Umurbrogol Ridge. The First Marine Regiment is withdrawn after a week, having sustained 56 percent casualties, and the 81st Infantry Division relieves the marine division on October 20. Fighting ends on November 25. American casualties are 1,460 killed and 7,711 wounded.

Alligator amtracs churn toward Peleliu on D-Day while *(far left)* an LSM(R)—Landing Ship Medium, Rocket—lays down a covering barrage. *Official U.S. Navy photograph.*

September 15.   The carrier *Shangri-la* (CV 38) is commissioned.

September 16.   The 20,000-ton, Japanese escort carrier *Unyo* is sunk by the submarine *Barb* (SS 220), Commander Eugene B. Fluckey, in the South China Sea. Another torpedo in the same salvo destroys the 11,000-ton tanker *Azusa*.

September 17–September 20.   **Seizure of Angaur.** Amphibious forces (Task Group 32.2) commanded by Rear Admiral W. H. P. ("Spike") Blandy land the 81st Infantry Division on the southernmost of the Palau Islands. Although organized resistance is declared to have ended on September 20, fighting continues in the interior of the island until October 23. In the meanwhile, army engineers have constructed an airfield to support the invasion of the Philippines.

September 21–22.   Aircraft from Vice Admiral Marc A. Mitscher's Task Force 38 attack Japanese airfields and shipping at Luzon, in the Philippines.

September 23.   **Ulithi.** The undefended atoll of Ulithi, halfway between and somewhat north of the Carolines and the Palaus, is occupied by a regiment of the 81st Infantry Division, landed by Rear Admiral W. H. P. Blandy's Task Group 32.2. This atoll replaces Eniwetok as the principal advanced base of the Pacific Fleet.

September 24.   Vice Admiral Mitscher's Task Force 38 switches its attention to Japanese positions on the Visayan islands in the central Philippines.

September 29.   In a meeting in San Francisco, Admirals Nimitz and Forrest P. Sherman finally persuade Admiral King that his plan of invading Formosa is impractical. The army cannot supply enough men. The next three objectives in the war against Japan will be Luzon, Iwo Jima, and Okinawa.

October 3.   The destroyer escort *Shelton* (DE 407), Lieutenant Commander L. G. Salomon, USNR, is torpedoed and sunk by a Japanese submarine north of Morotai, Netherlands East Indies. The destroyer escort *Richard M. Rowell* (DE 403) and carrier aircraft then attack and destroy the American submarine *Seawolf* (SS 197), Commander Albert M. Bontier, under the impression that she is Japanese.

October 3.   The joint chiefs of staff authorize General MacArthur to move on to Luzon and direct Admiral Nimitz to prepare to invade Iwo Jima and Okinawa.

October 9.   The carrier *Randolph* (CV 15) is commissioned.

October 10–15.   Aircraft of Vice Admiral Marc A. Mitscher's Task Force 38 deliver a series of heavy attacks against Japanese positions on Okinawa, the Ryukyus, Formosa, the Pescadores, and Luzon.

October 17.   The submarine *Escolar* (SS 294), Commander W. J. Millican, is lost sometime after communicating with the submarine *Perch* (SS 313) on this date. She probably hit a mine.

October 17.   A task force commanded by Rear Admiral Arthur D. Struble lands the 6th Ranger Battalion to destroy small Japanese posts on Suluan and Dinagat islands in the mouth of Leyte Gulf. It was feared that these installations might give warning of the invasion, which is just what happens.

October 17.   **Operation SHO-1.** Informed by the unit on Suluan Island of the appearance of American ships in Leyte Gulf, Admiral Soemu Toyoda, commander-in-chief of the Japanese Combined Fleet, activates Plan SHO-1 for the defense of the Philippines. SHO is the Japanese word for victory.

October 17–18.   Third Fleet carrier planes pound Japanese positions on Luzon.

October 19.   Battleships and cruisers of the fire support units of Vice Admiral Thomas C. Kinkaid's Seventh Fleet shell the landing beaches on Leyte Gulf.

October 20.   **Invasion of the Philippines.** MacArthur's promise to return to the Philippines is made good and the pincers of the dual advance in the Pacific close on the east coast of the island of Leyte. Shielded by the fast carriers and battleships of Admiral Halsey's Third Fleet, the Seventh Fleet ("MacArthur's Navy") lands four divisions of Lieutenant General Walter P. Krueger's Sixth Army on the shores of Leyte Gulf.

October 23.   Off Palawan, the submarines *Dace* (SS 247), Commander Bladen D. Claggett, and *Darter* (SS 227), Commander David H. McClintock, encounter the Japanese First Striking Force, the most powerful of the enemy fleet units converging on the Philippines. The *Dace* sinks the heavy cruiser *Maya*. *Darter* sinks the heavy cruiser *Atago*, flagship of the force commander, Vice Admiral Takeo Kurita, and seriously damages the heavy cruiser *Takao*, which returns to port.

October 24.   The submarine *Darter* (SS 227), Commander David H. McClintock, is scuttled after running ashore on Bombay Reef off Palawan. The *Dace* (SS 247) rescues her crew.

October 24.   **Loss of the Tang.** The submarine *Tang* (SS 306), Commander Richard H. O'Kane, is lost off the coast of Formosa when one of her own torpedoes circles back to sink her. The top-scoring American submariner of the war in terms of ships sunk (31 cred-

Ships of the American armada assembled at Seeadler Harbor off Manus Island in the Admiralties prior to the invasion of the Philippines. *Official U.S. Navy photograph.*

ited during the conflict, 24 according to a postwar survey), O'Kane survives to receive the Medal of Honor.

October 24.   The submarine *Shark* (SS 314), Commander Edward N. Blakely, is lost in the Philippines sometime after communicating with the submarine *Seadragon* (SS 194) on this date.

October 24.   **Beginning of the Battle of Leyte Gulf: Battle of the Sibuyan Sea.** In accordance with Plan SHO-1, the Imperial Japanese Navy stakes everything on the "decisive battle" to which its doctrine is devoted. There is really little choice in the matter. The loss of the Philippines would cut Japan off from her Southern Resources Area in Southeast Asia, without which her already crippled war economy will collapse. The Japanese hope to annihilate the American amphibious force, Admiral Kinkaid's Seventh Fleet, and thereby repel the invasion of Leyte. To do so, however, they must first destroy or decoy Admiral Halsey's Third Fleet. Realizing that their lack of carrier pilots

makes the former impossible, they have decided to use their carriers as bait to accomplish the latter. A "Northern Force" (as the Americans name it) of four carriers, two hybrid battleship-carriers, three light cruisers, and eight destroyers under Vice Admiral Jisaburo Ozawa is to advertise its presence off the northern coast of Luzon, luring Halsey away from the beachhead. Simultaneously, two powerful surface forces will converge on Leyte Gulf from the west—Vice Admiral Takeo Kurita's "Center Force" of the superbattleships *Musashi* and *Yamato*, battleships *Kongo, Haruna,* and *Nagato*, twelve cruisers, and fifteen destroyers via the San Bernardino Strait; and a "Southern Force" in two echelons of two battleships, four cruisers, and eleven destroyers under Vice Admirals Shoji Nishimura and Kiyohide Shima, via the Surigao Strait. The result of this strategy is four interlocking actions jointly comprising the largest naval battle ever fought. It begins around noon on this date, when planes from the Third

The Battle of the Sibuyan Sea. The *Musashi*, one of the two *Yamato*-class superbattleships of Admiral Kurita's Center Force, under heavy attack from the planes of Task Force 38. *Official U.S. Navy photograph.*

Fleet attack Kurita's Center Force on its passage through the Sibuyan Sea, sinking the superbattleship *Musashi* and the destroyer *Wakaba* and disabling the cruiser *Myoko*.

October 24–25.   **Battle of Surigao Strait.** After dark, Admiral Nishimura's Southern Force fights its way through the Surigao Strait under attack from 39 PT boats and the five destroyers of Captain Jesse G. Coward's Desron 54. The latter sink the battleship *Fuso* and the destroyers *Michishio* and *Yamagumo* and disable two other destroyers. Pressing on with the damaged battleship *Yamashiro,* heavy cruiser *Mogami,* and destroyer *Shigure,* Nishimura nears the eastern end of the strait to encounter a battle line composed of the six old battleships of the Seventh Fleet's fire support force—the *California* (BB 44), *Maryland* (BB 46), *Mississippi* (BB 41), *Pennsylvania* (BB 38), *Tennessee* (BB 43), and *West Virginia* (BB 48), under Rear Admiral Jesse B. Oldendorf. The *Yamashiro* is sunk and the *Mogami* seriously damaged. She and the *Shigure* withdraw. Vice Admiral Shima's echelon, two heavy cruisers, one light cruiser, and seven destroyers, enters the strait around this time, sizes up the situation and retires. Two of Nishimura's cripples, the *Mogami* and de-

stroyer *Asagumo,* are sunk after daybreak. Only one American ship, the destroyer *Albert W. Grant* (DD 649), is seriously damaged.

October 24.   Land-based Japanese planes sink the carrier *Princeton* (CVL 23), Captain W. H. Buracker, off Luzon.

October 25.   **Battle off Samar.** On the afternoon of the 24th (much later than the Japanese had hoped), Halsey's planes spot the Japanese Northern Force off Luzon. Accepting his pilots' exaggerated reports of the damage inflicted on the Center Force in the Battle of the Sibuyan Sea, Halsey takes the entire Third Fleet north after Ozawa's carriers. Because of a misunderstanding in communications, Admiral Kinkaid assumes that Halsey has left a force to guard San Bernardino Strait and does not try to cover it with the Seventh Fleet. Thus it is that at dawn Admiral Kurita's Center Force steams peacefully through the strait and opens fire on the six little escort carriers of Admiral Clifton F. ("Ziggy") Sprague's "Taffy 3" off the island of Samar. Sprague launches his planes, makes smoke, and retires at his best speed, a paltry 18 knots, calling for help. Unfortunately, the only units near are other "taffies." As the Center Force gains on his carriers, Sprague sends his three destroyers and four destroyer escorts to deliver torpedo attacks against the enemy battleships, a death-ride in which the destroyers *Hoel* (DD 533), Commander L. S. Kintberger, and *Johnston* (DD 557), Commander E. E. Evans, and the destroyer escort *Samuel B. Roberts* (DE 413), Lieutenant Commander R. W. Copeland, USNR, are sunk. The damage is not all on the American side, however. The heavy cruisers *Chikuma, Chokai,* and *Suzuya* take bomb and torpedo hits to which they will succumb before noon; but Kurita keeps coming. The *Gambier Bay* (CVE 73), Captain W. V. R. Vieweg, is the first of the carriers to be sunk by gunfire. Then, incredibly, Center Force reverses course. Admiral Kurita has mistaken the escort carriers for fleet carriers and, rattled by the attacks of the taffies' aircraft and destroyers, decides to break off the action. He may also be disoriented by the events of the last two days, during which he has lost two flagships. Shortly after noon, Center Force retires through San Bernardino Strait.

October 25. **Battle off Cape Engaño.** The planes of Admiral Halsey's Third Fleet have already begun attacking Ozawa's Northern Force when a message from Admiral Nimitz regarding the situation at San Bernardino Strait prompts Halsey to turn back south with his fast battleships. He leaves most of Mitscher's carriers with a cruiser-destroyer screen to pursue the Japanese. All four enemy carriers—the *Chitose, Chiyoda, Zuiho,* and *Zuikaku*—and the destroyer *Akizuki* are sunk in the course of the day. The cruiser-destroyer force overtakes and sinks the destroyer *Hatsuzuki,* and Commander Joseph B. Icenhower's submarine *Jallao* (SS 368) sinks the light cruiser *Tama.* This action concludes the Battle of Leyte Gulf, in which (including the approach and mopping up) the Imperial Japanese Navy loses four carriers, three battleships, eight cruisers, and eight destroyers and ceases to exist as an effective fighting force.

October 26. **First kamikaze attacks.** Japanese pilots in the Philippines fly the first deliberate suicide missions of the war. The escort carrier *St. Lo* (CVE 63), Captain

The Battle off Samar: Japanese shells straddle the doomed escort carrier *Gambier Bay,* as seen from the *Kitkun Bay,* another of the escort carriers in Taffy 3. *Official U.S. Navy photograph.*

F. J. McKenna, is crashed by a kamikaze in Leyte gulf and so badly damaged that she must be sunk. Four other escort carriers are also hit. The kamikaze plane will prove to be the most effective anti-ship weapon of World War II.

October 26. Two destroyers of the Japanese Center Force retiring from the Battle of Leyte Gulf are sunk, the *Hayashimo* by air attack and the *Nowaki* in a separate, surface action.

October 26. Planes from Rear Admiral Thomas L. Sprague's Taffy 2 catch a Japanese force retiring through the Visayan Sea after landing reinforcements on Leyte and sink the light cruiser *Kinu* and the destroyer *Uranami*.

October 26–November 5.   **Kamikaze attacks.** During this period off Leyte, Japanese suicide planes damage the carriers *Belleau Wood* (CVL 24), *Franklin* (CV 13), *Intrepid* (CV 11), and *Lexington* (CV 16), escort carrier *Suwanee* (CVE 27), light cruiser *Denver* (CL 58), and several destroyers and sink the destroyer *Abner Read* (DD 526), Commander A. M. Purdy. The destroyer escort *Eversole* (DE 404), Lieutenant Commander George E. Marix, is sunk by a Japanese submarine on October 28.

October 27. The Japanese light cruiser *Abukuma,* the only unit of Admiral Shima's force to be damaged in the Battle of Surigao Strait, is sunk by air attack off Negros Island.

November 5–6. Carrier aircraft from Vice Admiral J. S. McCain's Task Group 38.1 conduct heavy strikes against Japanese positions on Luzon and sink the heavy cruiser *Nachi* in Manila Bay.

November 7. The submarine *Albacore* (SS 218), Lieutenant Commander Hugh R. Rimmer, strikes a mine and is lost with all hands off the Japanese Home Island of Hokkaido.

November 8. The submarine *Growler* (SS 215), Commander Thomas B. Oakley, Jr., is destroyed while attacking a Japanese convoy on her 11th war patrol.

November 11. Third Fleet aircraft sink the Japanese destroyers *Hamanami, Naganami, Shimakaze,* and *Wakatsuki* off Ormoc Bay, Leyte.

November 13. The Japanese light cruiser *Kiso* and destroyers *Akebono, Akishimo, Hatsuharu,* and *Okinami* are sunk by Third Fleet air strikes in Manila Bay.

November 17. The 21,000-ton Japanese escort carrier *Shinyo* is sunk by the submarine *Spadefish* (SS 411), Commander Gordon Underwood, in the Yellow Sea.

November 21. **The Kongo.** Northwest of Formosa, the submarine *Sealion* (SS 315), Commander Eli T. Riech, sinks the Japanese battleship *Kongo* and destroyer *Urakaze.* The *Kongo* is the first enemy battleship to fall victim to an American submarine.

November 24. U.S. Army Air Force B-29 bombers make their first attack on Tokyo from the newly won airfields in the Marianas.

November 25. The Japanese heavy cruiser *Kumano* and cruiser *Yasojima* are sunk during Third Fleet air strikes on Luzon.

November 26. The carrier *Bon Homme Richard* (CV 31) is commissioned.

November 29. **The Shinano.** The 59,000-ton Japanese carrier *Shinano* is sunk off Tokyo Bay on her maiden voyage by the submarine *Archerfish* (SS 311), Commander Joseph F. Enright. The largest carrier in the world, she had been laid down as a sistership to the superbattleships *Musashi* and *Yamato.* This single sinking makes the *Archerfish*'s patrol the most successful of the war in terms of tonnage destroyed.

December 2–3. **Action in Ormoc Bay.** After nightfall three destroyers—the *Allen M. Sumner* (DD 692), *Cooper* (DD 695), and *Moale* (DD 693)—are sent to attack a Japanese convoy reported to be landing reinforcements at Ormoc Bay on Leyte. Despite heavy attacks by land-based enemy aircraft, they sink the destroyer *Kuwa* and several small transports. The *Cooper,* Commander M. A. Peterson, is torpedoed and sinks with the loss of 191 lives.

December 7. The conquest of Leyte continues when Rear Admiral Arthur D. Struble's Task Group 78.3 lands two regiments of the 77th Infantry Division at Ormoc Bay. Enemy resistance ashore is light, but persistent kamikaze attacks damage the destroyer *Mahan* (DD 364), Commander E. G. Campbell, so badly that she has to be sunk. Several other vessels are also hit.

December 11. The destroyer *Reid* (DD 369), Commander S. A. McCornock, is sunk by Japanese suicide planes off the Ormoc beachhead.

December 15. **Fleet Admiral.** This new, five-star rank, created a day earlier, is conferred upon Admirals William D. Leahy, chairman of the joint chiefs of staff; Ernest J. King, chief of naval operations; and Chester W. Nimitz, commander of the Pacific Fleet. The Third Fleet's Commander, William F. Halsey, is promoted to the rank after the war.

December 15. **Landing on Mindoro.** Rear Admiral Arthur D. Struble's Visayan Attack Force lands a reinforced army division on the central Philippine island of Mindoro. The operation is unopposed except by kamikazes, which damage several ships.

December 18.   **Philippine typhoon.** Off the east coast of the Philippines, Admiral Halsey's Third Fleet is caught in a terrific storm. Three destroyers capsize—the *Hull* (DD 350), Lieutenant Commander J. A. Marks, *Monaghan* (DD 354), Lieutenant Commander F. B. Garrett, Jr., and *Spence* (DD 512), Lieutenant Commander J. P. Andrea—and numerous vessels, including eight small carriers are damaged; 765 men drown. A court of inquiry finds Halsey principally responsible for failing to get out of the path of the typhoon.

December 19.   Commander Louis D. ("Sandy") McGregor's submarine *Redfish* (SS 395) sinks the Japanese escort carrier *Unryu* in the East China Sea.

December 21.   The submarine *Scamp* (SS 277), Commander John C. Hollingsworth, is reported overdue and presumed lost. She was probably sunk by a Japanese coast defense vessel south of Tokyo Bay on November 11.

1945

January 2–6.   **Advance to Lingayen Gulf.** Task Group 77.2, the support force for the invasion of Luzon, sails from Leyte Gulf to the landing site on Lingayen Gulf under the command of Vice Admiral Jesse B. Oldendorf. It consists of the battleships *California* (BB 44) (flag), *Colorado* (BB 45), *Mississippi* (BB 41), *New Mexico* (BB 40), *Pennsylvania* (BB 38), and *West Virginia* (BB 48), 12 escort carriers, 6 cruisers, 33 destroyers, and assorted other vessels. The movement is opposed by land-based Japanese kamikaze planes, which fatally damage the escort carrier *Ommaney Bay* (CVE 79), sink the destroyer *Hovey* (DD 208), and inflict varying degrees of damage on 23 other vessels. Rear Admiral Theodore E. Chandler, commanding Cruiser Division 4, is mortally wounded by a kamikaze crash on the *Louisville* (CA 28), and Lieutenant General Herbert Lumsden, the British liaison officer at General MacArthur's headquarters, is killed by a hit on the battleship *New Mexico* (BB 40).

January 2–9.   Admiral Thomas C. Kinkaid's Seventh Fleet attack force (TF 77) follows the same course taken by Admiral Oldendorf's task group to Lingayen Gulf. The kamikazes' concentration on the latter gives the attack force a relatively easy passage, although the escort carriers *Kadashan Bay* (CVE 76) and *Kitkun Bay* (CVE 71) are disabled by suicide planes.

January 3–9.   In support of the Luzon landings, Task Force 38 of Admiral W. F. Halsey's Third Fleet delivers a series of carrier air strikes on Japanese airfields and other installations on Formosa (January 3–4 and 9) and Luzon (January 6–7). Despite consistently bad weather, more than 3,000 sorties are flown, and large numbers of enemy aircraft are destroyed, mostly on the ground.

U.S. troops landing at Lingayen Gulf on the island of Luzon, January 9, 1945. *Official U.S. Coast Guard photo.*

January 5.   Cruiser Division 5, Rear Admiral Allan E. ("Hoke") Smith, shells Japanese positions on Iwo Jima, Chichi Jima, and Haha Jima in the Bonin Islands, while far to the north, a similar force under Rear Admiral J. L. McCrea bombards Paramushiro in the Kuriles.

January 7–8.   Vice Admiral Oldendorf's Bombardment and Fire Support Group (Task Group 77.2) delivers an intensive shore bombardment of the landing beaches on Lingayen Gulf. The destroyer minesweeper *Palmer* (DMS 5) is sunk by a conventional Japanese air attack, and the cruiser HMAS *Australia* is damaged by kamikazes.

January 9.   **Invasion of Luzon.** The Seventh Fleet, Vice Admiral Thomas C. Kinkaid, lands four divisions of Lieutenant General Walter Krueger's Sixth Army at Lingayen Gulf. The beaches are lightly defended, Japanese General Tomoyuki Yamashita having withdrawn most of the island's 250,000 defenders to the mountainous interior, and 68,000 American troops are safely ashore by nightfall.

January 10–20.   **Action in the South China Sea.** Following operations covering the invasion of Luzon, Admiral Halsey is authorized to penetrate the South China Sea, an operation he has long advocated. The Third Fleet's attacks commence with a spectacularly successful strike on the coast of Indochina, where approximately 132,700 tons of enemy shipping—29 merchantmen and 15 small naval vessels—are destroyed on January 12. Formosa, the Pescadores, Hong Kong, Hainan, and Canton are attacked on January 15–16.

January 12.   The submarine *Swordfish* (SS 193), Commander Keats E. Montross, is lost sometime after exchanging signals with the *Kete* (SS 369) early this morning. She had been sent to conduct a photographic reconnaissance of Okinawa.

January 21–22.   Carrier aircraft of the Third Fleet's Task Force 38, Vice Admiral John S. McCain, attack Formosa and Okinawa. The carrier *Ticonderoga* (CV 14) is badly damaged by a kamikaze, and the *Hancock* (CV 19) is hit by a torpedo plane during these raids.

January 25.   Japanese positions on Iwo Jima, one of the Bonin/Volcano Islands, are bombarded by surface forces, including the battleship *Indiana* (BB 58), under the command of Rear Admiral Oscar C. Badger.

January 26.   Admiral Raymond A. Spruance relieves Admiral William F. Halsey in command of the Third Fleet, which is redesignated the Fifth Fleet.

January 27.   The 1st Cavalry Division and the 32nd Infantry Division are landed at Lingayen Gulf to reinforce General Krueger's Sixth Army.

January 28.   The carrier *Antietam* (CV 36) is commissioned.

January 29.   The cargo ship *Serpens* (AK 97) blows up while being loaded with depth charges at Guadalcanal in the Solomons. Of 255 men aboard, all but 2 are killed.

January 29.   The Seventh Fleet's Amphibious Group 9, Rear Admiral Arthur D. Struble, lands Major General C. P. Hall's XI Army Corps—30,000 men—near San Antonio, at the neck of the Bataan Peninsula on Luzon. No opposition is encountered.

January 31.   The 11th Airborne Division, Major General J. M. Swing, is landed at Nasugbu, just south of the entrance of Manila Bay, by Rear Admiral William M. Fechteler's Amphibious Group 8.

February 1.   Prodded by General MacArthur, the XIV Army Corps, Major General Oscar W. Griswold, launches a strong attack towards Manila.

February 3.   **Liberation of Manila.** Supported by marine corps aviation, elements of the 1st Cavalry Division fight their way into Manila, liberating the 3,700 half-starved American POWs at the Santo Tomás camp. The capital's garrison, 18,000 mostly naval personnel under Rear Admiral Sanji Iwabuchi, withdraw into the Walled City, where more than 90 percent of them will die fighting. The last pockets of resistance are eliminated on March 4.

February 4–11.   **Yalta Conference.** The Big Three—Roosevelt, Churchill, and Stalin—meet in the Crimea to make plans for the postwar world. Upon Roosevelt's urging, Stalin agrees to enter the war against Japan in exchange for the southern (Japanese) half of the Sakhalin Peninsula, the Kurile Islands, and other Far Eastern concessions. He also promises to hold "free and unfettered" elections in Poland and the other Eastern European countries occupied by the Red Army—a promise his subsequent disregard of which will precipitate the Cold War—and to send delegates to the charter meeting of the United Nations in San Francisco.

February 9–12.   The submarine *Batfish* (SS 310), Commander John K. ("Jake") Fyfe, sets a record by sinking three Japanese submarines in four days: the *RO-115* on the 9th, *RO-112* on the 11th, and *RO-113* on the 12th.

February 13.   Supported by the light cruisers of Rear Admiral R. S. ("Count") Berkey's Close Covering Group (Task Group 77.3), minesweepers begin to clear Manila Bay.

February 15.   Rear Admiral Arthur D. Struble's Amphibious Group 9 lands the 151st Regimental Combat Team, Major General W. C. Chase, at Mariveles, on the tip of the Bataan Peninsula. This unit pushes north against light opposition to link up with army forces advancing to the south. The peninsula is secured on February 21.

February 16. The submarine *Barbel* (SS 316), Lieutenant Commander Conde L. Raguet, is reported overdue and presumed lost. She was probably sunk by a Japanese plane while on patrol in the Philippines on February 4.

February 16–27. Recapture of Corregidor. A combined airborne and amphibious assault overcomes the 5,200 Japanese garrisoning "The Rock" in Manila Bay. Only 200 of the defenders are made prisoner. American casualties are 225 killed and 405 wounded.

February 16. The pre-invasion bombardment of Iwo Jima is begun by the Fifth Fleet battleships and escort carriers under the command of Rear Admiral William H. P. ("Spike") Blandy.

February 16–March 1. Mitscher's raids. Carrier aircraft of Vice Admiral Marc A. Mitscher's Task Force 58 strike Japanese installations around Tokyo (February 16–17), at Iwo Jima (February 19–23), Tokyo again (February 25), and in the Ryukyu Islands (March 1). An estimated 300,000 tons of enemy merchant shipping and 648 aircraft are destroyed. Mitscher's armada includes 11 fleet carriers—the *Bennington* (CV 20), *Bunker Hill* (CV 17), *Enterprise* (CV 6), *Essex* (CV 9), *Hancock* (CV 19), *Hornet* (CV 12), *Lexington* (CV 16), *Randolph* (CV 15), *Saratoga* (CV 3), *Wasp* (CV 18), and *Yorktown* (CV 10)—4 escort carriers, 8 battleships, 18 cruisers, and 75 destroyers.

February 19. Iwo Jima (Operation Detachment). The eight-square-mile volcanic island of Iwo Jima, approximately 660 miles south of Tokyo, is to be captured for use as a forward airfield to support the bomber offensive against Japan. It is defended by 21,000 Japanese troops ably commanded by Lieutenant General Tadamichi Kuribayashi. Although the beaches are strongly fortified, Kuribayashi has concentrated most of his forces in an intricate complex of static positions, containing more than 730 separate strongpoints, around Mount Suribachi on the narrow southern tip of the island and the high ground on the northern end. The assault is made by the V Amphibious Corps, Major General Harry Schmidt, USMC, from Task Force 53, Rear Admiral Harry W. Hill, under the overall command of Vice Admiral Rich-

Before Iwo Jima: Lieutenant General Holland M. Smith, USMC, delivers a briefing attended by *(front row, left to right)* Rear Admiral Louis E. Denfield, Vice Admiral Richmond Kelly Turner, Secretary of the Navy James V. Forrestal, and Rear Admiral Harry W. Hill. *U.S. Naval Institute Collection.*

mond Kelly Turner, Commander, Joint Expeditionary Force (Task Force 51), and Lieutenant General Holland M. Smith, USMC, Commander Expeditionary Troops (Task Force 56). On this date the 4th and 5th Marine Divisions, Major Generals Clifton B. Cates and Keller E. Rockey, respectively, land on the east coast of the island. Despite 74 consecutive days of bombing by the Seventh Air Force from the Marianas and 3 days of the heaviest naval bombardment of the Pacific War, the majority of the island's dug-in defenses remain effectively intact. More than 2,300 marines are killed or wounded the first day. The corps is in for one of the hardest fights in its history.

February 21. At twilight the escort carrier *Bismarck Sea* (CVE 95), Captain J. L. Pratt, is hit by a kamikaze pilot off Iwo Jima. She sinks three hours later with the loss of 218 of her 943 officers and men.

February 23. On Iwo Jima, men of the 2nd Battalion, Twenty-eighth Marines, raise the American flag over Mount Suribachi. Secretary of the Navy James V. Forrestal, who is present on the beach, assures Lieutenant General Holland M. Smith, "The raising of that flag means a Marine Corps for the next 500 years."

February 24. The 3rd Marine Division, Major General Graves B. Erskine, enters the battle for Iwo Jima. One of its regiments had landed three days earlier.

February 28. Capture of Palawan. Rear Admiral William M. Fechteler's Amphibious Group 8 lands the 186th Regimental Combat Team, Brigadier General Harold H. Haney, at Puerto Princessa on

Marines advance across the black sands of Iwo Jima, with Mount Suribachi looming in the background, February 19, 1945. *Defense Department photo (Marine Corps).*

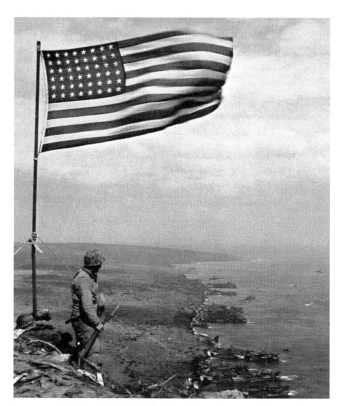

The American flag floats over Mount Suribachi, far above the landing beaches. *Official U.S. Coast Guard photo.*

the Philippine island of Palawan. The island is secured on April 22.

March 2.   Okino Daito (also called Borodino Island) in the Ryukyus is bombarded by a cruiser-destroyer force under Rear Admiral F. E. M. Whiting from Task Group 58.

March 10.   In the Philippines the 41st Division, Major General Jens Doe, is landed at Zamboanga, on the southwestern spur of the island of Mindanao, by Rear Admiral Forrest B. Royal's Amphibious Group 6. Organized resistance by the area's 8,300 defenders ends on March 24.

March 11.   **Crossing the Rhine.** In anticipation that the Germans will destroy the bridges over the Rhine and that the army's own assault boats may be unable to master the river's 8-knot current, four navy boat units have been organized under Commander William J. Whiteside to carry out the river crossings. Each of these units consists of 218 officers and men with 24 LCVPs (Landing Craft, Vehicle Personnel). A number of LCMs (Landing Craft, Mechanized) are later attached. Even though the bridge at Remagen is captured intact on March 7, the navy boats perform valuable service. Between March 11 and 27, Boat Unit 1 ferries 14,000 troops and 400 vehicles across the Rhine

LCMs ferrying tanks across the Rhine, March 24, 1945. *Official U.S. Navy photograph.*

at Bad Neuenahr. Other crossings are made, often under heavy fire, at Boppard, Oberwesel, Oppenheim, and Mainz.

March 15.   **British Pacific Fleet.** The newly reconstituted British Pacific Fleet, under the tactical command of Vice Admiral Sir H. Bernard Rawlings, RN, begins operations with the U.S. Pacific Fleet, into which it is incorporated as Task Force 113 (combat units) and Task Force 112 (service squadron). Its fighting ships include the battleships *King George V* and *Howe* and the carriers *Indefatigable, Indomitable, Illustrious,* and *Victorious,* which will serve with distinction off Okinawa and Japan in the closing months of the war.

March 18.   The 40th Infantry Division, Major General Rapp Brush, is landed on the island of Panay, in the Philippines, by Rear Admiral Arthur D. Struble's Task Group 78.3. The city of Ilo-Ilo is occupied the next day, and the island is secured on June 4.

March 18–21.   **Raids on the Home Islands.** Kyushu, southernmost of the Japanese Home Islands, is attacked by carrier planes from Vice Admiral Marc A. Mitscher's Task Force 58.

March 19.   **The ordeal of the Franklin.** Ninety miles off the coast of Japan the carrier *Franklin* (CV 13), Captain Leslie H. Gehres, flagship of Rear Admiral R. E. Davison's Task Group 58.2, is hit twice by an enemy bomber. One of the bombs penetrates her hangar deck, igniting armed planes, gasoline fuel, and ready ammunition, and turning the interior of the ship above the engine spaces into a raging inferno. Of her approximately 3,450 crewmen, 724 are killed and 265

wounded, but through almost superhuman efforts, the ship is saved. No other American carrier has ever survived such punishment, and no other American warship has sustained such casualties and remained afloat.

March 20.   The submarine *Kete* (SS 369), Lieutenant Commander Edward Ackermann, is lost somewhere between Japan and Okinawa after making her last radio report on this date.

March 23–April 1.   Aircraft of Vice Admiral Marc A. Mitscher's Task Force 58 carry out pre-invasion strikes on Okinawa.

March 24.   **Iwo Jima secured.** The last Japanese positions on Iwo Jima are destroyed. Of the island's 21,000 defenders, only 216 survive its fall. The V Amphibious Corps has lost 5,981 men killed and 19,920 wounded. These are by far the highest casualties ever suffered by the marine corps in a single battle. But they have not been in vain. Before the end of the war no less than 2,251 army air force bombers, carrying 24,761 crewmen, will make emergency landings on the island's airfields.

March 26.   **On to Okinawa.** The pre-invasion bombardment of Okinawa, in the Ryukyu Islands, is begun by Rear Admiral Morton L. Deyo's Gunfire and Covering Force (Task Force 54), consisting of 10 battleships—the *Tennessee* (BB 43) (flag), *Arkansas* (BB 33), *Colorado* (BB 45), *Idaho* (BB 42), *Maryland* (BB 46), *Nevada* (BB 36), *New Mexico* (BB 40), *New York* (BB 34), *Texas* (BB 35), and *West Virginia* (BB 48)—7 heavy and 3 light cruisers, and 32 destroyers and destroyer escorts.

March 26.   The destroyer *Halligan* (DD 584), Lieutenant Commander T. E. Grace, sinks with heavy loss of life off Okinawa after striking a mine.

March 26.   Rear Admiral I. N. Kiland's Task Group 51.1 lands the 77th Infantry Division, Major General W. H. Arnold, on six islands of the Kerama Retto group, approximately 10 miles off the southeastern coast of Okinawa. The occupation of these islands is virtually unopposed.

March 26.   **Capture of Cebu.** In the Philippines the Americal Division, Major General William H. Arnold, is landed by Captain Albert T. Sprague's Task Group 78.2 on the island of Cebu. The island is defended by 14,500 Japanese under Major General Takeo Manjome and Rear Admiral Kaku Harada. By April 12, 5,500 of these troops have been killed and the remainder driven into the mountains, where they are left until the end

The *Franklin* is wracked by one of a series of secondary explosions that followed the bomb hit on her hangar deck. *Official U.S. Navy photograph.*

of the war. American battle casualties are 410 dead and 1,700 wounded.

March 27.   The submarine *Trigger* (SS 237), Commander David R. Connole, is lost on her 12th Pacific war patrol sometime after sinking a small Japanese merchantman on this date.

March 27–April 5.   Supported by destroyers and rocket-firing PT boats, a battalion landing team of the 151st Regimental Combat Team destroys the Japanese garrison of Caballo Island, in Manila Bay.

March 29.   Rear Admiral A. D. Struble's Task Group 78.3 lands the 185th Regimental Combat Team under Major General Rapp Brush on the northwestern shore of Negros Island. The Japanese cease to contest the area, withdrawing into the mountainous interior, on June 4.

The *Franklin,* viewed from the cruiser *Santa Fe. Official U.S. Navy photograph.*

April 1.   Invasion of Okinawa (Operation Iceberg). As a preliminary to and staging area for the anticipated invasion of Japan, American forces plan to seize Okinawa in the Ryukyus, some 325 miles south of Kyushu, nearest of the enemy's Home Islands. A narrow, mountainous island, 60 miles long and from 2 to 18 miles in width, Okinawa is garrisoned by more than 115,000 troops of Lieutenant General Mitsuru Ushijima's Thirty-Second Army and Rear Admiral Minoro Ota's naval base force. Shunning the traditional Japanese strategy of attempting to repel an invasion at the water's edge, Ushijima has concentrated his forces in the rocky southern third of the island. The invasion, the largest and most complex of the Pacific war, is conducted by Admiral Raymond A. Spruance's Fifth Fleet. As usual, Vice Admiral Richmond Kelly Turner commands the Joint Expeditionary Force (Task Force 51). The landing force, designated the Tenth Army, is commanded by Lieutenant General Simon Bolivar Buckner, Jr., USA. It consists of the III Amphibious Corps, under Major General Roy S. Geiger, USMC, and the XXIV Corps, under Major General John S. Hodge, USA—more than 183,000 men altogether. Little resistance is encountered during the first three days after the landing, and the 1st and 6th Marine Divisions

continue to clear the northern end of the island without undue difficulty, but on April 4, the XXIV Corps, which has wheeled south, comes up against General Ushijima's Machinato Line. The land battle for Okinawa has begun.

April 1.   Awa Maru incident. The *Awa Maru,* a Japanese passenger ship of 11,600 tons, has been granted safe conduct by the United States government to deliver Red Cross supplies to POW camps in Malaya and the Netherlands East Indies. On this date she is torpedoed and sunk in the Formosa Strait, en route back to Japan, by the submarine *Queenfish* (SS 393), Commander C. E. Loughlin. Loughlin delivered a radar attack in a dense fog under the misimpression that the ship was an enemy destroyer. Found guilty of negligence by a court-martial, he receives a letter of admonition, but still goes on to attain the rank of rear admiral.

April 6.   Operation TEN-GO. The Japanese respond to the invasion of Okinawa with Operation TEN-GO, a massed air attack on the American amphibious force. Admiral Soemu Toyoda, commander of the Japanese Combined Fleet, had hoped to concentrate 4,500 planes. In the event, he is able to assemble only 669, including 355 kamikazes; however, these succeed in doing great damage. The destroyers *Bush*

LSM(R)s—Landing Ship Medium, Rockets—fire a salvo at Japanese positions on Okinawa. *Official U.S. Navy photograph.*

A marine flamethrowing tank douses a Japanese cave on Okinawa. *U.S. Marine Corps photograph.*

(DD 529), Commander R. E. Westholm, and *Calhoun* (DD 801), Commander G. R. Wilson, and destroyer minesweeper *Emmons* (DMS 22), Lieutenant Commander E. N. Foss, USNR, and the cargo ships *Hobbs Victory* and *Logan Victory* are sunk, and 12 other vessels are damaged, 4 of them—the destroyers *Leutze* (DD 481), *Morris* (DD 417), and *Newcomb* (SS 586), and the destroyer escort *Witter* (DE 636)—so badly that they have to be scrapped. Nine more mass kamikaze attacks will follow in the course of the Okinawan campaign. The Japanese call these raids *kikusui*—"floating chrysanthemums."

April 7.   **Battle of the East China Sea.** As an element of Operation TEN-GO, on the afternoon of April 6 a Japanese surface force consisting of the 68,000-ton superbattleship *Yamato*, light cruiser *Yahagi*, and eight destroyers sets out from the Inland Sea on a suicide sortie to attack the American amphibious fleet off Okinawa. No air cover is provided. Attacked by successive waves of close to 300 carrier planes from Vice Admiral Mitscher's Task Force 58 on the afternoon of April 7, the *Yamato* capsizes after two hours' pounding, during which she is hit by at least five bombs and eleven torpedoes. Only 269 of her 2,767 crewmen survive. The *Yahagi* and four destroyers are also sunk. The force commander, Vice Admiral Seiichi Ito, and the *Yamato*'s Captain Kosaku Ariga go down with the battleship. This is the last sortie of the Imperial Japanese Navy. American losses are 10 aircraft and 12 men.

April 7.   The Japanese light cruiser *Isuzu* is torpedoed and sunk by the submarines *Gabilan* (SS 252), Commander William B. Parham, and *Charr* (SS 328), Commander Francis D. Boyle, off Bima Bay, Soembawa, Netherlands East Indies.

April 11.   **Capture of Bohol.** The 164th Infantry Regiment is ferried in landing craft from Cebu to the neighboring Philippine island of Bohol. Fighting ends with the destruction of the Japanese garrison on April 20.

April 12.   President Franklin D. Roosevelt dies of a cerebral hemorrhage at Warm Springs, Georgia. He is succeeded by Vice President Harry S. Truman.

April 12–13.   **Second kikusui raid.** A force of 185 kamikaze planes accompanied by 150 fighters and 45 torpedo bombers attacks the American fleet off Okinawa. The heaviest blows fall on the destroyers of the radar picket screen. The *Mannert L. Abele* (DD 733), Commander A. E. Parker, is sunk by a piloted (*baka*) bomb and *LCS(L) 33* by a kamikaze; 9 other vessels are hit. Task Force 58's combat air patrol and the ships themselves claim to have downed 298 enemy aircraft.

The Battle of the East China Sea: an enormous pillar of smoke marks the spot where the Japanese superbattleship *Yamato* has just gone down. *Courtesy National Archives.*

April 12–20.   The submarine *Snook* (SS 279), Commander John F. Walling, is lost in the vicinity of Formosa between these dates.

April 16.   **Third kikusui raid.** Some 165 kamikazes attack the destroyer pickets off Okinawa. The *Pringle* (DD 477), Lieutenant Commander J. L. Kelley, is sunk. Commander Frederick J. Benton's *Laffey* (DD 724) is crashed by six aircraft and hit by four bombs. Every one of her guns is disabled, and 103 of her crewmen are killed or wounded, but almost miraculously, the ship is saved. The carrier *Intrepid* (CV 11), 4 destroyers, and 2 landing craft are damaged, some seriously.

April 16.   Task Force 53, Rear Admiral L. F. Reifsnider, lands Major General A. D. Bruce's 77th Division on Ie Shima, a small island off the west coast of Okinawa. Determined Japanese resistance is crushed by April 21.

April 16.   The carrier *Boxer* (CV 21) is commissioned.

April 17.   **Mindanao campaign.** The X Army Corps, Major General F. C. Silbert, is landed by Rear Admiral A. G. Noble's Task Group 78.2 on the west coast of the Philippine island of Mindanao. The 41st Infantry Division had seized Zamboanga, on the island's southwestern spur, on March 10. Several unopposed, subsidiary landings are made before organized resistance by Mindanao's 43,000 Japanese defenders is overcome on June 30.

April 24.   The destroyer escort *Frederick C. Davis* (DE 136), Lieutenant J. R. Crosby, USNR, is sunk in the central Atlantic by the *U-546*. The other destroyer escorts of the hunter-killer group to which the "Fighting Freddy" belonged then sink the U-boat.

August 24.   On Okinawa, the army's XXIV Corps breaks through the Machinato Line. General Ushijima withdraws to his next prepared position, where the American advance is halted on April 28.

April 26.   In the Philippines, Task Unit 78.3.3, Commander W. V. Deutermann, lands the 164th Infantry Regiment on the southeast side of the island of Negros. The 40th Division had been landed on the northwestern coast on March 29. The last enemy resistance is overcome on June 12. This action completes the liberation of the Southern Visayas.

April 27–28.   The cargo ship *Canada Victory* is sunk off Okinawa in the fourth mass kamikaze raid. Three destroyers and the hospital ship *Comfort* (AH 6) are damaged.

April 30.   Adolf Hitler commits suicide in the *Fuehrerbunker* in Berlin. Grand Admiral Karl Doenitz, supreme commander of the German Navy, is his designated successor as chief of state.

May 1.   On Okinawa, the III Amphibious Corps, having completed the conquest of the northern end of the island, is moved south to reinforce the XXIV Army Corps in attacking the Shuri Line.

May 1.   **Back to Borneo.** General MacArthur has been directed to expel the Japanese from the oil-rich island of Borneo, now in the backwaters of the Pacific war. Australia agrees to furnish the necessary land forces. On this date Rear Admiral F. B. Royal's Task Group 78.1 lands the 26th Brigade of the 9th Australian Division, Brigadier General David A. Whitehead, on Tarakan, a small, oil-producing island off the northeast coast of Borneo. Organized resistance is overcome on June 14.

May 3.   The submarine *Legarto* (SS 371), Commander Frank D. Latta, is destroyed, probably by the minesweeper *Hatsutaka*, while attacking a Japanese convoy in the Gulf of Siam.

May 3–4.   **Fifth kikusui attack.** Attacks by 124 kamikaze planes on the radar pickets off Okinawa sink the destroyers *Little* (DD 803), Commander Madison Hall, *Luce* (DD 522), Commander J. W. Waterhouse, and *Morrison* (DD 560), Commander J. R. Hansen, and three landing ships. The light cruiser *Birmingham* (CL 52), escort carrier *Sangamon* (CVE 26), destroyer *Ingraham* (DD 694), the destroyer minelayers *Aaron Ward* (DM 34) and *Shea* (DM 30), and the destroyer minesweeper *Macomb* (DMS 23) are damaged.

May 7.   Germany surrenders unconditionally.

May 8.   **V-E Day.** President Truman and Prime Minister Churchill proclaim the end of the war in Europe.

May 9.   The destroyer escort *Oberrender* (DE 344), Lieutenant Commander Samuel Spencer, USNR, is damaged beyond repair by a Japanese aircraft off Okinawa.

May 11.   Off Okinawa, 150 kamikazes deliver the sixth *kikusui* raid on the ships of the Fifth Fleet. Vice Admiral Mitscher's flagship, the carrier *Bunker Hill* (CV 17) is crashed by two planes and badly damaged, losing 396 men killed and 264 wounded. The destroyers *Evans* (DD 552) and *Hugh W. Hadley* (DD 774), and a landing ship are also hit.

May 13–14.   The carrier planes of Task Group 58.1, Rear Admiral J. J. ("Jocko") Clark, and Task Group 58.3, Rear Admiral Forrest P. Sherman, strike airfields on the Japanese Home Islands of Kyushu and Shikoku.

May 14.   The carrier *Enterprise* (CV 6), to which Admiral Mitscher had transferred his flag after the disabling of the *Bunker Hill* (CV 17) on May 11, is seriously damaged by a kamikaze plane off Okinawa.

The *Bunker Hill,* crashed by two kamikazes on the morning of May 11, 1945. *Courtesy National Archives.*

May 16.   The Japanese heavy cruiser *Haguro* is sunk in the Malacca Strait by five British destroyers in the last surface action of the war.

May 18.   The destroyer *Longshaw* (DD 559), Lieutenant Commander C. W. Becker, is destroyed by enemy artillery fire after running aground off Okinawa.

May 21.   Ashore on Okinawa, advances by the 6th Marine Division and the 96th Infantry Division compel the Japanese to abandon the Shuri Line. General Ushijima executes a skillful withdrawal to his last line of defense, along the Yaeju Dake Escarpment.

May 23–25.   The seventh *kikusui* attack off Okinawa is made by 165 kamikazes. The high-speed transport *Bates* (APD 47) and a landing ship are sunk, and seven other vessels are damaged, the high-speed transport *Barry* (APD 29) beyond repair.

May 27–29.   The destroyer *Drexler* (DD 741), Commander R. L. Wilson, sinks with the loss of 158 lives after being crashed by two kamikazes during the eighth *kikusui* raid. Three other destroyers and several additional vessels are hit.

May 27.   Admiral Halsey relieves Admiral Spruance off Okinawa, whereupon the Fifth Fleet again becomes the Third Fleet. Vice Admiral J. S. McCain relieves Vice Admiral Mitscher in command of Task Force 38 the following day.

June 2–3.   Aircraft of Rear Admiral Arthur W. Radford's Task Group 38.4, consisting of the carriers *Intrepid*

(CV 11) and *Yorktown* (CV 10) and the light carriers *Independence* (CVL 22) and *Langley* (CVL 27), with heavy surface forces, attack Japanese air bases on Kyushu.

June 3.   The carrier *Lake Champlain* (CV 39) is commissioned.

June 3–7.   The 50 kamikazes committed to the ninth *kikusui* attack at Okinawa achieve only meager results, damaging two minesweepers and a landing craft.

June 5.   **Okinawan typhoon.** Thirty-six vessels are damaged when the Third Fleet is caught in a typhoon off Okinawa. A court of inquiry finds that Admiral Halsey and Vice Admiral McCain exercised poor judgment on the approach of the storm, and Secretary of the Navy Forrestal seriously considers relieving Halsey of command.

June 8.   The Kanoya airfield on Kyushu, in the Japanese Home Islands, is attacked by aircraft from Rear Admiral Arthur W. Radford's Task Group 38.4.

June 8.   The British submarine *Trenchant,* Commander Arthur R. Hezlet, RN, sinks the Japanese heavy cruiser *Ashigara* off the northern coast of Java.

June 9–20.   **Operation Barney.** Vice Admiral Charles A. Lockwood, Commander Submarines, Pacific Fleet, sends "Hydeman's Hellcats," a wolf-pack of nine submarines under Commander Earl T. Hydeman in the *Sea Dog* (SS 401), to attack Japanese shipping in the Sea of Japan. Between these dates the Hellcats sink 28 Japanese ships totaling 54,784 tons, making this one of the most successful patrols of the war. One boat, the *Bonefish* (SS 223), Lieutenant Commander Lawrence Edge, is lost.

June 10.   **Landing on Brunei.** The reconquest of Borneo (see May 1) continues with the landing of a brigade of the 9th Australian Division, Major General G. T. Wooten, by Rear Admiral F. B. Royal's Task Group 78.1 at Brunei Bay, on the northwestern coast of the island. The area is secured by July 1.

June 10.   The destroyer *William D. Porter* (DD 579), Commander C. M. Keyes, sinks off Okinawa as a result of underwater damage sustained when a kamikaze crashes beside her. Not a single life is lost.

June 14.   On Okinawa, army and marine forces breach the final Japanese line of defense. Although the enemy continues to fight as fiercely as ever, it is obvious that the end is near.

June 16.   A kamikaze plane sinks the destroyer *Twiggs* (DD 591), Commander George Philip, off Okinawa. She is the 12th destroyer lost to date in the campaign. Every one of her twenty-two officers is killed or wounded.

June 18.   Lieutenant General S. B. Buckner, Jr., USA, is killed by an artillery burst at a forward observation post on Okinawa. He is succeeded in command of the Tenth Army by Major General Roy S. Geiger, the first marine ever to command a field army.

June 21.   **Okinawa secured.** General Geiger announces the end of organized resistance on the island. General Ushijima commits hara-kiri a few hours later. The battle for the island has cost the Tenth Army 7,613 dead and 31,807 wounded, almost equally divided between the army and the marines. Japanese losses are 107,500 killed and 7,400 captured. At sea, the U.S. Navy has had more than 4,900 men killed and 4,824 wounded, which makes the battle for Okinawa the bloodiest in its history. A total of 243 vessels have been damaged, and another 36 have been sunk, mostly by kamikazes.

June 21–22.   **Last kikusui attack.** The last mass kamikaze raid of the Okinawa campaign is made by 45 planes, which succeed only in sinking one landing ship and damaging four other vessels.

July 1.   **Landing at Balikpapan.** The last major amphibious operation of the war occurs when Rear Admiral A. G. Noble's Task Group 78.2 lands the 7th Australian Division, Major General E. J. Milford, at Balikpapan, on the southeast coast of Borneo, after a 16-day pre-invasion bombardment by an American, Australian, and Dutch cruiser-destroyer force under Rear Admiral R. S. Riggs. The town of Balikpapan, the center of Borneo's oil production, is captured on July 5, and Japanese resistance in the region ceases on July 22.

July 1.   **Operations against the Home Islands.** Task Force 38, Vice Admiral John S. McCain, sorties from Leyte Gulf to begin attacks on the Japanese Home Islands. It will operate in Japanese waters until the close of the war.

July 10.   Carrier aircraft of Task Force 38 strike Japanese airfields on the Tokyo plain. They have the sky to themselves, the Japanese having decided to husband their remaining aircraft for a mass attack on the anticipated invasion of the Home Islands.

July 14.   The first major shore bombardment of the Japanese Home Islands is delivered by Rear Admiral John F. ("Big Jack") Shafroth's Task Unit 34.81 against the Japan Iron Company plant at Kamaishi, Honshu. Engaged are the battleships *Indiana* (BB 58), *Massachusetts* (BB 59), and *South Dakota* (BB 57), heavy cruisers *Chicago* (CA 136) and *Quincy* (CA 71), and nine destroyers. The plant is put out of action.

July 14–15.   Closing to within 80 miles of the Japanese coast, the carriers of Task Force 38 launch 1,391 sorties against targets in northern Honshu and Hokkaido. These areas, outside the range of air force B-29s flying from the Marianas, have never before been attacked. Heavy damage is done, especially to merchant shipping.

July 15.   The Nihon Steel Company and Wanishi Ironworks plants at Muroran, Hokkaido, are shelled by Task Unit 34.8.2, Rear Admiral Oscar C. Badger, consisting of the fast battleships *Iowa* (BB 61), *Missouri* (BB 63), and *Wisconsin* (BB 64), two light cruisers, and nine destroyers. A total of 860 16-inch shells are fired during an hour's bombardment.

July 16.   The first atomic device is successfully exploded in a test at Alamagordo, New Mexico.

July 17–18.   Planes of Task Force 38 hit targets around Tokyo Bay, concentrating on the Yokosuka Naval Base.

July 17–18.   On this evening Admiral Badger's Task Unit 34.8.2, reinforced by the battleships *Alabama* (BB 60) and *North Carolina* (BB 55), bombards six industrial targets at Hitachi, 80 miles north of Tokyo.

July 24.   Off Luzon, the destroyer escort *Underhill* (DE 682), Lieutenant Commander R. M. Newcomb, USNR, is sunk with the loss of 112 lives, either by the Japanese submarine *I-53* or by a *kaiten* (piloted torpedo) released by the submarine.

July 24–28.   Task Force 38 launches some of the heaviest raids in the war against the Japanese naval bases at Kure and Kobe, on the Inland Sea, sinking the battleships *Haruna*, *Hyuga*, and *Ise,* the heavy cruisers *Aoba* and *Tone,* and the fleet carrier *Amagi,* and damaging the carriers *Katsuragi* and *Ryuho.*

July 25.   **Potsdam Declaration.** A statement issued by the Big Three in conference at Potsdam, Germany, calls upon Japan to surrender unconditionally or face "utter destruction." This is an implicit reference to the atomic bomb, the existence of which the Japanese (and the Russians) are yet unaware. Radio Tokyo rejects the ultimatum.

July 28.   The destroyer *Callaghan* (DD 792), Commander C. M. Bertholf, is sunk by a kamikaze while on picket duty off Okinawa; 120 of her crewmen are killed or wounded. She is the 13th and last destroyer lost during the Okinawa campaign.

July 29.   **The tragedy of the Indianapolis.** Two days after leaving Guam on an unescorted voyage to Leyte Gulf, the heavy cruiser *Indianapolis* (CA 35), Captain Charles B. McVay III, is sunk by the Japanese submarine *I-58,* Lieutenant Commander Mochitsura Hashimoto, or, it

A Japanese *Tone*-class cruiser under attack by the aircraft of Task Force 38 at the Kure Naval Base on Honshu, July 24, 1945. *Official U.S. Navy photograph.*

has been argued, by a *kaiten* released by this boat. Some 800 to 850 men succeed in abandoning the ship, but her SOS is unheard, and through a succession of tragic oversights, her loss goes unnoticed until August 2, when a group of survivors is accidentally sighted by a patrol plane. Only 316 men are then saved.

July 29–30.   Three small naval vessels and 12 merchantmen are sunk by planes of Task Force 38 in attacks on the Maizuru Naval Base on the Sea of Japan, and on the northern coast of Honshu.

July 30.   The British midget submarines *XE-1*, Lieutenant J. E. Smart, RN, and *XE-3*, Lieutenant I. E. Fraser, RN, attach charges that sink the Japanese heavy cruiser *Takao* (previously damaged by American aircraft) in the harbor at Singapore.

August 6.   **Hiroshima.** The B-29 *Enola Gay* drops an atomic bomb on Hiroshima, a city of approximately 500,000 on southern Honshu. More than 70,000 people are killed.

August 6.   The submarine *Bullhead* (SS 332), Lieutenant Commander Edward R. Holt, Jr., is sunk by a Japanese plane in the Lombok Strait.

The cruiser *Indianapolis. U.S. Naval Institute Collection.*

August 8.   The Soviet Union declares war on Japan.

August 9.   More than 251 Japanese aircraft are destroyed and 141 damaged on airfields on northern Honshu by carrier strikes from Task Force 38.

August 9.   **Nagasaki.** A second atomic bomb is dropped on Japan, this time on Nagasaki, a seaport on Kyushu. Approximately 20,000 people are killed.

August 10.   Task Force 38 continues its strikes on northern Honshu.

August 12.   The battleship *Pennsylvania* (BB 38) becomes the last major American warship to be damaged in World War II when she is hit by a Japanese torpedo plane in Buckner Bay, Okinawa.

August 13.   Planes of Task Force 38 attack Japanese airfields on the Tokyo plain, destroying 254 enemy aircraft and damaging 149 more. Another 18 planes are shot down by the carriers' combat air patrol.

August 14.   Japan surrenders unconditionally. The Japanese government, however, had been given to understand that no measures would be taken against the emperor.

August 15.   **V-J Day.** The last air strike of the war is launched at 4:15 by the carriers of Task Force 38. News of the Japanese surrender leads to the recall of a second wave already approaching the Japanese coast.

August 16.   Vice Admiral Aubrey W. Fitch becomes 34th superintendent of the Naval Academy.

August 30.   Covered by the guns of the Third Fleet, U.S. Army occupation forces begin landing in Tokyo Bay.

September 2.   The Japanese instrument of surrender is signed aboard the battleship *Missouri* (BB 63) in Tokyo Bay. General Douglas MacArthur signs on behalf of the Allied Powers, Fleet Admiral Chester W. Nimitz for the United States.

September 10.   The carrier *Midway* (CVB 41) is commissioned.

October 27.   The carrier *Franklin D. Roosevelt* (CVB 42) is commissioned.

November 6.   The first carrier landing by a jet aircraft is made by a Ryan FR-1 Fireball aboard the escort carrier *Wake Island* (CVE 65).

November 18.   The carrier *Princeton* (CV 37) is commissioned.

December 8.   The carrier *Tarawa* (CV 40) is commissioned.

December 15.   Fleet Admiral Chester W. Nimitz becomes the 10th chief of naval operations.

1946

January 1.   The U.S. Coast Guard, which has operated under the navy since November 1941, is returned to the Treasury Department.

January 29.   Rear Admiral Richard E. Byrd flies off the *Philippine Sea* (CV 47) with six R4D transports to assume personal command of Operation Highjump, the most thorough attempt to date to map the Antarctic.

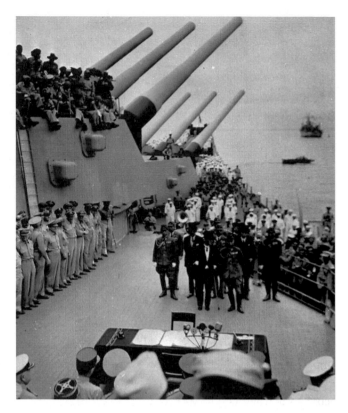

The Japanese delegation awaits the beginning of the surrender ceremony aboard the battleship *Missouri* in Tokyo Bay, September 2, 1945. *Official U.S. Navy photograph.*

March 2.   The carrier *Kearsarge* (CV 33) is commissioned.

April 5–14.   The battleship *Missouri* (BB 63) calls at Istanbul, Turkey, and Athens, Greece, in a powerful demonstration of American interest in the eastern Mediterranean.

April 11.   The carrier *Leyte* (CV 32) is commissioned.

May 11.   The carrier *Philippine Sea* (CV 47) is commissioned.

June 13.   The Navy Flight Demonstration Squadron, the Blue Angels, gives its first performance.

July 14.   The carrier *Saipan* (CVL 48) is commissioned.

August 8–October 4.   The carrier *Franklin D. Roosevelt* (CVB 42) deploys to the Mediterranean. A visit to Athens, reinforcing that of the *Missouri* six months earlier, shows American support for the pro-Western Greek government, which is involved in a bitter civil war against Communist insurgents.

August 13.   **Holloway Plan.** At the end of World War II it was evident that the Naval Academy, as traditionally constituted, would be unable to produce the annual output of ensigns needed by a truly global navy. In

August 1945 a board was convened under the presidency of Rear Admiral James L. Holloway, Jr., to consider the problem of officer education and training. It recommended retaining the Naval Academy in its existing format and developing a complementary source of junior officers by establishing a "regular" NROTC program with pay. Congress approved, and on this date President Harry S. Truman signs the Holloway Plan into law.

October 1.   **Genesis of the Sixth Fleet.** A new command, U.S. Naval Forces, Mediterranean, is established. It will be redesignated the Sixth Task Fleet in 1948 and the Sixth Fleet in February 1950.

November 3.   The carrier *Valley Forge* (CV 45) is commissioned.

1947

January 15.   Rear Admiral J. L. Holloway, Jr., becomes 35th superintendent of the Naval Academy.

February 9.   The carrier *Wright* (CVL 49) is commissioned.

March 12.   **Truman Doctrine.** In an address to Congress requesting emergency funds to help the Greek government in its civil war against the Communists, President Harry S. Truman declares that it should be the policy of the United States "to support free peoples who are resisting attempted subjugation by armed minorities or outside pressure." This concept will become one of the cornerstones of American foreign policy in the Cold War.

March 15.   Ensign John W. Lee becomes the first black to receive a commission in the regular navy.

May 1.   The *Cusk* (SS 348) becomes the first U.S. submarine to launch a missile. The missile is a Loon, the American naval version of the German V-1.

June 5.   **Marshall Plan.** Secretary of State George C. Marshall, speaking at the Harvard commencement, announces that the United States will provide economic aid to assist the recovery of the war-torn nations of Europe. The Soviet Union and her satellites refuse to participate in the program.

July.   **"X." Article.** George F. Kennan, a foreign service officer at the Moscow Embassy and a veteran observer of Soviet affairs, considers the problem of Soviet-American relations in an article, "Sources of Soviet Conduct," in *Foreign Affairs* magazine. In view of Kennan's official position, the article is signed simply "X." It concludes that the United States should adopt a policy of "patient but firm . . . containment" of Soviet expansionism by the "application of counterforce at a series of constantly shifting geographical and political points corresponding to the shifts . . . of Soviet policy." Although Kennan will later insist that this concept has been misinterpreted as a purely military prescription, together with the Truman Doctrine and the Marshall Plan, "containment" will form the foundation of American strategy in the Cold War.

September 6.   The carrier *Midway* (CVB 41) successfully conducts the first American launching of a V-2 ballistic missile.

September 18.   **NSA 47.** The National Security Act of 1947 becomes effective, unifying the departments of the army, navy, and air force under the aegis of a single Department of Defense (originally called the National Military Establishment).

September 18.   John L. Sullivan becomes 49th secretary of the navy, which NSA 47 has made a subcabinet post.

September 23.   Former secretary of the navy James V. Forrestal enters office as the first secretary of defense.

October 1.   The carrier *Coral Sea* (CVB 43) is commissioned.

December 15.   Admiral Louis E. Denfeld becomes the 11th chief of naval operations.

1948

January 1.   Major General Clifton B. Cates becomes 19th commandant of the marine corps.

February 24.   **Czech coup.** The democratic, neutralist government of Czechoslovakia is overthrown by a coup conducted by native Communists with the evident support of the Soviet Union. For many Americans the spectacle of this once-free country being dragged behind the Iron Curtain confirms the existence of the Cold War.

March 31–May 12, 1949.   **Berlin Airlift.** Beginning on this date Soviet authorities progressively impede the flow of traffic to West Berlin, deep in the Soviet occupation zone, until on June 24 they halt all land transport to the city. The western powers respond to the blockade with a massive airlift, unprecedented in history, which successfully supplies the million-plus inhabitants of Free Berlin with the necessities of life. Two navy transport squadrons participate in this humanitarian operation.

May 6.   Fighter Squadron 17A, the first all-jet navy squadron, qualifies for carrier landings aboard the light carrier *Saipan* (CVL 48). It is equipped with FH-1 Phantoms.

June 12.   The Women's Armed Services Integration Act (Public Law 25) authorizes women to serve in regular navy and marine corps, not just the reserve.

1949

March 28.   Louis Johnson becomes the second secretary of defense.

April 4.   **NATO.** The North Atlantic Treaty Organization, a defensive military alliance, is established by the United States, Great Britain, France, Italy, Canada, Belgium, Portugal, the Netherlands, Denmark, Norway, and Iceland. This is the first peacetime military alliance into which the United States has entered.

April 23.   **Cancellation of the United States.** Secretary of Defense Johnson announces the cancellation of the supercarrier *United States* (CVA 58), a decision about which neither Secretary of the Navy Sullivan nor the chief of naval operations, Admiral Louis E. Denfeld, were previously informed. Secretary Sullivan resigns in protest.

May 25.   Francis P. Matthews enters office as 50th secretary of the navy.

June 3.   Ensign Wesley A. Brown becomes the first black graduate of the U.S. Naval Academy.

August 9.   An aircraft ejection seat is used for the first time when Lieutenant J. L. Furin ejects from an F2H Banshee jet fighter traveling more than 500 knots.

August 26.   The submarine *Cochino* (SS 345) is lost off the coast of Norway.

October 1.   **MSTS.** The army and navy transportation service are combined to form the Military Sea Transportation Service, which will operate under the control of the secretary of the navy.

October 5.   **"Revolt of the Admirals."** Congressman Carl Vinson, chairman of the House Naval Affairs Committee, opens hearings on defense policy in which the navy and marine witnesses assert that the needs of the sea services are being ignored, citing in particular the abrupt cancellation of the supercarrier *United States* (CVA 58). The highlight of the hearings is a forceful presentation by the chief of naval operations, Admiral Louis E. Denfeld. The committee's report, issued on March 2, 1950, supports the navy's position.

November 1.   With the approval of President Truman, Admiral Denfeld is relieved of duty as chief of naval operations by Secretary of the Navy Matthews, to whom his testimony before the Vinson committee was most unwelcome.

November 2.   Admiral Forrest P. Sherman becomes the 12th chief of naval operations.

1950

February 12.   **Sixth Fleet.** The U.S. naval forces that have been operating in the Mediterranean since 1946 are officially designated the Sixth Fleet.

April 28.   Vice Admiral Harry W. Hill becomes the 36th superintendent of the U.S. Naval Academy.

June 25.   **Beginning of the Korean War.** Before dawn, six North Korean infantry divisions and three Border Constabulary brigades, supported by approximately 100 Russian-made T-34 tanks, invade the Republic of Korea.

June 25.   The United Nations Security Council adopts a resolution condemning the invasion of South Korea.

June 26.   The destroyers *De Haven* (DD 727) and *Mansfield* (DD 728) evacuate 700 American and foreign citizens from Inchon, South Korea.

June 27.   President Harry S. Truman authorizes General Douglas MacArthur, Commander-in-Chief, Far East, to use American air and naval forces in support of South Korea.

June 27.   The United Nations Security Council issues a second resolution condemning North Korean aggression and recommends that the U.N. members assist South Korea in repelling the attack.

June 28.   North Korean forces occupy Seoul, the capital of South Korea.

June 29.   **First fire support.** The cruiser *Juneau* (CL 119), Captain Jesse D. Sowell, delivers the first naval gunfire support of the Korean War, shelling an enemy troop concentration at Okkye on the east coast.

June 30.   President Truman authorizes the employment of U.S. ground forces in Korea. Advance elements of the 24th Division are airlifted to the peninsula from Japan this same day. Ships of the Military Sea Transportation Service begin embarking the main body on July 1.

July 2.   The only purely naval action in which an American warship is involved during the Korean War is fought off Chumunjin, on the east coast, when four North Korean torpedo boats attack the cruisers

The light cruiser *Juneau* at anchor in Kagoshima Wan, Japan, on June 25, 1950. *Official U.S. Navy photograph.*

Juneau (CL 119) and HMS *Jamaica* and the frigate HMS *Black Swan*. Three of the torpedo boats are destroyed; none of the allied ships are hit.

July 3–4. **First air strikes.** Two units of Vice Admiral Arthur D. Struble's Task Force 77, the carriers *Valley Forge* (CV 45), Captain L. K. Rice, and HMS *Triumph*, Captain A. D. Torless, DSO, deliver the first naval air strikes of the Korean War, attacking military installations in the North Korean capital of Pyongyang. The F-9F2 Panther fighters launched by the *Valley Forge* are the first navy jets to enter combat. They also score the first jet victories, downing two propeller-driven YAK-9 fighters.

July 4. President Truman proclaims a blockade of the coast of North Korea.

July 7. General Douglas MacArthur is appointed Supreme Commander of U.N. forces in Korea.

July 9. The South Korean navy is placed under the command of Commander Michael J. Luosey, USN.

July 11. **First raid.** After nightfall, Commander W. B. Porter leads a party of 10 seamen and marines from the cruiser *Juneau* (CL 119) to successfully destroy a railroad tunnel at Rashin, North Korea. Many similar operations are carried out in the course of the conflict by U.S. naval forces and U.S., British, and South Korean marines.

July 18–19. Amphibious Group One, Rear Admiral James H. Doyle, lands the 1st Cavalry Division at Pohang, on the southeastern coast of Korea. The arrival of this force is instrumental in halting the North Korean advance at an irregular, defensive perimeter extending 35 to 80 miles inland from the port of Pusan on the southeastern tip of the Korean peninsula.

July 18. Aircraft from the *Valley Forge* (CV 45) destroy the oil refinery at Wonsan, North Korea.

July 25. **Blockade of Korea.** Task Force 96.5 is organized to conduct the blockade of Korea. The U.S. Navy covers the east coast; the west coast is assigned to British Commonwealth forces (Task Group 96.53) under Rear Admiral William G. Andrewes, RN, who will be knighted in February 1951.

July 25. **Close air support.** In response to an urgent request from Lieutenant General Walton H. Walker, commanding the U.S. Eighth Army, the carriers of Task Force 77 begin the unaccustomed task of providing tactical air support for the army forces holding the hard-pressed Pusan Perimeter. These operations, in which the carrier *Philippine Sea* (CV 47) joins on August 5, continue into September.

July 25. The hospital ship *Benevolence* (AH 13) sinks with the loss of 13 lives following a collision with the SS *Mary Luckenbach* of San Francisco. She had been recommissioned to serve in the Korean War.

August 2. The 1st Provisional Marine Brigade, Brigadier General Edward A. Craig, lands at Pusan. It had sailed from San Diego on July 14, the first unit to leave the United States for Korea.

August 7. The marines enter action in Korea, counterattacking in the direction of Chinju and Sachon from the southwestern end of the Pusan Perimeter. Chinju is captured and the marines are poised to take Sachon when on August 12 they are diverted 75 miles to the north to repel an enemy offensive across the Naktong River. During this and subsequent actions the brigade receives valuable close air support from Marine Fighter Squadrons (VMF) 214 and 323, embarked on the escort carriers *Badoeng Strait* (CVE 116) and *Sicily* (CVE 118) of Rear Admiral Richard W. Ruble's Carrier Division 15. These squadrons also support U.S. and South Korean army units.

August 15.   **Battle of the Naktong.** The 1st Provisional Marine Brigade counterattacks the 4th North Korean People's Army division, which has established a bridgehead south of the Naktong River, within the Pusan Perimeter, and hurls it back across the river, capturing 34 guns.

August 16.   The 3rd Republic of Korea Division, encircled while fighting a delaying action near Yonghae, on the east coast of Korea, is evacuated by four landing ships covered by the cruiser *Helena* (CA 75) and escorting destroyers.

August 23.   In a dramatic conference in Tokyo, General MacArthur persuades Admiral Forrest P. Sherman, the chief of naval operations, and General J. Lawton Collins, army chief of staff, to support his plan for an amphibious assault at Inchon, on the west coast of Korea.

September 3–5.   **Second battle of the Naktong.** Between September 1 and 3, a Communist offensive spearheaded by the 9th North Korean People's Army Division pushes back the U.S. 2nd Infantry Division and reestablishes a bridgehead across the Naktong. The 1st Provisional Marine Brigade, which had been withdrawn to take part in the planned Inchon invasion, is sent to seal the breach. The marines eliminate the bridgehead in three days of heavy fighting.

September 12.   **Task Force 95.** The units conducting the blockade of Korea are reorganized as Task Force 95, the United Nations Blockading and Escort Force. The blockade of the west coast remains a British Commonwealth responsibility, as it will throughout the war.

September 15.   **Inchon invasion.** General MacArthur launches an amphibious operation of unexcelled audacity at Inchon, the port of Seoul, 150 miles behind enemy lines. A less promising location for a landing can hardly be imagined: the tidal range at Inchon is in excess of 30 feet; the narrow, twisting channel through the mud flats to the harbor could be blocked by a single ship; and the "beach" is a big-city waterfront. For these very reasons, MacArthur is confident that the invasion will achieve strategic surprise. His gamble

The Inchon invasion: First Lieutenant Baldomero Lopez, a platoon leader in the 3rd Marines, leads his men over the seawall. He was killed minutes later, smothering a grenade with his body, and posthumously awarded the Medal of Honor. *U.S. Marine Corps photograph.*

works to perfection. A two-day preliminary bombardment is carried out by the naval attack force, Amphibious Group One, commanded by Rear Admiral James H. Doyle. The landing force, army Major General Edward M. Almond's X Corps, consists of the 7th Infantry Division and the hastily constituted 1st Marine Division, under Major General O. P. Smith. The marines spearhead the assault, capturing the offshore island of Wolmi-do on the morning tide and landing at Inchon at 5:30 P.M. By nightfall the marines have secured their objectives at a cost of 22 dead and 174 wounded. The 7th Infantry Division follows them ashore on the 17th. Simultaneously, the forces in the Pusan Perimeter begin a drive north.

September 17.   The 3rd Battalion of Colonel R. L. Murray's Fifth Marine Regiment captures Kimpo Airfield, midway between Inchon and Soul.

September 18.   A detachment of 725 South Korean troops is evacuated from an unsuccessful east coast landing at Samchok by auxiliary vessels supported by the battleship *Missouri* (BB 63), cruiser *Helena* (CA 75), and four destroyers.

September 21.   General George C. Marshall becomes the third secretary of defense.

September 21–22.   Colonel Lewis B. ("Chesty") Puller's First Marine Regiment captures Yongdungpo, on the Han River opposite Seoul.

September 25.   **Capture of Seoul.** The 1st Marine Division and elements of the 7th Infantry Division enter Seoul.

September 25.   The carrier *Oriskany* (CV 34) is commissioned.

September 26.   **Destruction of the North Korean Army.** At 11:45 P.M. the 1st Cavalry Division, leading the Eighth Army's advance from the Pusan Perimeter, links up with units of the 7th Infantry Division south of Seoul. The North Korean Army, whose principal supply lines ran through Seoul, soon ceases to exist as an organized fighting force.

September 27.   The joint chiefs of staff authorize General MacArthur to pursue the North Korean Army north of the 38th Parallel.

September 29.   The minesweeper *Magpie* (AMS 25), Lieutenant (jg) Warren G. Person, is destroyed by a mine off Chuksan, North Korea. She is the first navy vessel lost in the war.

October 1.   General MacArthur calls upon North Korean Premier Kim Il Sung to surrender his forces to avoid useless loss of life.

October 4.   The Political Committee of the U.N. General Assembly resolves that all steps shall be taken for the establishment of a unified, democratic Korea.

October 9.   **Invasion of North Korea.** General MacArthur issues a second surrender ultimatum to the North Korean government. U.S. forces cross the 38th Parallel into North Korea this same day.

October 10.   **Wonsan: the battle of the mines.** Minesweepers begin clearing the harbor of Wonsan, on the east coast of North Korea, in preparation for a landing by the U.S. X Corps scheduled for October 20.

October 12.   The minesweepers *Pirate* (AM 275), Lieutenant Commander Bruce Hyatt, and *Pledge* (AM 277),

An F4U-4 Corsair from the *Philippine Sea* flies a combat air patrol over ships off Inchon, October 1950. *Official U.S. Navy photograph.*

Lieutenant Richard O. Young, are sunk by mines in Wonsan harbor. It is learned that the harbor is defended by approximately 3,000 mines, both contact and magnetic. Lanes through the minefields are finally opened on October 25, five days behind schedule.

October 19.   U.S. forces occupy the North Korean capital of Pyongyang.

October 26.   The 1st Marine Division lands unopposed at Wonsan. The city had been captured by South Korean troops advancing overland on October 10.

October 29–November 8.   The 7th Infantry Division, originally scheduled to land at Wonsan, is put ashore at Iwon, where no mines have been found.

November 1.   For the first time, Russian-built MiG-15 jet fighters based in Manchuria cross the Yalu River to attack U.N. aircraft.

November 2–7.   Colonel Homer L. Litzenberg's Seventh Marine Regiment, spearheading the 1st Marine Division's advance towards the Yalu, shatters a series of attacks by the 124th Chinese Communist Division.

November 2–20.   Minesweeping forces under Commander Stephen M. Archer clear the harbor of Chinnampo, the port city of Pyongyang, without a single casualty.

November 5.   General MacArthur officially notifies the United Nations of the presence of Chinese troops in North Korea.

November 8.   **Attacking the Yalu bridges.** The aircraft of Vice Admiral Arthur D. Struble's Carrier Task Force 77 are ordered to attack the Yalu River bridges near Chongsonjin. This is the first of many bridge-busting assignments. All are complicated by the fact that the aircraft are allowed to attack only the Korean end of the bridges.

November 9.   **First MiG kill.** Lieutenant Commander W. T. Amen, flying an F9F-2 Panther jet from the *Philippine Sea* (CV 47), downs a MiG-15 to become the first navy pilot to destroy an enemy jet fighter.

November 13.   The Seventh Marines reach the village of Hagaru-Ri, on the southern end of the Chosin Reservoir.

November 21.   The 7th Infantry Division's 17th Regimental Combat Team reaches the Manchurian border at Hyesanjin.

November 24.   **U.N. offensive.** U.N. forces launch an offensive intended to complete the occupation of North Korea.

November 25.   **Chinese intervention.** Approximately 300,000 Chinese Communist regular troops have entered North Korea, largely undetected by the widely separated U.N. columns advancing along the roads on the eastern and western sides of the peninsula. On this date around 180,000 of these troops attack the American and South Korean forces in the west.

November 27–28.   **Battle of the "Frozen Chosin."** Eight Chinese divisions attack 1st Marine Division positions to the west and south of the Chosin Reservoir. The marines hold their ground, but the Chinese cut the road between the marines' main body at Yudam-Ni, division headquarters 14 miles to the south at Hagaru-Ri, and from Hagaru-Ri south.

November 29.   The X Corps commander, Major General Edward M. Almond, USA, orders the 1st Marine Division to fall back to Hamhung.

November 29.   Task Force Drysdale, a composite formation of U.S. marines and infantry and 41st Independent Commando, Royal Marines—the whole under Lieutenant Colonel R. M. Drysdale, Royal Marines—fights its way north from Koto-Ri against heavy opposition to reinforce the marine battalion defending Hagaru-Ri.

December 3.   After 79 hours of almost uninterrupted combat, the main body of the 1st Marine Division completes its withdrawal from Yudam-Ni to Hagaru-Ri.

December 3–7.   U.S. naval forces evacuate 3,834 military personnel and 7,009 civilian refugees from Wonsan, on the east coast of North Korea.

December 4.   **Ensign Jesse L. Brown.** The navy's first black pilot, Ensign Brown is forced to make a crash-landing near Hagaru-Ri when his plane is hit by enemy ground fire while flying a close-support mission from the carrier *Leyte* (CV 32). Observing that Brown is unable to get out of his cockpit, one of his squadron

A marine column during the breakout from the Chosin Reservoir. *Defense Department photo (Marine Corps).*

mates, Lieutenant (jg) Thomas J. Hudner, fearlessly lands to help him. Brown dies before he can be removed from the wreckage. Hudner, who is rescued by helicopter, is awarded the Medal of Honor. Ensign Brown is posthumously decorated with the Distinguished Flying Cross.

December 5.   One the west coast of Korea, U.S. and British Commonwealth naval forces evacuate 7,700 U.S. and South Korean troops from Chinnampo.

December 6.   The 1st Marine Division begins its break-out south from Hagaru-Ri.

December 7.   U.S. naval forces begin the evacuation of Inchon. By the time the port is closed on January 5, 1951, some 32,400 troops and 57,700 tons of supplies have been transported to the south.

December 9.   **Marines break out.** Leading elements of the 1st Marine Division, attacking through Funchilin Pass, link up with marine units pushing north to meet them from Chinhung-Ni. The withdrawal from the Chosin Reservoir, one of the epic fighting retreats of all time, is complete. The marines have suffered 4,400

battle casualties, including 730 dead. Chinese losses are estimated at 37,500.

December 9.   General MacArthur orders the X Corps to be evacuated from North Korea from the port of Hungnam. Vice Admiral C. Turner Joy, Commander, U.S. Naval Forces, Far East, assigns Rear Admiral James H. Doyle, Commander, Task Force 90, the responsibility of carrying out the operation.

December 10–24.   **Hungnam evacuation.** Rear Admiral Doyle's Task Force 90 conducts an exemplary amphibious operation in reverse, evacuating 105,000 U.S. and South Korean troops, including the 1st Marine Division, 91,000 civilian refugees, and 350,000 tons of supplies and equipment from the port of Hungnam. Air and fire support for the evacuation, with which the enemy does not try to interfere, is provided by the carriers *Leyte* (CV 32), *Philippine Sea* (CV 47), *Princeton* (CV 37), *Valley Forge* (CV 45), *Badoeng Strait* (CVE 116), *Bataan* (CVL 29), and *Sicily* (CVE 118), and a surface force consisting of the battleship *Missouri* (BB 63), two heavy cruisers, eight destroyers, and three rocket ships.

The end at Hungnam: demolition charges destroy harbor installations upon the completion of the evacuation. The ship in the foreground is the fast transport *Begor. Official U.S. Navy photograph.*

1951

January 1–15. Communist armies numbering approximately 500,000 men, mostly Chinese, push U.N. forces approximately 50 miles south of the 38th Parallel, recapturing Seoul.

January 29. Carrier Task Force 77 is directed to begin a bombing offensive against the railway system and bridge network along the east coast of North Korea. Its commander, Vice Admiral Arthur D. Struble, had unsuccessfully protested the assignment, asserting that the carrier planes could best be used for close support.

February 2. The minesweeper *Partridge* (AMS 31), Lieutenant (jg) B. M. Clark, is sunk by a mine while sweeping southeast of Wonsan. She is the last minesweeper lost in the Korean conflict.

February 16. Siege of Wonsan. U.S. forces begin an unprecedented, 861-day naval siege of Wonsan, North Korea's principal sea port and a major communications center. A total of seven harbor islands are eventually occupied by U.N. forces—mainly South Korean marines—and U.S. warships maintain a constant presence off the city, shelling traffic and batteries ashore. The position also offers a haven to damaged U.N. aircraft; helicopters from *LST 799* rescue 24 U.S., British, and South African airmen from Wonsan harbor or nearby locations between March 1951 and November 1952, and an emergency airfield is constructed on Yo-do Island in the summer of 1952.

March 7–31. A U.N. counteroffensive, Operation Ripper, drives the Communists back to the 38th Parallel. Seoul is reoccupied on March 14.

March 8. The North Korean port of Songjin is put under siege by U.N. naval forces.

April 1. The bridge at Songjin, North Korea, is destroyed by the first navy jet bombing attack of the Korean War. It was delivered by Fighter Squadron (VF) 191 from the *Princeton* (CV 37).

April 7. Covered by fire from the cruiser *St. Paul* (CA 73) and two destroyers, 250 men of 41st Independent Commando, Royal Marines, destroy a section of railroad near Chongjin, on the east coast of North Korea.

April 11. Relief of MacArthur. President Truman relieves General MacArthur of command. MacArthur had made no secret of his dissatisfaction with the constraints the president established for the conduct of the war. He is succeeded by Lieutenant General Matthew B. Ridgeway.

April 22–May 1, May 14–20. Communist spring offensives. Two successive enemy offensives are repulsed with heavy losses.

April 26. U.S. naval forces put the North Korean port of Hungnam under siege.

May 20. The battleship *New Jersey* (BB 62), recommissioned for the Korean War, reaches the theater of operations and delivers her first bombardment against the east coast town of Kangsong.

May 22–31. U.N. counteroffensive. A general offensive by the U.S. Eighth Army, South Korean, and other U.N. troops pushes the enemy back all along the front. By this time the Communist forces have sustained an estimated 200,000 casualties in a matter of months and are apparently on the verge of collapse. However, fear of widening the war leads the Truman administration to prohibit another all-out drive into North Korea.

June 5–September 20. Operation Strangle. The planes of Carrier Task Force 77 and the 1st Marine Air Wing are directed to support the Fifth Air Force in an attempt to choke the enemy frontlines by cutting eight key supply routes across a degree of latitude on the Korean peninsula. The effort is not successful.

June 12. The destroyer *Walke* (DD 723) is heavily damaged by a mine off Hungnam, North Korea, losing 26 men killed and 35 wounded.

June 23. Soviet U.N. Ambassador Jacob Malik proposes opening cease-fire negotiations in Korea. The Soviet initiative is often interpreted as a testimonial to how badly Communist forces had been hurt.

July 10. Korean truce talks. Negotiations begin at Kaesong, inside Communist lines. The chief U.N. delegate is Vice Admiral C. Turner Joy, commander of U.S. Naval Forces, Far East, since the start of the war. The talks break down in August, but are resumed at Panmunjon, a village between the lines, on November 12.

July 31. Dan A. Kimball becomes 51st secretary of the navy.

August 16. Admiral William A. Fechteler becomes the 13th chief of naval operations.

August 25. Fighters from the carrier *Essex* (CV 9) escort air force B-29 Superfortresses on an attack on Rashin, North Korea, a major rail center only a few miles south of the Soviet border.

September 17. Robert A. Lovett becomes the fourth secretary of defense.

November 6. A P2V Neptune navy patrol plane is shot down on a routine mission over the international waters off the coast of Siberia.

F9F Panther jets from the *Boxer* over Wonsan, July 1951. *Official U.S. Navy photograph.*

The battleship *New Jersey* fires a full salvo in support of troops near the 38th Parallel, November 1951. *Official U.S. Navy photograph.*

1952

January 1.   Lieutenant General Lemuel C. Shepherd, Jr., becomes the 20th commandant of the marine corps.

January 11.   **Projects Package and Derail.** The seaborne artillery of Task Force 95 and aircraft of Task Force 77 begin to concert attacks against selected targets on the coastal rail lines of North Korea.

January 29.   LSTs of Task Force 90 complete the evacuation, begun in mid-December, of more than 20,000 civilians from islands off the west coast of Korea that have come under Communist attack.

February 19.   Off Songjin, on the east coast of North Korea, an amphibious assault on the U.N.-held islands of Kil-chu and Myongchon by enemy troops embarked in 45 sampans is broken up by the destroyer *Shelton* (DD 790), the New Zealand frigate *Taupo,* and the minesweeping destroyer *Endicott* (DMS 35). Several sampans reach Kil-chu, but the landing force is killed or captured by the island's defenders, a company of South Korean marines commanded by First Lieutenant Joseph Bartos, USMC.

April 21.   Thirty men are killed by a powder fire in the No. 1 8-inch turret of the cruiser *St. Paul* (CA 73) off Kojo, North Korea.

April 26.   **Hobson disaster.** The destroyer minesweeper *Hobson* (DMS 26), Lieutenant Commander W. J. Tierney, sinks with the loss of 176 lives following a collision with the carrier *Wasp* (CV 18) during exercises in the Atlantic.

April 28.   The U.S. Navy decides to install the steam-catapult aircraft-launching system developed by the Royal Navy in American carriers.

June 14.   The keel of the world's first nuclear-powered submarine, the *Nautilus* (SSN 571), is laid at the Electric Boat Company at Groton, Connecticut.

June 23.   **Suiho strike.** Thirty-five AD Skyraiders and an equal number of F9F-2 Panther jets from the carriers *Boxer* (CV 21), *Philippine Sea* (CV 47), and *Princeton* (CV 37) join air force Thunderjets in an attack on the heavily defended hydroelectric power plant at Suiho, North Korea, the fourth-largest such facility in the world. It is rendered unserviceable. The raid is part of a two-day aerial offensive against North Korea's 13 major power plants.

Marines hug the side of their trench as an enemy mortar shell explodes on its lip, April 1952. *Official U.S. Navy photograph.*

Ordnancemen arm Corsairs aboard the *Bataan*, summer 1952. *Official U.S. Navy photograph.*

September 1.   The first prototype Sidewinder air-to-air missile is fired at the Naval Ordnance Test Station at Inyokern, California.

September 9.   Marine Captain Jesse G. Folmar destroys a MiG-15 with his F4U Corsair. He is the first pilot to down an enemy jet while flying a propeller-driven aircraft.

October 8.   Twelve F2H-2 Banshee jets from the carrier *Kearsarge* (CV 33) escort 10 air force B-29 Superfortresses in an attack on the rail center at Kowon, North Korea. This is the second and last time in the Korean conflict that navy fighters cover B-29s.

October 9–July 1953.   **Cherokee Strikes.** Dissatisfied with the scarcity of profitable targets in North Korea, Vice Admiral J. J. ("Jocko") Clark, the Seventh Fleet commander, initiates a battle-front bombing campaign against enemy supply facilities outside the range of U.N. artillery. The campaign, named after the admiral's Indian ancestry and enthusiastically welcomed by the Eighth Army, soon absorbs almost

July 11.   **Pyongyang raid.** Ninety-one aircraft from the carriers *Bon Homme Richard* (CV 31) and *Princeton* (CV 37) collaborate with air force, marine, Australian Air Force and British carrier planes to hit some 40 military targets in and around the North Korean capital of Pyongyang.

July 12–22.   Marine Major John H. Glenn, Jr., the future astronaut, destroys three MiGs while serving on exchange duty with the Fifth Air Force.

July 27–28.   Carrier aircraft of Task Force 77 strike two major industrial targets in North Korea, the lead and zinc mill at Sindok, and the magnesite plant at Kilchu.

August 4.   Vice Admiral C. Turner Joy becomes 37th superintendent of the Naval Academy.

August 29.   **All United Nations Air Effort.** Planes from the carriers *Boxer* (CV 21) and *Essex* (CV 9) participate in the biggest bombing raid in the war to date, an attack on Pyongyang by more than 1,000 U.N. aircraft.

August 30.   The ocean tug *Sarsi* (ATF-111) is sunk by a mine while patrolling off Hungnam. She is the last U.S. naval vessel lost in the Korean conflict.

September 1.   The oil refinery at Aoji, North Korea, only eight miles from the Soviet border, is destroyed by 144 planes from the carriers *Boxer* (CV 21), *Essex* (CV 9), and *Princeton* (CV 37). This is the largest carrier raid of the war.

An AD Skyraider from the *Princeton* attacking marshalling yards near Kowon, North Korea, October 1952. Note the complete destruction of the bridge at lower left. *Official U.S. Navy photograph.*

half the carrier air effort and continues until the end of the war.

November 1.   The first shipboard firing of the Regulus I missile is made from the missile ship *Norton Sound* (AVM 1) at the Naval Air Test Center at Point Mugu, California.

November 18.   **Dogfight off Chongjin.** Three F9F-5 Panther jet fighters from the carrier *Oriskany* (CV 34) engage seven, presumably Soviet MiG-15s 90 miles southwest of Vladivostok. Two of the MiGs are definitely destroyed. No American planes are lost.

1953

January 18.   A navy P2V Neptune patrol plane is shot down by ground fire from a Communist-held island in the Straits of Taiwan.

January 22.   Landing tests begin on the navy's first angled-deck carrier, the *Antietam* (CV 36).

January 28.   **Terrier.** The first shipboard launching of a Terrier surface-to-air missile is made by the *Mississippi* (AG 128, formerly BB 41) off Cape Cod, Massachusetts.

January 28.   Charles E. Wilson becomes the fifth secretary of defense.

February 4.   Robert B. Anderson becomes 52nd secretary of the navy.

March 6.   The *Tunny* (SSG 282) is recommissioned as the navy's first missile-firing submarine. A veteran of World War II, she has been equipped with the navy's surface-launched Regulus I missile.

March 13.   Aircraft from Task Force 77 deliver a devastating attack against the industrial section of Chongjin, North Korea.

June 11.   With the truce talks apparently nearing a conclusion, the navy completes the evacuation of 19,425 Korean civilians from west coast islands north of the 38th Parallel.

June 15.   The carrier *Princeton* (CVA 37) establishes a Korean War record by launching 184 sorties against enemy positions in a single day.

July 11.   **Marine ace.** Major John F. Bolt, a marine pilot flying an F-86 Sabrejet on exchange duty with the Fifth Air Force, shoots down his fifth and sixth MiG-15s.

July 16.   **Navy ace.** Obsolete North Korean aircraft have begun nighttime, nuisance raids on Seoul. These

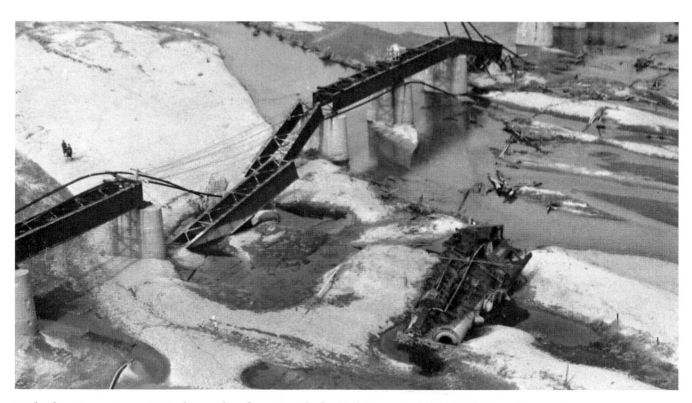

Bridge busting, summer 1953: the results of an air strike by Task Force 77. *Official U.S. Navy photograph.*

planes, derisively known as "Bedcheck Charlies," fly so slowly and at such low altitudes that Fifth Air Force jets are unable to intercept them, and in June a detachment of navy night pilots and four F4U-5N Corsairs are lent to the air force to counter the raids. Between June 29 and this date, Lieutenant Guy P. Bordelon destroys five Charlies, thus becoming the only navy ace of the Korean conflict and the first navy nightfighter ace ever.

July 27.   **Korean Armistice.** A cease-fire agreement, effective at 10:00 P.M. on this date, is signed by U.N. and Communist negotiators at the village of Panmunjon.

August 17.   Admiral Robert B. ("Mick") Carney becomes the 14th chief of naval operations.

September 2.   The navy announces plans to refit the *Midway*-class carriers with steam catapults and angled decks.

October 16.   An explosion and fire wrack the carrier *Leyte* (CV 32) in Boston Harbor, killing 37 men.

1954

May 3.   Charles S. Thomas assumes office as 53rd secretary of the navy.

May 26.   The carrier *Bennington* (CV 20) is damaged by an explosion and fire off Newport, Rhode Island; 103 men are killed and 201 injured.

May 27.   The chief of naval operations approves a program to completely modernize the *Essex*-class carriers by the installation of angled flight decks, enclosed bows, and other improvements.

July 26.   Near Hainan Island, in the South China Sea, two Communist Chinese LA-7-type aircraft attack two AD-1 Skyraiders that are searching for survivors from an Air Cathay flight shot down on July 24. Return fire from the Skyraiders destroys both planes.

August 11.   Chinese Communist Foreign Minister Chou En-lai declares the Nationalist-held Formosa must be "liberated." President Eisenhower replies that it will be necessary to "run over the Seventh Fleet" to do so.

August 12.   Rear Admiral Walter F. Boone becomes the 38th superintendent of the Naval Academy.

August 16–May 18, 1955.   **Operation Passage to Freedom.** According to the terms of the Geneva Accords, which ended the French Indochina War, Vietnamese who do not wish to live in the Communist-controlled north may move to the south. U.S. Navy units under Rear Admiral Lorenzo Sabin assist that emigration,

transporting 293,002 civilians and 17,846 military personnel.

September 4.   Two MiG fighters shoot down a PV2 Neptune reconnaissance aircraft of Patrol Squadron 19 on a routine flight over international waters off the coast of Siberia. Nine of the plane's ten crewmen are rescued.

September 8.   **SEATO.** In Manila, the United States and seven other nations—Great Britain, France, Australia, New Zealand, Pakistan, Thailand, and the Philippines—sign a collective defense treaty that provides the basis for the Southeast Asia Treaty Organization. Cambodia, Laos, and South Vietnam are later included in its protocols. Unlike NATO, however, SEATO does not establish an allied army or an integrated command.

September 13.   President Eisenhower orders the Seventh Fleet to provide logistic support to the Nationalist Chinese forces defending the coastal islands of Matsu and Quemoy.

September 30.   **The Nautilus.** The navy's first nuclear-powered ship, the submarine *Nautilus* (SSN 571), is commissioned at Groton, Connecticut.

1955

January 17.   **"Underway on nuclear power."** With these words, Commander Dennis Wilkinson reports the successful start of the first trial run of the *Nautilus* (SSN 571).

February 6–13.   **Evacuation of the Tachens.** The Seventh Fleet, Vice Admiral A. M. Pride, evacuates 29,000 Nationalist Chinese civilians and troops from the Tachen Islands, off the coast of China. The operation is covered by a carrier task force consisting of the *Essex* (CV 9), *Kearsarge* (CV 33), *Midway* (CVA 41), *Wasp* (CV 18), and *Yorktown* (CV 19).

June 22.   A P2V Neptune reconnaissance plane of Patrol Squadron 9, damaged by fire from two Soviet MiG-15 fighters while over international waters, crashes without loss of life on St. Lawrence Island in the Bering Strait.

August 17.   Admiral Arleigh A. Burke becomes the 15th chief of naval operations.

September 13.   President Eisenhower directs the Department of Defense to develop a ballistic missile with a range of 1,500 miles and the capability of being launched from both land and sea.

The *Forrestal* on maneuvers in the Caribbean, February 1956. *Official U.S. Navy photograph.*

October 1.   **New carriers.** The *Forrestal* (CVA 59), lead ship of a class of six new carriers—the first built since World War II—is commissioned at Norfolk, Virginia. Specifically designed to operate jet aircraft, these "super carriers" displace 59,630 tons.

November 8.   The Joint Army-Navy Missile Committee is established to oversee development of the intermediate range ballistic missile later designated the Jupiter.

November 17.   The navy creates a Special Projects Office under Rear Admiral William F. Raborn, Jr., to direct the development of a shipboard launching system for ballistic missiles.

November 28.   Secretary of the Navy Thomas sets a target date of 1965 for the completion of the solid-fuel ballistic missile for use by submarines.

1956

January 1.   General Randolph McC. Pate becomes 21st commandant of the marine corps.

January 10.   **Nuke school.** The navy's first nuclear power school is established at the submarine base at New London, Connecticut.

March 12.   Attack Squadron 83, the first to be equipped with air-to-air missiles, deploys to the Mediterranean aboard the carrier *Intrepid* (CVA 11). Its F-8 Crusaders carry Sparrow missiles.

March 16.   Rear Admiral W. R. Smedberg III becomes 39th superintendent of the Naval Academy.

April 14.   The carrier *Saratoga* (CVA 60) is commissioned.

June 25.   Fleet Admiral Ernest J. King dies in Portsmouth, New Hampshire, at the age of 77.

The *Nautilus* on her sea trials. *Official U.S. Navy photograph.*

July 20.   The first amphibious assault ship, the *Thetis Bay* (CVAH-1, later redesignated LPH-1) is commissioned. Vessels of this type carry a marine battalion (approximately 2,000 men) and helicopters to land them on hostile coasts.

August 22.   A Japan-based P4M Mercator reconnaissance plane is shot down while flying a routine patrol over international waters off the coast of China. There are no survivors.

October 29–November 3.   **Suez Crisis.** Ships of the Sixth Fleet join U.S. military aircraft in evacuating American citizens from Egypt, Israel, and Syria when war breaks out in the Middle East. A total of 2,213 Americans are extracted, 1,680 by sea and 533 by air.

October 31.   Seven officers and men headed by Rear Admiral G. J. Dufek, Commander Naval Support Force, Antarctic, become the first persons to set foot at the South Pole since Captain Robert Scott, RN, reached there in 1912. They land in the R-4D twin-engined transport *Que Sera Sera*.

December 3.   **Polaris approved.** The navy is authorized to pursue the development of the compact, solid-fuel Polaris missile and to withdraw from the liquid-fuel Jupiter missile project to which the army is committed. Approval for this program had been requested on November 9.

December 18.   The Joint Army-Navy Missile Committee is disbanded.

December 19.   Admiral William F. Raborn's Special Projects Office is assigned the responsibility of developing the complete Polaris missile system, which is accorded the navy's highest priority.

1957

February 8.   The Chief of Naval Operations, Admiral Arleigh Burke, sets a deadline of January 1965 for the deployment of a solid-fuel missile with a 1,500-mile range suitable for launching from a submerged submarine. A few months later the deadline is moved up to January 1963.

March 11.   Rear Admiral Richard E. Byrd dies at the age of 68. He was the first man to fly over both the Poles.

March 17.   **Vanguard I.** The navy's first satellite is launched from Cape Canaveral, Florida. It weighs $3\frac{1}{2}$ pounds.

April 1.   Thomas S. Gates becomes the 54th secretary of the navy.

August 10.   The carrier *Ranger* (CVA 61) is commissioned.

August 12.   Lieutenant Commander Don Walker lands an F3D Skyknight aboard the carrier *Antietam* (CV 36) in the first test of the automatic carrier landing system.

October 9.   Neil H. McElroy becomes the sixth secretary of defense.

December 9.   Secretary of Defense McElroy advances the deadline for the development of the Polaris submarine missile system to 1960. The preliminary design of the submarine itself has just been completed.

1958

January.   The first three Polaris fleet ballistic-missile submarines are put under construction. The lead ship, the *George Washington* (SSBN 598), had been laid down as the nuclear-powered attack submarine *Scorpion*. To accommodate Polaris missile-launching tubes, she is cut in two and lengthened by the insertion of a 130-foot section amidships.

March 7.   The *Grayback* (SSG 574), the first submarine designed with the capability of launching guided missiles, is commissioned. She must surface to fire her jet-powered Regulus II missiles, however, and the program is abandoned in favor of Polaris.

May 28.   The *Galveston* (CLG 3, originally CL 93), the first cruiser equipped with the Talos antiaircraft missiles, is commissioned.

May 28.   The submarine *Stickelback* (SS 415) is sunk without loss of life in a collision with the destroyer *Silverstein* (DE 534) off Pearl Harbor.

June 27.   Rear Admiral Charles L. Melson becomes the 40th superintendent of the Naval Academy.

July 15.   **Lebanon landing.** At the request of Lebanese President Camille Chamoun, U.S. forces commanded by Admiral J. L. Holloway, Jr., land at Beirut to support his government, which is threatened by both civil war and the prospect of foreign invasion. Two of the Sixth Fleet's three marine battalion landing teams are ashore within 24 hours. The third follows shortly. Within a few days the marines are joined by a reinforced airborne brigade flown from West Germany, and a USAF composite strike group arrives from the United States to support the Sixth Fleet carriers *Essex* (CVA 9), *Saratoga* (CVA 60) and *Wasp* (CVS 18). Peace is maintained. The feared invasion does not materialize, and American negotiators bring the civil war to an end by arranging an election satisfactory to all parties. The last American troops are withdrawn on October 25.

August 3.   **First under the ice.** The nuclear submarine *Nautilus* (SSN 571), Commander William R. Anderson, becomes the first ship to reach the North Pole, beneath which she passes on a 4-day, 1,830-mile voyage under the polar ice from the Pacific to the Atlantic, where she surfaces on August 7.

August 11.   **Surface at the Pole.** At 6:47 P.M., the *Skate* (SSN 578), Commander James F. Calvert, becomes the first submarine to surface at the North Pole. She does so again on August 17 in the course of a Arctic voyage of exploration that lasts from July 30 to September 22.

August 23.   **Matsu and Quemoy crisis.** Communist China begins an intensive artillery bombardment of the Nationalist-held offshore islands of Matsu and Quemoy. President Eisenhower orders the Seventh Fleet to assist the Nationalists in supplying the 100,000-man garrison of Quemoy, which it does by escorting their transports to the three-mile territorial limit. The president also reminds the Communists of a congressional resolution authorizing him to defend Formosa and deploys a six-carrier task force around the island. The crisis has cooled by December.

October 24.   The transport *Kliensmith* (APD 134), supported by the carrier *Franklin D. Roosevelt* (CVA 42),

Marines go ashore near Beirut, Lebanon, July 15, 1958. *Defense Department photo (Marine Corps).*

evacuates 56 American citizens and 3 foreign nationals from Nicara, Cuba, as Castro's revolution nears a climax.

1959

January 10.   The carrier *Independence* (CVA 62) is commissioned.

February 24.   The navy announces plans to scrap 43 obsolete warships, including the battleships *California* (BB 44), *Colorado* (BB 45), *Maryland* (BB 46), *Tennessee* (BB 43), and *West Virginia* (BB 48). The four fast battleships of the *Iowa* class are retained.

June 8.   William B. Franke becomes the 55th secretary of the navy.

June 16.   Two MiG fighters attack and damage a P4M navy reconnaissance plane during a routine mission over international waters off the coast of Korea.

July 20.   Fleet Admiral William D. Leahy dies, aged 84, at Bethesda, Maryland.

August 16.   Fleet Admiral William F. ("Bull") Halsey dies at the age of 76.

December 1.   **Antarctic Treaty.** Twelve nations, including the United States and the Soviet Union, pledge that they will not undertake any kind of military activities in Antarctica.

December 2.   Thomas S. Gates, Jr., becomes the seventh secretary of defense.

December 31.   **First fleet ballistic-missile submarine.** The *George Washington* (SSBN 598) is commissioned.

1960

January 1.   General David M. Shoup becomes 22nd commandant of the U.S. Marine Corps.

April 13.   Navy Transit IB, the navy's first navigational satellite, is launched from Cape Canaveral, Florida.

May 6.   The Cuban cutter *Oriente* fires on the submarine *Sea Poacher* (SS 406) in San Nicholas Channel.

May 10.   **Around the world submerged.** The nuclear-powered submarine *Triton* (SSN 586), Commander Edward L. Beach, becomes the first vessel to circumnavigate the earth submerged. Her voyage, which lasts for 84 days and covers 41,519 miles, closely follows the route taken by Magellan in the first conventional circumnavigation almost 350 years before.

The launching of the *George Washington* at Groton, Connecticut, June 9, 1959. *Courtesy General Dynamics Corporation.*

Commander Edward L. Beach on the bridge of the *Triton*. *Official U.S. Navy photograph.*

June 22.   Rear Admiral John F. Davidson becomes the 41st superintendent of the Naval Academy.

July 19.   The destroyers *Ammen* (DD 527) and *Collett* (DD 730) collide off Long Beach, California. Eleven of the *Ammen's* crewmen are killed, twenty injured, and the ship is damaged beyond repair.

July 20.   **First Polaris launch.** Off Cape Canaveral, Florida, the *George Washington* (SSBN 598) successfully conducts the first submerged launchings of the new Polaris A-1 missile.

The second of two Polaris missiles launched by the *George Washington* on July 20, 1960, breaks the surface. The upright object at lower right is the tip of a radio antenna temporarily mounted on the submarine to receive telemetry data from the missile. *Official U.S. Navy photograph.*

September 10.   The *Charles F. Adams* (DDG 2), the lead ship of a new class of 4,500-ton general-purpose destroyers, is commissioned. The first ships equipped with Tartar missiles, 23 of them will join the fleet between 1960 and 1963.

November 1.   Prime Minister Harold Macmillan announces the British government's decision to allow Polaris submarines to be based at Holy Loch, Scotland.

November 15.   **First Polaris patrol.** The *George Washington* (SSBN 598) sails from Charleston, South Carolina, on the navy's first operational Polaris submarine patrol. She carries 16 Polaris A-1 nuclear missiles, which have a range of 1,200 nautical miles.

November 19.   The carrier *Constellation* (CVA 64) is swept by fire while under construction at the Brooklyn Navy Yard. Fifty workers are killed and 150 injured. Damage to the ship is estimated at $75,000,000.

1961

January 12.   In the budget proposed for Fiscal Year 1962, President Eisenhower projects a navy of 817 ships (625,000 personnel) and a marine corps of three divisions and three air wings (175,000 personnel).

January 20.   President Kennedy names Robert S. McNamara the eighth secretary of defense and John B. Connally, Jr., the 56th secretary of the navy.

April 17–20.   **The Bay of Pigs.** A force of 1,400 Cuban exiles, secretly trained by U.S. personnel in Guatemala and equipped with obsolete American equipment, lands at the Bay of Pigs, on the southwestern coast of Cuba, to overthrow the Communist government of Fidel Castro. Due in part to the failure of preliminary air strikes to eliminate the Cuban air force, the invasion is a disaster. Virtually the entire exile brigade is killed or captured. American naval units are standing offshore, in position to assist the exiles, but President Kennedy decides that to intervene would only worsen the situation. The debacle is a heavy blow to American prestige. Some months later the captured Cubans are ransomed with American medical supplies.

April 29.   The first missile-armed aircraft carrier, the *Kitty Hawk* (CVA 63), is commissioned at Camden, New Jersey.

May 5.   **First man in space.** Commander Alan B. Shepard, Jr., reaches an altitude of 116.5 miles in the Mercury capsule Freedom 7 on a suborbital flight from Cape Canaveral, Florida. He is picked up in the Atlantic, 302 miles downrange, by a helicopter from the carrier *Lake Champlain* (CVS 39).

August 1.   Admiral George W. Anderson, Jr., becomes the 16th chief of naval operations.

August 26.   The *Iwo Jima* (LPH 2), the first vessel built from the keel up as an amphibious assault ship, is commissioned.

September 10.   The world's first nuclear-powered, guided-missile cruiser, the *Long Beach* (CGN 9), is commissioned.

October 23.   The first firing of the Polaris A-2 missile from a submerged submarine takes place aboard the *Ethan Allen* (SSBN 608). The range of this new missile is 1,500 miles.

October 27.   The carrier *Constellation* (CVA 64) is commissioned.

November 16.   **Increased aid to South Vietnam.** Acting upon a report by General Maxwell D. Taylor, President Kennedy decides to increase the number of American military advisers to the Republic of South

Commander Alan B. Shepard, Jr., soon after landing from his suborbital flight. *Courtesy National Aeronautics and Space Administration.*

Vietnam, whose existence is threatened by a Communist insurgency sponsored by North Vietnam.

November 25. **First nuclear-powered carrier.** The *Enterprise* (CVAN 65) is commissioned at Newport News, Virginia. Truly termed "the largest moving structure ever built by man," she is 1,123 feet in length, displaces 85,830 tons, and carries a crew of 4,600. Her flight deck covers four and one-half acres. On trials she achieves a speed of more than 35 knots.

November 28. **ASROC.** The antisubmarine rocket (ASROC) weapons system is formally approved.

1962

January 1. **Creation of the SEALs.** Two Sea Air Land (SEAL) operating teams are established for the purpose of conducting unconventional warfare at sea and in coastal and riverine areas.

January 4. Fred Korth becomes the 57th secretary of the navy.

February 8. The U.S. Military Assistance Advisory Group (MAAG) in South Vietnam, which had been established in 1956, is reorganized as the U.S. Military Assistance Command, Vietnam (MACV), under the command of Lieutenant General Paul Harkins.

February 20. **First American orbital flight.** Lieutenant Colonel John H. Glenn, Jr., USMC, makes three orbits of the earth, at an average speed of 17,400 miles per hour in the Project Mercury capsule Friendship 7. He travels 81,000 miles, attaining a maximum altitude of 162 miles, in 4 hours and 55 minutes. Landing in the Atlantic, he is recovered by the destroyer *Noa* (DD 841).

April 12. Three ships of the Seventh Fleet Amphibious Group, the *Valley Forge* (LPH 8), *Navarro* (APA 215), and *Point Defiance* (LSD 31), land marines in Thailand to help support the independence of that country.

May 24. **Second orbital flight.** Lieutenant Commander M. Scott Carpenter completes three orbits in the Aurora 7.

August 7. **First Polaris A-3.** The first flight model of this missile, capable of traveling 2,500 miles, is launched at Cape Canaveral, Florida.

The *Enterprise. Official U.S. Navy photograph.*

August 17.   The *Long Point* (PC(H)1), the navy's first hydrofoil patrol craft, is launched at Seattle, Washington.

August 18.   Rear Admiral Charles C. Kirkpatrick becomes the 42nd superintendent of the U.S. Naval Academy.

August 31.   **The end of LTA.** The decision to terminate the navy's lighter-than-air program was announced on November 30, 1961. Almost a year later, the last airship flight is made from the historic Naval Air Station, Lakehurst, New Jersey.

October 3.   Commander Walter W. Schirra completes an orbital flight of more than 160,000 miles in 10 hours and 46 minutes in the Mercury-Atlas Sigma 7 capsule.

October 6.   **First nuclear-powered, guided-missile frigate.** The *Bainbridge* (DLGN 25) is commissioned.

October 14.   **Beginning of the Cuban Missile Crisis.** An American U-2 reconnaissance plane photographs a Soviet nuclear missile site under construction at San Cristóbal, 100 miles west of Havana, Cuba.

October 16.   The U-2 photographs are presented to President Kennedy. Soon afterwards it is also learned that Soviet Il-28 bombers are being assembled on Cuban airfields.

October 16–20.   **What to do?** The president's closest advisers, later designated the Excomm (Executive Committee of the National Security Council) hold marathon meetings to frame an appropriate response to the Soviet challenge. The joint chiefs of staff are unanimous in recommending a surgical air strike, a course a number of the civilians also urge. Kennedy's reluctance to adopt so drastic a decision is reinforced by his military advisers' admission that they cannot guarantee to eliminate all of the missiles with a first strike. In the end, he chooses the more flexible option of imposing a naval blockade, which, since the United States and Cuba are not at war, will be called a quarantine.

October 22.   **Quarantine of Cuba.** President Kennedy appears on national television to announce that he is imposing a naval quarantine, effective October 24, to block the entry of Soviet offensive weapons into Cuba. To carry out the quarantine, Task Force 136 is organized under Vice Admiral Alfred G. Ward, Commander, Second Fleet, and Commander, Strike Fleet Atlantic. It consists of the support carrier *Essex* (CVS 9), the heavy cruisers *Newport News* (CA 148) and *Canberra* (CAG 2), several squadrons of destroyers, and the necessary support ships. At the same time, Task Force 135 is established under Rear Admiral John T. Hayward, Commander, Carrier Division 2. Formed around the nuclear carrier *Enterprise* (CVAN 65), it stands ready to come to the defense of the U.S. naval base at Guantánamo. Rear Admiral Robert J. Stroh's Carrier Division 6, with the *Independence* (CVA 62), is also in position to intervene.

October 23.   The United Nations Security Council holds an emergency session to consider a charge by the United States that the Soviet Union is threatening the peace. On the same day, the Organization of American States approves the use of force in carrying out the quarantine of Cuba by a vote of 19–0, Uruguay abstaining.

October 24.   The quarantine goes into effect. Reconnaissance has revealed that 25 Soviet vessels are en route to Cuba, but at mid-morning all but one of those nearing the blockade stop dead in the water. Several hours later, they reverse course.

October 25.   On the quarantine line, the destroyer *Gearing* (DD 710) stops the Soviet tanker *Bucharest,* but allows her to proceed to Cuba upon learning that she is carrying only oil.

October 26.   The destroyers *Joseph P. Kennedy, Jr.* (DD 850) and *John R. Pierce* (DD 753) halt and board a Soviet-chartered, Lebanese-flag freighter, the SS *Marucla.* After her cargo is inspected, she is allowed to continue to Havana.

October 26.   At 6:00 P.M. President Kennedy receives an emotional letter from Soviet Premier Khrushchev, which states that the missiles had been placed in Cuba only to deter an American invasion and promises to remove them if the United States will pledge to lift the blockade and not attack Cuba.

October 27.   Before Kennedy has replied to Khrushchev's letter, an American U-2 is shot down over Cuba by a surface-to-air missile, and a second letter is received from Khrushchev. In this communication, the Soviet leader couples a demand for the withdrawal of American missiles from Turkey to his previous terms for the withdrawal of Soviet missiles from Cuba. For several grim hours it appears as though the situation has reached an impasse. Then the president's brother, Attorney General Robert F. Kennedy, suggests that the president agree to the conditions of Khrushchev's first letter and simply ignore the second. This is done. At the same time, Robert Kennedy privately informs Soviet Ambas-

The Soviet ship *Volgoles,* closely observed by the radar picket *Vesole* and a navy P2V Neptune patrol plane, on her way home with a deckload of missiles at the conclusion of the Cuban Missile Crisis, November 9, 1962. *Official U.S. Navy photograph.*

sador Dobrinin that the president was already planning to remove the missiles from Turkey.

October 28.   **The crisis resolved.** Khrushchev notifies Kennedy that he is ordering the Soviet missiles and bombers in Cuba to be withdrawn. The most dangerous, direct Soviet-American confrontation to date in the Cold War is over.

November 8.   The Department of Defense announces that the Cuban missile bases have been dismantled.

November 20.   President Kennedy states that, having received Premier Khrushchev's promise to recall all Soviet bombers from Cuba within 30 days, he has ended the quarantine of the island.

1963

April 10.   **Loss of the Thresher.** The nuclear submarine *Thresher* (SSN 593), Lieutenant Commander John W. Harvey, is reported overdue and presumed lost with all hands, 129 officers, men, and civilian technicians, approximately 240 miles east of Cape Cod, Massachusetts. Apparently the disaster resulted from a reactor shut-down during a dive. The boat's auxiliary engines were unable to check her descent, and she was crushed by the pressure of the ocean depths. On October 1, 1964, the navy announces that the main wreckage has been located by the deep-submergence vehicle *Trieste II.*

April 23.   The *Lafayette* (SSBN 616), the lead ship of a new class of fleet ballistic-missile submarines, is commissioned.

August 1.   Admiral David L. McDonald becomes the 17th chief of naval operations.

October 26.   A Polaris A-3 missile is fired from a submerged submarine for the first time by the *Andrew Jackson* (SSBN 619).

November 1–2.   President Ngo Dinh Diem of South Vietnam is overthrown and killed by a military coup, leading to 18 months of political instability that greatly complicate the American efforts to aid the country in resisting the Viet Cong insurgency.

November 29.   Paul H. Nitze becomes the 58th secretary of the navy.

December 4.   **SUBROC.** The navy announces that it is developing a rocket-powered guided missile, capable of being fired underwater from a conventional torpedo tube and armed with a nuclear depth bomb to destroy enemy submarines at long range.

The *Thresher. Official U.S. Navy photograph.*

1964

January 1.   General Wallace M. Green, Jr., becomes the 23rd commandant of the marine corps.

January 11.   Rear Admiral Charles S. Minter, Jr., becomes the 43rd superintendent of the U.S. Naval Academy.

January 13.   During a revolution in Zanzibar, the destroyer *Manley* (DD 940) evacuates 55 American citizens and 36 other persons.

February 1.   **Admiral Rickover is extended.** Vice Admiral Hyman G. Rickover, assistant chief of the Bureau of Ships for Nuclear Propulsion and Director of Naval Reactors in the Atomic Energy Commission, reaches the mandatory retirement age of 64, but at the request of the president remains on active duty as a retired officer. He will receive biennial extensions for the next 15 years.

May 13.   **First nuclear-powered task group.** In the Mediterranean, the Sixth Fleet forms the world's first task group of nuclear-powered ships. Commanded by Rear Admiral Bernard M. Strean, it consists of the attack carrier *Enterprise* (CVAN 65), the guided-missile cruiser *Long Beach* (CGN 9), and the guided-missile frigate *Bainbridge* (DLGN 25).

June 6.   An RF-8 reconnaissance plane piloted by Lieutenant Charles F. Klusmann from the carrier *Kitty Hawk* (CVA 63) is shot down by Communist insurgents over the Plaine des Jarres, Laos. Lieutenant Klusmann parachutes to safety, but later waves off a rescue helicopter, fearing that it will also be shot down. Captured by the Communists, he escapes on September 1 and is awarded the Distinguished Flying Cross.

June 7.   An F-8 Crusader fighter from the *Kitty Hawk* is shot down while escorting a reconnaissance plane over the Plaine des Jarres, Laos.

July 31.   **Operation Sea Orbit.** All-nuclear Task Force One, consisting of the carrier *Enterprise* (CVAN 65), guided-missile cruiser *Long Beach* (CGN 9), and guided-missile frigate *Bainbridge* (DLGN 25), departs Gibraltar for a 30,565-nautical-mile unreplenished circumnavigation of the globe. The exercise concludes when the task force enters Charleston, South Carolina, on October 1.

August 2.   **Tonkin Gulf incident.** The destroyer *Maddox* (DD 731), Captain Herbert L. Ogier, is attacked at 3:08 P.M. local time by three North Vietnamese patrol boats while operating in international waters 30 miles off the coast of North Vietnam. The *Maddox* opens fire and calls on the carrier *Ticonderoga* (CVA 14), which sends four F-8E Crusaders to her assistance. The engagement lasts 21 minutes, during which the *Maddox* evades two torpedoes and one of the enemy boats is sunk.

August 4.   **Second Tonkin Gulf incident.** Beginning at 9:30 P.M., the *Maddox* and the *Turner Joy* (DD 951), Commander Robert C. Barnhart, patrolling together in the Gulf of Tonkin, pick up radar contacts that are identified as North Vietnamese patrol boats. The contacts persist for four hours, during which both ships take them under fire and maneuver to evade torpedoes. Aircraft launched from the *Ticonderoga* are unable to locate the enemy in the darkness. Afterwards there is speculation that the contacts were only radar blips.

Operation Sea Orbit *(from left to right)*: the frigate *Bainbridge,* cruiser *Long Beach,* and carrier *Enterprise. Official U.S. Navy photograph.*

The *Maddox. Official U.S. Navy photograph.*

August 5.   **First naval strike on North Vietnam.** In retaliation for the attacks on the *Maddox* and the *Turner Joy,* President Johnson orders aircraft from the *Constellation* (CVA 64) and *Ticonderoga* (CVA 14) to attack naval bases, patrol boats, and oil depots along 100 miles of the North Vietnamese coast. A total of 64 sorties are flown, during which 25 patrol boats are damaged or destroyed and an estimated 90 percent of the petroleum in the target areas is set ablaze. The strikes last for four hours. The *Constellation* loses two planes: an A-1H Skyraider, whose pilot, Lieutenant (jg) Richard A. Sather, is the first navy pilot to be killed in Vietnam, and an A-4E Skyhawk, whose pilot, Lieutenant (jg) Everett Alvarez, becomes the first navy POW.

August 7.   **Tonkin Gulf (Southeast Asia) Resolution.** Congress relinquishes its war-making powers to the president by authorizing him to "take all necessary measures to repel any armed attack against the forces of the United States . . . [and] to assist any member or protocol state" of the Southeast Asia Treaty Organization. The resolution passes in the House of Representatives by a vote of 416–0 and in the Senate by 88–2. It is on the basis of this legislation that President Johnson will commit U.S. forces to an ever-expanding role in Vietnam.

September 18.   After nightfall in the Gulf of Tonkin the destroyers *Morton* (DD 948) and *Parsons* (DD 949) open fire on four radar contacts believed to be attacking torpedo boats. The destroyers are undamaged; the effect of their fire is unknown.

September 28.   The first deployment of the Polaris A-3 occurs when the *Daniel Webster* (SSBN 626), armed with these missiles, departs Charleston, South Carolina, for a two-month patrol.

November 1.   **Bien Hoa incident.** The Viet Cong mortar the South Vietnamese air base at Bien Hoa. Four American servicemen are killed, 72 are wounded, and 28 American aircraft are damaged or destroyed.

December 6.   The completion of the last of three salt-water conversion plants makes the U.S. naval base at Guantánamo Bay, Cuba, independent of any outside water supply. The government of Fidel Castro had cut off the flow of fresh water to the base on February 6 and offered to restore it on March 4, but the offer was refused.

December 24.   A Viet Cong bomb explodes outside the Brink Bachelor Officers' Quarters in Saigon, killing two Americans and wounding 51 Americans and South Vietnamese.

December 26.   The first fleet ballistic-missile submarine patrol made in the Pacific begins when the *Daniel Boone* (SSBN 629) departs Guam armed with the Polaris A-3.

December 31.   At year's end, there are 23,000 U.S. servicemen in South Vietnam.

1965

January 23.   The aircraft carrier *America* (CVA 66) is commissioned.

February 7.   Eight American servicemen are killed and 126 wounded by a Viet Cong attack on a barracks at Pleiku, South Vietnam.

February 7.   **Flaming Dart I.** In retaliation for the Pleiku incident, barracks and facilities near Dong Hoi, North Vietnam, are attacked by 83 planes from the carriers *Coral Sea* (CVA 43), *Hancock* (CVA 19), and *Ranger* (CVA 61). One aircraft is lost. Simultaneously, the South Vietnamese Air Force hits North Vietnamese installations at Vinh.

February 10.   Twenty-three Americans are killed and twenty-one injured when the Viet Cong bomb an enlisted men's barracks at the helicopter base at Qui Nhon.

February 11.   **Flaming Dart II.** North Vietnamese military installations near Chan Hoa are attacked by 99 aircraft from the *Coral Sea* (CVA 43), *Hancock* (CVA 19), and *Ranger* (CVA 61), while the South Vietnamese Air Force strikes Vit Thu Lu. An F-8D Crusader from the *Coral Sea* is lost.

March 2.   **Rolling Thunder.** U.S. Navy and Air Force planes begin sustained bombardment of military targets in North Vietnam. These raids are an application of the strategic theory of graduated response, according to which pressure will be incrementally increased until the North's "ouch level" is reached, and it will terminate its support of the Viet Cong. The campaign continues until October 31, 1968. Unfortunately, the pressure applied does not produce the desired result. North Vietnam's "ouch level" will be not be reached until the Linebacker II B-52 strikes of December 1972.

March 8.   **Marines land at Da Nang.** Using the authority conferred on him by the Tonkin Gulf Resolution, President Johnson orders the 9th Marine Expeditionary Brigade, 3,500 men commanded by Brigadier General Frederick J. Karch, ashore to assume responsibility for the security of the air base at Da Nang, South Vietnam. This is the first commitment of American ground combat troops in the Vietnam War. Without realizing it, the United States has entered its longest foreign war.

March 11.   **Operation Market Time.** The operation that will be named Market Time begins when the Seventh Fleet destroyers *Black* (DD 666) and *Higbee* (DD 806) are ordered to the coastal zone of Vietnam to inspect native junk traffic in order to prevent the infiltration of men and arms to the south. Many more vessels as well as patrol planes are soon assigned to this mission, Task Force 71 (the Vietnam Patrol Force) being established to conduct it. By the end of November, Market Time ships have made 73,000 junk sightings, of which approximately 15,000 have been visually inspected at close quarters and another 6,000 boarded and searched.

March 15.   Aircraft from the *Hancock* (CVA 19) and *Ranger* (CVA 61) attack an ammunition depot at Phu Qui, 100 miles south of Hanoi. One plane and its pilot are lost.

March 23.   The first two-man Gemini space capsule, the Molly Brown, completes three orbits of the earth. Aboard are Lieutenant Colonel Virgil Grissom, USAF, and Lieutenant Commander John Young.

March 26.   Four radar sites in North Vietnam are attacked by 40 planes from the *Hancock* (CVA 19) and *Coral Sea* (CVA 43). Two aircraft are lost, but both pilots are rescued.

April.   **Naval air war in Vietnam.** From this time forward, strikes involving from 4 to 100 aircraft are flown al-

An A-1 Skyraider on the catapult of the *Hancock*, ready to be launched on a strike against North Vietnam, March 1965. *Official U.S. Navy photograph.*

most daily from carriers at Yankee Station in the South China Sea, attacking military targets, transportation facilities, and power stations in North Vietnam. Altogether, in the course of the year navy planes will fly more than 55,000 sorties in Vietnam. The U.S. Air Force will fly 50,000.

April 9.   Four F-4 Phantom fighters, flying cover for a raid on North Vietnam, are attacked by several MiG-17s, nationality undetermined, about 35 miles south of Hainan Island. One MiG is believed downed, and one F-4 fails to return.

April 10.   **Marine air to Vietnam.** Marine Fighter Attack Squadron (VMFA) 531 is based at Da Nang. Other squadrons soon follow.

April 14.   The 3rd Battalion, Fourth Marines, lands near Da Nang, bringing the strength of American ground combat troops in South Vietnam to 8,000.

April 15.   Navy and marine aircraft from the *Coral Sea* (CVA 43) and *Midway* (CVA 41) join U.S. and South Vietnamese air force planes in attacking Viet Cong positions in South Vietnam. This is the first time naval aircraft have been used against targets inside the country.

April 15.   Ten aircraft from the same two carriers fly the first reconnaissance mission over North Vietnam.

April 22.   **First ground action in Vietnam.** Near Da Nang, marines engage in a fire fight with the Viet Cong. No marines are killed or seriously wounded.

April 28. **Dominican intervention.** A 400-man expeditionary force of the 3rd Battalion, Sixth Marines, is airlifted into Santo Domingo, the capital of the Dominican Republic, where a revolution that began on April 25 is believed to endanger American citizens.

April 29. Reinforcements raise the strength of marine forces in the Dominican Republic to 1,600. They will be organized as the 4th Marine Expeditionary Brigade.

May 3. **First army combat unit to Vietnam.** Leading elements of the 173rd Airborne Brigade begin to land at Saigon. The arrival of this unit will raise the total number of U.S. personnel in South Vietnam to 36,000.

May 3–7. **III MAF.** In Vietnam the 9th Marine Expeditionary Brigade is reinforced and reorganized as the III Marine Amphibious Force, under Lieutenant General Lewis W. Walt. The marines will be responsible for the northernmost of the four military districts into which the country is divided, five provinces comprising the I Corps Tactical Zone.

May 5. Mediators of the Organization of American States persuade the warring Dominican factions to sign a cease fire, despite which fighting continues in Santo Domingo.

May 7. **Chu Lai airfield.** The 1st and 2nd Battalions, Fourth Marines, and several hundred Seabees land at Chu Lai, South Vietnam, and commence construction of a marine field. It becomes operational on June 1.

May 11. With the arrival of elements of the army's 82nd Airborne Division, the number of U.S. troops in the Dominican Republic rises to more than 11,000, including 6,000 marines.

May 12–18. **First Vietnamese bombing pause.** President Johnson suspends air attacks on North Vietnam and calls upon its government to negotiate. There is no response.

May 16. **Dixie Station.** A single-carrier station is established approximately 100 miles southeast of Cam Ranh Bay, from which strikes can be launched in support of allied forces inside South Vietnam. It is discontinued 15 months later, following the buildup of air strength ashore.

May 20. **First shore bombardment of the Vietnam conflict.** Units of the Seventh Fleet begin to deliver the navy's first fire-support missions since the Korean War. The use of naval gunfire in South Vietnam had been authorized on May 14.

May 26–June 6. **Dominican wind-down.** Arrangements having been made through the Organization of American States to have an Inter-American peace-keeping force replace U.S. troops in the Dominican Republic, the marines are withdrawn. In the course of the crisis they have lost 10 men killed and 26 wounded in scattered street fighting in Santo Domingo. Elements of the 82nd Airborne remain to form part of the Inter-American force.

June 9. **Development of Cam Ranh Bay.** The army's 35th Engineer Group lands to begin construction of a major port facility at Cam Ranh Bay, South Vietnam.

June 12. Rear Admiral Draper L. Kauffman becomes the 44th superintendent of the Naval Academy.

June 17. **First confirmed MiG kills of the Vietnam War.** Some 50 miles south of Hanoi two F-4B Phantoms of the *Midway*'s VF-21 are attacked by four MiG-17s and shoot down two with Sparrow air-to-air missiles.

June 19. Youthful Air Vice Marshal Nguyen Cao Ky becomes premier of South Vietnam, effectively ending the political instability that has plagued the country since the overthrow of President Diem in November 1963.

June 20. Over North Vietnam, two MiG-17s attack four propeller-driven A-1H Skyraiders (popularly known as Spads) from the *Midway* (CVA 41). A Skyraider destroys one of the enemy with 20-mm cannon fire.

July 20–August 1. **The coast guard in Vietnam.** Seventeen 82-foot coast guard cutters, organized as Coast Guard Division 1, arrive in South Vietnam and begin monitoring coastal shipping as part of the campaign (Operation Market Time) to prevent the infiltration of supplies to the Viet Cong. Each boat carries a crew of two officers and nine men.

July 28. In a television address to the nation, President Johnson announces that he has ordered 1st Cavalry Division (Airmobile) and other, smaller units to South Vietnam. The arrival of these forces will increase the American commitment to approximately 125,000 men.

August 1. The responsibility for the conduct of Operation Market Time is transferred to Rear Admiral Norvell G. Ward, Naval Component Commander, Military Advisory Command, Vietnam, and the units involved are reorganized as Task Force 115 (Coastal Surveillance Force).

August 11–12. **First SAMs.** The first navy plane definitely known to have been downed by a surface-to-air missile, an A-4E Skyhawk from the *Midway* (CVA 41), is lost over North Vietnam. The first American aircraft destroyed by a SAM was an Air Force F-4 on July 24.

August 13. Five aircraft—an A-1 Skyraider, two A-4 Sky-hawks, and two F-8 Crusaders—from the *Coral Sea* (CVA 43) and *Midway* (CVA 41) are shot down over North Vietnam by conventional ground fire while searching for SAM sites in the worst day of the naval air war to date.

August 18. **Operation Starlite.** The marines launch their first large-scale amphibious assault in Vietnam on the Van Tuong Peninsula 14 miles south of Chu Lai. Supported by marine air and naval gunfire from the cruiser *Galveston* (CLG 3) and two destroyers, 4,000 men of the Third, Fourth, and Seventh Marines go ashore over the beach and by helicopter. Regimental Landing Team 7 virtually destroys the Viet Cong 1st Regiment, killing 964 of the enemy and taking 125 prisoner. This is the first major action between U.S. troops and the Viet Cong main force and the largest battle Americans have fought since the Korean War. Marines losses are approximately 50 killed and 125 wounded.

August 28. **Aquanauts.** Three teams of 10 men each spend 15 days in Sealab II, 205 feet below the surface off La Jolla, California. Commander M. Scott Carpenter, who is also an astronaut, remains in the capsule for 30 successive days.

October 15. The U.S. Naval Support Activity, Da Nang, is organized under the Commander, Service Force, Pacific Fleet, to provide logistic support for the war effort in South Vietnam.

October 17. An A-6 Intruder and four A-4E Skyhawks from the *Independence* (CVA 62) destroy a North Vietnamese SAM site at Kep 37 miles north of Hanoi without loss to themselves. This is the first successful strike on an enemy missile site.

October 31. **Swift Boats.** The first two Swift Boats to arrive in Vietnam exchange fire with the enemy within hours. These are 50-foot, aluminum-hulled fast patrol craft (PCF) armed with three .50-caliber machine guns and an 81-mm mortar. They carry a crew of one officer and four enlisted men. By the end of the year the navy has ordered 104 of these craft. They will be used mostly in Operation Market Time.

December 2. **First nuclear-powered ship at war.** The *Enterprise* (CVAN 65) launches 118 sorties against targets in South Vietnam, thus becoming the first nuclear ship to engage in hostilities.

December 4. The Gemini VII space capsule carries Commander James A. Lovell, Jr., USN, and Lieutenant Colonel Frank Borman, USAF, on a record-breaking orbital flight of 14 days.

An A-4 Skyhawk releasing bombs over Vietnam, November 1965. *Official U.S. Navy photograph.*

A Swift Boat (PCF) of the brown-water navy on a river north of Saigon during Operation Giant Slingshot, February 1969. *Official U.S. Navy photograph.*

December 15. **First meeting in space.** The Gemini VIII capsule, manned by Captain Walter Schirra, USN, and Major Thomas P. Stafford, USAF, is launched and makes a rendezvous with Gemini VII. This is the first meeting of manned space vehicles in orbital flight.

December 18. **Birth of Operation Game Warden.** The U.S. Navy River Patrol Force (Task Force 116) is activated in South Vietnam with the mission of patrolling the Mekong Delta and the swampy area between Saigon and the sea designated the Rung Sat Special Zone. Initially its equipment consists of four large patrol landing craft (LCPLs). Later it is given control of the navy's river patrol boats, which begin to arrive in April 1966, and its activities are designated Operation Game Warden.

December 22.   The North Vietnamese thermal power plant at Uong Bi is hit by 100 aircraft from the *Enterprise* (CVAN 65), *Kitty Hawk* (CVA 63), and *Ticonderoga* (CV 14). Two planes are lost. This is the first raid on a purely industrial enemy target.

December 24.   **Bombing halt.** President Johnson orders the second pause in the air war against North Vietnam, which will not be resumed until January 31, 1966.

December 31.   On this date, there are 181,000 American troops in South Vietnam. A total of 1,365 U.S. servicemen have been killed in action there in the course of the year.

1966

January 31.   **End of the bombing halt.** After a 37-day pause, during which the U.S. government has tried unsuccessfully to open negotiations with North Vietnam, raids against military targets in that country are resumed.

February 14.   Off the coast of South Vietnam, *PCF 4* becomes the first Swift Boat lost in action when she is destroyed by an underwater explosion. Four of her crewmen are killed and two are wounded.

February 16.   The hospital ship *Repose* (AH 16) begins operations at Chu Lai, South Vietnam.

February 20.   Fleet Admiral Chester W. Nimitz, the navy's last five-star admiral, dies at the age of 81 at his home on Yerba Buena Island in San Francisco Bay.

February 26.   Nine more coast guard cutters reach South Vietnam. Organized as Coast Guard Division 13, they will be based at Vung Tau. There are now 26 cutters in the combat zone.

March 1.   The 5th Marine Division is reactivated. In the next 12 months the personnel strength of the corps is to be increased from 190,000 to 278,000.

March 31.   The 1st Marine Division joins the 3rd Marine Division in Vietnam. This is the first time since World War II that two marine divisions have been committed to the same war zone.

March 31.   **Arnheiter affair.** Lieutenant Commander Marcus Aurelius Arnheiter is abruptly relieved of command of the destroyer picket *Vance* (DER 387) on the gun line off Vietnam. Subsequently he protests that he has been victimized by a cabal of disloyal junior officers, and the incident attracts nationwide publicity. Hearings and suits continue for several years.

April 1.   A new command, U.S. Naval Forces, Vietnam, is created to control the operations of naval forces inside South Vietnam and certain coastal units. Its first chief is Rear Admiral Norvell G. Ward, formerly Naval Component Commander, Military Advisory Command, Vietnam. The latter title is abolished.

April 7.   An H-bomb lost when two U.S. Air Force planes collided off Palomares, Spain, is recovered by the navy after an intensive, 80-day search.

April 10.   **PBRs in Vietnam.** Two of the navy's new 31-foot, water-jet-propelled river patrol boats (PBRs) are assigned to Operation Game Warden.

April 11.   **First B-52 raids on North Vietnam.** U.S. Air Force B-52 bombers attack targets near the Mu Gia Pass, 65 miles south of Vinh.

April 17.   Off Vietnam, the heavy cruiser *Canberra* (CAG 2) becomes the first U.S. Navy vessel to relay an operational message via communications satellite, using the Syncom III to reach the Naval Communications Station in Honolulu, 4,000 miles away.

May 1.   **Administrative reorganization.** Four of the navy's traditional bureaus—Naval Weapons, Ships, Supplies and Accounts, and Yards and Docks—are reconstituted into six commands under the Office of Naval Material: Ordnance Systems, Air Systems, Ship Systems, Electronic Systems, Supply Systems,

A PBR in the Long Tau River, the main shipping channel between Saigon and the sea, January 1968. *Official U.S. Navy photograph.*

and Facilities Engineering. At the same time, the Office of Naval Material, the Bureau of Naval Personnel, and the Bureau of Medicine and Surgery are placed directly under the chief of naval operations.

May 9.   **First operations in the Mekong Delta.** Ten river patrol boats (PBRs) begin to patrol the Bassac River. By June 1967 the Mekong Delta River Patrol Group has grown to include 80 PBRs, six UH-1B Seawolf helicopter gunships, and three platoons of SEALs.

May 9.   **First operational air-cushion craft.** Three air-cushion patrol vehicles (PACVs), capable of more than 50 knots, join Operation Market Time off South Vietnam. They carry one .50-caliber machine gun. These are the first vessels of their kind to become operational in the U.S. Navy.

May 11.   **Market Time action.** The *Brister* (DER 327), coastal minesweeper *Vireo* (MSC 205), and coast guard cutter *Point Grey* (WPB 82324) concert action with the South Vietnamese Air Force to destroy a 120-foot steel freighter caught running arms to the Viet Cong. The vessel carried 50 tons of supplies.

May 22.   Swift Boat *PCF 41* is sunk by 57-mm recoilless rifle fire on the Dinh Ba River in the Rung Sat Special Zone.

June 3.   **Gemini IX.** Lieutenant Commander Eugene A. Cernan, USN, on a three-day mission with Lieutenant Colonel Thomas P. Stafford, USAF, becomes the second American to walk in space.

June 12.   **First F-8 kill.** The navy scores its first aerial victory of the year and the first ever won by an F-8 Cru-

sader when Commander Harold L. Marr, flying off the *Hancock* (CVA 19), destroys a MiG-17 over North Vietnam with a Sidewinder air-to-air missile.

June 20.   **More Market Time action.** Near the Co Chien River at the mouth of the Mekong Delta, the coast guard cutters *Point League* (WPG 82304) and *Point Slocum* (WPB 82313) encounter and receive fire from a 120-foot, steel-hulled trawler, which they drive aground ablaze. The Communist Chinese vessel is found to be carrying 250 tons of munitions destined for the Viet Cong. The *Point Slocum* takes a hit from a mortar shell in the course of the action.

June 29.   Forty-six planes from the *Constellation* (CVA 64) and *Ranger* (CVA 61) strike oil-storage plants on the outskirts of Hanoi and Haiphong, beginning a campaign to cripple the petroleum and oil storage and distribution system of North Vietnam. This is the nearest American bombs have fallen to either city.

July 1.   **Minesweeping.** Twelve 57-foot minesweeping boats (MSBs) of Mine Squadron 11 are constituted as Detachment Alpha, with the responsibility of keeping the Long Tau River shipping channel to Saigon clear of mines.

July 13.   Six MiG-17s are shot down, one by an F-4 Phantom from the *Constellation* (CVA 64) and five by air force planes. This raises the total of U.S. aerial victories in the war to 15.

July 15–August 3.   **Operation Hastings III.** In Quang Tri Province Task Force Delta—8,000 men of the III Marine Amphibious Force and 3,000 South Vietnamese troops—launch a sweep to intercept the movement of the North Vietnamese 324B Division south across the Demilitarized Zone. The enemy offensive is spoiled after heavy fighting in which 824 North Vietnamese are killed.

August 3.   Aircraft from the *Constellation* (CVA 64) deliver another attack against the oil depots at Haiphong. The Soviet Union later charges, and the United States denies, that the Soviet merchantman *Medyn* was hit by bullets fired by the planes.

August 6–22.   **Operation Colorado.** In a sweep through Quang Nam and Quang Tri provinces, a reinforced battalion of the Fifth Marines kills 170 Viet Cong.

August 7.   Seven U.S. aircraft, including a navy A-1 Skyraider, are lost over North Vietnam in the worst day of the air war to date.

August 20–29.   **Operation Allegheny.** A battalion of the Third Marines kills 117 Viet Cong in a drive in Quang Nam Province.

Operation Market Time: a Swift Boat examines two Vietnamese junks. *Official U.S. Navy photograph.*

August 23.   The SS *Baton Rouge,* a freighter chartered by Military Sea Transport Service (MSTS), strikes a mine in the Long Tau channel 20 miles east of Saigon. Seven crewmen are killed, and the ship is beached. She is the third vessel mined in or near Saigon since 1964.

August 29.   A-4 Skyhawks and A-6 Intruders from the *Constellation* (CVA 64) damage two enemy torpedo boats and sink a third. Communist China later protests that the ship sunk and one of those damaged were Chinese merchantmen. The United States replies that the vessels were not attacked until they fired on the planes.

August 30.   Navy crews are placed in the armed UH-1B Seawolf helicopters being used in support of Operation Game Warden. Previously the Hueys had been flown by army personnel.

September 11.   Navy and air force pilots fly a record 171 missions over North Vietnam without losing a single plane. The previous record of 156 missions was set on August 26.

September 11.   The Viet Cong ambush two river patrol boats on the Co Chin River. One crewman is killed. He is the first American fatality in Operation Game Warden.

September 15.   **Gemini XI.** Navy astronauts Commander Charles Conrad and Lieutenant Commander Richard F. Gordon are recovered in the Atlantic by the USS *Guam* (LPH 9) after a 71-hour spaceflight.

September 17–27.   **Operation Golden Fleece 7-1.** A battalion of the Seventh Marines kills 244 Viet Cong and protects villagers harvesting an estimated 7,620 tons of rice in Quang Ngai Province.

September 22.   The Mine Force suffers its first casualties when two minesweeping boats come under recoilless rifle and rocket fire on the Long Tau River. One crewman is killed and eleven wounded by a hit on the pilothouse of *MSB 15*.

October 9.   **Two MiG kills.** A MiG-21 is shot down by an A-1 Skyraider from the *Intrepid* (CVS 11) over the Phy Ly Bridge, 35 miles south of Hanoi, and a second MiG-21 is downed by an F-8 Crusader from the *Oriskany* (CVA 34).

October 25.   **Operation Sea Dragon.** The Seventh Fleet begins to attack supply vessels on the coast of North Vietnam. Some 230 enemy watercraft are sunk in a month. By the end of the first year of the operation this figure has risen to 2,000.

October 26.   **Fire on the Oriskany.** Off Vietnam, a parachute flare ignites a fire on the hangar deck of the *Oriskany* (CVA 34), in which 44 officers and men are lost.

October 31.   **Largest riverine action.** On the Mekong River, 10 miles west of My Tho, eight Operation Game Warden river patrol boats supported by navy Seawolf helicopter gunships destroy 51 junks and sampans and capture 6 more in an engagement lasting three hours. There are no American casualties.

October 31.   *MSB 54* becomes the first U.S. minesweeping boat lost in the war when she is sunk by a mine in the Long Tau River. Of her seven crewmen, two are missing and four wounded.

November 15.   **Gemini XII.** The last space flight of the Gemini series is completed by Captain James A. Lovell, USN, and Lieutenant Colonel Edwin E. Aldrin, Jr., USAF.

November 18.   For the first time in the Vietnam War, navy ships shell a target that has not fired first when the destroyers *John R. Craig* (DD 885) and *Hamner* (DD 718) bombard a radar site two miles north of the Demilitarized Zone.

November 23.   The destroyers *Mullany* (DD 528) and *Warrington* (DD 843) sink or damage 47 of a convoy of 60 supply barges off the coast of North Vietnam.

December 11.   **Fight in the Mekong Delta.** In the second-largest riverine action to date, two patrol boats discover 40 sampans in a canal off the Mekong River west of My Tho and observe large numbers of uniformed Viet Cong ashore, evidently waiting to cross. In the ensuing engagement the patrol boats sink 28 sampans and kill 9 enemy soldiers.

December 23.   **First hit by a North Vietnamese shore battery.** Two men are killed and four wounded when the destroyer *O'Brien* (DD 725) is hit twice by shore batteries approximately three miles north of Dong Hoi. Although ships have been fired on before, and the *Ingersoll* (DD 652) was struck by fragments from near misses on December 5, this is the first time a U.S. vessel has taken a direct hit.

At year's end, there are 385,000 U.S. troops in South Vietnam.

1967

January 13.   **Master chief petty officer of the navy.** Master Chief Gunner's Mate Delbert D. Black is appointed the first Senior Enlisted Adviser of the Navy, a position analogous to the Sergeant Major of the Army. The title is soon changed to master chief petty officer of the navy.

January 27.   **Apollo tragedy.** At Cape Kennedy, a flash fire in a training session in the Apollo 1 spacecraft results in the death of three astronauts: Lieutenant Colonel Virgil I. Grissom, USAF; Lieutenant Colonel Edward H. White, USAF; and Lieutenant Commander Roger B. Chaffee, USN.

February 1–March 18.   **Operation Prairie II.** Three marine battalions, later increased to five, make a sweep through northern Quang Tri Province, killing 693 enemy troops. Marine losses are 93 dead and 483 wounded.

February 4.   River patrol boat *PBR 113* becomes the first of her class lost to enemy fire when she is damaged beyond repair by a grenade while patrolling the Co Chien River.

February 16.   **Operations in the Rung Sat Special Zone.** In cooperation with units of the U.S. 9th Infantry Division, River Assault Squadron 1 begins offensive operations in the Rung Sat Special Zone.

February 16–March 3.   **Operation Deckhouse VI.** In a two-phase operation beginning 60 miles south of Chu Lai, the Seventh Fleet Special Landing Force accounts for 280 enemy dead.

February 26.   **First mining of North Vietnam.** A-6 Intruders from the *Enterprise* (CVAN 65) drop mines in the rivers in the panhandle of North Vietnam. The United States announces that the mines pose no danger to "deep water maritime traffic."

February 28.   The Mekong Delta Mobile Riverine Force (Task Force 117) is established.

March 9–11.   **Gunnery duels.** The heavy cruiser *Canberra* (CAG 2) and destroyers *Ingersoll* (DD 652) and *Keppler* (DD 765) engage and silence numerous shore batteries while shelling coastal targets around Vinh, North Vietnam. The *Keppler* is hit on March 11, but none of her crewmen are killed.

March 11.   **Walleye.** The first television-guided air-to-surface glide bomb (Walleye) used in combat is employed by aircraft from the *Oriskany* (CV 34) in an attack on the barracks at Sam Son, North Vietnam.

March 14.   A steel-hulled North Vietnamese trawler carrying arms to the Viet Cong is spotted by a P-2 Neptune on Market Time patrol and beaches herself after being intercepted by the *Brister* (DER 327), USCG cutter *Point Ellis* (WPB 82330) and *PCF 78*. Tons of munitions are captured.

March 20–April 1.   **Operation Beacon Hill I.** In the third amphibious landing of the year, a Special Landing Force of the 1st Battalion, Fourth Marines, attacks

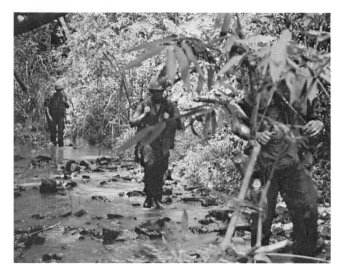

Marines advance along a streambed south of the Cam Lo River in Operation Prairie III, late March 1967. *Defense Department photo (Marine Corps).*

enemy positions in Quang Tri Province a few miles south of the Demilitarized Zone. The Viet Cong and North Vietnamese lose 334 dead.

April 1.   **Coast guard transferred.** The coast guard is incorporated into the newly established Department of Transportation after 177 years as part of the Treasury Department.

April 10.   The *Sanctuary* (AH 17) becomes the second hospital ship to commence operations in Vietnam.

April 20.   Aircraft from the *Kitty Hawk* (CVA 63) and the *Ticonderoga* (CVA 14) attack power plants 2.1 and 1.1 miles from the heart of Haiphong. This is the closest planes have ever struck to the center of the city.

April 21–May 12.   **Operation Beacon Star.** A sweep through Thua Thien Province by the Special Landing Force of the Seventh Fleet leaves 764 enemy dead.

April 24–May 5.   **Battle for Hill 861 and Hills 881 North and 881 South.** A major battle erupts when North Vietnamese troops attack the Third Marine Regiment at Khe Sanh, just south of the Demilitarized Zone near the Laotian border. The marines count 554 enemy dead and estimate that another 600 have been killed and carried off. They lose 138 dead and wounded.

April 24.   **First attacks on enemy airfields.** A-4 Skyhawks, A-6 Intruders, and F-4 Phantoms from the *Bon Homme Richard* (CVA 31) and the *Kitty Hawk* (CVA 63) hit the North Vietnamese jet base at Kep, 37 miles northeast of Hanoi, while air force planes hit Hoa Lac, 19 miles to the west of it. At Kep, two MiG-17s are downed while attempting to take off.

April 27.   Rear Admiral Norvell G. Ward is relieved by Rear Admiral Kenneth L. Veth as Commander, U.S. Naval Forces, Vietnam.

April 28–May 13.   **Operation Beaver Cage.** The 1st Battalion, Third Marines, lands to sweep a long-established enemy stronghold 25 miles south of Da Nang. More than 200 Viet Cong are killed.

May 1.   A-4 Skyhawks from the *Bon Homme Richard* (CVA 31) and *Kitty Hawk* (CVA 63) destroy two MiG-17s in aerial combat and four more on the ground in a second attack on the jet field at Kep.

May 13–July 16.   **Operation Crockett.** In Quang Tri Province, the Twenty-sixth Marines account for 206 enemy dead.

May 15.   The number of coast guardsmen in Vietnam is doubled by the arrival of three 311-foot cutters, each of which carries a crew of 150 officers and men: the *Barataria* (WHEC 381), the *Bering Strait* (WHEC 382), and the *Gresham* (WHEC 387).

May 19.   Four MiG-17s are downed by F-8 Crusaders from the *Bon Homme Richard* (CVA 31) flying cover for A-4 Skyhawks attacking a thermal power plant 1.1 miles from the center of Hanoi.

May 20–28.   **Operation Hickory.** In Quang Tri Province, battalions of the 3rd Marine Division kill 445 enemy troops.

May 27.   The *Truxtun* (DLGN 35), the navy's second nuclear-powered, guided-missile frigate is commissioned at Camden, New Jersey.

May 31.   **Operation Prairie IV.** Another sweep through Quang Tri Province by the 3rd Marine Division yields 489 enemy dead. Marine casualties are 164 killed and 999 wounded.

May 31.   Lieutenant General Robert E. Cushman relieves Lieutenant General Lewis W. Walt as commander of the III Marine Amphibious Force. There are 75,000 marines in South Vietnam at this time.

June 1–July 14.   **Operations Cimarron and Buffalo.** The Thirtieth Marines, 3rd Marine Division, launch a major drive in Quang Tri Province—Operation Cimarron—which continues after July 2 as Operation Buffalo. Some 1,290 of the enemy are killed.

June 2.   **Soviets protest.** The Soviet Union complains that the Soviet merchant ship *Turkestan* was attacked by American aircraft in port at Cam Pha, North Vietnam. One crewmen is said to have been killed and several wounded.

June 5.   **Operation Union II.** At its conclusion, a drive through Quang Nam and Quang Tin provinces by two battalions of the Fifth Marines has killed 701 enemy soldiers.

June 8.   **Attack on the Liberty.** During the Arab-Israeli War the "technical research" (actually, signals intelligence) ship *Liberty* (AGTR 5) is repeatedly attacked by Israeli fighters and torpedo boats while operating in international waters north of the Sinai Peninsula. Of her 297 crewmen, 34 are killed and 171 wounded. Israel apologizes for the attack, claiming that the *Liberty* was mistaken for an Egyptian vessel, and pays $3,323,500 compensation to the families of the men killed. In reply to the Israeli apology, the U.S. State Department condemns the attack as a "literally incomprehensible . . . act of military recklessness reflecting wanton disregard of human life." Captain William L. McGonagle, the ship's commanding officer, is awarded the Medal of Honor for his conduct during the attack.

June 25.   Swift Boat *PCF 97* is sunk by recoilless rifle and automatic weapons fire on the east coast of Ca Mau Peninsula. Miraculously, only one man is wounded. This is the third Swift Boat lost in action.

June 30.   The Soviet government protests that the Soviet merchant ship *Mikhail Frunze* has been hit by bombs during an American bombing raid on Haiphong the previous day.

July 15.   A 120-foot, steel-hulled trawler that ignores the challenge of navy and coast guard vessels on Market Time patrol is driven ashore at Cape Batangan, 11 miles north of Quang Ngai City. She is found to be carrying arms and ammunition for the Viet Cong.

July 21.   Three MiG-17s are shot down by F-8 Crusaders from the *Bon Homme Richard* (CVA 31) during a raid on the oil storage plant at Ta Xa, 30 miles north of Haiphong. Pilots from this carrier have now knocked down nine MiGs.

July 29.   **Fire on the Forrestal.** Off the coast of Vietnam, a conflagration breaks out on the flight deck of the *Forrestal* (CVA 59) when a rocket goes off as aircraft are being readied for launching. Fires burn for eight hours, during which 134 crewmen are killed and 21 aircraft destroyed. The carrier had begun operations on her first Vietnam deployment on July 26.

August 1.   Admiral Thomas H. Moorer becomes the 18th chief of naval operations.

Operation Sea Dragon: the cruiser *St. Paul* is taken under fire while shelling the railway yard at Cong Phu, 25 miles south of Thanh Hoa, August 4, 1967. *Official U.S. Navy photograph.*

A monitor, the capital ship of the riverine assault force, engaging an enemy position in the Mekong Delta with her 40-mm cannon, October 6, 1967. *Official U.S. Navy photograph.*

August 1.   The New Jersey to be reactivated. The decision is made to bring the battleship *New Jersey* (BB 62) back into service to add the weight of her shells to the gun line off Vietnam. The four mothballed *Iowa*-class battleships possess the last 16-inch naval guns in the world.

August 10.   Two MiG-21s are downed by F-4 Phantoms from the *Constellation* (CVA 64) during an attack on a truck park south of Hanoi.

August 30.   The carriers of Task Force 77 begin a campaign to isolate the port of Haiphong with an attack by the air wing of the *Oriskany* (CV 34) on one of four major bridges linking the city to Hanoi.

September 1.   Paul R. Ignatius becomes the 59th secretary of the navy.

September 3.   General Nguyen Van Thieu is elected president of South Vietnam. He will remain in power until the fall of the country in April 1975.

September 28.   A PBR is sunk by a single rocket hit in a canal off the Mekong River. Two of her crewmen are killed and four wounded.

October 25.   Carrier pilots destroy or damage at least 10 MiGs on the ground in a strike on the Phuc Yen airfield.

October 26.   An F-4 Phantom from the *Constellation* (CVA 64) downs a MiG-21 south of Hanoi.

October 30.   Some 35 miles northeast of Hanoi two F-4 Phantoms from the *Constellation* (CVA 64) have a dogfight with four MiG-17s. One of the MiGs is dropped by an air-to-air missile.

November 1–February 28, 1969.   Operation Kentucky. In 16 months, this 3rd Marine Division operation produces 3,821 enemy dead. American casualties are 520 killed and 3,079 wounded.

November 5–December 9, 1968.   Operation Napoleon Saline. Battalions of the 3rd Marine Division, the army's 196th Light Infantry Brigade and the 1st Brigade, 5th Infantry Division (Mechanized) kill 3,495 enemy troops in operations east of Gio Linh. American losses are 395 killed and 1,680 wounded.

November 14.   Major General Bruno Hochmuth, commander of the 3rd Marine Division, is killed when his UH-1E helicopter crashes five miles northwest of Hue.

December 4.   In Dinh Tuong Province, 66 miles south of Saigon, the Mobile Riverine Force kills 235 Viet Cong in a day's fighting.

December 14.   A MiG-21 is downed by an air-to-air missile launched by an F-8 Crusader from the *Oriskany* (CVA 34) in a dogfight between four MiGs and four navy planes.

December 31.   As of this date, the strength of American forces in South Vietnam is 486,000.

1968

January 1.   General Leonard F. Chapman, Jr., becomes the 24th commandant of the marine corps.

January 1–5.   Five naval aircraft are downed over North Vietnam in one of the worst weeks of the air war.

January 15–18.   President Johnson suspends the bombing of targets in the vicinity of Haiphong, North Vietnam.

January 21.   **Siege of Khe Sanh.** In western Quang Tri Province the combat base at Khe Sanh, garrisoned by the 3,500 men of Colonel David E. Lownd's Twenty-sixth Marines, is isolated from overland access when North Vietnamese forces cut Route 9. In the following days the 1st Battalion, Ninth Marines, a South Vietnamese Ranger battalion, and two additional 105-mm batteries are air-lifted in to reinforce the defense. By January 29, Khe Sanh's garrison is 6,000 strong. Surrounding it are 15–20,000 troops of the North Vietnamese 324B and 325C Divisions. At least superficially, the situation bears a worrisome resemblance to that which resulted in the French disaster at Dienbienphu in 1954. The key difference is air power. The North Vietnamese never succeed in closing Khe Sanh's airfield; only four transports are shot down in the course of the siege, which lasts until early April; and American aircraft, ranging from air force B-52s to Seventh Fleet F-4s, drop 100,000 tons of bombs on enemy positions ringing the base.

January 22.   **Pueblo affair.** The intelligence collection ship *Pueblo* (AGER 2), Lieutenant Commander Lloyd M. Bucher, is surrounded and fired on by North Korean patrol boats in international waters off the east coast of North Korea. One crewman is mortally wounded and three others, including Bucher, are hit. The *Pueblo*'s only weapons, a pair of .50-caliber machine guns, are frozen fast beneath their tarpaulins on the ship's bridge, and there are no U.S. naval or air forces close enough to come to her assistance. Bucher accedes to the North Korean boats' demand to follow them into Wonsan harbor.

January 30–31.   **Tet Offensive.** North Vietnam chooses the most important Vietnamese holiday, the lunar new year (Tet), to launch its largest offensive of the war. In the past a tacit truce has been observed during this period, and about half of South Vietnam's 730,000-man army is on leave. Within a period of 48 hours, attacks are made on Saigon, Hue, Quang Tri, Da Nang, Kontum, and virtually every other major

The western perimeter of Khe Sanh. *Defense Department photo (Marine Corps).*

The *Pueblo. Official U.S. Navy photograph.*

city in South Vietnam—36 of 44 provincial capitals (10 of which are briefly occupied), 5 of 6 autonomous cities, and 23 military airfields and installations. Television coverage centers American domestic attention on Saigon, where a suicide squad of 15 sappers penetrates the U.S. embassy, killing 5 servicemen before being wiped out. In purely military terms the effort ends in a major defeat for North Vietnam. Some 32,000 North Vietnamese and (mostly) Viet Cong troops—at least half the attacking force—are killed and 5,800 captured, against 1,000 American and 2,800 South Vietnamese combat deaths. A popular uprising against the Americans, for which Tet was expected to provide the impetus, fails to occur, and Hue is the only important position the attackers succeed in holding for any length of time. But the offensive's psychological impact on the American people, as transmitted by their television screens, transforms North Vietnam's military defeat into political victory. American public opinion turns strongly against the continuation of the war.

January 31–March 2.   **Recapture of Hue.** A battalion of the Fifth Marines aids South Vietnamese troops to recover the former imperial capital. Marine casualties are 142 dead and 857 wounded. While they held the city the North Vietnamese had executed 5,000 civilian "political enemies."

February 29–March 2.   Three North Vietnamese trawlers attempting to land arms in South Vietnam are intercepted and destroyed by eight Coast Guard cutters and several of the Brown Water Navy's small combatants. A fourth trawler turns back.

March 1.   Clark M. Clifford becomes the ninth secretary of defense.

March 31.   **Bombing limitation.** President Johnson declares that he will not seek reelection and calls for the beginning of peace talks. As a token of good faith, he orders the bombing of North Vietnam restricted to the panhandle south of the 20th parallel.

April 3.   Radio Hanoi announces the willingness of the government of North Vietnam to discuss conditions for holding peace talks.

April 6.   The battleship *New Jersey* (BB 62) is recommissioned.

April 10.   **Farewell to the Skyraiders.** The propeller-driven A-1 Skyraider, which entered service in 1945, is removed from the navy's aircraft inventory.

April 14.   **Relief of Khe Sanh.** The U.S. 1st Air Cavalry Division and a South Vietnamese battalion reestablish over-land contact with the marine garrison of Khe Sanh in Operation Pegasus/Lam Son 207. It is estimated that in the course of the siege approximately 10,000 North Vietnamese have been killed; the defenders' casualties are 205 dead and about 800 wounded.

April 15–February 28, 1969.   **Operation Scotland II.** In Quang Tri Province this operation by the 3rd Marine Division claims a total of 3,304 enemy dead. American losses are 463 killed and 2,553 wounded.

May 3.   The government of North Vietnam agrees to begin preliminary peace talks in Paris.

A UH-1B Seawolf helicopter provides air cover for a squadron of PBRs on the Cho Gao Canal in the Mekong Delta. *Official U.S. Navy photograph.*

May 18–October 23.   **Operation Mameluke Thrust.** 2,728 enemy troops are killed in an operation launched by the 1st Marine Division and the 26th Marine Regimental Landing Team 25 miles to the west and south of Da Nang. Marine losses are 267 killed and 1,730 wounded.

May 21.   **Loss of the Scorpion.** The nuclear-powered attack submarine *Scorpion* (SSN 589), Commander Francis A. Slattery, returning to Norfolk, Virginia, from training operations with the Sixth Fleet in the Mediterranean, is last heard from at 11:03 P.M. EDT. She is declared to be presumed lost with all hands (99 officers and men) on June 5. Wreckage is finally located and photographed in more than 10,000 feet of water 400 miles southwest of the Azores by the Military Sea Transportation Service oceanographic research ship USNS *Mizar* (T-AGOR 11) on October 30. The cause of the disaster cannot be determined, but foul play is ruled out.

June 10.   The South Vietnamese navy assumes responsibility for sweeping command-detonated mines from the Long Tau River channel to Saigon. Fourteen U.S. vessels are turned over to it for this purpose. This event marks the beginning of the turn-over program through which the South Vietnamese Navy is to be trained and equipped to fight the brown-water war on its own.

June 16.   The cruiser *Boston* (CAG 1) and the Australian guided-missile destroyer *Hobart* are slightly damaged and Swift Boat *PCF 19* is sunk by U.S. Air Force planes that mistake them for low-flying enemy helicopters.

June 22.   Captain Lawrence Heyworth, Jr., becomes 45th (temporary) superintendent of the Naval Academy.

June 26.   **Dogfight.** Three F-8 Crusaders from the *Bon Homme Richard* (CVA 31) tangle with two MiG-21s over North Vietnam. One MiG is downed by an air-to-air missile.

July 6.   The first North American OV-10A Broncos, small, propeller-driven aircraft especially designed for counter-insurgency warfare, begin operations with marine squadrons at Da Nang.

July 9.   The Army-Navy Mobile Riverine Force, now 18 months old, commences operations on the Co Chien River, the only branch of the Mekong on which it was not already active.

July 12.   **The last seaplane.** The navy's last operational seaplane, a P-5 Marlin, is retired in ceremonies at Patuxent Naval Air Station.

July 20.   Rear Admiral James F. Calvert becomes the 46th superintendent of the Naval Academy.

July 22.   **306 missions.** Commander Samuel R. Chessman, 42, commanding officer of the Attack Squadron 195 aboard the *Ticonderoga* (CVA 14) flies his 306th Vietnam combat mission, breaking the record of 305 set by his predecessor, Commander Charles Hathaway, in April 1967. Chessman also flew 77 combat missions in Korea.

July 29.   **Operation Game Warden expanded.** Patrols are extended to the upper reaches of the Mekong and Bassac rivers, so that Game Warden now covers the delta waterways from the Cambodian border to the sea.

July 29.   Four F-8 Crusaders from the *Bon Homme Richard* (CVA 31) engage an equal number of MiG-17s in a five-minute dogfight northwest of Vinh. One MiG is shot down.

September 7.   The *John F. Kennedy* (CVA 67), a conventionally powered, *Forrestal*-class carrier, is commissioned.

September 18.   In Quang Tin Province, 35 miles south of Da Nang, Swift Boat *PCF 21* destroys or damages 44 junks and 4 sampans and kills four Viet Cong.

September 19.   An F-8 Crusader from the *Intrepid* (CVS 11) kills a MiG-21 northwest of Vinh. This victory, the navy's 29th and the last officially credited to an F-8, is the 110th scored by U.S. forces so far in the war.

September 29.   **Back to the war.** The battleship *New Jersey* (BB 62) begins operations off the coast of Vietnam, firing 20 of her 16-inch shells at enemy positions north-northwest of Con Thien near the northern boundary of the Demilitarized Zone.

September 29.   Vice Admiral Elmo R. Zumwalt, Jr., relieves Rear Admiral Kenneth L. Veth as Commander, U.S. Naval Forces, Vietnam.

October 6–19.   **Operation Maui Peak.** More than 350 enemy are killed in a search-and-clear operation around An Hoa by battalions of the 1st Marine Division and the South Vietnamese 51st Regiment.

October 15.   **Operation Sealords.** The previously independent efforts of Operation Game Warden forces and the Army-Navy Mobile Riverine Force are concerted in a joint operational plan against the enemy in the Mekong Delta. Sealords stands for "South East Asia Lake, Ocean, River, Delta Strategy."

October 23–December 7.   **Operation Henderson Hill.** Battalions of the 1st Marine Division kill 700 enemy troops and detain 94 suspects in a sweep a few miles west of Hoi An. Marine losses are 35 killed and 231 wounded.

A monitor leads two armored troop carriers along a canal in the Mekong Delta. *U.S. Naval Institute Collection.*

October 29.   Seven Swift Boats, the Market Time support ship *Washoe County* (LST 1165), coast guard cutter *Wachusett* (WHEC 44) and South Vietnamese Air Force A-1 Skyraiders cooperate in a surprise attack against enemy positions in the Cua Lon–Bo De river areas of the extreme southern tip of South Vietnam. In five hours 242 enemy junks and sampans and 167 structures are damaged or destroyed. U.S. casualties are five wounded.

October 31.   **Bombing halt.** President Johnson orders a complete cessation of all air, sea, and land bombardment of North Vietnam, effective at 8:00 A.M. EST November 1. Previous to this announcement there had been nine separate bombing pauses since June 1965. After each pause American pilots found that the North Vietnamese had used the respite to repair and improve their air-defense system.

November 1–30.   **The New Jersey on the gun line.** In her first full month in action, the battleship *New Jersey* (BB 62) destroys 182 enemy bunkers, more than 800 other structures, 15 cave complexes, and 9 sampans.

November 20–December 9.   **Operation Meade River.** In a sweep through Quang Nam Province, battalions of the 1st Marine Division kill 841 enemy soldiers and detain 2,710 suspects. U.S. losses are 107 killed and 385 wounded.

December 6.   **Operation Giant Slingshot.** The brown-water navy's activities are expanded by the initiation of regular patrols on the Vam Co Dong and Vam Co Tay rivers, which extend westward from their divergence 23 miles south of Saigon in a Y- or slingshot-shaped configuration to enclose the "Parrot's Beak" of the Cambodian border. In the first year, forces committed to the operation kill 1,894 enemy troops and capture 517 tons of supplies.

December 7–March 8, 1969.   **Operation Taylor Common.** Battalions of the 1st Marine Division conduct a search-and-clear operation 10 miles west of An Hoa. Losses of 1,398 dead are inflicted on the enemy at a cost of 151 killed and 1,324 wounded.

December 23.   The 82 crewmen of the intelligence ship *Pueblo* (AGER 2), which was seized by North Korea on January 22, are released.

December 23.   Attacking enemy base camps in An Xuyen Province, never previously disturbed by naval forces, a task force of four Swift Boats supported by army gunship helicopters destroy or damage 167 sampans, 125 structures, and 8 bunkers.

1969

January 13.   **Operation Bold Mariner.** The largest amphibious assault of the Vietnam War is made when more than 2,500 marines from the Seventh Fleet Amphibious Force land on the Batangan Peninsula, a Viet

Two A-6A Intruders from the *Constellation* on a bomb run. *Official U.S. Navy photograph.*

Cong stronghold 10 miles north of Quang Ngai City in the I Corps area. The operation is supported by fire from the battleship *New Jersey* (BB 62) and two destroyers. U.S. Army and South Vietnamese troops are positioned inland in an attempt to trap the enemy on the peninsula. Some 12,000 Vietnamese are screened, and 239 Viet Cong are killed.

January 14.   **Fire on the Enterprise.** Seventy miles south of the Hawaiian island of Oahu, fire breaks out when a rocket ignites on the flight deck of the nuclear-powered carrier *Enterprise* (CVAN 65). The blaze is brought under control in 45 minutes, but 28 crewmen have been killed and 65 injured.

January 22.   Melvin R. Laird becomes the tenth secretary of defense.

January 22–March 19.   **Operation Dewey Canyon I.** More than 1,600 of the enemy are killed during an extremely successful sweep through the Da Krong valley in southwestern Quang Tri Province by Colonel Robert H. Barrow's Ninth Marines.

January 25.   **Truce talks.** In Paris, representatives of the United States and North Vietnam begin formal negotiations to end the Vietnam War.

January 31.   John H. Chafee becomes the 60th secretary of the navy.

January 31.   The strength of U.S. forces in Vietnam reaches a peak of 542,000.

February 1.   In the Mekong Delta, twenty-five U.S. river gunboats, representing two complete river assault and interdiction divisions, are transferred to the South Vietnamese Navy.

March 5.   The *Ticonderoga* (CVA 14) begins her fifth tour off Vietnam, the first carrier to reach this number.

March 15.   **Operation Maine Crag.** The Third Regiment, 3rd Marine Division, begins a search-and-clear operation six miles south of Khe Sanh. By the time the operation ends on May 2, marines have killed 157 Viet Cong, detained 52 suspects, and captured 465 weapons. Their losses are 17 killed and 104 wounded.

March 25.   The air component of the River Patrol Force is reinforced by the arrival of Light Attack Squadron (VAL) 4, which is based at Vung Tau and Binh Thuy. Its OV-10A Broncos will fly in support of the river patrol boats.

March 26.   Lieutenant General Herman Nickerson, Jr., relieves Lieutenant General Cushman as commander of the III MAF.

March 27.   In her most effective single day's shelling, the battleship *New Jersey* (BB 62) destroys or damages 72 enemy bunkers around Phan Thiet in the II Corps area.

March 31.   The *New Jersey* (BB 62) leaves the gun line at the conclusion of a six months' tour off Vietnam.

March 31–May 29.   Operation Oklahoma Hills. The Seventh Marines search and clear an area 20 miles southwest of Da Nang. The enemy loses 596 dead; marine casualties are 53 killed and 482 wounded.

April 14.   EC-121 Incident. An unarmed, four-engined EC-121 aircraft of Fleet Air Reconnaissance Squadron 1 carrying a crew of 31 is shot down by North Korean aircraft while on a routine mission over the Sea of Japan. She disappears from U.S. radar screens at 11:50 P.M. EST, in a position approximately 90 miles southeast of Chongjin. An intensive air-sea search is mounted. Two bodies, as well as wreckage, are found on April 17, but there are no survivors.

April 18.   The *Bon Homme Richard* (CVA 31) begins her fifth tour off Vietnam.

April 20.   Show of force. In response to the North Korean attack on the EC-121 aircraft, Task Force 71 is organized under the command of Rear Admiral Malcolm W. Cagle to make a naval demonstration in the Sea of Japan. Initially it consists of 23 combatant vessels, including the carriers *Enterprise* (CVAN 65), *Ranger* (CVA 61), *Ticonderoga* (CVA 14), and *Hornet* (CVS 12), and is strengthened on April 23 by another six destroyers. The *New Jersey* (BB 62), en route home from Vietnam, is ordered back to Japan.

April 26.   At the end of its demonstration, Task Force 71 passes through the Straits of Tsushima into the Yellow Sea and is soon deactivated.

May 3.   The Triton (SSN 586) is decommissioned. The first submarine to circumnavigate the globe submerged and the largest nuclear submarine built to date is decommissioned at Groton, Connecticut.

May 5.   Operation Daring Rebel. Marine Battalion Landing Team 1/26 joins South Vietnamese and South Korean forces in an amphibious operation 20 miles south of Da Nang. Commanded by the Seventh Fleet's Amphibious Force Alpha, the operation terminates on Barrier Island on May 20. The marines kill 105 Viet Cong at a cost to themselves of 2 dead and 51 wounded. Overall, 7,000 Vietnamese are detained for questioning, and 200 enemy cadre are captured.

May 15.   The *Guitarro* (SSN 665), a nuclear submarine being built at the San Francisco Bay Naval Shipyard (Vallejo), sinks at dockside in 35 feet of water. The report of Special House Armed Service Subcommittee convened to investigate the accident charges "culpable negligence" on the part of shipyard workers responsible for it.

May 16.   The *Point Garnet* (WPB 82310) and *Point League*

(WPB 82304) become the first coast guard cutters to be transferred to the South Vietnamese Navy. They raise to 101 the number of vessels turned over to the South Vietnamese since June 1968.

June 1.   Progress of Vietnamization. The South Vietnamese Navy assumes full responsibility for patrolling the Fourth Coastal Zone, which extends more than 400 miles along the South China Sea and the Gulf of Thailand.

June 2.   Lieutenant General Lewis W. Walt, assistant commandant of the marine corps, is promoted to full general. This is the first time in its history that the corps has been authorized two four-star posts.

June 2.   Evans disaster. The destroyer *Frank E. Evans* (DD 754) is struck and cut in two by the Australian aircraft carrier *Melbourne* (R 21) in the South China Sea approximately 650 miles southwest of Manila at 4:15 A.M. June 3, Philippine time. The two ships are engaged in a SEATO naval exercise. The bow section of the *Evans* sinks in two minutes with the loss of 74 of her 273 crewmen. Her aft section is quickly secured alongside the *Melbourne*. There are no Australian casualties. On June 9, a Joint Board of Investigation composed of three American and three Australian naval officers begins hearings at the Subic Bay Naval Base. It finds that primary responsibility for the collision rests with the destroyer, but that the carrier is partly to blame. The *Evans*'s captain and officer of the deck are court-martialed, found guilty of dereliction in the performance of duty, and reprimanded. The commander of the *Melbourne*, Captain J. P. Stephenson, is honorably acquitted by a Royal Australian Navy court-martial. In September, Australia donates $32,500 to the 26 children whose fathers were lost on the *Evans*.

June 8.   First troop withdrawals from Vietnam. While meeting with South Vietnamese President Nguyen Van Thieu at Midway Island, President Nixon announces that 25,000 U.S. combat troops will be withdrawn from Vietnam by August 31.

July 1.   Strength of the fleet. At the start of Fiscal Year 1970 the U.S. Navy has 886 vessels in active commission. Their average age is 17 years.

July 10.   OV-10A Bronco aircraft attached to the River Patrol Force sink six Viet Cong boats that are seeking to evade river patrol boats off Kien Giang Province in the Gulf of Thailand. Twelve of the enemy are killed.

July 20.   Moon landing. The Apollo 11 capsule lands on the moon. The first man to walk on the lunar surface is former navy fighter pilot Neil A. Armstrong. On its return to earth the spacecraft is recovered by the carrier *Hornet* (CVS 12).

August 5.   First POWs released. North Vietnam releases the first three American prisoners of war: Lieutenant Robert F. Frishman, USNR; Seaman Douglas B. Hegdahl, USN; and Captain Wesley L. Rumble, USAF. Lieutenant Frishman, a pilot in Attack Squadron 121, was shot down and captured on October 24, 1967; Seaman Hegdahl was captured on April 6, 1967, after falling overboard from the cruiser *Canberra* (CAG 2) in the Gulf of Tonkin. In a press conference at Bethesda Naval Hospital on October 3, they report that American POWs are being beaten and tortured by the North Vietnamese.

August 21.   Defense cuts. Secretary of Defense Laird announces that up to $3 billion will be shaved from defense expenditures for Fiscal Year 1970. Part of the savings is to be realized by deactivating more than 100 naval vessels, including the battleship *New Jersey* (BB 62).

September 16.   Troop withdrawals. President Nixon announces that 35,000 more troops will be withdrawn from Vietnam by December 15. This figure includes 5,200 navy personnel and 18,500 marines. The number of American forces left in Vietnam will be 484,000.

October 10.   Eighty U.S. Navy river patrol boats (PBRs) are turned over to the South Vietnamese Navy. The largest single transfer to date, this raises to 229 the total number of vessels turned over to the Vietnamese since June 1968.

October 26.   The carrier *Coral Sea* (CVA 43) begins her fifth tour off Vietnam.

November 14.   Apollo 12.   America's second moon-shot is manned by an all-navy crew: Commander Charles Conrad (mission commander), Commander Richard Gordon (command module pilot), and Lieutenant Commander Alan Bean (lunar module pilot). Their capsule is recovered in the Pacific by the *Hornet* (CVS 12) on November 24, and all astronauts are promoted to the rank of captain by President Nixon during a telephone conversation aboard the carrier.

November 15.   The antiwar movement's "November Vietnam Moratorium" produces massive demonstrations in Washington and San Francisco.

November 29.   In the Mekong Delta, the U.S. My Tho Naval Base is turned over to the navy of South Vietnam. This is the first naval base to be transferred.

December 13.   Admiral Raymond A. Spruance, commander of the American naval forces at the Battles of Midway and the Philippine Sea, dies at his home in Pebble Beach, California, at the age of 83.

December 15.   President Nixon directs the withdrawal of another 50,000 men from Vietnam, bringing the total ordered home in 1969 to 110,000.

December 17.   The New Jersey (BB 62) is decommissioned. The ceremony occurs at the Naval Inactive

OV-10A Broncos of Light Attack Squadron (VAL) 4 over the Rung Sat Special Zone. *Official U.S. Navy photograph.*

Ship Maintenance Facility in Bremerton, Washington. In his address, the ship's commanding officer, Captain Robert C. Peniston, enjoins the battleship to "rest well but sleep lightly." His words are prophetic. Thirteen years later the *New Jersey* will return to service.

December 30.   In a typical riverine action, a patrol boat on the Saigon River surprises a body of enemy troops making a crossing 17 miles north of the capital. She takes them under fire and also calls for a helicopter gunship. Twenty-seven of the enemy are killed and one captured. American casualties are nil.

1970

January 1.   On the Saigon River, 25 miles northwest of the city, U.S. and South Vietnamese naval forces fight throughout New Year's night to defend a sunken South Vietnamese river patrol boat from the enemy, whose swimmers make six attempts to destroy it. Later, twelve enemy dead are counted, and the patrol boat is salvaged.

January 9.   A Sealords patrol encounters enemy forces estimated at battalion strength in Tay Ninh Province. Navy Seawolf helicopter gunships and OV-10 Bronco aircraft are called in. A total of 32 Viet Cong are killed.

January 28.   Near Vung Tau, in South Vietnam's III Corps area, the destroyer *Mansfield* (DD 728) heavily damages enemy positions while firing in close support of the 1st Australian Task Force.

February 3.   Merchant shipping on the Long Tau River in the Rung Sat Special Zone comes under enemy small arms and rocket fire for the first time in six months. No serious damage is done.

February 14.   Three 82-foot coast guard cutters are transferred to the South Vietnamese Navy. Six others follow later in the year.

February 28.   At Da Nang, 11 Swift Boats are transferred to the South Vietnamese Navy, which now takes over all coastal patrols operating off the country's five northern provinces.

March 7.   In the IV Corps area, the South Vietnamese Navy assumes control of Operation Tran Hung Dao I, which had been established in February 1969 to interdict the infiltration of enemy personnel and supplies from Cambodia.

March 9.   Lieutenant General Keith B. McCutcheon relieves Lieutenant General Nickerson as commander of the III MAF.

March 14.   The hospital ship *Repose* (AH 16) leaves South Vietnam after four years of almost uninterrupted service there.

March 16.   Four U.S. Navy support ships and two more coast guard cutters are transferred to the South Vietnamese Navy at Da Nang. The coast guard decommissions the second of the three divisions it had operated in Vietnam. Only the 13th Division, which operates in the Mekong Delta, remains active.

March 18.   The left-leaning, neutralist Cambodian government of Prince Sihanouk is overthrown in a bloodless coup by General Lon Nol, whose anticommunist stance attracts the sympathy of the Nixon administration.

March 28.   **MiG kill.** An F-4 Phantom fighter escorting an unarmed reconnaissance plane, both from the *Constellation* (CVA 64), destroys a MiG-21 near Thanh Hoa, North Vietnam. This is the navy's first aerial victory in 16 months, as enemy aircraft seldom venture into airspace in which U.S. planes are authorized to operate.

March 28.   On the gun line, the destroyer *Orleck* (DD 886) damages or destroys 44 enemy structures while firing in support of the South Vietnamese 21st Infantry Division near Rach Gia in the IV Corps area. In the course of the week ending April 3, the *Orleck,* other Seventh Fleet destroyers, and the coast guard cutters *Chase* (WHEC 718) and *Dallas* (WHEC 716) hit 105 enemy structures, 48 bunkers, and 22 sampans.

April 20.   **Troop withdrawals.** President Nixon announces plans to withdraw 150,000 U.S. servicemen from Vietnam during the next 12 months. This will leave approximately 285,000 in the country.

April 29–June 30.   **Invasion of Cambodia.** American and South Vietnamese forces launch spoiling attacks into six Communist staging areas, one no more than 33 miles from Saigon, inside the Cambodian border. Great quantities of munitions and supplies are captured or destroyed.

May 4.   **Kent State.** The invasion of Cambodia sparks antiwar demonstrations throughout the United States. At Kent State University, where the Ohio National Guard has been sent to maintain order after the burning of the ROTC building, a detachment of guardsmen open fire on a group of protesters. Four students are killed. The tragedy provokes a new wave of campus disorders. By the week's end, 450 colleges or universities are closed by student or faculty strikes.

May 5.   Operation Giant Slingshot, the joint U.S.–South Vietnamese navy patrol of the Vam Go Dong and Vam Co Tay rivers north of Saigon, is turned over to the South Vietnamese in ceremonies at Ben Luc. Since its inception in December 1968, forces in the operation have engaged in 1,200 fire fights and killed more than 2,400 enemy troops.

May 6.   **The navy in Cambodia.** A flotilla of 40 U.S. river patrol boats enters Cambodia on the Kham Span River, some 65 miles northwest of Saigon. It comes under fire less than two miles inside the border.

May 8.   A force of 100 U.S. and South Vietnamese patrol boats move up the Mekong River into Cambodia. The U.S. boats are to stay inside the 21.7-mile limit President Nixon has established for the American penetration of Cambodia.

May 12.   In the Gulf of Thailand, U.S. and South Vietnamese vessels establish a blockade of the Cambodian coastline west to Sihanoukville to prevent North Vietnamese and Viet Cong vessels from reaching Cambodia.

June 23.   **Vietnamization of the riverine force.** The U.S. transfers 273 river patrol craft to the South Vietnamese Navy, raising the total vessels turned over to date to 525. The 125 boats still being operated by the U.S. Navy are scheduled to be transferred in December.

July 1.   Admiral Elmo R. Zumwalt becomes the 19th chief of naval operations, relieving Admiral Thomas H. Moorer, who has been named chairman of the joint chiefs of staff. At the age of 49, Zumwalt is both the youngest four-star admiral and the youngest CNO in the history of the navy. He will also become one of the most controversial.

July 22.   Sixty South Vietnamese are graduated from the U.S. Navy's Officer Candidate School at Newport, Rhode Island. They are the first class of South Vietnamese to attend.

August 3.   **Poseidon.** The first submerged launching of the navy's new, multi-warhead Poseidon nuclear missile is made by the fleet ballistic submarine *James Madison* (SSBN 627) off Cape Kennedy. A Russian surface ship closely observes the proceedings.

September 14.   A Pentagon report places the strength of the South Vietnamese Navy at 35,000 men and 1,500 vessels, including 600 U.S. river patrol boats transferred since the beginning of Vietnamization.

September 17.   The navy announces plans to deactivate 58 ships, including the carrier *Shangri-La* (CVS 38). Together with previous deactivations, this raises the number of ships retired from active service since January 1969 to 286.

October 29.   Secretary of the Navy Chafee states that under current projections the U.S. Navy will have fewer than 700 ships in July 1971, a net reduction of 234 vessels since his entry into office, and warns that any further reduction would be dangerous.

November 20.   **POW rescue mission.** A U.S. commando force lands from helicopters 23 miles west of Hanoi in an attempt to free American POWs. Unfortunately, the POWs had been moved from the area a few days earlier.

December 15.   The State Department announces that a $19 million naval communications facility will be constructed on the British island of Diego Garcia in the Indian Ocean.

December 31.   **Repeal of the Tonkin Gulf Resolution.** Having passed the Senate by a vote of 81–10 on June 24, the repeal of the resolution through which President Johnson introduced U.S. troops into Vietnam is approved by the House. President Nixon signs the bill into law on January 14, 1971.

1971

January 6.   **Harrier.** The marine corps accepts the first of its new, close-support, V/STOL aircraft, the British-built AV-8A Harrier.

February 8–March 25.   **Attack into Laos (Operation Lam Son 719/Dewey Canyon II).** A force of 16,000 South Vietnamese troops cross the Laotian border slightly south of the Demilitarized Zone in an operation designed both to disrupt a Communist build-up in the area and to demonstrate the capability of the South Vietnamese Army. No American ground troops enter Laos, but many South Vietnamese units are lifted into (and out of) the country in U.S. army helicopters, and the U.S. Air Force and 1st Marine Air Wing provide massive air support. The results of the operation are mixed. Although the South Vietnamese inflict heavy losses on the enemy and capture large quantities of arms and ammunition, their withdrawal, begun on schedule on March 10, is often disorderly, and they suffer roughly 50 percent casualties.

February 11.   The navy's traditional practice of enlisting Filipinos to serve as mess stewards is abolished by Admiral Zumwalt.

February 11.   The United States and the Soviet Union sign a treaty prohibiting the deployment of nuclear weapons on the ocean floor.

April 1.   **First Poseidon deployment.** The *James Madison* (SSBN 627) departs Charleston, South Carolina, on an operational patrol armed with the new missiles.

April 7.   President Nixon announces that 100,000 troops will be withdrawn from South Vietnam in the course of the year.

April 12.   A navy gunboat, two coast guard cutters, a South Vietnamese patrol craft, and two navy aircraft collaborate to sink a 160-foot North Vietnamese trawler discovered attempting to slip through the surveillance line off the southernmost coast of South Vietnam.

April 14.   The wind-down of the marines' war in Vietnam is symbolized by the deactivation of the Third Marine Amphibious Force (III MAF) and the withdrawal of the 1st Marine Aircraft Wing from Da Nang.

April 24.   Approximately 200,000 protesters stage a giant antiwar rally in Washington, D.C.

April 28.   **First black admiral.** The navy announces the selection of 49 new rear admirals, including Captain Samuel L. Gravely, Jr., the first black to reach that rank.

May 1.   The hospital ship *Sanctuary* (AH 17) sails from Da Nang for home after four years in Vietnam.

June 26.   **Marine withdrawal completed.** The 3rd Marine Amphibious Brigade, the last marine combat unit in South Vietnam, departs from Da Nang.

August 19.   In Vietnam, ships of the Seventh Fleet shell enemy rocket and mortar positions in the southern half of the Demilitarized Zone.

August 26.   America's first man in space, astronaut Alan B. Shepard, is promoted to the rank of rear admiral. His selection had been announced on April 28.

October 1.   The carrier *Constellation* (CVA 64) sails from San Diego on her sixth deployment off Vietnam. The antiwar movement had staged a well-publicized campaign to "Keep Connie Home."

November 12.   President Nixon announces that another 45,000 troops will be withdrawn from Vietnam by February 1, 1972. At the end of 1971 there will be fewer than 175,000 American servicemen still in the country.

December 11.   Full-fledged war began between India and Pakistan on December 4. On this date, a task force formed around the *Enterprise* (CVAN 65) is ordered from the coast of Vietnam to the Bay of Bengal, where, if necessary, it can evacuate American citizens from East Pakistan.

December 31.   The ropewalk at the Boston Naval Shipyard, the navy's only rope-making activity, is closed after 147 years in operation. Hereafter the navy's rope will be made by private firms.

1972

January 1.   General Robert E. Cushman, Jr., becomes 25th commandant of the marine corps.

January 13.   President Nixon announces that another 70,000 troops are to be withdrawn from South Vietnam. Only 69,000 will be left there by May 1.

January 19.   Over North Vietnam, an F-4 Phantom from the *Constellation* (CVA 64) downs a MiG-21. This victory, the navy's first since March 1970, is also the first scored by the team of Lieutenant Randall F. Cunningham, pilot, and Lieutenant (jg) William Driscoll, radar intercept officer, who will become the first American aces of the Vietnam War.

March 28.   Two F-4 Phantoms from the *Coral Sea* (CV 43) destroy a MiG-17.

March 30.   **Spring offensive.** North Vietnam launches a massive conventional invasion of the south, sending three divisions across the Demilitarized Zone.

April 1.   The navy's last in-country combat unit, Light Attack Squadron (VAL) 4, is withdrawn from South Vietnam.

April 6.   In response to the North Vietnamese invasion, the United States resumes the aerial bombing and naval bombardment of North Vietnam. Marine air squadrons are sent to Da Nang to provide close support for the South Vietnamese.

April 17.   **Linebacker.** Following orders from President Nixon, B-52s hit North Vietnam above the 20th parallel for the first time since March 1968.

April 25.   John Warner becomes the 61st secretary of the navy.

April 27.   **First woman admiral.** Captain Alene B. Duerk, a nurse, is the first woman promoted to the rank of rear admiral.

May.   Navy pilots have their best month of the war, downing a total of 16 MiGs. In addition, the cruiser *Chicago* (CG 11) knocks down an unidentified enemy aircraft with a Talos surface-to-air missile.

May 1.   The North Vietnamese capture Quang Tri City.

May 8.   **Mining of North Vietnam.** Confronted by North Vietnamese intransigence at the Paris peace talks and the continuation of the enemy spring offensive, President Nixon orders the navy to carry out existing plans for mining the harbors of North Vietnam. A-6 Intruders from U.S. carriers sow mines at Haiphong, Hon Gai, Cam Pha, Thanh Hoa, Vinh, Quang Khe, and Dong Hoi. Neutral shipping is given a grace period to clear North Vietnamese waters by a 72-hour delay in the activation of the mines. The flow of seaborne supplies to North Vietnam ceases overnight.

May 8.   Rear Admiral Rembrandt C. Robinson, commander, Cruiser-Destroyer Flotilla 11, becomes the first flag officer killed in the Vietnam War when his helicopter crashes in the Gulf of Tonkin.

May 8.   Lieutenant Randall J. Cunningham and Lieutenant (jg) William Driscoll score their second aerial victory, destroying a MiG-17 with a Sidewinder air-to-air missile.

May 10.   **Navy aces.** Carrier pilots shoot down seven MiGs, three of which fall to Cunningham and Driscoll, making them the first American aces of the war.

May 15.   The United States relinquishes Okinawa, which it has ruled since World War II, to Japan.

May 26.   **SALT I.** The United States and the Soviet Union conclude two strategic arms limitations agreements. The first limits each country to the construction of two anti-ballistic missile (ABM) systems; the second establishes ceilings on the number of land- and sea-based intercontinental ballistic missiles (ICBMs) to be deployed during the next five years. Strategic Arms Limitation Talks between the two countries had begun in November 1969.

June 16.   Vice Admiral William P. Mack, former commander of the Seventh Fleet, becomes 47th superintendent of the U.S. Naval Academy.

June 25.   **Success in South Vietnam.** South Vietnamese troops break the siege of An Loc, in the III Corps area, signaling the defeat of the North Vietnamese spring offensive. Although no U.S. ground forces have been engaged, American air power has made a crucial, perhaps decisive, contribution to the victory.

June 30.   The nomination of Admiral Thomas Moorer to serve a second, two-year term as chairman of the joint chiefs of staff is approved by the Senate.

July 26–27.   Congress authorizes the construction of a fourth nuclear-powered carrier.

August 27.   **Shelling Haiphong.** A four-ship surface action group with the Seventh Fleet commander, Admiral James L. Holloway III, embarked delivers a night bombardment of the North Vietnamese port

Lieutenant Randall F. Cunningham and Lieutenant (jg) William P. Driscoll in the office of Secretary of the Navy John W. Warner in June 1972, a month after scoring their fifth victory. Cunningham holds a model of the navy's new fighter, the F-14 Tomcat. *Official U.S. Navy photograph.*

of Haiphong. Two enemy torpedo boats that engage the force are sunk.

September 22.   Commander Dennis R. Weichmann sets a naval aviation record when he returns from his 501st combat mission over Vietnam.

October 11.   Nineteen sailors are killed and ten wounded (one mortally) by an explosion in an 8-inch turret on the all-gun cruiser *Newport News* (CA 148) during a fire mission off the coast of Vietnam.

October 23.   Bombing raids on North Vietnam above the 20th parallel are halted by order of President Nixon in anticipation of peace.

October 26.   Presidential Adviser Henry Kissinger, who has been conducting the Paris peace talks, announces that "peace is at hand"; the remaining differences between the United States and North Vietnam should be resolved in one or more negotiating session.

December 6.   The last scheduled moon flight is made by Captain Eugene A. Cernan, Commander Ronald E. Evans, and a civilian, Dr. Harrison H. Schmidt.

December 18.   The American anticipation of imminent peace is confounded when the North Vietnamese delegation walks out of the Paris peace talks.

December 19–30.   **Linebacker II.** President Nixon bombs the enemy back to the negotiating table by the resumption of B-52 strikes throughout North Vietnam. In eleven days, the B-52s fly a total of 729 sorties—389 from Guam and 340 from U Tapao airfield in Thailand. By this time, the air defenses of the Hanoi-Haiphong area are probably the densest in the world and 15 B-52s are lost, all to SAM missiles, six on December 20 alone. The enemy defenses are gradually overcome, however, and no planes are downed during the last three days of the raids.

1973

January 3.   In Paris, the North Vietnamese delegation announces its readiness to resume peace talks.

January 5.   In a personal letter to South Vietnamese President Thieu, President Nixon promises that the United States will take "swift and severe retaliatory action" should North Vietnam violate the terms of a peace accord.

January 12.   **Last MiG kill.** Lieutenant Walter Kovaleski and his radar intercept officer, Lieutenant James Wise, flying an F-4 Phantom off the *Midway* (CVA 41), score the last American aerial victory of the Vietnam War, destroying a MiG-17 with two Sidewinder missiles over the Gulf of Tonkin. In the course of the conflict, navy pilots have shot down 59 MiGs and 2 AN-2 biplane transports. By a twist of fate, two days later Lieutenant Kovaleski and another RIO, Ensign Dennis Plautz, become the last American fliers downed in the war when their plane is hit by antiaircraft fire. Happily, they eject over the ocean and are rescued by a navy helicopter.

January 15.   In anticipation of peace, President Nixon suspends all offensive operations against North Vietnam.

January 27.   **Paris Accords.** Dr. Henry Kissinger and Le Duc Tho, chief North Vietnamese negotiator, formally sign the agreement ending direct American participation in the Vietnam War. The terms call for a cease-fire throughout South Vietnam; the withdrawal of U.S. forces; and the release of all American prisoners of war within 60 days.

January 30.   Elliot L. Richardson becomes the 11th secretary of defense.

February 17.   **Return of the POWs.** The first group of American POWs released by North Vietnam arrives in California as the nation celebrates their return. A total

of 591 U.S. servicemen are repatriated; more than 800 remain missing.

February 24–July 18.   **Operation Endsweep.** In conformity with the terms of the Paris Accords, a squadron of four ocean minesweepers and Helicopter Mine Countermeasures Squadron 12, organized as Task Force 78, sweep North Vietnamese waters of the mines laid in May 1972.

March 20.   American air power covers a convoy of eight supply ships that proceed up the Mekong River to the besieged Cambodian capital of Phnom Penh.

March 29.   The last American troops leave South Vietnam.

April 10.   U.S. forces begin airlifting gasoline and oil into Phnom Penh.

May 25.   **Skylab I.** An all-navy crew, consisting of Captain Charles P. Conrad, Jr., Commander Joseph P. Kerwin, and Commander Paul J. Weitz, begins a 28-day mission aboard America's first space laboratory. The unmanned Skylab capsule was launched on May 14.

June 22.   The three Skylab I astronauts splash down in the Pacific.

June 29.   Congress passes a resolution banning the continuation after August 15 of bombing in Cambodia, where American air power is being used to support the government against the Communist Khmer Rouge.

July 3.   James R. Schlesinger assumes office as the 12th secretary of defense.

August 15.   With the cessation of bombing in Cambodia, in accordance with the congressional resolution of June 29, American military operations in Southeast Asia come to an end.

September 1.   The last American combat unit is withdrawn from the Southeast Asian mainland when a marine F-4 squadron leaves Thailand.

September 5.   **Skylab II.** A new record for time in space is set by navy Captain Alan L. Bean in the second Skylab mission. The previous record of 49 days, 3 hours, and 37 minutes had been held by Captain Charles P. Conrad, Jr.

November 7.   **War Powers Act.** In a measure intended to prevent the president from conducting undeclared wars, Congress passes a resolution requiring that the president notify it with 48 hours of committing American forces to combat or "situations where imminent involvement in hostilities is clearly indicated by the circumstances," and that such forces must be withdrawn within 60 days unless it is declares war or authorizes an extension of the 60-day period.

November 19.   Vice Admiral Hyman G. Rickover, USN (Retired), is promoted to four-star rank.

Vice Admiral Hyman Rickover is congratulated on his promotion to four-star rank by President Richard M. Nixon and Secretary of the Navy Warner. *Official U.S. Navy photograph.*

1974

February 8. **Skylab III.** The three Skylab III astronauts are recovered by the *New Orleans* (LPH 11) in the Pacific approximately 150 miles west of San Diego.

April 24. **Clearing the Suez.** U.S. Task Force 65 begins clearing the Suez Canal of mines and vessels laid and sunk in it by Egypt during the 1972 Mideast War. The minesweeping is completed on June 3, and most major obstructions have been removed by mid-December.

June 20. J. William Middendorf II is nominated by the president to become 62nd secretary of the navy.

July 1. Admiral James L. Holloway III becomes the 20th chief of naval operations.

July 1. The Boston Naval Shipyard is closed after 174 years in operation. It was the navy's oldest facility.

July 2. Admiral Thomas H. Moorer retires after four years as chairman of the Joint Chiefs of Staff. His successor is air force General George S. Brown.

July 22. U.S. Marine and Royal Navy helicopters evacuate more than 400 American, British, and other foreign citizens from the British base at Dhekelia on the southern coast of Cyprus. Turkish forces had invaded the island on July 20.

July 25. **Trident.** The General Dynamics Corporation is awarded the contract to begin construction of the first nuclear-powered, fleet ballistic-missile Trident submarine.

November 24. The *Constellation* (CVA 64) becomes the first American aircraft carrier to enter the Persian Gulf since 1948.

1975

March 3. The Navy Department announces that as of 30 June 1976 the strength of the fleet will have dropped to 490 ships.

March 5. **North Vietnamese spring offensive.** North Vietnam launches a strong conventional offensive in the central highlands of South Vietnam. The early success of the attack leads South Vietnamese President Thieu to order his forces to withdraw from Kontum, Pleiku, and Darlac provinces. The retreat quickly degenerates into a rout, and in a few weeks the northern two-thirds of the country is abandoned to the North Vietnamese.

March 25. Army Chief of Staff General Frederick C. Weyland is sent to South Vietnam to evaluate the military situation.

April 1. General Lon Nol, head of the Cambodian government, flees the country as Communist forces tighten their grip on Phnom Penh.

April 8. General Weyland, returned from his fact-finding mission to South Vietnam, reports to Congress that without major American military assistance the country will fall. No such assistance is authorized.

April 9–11. In Laos, heavy fighting breaks out between government forces and the Communist Pathet Lao.

April 10–15. **Fall of Xuan Loc.** Thirty miles east of Saigon the town of Xuan Loc, where the best remaining South Vietnamese Army units have made a strong stand, is overrun by numerically superior enemy forces.

April 12. **Operation Eagle Pull.** American embassy personnel are evacuated from Phnom Penh, Cambodia's besieged capital, by the CH-53 Sea Stallions of Heavy Marine Helicopter Squadrons (HMH) 462 and 463.

April 17. Phnom Penh falls to the Khmer rouge.

April 21. South Vietnamese President Thieu resigns in an emotional television address, during which he denounces the United States for abandoning his country.

April 26–27. In anticipation of the fall of Saigon, some 6,000 Americans, South Vietnamese whose associations with Americans would compromise them in enemy eyes, and other nationalities are flown out of Tan Son Nhut airfield on C-130 and C-141 transports.

April 29.   North Vietnamese artillery opens fire on Tan Son Nhut airfield, making further evacuation flights impossible.

April 29–30.   **Operation Frequent Wind.** In 18 hours, navy and marine helicopters from Seventh Fleet carriers evacuate almost 9,000 people from Saigon: 1,373 Americans and 6,422 of other nationalities, plus 989 marines who were inserted to cover the operation. A-6, A-7, and F-14 fighter aircraft and A-1 and AC-119 gunships from the *Coral Sea* (CVA 43), *Enterprise* (CVAN 65), *Hancock* (CVA 19), and *Midway* (CVA 41) provide air support. The final flights are made from the rooftop of the American embassy, where U.S. Ambassador Graham Martin is among the last to leave.

April 30.   **Fall of Saigon.** As North Vietnamese tanks roll into the city, General Duong Van Minh, who succeeded President Thieu on April 28, announces the unconditional surrender of South Vietnam.

May 3.   The 81,600-ton, nuclear-powered carrier *Nimitz* (CVAN 68) is commissioned. America's second nuclear-powered carrier, she carries approximately 100 aircraft and helicopters and has a speed in excess of 30 knots.

May 12–15.   **Mayaguez Incident.** On May 12, the American container ship *Mayaguez* is fired upon and seized while en route from Hong Kong to Sattahip, Thailand,

by a gunboat of the Cambodian Communist (Khmer Rouge) regime. President Gerald R. Ford warns that "serious consequences" will follow unless the ship and her 40 crewmen are released immediately, and a battalion of marines is flown from Okinawa to U Tapao air base in Thailand. On May 15, a rescue operation is mounted. It centers on Koh Tang Island, 34 miles from the Cambodian coast, off which the *Mayaguez* is anchored and on which her crew is believed to be held. While planes from the *Coral Sea* (CVA 43) hit air and naval bases on the Cambodian mainland, a party of 60 marines and sailors from the *Harold E. Holt* (DE 1074) board the *Mayaguez,* which is discovered to be deserted, and a company of marines in helicopters from U Tapao assaults Koh Tang. In the meanwhile, the Cambodians have decided to release the American seamen, who are being carried back to their ship when the attack begins. The marines meet strong resistance at Koh Tang. By the time they are withdrawn that evening, 15 servicemen have been killed, 3 are missing, 50 have been wounded, 3 of their helicopters have been shot down, and 10 have been damaged. The *Mayaguez* resumes her voyage.

June 5.   **Reopening of the Suez Canal.** The guided-missile cruiser *Little Rock* (CLG 4), flagship of the Sixth Fleet, is the only foreign naval vessel in the official

The *Nimitz* during her sea trials. *Official U.S. Navy photograph.*

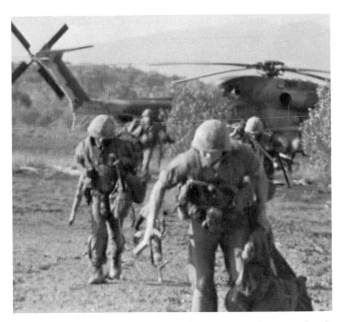

The *Mayaguez* incident: marines landing on Koh Tang Island. *U.S. Air Force photo.*

flotilla that first transits the canal. U.S. forces had cleared the waterway of the mines and hulks that had kept it closed since the Mideast War. The clearing operation officially ends on July 23.

July 1.   General Louis H. Wilson, Jr., who won the Medal of Honor on Guam in 1944, becomes the 26th commandant of the marine corps.

August 1.   Rear Admiral Kinnaird R. McKee becomes the 48th superintendent of the Naval Academy.

August 23.   **Fall of Laos.** The Pathet Lao complete the conquest of Laos. All of the states of Indochina are now under Communist rule.

September 20.   **Spruance class.** The *Spruance* (DD 963), lead ship of a new class of 30 destroyers, is commissioned at Pascagoula, Mississippi. These 7,400-ton vessels are the navy's first gas turbine-powered destroyers.

November 20.   Donald H. Rumsfeld becomes the 13th secretary of defense.

November 22.   **Belknap disaster.** In the Mediterranean, the guided-missile cruiser *Belknap* (CG 26) collides with the carrier *John F. Kennedy* (CV 67). Six of the *Belknap*'s sailors are killed, one dies later, and 24 require hospitalization. One man is killed on the *Kennedy.* In the ensuing investigation, the *Belknap*'s officer of the deck is found guilty of negligence and disobedience of orders.

1976

February 12.   Captain Fran McKee becomes the navy's first woman line officer selected for promotion to the rank of rear admiral.

March 28.   **Tomahawk.** The first successful launch of the Tomahawk cruise missile is made from an A-6 Intruder off the coast of California. A second 315-mile flight is made over the Pacific on April 26.

June 20.   Elements of the Sixth Fleet evacuate U.S. and other civilians endangered by factional strife from Beirut, Lebanon. The process is repeated on July 27.

July 6.   **First women at the Naval Academy.** At Annapolis, 81 women are sworn into the Academy's Class of 1980.

August 28.   In the Ionian Sea, a submerged Soviet Echo II–class submarine collides with the frigate *Voge* (FF 1047). Both vessels suffer damage: the *Voge* to her propeller, the submarine (which surfaces) to her sail. One American sailor is injured. A U.S. Navy investigation concludes that the submarine was at fault.

September 14.   The carrier *John F. Kennedy* (CV 67) and the destroyer *Bordelon* (DD 881) collide during night operations 100 miles north of Scotland. Six of the destroyer's crewmen are injured. The cost of repairing the *Bordelon* is deemed uneconomical, and she is decommissioned in February 1977.

October 7.   **Naval districts consolidated.** The number of naval districts is reduced from twelve to four. Their headquarters are located in Seattle, Washington; Great Lakes, Illinois; Philadelphia, Pennsylvania; and Washington, D.C.

November 13.   **Los Angeles class.** The *Los Angeles* (SSN 688), lead ship of the navy's newest class of nuclear attack submarines, is commissioned at Newport News, Virginia. The largest SSNs built to date, these vessels—360 feet in length—have a submerged speed of more than 30 knots and are armed with Tomahawk, Sub-Harpoon, and SUBROC missiles.

1977

January 10.   Admiral Arleigh A. Burke, former chief of naval operations, is awarded the Medal of Freedom, the United States' highest civilian decoration.

January 18.   The first successful launch of the navy's new, long-range Trident ballistic missile is made at Cape Canaveral, Florida.

The *Los Angeles*. *Courtesy Newport News Shipbuilding Company.*

January 21.   Dr. Harold R. Brown becomes the 14th secretary of defense.

February 14.   W. Graham Clayton, Jr., enters office as 63rd secretary of the navy.

May 9.   The navy announces that during Fiscal Year 1978 the strength of the fleet will reach a low of 462 active vessels.

June 28.   The guided-missile cruiser *California* (CGN 36) and submarine *Billfish* (SSN 676) are among 150 British and foreign vessels that participate in Queen Elizabeth's Silver Jubilee Naval Review off Portsmouth, England.

September 7.   **Panama Canal Treaty.** President Jimmy Carter and Panamanian President Omar Torrijos sign treaties that recognize Panamanian sovereignty over the Canal Zone and provide for the transfer of the canal to Panama.

October 3.   **SALT I expires.** The 1972 Strategic Arms Limitation Agreements between the United States and Soviet Union expires, but both counties declare that they will continue to adhere to its provisions during the negotiating of a second treaty.

October 18.   The *Dwight D. Eisenhower* (CVN 69) is commissioned. She is the navy's third nuclear-powered carrier and the second of the *Nimitz* class.

December 17.   **Perry class.** The *Oliver H. Perry* (FFG 7), lead ship of a new class of 50 guided-missile frigates, is commissioned. The most numerous class of U.S. warships built since World War II, the *Perrys* are designed primarily for convoy escort and related duties.

1978

February 1.   The first submarine launch of a Tomahawk cruise missile is made from the *Barb* (SSN 596) off the coast of California.

February 9.   A new era in naval communications begins with the launching of the first satellite of the navy's Fleet Satellite Communications System.

March 11.   The *Abraham Lincoln* (SSBN 602) becomes the first ballistic-missile submarine to complete 50 operational patrols. In the 17 years since her commissioning, she has spent more than 8 ½ years submerged and steamed more than 420,000 miles.

April 6.   Colonel Margaret A. Brewer is nominated by President Carter to become the first woman brigadier general in the marine corps.

July 1.   Admiral Thomas B. Hayward becomes the 21st chief of naval operations.

August 28.   Rear Admiral William P. Lawrence becomes 49th superintendent of the U.S. Naval Academy.

October 20.   The commandant of the marine corps is designated a full member of the joint chiefs of staff.

October 20.   **Cuyahoga disaster.** The coast guard training cutter *Cuyahoga* (WIX 157) is sunk in a collision with the 521-foot Argentine freighter *Santa Cruz II* in the Chesapeake Bay. Eleven coast guardsmen lose their lives; the freighter rescues eighteen others. The captain of the *Cuyahoga,* found guilty of dereliction of duty, receives a letter of reprimand and is demoted 200 places on the seniority list.

November 1.   **Women at sea.** Nine women ensigns are assigned to five non-combatant vessels of the Atlantic Fleet. This is the first time in history women have been assigned to vessels other than hospital ships and troop transports. Such assignment was authorized by the Department of Defense appropriations act for Fiscal 1979, which also allowed for the assignment of women to temporary duty of up to 180 days on combat ships provided no combat is foreseen.

October 25.   Edward Hidalgo becomes 64th secretary of the navy.

November 4.   **Iranian hostage crisis.** A mob of Muslim "students," adherents of the Ayatollah Khomeini's fundamentalist revolution, storms the U.S. Embassy at Teheran and seizes the Americans in the compound, including 14 marine guards. The students announce that they will release their hostages if the United States will extradite the deposed shah, who is undergoing medical treatment in New York, for trial by a revolutionary tribunal.

November 19.   The Iranians occupying the Teheran embassy free three American hostages: a woman and two black marines.

November 20.   Ten more of the Americans taken hostage at the Teheran embassy are freed. Fifth-three remain in captivity.

November 21.   A marine guard and an army warrant officer are killed when a mob burns the U.S. Embassy at Islamabad, Pakistan.

December 2.   A mob storms the U.S. Embassy at Tripoli, Libya. The embassy personnel escape unharmed.

December 5.   **RDF.** The marines announce that the corps is organizing three brigades to form a part of joint-services Rapid Deployment Force (RDF), which is to be maintained in instant readiness for operations anywhere on the globe. Later in the month marine Major General P. X. Kelley is designated force commander.

1979

February 6.   Six U.S. vessels evacuate 200 American citizens and 240 other persons from the ports of Bandar Abbas and Char Bahar in revolution-wracked Iran.

April 1.   Twenty-six-year-old Lieutenant (jg) Beverly Kelly, USCG, becomes the first woman ever to captain a U.S. warship when she assumes command of the coast guard cutter *Cape Newagen* (WPB 95318).

June 18.   **SALT II.** In Vienna, Austria, the second Strategic Arms Limitations Treaty is signed by President Jimmy Carter and Soviet President Leonid Brezhnev. It is later rejected by the U.S. Senate.

June 28.   General Robert H. Barrow becomes the 27th commandant of the U.S. Marine Corps.

September 30.   At midnight, the United States relinquishes the Panama Canal Zone to the Panamanian government.

1980

January 10.   Ensign Roberta L. McIntyre becomes the first woman to earn the badge of a surface warfare officer.

January 28.   **Blackthorn disaster.** The coast guard buoy tender *Blackthorn* (WLB 91) sinks with the loss of 23 lives following a collision with the tanker *Capricorn* in Tampa Bay, Florida. The National Transportation Safety Board rules that the *Blackthorn* was chiefly at fault.

March 1.   The repair ship *Vulcan* (AR 5) completes the first regular, six-months' deployment of a U.S. naval vessel in which women formed part of the ship's company. There were 57 females in her crew.

April 7.   As the hostage crisis enters its fifth month, the United States severs diplomatic relations with Iran.

April 24.   **Operation Blue Light.** A daring attempt to rescue the hostages ends in disaster. Six Air Force C-130 transports from Egypt and eight navy RH-53D helicopters from the *Nimitz* (CVN 68) carry a joint services commando to rendezvous at Desert One, a staging point 200 miles from Tehran. Unfortunately, two of the helicopters are forced to turn back as a result of mechanical difficulties, and a third conks out at Desert One. As a minimum of six helicopters is needed for the rescue, the mission commander, Colonel Charles Beckwith, USA, cancels the operation. During the withdrawal from the landing site, a helicopter and a transport collide on the ground, and five airmen and three marines are killed.

May 28.   Fifty-five midshipmen of the 770-strong Class of 1980 become the first women to graduate from the U.S. Naval Academy.

December 22.   The nuclear-powered carrier *Dwight D. Eisenhower* (CVN 69) and her escorts, the nuclear-powered, guided-missile cruisers *South Carolina* (CGN 37) and *Virginia* (CGN 38), return from the troubled Indian Ocean–Persian Gulf area after the navy's longest deployment since World War II—251 days. At one point the *Eisenhower* was at sea for 152 consecutive days.

1981

January 20.   After 444 days of captivity, the Americans remaining hostage from the seizure of the Tehran embassy are released by Iran on the day Ronald Reagan takes office as president of the United States.

January 20.   The Senate confirms the appointment of Caspar M. Weinberger as the 15th secretary of defense.

February 5.   John F. Lehman, Jr., assumes office as 65th secretary of the navy. In testimony before the Senate Armed Forces Committee he states that the navy must build back to an active fleet of 600 ships, including 15 carrier groups.

March 4.   **Defense build-up.** Secretary of Defense Weinberger unveils the Reagan administration's defense budgets for Fiscal Year 1981 and 1982, proposing increases of 11 percent and 15 percent, respectively, over the previous administration's proposals. The 1981 budget includes funds for the reactivation of the battleships *New Jersey* (BB 62) and *Iowa* (BB 61) and the carrier *Oriskany* (CV 34).

April 9.   While running submerged, the fleet ballistic-missile submarine *George Washington* (SSBN 598) collides with the 2,350-ton Japanese merchantman *Nissho*

Maru approximately 110 miles south of Sasebo, Japan. The submarine is essentially undamaged; the merchant ship sinks with the loss of two of her fifteen crewmen. A navy investigation finds that the submarine was at fault. Her captain is relieved of command and issued a letter of reprimand.

April 27.   The 37-year-old carrier *Intrepid* (CVS 11), which has served in World War II, Korea, and Vietnam, is transferred to the Intrepid Museum Foundation of New York City for conversion into a sea-air-space museum.

May 28.   Fourteen men are killed and forty-eight injured when a twin-engined, marine EA-6B Prowler crashes while attempting to land on the carrier *Nimitz* (CVN 68) off the coast of Florida.

June 27.   The navy's 2,000th fleet ballistic-missile patrol is completed by the *James K. Polk* (SSBN 645).

August 19.   **Gulf of Sidra incident.** Two F-14 Tomcats from the carrier *Nimitz* (CVN 68) shoot down two Libyan SU-22 Fitter fighters that open fire on them over international waters some 60 miles off the coast of Libya. The Libyan government of Colonel Omar Khadafi has claimed the entire Gulf of Sidra as its territorial waters, a pretension the United States refuses to recognize.

August 22.   Vice Admiral Edwin C. Waller III becomes 50th superintendent of the U.S. Naval Academy.

October 1.   The last Polaris missile patrol is completed by the *Robert E. Lee* (SSBN 601).

November 11.   **Ohio class.** The first of the navy's new, nuclear-powered, fleet ballistic-missile submarines, the *Ohio* (SSBN 726), is commissioned at Groton, Connecticut. She was originally scheduled for delivery in April 1979. Seven others of her class are under construction or on order. These ships are by far the largest submarines ever built, having a submerged displacement of 18,700 tons. They are armed with 24 Trident I nuclear missiles, each of which carries more than 14 independently targeted reentry vehicles (MIRV) and has a range of more than 4,000 nautical miles.

November 13.   **Admiral Rickover is retired.** The navy announces that 81-year-old Admiral Hyman Rickover, head of the navy's nuclear propulsion program for more than three decades, has been appointed presidential adviser on nuclear science and will not be retained on active duty when his current extension ends on January 31, 1982. He is succeeded by Admiral Kinnaird R. McKee.

An F-14 Tomcat. *Official U.S. Navy photograph.*

1982

January 17.   The submarine *Ohio* (SSBN 726) successfully fires her first Trident I missile while submerged off Cape Canaveral, Florida.

March 1.   **The last Polaris.** The navy's last Polaris fleet ballistic-missile submarine, the *Robert E. Lee* (SSBN 601), is redesignated an attack submarine (SSN 601), marking the end of the Polaris system after 21 years in service.

March 13.   The *Nimitz*-class supercarrier *Carl Vinson* (CVN 70) is commissioned, giving the navy a total of 14 carriers.

June 6.   Israel invades Lebanon with the object of eliminating the Palestine Liberation Organization (PLO), an action that brings the Middle East to a boil.

June 20.   In the South China Sea, an unidentified vessel opens fire with a machine gun on three U.S. naval vessels—the guided-missile cruiser *Sterett* (CG 31) and destroyers *Lynde McCormick* (DDG 8) and *Turner Joy* (DD 951)—which are returning from the U.S.-Thai exercise Cobra Gold '82. The *McCormick* responds with her machine gun, deliberately aiming high, and the foreign craft ceases fire. She is probably Vietnamese.

June 24–25.   Nearly 600 American and foreign citizens are evacuated from Juniyah, near Beirut, Lebanon, where the Israeli Army is engaged in pitched combat with the PLO, by the amphibious transport *Nashville* (LPD 13) and landing ship *Hermitage* (LSD 34).

July 1.   Admiral James D. Watkins becomes the 22nd chief of naval operations.

July 6.   President Reagan states that he has conditionally approved the deployment of U.S. Marines to join a Multinational Peace-Keeping Force in Beirut, Lebanon, to safeguard the evacuation of the PLO in the event a cease-fire agreement is reached.

August 25.   **Peace-keeping in Lebanon.** A force of approximately 800 marines from the 32nd Marine Am-

phibious Unit lands at Beirut, Lebanon, under Colonel James M. Mead to cooperate with French and Italian detachments in supervising the departure of the PLO. More than 12,000 Palestinians are evacuated in a 10-day period ending September 10. The merchant ships in which they sail are convoyed by 11 cruisers, frigates, and destroyers of the U.S. Sixth Fleet.

September 10.   The evacuation of the PLO completed, the 32nd Marine Amphibious Unit is withdrawn from Beirut.

September 15.   The battleship *Iowa* (BB 61) enters the Avondale Shipyards, at Pascagoula, Mississippi, for modernization. She is scheduled to join the fleet in June 1984.

September 20.   President Reagan announces that U.S. forces will return to Beirut in a peace-keeping mission to assist the Lebanese government in retaining control of the city.

September 29.   **Return to Lebanon.** The 32nd Marine Amphibious Unit, 1,200 men under Colonel James M. Mead, lands at Beirut, where 2,200 French and Italian troops are already present, to form a Multinational Peace-Keeping Force.

December 28.   **The New Jersey.** The battleship *New Jersey* (BB 62), a veteran of World War II, Korea, and Vietnam, is recommissioned at Long Beach, California. Her modernization includes the installation of 16 Harpoon missiles with a range of 50–60 miles and 32 Tomahawk cruise missiles with ranges up to approximately 500 miles.

Marines on patrol in Beirut, Lebanon, October 1982. *Official U.S. Navy photograph.*

1983

January 1.   **USCentCom.** The U.S. Central Command is activated to respond to threats to American security interests in the Middle East, including the Persian Gulf. An extension of the Rapid Deployment Force, its contingent authority includes the deployment of marine forces.

April 18.   A truck bomb explodes outside the U.S. Embassy in Beirut, Lebanon, killing 61 persons. A marine is among the 17 American dead, and 8 other marines are wounded.

May 17.   Israel signs an agreement with Lebanon, providing for the withdrawal of foreign armies from the latter country; but Syria, which also has moved sizable forces into Lebanon, refuses to join the accord.

June 26.   General Paul X. Kelley becomes the 28th commandant of the marine corps.

July 26.   **Naval demonstration.** The carrier *Ranger* (CV 61) leads a battle group that conducts a two-week demonstration off the west coast of Central America, where the United States is attempting to check the spread of Communism. Later in the summer, another carrier group headed by the *Coral Sea* (CV 43) exercises off the east coast and the battleship *New Jersey* (BB 62) off the west.

August 29.   The first two marines to die in Lebanon as a result of enemy fire are killed during a rocket, artillery, and mortar attack on the marine positions around the Beirut International Airport.

August 31.   Rear Admiral Charles R. Larson becomes 51st superintendent of the U.S. Naval Academy.

September 1.   **KAL atrocity.** Soviet fighters shoot down Korean Air Lines Flight 007—a Boeing 747 jetliner—en route from Anchorage, Alaska, to Seoul, Korea, after it strays into Soviet airspace over the Kamchatka Peninsula and Sakhalin Island. All 261 persons aboard, including U.S. Representative Larry McDonald, are killed. U.S. naval forces participate in the search for survivors and, after it is clear that there are none, for the wreckage of the plane.

September 8.   **Fire Support in Lebanon.** The Sixth Fleet frigate *Bowen* (FF 1079) becomes the first vessel to fire in support of the marines at Beirut, using her 5-inch gun against a position from which the Syrian-supported Druze militia had shelled marine positions.

September 19.   What will be widely perceived as a major shift in U.S. policy in Lebanon occurs when the nuclear guided-missile cruiser *Virginia* (CGN 38) and destroyer *John Rodgers* (DD 983) fire 338 rounds from their 5-inch guns in support of Lebanese Army forces defending the strategically important village of Sug el Gharb in the Shouf Mountains east of Beirut. Until now Sixth Fleet ships had fired only in response to attacks on U.S. positions.

September 25.   The battleship *New Jersey* (BB 62) takes station off Beirut, Lebanon.

October 23.   **Beirut bombing.** Around 6:25 A.M. on this Sunday morning a Mercedes truck loaded with 12,000 pounds of high explosive crashes through the barricades outside the headquarters building of the 24th Marine Amphibious Unit assigned to the Multinational Peace-keeping Force in strife-torn Lebanon. Inside the lobby of the building the suicide-driver detonates the charge. A total of 241 Americans die and 70 are wounded as a result of the blast. Minutes later, 58 members of the French contingent are killed when a second truck rams into their quarters.

October 25.   **Landing on Grenada (Operation Urgent Fury).** On October 19, a radical Marxist military coup overthrows the government of the 133-square mile, eastern Caribbean island of Grenada, a former British colony and Commonwealth nation. This event and subsequent developments arouse official apprehension over the safety of the approximately 1,000 U.S. citizens on the island, mostly students at St. George's University Medical School. A task force of 12 ships, including the carrier *Independence* (CV 62) and the amphibious assault ship *Guam* (LPH 9), en route to Lebanon with 1,900 men of the 22nd Marine Amphibious Unit to relieve the troops there, is diverted to the area. On October 22, the Organization of Eastern Caribbean States, fearful that Grenada will become a Cuban-Soviet outpost, formally asks the United States to intervene. Two days later, President Reagan orders American forces to occupy the island. The mission commander is Vice Admiral Joseph Metcalf III. Operations begin before dawn on October 25 when a SEAL team infiltrates the Grenadan capital of St. George's to secure Government House, where Governor General Sir Paul Scoon has been held since the coup. At 5:36 A.M., 400 marines from the *Guam* land in helicopters to seize Pearls Airport, Grenada's only operational airfield. Half an hour later, C-5A and C-130 transports from Barbados drop army ranger parachutists over the unfinished 9,000-foot airstrip being built by Cuban forces at Point Salinas. Despite unexpectedly stiff resistance from some of the 784 Cuban troops on the is-

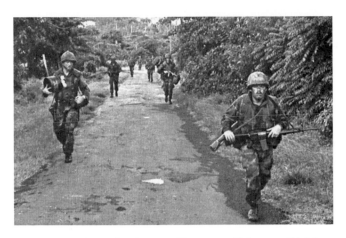

Marines on Grenada. *Courtesy History and Museums Division, Headquarters, U.S. Marine Corps.*

land, the airfield and the medical school's True Blue campus are secured by 8:50 A.M. At 7:50 P.M., 250 marines from the *Guam* make an amphibious landing at Grand Mal Bay, just north of St. George's. By nightfall 1,900 American troops have reached the island.

October 26. At 7:12 A.M., marine forces reach Government House at St. George's, where the SEALs, landed the day before, have been besieged. Governor General Scoon and 32 other government officials are, at their own request, flown to safety on the *Guam*. American medical students from the True Blue campus begin to be evacuated from the Point Salinas airfield at 9:00 A.M. Resistance from several hundred Cubans and an unknown number of Grenadan troops outside the medical school campus at Grande Anse is overcome around 4:00 P.M. None of the students have been harmed.

October 27. **Grenada secured.** Admiral Wesley McDonald, commander of the Atlantic Fleet, announces that all major military objectives on the island have been secured, though pockets of resistance remain. Some 638 Cubans have been made prisoner. By this time the flow of reinforcements has raised the strength of U.S. forces on Grenada to 500 marines, 500 rangers, and 5,000 paratroopers of the 82nd Airborne Division. American casualties in the course of the operation are 18 killed and 116 wounded. The Cubans lose 24 dead and 59 wounded; 45 Grenadan soldiers are also killed. The results of the operation prove that the concerns prompting this action were fully justified. American students and foreign service officers on the island testify that they felt their situation to be distinctly dangerous, and evidence of a Communist military build-up is unmistakable. Discoveries include the presence of 49 Russians, 24 North Korean, and 13 Eastern European diplomats and advisers; warehouses crammed with arms and military equipment; and documents revealing plans for a garrison of 6,800 Cuban troops. The majority of Grenadans greet the Americans as liberators.

November 1. Six men are killed and thirty-five injured when fire breaks out in the engine room of the carrier *Ranger* (CV 61) in the Arabian Sea.

November 1. Retired Admiral Hyman G. Rickover receives his second congressional gold medal. He and President Zachary Taylor are the only persons ever to be awarded two congressional medals.

November 8. Captain Grace M. Hopper, a pioneer in the creation of computer-programming languages, is promoted to commodore at age 76. She will retire as a rear admiral in 1986.

November 17. The Soviet Krivak I-class guided-missile frigate *Razyashchiy* collides with the destroyer *Fife* (DD 991) in the Arabian Sea. The *Fife* had moved to head off the Soviet ship when she approached too near the carrier *Ranger* (CV 61). No one is injured on the destroyer, which suffers minor damage. The *Razyashchiy* appears unharmed.

November 28. The Navy Department announces that the battleship *New Jersey* (BB 62), which has been diverted to Lebanese waters from a Western Pacific cruise originally scheduled to end in September, will be retained off Beirut, although her crew may be rotated.

December 4. **Action in Lebanon.** On December 3, Syrian antiaircraft and surface-to-air missile batteries fire on U.S. naval reconnaissance aircraft over the Bekaa Valley, 20 miles east of Beirut. In retaliation, 16 A-6 Intruders and 12 A-7 Corsairs from the carriers *Independence* (CV 62) and *John F. Kennedy* (CV 67) strike six Syrian positions in the mountains overlooking the valley. Two aircraft are lost. Later, eight marines are killed when the Syrian-sponsored Druze militia shell their perimeter around the Beirut International Airport. U.S. warships respond by bombarding the Druze positions.

December 14. The *New Jersey* (BB 62) fires 11 shells from her 16-inch guns at hostile positions inland of Beirut. These are the first 16-inch shells fired for effect anywhere in the world since 1969.

1984

January 3.   Lieutenant Robert O. Goodman, the bombardier-navigator of one of the carrier planes (an A-6E Intruder) shot down by Syrian forces in Lebanon on December 4, 1983, is released from captivity following a meeting between the American Reverend Jesse Jackson and Syrian President Haffez Assad. Goodman's pilot, Lieutenant Mark A. Lange, was mortally wounded in the crash of their plane.

February 7.   **Redeployment in Lebanon.** President Reagan announces his decision to withdraw the 1,600 Marines who form part of the Multinational Peacekeeping Force in Beirut to ships standing off the Lebanese coast.

February 7.   Navy Captain Bruce McCandless uses the manned maneuvering unit (MMU) to make the first untethered walk in space from the Challenger space shuttle.

February 8.   The battleship *New Jersey* (BB 62) fires 270 16-inch shells at Druze and Syrian positions in the Bekaa Valley east of Beirut. This is by far the heaviest shore bombardment conducted since the Korean War. Eight batteries on the receiving end disappear from the Syrian order of battle.

February 9.   The destroyer *Moosbrugger* (DD 980) fires approximately 150 shells at Syrian artillery positions east of Beirut.

February 14.   Syrian-occupied territory east of Beirut is shelled by the guided-missile destroyer *Claude V. Ricketts* (DDG 5) and other ships of the Sixth Fleet.

February 26.   The 22nd Marine Amphibious Unit completes its withdrawal from Beirut, leaving only the marine embassy guard.

March 21.   The carrier *Kitty Hawk* (CV 63) collides with a surfacing, Soviet Victor I-class nuclear submarine during night exercises in the Sea of Japan. The carrier sustains minor damage. A Soviet salvage vessel tows the submarine to the Vladivostok naval base.

April 2.   At midday in the South China Sea the Soviet carrier *Minsk* fires eight signal flares at the frigate *Harold E. Holt* (FF 1074) when the latter passes along her starboard side at a distance of approximately 300 meters. Three of the flares strike the *Holt,* but no one is injured.

April 28.   The battleship *Iowa* (BB 61) is recommissioned.

May 5.   The battleship *New Jersey* (BB 62) completes her first post-reactivation deployment, on which she sailed on June 9, 1983. Originally scheduled for a three

months' cruise in the Western Pacific, she was diverted to Central America in June and to the Mediterranean in September. Upon her return home, she has steamed 76,000 nautical miles in 322 days.

June 25–26.   F-14 Tomcats from the *Saratoga* (CV 60) fly over the Gulf of Sidra in demonstration of the United States' rejection of Libya's claim to sovereignty over the 30,000-square-mile body of water (see August 19, 1981). The Libyan government protests.

August 4–September 18.   **Red Sea mine hunting.** Following an Egyptian request of July 29, the U.S. Navy joins a multinational effort to locate mines which have mysteriously appeared in the Gulf of Suez. The USNS *Harkness* (T-AGS 32), a Military Sealift Command hydrographic survey ship, begins operations on August 4. She is joined by the amphibious transport dock *Shreveport* (LPD 12) and four RH-53D Sea Stallions of Helicopter Mine Countermeasures Squadron 14 on August 17. Meanwhile, on August 8, Saudi Arabia asks for assistance in sweeping the approaches to Jidda and Yanbu on the southern Red Sea. Three more Sea Stallions begin searches there on August 15 and are joined by the *La Salle* (AGF 3), flagship of the commander, Middle East Force, on August 20. British, French, Italian, and Netherlands vessels are also engaged. U.S. forces find no mines, but French and Italian units detonate a number and the British recover one, which proves to have been manufactured in the Soviet Union no later than 1981. Although the Islamic Jihad terrorist organization claims responsibility, the U.S. and Egyptian governments conclude that the mines were probably laid by the Libyan roll-on/roll-off cargo ferry *Ghat* in July.

September 20.   Twenty-three persons are killed and several dozen others, including U.S. Ambassador Reginald Bartholomew and four marine guards, are wounded when a suicide-driver explodes a truck bomb outside the U.S. Embassy Annex in East Beirut, Lebanon.

November 28.   **Weinberger Doctrine.** In an address entitled "The Uses of Military Power" to the National Press Club, Secretary of Defense Weinberger proposes what becomes known as the Weinberger Doctrine— six principles to govern the commitment of U.S. forces to combat abroad. These are (1) U.S. forces should not be committed unless the matter is deemed vital to the national interest; (2) if troops are committed, it should be with the clear intention of winning; (3) political and military goals should be clearly defined; (4) the relationship between the scale of the commitment and

An RH-53D Sea Stallion of Helicopter Mine Countermeasures Squadron 14 sweeping for mines in the Red Sea. *Official U.S. Navy photograph.*

the goals sought should be continually reassessed; (5) troops should not be committed unless there is reasonable assurance that the action will be supported by the American people and their elected representatives; and (6) the commitment of combat forces should be a last resort.

December 2–4.   Following exercise FleetEx 85-1, which ends on December 1, the *Carl Vinson* (CVN 70) and *Midway* (CV 41) carrier battle groups operate together in the Sea of Japan, approaching to within 50 nautical miles of Vladivostok. At least 100 Soviet aircraft and some surface vessels appear in what one source describes as the most vigorous Soviet response to any such American naval movement to date.

1985

February 2.   The State Department announces that New Zealand has denied permission for the destroyer *Buchanan* (DDG 14) to pay a port call to that country at the conclusion of ANZUS Exercise Sea Eagle, on grounds that nuclear-powered or nuclear-armed vessels are unwelcome. Later, New Zealand suggests that another ship be substituted. The United States declines to accept this proposal, conforming to a policy, shared by the United Kingdom, of refusing to confirm or deny the presence of nuclear weapons on its ships.

February 7.   Colonel Gail M. Reals becomes the first female marine selected for promotion to the rank of brigadier general in competition with male marines.

May 20.   **Walker case.** The most sensational spy scandal in the navy's history begins to unfold when 47-year-old, retired Chief Warrant Officer John A. Walker, Jr., is arrested and charged with selling secret information to the Soviets. The FBI had kept Walker under surveillance for six months following a tip from his ex-wife Barbara. Other members of Walker's spy ring are arrested soon afterwards: his 22-year-old son, Seaman Michael L. Walker, on May 22; his older brother, retired Lieutenant Commander Arthur J. Walker, on May 28; and retired Senior Chief Radioman Jerry A. Whitworth on June 3. A communications specialist with a top-secret crypto clearance who had served in a number of highly sensitive positions in the course of his navy career (1955–1976), Walker had begun selling classified materials to the Soviets around 1967. Ideology apparently had nothing to do with his treason; his motives were purely pecuniary. Whitworth, who had met Walker when both were on the staff of the radioman school at San Diego, entered the conspiracy between 1970 and 1975 and collaborated in it until his retirement in 1983. Like Walker, he had wide exposure to the navy's cryptographic machines and systems. Arthur Walker, who had retired from the navy in 1973, joined his brother's espionage net in 1980, obtaining a position as an engineer with a defense contractor, VSE Corporation, from whose offices he removed documents on naval matters. Michael Walker, a yeoman aboard the *Nimitz* (CVAN 68), was initiated into the conspiracy in 1983. At the time of his arrest, he is found to have 14 pounds of classified documents stashed behind an air conditioner near his bunk. During the ensuing trials, the prosecution contends that the Walker ring's activities constituted a major breach of national security. Arthur Walker, found guilty of all seven counts of espionage with which he is charged, is sentenced to life imprisonment on November 12. Whitworth is sentenced to 365 years in August 1986. John Walker plea-bargains on behalf of himself and his son, both of whom face multiple life sentences, offering to cooperate with the government if it will ask the court to sentence him to a single life term and Michael to 25 years. In this case, he would become eligible for parole in ten years and his son in eight. Attorney General Edwin Meese, Secretary of Defense Weinberger, and Secretary of the Navy Lehman approve the bargain, and the two Walkers are sentenced to these terms on November 6, 1986. U.S. District Judge Alexander Harvey II adds that he will recommend that they be denied parole.

June 14.   **Hijacking of TWA 847.** TransWorld Airlines Flight 847 is seized by Palestinian terrorists after taking off from Athens, Greece. The hijackers order the plane to land in Beirut. There on June 15 they murder one of the 37 American passengers, Steelworker 2nd Class Robert D. Stetham, a navy diver, and dump his body on the runway. Predictable demands that Israel free a number of imprisoned terrorists have in the meantime been rejected. The *Nimitz* (CVAN 68) battle group and amphibious vessels carrying 1,800 men of the 24th Marine Amphibious Unit arrive off Beirut on June 17. U.S. forces do not intervene in the incident, however, and after a second round-trip flight to Algiers the terrorists abandon the aircraft, taking the Americans aboard into the Beirut area as hostages. Negotiations secure the passengers' release on June 30. Inability to identify the parties responsible for the outrage prevents the United States from taking retaliatory action.

June 19.   Four marine sergeants serving in the embassy guard detachment in El Salvador are killed in a terrorist attack at a sidewalk café in San Salvador.

June 19.   This date is designated by President Reagan as National POW/MIA Recognition Day.

July 30.   **Maritime prepositioning.** Maritime Prepositioning Squadron (MPS) 1 becomes operational. The prepositioning concept is designed to facilitate rapid deployment by keeping squadrons of cargo ships, each carrying vehicles and supplies sufficient to support a 16,500-man Marine Amphibious Brigade (MAB) for 30 days ashore, permanently on station overseas. A total of 13 new or converted commercial vessels is planned. They are to be organized in three squadrons and contract-manned by the Military Sealift Command. MPS 1 is deployed in the eastern Atlantic in support of the 6th MAB. MPS 2, which becomes operational on December 31, deploys to the Indian Ocean in support of the 7th MAB. MPS 3 is scheduled to deploy to the western Pacific in support of the 1st MAB. The MPS concept originated in 1978, and an interim, Near-Term Prepositioning Force had previously been deployed.

August 28.   The navy unveils its new Surface Warfare Insignia, consisting of a ship's bow issuing from a pair of crossed swords.

August 29–September 20.   **Ocean Safari '85.** Ships from ten nations—the United States, Belgium, Canada, Denmark, France, the Federal Republic of Germany, the Netherlands, Norway, Portugal, and the United Kingdom—participate in the largest NATO exercise held to date. Altogether, 157 vessels and 70,000 servicemen (21,000 American) are involved.

October 1.   Admiral William J. Crowe, Jr., USN, becomes Chairman of the Joint Chiefs of Staff.

October 7.   **Achille Lauro hijacking.** At approximately 1:00 P.M. (local time), the Italian cruise ship *Achille Lauro* is seized while en route from Alexandria to Port Said, Egypt, by four Palestinian terrorists who had boarded the vessel under false passports at Genoa on October 3. The hijackers, armed with AK-47 assault rifles and hand grenades, segregate the Americans and Britons among the 438 passengers and order the ship to proceed to Syria. Almost as an afterthought, they broadcast a demand for Israel to release 50 terrorists it is holding. Israel refuses and U.S. and Italian warships begin shadowing the liner. The United States also rushes a SEAL team and a Delta Force commando to the Mediterranean and urges the governments of Cyprus, Lebanon, and Syria—the countries where it is deemed most likely the terrorists will seek asylum—not to permit the ship to enter their ports.

October 8.   The *Achille Lauro* requests permission to enter the Syrian port of Tartus. When this is denied, the terrorists murder one of the passengers, Leon Klinghoffer, a physically disabled, 69-year-old New Yorker, and threaten that other killings will follow unless they are allowed to dock. Klinghoffer was evidently singled out because he was American and Jewish. In the meantime, PLO leader Yasser Arafat has denounced the hijacking and sent Abul Abbas, a member of the PLO executive committee and general-secretary of the Palestine Liberation Front, to which the hijackers belong, to Egypt to aid in negotiations. Abbas radios orders to his followers to have the ship return to Egypt. Later he tells newsmen that the seizure of the *Achille Lauro* was an accident; the Palestinians panicked when a steward surprised them cleaning their guns. Their real mission had been to make a suicide attack at Ashod, Israel, where the ship was to call after leaving Port Said.

October 9.   Over the strenuous objections of U.S. Ambassador Nicholas Veliotes, the Egyptian government makes a deal with the *Achille Lauro* hijackers, promising them safe conduct to a destination of their choice in exchange for the release of the liner and its passengers and crew. The ship's captain, Gerardo de Rosa, had previously been compelled to announce that no one aboard had been harmed. At 5:00 P.M. (local time) the terrorists are taken off the ship, which enters Port Said at 8:00. The murder of Leon Klinghoffer is then reported.

October 10.   **"We Bag the Bums!"** is the headline with which the *New York Daily News* announces the capture of the *Achille Lauro* hijackers. Upon learning of the Klinghoffer killing, Ambassador Veliotes demands that Egypt prosecute the terrorists. Egyptian authorities reply that, unfortunately, it is too late; they have already left the country. Almost simultaneously, U.S. intelligence learns that in fact the Palestinians are at the Egyptian Al Maza military airfield, from which they are to be flown out in an EgyptAir Boeing 737. The National Security Council develops a plan to force the aircraft to land at the U.S. Naval Air Station at Sigonella, Sicily. President Reagan approves the operation, with the proviso that innocent lives must not be endangered. The EgyptAir plane is schedule to take off around 10:00 P.M. (local time). Commencing at 8:15, the carrier *Saratoga* (CV 60) launches two E-2C Hawkeye early-warning aircraft, an EA-6B Prowler electronic-warfare aircraft, and seven F-14 Tomcat fighters, the latter of which refuel in the air from KA-6D tankers. The EgyptAir 737 is intercepted over the Mediterranean south of Crete and escorted to Sigonella, where it sets down around 12:30 A.M. on October 11. The United States reluctantly turns the hijackers over to Italy for prosecution. Abul Abbas is also discovered aboard the plane but, despite American insistence that he should also be charged, the Italian government releases him two days later. The four hijackers are tried by Italian courts, initially for illegal possession of firearms and explosives, for which they are sentenced to from four to nine years of imprisonment on November 18.

November 8.   The rank of commodore is superseded by that of rear admiral (lower half).

December 21.   A Soviet news report reveals that, after 30 years as a commander in chief of the Soviet Navy, Fleet Admiral Sergei Gorshkov has been replaced by Admiral Vladimir N. Chernavin.

December 27.   **Airport atrocities.** Palestinian terrorists open fire on travelers in the lobbies of the Rome and Vienna international airports, killing 18 persons, including 5 Americans, and wounding 110 others.

1986

January 7.   President Reagan severs American economic ties with Libya and orders U.S. citizens to leave that country.

January 12.   The SS *President Taylor*, a U.S.-flagged container ship owned by American President Lines, is stopped by an Iranian naval vessel in international waters approximately 30 miles south of Fujaira, United Arab Emirates, and searched by a boarding party. The Iranians explain that they suspect the *Taylor* is carrying military material to Iraq. Finding none, they release the ship after two hours without injury to her 43 crewmen. No U.S. naval vessels or aircraft are in the vicinity at the time. A similar incident is probably averted by the presence of the destroyer *David R. Ray* (DD 971) when an Iranian vessel hails another President Lines ship, the *President McKinley,* in the Gulf of Oman on May 12.

January 24–31.   The *Coral Sea* (CV 43) and *Saratoga* (CV 60) carrier battle groups conduct freedom of navigation exercises (Operation Attain Document I) in and near the Gulf of Sidra, demonstrating the longstanding U.S. refusal to recognize Colonel Khadafi's attempt to include the gulf in Libyan territorial waters (see August 19, 1981). A second exercise by the same two battle groups (Operation Attain Document II) is held February 10–15.

January 29.   **Challenger disaster.** The *Challenger* space shuttle explodes 79 seconds after launching from Cape Canaveral, Florida. All seven astronauts are killed. Among them is Commander Michael J. Smith (USNA 1967), the shuttle pilot.

March 22.   The medium harbor tug *Secota* (YTM 415) sinks with the loss of two lives when she loses power and collides with the stern planes of the Trident submarine *Georgia* (SSBN 729) after completing a personnel transfer near Midway Island. The *Georgia* suffers no damage.

March 24.   **Action in the Gulf of Sidra.** On March 23, three carrier battle groups—those of the *America* (CV 66), *Coral Sea* (CV 43), and *Saratoga* (CV 60)— approach the Gulf of Sidra on another freedom of navigation exercise (Attain Document III). Navy aircraft cross Colonel Khadafi's "Line of Death" (32°30′ north latitude) delineating what Libya claims as territorial waters at 11:01 P.M. (local time) that day and a surface action group consisting of the cruiser *Ticonderoga* (CG 47), guided-missile destroyer *Scott*

Commander Michael J. Smith, USN, the pilot of the *Challenger*. *Official NASA photograph.*

(DDG 995), and destroyer *Caron* (DD 970) do so at noon on March 24. Between 1:52 and 6:45 P.M. four SA-5 Gammon and one SA-2 Guideline missiles are launched from coastal installation near Sirte, apparently at the surface action group's combat air patrol, and two Libyan Air Force MiG-25s are intercepted and turned back upon entering the exercise area. A sixth missile is probably fired at 7:14. Vice Admiral Frank B. Kelso II, commanding the Sixth Fleet, thereupon declares that all military units departing Libyan waters or air space are to be considered hostile. Shortly past 8:30, a Libyan La Combattante missile patrol boat, discovered heading towards the surface action group from the port of Misratah, is severely damaged by a Harpoon missile and Rockeye Mk-20 cluster bomb launched by two of the *America*'s A-6E Intruders. When the Sirte missile site reactivates its target-acquisition radar around 9:00, it is attacked by a pair of A-7E Corsair IIs from the *Saratoga*. Two HARM (high-speed, anti-radiation) missiles are launched and the transmissions cease. The radars come on again several hours later and two of the *Saratoga*'s Corsairs launch another two HARMs at 12:47 A.M., after which the site remains inactive. Meanwhile, at 10:30 P.M. an A-6 has damaged a second Libyan vessel, this one a Nanuchka II–class guided-missile corvette, with Rockeye Mk-20 cluster bombs. The corvette takes refuge beside a neutral merchant ship and later limps back to Benghazi.

March 25.   At 8:00 A.M. (local time), a second Nanuchka-class corvette, also based on Benghazi, is attacked by an A-6E from the *Coral Sea* (CV 43) and another from the *Saratoga* (CV 60) upon being detected entering international waters. The disabled vessel, dead in the water and burning fiercely, launches life rafts and U.S. forces allow Libyan vessels to conduct rescue operations. No further units attempt to go beyond the 12-mile limit recognized by the United States as Libyan territorial waters.

March 27.   At 3:00 P.M. (local time) U.S. forces withdraw from the Gulf of Sidra, in which the surface action group has spent 75 consecutive hours below the Line of Death. The exercise was scheduled to last three more days, but the unchallenged navigation of the gulf during the past 48 hours is deemed sufficient refutation of Libyan claims to sovereignty over these waters.

April 3.   Four U.S. citizens are killed when a bomb explodes aboard a TWA flight from Rome to Athens. Colonel Khadafi congratulates the terrorists, apparently Syrian, and promises, "We shall escalate the violence against American targets, civilian and non-civilian, throughout the world."

April 5.   A bomb explodes in La Belle discotheque, a West Berlin nightspot popular with U.S. military personnel, killing an American soldier and a Turkish civilian and wounding 229 others, including 78 Americans. U.S. intelligence links the outrage to Libya.

April 15.   **Raid on Libya (Operation Eldorado Canyon).** In response to the disco bombing, President Reagan authorizes a retaliatory strike on Libya. Five targets are selected. To reduce the efficiency of the Libyan air defenses, the attack is to be made after nightfall. This decision creates a problem, as the United States possesses only two tactical aircraft capable of precision night bombing, the air force F-111 and the navy A-6E Intruder; and the *America* (CV 66) and *Coral Sea* (CV 43) have only 18 Intruders—too few to hit all five targets simultaneously. The United States therefore requests the permission of the United Kingdom to launch F-111s from airfields in England. Prime Minister Margaret Thatcher grants this request, but neither the

A Libyan Nanuchka II–class corvette in flames following attacks by American carrier aircraft in the Gulf of Sidra on March 25, 1986. *Official U.S. Navy photograph.*

French nor the Spanish government, are willing to let the planes transit their airspace. This increases the F-111s' round trip from 3,000 to 6,000-plus miles and necessitates four inflight refuelings en route to Libya. All aircraft are to be on target at 2:00 A.M. (local time). A few minutes after 6:30 P.M. on April 14, 24 F-111s of the 48th Tactical Fighter Wing take off from Royal Air Force Station Lakenheath and 5 EF-111 electronic warfare planes of the 20th Tactical Fighter Wing from RAF Upper Heyford. The carriers launch their aircraft between 12:45 and 1:20 A.M. Prior to the bombing runs, navy A-7 Corsairs and F/A-18 Hornets deliver preemptive strikes on Libyan SAM sites and EA-6B Prowler electronic warfare aircraft join the USAF EF-111s in jamming Libyan radar. Other Hornets and F-14 Tomcats fly combat air patrol over the carriers and E-2C Hawkeye early warning aircraft are airborne to alert fighters in the event that any Libyan MiGs rise to oppose the strikes. Three of the five targets are located in the Tripoli area, which is allocated to the air force. Its major effort is against the Bab al Azizia (Tarabalus) Barracks, believed to be the headquarters of Libyan terrorist activities. Due to stringent rules of engagement, only four F-111s release their ordnance and one reports bombing long. Nevertheless, substantial damage is inflicted. Five of the six planes assigned to the Tripoli Military Airfield complete their mission, destroying two Il-76 transports and damaging several others. All three of the F-111s ordered to attack the Sidi Bilal naval base, a terrorist commando training center, hit their target.

To the east, navy planes strike targets around Benghazi. Six A-6Es from the *America* bomb the Al Jumahiriya Military Barracks. Two of the eight that the *Coral Sea* launches against the Benina Military Airfield are forded to abort, but the others execute a highly successful attack, destroying at least three MiG-25s, an F-27 Friendship transport, a small plane, and two military helicopters, and damaging six or more other aircraft. The attackers are outbound in 12 minutes. No Libyan interceptor has become airborne during the raid and none of the missiles launched by the ground defenses have scored. The Intruders are back aboard their carriers by 2:53 A.M. One F-111 and its two crewmen are lost over the Mediterranean, probably during the approach. The great care taken to pinpoint targets has been largely successful and only three bombs impacted in civilian areas—one, ironically, near the French embassy. Libya later announces that 37 persons have been killed and 93 wounded, but does not specify the status of these casualties. The wounded apparently include Colonel Khadafi, who was at the Azizia Barracks at the time of the attack.

April 16–18.   The carrier task force remains off the Libyan coast. The angry MiGs many anticipate the morning after the raid do not appear; the only Libyan response is to launch two Soviet-made SS-1 missiles towards the Italian island of Lampedusa, the site of a U.S. Coast Guard navigational aid facility. Both fall short of the island. In succeeding years, the incidence of Libyan-connected terrorist activities shows a drastic decline.

May 6.   Three submarines surface together at the North Pole for the first time ever. They are the *Archerfish* (SSN 678), *Hawkbill* (SSN 666), and *Ray* (SSN 653). The operation is part of Exercise Icex I-86, designed to "test submarine force readiness under Arctic conditions without logistics support."

May 10.   The *Missouri* (BB 63) is recommissioned. She is the third battleship to rejoin the fleet since 1982.

May 13.   **First battleship battle group overseas deployment.** The *New Jersey* (BB 62) sails for the western

Pacific from her home port of Long Beach, California, accompanied by the cruiser *Long Beach* (CG 9), destroyer *Merrill* (DD 976), and frigate *Thatch* (FFG 43). This is the first foreign deployment of a battleship battle group to be made since the reactivation of the big ships began. The *New Jersey* returns to Long Beach on October 20.

June 30.   Admiral Carlisle H. Trost becomes the 23rd chief of naval operations.

July 8.   Admiral Hyman G. Rickover, USN (Ret.), father of the nuclear navy, dies at the age of 86.

August 19.   Rear Admiral Ronald F. Marryott is appointed 52nd superintendent of the U.S. Naval Academy.

October 1.   **Defense reorganization.** The Goldwater-Nichols Defense Reorganization Act becomes law. Intended to improve the functioning of the Department of Defense, it increases the authority of the chairman of the Joint Chiefs of Staff, designating him the principal military adviser to the President, the National Security Council, and the Secretary of Defense, through whom the recommendations of the other chiefs are to be presented, and making the Joint Staff responsible to him rather than to the JCS as a whole. It also establishes the post of vice chairman of the JCS. Other provisions, designed to harmonize the conduct of joint operations, include an increase in the authority of commanders in chief over component service commanders and the creation of a career category of "joint specialty" officers.

October 25.   The navy's fifth nuclear-powered carrier, the *Theodore Roosevelt* (CVN 71) is commissioned. She raises the number of active carriers to 15, of which 14 are considered deployable and 1, the *Independence* (CV 62), is undergoing a service life extension program (SLEP) at the Philadelphia Naval Shipyard. Two other nuclear-powered carriers remain under construction: the *Abraham Lincoln* (CVN 72) and the *George Washington* (CVN 73).

1987

January 10.   **Sex for secrets scandal.** The marine corps announces the arrest of Sergeant Clayton J. Lonetree, 25, who is accused of having betrayed secrets in exchange for the sexual favors of a KGB agent while serving as a guard at the Moscow embassy between September 1984 and March 1986. Two other former Moscow embassy guards are subsequently arrested, but the espi-

onage charges against them are dropped. On August 24, a court martial finds Lonetree guilty of 13 counts of espionage and sentences him to 30 years' confinement, loss of rank, and a $5,000 fine. He is believed to be the first member of the marine corps ever convicted of such an offense. Later, his sentence is reduced to 25 years (which makes him eligible for parole in eight years and three months) and his fine lifted in exchange for his cooperation in making full disclosure of his activities.

March 7.   **Tanker War.** In response to an overture from the government of Kuwait, the Reagan administration agrees to provide naval protection for 11 Kuwaiti Oil Company supertankers to be reflagged under American colors. The Kuwaiti request is prompted by the "Tanker War" in the Persian Gulf, an outgrowth of the conflict which has been under way between Iran and Iraq since September 1980. Iraq, whose oil terminal was destroyed early in the war, began attacking ships—mainly tankers—serving Iranian ports in 1981. Three years later, Iran initiated its own attacks on shipping, hoping thereby to deter the southern Gulf states. Kuwait, and Saudi Arabia from continuing their support of Iraq and to discourage the delivery of war materials to that country. In 1986 approximately 111 attacks (sources vary) were made on merchant ships in the Persian Gulf.

April 10.   James H. Webb becomes 66th secretary of the navy, succeeding John W. Lehman, Jr., who has announced his intention to return to private enterprise. A graduate of the Naval Academy Class of 1968, highly decorated marine veteran of the Vietnam War, and best-selling novelist, Webb had been serving as assistant secretary of defense for reserve affairs. During his seven years as secretary, Lehman presided over a major build-up aimed at restoring the strength of the fleet to 600 active ships. He also sponsored the adoption of a controversial "Maritime Strategy," which, in the event of war with the East Bloc, calls for U.S. naval forces to advance into the North Sea to prevent Soviet submarines from reaching the Atlantic and later to employ carrier battle groups to attack the peripheries of the Soviet Union.

April 15.   **SOCOM and the SEALs.** The Special Operations Command (SOCOM) created by the FY 1987 defense authorization passed by Congress on October 15, 1986, becomes functional with the appointment of its first commanding officer. The new organization, which will be given control of its own budget on January 24, 1989, brings all of the military services' special forces under a unified command structure. This includes the navy's SEALs. However, the navy continues to coordinate SEAL selection, training, and requirements, as well as policy guiding their deployment, and almost half the force remains forward-deployed with the fleet.

May 5.   **Iran-Contra affair.** House and Senate committees open nationally-televised hearings into the Iran-Contra scandal—the secret sale of arms to Iran, which was undertaken by the National Security Council (NSC) in an attempt to consolidate relations with supposed moderates within the Ayatollah Khomeini's radical regime but soon degenerated into an arms-for-hostages exchange for American citizens held by Iranian-backed terrorists; the diversion of the profit from these transactions to support the Contra resistance to the Sandinista government of Nicaragua after the Boland Amendment prohibited the use of federal funds for that purpose; and the unsuccessful cover-up of both activities. Public interest in the proceedings reaches a peak with the appearance of marine Lieutenant Colonel Oliver L. North, an NSC staffer whom previous witnesses have identified as the key operational figure in the affair. Attractive, articulate, and impassioned, North quickly becomes the best-known lieutenant colonel in the corps's history, creating a legion of admirers in a spontaneous outburst of "Olliemania," while others view him as the loose cannon of American foreign policy. In six days (July 7–10, 13–14) of spellbinding testimony under a grant of limited immunity, he lectures the committees on the necessity for covert operations ("I think it is very important for the American people to know that this is a dangerous world"), admits his part in the cover-up, and not only acknowledges but defends ("I thought it was neat!") the use of Iranian funds to finance the Contras, to whose cause he is deeply devoted. But he insists that he kept the national security adviser, Vice Admiral John M. Poindexter, fully informed of the diversions and assumed that they had been approved by President Reagan. This assumption is subsequently refuted by Poindexter, who testifies that he did not tell the president of them. North and Poindexter (both of whom have in the meantime retired from the service) are indicted by a federal grand jury on March 16, 1988. Poindexter's predecessor as national security adviser, Lieutenant Colonel Robert C. McFarlane, USMC (Ret.), under whom the arms deal originated, has also been drawn into the scandal. He pleads guilty to four misdemeanor counts of withholding information from Congress and is sentenced on March 3, 1989, to two years' probation, a $20,000 fine, and 200 hours of community service.

On May 4, 1989, North is found guilty of three felony counts: obstructing Congress, unlawfully mutilating government documents, and accepting an illegal gratuity—a security fence for his home, provided by a businessman involved in the arms sales after North's life had been threatened by terrorist Abu Nidal. On July 6, he is sentenced to three years' probation, a $150,000 fine (which he is not required to pay), and 1,200 hours of community service. A year later, however, the District of Columbia court of appeals overturns his conviction for destroying documents and suspends the other two on grounds that the trial judge had failed to ensure that witnesses had not refreshed their memories with North's testimony at the congressional hearings. Admiral Poindexter is convicted on April 7, 1990, of five felony counts: two counts of obstructing Congress, two of making false statements to Congress, and one of conspiracy to obstruct Congress. On June 12, he is sentenced to six months in prison. The sentence is appealed.

May 17.   **The Stark.** Thirty-seven crewmen are killed when the Perry-class frigate *Stark* (FFG 31), on radar picket duty in the Persian Gulf 80 miles northeast of Bahrain, is hit by two Exocet missiles launched by an Iraqi F-1 Mirage. The *Stark* is alerted of the F-1's approach by an E-3 AWACs aircraft at 8:00 P.M. local time; her CO, Captain Glenn R. Brindel, has been notified by 8:05; and the frigate acquires the F-1 on her own air-search radar at a range of 70 miles at 8:58. At this time, the ship's super-rapid blooming offboard chaff (SRBOC) launchers are not armed, her Phalanx anti-missile Gatling gun is turned off, and her .50-caliber machine guns are unloaded. The F-1 turns towards the *Stark* at 9:05 and launches its first missile at a range of 22.5 nautical miles at 9:07. At 9:08 the ship's tactical action officer, Lieutenant Basil Moncreif, requests the aircraft to identify itself and gives orders for the chaff launcher to be armed and the Phalanx placed on "standby mode." The first missile strikes the *Stark*'s port side at 9:09; the second, launched from 15.5 miles, 20 to 30 seconds later. Both are sighted by lookouts before impact, but neither was detected by the ship's radar or electronic countermeasures systems.

A port-quarter view of the *Stark* the morning after she was hit by two Iraqi Exocets. *Official U.S. Navy photograph.*

Damage control is magnificent. Although fires reach a temperature of 1800 degrees F, melting parts of the aluminum superstructure, and the weight of the water sprayed into the conflagration causes the vessel to list 16 degrees to port, the *Stark*'s men save their ship. In approximately 24 hours she is under tow to Bahrain and in July she sails for the United States. The Iraqi government apologizes for the attack, stating that the F-1's pilot misidentified the frigate as a tanker. The navy's investigation, made public on October 15, finds that the tragedy was the result of human error, not failure of the *Stark*'s defensive systems. Earlier, it had been announced that, in view of their "extraordinary and heroic" conduct after the hits, Captain Brindel and Lieutenant Moncreif would not be court-martialed; instead, they are given letters of reprimand and allowed to resign.

June 28.   General Alfred M. Gray becomes the 29th commandant of the marine corps.

July 21.   **Tanker escort (Operation Earnest Will).** The guided-missile cruiser *Fox* (CG 33), guided-missile frigate *Crommelin* (FFG 37), and guided-missile destroyer *Kidd* (DDG 993) conduct the first U.S. naval convoy of the reflagged Kuwaiti tankers, departing Khawr Fakkan anchorage, just north of Fujaira, United Arab Emirates, for Kuwait (see March 7). On July 24, one of the tankers, the 401,832 deadweight SS *Bridgeton,* Captain Frank C. Seitz, Jr., U.S. Merchant Marine, strikes what is subsequently determined to

Tanker convoy number 12: the liquefied petroleum tanker *Gas King* and guided-missile destroyer *Standley* as viewed from the amphibious transport *Raleigh* on October 21, 1987. *Official U.S. Navy photograph (PH2 [SW] Elliott).*

have been a moored, floating contact mine of czarist Russian design approximately 20 miles west of Farsi Island. The explosion of the 115-kilogram charge tears a 10-by-15-meter hole in the tanker's $1^{1}/_{8}$-inch steel plating, but there are no casualties and she is able to complete her voyage to Kuwait and take on a reduced cargo of oil. On the return voyage, the convoy is preceded by two 150-foot commercial fishing vessels towing minesweeping paravanes operated by naval personnel. The *Bridgeton* later undergoes a month's repair in Dubai. She is the fourth vessel known to have hit a mine in the Persian Gulf. No nation asserts responsibility for the incident, which Iran ascribes to "the hand of God." The U.S. Navy reacts by sending eight RH-53D minesweeping helicopters to patrol the Gulf from the amphibious assault ship *Guadalcanal* (LPH 7) and by the deployment of six ocean minesweepers, three each from the Atlantic and Pacific fleets. These vessels reach the Gulf in late October and early November. By year's end, U.S. naval forces have escorted a total of 56 tankers in 23 transits of the Persian Gulf.

September 21.   **Capture of the Iran Ajr.** Shortly past midnight, a U.S. Army special warfare MH-6 helicopter gunship operating from the guided-missile frigate *Jarrett* (FFG 33) discovers an Iranian landing craft, the *Iran Ajr,* laying mines in an anchorage used by tankers 50 miles northeast of Bahrain. The helicopter attacks with 2.75-in. rockets and machine-gun fire, killing three Iranians and disabling the *Iran Ajr,* which is seized and taken under tow by navy SEALs the next morning. Ten contact mines of the type struck by the *Bridgeton,* others of which have in the meantime been found in the Gulf, are still aboard. Twenty-six captured Iranians are released on September 26. Iran protests that the craft had been filled with foodstuffs.

October 8.   Four Iranian speedboats, one of which has fired on a U.S. helicopter, are attacked 15 miles south of Farsi Island by U.S. Army MH-6 helicopters based on the guided-missile frigate *Ford* (FFG 54). One of the boats is sunk and two others captured. Six of their crewmen, two of whom subsequently die of wounds, are made prisoner.

October 16.   The reflagged Kuwaiti tanker *Sea Isle City* is damaged 10 miles off Mina al-Ahmadi by a Silkworm missile launched from an Iranian installation on the Fao Peninsula. Eighteen of her crewmembers, including the American master, are wounded. Iran began using Silkworms—Chinese-built cruise missiles with a range of 50 nautical miles—in the tanker war in September of this year.

October 19.   **Attack on the Rashadat platforms.** U.S. forces respond to the attack on the *Sea Isle City* by shelling two old Iranian oil platforms 80 miles east-northeast of Qatar that are being used as communication centers, radar pickets, and bases for speedboats operating against merchant shipping. Iranian

SEALs boarding the *Iran Ajr. Official U.S. Navy photograph (PH3 Henry Cleveland).*

personnel present on the platforms are given 20 minutes to evacuate them. The guided-missile destroyers *Hoel* (DDG 993) and *Kidd* (DDG 993) and destroyers *John Young* (DD 973) and *Leftwich* (DD 984) then fire 1,085 rounds of high explosive and armor-piercing shells in an 85-minute bombardment that reduces both platforms to ruins.

November 24.   Frank C. Carlucci becomes the 16th secretary of defense.

December 8.   **INF.** President Reagan and Soviet General Secretary Gorbachev sign the Intermediate Nuclear Forces arms control agreement in Washington, D.C. By its terms, the United States is bound to eliminate 108 Pershing II and 462 ground-launched cruise missiles (570 warheads) from Western Europe; the Soviet Union, to eliminate 441 SS-20 three-warhead and 112 SS-4 single-warhead intermediate-range missiles and 120 SS-12/22 and 20 SS-23 shorter-range missiles (1,575 warheads). Despite the American advantage in the number of warheads involved, some Western leaders register concern that the removal of the U.S. nuclear deterrent from Western Europe may have a destabilizing effect on East-West relations. Tactical nuclear weapons remain and the navy's Tomahawk nuclear land-attack cruise missile is not covered by the agreement.

The *John Young* at the destruction of the Iranian oil platforms near Rashadat. *Official U.S. Navy photograph.*

December 12.   Eleven crew members of the Cypriot-flagged tanker *Pivot* are rescued by helicopters from the guided-missile destroyer *Chandler* (DDG 996) when their vessel is left in sinking condition following an attack by Iranian speedboats. Another 29 crewmen are evacuated by a CBS News helicopter.

December 25.   U.S. and Royal Navy helicopters from the frigates *Elrod* (FFG 55) and HMS *Scylla* work together to rescue 20 crewmen from the South Korean–flagged tanker *Hyundai* after she has been attacked by an Iranian frigate near Abu Musa Island, some 20 miles northwest of Sharjar.

1988

February 12.   The guided-missile cruiser *Yorktown* (CG 48) and the destroyer *Caron* (DD 970) are bumped by a Soviet frigate and destroyer, respectively, in international waters near Sebastopol, the Soviet Navy's Black Sea base.

February 17.   Marine Lieutenant Colonel William R. ("Rich") Higgins, the head of one of three U.N. Truce Supervision Organizations (UNTSO) monitoring the Israeli-Lebanese border, is kidnapped by terrorists while driving alone near the Lebanese port of Tyre. On July 31, 1989, a group calling itself the Organization of the Oppressed on Earth—presumably a front for the Iranian-backed, Muslim fundamentalist Hizballah (Party of God)—releases a shadowy, 30-second videotape of a hanging man said to be Colonel Higgins. An FBI forensic examination concludes that the identification is correct.

February 22.   Secretary of the Navy James H. Webb resigns in protest of what he considers to be Secretary of Defense Carlucci's lack of support of a 600-ship navy. His action was triggered by the latter's decision to mothball 16 elderly frigates. At year's end, the navy has 509 ships in the active fleet and 44 more in reserve.

March 24.   William L. Ball III, a former naval officer, enters office as 67th secretary of the navy.

April 14.   **Mining of the Sammy B.** The Perry-class guided-missile frigate *Samuel B. Roberts* (FFG 58) is severely damaged by a contact mine in a previously swept area of the Persian Gulf. Members of her crew sighted three mines anchored just below the surface prior to the explosion and the frigate is backing down when a fourth explodes under her hull. A 21-foot-long hole is torn in her bottom; the main engines are jarred off their mountings; the engine room floods; and

The *Samuel B. Roberts. Official U.S. Navy photograph.*

cracks are opened in her superstructure. Fortunately, no lives are lost and the performance of the damage-control party is outstanding. Parts of the superstructure are literally wired together and the ship is towed into port at Dubai, United Arab Emirates.

April 18.   **Operation Praying Mantis.** The largest purely naval action fought by the U.S. Navy since World War II occurs when the forces in the Persian Gulf are ordered to retaliate for the mining of the *Samuel B. Roberts.* The targets are the Sassan and Sirri armed oil platforms in the central and southern Persian Gulf, which are being used as command and control centers for attacks on merchant shipping, and the Iranian navy Saam-class frigate *Sabalan,* which has played an especially active role in these attacks. The battle opens at 8:04 A.M. (local time) when Surface Action Group (SAG) Bravo, consisting of the guided-missile destroyer *Lynde McCormick* (DDG 8), destroyer *Merrill* (DD 976), and amphibious transport dock *Trenton* (LPD 14), tackle the Sassan platform. Iranian personnel are given five minutes to leave the rig and some do so, but others remain and return fire with a 23-mm cannon. The gun is silenced by a direct hit by one of the *Merrill*'s 5-inch mounts and an Iranian tugboat is granted permission to take off the defenders. Members of Contingency Marine Air-Ground Task Force 2-88 from the *Trenton* and a Navy Explosive Ordnance Disposal Detachment board and complete the destruction of the facility. During this action an AH-1T Cobra from Marine Light Attack Helicopter Squadron 167 is lost with both crew members. These officers are the only American casualties in Operation Praying Mantis. What happened is unclear: the last transmission received from the Cobra reported that Iranian radar had locked onto it, but wreckage recovered on May 15 shows no sign of battle damage.

SAG Charlie, composed of the guided-missile cruiser *Wainwright* (CG 28), guided-missile frigate *Simpson* (FFG 56), and frigate *Bagley* (FF 1069), attacks the Sirri platform at approximately 8:15. The occupants are given time to abandon the platform before the start of the bombardment and subsequently shelling is suspended to allow Iranian vessels

Marines on top of the Sassan oil platform; note the 23-mm gun at upper right. *Official U.S. Navy photograph (Corporal Hyp).*

to evacuate the personnel who had elected to resist. The flames and secondary explosions enveloping the rig make it unnecessary to insert a SEAL demolition team which is standing by.

Meanwhile, SAG Delta, made up of the guided-missile destroyer *Joseph Strauss* (DDG 16), destroyer *O'Brien* (DD 975), and guided-missile frigate *Jack Williams* (FFG 24), approach the Strait of Hormuz in search of the *Sabalan*. Following the attack on the oil platforms, however, that vessel has returned to port at Bandar Abbas and anchored in a protected position between two large tankers. Around noon the slack is taken up by the *Joshan*, a 147-foot, Combattante-II-class fast patrol boat. Disregarding four radio warnings, she closes to within 13 miles of the *Wainwright* and launches a Harpoon anti-ship missile at her. The missile passes closely but harmlessly down the cruiser's starboard side. The *Wainwright* and the frigate *Simpson* reply with five SM-1 missiles (modified for surface-to-air firing), all of which are hits. Reduced to a flaming hulk and hammered by 5-inch and 76-mm shells from both ships, the *Joshan* soon sinks. An Iranian air threat materializes shortly before she goes down when an F-4 Phantom from Bandar Abbas heads towards the *Wainwright*. After the ship's warnings are again ignored, she fires two SM-2 anti-aircraft missiles, scoring a hit that sends the Phantom limping back to base.

Next to enter the fray on the Iranian side are five Boghammar speedboats from Abu Musa Island. After firing on two merchantmen, they attack the *Scan Bay*, a Panamanian jack-up barge with 15 American crewmen aboard anchored in the Mubarak oil field. Virtually instantaneous communications allow naval commanders to ask Washington for permission to intervene. President Reagan personally authorizes *Enterprise* (CVN 65) aircraft on the scene to attack. Two A-6 Intruders sink the lead Boghammar with Rockeye Mk-II cluster bombs, each of which disperses 247 bomblets. The other four boats race to beach themselves on Abu Musa.

The scale of the action increases in mid-afternoon when the 1,100-ton frigate *Sahand*, a sister ship of the *Sabalan*, sorties from Bandar Abbas in the direction of SAG Delta. The frigate opens the engagement by firing at an A-6 investigating her identity. The A-6 and six A-7 Corsairs respond by launching Walleye, Harpoon, and Skipper missiles and laser-guided bombs. The *Strauss* also launches a Harpoon. Three Harpoons, three Skippers, a Walleye, and several bombs hit the *Sahand*, detonating her magazines. The shattered frigate sinks several hours later. Her disastrous sortie is soon duplicated by the *Sabalan*, which enters the Strait of Hormuz and fires at the two A-6s that had driven off the Boghammars. The leading A-6 retaliates by releasing a Mk-82 500-lb. laser-guided bomb, which

The Iranian frigate *Sahand* ablaze. *Official U.S. Navy photograph.*

leaves the frigate dead in the water. The question of whether to finish off the ship is relayed to Washington. Secretary of Defense Carlucci instructs U.S. forces not to interfere with Iranian salvage efforts and later in the day tugs take the *Sabalan* in tow for Bandar Abbas. Operation Praying Mantis is over.

April 24.   The *Bonefish* (SS 582), one of the navy's last diesel submarines, is wracked by explosions and a fire in her battery compartment during exercises with the carrier *John F. Kennedy* (CV 67) and guided-missile frigate *Carr* (FFG 52) 160 miles west of Cape Canaveral. Three of her 92 crewmen are killed; the others are evacuated by the *Kennedy* and the *Carr.* The abandoned submarine, made fast alongside the *Carr*, is boarded by a salvage crew on April 26. The next day, the salvage ship *Hoist* (ARS 40) begins towing the *Bonefish* home to Charleston, South Carolina.

April 29.   Secretary of Defense Carlucci announces that henceforth U.S. naval vessels in the Persian Gulf will protect friendly, neutral merchant shipping in the vicinity of ships under their escort.

June 28.   The U.S. naval attaché to Greece, Captain William E. Nordeen, 52, is killed while driving to his office by the explosion of a command-detonated car bomb in an Athens suburb. A leftist terrorist group calling itself November 17 claims to have committed the outrage. The same group had earlier asserted its responsibility for the shooting death of Captain George Tsantes, chief of the naval section of the Joint U.S. Military Advisory Group to Greece, on November 15, 1983.

July 2.   Putting the new U.S. Persian Gulf policy into effect (see April 29), the frigate *Elmer B. Montgomery* (FF 1082) fires a warning shot at an Iranian speedboat which had fired at a Danish supertanker.

July 3.   **Iran Air tragedy.** Iran Air Flight 655, an A300 airbus en route from Bandar Abbas Airport to Dubai, United Arab Emirates, is destroyed at 10:55 A.M. (local time) by two SM-2 Standard surface-to-air missiles launched at a range of nine miles by the Aegis cruiser *Vincennes* (CG 49), Captain Will C. Rodgers III. All 290 persons aboard perish. It is the sixth-worst disaster in aviation history. Minutes earlier, the *Vincennes* and the frigate *Elmer B. Montgomery* (FF 1082) had been engaged in action with Iranian Boghammar speedboats which had fired on U.S. Navy helicopters. The airliner's failure to respond to seven requests from the *Vincennes* to identify itself—three transmitted over the civil air emergency frequency routinely monitored by commercial airliners and four over the military equivalent—leads the cruiser's captain to believe that is an Iranian Air Force F-14 on an attack run. (The difference in size between an airbus and an F-14 would not necessarily be evident on radar.) U.S. spokesmen refute the inevitable comparisons with the Soviet destruction of Korean Air Lines Flight 007 (see September 1, 1983) by pointing out that: (1) KAL 007 was not entering an area where combat was in progress; (2) it was not requested to identify itself by Soviet air defense; and (3) the Soviet fighter that shot it down had established visual contact. President Reagan expresses regret for the incident and later announces that the United States will offer compensation to the families of the dead. A navy investigation finds that through human error in the *Vincennes*'s combat information center the oncoming airbus's decreasing range was misinterpreted as decreasing altitude, causing Captain Rodgers to be told that the aircraft was diving towards his ship when in fact it was climbing away. The report concludes that the captain had acted prudently on the basis of the information at his disposal.

August 18.   Rear Admiral Virgil L. Hill, Jr., becomes the 53rd superintendent of the U.S. Naval Academy.

August 20.   **Close of the Gulf War.** Hostilities between Iran and Iraq end in a U.N.-sponsored ceasefire only a few days short of eight years after they began.

September 26.   In what is widely regarded as the first step in the reduction of U.S. naval activities in the Persian Gulf, President Reagan announces that classic convoy escort operations will be replaced by a looser, "zone defense" system.

September 28.   **War on Drugs.** Passage of the 1989 Defense Authorization Act brings the Department of Defense into the war on drugs by designating it the lead agency for the "detection and monitoring" of sea and air traffic brining illegal drugs to the United States. The actual apprehension of suspected smugglers will remain the responsibility of law enforcement agencies and the Coast Guard.

October 22.   The battleship *Wisconsin* (BB 64) is commissioned. She is the last of the four modernized *Iowas* to join the fleet.

December.   **End of Earnest Will.** The mission of U.S. naval forces in the Persian Gulf is reduced to monitoring U.S.-flag vessels in the region. From the commencement of convoy operations in July 1987 through the end of this month, navy vessels have escorted a total of 270 merchant ships in 136 convoys. Only one vessel, the *Bridgeton,* has been damaged while under escort (see July 21, 1987).

1989

January 4. In an incident reminiscent of that which occurred over the Gulf of Sidra on August 19, 1981, two VF-32 F-14 Tomcats from the *John F. Kennedy* (CV 67) down two Libyan MiG-23 Floggers over the central Mediterranean. Navy spokesmen report that the F-14s fired only after making repeated maneuvers in an attempt to avoid the Libyan planes.

March. **FMFM-1.** The marine corps issues Fleet Marine Force Manual 1, *Warfighting,* as an introduction to the operational doctrine championed by its commandant, General Al Gray. The manual, drafted by Captain John F. Schmitt, uses historical example to describe the advantages of "maneuver warfare"—as opposed to the strategy and tactics of attrition. It is required reading for marine officers and staff NCOs.

March 20. Eighteen marines and a navy corpsman are killed when their CH-53D Sea Stallion helicopter crashes near Pohang, South Korea, during Exercise Team Spirit 89.

March 21. **Trident II.** The first submerged test launch of the eight-warhead Trident II D-5 destined to replace the Trident C-4 in the ballistic-missile submarine fleet is made from the *Tennessee* (SSBN 734) off Cape Canaveral, Florida. It proves a spectacular failure as the missile turns cartwheels through the sky and has to be destroyed. In December, after design changes and further tests, the director of the navy's Strategic Systems Program, Rear Admiral Kenneth C. Malley, announces that the D-5 program is back on track.

March 21. Richard B. Cheney assumes office as 17th secretary of defense.

April 19. **Turret disaster in the Iowa.** The explosion of five powder charges being loaded in the center 16-inch gun of Number Two Turret of the battleship *Iowa* (BB 61) kills 47 officers and men—the entire turret crew—at the beginning of a practice firing off Puerto Rico. The disaster is destined to become the navy's most controversial accident in recent years. A naval Judge Advocate General Manual investigation is conducted by Rear Admiral Richard D. Milligan, supported by a Naval Sea Systems Command technical team headed by Captain Joseph D. Miceli. Initially,

Smoke pours from the *Iowa's* number two turret moments after the disaster. *Official U.S. Navy photograph (Lt. Thomas Jerrell).*

Admiral Milligan assumes that the tragedy was indeed an accident, but early in May he concludes that it may have been a deliberate act and the Naval Intelligence Service is called into the investigation. His initial report is signed on July 15 and, after being reviewed by the commander, Naval Surface Forces Atlantic, the commander of the Atlantic Fleet, and the chief of naval operations, is released to the press on September 7. It states that the explosion resulted from a willful human action, "most probably" performed by Gunner's Mate 2nd Class Clayton Hartwig, who is portrayed as an emotionally unbalanced young man distraught over the cooling of a close friendship with a recently married shipmate, Gunner's Mate 3rd Class Kendall Truitt. The possibility that the charges were ignited by a chemical incendiary device, mentioned in this report, is confirmed by Captain Miceli's report of October 27. According to the latter, scientific analysis of molecular particles embedded in the copper rotating band of the shell in the chamber revealed traces of brake fluid, steel wool fibers, and two organic chemicals not present in either the propellant or the bore cleaners used in the guns. The fact that the rammer in the gun had traveled 21 inches further than usual is considered consistent with this finding, as the overstroke would have ignited the explosive device (presumably contained in a plastic bag) and facilitated the spread of the heat and flames to the powder bags between which it was placed. Initially, the navy had theorized that the explosion had been set off by a timer-detonator device, but an FBI laboratory analysis of the bore residue performed at the navy's request rules that out. Several other possible causes for the explosion are investigated and eliminated: for example, that the powder had become overheated and unstable as a result of being stored in a barge—but the amount of stabilizer in the *Iowa*'s powder is found to be virtually identical to that of the same lot in magazines ashore; or that the compression caused by rammer's overstroke had in itself ignited the powder—but navy investigators are unable to ignite powder bags either by duplicating the overstroke in another gun or dropping them from a height of 100 feet. The customary causes of turret disasters, the presence in the chamber of hot particles or hot gases from the firing of the previous round, have never offered a clue to the *Iowa* tragedy, since no previous round had been fired.

The navy's report is buttressed by more than 20,000 tests and analyses and the concurrence of the Ballistic Research Laboratory at the army's Aberdeen Proving Ground. Nevertheless, it is received with skepticism by Congress and the press, not to mention Gunner's Mate Hartwig's family, who protest the characterization of him as a suicidal misfit, and Congress orders a review of the findings. The new tests are conducted at the Scania National Laboratory. Their results, made public in May 1990, cast the navy's conclusions into doubt. The laboratory's researchers find that the "foreign material" in the *Iowa*'s gun was left by gun lubricant and sea water, and, after 17 attempts, succeed in igniting a weighted stack of powder bags dropped from a height of three feet. Secretary of the Navy Garrett orders all four of the navy's battleships to stop firing their 16-inch guns and reopens the investigation of the explosion of the *Iowa*.

April 25.   **Program cuts.** Announcing the defense budget to Congress, Secretary of Defense Cheney reports the cancellation of funding for the V-22 Osprey—a tiltrotor aircraft combining the capabilities of a helicopter and a fixed-wing turboprop, with which the marine corps had planned to replace its venerable CH-46E and CH-53A/D assault support helicopters—and for the navy's F-14D, an advanced version of the Tomcat fighter. These and other cuts have been designed to pare $19.9 billion from defense spending for fiscal years 1990 and 1991. However, Congress reinserts funds to keep the Osprey alive in the defense budgets for both years.

May 15.   H. Lawrence Garrett, a veteran of 20 years' service in the navy's Judge Advocate General's Corps, en-

ters office as 68th secretary of the navy.

May 30.   A CH-46 Sea Knight helicopter crashes into the sea moments after taking off from the amphibious transport *Denver* (LPD 9) during night operations off Okinawa, killing 13 marines and a navy corpsman.

July 21–25.   Three Soviet Navy vessels—the Slava-class cruiser *Marshal Ustinov,* Sovremennyi-class destroyer *Otlichnyi,* and replenishment ship *Genrich Gassanov*—make a port call at Norfolk, Virginia. Their visit initiates the first major military exchanges between the two nations.

August 1.   **Marine Corps University.** The Marine Corps University is established in Quantico, Virginia. It will be responsible for directing all marine educational (not training) programs. These include the Basic and Amphibious Warfare Schools, the Command and Staff College, 17 noncommissioned officer's schools, and numerous other activities. General A. M. Gray, the corps' commandant, explains, "Our goal is . . . to offer a graduate-level program . . . by combining the Marine Corps University core curriculum with affiliated civilian universities." Groundbreaking is scheduled for 1991 and a 300,000-volume research center is planned.

August 4–8.   Returning the Soviet port call at Norfolk, the guided-missile cruiser *Thomas S. Gates* (CG 51) and guided-missile frigate *Kauffman* (FFG 59) visit the Soviet Black Sea Fleet base at Sebastopol.

September 16.   **Arleigh Burke class.** The guided-missile destroyer *Arleigh Burke* (DDG 51), lead ship of a projected class of 25, is launched at Bath, Maine. According to the unclassified version of the navy's Surface Warfare Plan, the *Burke* class is to become the navy's battle-force component, defined as "a multi-mission ship equipped with a phased-array radar, an Aegis-type battle management system, a vertical launch system of 90-120 cells, and an advanced . . . anti-submarine combat system." Next to the B-2 bomber and Strategic Defense Initiative anti-missile research, construction of the *Burke* class represents the largest program in the defense budget for fiscal years 1990 and 1991.

September 29.   Admiral William J. Crowe, Jr., chairman of the Joint Chiefs of Staff, retires in a ceremony held at the Naval Academy. He is succeeded by General Colin Powell, USA.

October 11.   During an Atlantic exercise, an officer is killed and a seaman wounded when the amphibious assault ship *Iwo Jima* (LPH 2) is struck by rounds fired from the Phalanx aboard the amphibious cargo ship *El Paso* (LKA 117).

October 17.   Navy and marine corps units participate in disaster relief and rescue activities in and around San Francisco after the bay area is shaken by an earthquake that registers nearly 7.0 on the Richter scale.

October 29.   A pilot making his first carrier landing and four others are killed when his plane crashes on the flight deck of the training carrier *Lexington* (AVT 16) off Pensacola.

October 30.   Five men are slightly injured when the pilot of an F-18 Hornet accidentally drops a 500-lb. bomb on the bow of the guided-missile cruiser *Reeves* (CG 24) during exercises in the Indian Ocean.

November 11.   The nuclear-powered carrier *Abraham Lincoln* (CVN 72), the fifth of the *Nimitz* class, is commissioned.

November 14.   **Safety stand down.** Following a succession of unrelated accidents in preceding weeks, the chief of naval operations, Admiral Carlisle Trost, orders every navy unit at sea and ashore to suspend normal operations for 48 hours to review basic safety procedures. Two days later, he testifies to Congress that with only 67 major mishaps (defined as involving loss of life or damage in excess of $1 million), the navy's year-to-date safety record compares favorably to the historically low total of 69 major mishaps in 1988. In a message to senior commanders on December 18, he calls for added emphasis on safety procedures, noting that the investigations of these accidents have revealed that on-scene supervision was "often inadequate."

November 17–20.   **Force reductions forecast.** Guidelines for fiscal savings issued by Secretary of Defense Cheney project a 13.8 percent overall reduction in the nation's military personnel—290,000 slots—by 1995. By service and in order of magnitude, the anticipated cuts are as follows: navy, 6.9 percent; marine corps, 7.7 percent; air force, 17.3 percent; and army, 17.6 percent.

December 2–3.   **Malta Summit.** A two-day summit between President George Bush and Soviet President Mikhail Gorbachev is scheduled to take place aboard the guided-missile cruiser *Belknap* (CG 26), flagship of the Sixth Fleet, and the Soviet guided-missile cruiser *Slava* in the Marsaxlokk Bay. Owing to high winds and seas brought on by a winter storm, the meetings are actually held in the Soviet luxury-liner *Maxim Gorky*. In the course of the negotiations, Gorbachev proposes the elimination of tactical nuclear weapons from all surface ships.

December 7.   The *New Jersey* (BB 62) enters the Persian Gulf for a five-day goodwill cruise. The first battleship in decades to sail in these waters, she subsequently pays port calls in Bahrain and the United Arab Emirates.

December 15.   **Crisis in Panama.** The United States has been trying to compel Panamanian strongman General Manuel A. Noriega to surrender power since 1988. Formerly chief of intelligence of the Panamanian Defense Force (PDF), Noriega had become the *de facto* ruler of Panama following the death of General Omar Torrijos in a plane crash in 1981. According to published reports, Noriega had been a CIA informant and continued for some time to support covert U.S. operations in Central America, facilitating support of the Nicaraguan Contras, but the relationship soured as he became identified with international drug trafficking. Early in February 1988, federal grand juries in Miami and Tampa, Florida, indicted him on charges of running drugs. On February 24, Panamanian President Eric A. Delvalle, whom Noriega had put in office, attempted to dismiss the general as commander of the PDF. The following day the National Assembly, packed with Noriega supporters, ousted Delvalle, who went into hiding; Minister of Education Manuel Solis Palma was appointed minister in charge of the presidency; and Noriega remained as powerful as ever. The Reagan administration reacted to these developments by the imposition of economic sanctions (March 11), including the withholding of fees for the use of the Panama Canal. It also entered into talks intended to encourage Noriega to release his hold on the country. These negotiations almost achieved their objective in May 1988, when Noriega's representatives tentatively agreed that he would leave Panama for nine months in return for dropping of the drug indictments against him, but collapsed upon Noriega's demand that the United States recognize the president of his choice and reduce the garrison of the Canal Zone. Meanwhile, a coup staged by PDF officers against Noriega had been crushed (March 16); the government had suppressed the opposition news media; the U.S. embargo had begun to undermine the Panamanian economy; and a number of public protests against the regime had taken place.

This was the situation prevailing when presidential elections supervised by teams of international observers, including former U.S. President Jimmy Carter, were held on May 7–9, 1989. Poll-watchers agreed that opposition candidate Guillermo Endara had defeated the Noriega candidate, Carlos Duque, by approximately 3 to 1. On May 10, however, Noriega nullified the election before the outcome was officially announced, alleging fraud and foreign interference. The next day, President Bush ordered another 1,900 U.S. troops to join those already stationed in the Canal Zone. The new units included 147 marines and 16 light armored vehicles from the 2nd Light Armored Infantry Battalion at Camp Lejeune, North Carolina.

On October 3, a group of PDF officers made a second unsuccessful attempt to overthrow Noriega. U.S. forces in the Canal Zone were asked to support the coup and complied to the extent of blocking two roads. In the aftermath of these events, relations between the United States and the Noriega regime grew increasingly tense. On December 15, the Panamanian National Assembly appointed by Noriega in October designates him "maximum leader" and declares that Panama is in a state of war with the United States.

December 16.   **Provocation in Panama.** Four unarmed American officers in civilian clothes driving to a restaurant in Panama City lose their way and are stopped at a PDF roadblock when they inadvertently approach PDF Headquarters. The threatening attitude of the PDF members and a crowd of civilians which quickly gathers prompts the Americans to speed away from the roadblock. The Panamanians open fire. Marine Lieutenant Robert Paz is mortally wounded and a sec-

ond officer is hit. A U.S. Navy lieutenant and his wife, stopped at the same roadblock, witness the incident. They are taken to a PDF office and held for four hours, during which the lieutenant is beaten and his wife is sexually threatened before being released.

December 17.   The 12,000 U.S. troops in the Canal Zone are put on heightened alert. In Washington, Secretary of Defense Cheney denounces the preceding day's events in Panama, declaring that General Noriega is responsible for creating "an atmosphere in which Panamanian Defense Forces feel free to fire on unarmed Americans." Neither he nor any other official suggests that the administration is considering a military response; but it is on this day that President Bush gives the orders that set Operation Just Cause in motion.

December 20.   **Invasion of Panama (Operation Just Cause).** Declaring that "General Noriega's reckless threats and attacks upon Americans . . . have created an imminent danger to the 35,000 American citizens . . . in Panama," President Bush appears on television at 7:00 A.M. EST to inform the nation that he has ordered American forces into Panama. The operation is directed by General Maxwell Thurman, USA, commander of the Southern Command. It began at 1:00 A.M., when armored vehicles and attack helicopters moved out from bases in the Canal Zone. At the same time, C-130 and C-141 transports flew in carrying

American light armored vehicles in Panama City shortly after the opening of Operation Just Cause. *Department of Defense photograph.*

7,000 troops of the 2nd Brigade of the 82nd Airborne Division from Fort Bragg, North Carolina, and the 7th Light Infantry Division from Fort Ord, California. The principal American objective is to apprehend General Noriega, which will necessitate neutralizing loyalist units of the 6,000-man PDF and the paramilitary bands of thugs the general calls Dignity Battalions— and which, inevitably, U.S. troops christen "Dingbats." A SEAL unit enters Panama City prior to the invasion with the mission of disabling aircraft and helicopters at Paitilla Airport, from which it is thought Noriega might seek to escape. Unfortunately, it bumps into three armored personnel carriers full of PDF troops and a spirited firefight ensues before the SEALs can accomplish their mission, at the cost of some delay and eleven killed and wounded. Overall, Panama City and its environs have been divided into four tactical areas, the southwestern of which is assigned to Task Force Semper Fidelis, 700 marines commanded by Colonel C. E. Richardson. Its primary mission is to secure the Bridge of the Americas, the principal causeway over the canal. A force of 110 marines is also assigned to take the PDF outpost at Arraijan, just outside the city. In the course of the latter operation, Corporal Garreth C. Isaak becomes the first member of U.S. forces—and the only marine—killed in Just Cause.

Heavy fighting takes place during the hours of darkness around PDF Headquarters—the Comandancia—which is soon reduced to a flaming ruin. Elsewhere resistance is relatively light and, though mopping-up operations continue, by 10:00 A.M. General Colin Powell, USA, Chairman of the Joint Chiefs of Staff, is able to declare the intervention a success. A new Panamanian government headed by Guillermo Endara, the real victor of the May election, was sworn into office an hour before the invasion began. General Noriega remains at large, however, and widespread looting has broken out in shopping areas not yet controlled by U.S. troops.

December 21.   A flare-up of fighting with Dignity Battalions in the middle-class San Miguelito district of Panama City before dawn marks the effective end of armed combat in Operation Just Cause, although scattered sniping persists throughout the afternoon. Three thousand fresh army troops arrive in Panama City, but looting continues in areas outside American control. Twenty-six U.S. citizens who had been held hostage by Noriega forces at the Panama City Marriott Hotel and other locations are released unharmed.

December 22.   President Bush offers a $1 million reward for information leading to the apprehension of General Noriega, who has disappeared, and dispatches another 2,500 army troops to join the 22,500 soldiers, marines, and airmen already in Panama. In succeeding days, American forces extend their control throughout the country. Most Panamanians welcome them warmly and the resistance occasionally encountered from Noriega loyalists is negligible. By the end of the operation, 23 U.S. servicemen have been killed and 324 wounded. One American and no fewer than 202 Panamanian civilians have also been killed. PDF and Dignity Battalion casualties are estimated to include at least 59 dead. Approximately 5,500 PDF and Dingbats are temporarily detained, more than 1,500 by Task Force Semper Fidelis.

December 24.   **Noriega is located.** In Panama City, the papal nuncio announces that a haggard ex-maximum leader has taken refuge in the Vatican diplomatic compound. It is later learned that the general had spent the days since the invasion driving around the city from one supposedly safe house to another. U.S. forces surround the complex while the government begins urging the Vatican to release him into American custody.

December 27–30.   The troops surrounding the Vatican Embassy subject it to round-the-clock, concert-volume rock and roll with the objective of driving out General Noriega, whose tastes in music reportedly run to the classical. The stratagem is abandoned at the request of the papal diplomats, who are also an involuntary audience.

1990

January 3.   **Noriega in custody.** Late in the day General Manuel Noriega, the deposed Panamanian dictator, walks out of the papal diplomatic compound in Panama City to surrender to U.S. troops. He is flown to Florida the same evening and arraigned on drug-trafficking charges in the federal court in Miami the next day.

January 25.   **Force reductions.** Unveiling the Pentagon budget for fiscal year 1991, Secretary of Defense Cheney discloses plans to retire 54 ships, including two of the navy's four battleships, the *Iowa* (BB 61) and the *New Jersey* (BB 62), and five nuclear attack submarines (in addition to the three already scheduled for deactivation in the FY 1990 budget). At the end of the fiscal year, the navy will have 546 ships in active commission. Personnel strength is to be cut back from 591,000 (in FY 1990) to 585,000. It is evident that in the new climate of fiscal austerity brought about by the ballooning federal deficit and the virtual disappearance of Cold War tensions—symbolized by the opening of the Berlin Wall on November 9, 1989—the objective of a 600-ship navy has become unattainable.

February 8.   It is announced that U.S. Secretary of State James A. Baker III and Soviet Foreign Minister Eduard Shevardnadze have agreed to a "declaratory approach" to sea-launched cruise missiles (SLCMs), decoupling them from the rules for counting nuclear warheads in the Strategic Arms Reduction Talks (START). According to this understanding, both sides will state the number of SLCMs that they plan to build in the next five years. The figures would be binding. The matter is by no means settled, however, as Soviet negotiators wish to place limitations on conventional as well as nuclear SLCMs, to include the number and type of vessels carrying them.

February 27.   Admiral David E. Jeremiah, USN, becomes the second Vice Chairman of the Joint Chiefs of Staff.

March 9.   The Department of Defense reports that to conduct its recently assigned responsibilities in the war on drugs it has budgeted $877 million for FY 1990 and $1.2 billion for FY 1991. These funds are to be used to expand the department's monitoring and detection activities in the Pacific; to increase air surveillance, especially in the Caribbean; to complete the aerostat radar screen across the southern border; and to train South American law enforcement officials.

April 30.   The carrier *Coral Sea* (CV 43) is decommissioned at Norfolk, Virginia. A veteran of 42 years' service, she had logged more steaming time and aircraft launches than any other carrier. Her retirement—earlier than previously scheduled—reduces the number of deployable carrier battle groups to 14, with the *Midway* (CV 41) slated for deactivation in FY 1991. Some analysts predict that in time the navy will revert to 12 carrier battle groups, the accepted number prior to the Reagan buildup of the early '80s.

May 8.   The guided-missile destroyer *Conyngham* (DDG 17) is damaged by a predawn fire caused by a fuel leak in one of her boiler rooms during operations approximately 100 miles southeast of Norfolk, Virginia. The ship's operations officer loses his life and 18 seamen are injured before the conflagration is subdued.

May 12.   In testimony before a Senate panel Roland Lehman, director of the Arms Control and Disarmament Agency, states that U.S. negotiators have concluded that it would not be in the national interest to enter talks about cutbacks in tactical nuclear weapons (cruise missiles) at sea. The possibility of such cutbacks had been raised by President Gorbachev at the Malta summit (see December 2–3, 1989) and by Soviet Marshal Sergei Akhromeyev in his testimony to Congress on May 8. Lehman adds that the administration is optimistic that this decision will not impede progress in the reduction of strategic nuclear weapons.

June 20.   Conducting flight operations off the east coast of Japan, the carrier *Midway* (CV 41) is rocked by two explosions set off by a fire that breaks out in a storeroom six decks below her flight deck. Sixteen seamen are injured and two are killed.

June 25.   The Pentagon announces that the guided-missile carrier *Yarnell* (CG 17) and guided-missile frigate *Kauffman* (FFG 59) will become the first U.S. Navy ships to visit Poland in 45 years when they make a port call at Gdansk, June 27–29.

June 29.   Admiral Frank B. Kelso II succeeds Admiral Carlisle A. H. Trost to become 24th chief of naval operations. As has become customary in recent years, the ceremony is held at the U.S. Naval Academy.

August 2.   **Iraq invades Kuwait.** Under orders of President Saddam Hussein, an Iraqi force of 100,000 troops and 350 tanks invades and quickly overruns the tiny Persian Gulf emirate of Kuwait, whose entire armed forces number 20,300 men. The Kuwaiti ruler, Sheikh Jaber al-Ahmed al-Sabah, escapes to Saudi Arabia. Although Kuwait had supported Iraq in its eight-year war with Iran, since the cessation of hostilities in September 1988 Iraq had adopted an increasingly belligerent stance towards its oil-rich neighbor, demanding that Kuwait waive repayment of its estimated $15 billion of war loans to Iraq; give $2.4 billion in compensation for oil supposedly tapped from Iraqi frontier fields; and observe the Organization of Petroleum Exporting Countries (OPEC) oil production quota, Kuwait's disregard of which is held to have contributed to the depression of the world price of oil. Kuwait had agreed to reduce its oil production at the OPEC conference at Geneva in July, and representatives of the two countries met to discuss their remaining differences on August 1, but Iraqi intransigence caused the talks to collapse after two hours. The invasion takes place the following morning.

Despite the evident tensions, the Iraqi action takes most of the world by surprise: first, as an almost unprecedented aggression by one Arab state against another; and, second, because of the promise that Saddam Hussein had given Egyptian President Hosni Mubarak less than a month earlier that he would not attack Kuwait in the immediate future. Iraq's claim that it has entered Kuwait in response to the invitation of a revolutionary "Free Interim Government" meets with universal disbelief. President Bush, describing the invasion as an act of "naked aggression," signs an order freezing Iraqi assets, barring Iraqi access to Kuwaiti assets, and blocking Iraqi imports. The U.N. Security Council condemns the invasion and calls upon Iraq to withdraw at once.

August 3. Launching what will prove to be a diplomatic tour de force to isolate Iraq, the Bush administration proposes that the U.N. Security Council adopt far-reaching economic and military sanctions against the aggressor. At the same time, it calls upon America's NATO allies to join in its embargo against Iraqi imports (including oil) and issues an unusual, joint declaration with the Soviet Union condemning the invasion of Kuwait and demanding that Iraq withdraw. The Soviet Union also announces that it is suspending arms sales to Iraq, and Britain and France freeze Iraqi and Kuwaiti assets.

The U.S. response is not confined to diplomatic channels, however. The *Eisenhower* (CVN 69) carrier battle group is directed to proceed from the Mediterranean into the Red Sea and the carrier *Independence* (CV 62) battle group, conducting exercises off the Indian Ocean island of Diego Garcia, is ordered to join the vessels of the Joint Task Force, Middle East, already in the Persian Gulf region. It reaches there three days later.

Radio Baghdad's report that Iraqi forces will begin withdrawing from Kuwait on August 5 reassures no one. Instead, the massing of armor along the emirate's southern border exacerbates apprehensions that Iraq may invade Saudi Arabia, whose armed forces, 55,000 strong, would be no match for its nearly 1,000,000. In Iraq and Kuwait, Saddam Hussein controls 20 percent of the world's known oil reserves. With the addition of Saudi Arabia, he would control 45 percent.

August 5. Referring to the seizure of Kuwait, President Bush declares that Iraq's "brutal . . . aggression . . . will not stand." His campaign to rally the world community to concerted action achieves a major success

when the European Economic Community and Japan declare an embargo on Iraqi oil and freeze Iraqi and Kuwaiti assets. Inside the region, the Iraqi puppet government responds by threatening to take foreign nationals hostage or to nationalize foreign properties. The fate of the 21,000 foreigners in Iraq and Kuwait—including an estimated 3,500 Americans and 4,500 Britons—will be a major source of concern throughout the following months.

August 5.   Liberian evacuation (Operation Sharp Edge). Since December 1989 the west African nation of Liberia has been convulsed by a bloody, three-way civil war between President Samuel K. Doe and rebel leaders Charles McArthur Taylor and Prince Yormi Johnson. Late in May, as Taylor's troops neared Monrovia, the capital, an American amphibious ready group of four ships with 2,100 marines aboard was positioned off the coast to evacuate U.S. citizens if the need arose. The United States also offered to evacuate President Doe to a third country. He declined to depart and at the end of July, after rebel forces advanced to within several hundred yards of the heavily fortified presidential mansion, the conflict settled into a stalemate. On August 4, Prince Johnson threatens to begin taking foreign nationals hostage—starting with American, British, Lebanese, and Indian citizens—as a means of forcing great-power intervention. The number of Americans in Liberia is estimated at 370. That evening, President Bush orders the 22nd Marine Expeditionary Unit to launch a rescue mission. The next morning, a reinforced rifle company of 225 marines from the am-

Marines placing sandbags inside the American Embassy compound in Monrovia, Liberia, August 6, 1990. *Official U.S. Navy photograph (JO2 William G. Davis III).*

phibious assault ship *Saipan* (LHA 2) lands by helicopter to join the 12-man marine guard in the American Embassy compound. The unopposed movement is made by 11 CH-46 Sea Knight and CH-53 Sea Stallion helicopters escorted by 4 AH-1 Cobra attack helicopters and 2 Harrier VSTOL aircraft. A total of 73 people, mostly diplomatic personnel and their dependents, are flown to the American ships. The marines remain to guard the embassy compound. On August 8, Prince Johnson releases 22 hostages, including 1 American, that he had taken on the 6th. Captured by Johnson's forces on September 9, President Doe either dies of wounds or is executed a day later.

August 6.   **Saudi Arabia asks for help.** Secretary of Defense Cheney arrives in Saudi Arabia together with General H. Norman Schwarzkopf, USA, commander of the Central Command, and other officials to meet with King Fahd. The secretary's briefing on the strength of Iraqi forces in Kuwait, based on satellite intelligence, leads the Saudi ruler to the unprecedented decision to request the deployment of American ground troops to his reclusive kingdom. Meanwhile, the American diplomatic offensive accomplishes another key objective when the U.N. Security Council votes to impose a complete trade embargo on Iraq.

August 8.   **Operation Desert Shield.** In accordance with a decision reached by President Bush the preceding day, the American armed forces begin what will be by far their largest overseas deployment since the Vietnam War and the greatest airlift in history. The first elements of the Central Command—5,000 army troops—emplane to take up "defensive positions" in Saudi Arabia, while Maritime Prepositioning Ship (MPS) Squadron 2 sails from Diego Garcia carrying supplies sufficient to support a marine expeditionary brigade for 30 days. The other two MPS squadrons also deploy for Desert Shield, MPS Squadron 1 from European ports and MPS Squadron 3 from Saipan and Guam. The rapid arrival of these squadrons in Saudi Arabia, where three marine brigades are put ashore in two weeks, is one of the great opening successes of the operation. The American show of force is counterpointed by the progressive economic isolation of Iraq as Turkey joins Saudi Arabia in shutting the pipelines that carry Iraqi oil across its territory. With these overland outlets closed the only way that Iraq can export its oil is by tanker traffic through the Persian Gulf. Experts estimate that choking off all three outlets

would cause the Iraqi economy to collapse in a matter of months. Apparently unperturbed by these developments, Iraq announces that it has annexed Kuwait.

August 9.   Britain, France, and Australia announce that they will send warships to the Persian Gulf, and Secretary of State Baker tells reporters that the Soviet Union will dispatch naval forces to participate in any blockade established to uphold the U.N. economic sanctions. In Cairo, the Arab League holds an emergency meeting called by President Mubarak, who asks its member states to organize an Arab peace-keeping force in Saudi Arabia. In an apparent attempt to counter the Egyptian initiative, Saddam Hussein issues an appeal to all Arabs to overthrow the "emirs of oil," "rescue" the holy places in Saudi Arabia, and attack Western troops in the area.

August 10.   While President Bush formally notifies Congress of the deployments to Saudi Arabia in accordance with the War Powers Act, unnamed Pentagon sources state that the strength of the forces committed to Desert Shield may reach 200,000 to 250,000 men and women. Secretary of State Baker addresses another major American concern by stating that the government is disturbed that foreign nationals, including U.S. citizens, are not being allowed to leave Iraq and Kuwait. Iraq suffers another diplomatic defeat when 12 of the 20 nations attending the Arab League conference at Cairo support a seven-point resolution condemning the invasion of Kuwait and pledging to send forces to help defend Saudi Arabia.

August 11.   The hospital ship *Comfort* (T-AH 20) sails from Baltimore for Norfolk and the Persian Gulf. She is the first hospital ship to be fully activated since the Vietnam War. A second hospital ship, the *Mercy* (T-AH 19), leaves San Diego for the Gulf a few days later.

August 12.   **Naval quarantine of Iraq.** President Bush announces that U.S. naval forces have established a quarantine of Iraq to enforce the U.N. economic embargo.

August 12.   In his first essay at diplomacy, Saddam Hussein offers to withdraw from Kuwait in return for the lifting of economic sanctions against Iraq, the withdrawal of U.S. and other foreign forces from Saudi Arabia, and the Israeli evacuation of occupied territories on the West Bank of the Jordan and in the Gaza Strip—a proposal the U.S. government "categorically rejects."

August 13.   **Production cutbacks.** Secretary of Defense Cheney discloses that, in view of the lessening of the Soviet threat and the deficit problem, the production

The *Eisenhower* passing though the Suez Canal on her way back to the Mediterranean following a Red Sea deployment in support of Operation Desert Shield, August 22, 1990. *Official U.S. Navy photograph (PH3 Frank A. Marquart).*

rate of the navy's new and expensive *Seawolf* nuclear attack submarine and *Arleigh Burke* Aegis missile destroyer will be slowed. From FY 1991 through 1994, the navy will purchase 16 destroyers rather than the 25 originally programmed, while the submarines will be acquired at the rate of 3 every two years rather than 10 every three years. It is estimated that these slowdowns will save $2.2 billion from the 1991 budget and a total of $7 billion through 1994.

August 14.   Responding to evidence that Iraqi trade is still flowing through the Jordanian Red Sea port of Aqaba, President Bush says that the United States may extend its naval quarantine to that port. American resolve is underlined by the news that Secretary Cheney may ask the President to call up the reserves and that the carrier *John F. Kennedy* (CV 67) battle group of eight vessels is being sent to the Mideast.

In a shrewd initiative, Saddam Hussein moves to repair relations with Iran, promising to release the Iranian POWs Iraq is still holding and to evacuate occupied Iranian territory. A different sort of Iraqi initiative is unveiled by a foreign ministry official who tells ABC News that the U.S. citizens in Iraq will be held as "detainees" until the crisis has ended.

August 15.   President Bush authorizes U.S. naval commanders to use "minimum force necessary" to maintain the quarantine of Iraq.

August 18.   **Human shields.** In the Gulf of Oman, the guided-missile frigate *Reid* (FFG 30) fires six warning shots across the bow of an Iraqi tanker that ignores orders to halt, and the frigate *Bradley* (FF 1041) fires three shots across the bow of a second Iraqi tanker in the Persian Gulf. Following instructions that the Iraqi government has given its shipping to refuse compliance with the quarantine, the tankers continue on course shadowed by the U.S. vessels, which make no further attempt to stop them, and dock at Aden, Yemen, on August 21.

In other developments during the course of an eventful day, President Bush decides to call up an unspecified number of specialist personnel from the reserves; the Iraqi government describes the embargo as an act of war; and Iraqi Foreign Minister Tariq Aziz announces that the foreign "detainees" will be dispersed as "human shields" among military installations and strategic facilities, although they "will not be treated in a harsh or hostile manner." The U.N. Security Council asks Secretary General Javier Pérez de Cuéllar to take all necessary measures to assure the release of the hostages.

August 19.   Saddam Hussein offers to free all his foreign hostages if the United States will withdraw from the Persian Gulf and guarantee that the economic sanctions against Iraq will be lifted.

August 20.   Iraq demands that all the embassies in Kuwait must close by August 24.

August 22.   **Reserve call-up.** President Bush signs orders calling up the reserves. The exact number is released a day later: 46,700 troops in specialist areas such as food and water handling, construction, intelligence, and medical services. The American press reports that as of this date there are approximately 30,000 U.S. soldiers and 10,000 marines on the ground in Saudi Arabia. The latter includes advanced elements of the 1st Marine Expeditionary Brigade (MEB) from Camp Pendleton, California, and the 7th MEB from Twentynine Palms, California. Also present, besides the Saudi armed forces, are 5,000 Egyptian and 1,000 Moroccan troops. Confronting them in Kuwait are an estimated 150,000 Iraqis with 1,000 tanks. At least 200,000 U.S. troops, including 45,000 marines (a quarter of the corps), are expected to reach the Arabian peninsula by the beginning of October. Tactical air su-

periority has already been achieved and a formidable naval force is assembled in the region.

August 23.   Iraq orders all foreign embassies in Kuwait to close within 24 hours. The United States and thirty of the other 65 nations maintaining embassies in the occupied kingdom announce that they will not comply. By the beginning of October, however, shortages of supplies will have forced all except a handful to be evacuated. In Iraq, officials turn away two U.N. envoys sent to urge the release of the hostages.

August 24.   While U.S. ambassador Nathaniel Howell and a skeleton staff remain in the embassy compound in Kuwait City, approximately 100 diplomatic personnel and dependents, including the marine guard, proceed to Baghdad with the understanding that they will be allowed to leave Iraq. They are, however, held there. In a bizarre public relations ploy, Saddam Hussein appears on Iraqi television with a group of British hostage families, whose role as "human shields" he describes as "guardians of peace." The effect of the telecast, at least in Western lands, is highly counterproductive.

August 25.   **"Minimal force" approved.** American diplomacy achieves another success when the U.N. Security Council votes 13–0 with 2 abstentions, to approve the use of "minimal force" to uphold the economic embargo of Iraq. This is the first time in its history that the United Nations has resolved to support economic sanctions with force. In Kuwait City, Iraqi forces shut off electrical power and water to all the embassies. Troops also take position outside the U.S. and 25 other embassies.

August 26.   The commander-in-chief of the U.S. Central Command, General H. Norman Schwarzkopf, formally establishes his headquarters in Riyadh, Saudi Arabia.

August 27.   Iraq releases 52 dependents of the U.S. Kuwait embassy personnel held in Baghdad, but retains three young men over the age of 18 as well as the other adult males.

American news media reports that Iraq has ordered its merchant ships to comply with the orders of the naval vessels maintaining the blockade. Washington authorities are unable to confirm this statement, but subsequent events indicate that some such instruction must have been issued.

August 28.   In the first such action following the U.N. sanction of the use of force in the quarantine of Iraq, U.S. naval forces halt and board the Greek container ship

Zorba Express near the entrance to the Gulf of Aqaba. The Indian merchant ship *Kalidas* is halted in the same area. Both vessels are allowed to continue on their way after it is ascertained that their cargoes are not destined for Iraq.

Saddam Hussein makes another television appearance with a group of Western hostages, during which an American, Kevin Basner, urges him to release the foreign women and children. A few hours later, Saddam's Revolutionary Command Council announces that the women and children—including approximately 1,000 Americans—will be freed. Welcomed as this gesture is, it does little to defuse the crisis. On the same day, Baghdad reports that Kuwait has become the 19th province of Iraq.

August 29.   Japan announces that it will provide $1 billion, medical personnel, and non-lethal supplies to support the multinational effort in the Persian Gulf; the OPEC oil ministers agree to increase production to make up for the shortage caused by the embargo on Iraqi and Kuwaiti oil; the U.S. government authorizes the sale of an additional $3 billion of military equipment to Saudi Arabia; and a White House official confirms that the administration has rejected a secret Iraqi offer to release all foreign hostages and withdraw from Kuwait in return for the lifting of the embargo, greater access to the Persian Gulf, and complete control of the Rumaillah field, which extends into Kuwait. By now, the naval quarantine of Iraq is virtually airtight.

August 31.   To date, multinational force vessels have stopped approximately 350 ships and boarded 11, including an Iraqi tanker that the American cruiser *Biddle* (CG 34) allowed to proceed upon ascertaining that she was empty.

U.N. Secretary General Pérez de Cuéllar begins two days of talks with Iraqi Foreign Minister Tariq Aziz at Amman, Jordan. The meeting proves unproductive.

The first group of foreign women and children to be released in accordance with Iraq's four-day-old promise, 19 Italian nationals, reach Jordan.

September 1–2.   **Women and children released.** Three airliners leave Baghdad carrying more than 600 foreign citizens, mostly women and children, 102 of whom are Americans. Seven more evacuation flights follow from now until September 22. Their passengers include 1,900 U.S. citizens, leaving approximately 1,000, including about 80 men who are "detained" as "human shields," trapped in Iraq and Kuwait.

September 4.   President Bush dispatches Secretary of State Baker and Secretary of the Treasury Nicholas Brady on a mission to America's allies in Europe and the Middle East to seek economic and military support for the buildup in the Persian Gulf and financial assistance to poor nations hurt by the oil embargo. In the course of a whirlwind tour ending on September 15, the American envoys obtain pledges of more than $16 billion in aid, including $12 billion from Saudi Arabia, Kuwait, and the United Arab Emirates, and an additional $3 billion from Japan.

September 9.   **Helsinki Summit.** In a joint declaration at the close of a one-day conference in Helsinki, Finland, Presidents Bush and Gorbachev declare that the only acceptable solution to the Gulf crisis will be Iraq's full compliance with the U.N. Resolution of August 2—an unconditional withdrawal from Kuwait and the restoration of the legitimate government.

September 11.   In a televised address to a Joint Session of Congress, President Bush states that the Gulf crisis has forged "a new world order." By now, 26 nations have contributed forces to the military buildup in the region. More than 60 U.S. warships have reached the area and the navy has mobilized 42 of the 96 cargo ships in the Military Sealift Command Ready Reserve Force.

September 12.   The *Wisconsin* (BB 64) becomes the first battleship to conduct a practice firing with her 16-inch guns since the *Iowa* turret disaster of April 19, 1989. Secretary of the Navy Garrett had authorized her to do so on September 5, explaining that the Naval Sea Systems Command had determined that specific lots of propellant could be fired safely.

September 14.   **Iraqi embassy raids.** In Kuwait City, Iraqi troops force their way into the French, Belgian, Canadian, and Australian embassy compounds. Although they subsequently withdraw, this breach of the law of nations, condemned by the U.N. Security Council on September 16, provokes a sharp reaction from France (see September 15).

The British government announces that it is sending the 7th Armored Brigade—6,000 men and 120 tanks—to Saudi Arabia. This unit is the first sizable ground force to be deployed in the region by any Western power besides the United States.

September 15.   French President François Mitterand states that, in response to the Iraqi raid on its Kuwait City embassy, France is dispatching 4,000 ground troops— three regiments—with tanks and attack helicopters to

Saudi Arabia and that it will seek to extend the economic embargo of Iraq to include air traffic.

September 15.   In an interview at Dhahran, Saudi Arabia, the U.S. Air Force chief of staff, General Michael J. Dugan, tells newsmen that the Joint Chiefs of Staff has concluded that the best way to force Iraq out of Kuwait in case of war would be by a massive bombing campaign whose targets would include Saddam Hussein.

September 17.   Secretary of Defense Cheney relieves General Dugan as air force chief of staff, citing "lack of judgment" in his remarks to the press two days earlier.

September 25.   **Air embargo.** The U.N. Security Council votes 14–1 (Cuba opposing) to extend the economic embargo of Iraq to include air traffic—a measure pressed by France ever since the embassy break-in. The significance of the resolution—the eighth passed against Iraq in eight weeks—is largely symbolic, as there is no intention of forcibly interdicting air traffic. On the other hand, Secretary of State Baker and Soviet Foreign Minister Shevardnadze suggest that the United Nations could take military action to eject Iraq from Kuwait if other means fail.

Iraqi troop strength in Kuwait and southern Iraq is reported to have risen to 430,000—a 50 percent increase in the last two weeks.

October 1.   The *Independence* (CV 62) becomes the first U.S. carrier to actually enter the Persian Gulf since 1974.

October 1.   Addressing the U.N. General Assembly on the Gulf crisis, President Bush urges world leaders to stand firm against Iraqi aggression. He adds that Iraq's unconditional withdrawal from Kuwait could "create new opportunities" for a lasting reconciliation between Iraq and Kuwait, stability in the Persian Gulf, and a settlement between Israel and its Arab neighbors. These statements are widely interpreted as offering Saddam Hussein a diplomatic alternative to a military showdown.

October 4.   A White House official, speaking anonymously, states that Saddam Hussein is attempting to "mobilize" terrorist groups against the United States, its European allies, and Israel, and that the United States has warned Saddam that he will be held personally responsible should any terrorist actions take place.

October 8.   The U.S. frigate *Reasoner* (FF 1063), British frigates *Battleaxe* and *London,* and Australian frigate *Adelaide* fire across the bow of the 5,885-ton Iraqi freighter *Al-Wasitti* when the latter refuses to halt for inspection in the Gulf of Oman. The vessel is then boarded and searched by Royal Marines from the *Battleaxe* and *London.* Found to be empty, she is allowed to proceed. This is the first time British ships have fired in the Gulf crisis.

October 11.   The first evacuation flight from Iraq in almost three weeks lands in London carrying 321 Westerners, including 123 Americans.

October 15.   Speaking in Dallas, Texas, President Bush suggests that Saddam Hussein ("Hitler revisited") could face a war crimes trial for atrocities committed by Iraqi forces in Kuwait.

October 20.   Since the commencement of the naval quarantine of Iraq on August 25, U.S. and allied warships have intercepted approximately 2,500 vessels and boarded 240.

October 25.   **Crackdown on sexual harassment.** Secretary of the Navy Garrett issues a memorandum directing commanders to take strong action to eliminate sexual harassment of women and sexual discrimination. He and Admiral Kelso, the chief of naval operations, also organize a task force charged with proposing new policies to improve the opportunities and quality of life for women in the navy. These measures are prompted by a rash of recent incidents and assaults.

October 26.   The battleship *Iowa* (BB 61) is decommissioned at Norfolk, Virginia. She is the first of the navy's four battleships to be returned to mothballs.

October 30.   Eight sailors are killed and two fatally injured when a steam line ruptures in the boiler room of the amphibious assault ship *Iwo Jima* (LPH 2) in the Persian Gulf. Their deaths raise to 26 the number of U.S. servicemen to die in the area since the commencement of Desert Shield.

November 8.   In testimony to Congress the chief of the Naval Sea Systems Command, Vice Admiral Peter M. Hekman, Jr., states the navy is considering mothballing its last two active battleships, the *Missouri* (BB 63) and *Wisconsin* (BB 64), unless "Middle East operations convincingly demonstrate their unique utility."

November 8.   **Reinforcements to the Persian Gulf.** With the initial deployment of U.S. forces to the Persian Gulf virtually completed, President Bush announces the dispatch of reinforcements that will raise the total, all-service troop strength from approximately 240,000 to 430,000. Naval forces in the region will be joined by three additional carrier battle groups and the battleship *Missouri* (BB 63); three carriers and the battleship *Wisconsin* (BB 64) are already present. On the ground, the four-and-a-half army divisions (more than 100,000 personnel) and I Marine Expeditionary Force (more than 45,000) will be reinforced by two-and-a-half armored divisions from Germany, plus assorted other troops (75,000 total) and another marine expeditionary force (at least 34,000 strong). Tank strength will increase from 800 to 2,000. An unspecified number of aircraft will be added to the 500 air force and marine corps fighter and attack aircraft presently based in Saudi Arabia. When these movements, expected to take two months, have been completed, roughly one-third of the U.S. Army and nearly half of the Marine Corps will be in the Middle East. The president states that, while he continues to hope that Iraq will peacefully withdraw from Kuwait, the commitment of these forces will create an "adequate offensive military option."

November 14.   The Bush administration announces that the ceiling on the number of reserve and National Guard troops called up to support Operation Desert Shield has been raised to 125,000. The naval reserve ceiling (included in this total) is lifted from 6,300 to 10,000.

November 18.   Iraq states that it will allow the Westerners trapped there and in Kuwait—estimated to number approximately 2,000—to depart between Christmas and March 25 "unless something would take place that mars the atmosphere of peace." President Bush characterizes the proposal as "a total ploy" designed to buy time.

November 19.   **Conventional Forces in Europe Treaty.** The thirty-four–nation Paris summit Conference on Security and Cooperation in Europe climaxes with the signing of an arms reduction treaty that is acclaimed as marking the end of the Cold War. More than 100,000 tanks, armored fighting vehicles, aircraft, and artillery pieces are to be scrapped by mid-1991. Most will come from Warsaw Pact inventories, effectively eliminating the threat of a massive Soviet mechanized thrust into Central Europe. For example, the number of tanks on both sides will stabilize at 20,000 (down 21,000 for the Warsaw Pact and 2,000 for NATO). A corollary nonaggression pact is also signed between the sixteen NATO and six Warsaw Pact nations.

November 27.   **Gulf crisis hearings.** In a measure reflecting heightened public concern prompted by the administration's deployment of an additional 200,000 troops to the Persian Gulf (see November 8), Con-

gressional committees open hearings on the Mideast crisis. On the same day, the administration is reported to be ready to ask the U.N. Security Council to authorize the use of force against Iraq unless the latter withdraws from Kuwait by January 1, 1991. In the ensuing hearings some witnesses, including two retired chairmen of the Joint Chiefs of Staff (Admiral William J. Crowe, USN, and General David C. Jones, USAF), recommend that economic sanctions should be given many more months to take effect. In contrast, Secretary of State Baker, Secretary of Defense Cheney, and General Colin Powell, USA, the current JCS chairman, testify that the sanctions are unlikely to move Saddam Hussein.

November 27.   To date, 4,162 ships have been intercepted, 500 boarded, and 19 diverted by U.S. and allied naval forces in the quarantine of Iraq.

November 29.   **The U.N. approves the use of force.** American diplomacy scores another striking success when the Security Council authorizes member nations to employ "all necessary means" to expel Iraq from Kuwait if it remains in occupation of the emirate after January 15, 1991. The deadline for the Iraqi withdrawal was extended from the January 1st date initially proposed by the United States in deference to Soviet wishes. The Security Council vote is 12-2-1, Cuba and Yemen opposing and China abstaining.

November 30.   **Bush proposes discussions.** In a surprise move, President Bush offers to send Secretary of State Baker to Baghdad for talks with Saddam Hussein and states that Iraqi Foreign Minister Tariq Aziz would be welcome in Washington on the week of December 10. The President emphasizes that the invitation does not signify any softening of the U.S. insistence upon Iraq's complete and unconditional evacuation of Kuwait. Plans are soon settled for Aziz to meet with Bush on December 17, but on December 9 Saddam Hussein refuses to see Baker before January 12, which the President rejects as too close to the withdrawal deadline. The United States declares that Aziz will not be received unless a date has been set for Baker's visit, and on December 15 Iraq cancels his trip.

December 3.   **End of Operation Sharp Edge.** The evacuation of American and other foreign citizens from Monrovia, Liberia, which began on August 5, 1990, is officially terminated. The Liberian civil war has ended in a cease-fire signed on 28 November. A total of 226 U.S. citizens and 2,213 other foreigners from 59 countries have been evacuated.

December 6. **All hostages released.** The Iraqi News Agency reports that Saddam Hussein has proposed, pending the (rubber-stamp) approval of the Iraqi National Assembly, to free all of the foreign hostages. The assembly duly approves their release the next day.

December 7. The State Department announces that the skeleton staff manning the U.S. embassy in Kuwait will be withdrawn as soon as it completes the process of assisting Americans who wish to leave the country. Officially, the embassy will remain open but "vacated."

December 9. Approximately 400 former hostages, including 152 Americans and 101 Britons, fly out of Baghdad on a U.S.-chartered Iraqi Airways jet. Twenty-one other Americans left a day earlier on an aircraft chartered by former Secretary of the Navy John Connally, who had been conducting private negotiations for the hostages' release.

December 10. **A-12 probe.** Susan Crawford, the Pentagon's inspector general, informs the House Armed Services Committee that the government is conducting a criminal investigation into the overpayment of progress payments on the A-12 Avenger stealth attack aircraft being developed for the navy by McDonnell Douglas and General Dynamics. Months earlier it had been revealed that the program was running eighteen months behind schedule and $1 billion over its $4.7 billion budget.

December 13. **Last flight out.** Ambassador Nathaniel Howell and his staff vacate the U.S. embassy in Kuwait to board the last American charter flight from Baghdad. The plane carries 31 U.S. citizens and family members and 63 other evacuees. More than 200 Americans have been flown out since December 8, including 66 who were hiding in Kuwait. The latter have high praise for the Kuwaitis who helped them avoid the Iraqi dragnet and state that the Kuwaiti resistance is still active. About 500 Americans remain in Iraq and Kuwait, mostly children from mixed-citizenship marriages.

December 19. In London, Amnesty International issues an 82-page report charging that Iraqi occupation forces have killed and tortured hundreds of Kuwaitis.

December 21. Twenty-one seamen returning to the Saratoga (CV 60) from liberty in Haifa, Israel, are drowned when the chartered ferry Tuvia capsizes while approaching the carrier. Eighty-two others survive.

December 26. The 11,300-ton Iraqi freighter Ibn Khaldoon, bound for Basra, Iraq, with a cargo of foodstuffs, is boarded in the Arabian Sea by helo-borne American and Australian forces. Some of the ship's crew members and embarked peace activists attempt to resist the seizure but are deterred by stun grenades. The freighter is compelled to anchor off Oman.

December 27. **First female skipper.** Lieutenant Commander Darlene Iskra becomes the first woman to captain a U.S. naval vessel when she assumed command of the salvage ship Opportune (ARS 41) at Naples, Italy.

1991

January 3. In "one last attempt to go the extra mile for peace," President Bush proposes a meeting between Secretary of State Baker and Iraqi Foreign Minister Aziz in Switzerland between January 7 and 9. On January 4, Iraq announces that it will send Aziz to talk with Baker in Geneva on January 9. In reporting the acceptance of his offer, the President declares that "there can be no compromise or negotiations on the U.S. objective."

January 4. The Soviet freighter Dmitri Firmanov is halted in the Red Sea by the Spanish frigate Infanta Christina and detained after a search by U.S. and Spanish boarding parties turns up a considerable amount of military equipment not on her cargo manifest. The ship had been bound for the Jordanian port of Aqaba, which is widely regarded as a delivery terminal for goods destined for Iraq. State Department officials remark that presumably the shipment was an act of private enterprise rather than a reflection of a change in Soviet policy.

January 5. **Mogadishu evacuation (Operation Eastern Exit).** A civil war in Somalia, on the Horn of Africa, reaches Mogadishu, the country's seacoast capital, endangering the approximately 500 foreign nationals, including 70–80 U.S. diplomats and citizens, present there. The opposing forces are those of President Mohammed Siad Barre, who has held power since 1969, and the United Somali Congress, one of three rebel factions that took arms against him in 1988 and 1989. Two vessels assigned to Operation Desert Shield—the amphibious assault ship Guam (LPH 9) and amphibious transport dock Trenton (LPD 14), with marines and helicopters of the 4th Marine Expeditionary Brigade embarked—are dispatched to evacuate the Americans. Two CH-53E Sea Stallion helicopters carrying a reinforced rifle platoon of 60 marines lift off the *Trenton* at 2:45 A.M. (local time) approximately 460 miles from Mogadishu and reach the U.S. embassy compound at 6:10 A.M., having refueled twice from KC-130 tankers en route. The first 62 evacuees are on their way to the *Trenton* in the two helicopters by 7:30. The *Guam* reaches Mogadishu less than 24 hours later and four waves of five CH-46 Sea Knight helicopters extract 200 American and other foreign citizens (including the Soviet ambassador) and the marine platoon, leaving the compound empty. In a separate operation, Italy evacuates 189 foreigners in two C-130 transport planes. Virtually all of the others are extracted by French and Italian efforts on January 8 and 12.

January 7.   **Cancellation of the A-12.** Secretary of Defense Cheney gives the coup de grâce to the navy's behind-schedule, over-budget A-12 Avenger stealth aircraft (see December 10, 1990). At a project cost of $52 billion, it is the largest defense contract ever canceled.

January 8.   President Bush sends a message to Congress requesting the passage of a resolution authorizing him to take forcible action in the event that Iraq fails to withdraw from Kuwait.

January 9.   **Geneva meeting.** Nearly six-and-a-half hours of talks between Secretary of State Baker and Iraqi Foreign Minister Tariq Aziz on the Gulf crisis prove altogether unproductive. Aziz also refuses to deliver a letter from President Bush to Saddam Hussein. Many observers regard the outcome of the discussions as raising the prospect of armed conflict to a near-certainty. In Iraq, Saddam Hussein declares that if war comes Americans "will swim in their own blood."

January 12.   **Congress authorizes the use of force.** The House and Senate pass resolutions authorizing President Bush to employ force to bring about Iraq's compliance with the U.N. resolution calling for the evacuation of Kuwait. The votes are 250–183 and 52–47, respectively. On the same day, the last six American diplomats vacate the Baghdad embassy.

January 13.   Another attempt to achieve a peaceful solution to the Gulf crisis fails when U.N. Secretary General Pérez de Cuéllar spends two-and-a-half hours in Baghdad in fruitless discussion with Saddam Hussein.

January 14.   The U.S. government warns of the possibility of a worldwide wave of Iraqi-inspired terrorist attacks in the event of war.

January 15.   **Time runs out.** The U.N. deadline for the Iraqi withdrawal from Kuwait expires at midnight EST (8:00 A.M., January 16, Gulf time).

January 16.   **War with Iraq (Operation Desert Storm).** "The liberation of Kuwait has begun." With these words at 7:06 P.M. EST Presidential Press Secretary Marlin Fitzwater confirms that the American-led coalition has initiated military action against Iraq. Television viewers had become aware of the commencement of hostilities at 6:40, when Western newsmen broadcasting live from Baghdad reported seeing "flashes in the sky" and hearing explosions.

When war comes, there are an estimated 615,000 to 660,000 allied personnel with more than 3,200 tanks, upwards of 2,200 aircraft, and approximately 175 naval vessels in the theater of operations. Although no fewer than 28 nations have contributed to the buildup, the majority of the forces—425,000 servicemen and women—are American. These include 245,000 U.S. Army troops with 2,000 tanks and 75,000 marines with 200 tanks ashore in Saudi Arabia; 1,800 aircraft, including 450 from the navy's carriers and 300-plus of the shore-based 3rd Marine Air Wing; and 108 warships in the Persian Gulf and nearby waters. Other major ground contingents have been provided by Great Britain, Egypt, Saudi Arabia, Syria, and France. Britain, France, and Italy also dispatch a total of almost 40 naval vessels to the area. Also present in the allied armada east of Suez are from one to four ships from Argentina, Australia, Belgium, Canada, Denmark, Greece, the Netherlands, Norway, Portugal, the Soviet Union, Spain, and Turkey. Germany, whose constitution prohibits deployments outside the NATO area, has sent eight ships to the eastern Mediterranean to relieve allied vessels there.

Iraq's navy is insignificant and her 730-plane air force is clearly outclassed; only her 60-some Mirage F-1s and MiG-29s are state of the art. Saddam Hussein's military might is concentrated in his army—the fourth largest in the world: a nominal total of 555,000 regulars and 490,000 reservists, all of which have presumably been mobilized, with powerful artillery. He also possesses more than 4,000 tanks, including 500 modern Soviet-made T-72s, but many of the remainder belong in museums. The hard core of the Iraqi Army is composed of the Republican Guard, an elite, all-volunteer force with an estimated strength of 125,000 men organized into eight divisions and dug in as a strategic reserve along the Iraqi-Kuwaiti border. Most of the balance of the estimated 545,000 enemy troops in the Kuwait Theater of Operations are positioned in elaborate entrenchments

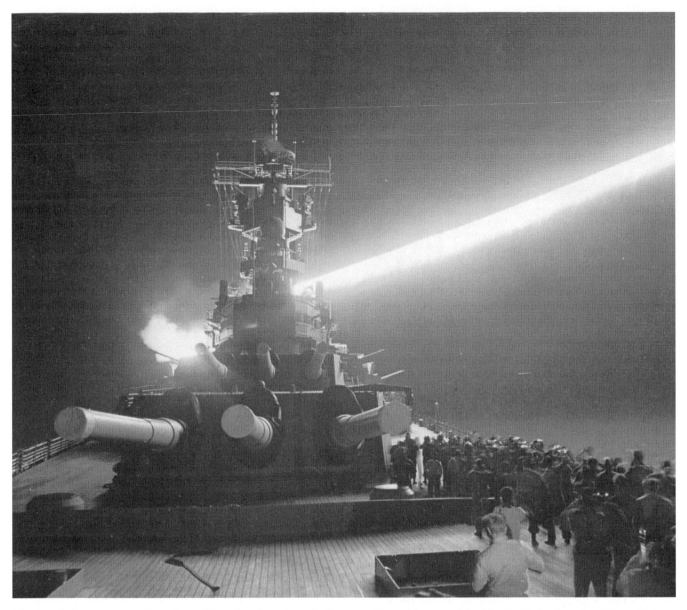

The battleship *Wisconsin* launches a Tomahawk cruise missile toward Iraq. *Photograph by John R. McCutchen,* San Diego Union.

on the southern frontiers of Iraq and Kuwait.

The conflict opens (about 2:40 A.M., Thursday, January 17, local time) with a surgical strike against Iraqi military, political, communications, and industrial installations by 1,700 American and allied aircraft, supplemented by a rain of Tomahawk II land-attack cruise missiles from the battleships *Missouri* (BB 63) and *Wisconsin* (BB 64) and other U.S. vessels in the Persian Gulf, the Red Sea, and the eastern Mediterranean. U.S. Air Force and Marine Corps fighter-attack planes take off from bases in central and eastern Saudi Arabia, while naval aircraft fly from the carriers *Midway*

(CV 41) and *Ranger* (CV61) in the Persian Gulf and the *America* (CV 66), *Kennedy* (CV 67), *Roosevelt* (CVN 71), and *Saratoga* (CV 60) in the Red Sea. British, French, Kuwaiti, and Saudi aircraft also participate in the operation. More than 160 sites throughout Iraq are hit. Targets include airfields; surface-to-air missile (SAM) sites; command and communications centers; chemical, biological, and nuclear plants; conventional munitions works; bridges; oil refineries; and launchers for the Soviet-made Scud-B ballistic missiles with which Saddam Hussein has threatened to bombard Israel. (Iraq is estimated to have 32 fixed and 36 mobile

A flight of A-7E Corsair IIs from the *John F. Kennedy* peeling off during Operation Desert Storm. *Official U.S. Navy photograph.*

launchers and anywhere from 300 to 3,000 Scuds in inventory.) At the same time, U.S. Air Force B-52 Stratofortresses begin bombing the Republican Guard. Some 1,400 sorties (half combat, half support) are flown and 104 Tomahawks launched during the first 24 hours of the war. U.S. authorities report that 80 percent of the aircraft release their ordnance over their targets and that the Tomahawks score 90 percent hits.

Shortly before the air attack opens, allied special forces and U.S. Army AH-64A helicopter gunships destroy two Iraqi air defense command centers. The effects of this strike and powerful electronic countermeasures equipment aboard navy EA-6B Prowlers and air force F-4G Wild Weasels render the enemy air-defense system almost totally ineffective. No opposition is offered by the Iraqi Air Force; the relatively few enemy planes to become airborne flee north. Only four allied aircraft are lost: an F/A-18 Hornet (hit by a SAM) from the *Saratoga,* two British Tornado GR-1 fighter-attack planes, and a Kuwaiti F-4 Phantom. The navy pilot, Lieutenant Commander Michael S. Speicher, is the first U.S. serviceman to die in the conflict.

January 17.   **First Scuds hit Israel.** The allied air offensive continues at the rate of 2,000 sorties a day. Resistance remains minimal and only three aircraft are lost: an A-6E Intruder from the *Saratoga* (CV 60); a U.S. Air Force F-15E Eagle, and an Italian Tornado. The opportunity to establish an air front over northern Iraq opens when the Turkish National Assembly votes to permit U.S. planes to fly attacks from Turkish soil. The first missions are launched from the NATO base at Incirlik on January 18.

However, allied elation over the success of the air war is diminished when Saddam Hussein fulfills a promise he has made time and again during the crisis: that, in the event of hostilities, he will attack Israel. At 7:15 P.M. EST (2:15 A.M., January 18, local time), seven Scud missiles strike that country, two in Tel Aviv. Fortunately, fears that they contain chemical warheads turn out to be unfounded and only 12 persons are injured, none seriously. An eighth Scud launched at the air base at Dhahran is destroyed by a U.S. Army Patriot air-defense missile, one of the techno-stars of the war. Although subsequently both Egypt and Saudi Arabia acknowledge Israel's right to retaliate, American leaders are apprehensive that any such action would fragment the Arab coalition against Iraq and urge Israel to refrain. After prolonged deliberations, Prime Minister Yitzhak Shamir announces that, at least for the moment, Israel will not respond. In succeeding days, allied aircraft redouble their efforts to eliminate the Scud launchers.

January 17–February 23.   **Air war.** During these weeks coalition forces continue the bombing offensive against Iraq at an average rate of almost 1,200 combat missions a day. Approximately 85 percent of them are flown by American aircraft. Beginning on January 24, the emphasis changes from the strategic bombing of the interior of Iraq to tactical bombing of enemy fortifications and facilities in the Kuwait Theater of Operations. The latter include the positions occupied by the Republican Guard in southern Iraq. Allied command of the air remains virtually uncontested. Never in history has an army passively endured such a pounding.

January 18.   The guided missile frigate *Nicholas* (FFG 47) and a Kuwaiti patrol boat assisted by U.S. Army UH-58 special operations helicopters recapture eleven Kuwaiti offshore oil platforms from which Iraqi troops were firing on allied aircraft. Five Iraqis are killed and twenty-six captured. There are no allied casualties.

January 19.   Naval history is made when the *Louisville* (SSN 724) fires a Tomahawk at Iraq, thus becoming the first submarine to launch a cruise missile in combat.

Three more Scuds strike Tel Aviv. There are no fatalities and, after lengthy discussions, the Israeli government again agrees to refrain from retaliating and thereby playing into Saddam Hussein's hands. For its part, the United States airlifts two Patriot air-defense batteries and crews to Israel from Germany. Israel had been supplied with two Patriot batteries shortly before the war, but their crews are still in training. The Patriots will not succeed in stopping every incoming Scud, but hereafter the prospect that Israel will take independent action against Iraq recedes.

January 20.   Iraqi television runs tapes of seven captured airmen—three Americans, two Britons, an Italian, and a Kuwaiti. Among the Americans is a naval officer, Lieutenant Jeffrey N. Zaun, an A-6 navigator-bombardier from the *Saratoga* (CV 60). Several of the airmen, who appear to have been beaten, condemn the war. The next day, the Iraqi government announces that the prisoners will be dispersed as "human shields" among potential target sites. These violations of the Geneva conventions are protested by the allied governments, as well as the International Red Cross. Four other POWs are shown on Baghdad television up to January 26, when the Iraqi Ministry of Information announces that the practice will cease.

Despite heavy cloud cover, allied fliers log 2,300 sorties. General H. Norman Schwarzkopf states that by now Iraq's nuclear reactors have been destroyed, as have all its fixed Scud launchers and 16 to 20 mobile launchers. Unfortunately, it appears that Iraq has the ability to improvise mobile launchers from eight-wheel trucks. Although the frequency of attacks declines as allied aircraft destroy more and more launchers, Iraq will remain able to fire several missiles—one of which inflicts heavy American casualties—in the final week of the war.

January 21.   To date, U.S. vessels have made approximately 7,000 interceptions and 830 boardings in the quarantine of Iraq.

January 23–24.   U.S. Navy A-6 Intruders sink an Iraqi tanker and an accompanying hovercraft that were monitoring allied air activity over the northern Persian Gulf. Two Iraqi minelayers are also attacked off the coast of Kuwait. One minelayer is sunk and the other goes down after running into a newly laid mine. Twenty-two of the ships' crews are rescued by a helicopter from the guided-missile frigate *Curts* (FFG 38). During this operation the helicopter draws fire from Iraqi troops on the tiny Kuwaiti island of Qaruh. This detachment is then attacked by naval aircraft; three Iraqis are killed and the remaining twenty-nine surrender. The island, 35 miles offshore, thus becomes the first Kuwaiti territory to be liberated from Iraqi occupation.

Royal Saudi Air Force Captain Ayedh al-Shamrani scores a double victory when his Sidewinders splash two of three Exocet-armed Iraqi Mirage F-1s as they approach coalition vessels in Saudi waters. The third Mirage jettisons its Exocet and flees. The Saudi airman's F-15 had been vectored to intercept the Iraqis by a U.S. AWACS aircraft. This is the first and, so far as is known, the last attempted offensive employment of the Iraqi Air Force.

January 25.   **Eco-terrorism.** A giant oil slick, 20 miles long and 3 miles wide, is reported spreading southward through the Persian Gulf. The first source identified is the Sea Island Terminal, a tanker loading station off the Kuwaiti coast connected by underwater pipelines to the Al Ahmadi refinery complex, Kuwait's largest oil facility. Iraqi forces apparently opened the valves on January 22 with the objectives of fouling Saudi desalination plants and complicating an amphibious landing. To check the spill it will be necessary to set the oil ablaze as it pours into the gulf at Sea Island and to cut the pipelines leading there. The first of these objectives is serendipitously achieved by a U.S. Navy vessel shelling a minelayer near the terminal and on January 26 the second is accomplished by USAF F-111s dropping laser-guided bombs in a precision strike ashore. At that point the slick covers an area of 308 square miles; it also appears to have been fed by the cargo of an Iraqi tanker sunk by a coalition air strike and an unknown source on Iraq's Fao Peninsula. The total spill is estimated at 120 million gallons—more than ten times the amount dumped in Prince William Sound, Alaska, by the *Exxon Valdez* in 1989.

January 28.   **The great fly-out.** By this date a total of 69 Iraqi military aircraft—30 transports and 39 fighter-attack planes—have taken refuge in neighboring Iran. The Pentagon had first disclosed that substantial numbers of Iraqi planes were flying to Iran on January 26. The puzzling exodus continues in following days until by February 9 no fewer than 137 have fled there. Although on January 29 Saddam Hussein intimates that the planes may return to combat, on February 2 Iranian President Hashemi Rafsanjani promises that Iran will uphold its neutrality, strongly implying that he will not allow them to leave. Around the same time, American officers begin to express doubt that the Iraqi aircraft will attempt to reenter the war, given the obvious inexperience of their pilots and the maintenance problems they face in Iran. In fact, the planes stay put. After the disquieting outcome of the first week of the air war, Saddam Hussein evidently elected to preserve at least part of his air force by extricating it from conflict.

January 28.   **Scud score.** Iraq has fired 51 Scud missiles so far, 35 in the first week of the war; 26 were aimed at Saudi Arabia and 25 at Israel.

January 29.   **First ground action.** Iraqi mechanized forces initiate the first significant land battle of the war by launching four probes into Saudi Arabia between the deserted, gulf-coast city of Ras al Khafji and the town of Umm Hujul, 50 miles inland. An Iraqi battalion occupies Khafji on January 30, but is destroyed by Saudi and Qatari units supported by U.S. Marines and American helicopter gunships the next day. The Arab forces capture 429 Iraqis, kill or wound 67 more, and knock out 45 armored vehicles at a cost of 51 casualties. American losses are nil. At Umm Hujul the invaders are repulsed by elements of the 1st Marine Division in an action that continues until January 31. Sixty-one Iraqi tanks and personnel carriers are destroyed. Eleven marines die in the fighting on the 29th, seven when an American aircraft mistakenly attacks their light armored vehicle. They are the first Americans to be killed in ground combat in the Gulf War. Allied commanders are encouraged by the Iraqis' generally inept performance in these encounters.

At sea, U.S. Navy aircraft destroy three Iraqi patrol boats near Bubiyan Island and another three in the gulf, while Royal Navy helicopters sink two patrol boats and a minelayer. Elements of the 13th Marine Expeditionary Unit, deployed in the amphibious assault ship *Okinawa* (LPH 3), seize Umm al Maradim Island, 12 miles off the coast of Kuwait. This is the second Kuwaiti island to be liberated.

A marine Cobra gunship flies over a column of allied tanks during the battle of Khafji, January 31, 1991. *Associated Press photograph.*

February 1–2.   **Naval strikes.** Coalition air forces launch attacks on an Iraqi naval base and patrol boats found in three different locations. Since the beginning of the war, and mostly during the past week, allied naval vessels and helicopters have destroyed or attacked 70 Iraqi ships and landing craft, usually as the latter were attempting to leave port. According to prisoners, their vessels had been ordered to take refuge in Iran. Any possibility that Iraqi craft might attempt to mount an Exocet attack on allied surface forces is now considered to have been eliminated, a supposition subsequently proven correct.

February 4–9.   **Battleships in action.** The battleship *Missouri* (BB 63), upon whose deck the Japanese instrument of surrender was signed in 1945, fires her 16-inch guns in battle for the first time since the Korean War, dropping seven shells on prefabricated concrete bunkers being positioned in Kuwait under cover of darkness. She remains in action through February 6, firing another 44 rounds, which destroy an Iraqi SAM position, a radar site, and some artillery and hit a dug-in enemy unit with unknown results. On February 7, she is relieved by the battleship *Wisconsin* (BB 64), whose big guns fire for effect—also for the first time since Korea—through the evening of February 9.

February 4.   **Defense budget.** The Pentagon releases its budget—$290.8 billion—for Fiscal Year 1992. This figure includes $2.8 billion for a *Seawolf* nuclear attack submarine, but among the economies it projects is the retirement of the navy's last two active battleships, the *Missouri* (BB 63) and the *Wisconsin* (BB 64), by September 1991. Long-range plans call for reducing the navy from 545 to 451 ships by 1995.

February 6.   U.S. Air Force planes down four Iraqi aircraft attempting to flee to Iran. These interceptions raise the coalition's air-combat score to 35–0. Another 91 Iraqi aircraft have been confirmed destroyed on the ground.

February 8.   The battleship *New Jersey* (BB 62) is decommissioned at Long Beach, California.

February 13.   Some 400 Iraqi civilians, mostly women and children, are killed when two 2,000-lb Smart bombs dropped by a USAF Stealth aircraft destroy a reinforced-concrete bunker in Baghdad. Iraqi authorities protest that the structure was an air-raid shelter. American military spokesmen state that it was actually a command and control center from which U.S. intelligence satellites had detected military transmissions a

Three of the carriers that took part in the Gulf War *(from left to right)*: the *Saratoga, John F. Kennedy,* and *America.* They are escorted by the guided-missile cruisers *Thomas S. Gates, San Jacinto, Mississippi, Normandy,* and *Philippine Sea,* and the guided-missile destroyer *Preble. Official U.S. Navy photograph.*

few days earlier and that they had no idea civilians were being allowed to sleep in its upper levels.

February 15. A communiqué from Iraq's Revolutionary Command Council offers "to deal with resolution" with the U.N. demand to withdraw from Kuwait, but hedges the offer with conditions—such as the exclusion of the restoration of the legitimate government—that cause President Bush to call it a "cruel hoax."

February 17. The daily average of allied sorties over the Kuwait Theater of Operations has increased from 400 two weeks ago to 700 or 800 (and sometimes more) in recent days.

February 18. **Ships mined.** Two U.S. vessels—the new Aegis cruiser *Princeton* (CG 59) and the amphibious assault ship *Tripoli* (LPH 10)—are damaged by mines at locations approximately 10 miles apart in the northern Persian Gulf. Seven seamen are injured. The *Princeton* has a 16-foot hole blown in her hull and loses power for an hour before proceeding to a gulf port for damage assessment; the *Tripoli* remains on station after onboard repairs. These events lead to the discovery of an Iraqi minefield across a main shipping channel, to which U.S. and British minesweepers hasten. Approximately 80 mines have been found in the gulf to date.

February 18. **Soviet initiative.** On February 10, Soviet President Gorbachev announced his intention to send a special envoy to Baghdad for talks with Saddam Hussein, asserting that the scope of Gulf operations was threatening to exceed the U.N. mandate. Soviet Mideast expert Yevgeny Primakov reached Baghdad the next day and on February 13 it was reported that Iraqi Foreign Minister Tariq Aziz would journey to Moscow for consultations. Aziz and Deputy Prime Minister Saadoun Hammadi arrived there on February 17. On the basis of their discussions, Gorbachev today proposes a peace plan calling for the complete and unconditional Iraqi evacuation of Kuwait. The "unconditional" evacuation is, however, encrusted with numerous and, for Iraq, advantageous conditions. President Bush responds on February 19, thanking the Soviets for their efforts but declaring that the proposal "falls well short of what will be required" to end the war.

February 20. General Schwarzkopf states that the Iraqi army is "on the verge of collapse."

February 21. The Iraqi government gives conflicting signals: in a 40-minute broadcast, Saddam Hussein declares that his country is ready for a ground war, but Tariq Aziz returns to Moscow.

February 21–22. A 500-man marine reconnaissance patrol inside Kuwait provokes an engagement in which 33

Iraqi armored vehicles are destroyed and 200 prisoners taken. Allied special forces have been operating behind enemy lines for some time.

February 22.   **The last deadline.** President Bush sets a deadline of noon EST (8:00 P.M. Gulf time), Saturday, February 23, for Iraq to begin withdrawing from Kuwait. He further stipulates that the withdrawal must be completed within one week; the legitimate government is to be allowed to return to Kuwait; all prisoners and hostages are to be released within 24 hours; and Iraqi liaison officers are to be provided to assist coalition forces in locating booby traps and mines. Although the timing of his announcement suggests that the President is simply reacting to the Soviet peace initiative, in reality the administration had chosen February 23 as a likely date for opening the ground war more than a week earlier. Later in the day, after discussions with Tariq Aziz, President Gorbachev proposes another peace plan in which Iraq relaxes some of the conditions attached to the previous proposal. This offer is no more acceptable than its predecessor.

In Kuwait, Iraqi forces begin a systematic destruction of the country's oil facilities.

To date, other countries—principally Saudi Arabia, Kuwait, Japan, and Germany—have pledged $51 billion (and paid $14.9 billion) towards the American costs of the war.

February 24.   **The ground war: Day 1.** What Saddam Hussein has repeatedly prophesied to be the "Mother of Battles" opens at 4:00 A.M. Sunday Gulf time (8:00 P.M., Saturday, February 23 EST). Announcing its commencement in an internationally televised address, President Bush declares that, "I have complete confidence in the ability of the coalition forces swiftly and decisively to accomplish their mission." His confidence is not misplaced.

The units that advance north across the Saudi border belong to eleven nations; in descending order of theater strength, the United States (371,000), Saudi Arabia (40,000), Egypt (38,500), Great Britain (32,000), Syria (19,000), France (12,500), and the Gulf states of Bahrain, Kuwait, Oman, Qatar, and the United Arab Emirates (11,500). The U.S. Army component, 295,000 strong, consists of two corps with seven divisions, plus support troops: the VII Corps—comprised of the 1st Infantry Division (Mechanized), the 1st Cavalry Division, and the 1st and 3rd Armored Divisions, and the XVIII Airborne Corps—comprised of the 24th Infantry Division (Mechanized) and the 82nd and 101st Airborne Divisions. The 76,000-member I Marine Expeditionary Force, commanded by Lieutenant General Walter Boomer, includes the 1st Marine Division (Major General James M. Myatt) and the 2nd Marine Division (Major General William M. Keys), whose tank strength is increased by the Tiger Brigade of the army's 2nd Armored Division. In addition, 17,000 troops of the 4th and 5th Marine Expeditionary Brigades and the 13th Marine Expeditionary Unit are afloat in the Persian Gulf.

From the beginning of the war until the start of the offensive, the allies have suffered the following combat casualties (the U.S. component is shown in parentheses): killed, 43 (24); missing, 51 (30); known captured, 13 (9). The extent of enemy losses is conjectural. Prior to the ground offensive, 3,500 soldiers have surrendered. An unnamed Iraqi official has been quoted as stating that 20,000 persons were killed and 60,000 wounded during the first 26 days of the air war, but these figures do not distinguish between civilian and military casualties. Soon to become apparent is the fact that allied intelligence officers, assuming Iraqi divisions would be at full strength, have considerably exaggerated the number of enemy troops in the Kuwait theater. That number probably peaked at about 350,000—not the estimated 545,000—at the start of the war. Since then, perhaps as many as 100,000 have deserted.

Including a record 1,200 sorties over the Kuwait theater today, coalition air forces have flown more than 94,000 missions and dropped 60,000 tons of bombs. The Iraqi Air Force has long since disappeared from the military equation, with 135 of its aircraft confirmed destroyed, 137 in Iran, and the remainder grounded at home. American leaders calculate that during the 38-day aerial offensive, allied air power has destroyed 39 percent of the estimated 4,280 Iraqi tanks in the theater, 32 percent of the 2,870 armored personnel carriers, and 48 percent of the 3,110 artillery pieces. The relentless aerial bombardment has also been primarily responsible for the 20 to 50 percent desertion rates from which Iraqi divisions have suffered. A total of 41 coalition planes have been lost; 32 in combat (23 U.S., 6 British, 1 Italian, 1 Kuwaiti, and 1 Saudi) and 9 (7 U.S., 1 British, and 1 Saudi) in noncombat mishaps.

General Schwarzkopf's plan is based on a greater and a lesser deception. The lesser deception, provided by the marine expeditionary force in the gulf, keeps 6 of the 42 Iraqi divisions in the theater pinned to the coast to repel an amphibious invasion that is never launched. The greater diversion is produced by secretly shuttling almost all the U.S. Army's combat units, the British 1st Armoured Division, and the French 6th Light Armored Division beyond the western extremity of the heavily fortified Saddam Line, which runs 138 miles inland from the Persian Gulf along the southern border of Kuwait. These forces are to execute a great turning movement to the north and east with the objective of enveloping the entire Kuwait theater, including the Republican Guard divisions in reserve in southern Iraq.

The Iraqi expectation that coalition forces will try to break through the entrenched lines on the Kuwait front is not completely disappointed, however. The 1st and 2nd Marine Divisions strike northeast across the dogleg of the Kuwaiti border toward Kuwait City; to their right, a Saudi task force pushes up to the coast toward the capital; and to their left, a Pan-Arab (predominantly Egyptian and Syrian) force wheels eastward toward the same objective.

The plan works to perfection. In the west, American and French forces race virtually unopposed across the Iraqi desert, while on the Kuwait front the marines quickly burst through the Saddam Line, many of whose dazed defenders have been anxiously awaiting the opportunity to surrender. Whole battalions do so en masse. By day's end, more than 14,000 prisoners have been taken. Five American and four allied personnel are reported killed in action, an extraordinarily small number in regard to the magnitude of the operations under way.

In Kuwait City, Iraqi troops begin executing civilians in what a Central Command spokesman characterizes as "terrorism at its finest hour." In recent days, thousands of other Kuwaitis have been abducted to Iraq. The malicious destruction of Kuwait's oil industry continues apace; by war's end, approximately 650 of the country's wells have been set ablaze.

February 25. **The ground war: Day 2.** Almost one-fourth of all the deaths American forces will suffer from enemy action occur when the warhead of a Scud which breaks up in flight plummets into the barracks of the 475th Quartermaster Group, an army reserve unit, at Dhahran, Saudi Arabia. Twenty-eight soldiers, including two women, are killed, and more than ninety wounded.

Elsewhere in the Kuwait theater, allied operations are officially described as a "tremendous success," and late in the day Baghdad broadcasts an order for Iraqi forces to withdraw from Kuwait. In the far west, the French 6th Light Armored Division captures the As Salman fort and airfield, 105 miles inside Iraq, and takes position to defend the flank of the coalition forces from any Iraqi units outside what is rapidly becoming the Kuwait pocket. In the north, American units reach the Euphrates, foreshadowing the imminent encirclement of the Iraqi army, and both British and American forces make contact with the Republican Guards who are trapped south of the river as a result of the bombing of bridges. In the east, armored elements of the 1st Marine Division destroy 50 to 60 Iraqi tanks in an action in the Burqan oil field near the Kuwait International Airport. Allied troops are pleasantly surprised by the continued absence of chemical weapons, which almost everyone had expected Iraq to employ.

In the gulf, 31 U.S. and Royal Navy ships, among them the battleships *Missouri* (BB 63) and *Wisconsin* (BB 64), shell enemy positions along the Kuwaiti coast and on Faylakah island, in the mouth of Kuwait Bay. Iraq launches its first Silkworm anti-ship missile of the war—according to British sources, at the *Missouri*. The missile is downed by two Sea Darts fired by the British destroyer *Gloucester*. Later a second Silkworm falls harmlessly into the sea.

Dispirited Iraqi troops continue to surrender in droves. By the morning of February 26, coalition forces are holding more than 30,000, after which they cease trying to keep count. Allied casualties remain almost unbelievably low. Four coalition planes, all American, are shot down. They prove to be the last fixed-wing aircraft lost in the war.

February 26. **The ground war: Day 3.** At daybreak, Iraqi forces begin a panic withdrawal from Kuwait City and, despite scattered sniping, by afternoon the Kuwaiti resistance is in effective control of the capital. North of the city a bumper-to-bumper stream of Iraqi military vehicles and stolen civilian cars and trucks, many crammed with loot, is devastated by allied air strikes. The next day, the city is formally liberated by Saudi and Kuwaiti troops, to whom the U.S. command has reserved that honor.

Elsewhere, the disintegration of the Iraqi army continues at an accelerating rate. In the afternoon elements of the 2nd Marine Division reach the highway from Kuwait City to Basra, in southern Iraq, blocking the Iraqi retreat from the capital, and the 1st Marine Division secures Kuwait International Airport after a fierce armored action in which more than 300 Iraqi tanks engaged are destroyed. In the north, U.S. and British forces have turned eastward to pin the retreating enemy between the Euphrates and the head of the Persian Gulf.

February 27.   **The ground war: Day 4 and victory.** The envelopment of the Iraqi army in the Kuwait theater is completed this morning when American and British forces reach the Euphrates in sufficient strength to prevent any crossings. Baghdad proposes to nullify its annexation of Kuwait in return for a cease-fire, but the United States and Britain spurn the offer because it ignores the other U.N. resolutions in force against Iraq. Military operations come to a climax in a great, day-long tank battle west of Basra in which American armor routs elements of the Republican Guard.

At 9:00 P.M. (1:00 P.M. EST) General Schwarzkopf goes before the television cameras at Central Command headquarters at Riyadh to deliver a spellbinding account of the course of the campaign. His remarks leave no doubt that organized Iraqi resistance is approaching an end. Twenty-six of the forty-two enemy divisions and 3,000 of the (at latest estimate) 4,700 tanks in the Kuwait theater have been put out of action—and "you can add 700 [tanks] to that as a result of the battle that's going on right now with the Republican Guard."

Among this bravura briefing's viewers is President Bush, who concludes that the time has come to bring the war to a close. In a television address beginning at 9:00 P.M. EST, the President announces that he has ordered offensive operations to be suspended in three hours. For the suspension to remain in effect, Iraq must cease fire; designate military leaders to meet with allied commanders within 48 hours; release all POWs and detainees; assist allied forces in locating mines; and comply with all U.N. resolutions.

February 28.   The 100-hour ground war comes to an end. Seldom if ever has an army as large as Iraq's been so thoroughly vanquished at so little cost to its foe. When the fighting stops at 8:00 A.M. (Gulf time), 40$^1/_2$ of the 42 Iraqi divisions in the Kuwait theater have been effectively destroyed. The number of Iraqi casualties is unknown. Saudi authorities estimate they may reach 85,000 to 100,000; 63,000 prisoners have definitely been taken. In contrast, allied casualties are amazingly light. According to statistics published today, the cost to the coalition of the ground offensive was 56 dead, evenly divided between American and allied troops. All told, 304 U.S. military personnel—296 men and 8 women—gave their lives in operations relating to the Gulf War, 122 as a result of enemy action and 182 in consequence of accidents or natural causes.

March 1.   Entering the U.S. Embassy in Kuwait City, Ambassador Edward W. Gnehm raises the flag that Ambassador Nathaniel Howell had brought out with him on December 13. In the United States, President Bush declares, "By God, we've kicked the Vietnam syndrome once and for all."

March 2.   **Cease-fire terms.** The U.N. Security Council passes a resolution setting the terms for a formal cease fire with Iraq. These call for Iraq to rescind its annexation of Kuwait and to accept liability for damages inflicted on Kuwait, other nations, individuals, and corporations; the return of all prisoners of war and civilian hostages; Iraqi assistance in locating mines and booby traps; and the withdrawal of allied forces as soon as possible upon the return of stability. The coalition is authorized to resume hostilities in the event Iraq fails to comply with these conditions, and the military and economic embargo of Iraq remains in effect. The vote is 11-3-1, Cuba opposing and China, India, and Yemen abstaining.

March 3.   **Truce talks.** General Schwarzkopf and Saudi Lieutenant General Khalid bin Sultan meet seven Iraqi senior officers at the captured Iraqi Air Force base at Safwan. The talks, originally scheduled to be held a day earlier, had been postponed at the request of Iraq. The Iraqis pledge their country's full compliance with the conditions of the U.N. resolution of March 2 and agree to an immediate "symbolic release" of a number of POWs.

March 4.   Iraq releases 10 of its prisoners—6 Americans, 3 Britons, an Italian, and a Kuwaiti. Among the Americans are 3 naval aviators, including Lieutenant Zaun (see January 20).

March 5.   Another 35 allied POWs—15 Americans, 9 Britons, 9 Saudis, 1 Kuwaiti, and 1 Italian—are released into the custody of the Red Cross in Baghdad. Bad weather prevents their departure for Riyadh until March 6, on which day 294 Iraqi POWs are flown to Baghdad. By week's end, the discovery of crash sites has reduced the number of Americans missing in action to 9, all aviators.

March 8–10.   The first American ground troops to return from the Gulf War receive heroes' welcomes upon their arrival in the United States.

First Division Marines roll into Kuwait International Airport in light armored vehicles on 27 February 1991, the final full day of Operation Desert Storm. A CH-53 Sea Stallion helicopter appears at right. *Department of Defense Still Media Records Center.*

March 31. **Dissolution of the Warsaw Pact.** In accordance with a decision reached on February 25, the members of the Warsaw Pact withdraw from the military alliance that had been imposed on them by the Soviet Union in 1955.

April 7–December 31, 1996.   **Aid to the Kurds (Operation Provide Comfort).** At the close of the Gulf War two oppressed minorities within Iraq, the Kurds in the north and the Shi'ite Muslims in the south, rebelled against Saddam Hussein. The uprisings scored some early successes, but within weeks both had been crushed. By the beginning of April more than a third of Iraq's Kurdish population is fleeing across the mountains along the country's northern frontiers. Approximately a million Kurds are allowed to enter Iran, but half a million are halted at the Turkish border. On April 7, the United States initiates Operation Provide Comfort to airdrop supplies to the refugees. Two days later British Prime Minister John Major proposes the insertion of an international force to create Kurdish "safe havens" in Iraq. President Bush endorses the idea, and on April 10, the United States, Great Britain, and France establish a no-fly zone above the 36th parallel. Any Iraqi aircraft detected north of this boundary will be subject to attack. By the end of May 20,000 U.S., British, French, Dutch, Spanish, and Italian troops have been deployed to southern Turkey and northern Iraq. Iraqi forces do not dispute their presence. The U.S. contingent, approximately 11,000 strong, includes the 24th Marine Expeditionary Unit (Special Operations Capable). The ground forces have been withdrawn from northern Iraq by July 15, but coalition aircraft will enforce the no-fly zone until Operation Provide Comfort is replaced by Operation Northern Watch in January 1997.

April 11.   The U.N. Security Council declares a permanent cease-fire formally ending the Gulf War. The economic sanctions imposed on Iraq in August 1990 remain in effect, and Saddam Hussein grudgingly agrees to neutralize existing stocks of chemical and biological weapons and to abort his program to develop nuclear weapons. Compliance with these requirements is to be monitored by U.N. arms inspectors. In the event, Iraq's repeated obstruction of the inspection process will give rise to much future unpleasantness.

April 30.   During the night of April 29–30, Cyclone Marian slams into the low-lying coast of Bangladesh with winds exceeding 145 miles per hour, killing 131,000 people and doing massive damage. When Prime Minister Khaleda Zia appeals for international assistance, American forces en route home from the Gulf War are diverted to the scene. Between May 15 and 29, an amphibious task force including the 5th Marine Expeditionary Brigade, aided by air force and army aircraft, delivers more than 4,500 tons of vitally needed supplies. Other units continue to render assistance until June 15. All told, Operation Sea Angel is estimated to have saved 30,000 lives.

June 15.   Rear Admiral Thomas C. Lynch becomes the 54th superintendent of the U.S. Naval Academy.

June 16–25.   On June 9, increased seismic activity in Mount Pinatubo, on the central Philippine island of Luzon not far from Clark Air Force Base, prompts a wise decision to move the base's population to the U.S. Naval Facility at Subic Bay, 21 miles from the volcano. Even before Pinatubo erupts on June 12, plans are made to transfer American dependents from overcrowded Subic. During Operation Fiery Vigil, 17 Seventh Fleet ships evacuate nearly 19,000 persons.

July 1.   General Carl E. Mundy, Jr., becomes the 30th commandant of the marine corps.

July 4.   The *Arleigh Burke* (DDG 51), name-ship of a new class of Aegis guided-missile destroyers, is commissioned at Norfolk, Virginia. Admiral Burke is present at the ceremony. The *Burke*s are intended to become the most numerous class of ships in the navy.

July 30.   Rolf Ekeus, chief of the U.N. arms inspectors in Iraq, reports that his teams have discovered four times as many chemical and biological weapons as Iraq had declared having.

July 31.   **START I.** At a meeting in Moscow, President Bush and President Gorbachev sign the Strategic Arms Reduction Treaty, which calls for cutting the U.S. and Soviet nuclear arsenals by 25 to 30 percent. According to the terms of the treaty, each nation is allowed 1,600 strategic nuclear delivery systems and 6,000 warheads, but warheads carried by aircraft are

The *Arleigh Burke* in high seas. *Official U.S. Navy photograph (PH3 James Collins).*

deliberately undercounted to encourage that mode of employment, since an aircraft is easier than a ballistic missile to recall. In reality, the United States will be left with approximately 9,000 warheads, and the Soviet Union with 7,000. The treaty contains rigorous provisions for on-site inspections.

September 8.   **Tailhook.** The worst scandal in the navy's history begins to unfold when Lieutenant Paula Coughlin, USN, a helicopter pilot serving as an admiral's aide, reports that she was groped during the Saturday night festivities at the 35th annual symposium of the Tailhook Association at Las Vegas, Nevada (September 5–8). A private, nonprofit organization dedicated to the support of "the aircraft carrier, sea-based aircraft . . . and aircrew," Tailhook has long enjoyed the approval of the Navy Department, and both the chief of naval operations and the secretary of the navy are among the 4,000 (2,000 registered) attendees. Unfortunately, the professional-development aspect of the symposium is eclipsed in the public perception by the bawdy revelries in a few of the squadron-sponsored hospitality suites on the third floor of the Las Vegas Hilton and the activities of the infamous "gauntlet" in the hallway outside them. Official support of the Tailhook Association is withdrawn, and major investigations are conducted by the Naval Investigative Service (NIS) and the Department of Defense Inspector General (DoD IG). The NIS investigation, held from October 11, 1991 to April 15, 1992, identifies 26 women (9 of whom decline to assist) as possible assault victims and 10 officers suspected of criminal behavior. The navy inspector general, who has conducted a parallel, noncriminal investigation, submits a complementary report on June 1, 1992, citing 33 officers for noncriminal abuses. The DoD IG investigation, requested on June 18, 1992, files reports on September 21, 1992 and April 13, 1993. It finds that 90 persons (including 7 males) were victims of indecent assault; charges 23 officers with indecent assault; accuses 117 officers of being "implicated" in indecent assault, improper conduct, or failure to restore good order; and alleges that 51 others made false official statements to investigators. The last Tailhook case is closed on June 3, 1994. By that date, 48 navy and marine corps officers have received nonjudicial punishment for indecent exposure, conduct unbecoming an officer, or making false statements, and 21 have been subject to lesser, administrative action. The remaining cases are dismissed for insufficient evidence. No one is court-martialed. The investigations' relatively muted outcome notwithstanding, Tailhook's consequences are profound. Careers are blighted or destroyed. The boorish behavior on the Hilton's third floor—by a statistically small portion of Tailhook attendees—reflects adversely on the navy as a whole, causing many observers to conclude that its institutional culture must be thoroughly overhauled. Sexual sensitivity training proliferates and the integration of women into the armed forces accelerates.

September 16.   All charges brought against retired marine Lieutenant Colonel Oliver L. North resulting from his involvement in the Iran-Contra affair are dropped.

September 16.   Despite the support of President Corazon Aquino, the Philippine senate rejects a treaty renewing the U.S. lease on the Subic Bay Naval Facility by a vote of 12 to 11. This decision ends a presence dating back to the Spanish-American War. The facility is formally relinquished on November 24, 1992.

September 27.   **Nuclear weapons reductions.** President Bush surprises the world by announcing that, since the Soviet Union no longer poses a creditable threat to Western Europe, the United States will withdraw its tactical nuclear weapons on the ground in Europe and Asia; take the Strategic Air Command's nuclear bombers off 24-hour alert; and remove all tactical nuclear weapons from the navy's surface vessels, attack submarines, and aircraft. The president adds that he hopes the Soviet Union will undertake corresponding weapons reductions. The next day President Gorbachev declares that the U.S. initiative will meet a positive response.

September 30.   The battleship *Wisconsin* (BB 64) is decommissioned.

November 15.   A federal appeals court reverses Rear Admiral John M. Poindexter's conviction on charges stemming from his role as a member of the National Security Council staff in the Iran-Contra affair.

December 8–21.   **Collapse of the USSR.** In the Soviet Union, the ties that bind have been steadily loosening ever since the breakaway of its former eastern European satellites. From August 19 to 21, President Gorbachev is detained by Communist hardliners in an attempted coup that fails when the Soviet military and special forces refuse to support it. Gorbachev's authority has been irreparably undermined, however, and Russian President Boris Yeltsin, who rallied resistance to the coup, emerges as Moscow's most powerful political figure. Gorbachev resigns as secretary general of the Communist Party of the Soviet Union on August 24, the same day that Ukraine declares its independence of the USSR. The Baltic republics of Estonia, Latvia, and Lithuania become independent on September 24, and on December 8, representatives of Russia, Ukraine, and Belarus (formerly Belorussia) declare that the Soviet Union is extinct and establish a loose federation called the Commonwealth of Independent States (CIS). Eight of the other former Soviet republics (but not the Baltic states and Georgia) join them in formalizing the new federation on December 21. Gorbachev resigns the presidency of the now nonexistent Soviet Union on the 25th. The free world has won the Cold War.

1992

February 1.   President Bush and President Boris Yeltsin sign a statement declaring that the United States and Russia "do not regard each other as potential enemies" and pledging to "work to remove any remnant of cold war hostility."

March 31.   The battleship *Missouri* (BB 63) is decommissioned.

June 22.   Secretary of the Navy H. Lawrence Garrett III resigns amid mounting media criticism of the navy's handling of the Tailhook scandal.

July 1–March 15, 1996.   **Aid to Bosnia (Operation Provide Promise).** The resurgence of suppressed nationalities in eastern Europe following the collapse of the Soviet colossus has spread to the Serb-dominated federation of Yugoslavia, which as organized at the end of World War II consisted of six republics: Serbia, Montenegro, Croatia, Slovenia, Bosnia-Herzegovina, and Macedonia. Between June 25 and December 23, 1991, four of the six—Croatia, Slovenia, Bosnia-Herzegovena, and Macedonia—opt for independence. The forcible opposition of the Yugoslav rump state, under the intransigent leadership of Serbian president Slobodan Milosevic, to the secession of all but Macedonia leads to a decade of violence and a substantial commitment of American forces. The fighting begins in Slovenia on June 27 and soon spreads to Croatia. By the time the European Community imposes an economic blockade on Yugoslavia on November 8, 12 cease-fires or other mediation attempts have failed. A new agreement negotiated by U.S. Special Envoy Cyrus Vance in January 1992 brings an end to large-scale hostilities, and a multinational U.N. Protection Force (UNPROFOR) is sent to Croatia to safeguard Serbian minorities. Croatia, Slovenia, and Bosnia-Herzegovina are recognized as independent states by the United Nations on May 22. In the meanwhile, however, fighting has broken out in Bosnia-Herzegovina, where on March 27 Bosnian Serb leaders proclaim the existence of a Serb Republic federated with Yugoslavia. Supported by the Yugoslav army, Bosnian Serb irregulars launch a barbaric campaign of "ethnic cleansing" of the Muslim and Croatian inhabitants. The U.N. Security Council calls upon all member states to provide humanitarian aid to Bosnia and on March 30 it imposes wide-ranging sanctions against Serbia, including an economic embargo and a ban on air traffic. On July 1 Washington orders the U.S. European Command to initiate relief flights into Bosnia. The first supplies are landed two days later. By the middle of the month, 16 nations have furnished aid. Navy carrier aircraft provide air cover for the air force transports that carry the American contributions until the commencement of Operation Deny Flight in April 1993.

July 4.   The nuclear-powered carrier *George Washington* (CVN 73), the sixth of the *Nimitz* class, is commissioned.

July 10.   General Manuel Noriega, the Panamanian strongman apprehended by U.S. forces at the conclusion of Operation Just Cause in January 1990, is sentenced to 40 years' imprisonment by a U.S. federal court in Miami, Florida, following his conviction on charges of drug trafficking, money laundering, and racketeering.

August 18–December 9.   **Aid to Somalia (Operation Provide Relief).** The overthrow of Mohammed Siad Barre, the long-time presidential dictator of Somalia, in January 1991 has plunged the impoverished nation into a state of anarchy as rival clans vie for power. Some observers estimate that by mid-1992 300,000 Somalis have starved to death and 1.5 million more are at risk. On this date President Bush directs U.S. Central Command to deliver 145,000 tons of food, medicine, and other vital supplies to the suffering Somalis. Ten days later Joint Task Force Provide Relief, composed primarily of U.S. Air Force personnel but initially commanded by marine Brigadier General Frank Libutti, commences supply flights from Mombasa, Kenya, to distribution sites in Somalia.

August 26.   **No-fly zone over southern Iraq (Operation Southern Watch).** In an attempt to protect the approximately 200,000 Shi'ite Muslim marsh dwellers in southern Iraq from attacks by Saddam Hussein, the U.N. Security Council establishes a no-fly zone, enforced by the United States, Great Britain, and France, below the 32nd parallel. Any Iraqi aircraft found south of this boundary are liable to be attacked. Coalition fighters continue to patrol the zone at the close of the decade.

September 14.   The U.N. Security Council authorizes the deployment of a protection force (UNPROFOR) to Bosnia-Herzegovina. There it will establish "safe areas" for Bosnian Muslims around six cities—Serajevo, Gorazde, Tuzla, Bihac, Srebenica, and Zepa, the last two of which subsequently fall.

September 22.   The U.N. General Assembly votes to expel Yugoslavia in condemnation of its role in the war in Bosnia-Herzegovina.

September 28.   **". . . From the Sea."** For more than four decades the naval service has viewed its principal missions in the context of the Cold War: to help deter the Soviet Union from attacking the West, and, should deterrence fail, to be prepared to fight a global nuclear war in which its command of the sea would be challenged by the Soviet fleet. The conclusion of the Cold War relegates these roles to history. This Department of the Navy white paper proposes to define new missions appropriate to a single-superpower world of declining military expenditures. Postulating that American command of the sea will remain uncontested for the foreseeable future, it holds that the sea services' primary role will be to support the projection of joint military force ashore in littoral areas during regional conflicts. A revised white paper, "Forward . . . From the Sea," released on November 9, 1994, emphasizes the deterrence of such conflicts by forward deployment (or, as it used to be called, gunboat diplomacy).

October 1. During an allied exercise in the Aegean Sea the carrier *Saratoga* (CV 60) accidentally fires two of her Sea Sparrow missiles. One strikes the bridge of the Turkish destroyer *Mauvenet,* killing her captain and four other crew members.

October 2. Sean O'Keefe becomes the 69th secretary of the navy.

December 9. **Intervention in Somalia (Operation Restore Hope).** On December 4, President Bush announces that the United Nations has accepted an American offer to safeguard the delivery of food and relief supplies in famine-stricken, strife-torn Somalia by sending troops to secure control of distribution centers. All forces are to be withdrawn by January 20, 1993. The first U.S. troops—Navy SEALs and recon marines, followed by elements of the 15th Marine Expeditionary Unit (Special Operations Capable)—come ashore at Mogadishu on this date. By the end of the month, more than 12,500 U.S. personnel are serving in Somalia, along with 6,000 other troops from 17 nations. The U.S. forces have accomplished their original, humanitarian mission, but Somalia remains in a state of anarchy and they will not be withdrawn in January.

December 27. A U.S. Air Force F-16D Fighting Falcon destroys an Iraqi MiG-25 that intrudes into the southern no-fly zone.

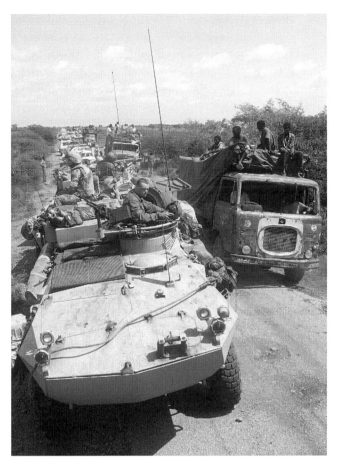

During Operation Restore Hope, a marine light armored vehicle escorts civilian workers delivering food near Baidoa, Somalia. *Official U.S. Navy photograph (PH1[AW] Joseph Dorey).*

1993

January 12. Marine PFC Domingo Arroya becomes the first U.S. serviceman to be killed in Somalia when his squad is ambushed by a Somali gang while on patrol near Mogadishu International Airport.

January 13. Thirty-five aircraft from the *Kitty Hawk* (CV 63) lead a coalition strike against 32 Iraqi SAM sites and air-defense control centers that, despite repeated warnings, have continued to direct their radars at planes patrolling the southern no-fly zone.

January 15–November 26, 1994. **Haitian migrant interdiction (Operation Able Manner).** On September 30, 1991, the legally elected president of Haiti, Jean-

Bertrand Aristide, who had entered office in February, was overthrown by the Haitian army. The chief of staff, General Manuel Cedras, held power until a civilian puppet government could be installed. In exile Aristide calls upon the international community for support. On October 11, 1991, the U.N. General Assembly demands that he be restored to office, and later that month the Organization of American States and the United States impose economic sanctions on Haiti. The shock to the Haitian economy produces a torrent of migrants who put to sea, often in poorly built, dangerously overcrowded vessels, with the aim of reaching the United States. Between September 1991 and January 1993 U.S. vessels interdict more than 40,000 migrants on the high seas. Operation Able Manner, carried out primarily by the U.S. Coast Guard, seeks to deter departures by maintaining patrols at the 12-mile limit of Haitian territorial waters, clearly visible from shore, as well as intercepting boats that manage to slip out. Some 25,177 migrants are taken into custody before democracy in Haiti is restored and the operation ends. Seventeen coast guard cutters and five naval vessels are employed.

January 17.   Three destroyers—the *Caron* (DD 970), *Hewitt* (DD 966), and *Stump* (DD 978)—launch a total of 45 Tomahawk cruise missiles at the Zaafaraniyah Nuclear Fabrication Facility near Baghdad, which is believed to be making parts for nuclear weapons. Forty-one missiles hit their targets.

January 18.   Seventy-five U.S., British, and French aircraft attack Iraqi SAM sites in the southern no-fly zone.

January 21.   Les Aspin becomes the 18th secretary of defense.

March 26.   **Mission creep in Somalia.** A trend already evident in December 1992 is confirmed by the U.N. Security Council's passage of Resolution 814, which transforms the United Nations' objective in Somalia from humanitarian relief to nation building. The latter is to include the disarmament of the clans' militias—private armies—a process that generates increasing friction in the region.

April 12–December 20, 1995.   **Air umbrella over Bosnia (Operation Deny Flight).** In response to a NATO recommendation, the U.N. Security Council passes Resolution 802, authorizing the imposition of a no-fly zone over Bosnia-Herzegovina to provide air cover for U.N. peacekeepers on the ground and to deny Bosnian Serb and Yugoslav forces the advantage of air support. U.S. Navy and Marine Corps aircraft flying from carriers in the Adriatic and the NATO air base at Aviano, Italy, take part in operation from the start. Operation Deliberate Force (see August 30, 1995) ends the campaign, which involves a total of 50,098 fighter, close air support, and strike sorties.

April 24.   The last U.S. Marine Corps units withdraw from Mogadishu. Marine strength in or offshore Somalia had peaked at 11,600 in January.

April 28.   Secretary of Defense Aspin announces that women will be allowed to fly combat aircraft and that he plans to recommend Congress lift the ban on the assignment of women to combat vessels.

May 4.   Lieutenant General Robert B. Johnston, USMC, formally transfers command of U.N. forces in Somalia to Turkish Lieutenant General Cevik Bir. Approximately four thousand U.S. Army troops remain in the country as part of Operation Restore Hope.

June 5.   In Mogadishu, Somalia, a detachment of Pakistani peacekeepers is ambushed and 24 of its members killed

by followers of General Mohamed Farah Aidid, one of the country's most powerful clan leaders. The U.N. Security Council responds with Resolution 837, which calls for the arrest of those responsible and the disarmament of "all Somalian parties." The ensuing search for Aidid will be conducted by elite U.S. Army troops requested by the senior U.N. official in Somalia, Special Envoy Jonathan Howe, a retired American admiral.

June 15–June 19, 1996.   **Adriatic blockade (Operation Sharp Guard).** To enforce a U.N. embargo on the shipment of arms to Yugoslavia and rival factions in Croatia and Bosnia, NATO Standing Naval Forces Mediterranean and other Western European Union naval formations establish a blockade in the Adriatic. Carrier- and land-based U.S. Navy and Marine Corps aircraft and navy surface ships and submarines, some with U.S. Coast Guard detachments embarked, participate in the operation. In November 1994 U.S. policy shifts to allow arms to reach the Bosnian Muslims. By the time the operation ends, some 73,000 vessels have been challenged and 7,200 inspected. The enforcement of the embargo on heavy weapons and military aircraft continues.

June 26.   The Aegis cruiser *Chancellorsville* (CG 62) and destroyer *Peterson* (DD 969) launch 23 Tomahawk cruise missiles at Iraqi Intelligence Service headquarters in Baghdad. The action is taken in response to the discovery that Iraq had plotted to assassinate former president George Bush during his visit to Kuwait in April. Sixteen Tomahawks score dead hits; four fall within the intelligence compound without striking their targets; and three impact adjacent residential districts.

The Aegis cruiser *Normandy* on patrol in the Adriatic during Operation Sharp Guard. *Official U.S. Navy photograph (PH1 David W. Hanselman).*

July 19.   President Clinton announces a new policy (effective on October 1) toward homosexuals in the armed forces, which is soon summarized as "Don't ask, don't tell." It states that although homosexual conduct will continue to constitute grounds for discharge, sexual orientation alone will not.

July 22.   John H. Dalton becomes the 70th secretary of the navy.

July 29.   In separate incidents, two navy EA-6B Prowlers fire high-speed antiradiation missiles (HARMs) at Iraqi SAM sites in the southern no-fly zone after being illuminated by the sites' target-acquisition radar.

September 1.   The Department of Defense releases its Bottom Up Review, a study intended to define the force levels sufficient to fight two major regional conflicts and one low-intensity conflict at the same time. The review calls for a 346-ship navy with 11 carrier battle groups, plus one training/reserve carrier battle group, and a marine corps of three divisions and three air wings with 174,000 active-duty personnel and 42,000 reserves. The proposed force contains far fewer than the 560 ships the Reagan administration had at the peak of its defense build-up, and it contains one carrier battle group fewer than the Bush administration had proposed.

September 11.   The 38-year-old *Forrestal* (CV 59), the navy's first "super carrier" (see October 1, 1955), is decommissioned.

October 3.   **Disaster in Mogadishu.** Task Force Ranger, approximately 400 U.S. Army airborne rangers and Delta Force commandos, is ambushed by a vastly superior number of Somalis during an attempt to seize General Mohamed Farah Aidid. Eighteen Americans are killed and 77 wounded in the most costly day's fighting for U.S. forces since the Vietnam War. Somali casualties are estimated at 300 dead and 700 wounded. The ensuing outcry in the United States prompts the Clinton administration to rethink its options.

October 7.   President Clinton announces that 1,700 more army troops are being sent to Somalia but that all U.S. forces will be withdrawn in six months. At the same time, the 13th and 22nd Marine Expeditionary Units (Special Operations Capable) are ordered to take station off Mogadishu.

October 18.   **Quarantine of Haiti (Operation Support Democracy).** The sanctions imposed by the United States and the Organization of American States in October 1991 have crippled the Haitian economy, but they have not achieved their objective of moving the Haitian military to accept the return of President Aristide; nor have negotiations conducted by the United States, the United Nations, the Organization of American States, and Aristide's own representatives. On this date, the U.S. Navy deploys Task Force 120 to establish an economic quarantine of Haiti. It is assisted by ships and aircraft of the U.S. Coast Guard and naval vessels from Argentina, Britain, Canada, France, and the Netherlands. The operation's most immediate effect is to exacerbate the migrant problem.

November 30.   President Clinton signs legislation authorizing the assignment of women to combat ships.

1994

February 3.   William J. Perry becomes the 19th secretary of defense.

February 27.   Lieutenant Shannon Workman, USN, is the first woman fighter pilot to become carrier qualified.

March 7.   Sixty-three women are detailed to the carrier *Dwight D. Eisenhower* (CVN 69), making them the first women to be permanently assigned to the crew of a combat vessel.

March 24.   **Withdrawal from Somalia.** In keeping with the program announced six months earlier, U.S. forces withdraw from Somalia in March. On this date, the last transport departs Mogadishu. The *Inchon* (LPH 12) and *Peleliu* (LHA 5) Amphibious Ready Groups are positioned offshore to support the movement, which, in the event, proceeds peacefully. Fifty-five marines of the fleet antiterrorist security team remain behind to guard the U.S. embassy until it is closed in September. Approximately 10,000 third-world U.N. troops also remain in Mogadishu.

April 9–12.   A task force of 330 marines from the 11th Marine Expeditionary Unit (Special Operations Capable) deployed in the *Peleliu* (LHA 5) Amphibious Ready Group, is flown 650 miles inland to Bujumbara, capital of the landlocked central African nation of Burundi, to safeguard the evacuation of foreign nationals fleeing the civil war in neighboring Rwanda (Operation Distant Runner). Some 230 persons, including 142 Americans, are assembled at the international airport and extracted by U.S. Air Force transports.

April 11.   In Bosnia, two marine corps F/A-18A Hornets bomb and strafe targets near the Gorazde safe area in support of U.N. peacekeepers.

April 23.   Admiral Jeremy M. ("Mike") Boorda becomes the 25th chief of naval operations. He is the first ex-enlisted man to attain the navy's highest post.

May 20–February 8, 1996.   The U.S. naval base at Guantánamo, Cuba, becomes the site of a major humanitarian operation, Sea Signal, as a tent city is erected to house the thousands of Haitian and, later, Cuban migrants being intercepted on the high seas until they can be processed for repatriation or asylum. Despite some unrest among the residents, order is maintained by U.S. Marines. At its peak population the camp contains some 30,000 people and during the operation more than 40,000 are processed.

June 1.   Marine Brigadier General Carol A. Mutter is promoted to the rank of major general, thereby becoming the first woman marine to wear two stars.

July 24–October 2.   Elements of the 15th Marine Expeditionary Unit (Special Operations Capable) are among 2,350 U.S. troops sent to support the United Nations' effort to aid a million refugees uprooted by a bloody civil war in Rwanda (Operation Support Hope).

August 1.   Admiral Charles R. Larson becomes the 55th superintendent of the U.S. Naval Academy, a position he had occupied as the 51st superintendent from 1983 to 1986. He will be the first man ever to perform two full tours in that post.

August 19–24.   A tightening of the U.S. policy granting asylum to refugees from Castro's Cuba launches a wave of would-be illegal emigrants who set out for Florida on anything that will float, including inner tubes. Operation Able Vigil is instituted to interdict the exodus. Like Able Manner, which it overlaps, the operation is jointly conducted by the U.S. Navy and Coast Guard. The crisis ends when the United States agrees to accept more emigrants and Castro pledges to curb unauthorized departures. By then, 30,224 Cubans have been intercepted by 38 cutters and 9 naval vessels in what is the coast guard's largest operation since the Vietnam War.

September 19.   **Intervention in Haiti.** Operation Support Democracy grows teeth as the United States prepares to implement U.N. resolutions calling for the restoration of Haitian President Jean-Bertrand Aristide—by force, if need be. The movement begins on September 12–13, when the carriers *Dwight*

D. Eisenhower (CVN 69) and *America* (CV 66) deploy to the Caribbean with elements of the 10th Mountain Division and army and navy helicopters embarked in place of their air wings. As finally constituted, Joint (Expeditionary) Task Force 190 numbers 24 ships and 20,000 troops, including 1,900 marines in Special Purpose Marine Task Force Caribbean. The Haitian military vows to fight, but at the last moment a U.S. negotiating team headed by former President Jimmy Carter, retired General Colin Powell, and Senator Sam Nunn convinces its leader, General Manuel Cedras, to bow out gracefully.

September 20.   Marines of Joint Task Force 190 land at Cap Haitien. Aside from a firefight in which 10 Haitian policemen are killed, the occupation is uneventful. The marines are relieved by members of the 10th Mountain Division 12 days later, and on March 31, 1995, U.S. units are replaced by the newly organized United Nations Mission in Haiti (UNMIH).

October 8–December 22.   **Deterring Iraq (Operation Vigilant Warrior).** President Clinton responds to the appearance of two Iraqi Republican Guard divisions just above the Kuwaiti border, allegedly on maneuvers, by warning Saddam Hussein not to underestimate American resolve and ordering U.S. forces into the region. The carrier *George Washington* (CVN 73) battle group reaches the Red Sea on December 10, and the *Tripoli* (LPH 10) Amphibious Ready Group, with the 15th Marine Expeditionary Unit (Special Operations Capable) embarked, takes position off Kuwait City. Additional naval forces, 20,000 members of the I Marine Expeditionary Force, the army's 4th Mechanized Division, and powerful air force formations are also ordered to the Persian Gulf. The Iraqi divisions withdraw.

October 25.   Navy Lieutenant Kara S. Hultgreen, the first woman pilot to become carrier-qualified in the F-14 Tomcat fighter, is killed when her F-14A loses power during an attempt to land on the *Abraham Lincoln* (CVN 72) while on exercises in the Gulf of Mexico. The aircraft's radar intercept officer survives.

November 21.   Marine corps aircraft supporting Operation Deny Flight take part in strikes against Ubdina airfield in Serb-occupied Croatia. Aircraft based at the airfield had attacked targets near the Bihac safe area in Bosnia.

1995

January 12. **Battleships stricken.** The four mothballed *Iowa*-class battleships are stricken from the Naval Vessel Register. This action would seem to spell an end to the battleship in the U.S. Navy, but events will prove that assumption incorrect.

February 27–March 3. **Evacuating Somalia (Operation United Shield).** Combined Task Force United Shield, commanded by Lieutenant General Anthony C. Zinni, USMC, covers the withdrawal of U.N. forces. A fleet of 21 ships from 6 nations stands offshore, including the *Essex* (LHD 2) Amphibious Ready Group and the Italian helicopter carrier *Garibaldi*. When only two units—a Pakistani regiment and a Bangladeshi battalion—are left, 1,850 U.S. Marines and 350 Italian marines land and establish a defensive perimeter to screen their embarkation. A few shots are fired and returned, but the evacuation is otherwise unopposed.

March 3. Lieutenant Commander Wendy Lawrence launches as a mission specialist aboard the Space Shuttle *Endeavour* and becomes the first woman naval aviator in space.

May 25–26. Marine corps aircraft take part in an attack on a Bosnian Serb ammunition dump near Pale, Bosnia.

June 8. **Rescue of Scott O'Grady.** On June 2, air force captain Scott O'Grady's F-16C Fighting Falcon was shot down by a Serb SAM while on an Operation Deny Flight patrol near Banja Luka, Bosnia. After six harrowing days on the ground, during which Serb search parties sometimes come within yards of his hiding places, O'Grady is rescued by a marine tactical recovery of aircraft and personnel (TRAP) team from the 24th Marine Expeditionary Unit (Special Operations Capable) embarked in the *Kearsarge* (LHD 3) Amphibious Ready Group in the Adriatic. The team's two CH-53E Sea Stallion helicopters are supported by AH-1 Cobra light-attack helicopters and AV-8 Harriers. Their return flight is made under fire from small arms, antiaircraft guns, and SAMs.

July 1. A new Fifth Fleet is established to exercise operational control over U.S. naval forces in the Persian Gulf and Indian Ocean. It is subordinate to U.S. Central Command.

July 30. General Charles C. Krulak becomes the 31st commandant of the marine corps.

August 4. Two EA-6B Prowlers from the carrier *Theodore Roosevelt* (CVN 71) and two marine corps F/A-18 Hornets from Aviano, Italy, launch high-speed antiradiation missiles (HARMs) at two Serb mobile SAM sites

A marine corps UH-1 Huey engaged in Operation United Shield lifts off from Moi International Airport at Mombasa, Kenya, where the U.S. Air Force maintained a logistical supply base. A CH-53 Sea Stallion appears at left. *Official U.S. Navy photograph (A1C Randy S. Mallard).*

Air Force Captain Scott O'Grady (center) immediately after landing on the *Kearsarge*. The helicopter is the CH-53 that plucked him from the hills of Bosnia. *Official U.S. Marine Corps photograph.*

near Knin and Ubdina, Croatia, after being illuminated by the sites' radar.

August 17.   **Deterring Iraq again (Operation Vigilant Sentinel).** The United States responds to Iraqi troop movements that threaten Kuwait and Jordan with another rapid deployment. The *Abraham Lincoln* (CVN 72) and *Independence* (CV 62) carrier battle groups and the *New Orleans* (LPH 11) Amphibious Ready Group, with the 13th Marine Expeditionary Unit (Special Operations Capable) embarked, take station off Kuwait, while the *Theodore Roosevelt* (CVN 71) stands ready in the eastern Mediterranean; U.S. Air Force units in Saudi Arabia are put on alert; and Maritime Prepositioning Squadron 2, carrying 30 days' supplies and equipment for 16,500 marines, is ordered from Diego Garcia to the Persian Gulf. The crisis gradually subsides.

August 30–September 21.   **Bombing campaign against the Bosnian Serbs (Operation Deliberate Force).** A mortar attack on Serajevo, the Bosnian capital and one of the four remaining (supposedly) safe areas, triggers a sustained NATO bombing offensive against Serb missile and radar sites, command posts, ammunition dumps, and communications facilities in southeastern Bosnia in an attempt to end the fighting. Carrier air wings from the *Theodore Roosevelt* (CVN 71) and, after September 12, the *America* (CV 66) and U.S. Marine Corps aircraft operating from Aviano, Italy, join U.S. Air Force and other NATO forces in the attacks. The

only allied loss occurs on the opening day, when a French Mirage 2000 is downed by a SAM. Its two crewmembers are captured and eventually released. A bombing pause is called on September 1, but diplomatic overtures prove fruitless and the campaign resumes on the 5th. On September 10, the Aegis cruiser *Normandy* (CG 60) enters the fray by launching 13 Tomahawk missiles, 11 of which strike within 10 feet of their aim points at an air-defense complex near Banja Luka. Altogether, a total of 3,515 sorties are flown and 48 targets with 338 aim points attacked. Coupled with an offensive by the Bosnian Muslims and the Croats in western Bosnia, the campaign encourages the Bosnian Serbs and their Yugoslav backers to enter negotiations that culminate in the signing of the Dayton Accords (see December 14).

September 26.   Marine First Lieutenant Sarah Deal completes training as a helicopter pilot and thereby becomes the corps's first woman aviator.

October 1.   The Marine Corps Warfighting Laboratory (MCWL)—originally the Commandant's Warfighting Laboratory—is activated at Quantico, Virginia. Its purpose is to develop and assess new concepts, tactics, and doctrine for possible adoption by the fleet marine force.

December 9.   The eighth *Nimitz*-class carrier, the *John C. Stennis* (CVN 74), is commissioned.

December 14.   **Dayton Accords.** This agreement, initialed by Serbian president Slobodan Milosevic and the presidents of Bosnia and Croatia at Dayton, Ohio, on November 21 and signed in Paris on this date, ends the war in Bosnia-Herzegovina. Under its provisions, the country becomes a federation of two nearly autonomous components, the Serb Republic and the Federation of Bosnia-Herzegovina, the latter inhabited mainly by Bosnians and Croats, and U.N. peacekeepers are relieved by a NATO Implementation Force (IFOR) whose 60,000 members include 20,000 U.S. troops.

1996

January 1.   Admiral Arleigh Burke, the three-time CNO often called the father of the modern navy, dies at the age of 94.

January 22.   **Battleships in contention.** The Department of Defense appropriations act signed on December 1, 1995, prohibits the use of any funds to restore to the

Naval Vessel Register the four *Iowa*s, which the navy declares are too expensive to maintain in mothballs. That provision notwithstanding, the defense authorization bill signed on this date requires the navy to reinstate the two best-preserved *Iowa*s in the register. The navy requests clarification, pending which the *Iowa* (BB 61) and *Wisconsin* (BB 64) are to be retained as Category B Mobilization Assets.

March 5–24.   When the People's Republic of China announces its intention to close part of the Taiwan Strait to conduct live-firing exercises on the eve of Taiwan's presidential election, the United States responds by hurrying the *Nimitz* (CVN 68) and *Independence* (CV 62) carrier battle groups to the scene. A Department of Defense official characterizes the deployment as a "physical manifestation of our commitment to defend Taiwan."

April 20.   The *Guam* (LPH 9) Amphibious Ready Group, with the 22nd Marine Expeditionary Unit (Special Operations Capable) embarked, is rushed to Monrovia, Liberia, after armed intruders enter the U.S. embassy compound there. Besides reinforcing the embassy guard, the marines supervise the evacuation of 49 U.S. citizens and more than 1,200 foreign nationals in Operation Assured Response.

May 16.   **Death of Admiral Boorda.** Admiral Jeremy M. Boorda, chief of naval operations, shoots himself in the midst of a journalistic investigation of his entitlement to wear "Combat V" devices on the ribbons of the Navy Commendation and Navy Achievement Medals. Boorda had been awarded the medals for services in the destroyer *John R. Craig* (DD 885) and the guided-missile frigate *Brooke* (FFG 1) off Vietnam in 1965 and 1971–73. He had stopped wearing the devices in 1995 when told by his staff judge advocate general that he did not qualify for them, but regulations in force at the time of the awards make the question a murky one. Following Boorda's death, Admiral Elmo R. Zumwalt, Jr., a former chief of naval operations who had commanded Naval Forces Vietnam from 1968 to 1970, states that the he was eligible for the devices, and Secretary of the Navy Dalton places a memorandum to that effect in Boorda's personnel file; but, despite the use of the words "combat operations" in the citation of the first medal and "combat mission" in that of the second, in June 1999 a review board rules that he was not authorized to wear them. In a last letter "To My Sailors," Boorda writes, "What I am about to do is not very smart but it is right for me.

The *Seawolf* on sea trials. *Electric Boat Corporation (Jim Brennan).*

. . . I don't expect any reporters to believe I could make an honest mistake. . . . I love our Navy so much, and you who are the heart and soul of our Navy, that I couldn't bear to bring dishonor to you." Under fire from critics who charged that he was sacrificing the navy's interests to the dictates of political correctness, Boorda had recently told family members that he intended to resign his position in August, midway through his tour as CNO.

May 21.   The 22nd Marine Expeditionary Unit (Special Operations Capable), embarked on the amphibious assault ship *Guam* (LPH 9), is directed to evacuate American and other nationals threatened by disturbances in the landlocked Central African Republic. During Operation Quick Response, marine Aerial Refueler Transport Squadron 252 extricates 208 U.S. citizens and 240 foreign nationals from the capital city of Bangui, 1,500 miles from the sea.

June 13.   **AAAV.** The marine corps awards General Dynamics a contract to develop prototypes of an Advanced Amphibious Assault Vehicle (AAAV). The new amphibian is to be capable of 20 to 25 knots at sea and 69 to 72 kilometers on hard road surfaces, and to carry 17 or 18 marines. Projections call for the corps to procure 1,013 AAAVs through the year 2012.

July 5.   The *Seawolf* (SSN 21) returns from her first sea trials. Admiral Bruce DeMars, director of the navy's nuclear propulsion program, describes her as "the fastest, the quietest, [and] the most heavily armed submarine in the world." Unfortunately at $2.1 billion each, the *Seawolf* is also the most expensive submarine in the world, and after much soul-searching Congress, which had originally called for twenty-eight submarines, caps the class at three.

July 10.   Promotion to the rank of vice admiral makes Patricia Tracey the first woman in the U.S. armed forces to wear three stars. Marine Major General Carol A. Mutter, who had been nominated for her third star seven weeks earlier than Admiral Tracey, is promoted to lieutenant general on July 23.

August 5.   Admiral Jay L. Johnson becomes the 26th chief of naval operations.

September 3–4.   **Missile attack on Iraq (Operation Desert Strike).** Troop movements suggest that Saddam Hussein is preparing to invade the Kurdish sanctuaries in northern Iraq under the protection of Operation Provide Comfort. The United States registers its disapproval by missile strikes against 15 air defense installations in southern Iraq. Thirty-one Tomahawks are launched from naval vessels—6 from the Aegis cruiser *Shiloh* (CG 67), 23 from the destroyers *Laboon* (DDG 58), *Russell* (DDG 59), and *Hewitt* (DD 966), and 2 from the submarine *Jefferson City* (SSN 759)—and 13 other cruise missiles from USAF B-52s flying from

Guam. U.S. analysts are disappointed in the results; although all the targets have been hit, none is completely destroyed.

September 4.   President Clinton extends the no-fly zone over southern Iraq from the 32nd to the 33rd parallel. Britain agrees to the extension, but France declines to participate in patrols above the original boundary.

1997

January 1.   **Operation Northern Watch.** The enforcement of the no-fly zone over northern Iraq, which originated under Operation Provide Comfort in 1991, is renamed Operation Northern Watch. France opts out, protesting that the operation will no longer be tied to protecting the Kurds. The United States and Great Britain continue to maintain the no-fly zone into the next century.

January 18.   **Super Hornet.** An F/A-18F makes the first Super Hornet carrier landing during sea trials aboard the *John C. Stennis* (CVN 74). The navy chose to develop the Super Hornet as its next-generation fighter-

The Aegis cruiser *Shiloh* launches its first Tomahawk cruise missile at Iraq from the northern Persian Gulf on the morning of September 3, 1996, the first day of Operation Desert Strike. *Official U.S. Navy photograph.*

attack aircraft following the cancellation of the A-12 in 1991. There are two models: the F/A-18E, a single seater, and the F/A-18F, a two seater. Much more than a mere upgrade of the F/A-18C/D Hornet, the new aircraft is 25 percent larger, mounts more weapons, and has significantly greater range, payload, surviv-ability, and growth capacity. Some 800–1,000 are ex-pected to be built before the advent of the Joint Strike Fighter in 2010.

January 24.   William S. Cohen becomes the 20th secretary of defense.

March 13–17.   Early this month Albania is plunged into an-archy by a catastrophic financial collapse. The 26th Marine Expeditionary Unit (Special Operations Capa-ble), embarked in the *Nassau* (LHA 4) Amphibious Ready Group in the Adriatic as a strategic reserve for the U.S. peacekeepers in Bosnia, is put on standby, and on the 13th U.S. Ambassador Mirisma Lima requests it to reinforce the Tirana embassy guard and begin evacuating American and other foreign nationals. Ma-rine helicopters touch down in the embassy's housing compound within two hours and commence airlifting refugees to the amphibious transport dock *Nashville* (LPD 13). The next day the choppers come under spo-radic ground fire, but this dwindles after an AH-1 Cobra eliminates an Albanian who is aiming a shoul-der-fired SAM. In all, 877 refugees are flown to safety in Operation Silver Wake. A marine detachment re-mains at the embassy until the arrival of a fleet an-titerrorist unit on April 29.

May 19.   Secretary of Defense Cohen announces the re-sults of the first Quadrennial Defense Review, a study undertaken to define the force levels needed to fight two simultaneous regional conflicts at any time be-tween this date and the year 2015. So far as the navy is concerned, it calls for the retention of 12 carrier bat-tle groups and 12 amphibious ready groups, and the construction of a tenth *Nimitz*-class carrier to replace the aging *Kitty Hawk* (CV 63). However, the number of surface warships is to be reduced from the current 128 to 116 and the number of attack submarines from 73 to 50.

May 30–June 4.   Rapacious soldiers run riot through the streets of Freetown, Sierra Leone, threatening the lives of several hundred American citizens, after a military revolt overthrows the legally elected government. By happy chance, the *Kearsarge* (LHD 3) Amphibious Ready Group, with the 22nd Marine Expeditionary Unit (Special Operations Capable) embarked, has been

An F/A-18 Super Hornet loaded for aerial combat. On each wingtip it carries an AIM-9 Sidewinder air-intercept missile. The next inboard weapon's station carries an AIM-7 Sparrow missile, and the next two each carry two AIM-120 AMRAAMs (Advanced Medium-Range Air-to-Air Mis-siles). *The Boeing Company.*

standing off Zaire since May 2, ready to evacuate Americans should the fighting in the civil war raging there approach Kinshasa, the country's capital. The force is rushed to Sierra Leone, and more than 22 countries request American assistance in extricating their nationals. Despite the military government's pro-hibition of foreign overflights, marines and sailors se-cure a landing zone on Freetown's harbor, and marine CH-53 Super Stallions begin ferrying foreigners to the *Kearsarge*. More than 2,500 persons, including 451 Americans, are evacuated in Operation Noble Obelisk.

July 21.   **Old Ironsides under sail.** Following a three-year, $12-million restoration, the historic frigate *Constitution* puts to sea under her own power for the first time in 116 years to celebrate her 200th anniversary.

1998

January 12.   Iraq's Saddam Hussein precipitates yet an-other crisis in the Persian Gulf by denying a U.N. in-spection team headed by Scott Ritter, a former U.S. Marine Corps captain, entry to a suspected weapons site. In the following weeks, more than 27,000 Amer-ican and British troops are concentrated in the region in readiness for action against Iraq. They include 2,200

The frigate *Constitution* under sail in Massachusetts Bay, July 21, 1997. *Official U.S. Navy photograph (JO2 Todd Stevens).*

members of the 24th Marine Expeditionary Unit (Special Operations Capable) deployed with the *Guam* (LPH 9) Amphibious Ready Group. U.N. Secretary General Kofi Annan defuses the crisis—for the time being—on February 23 by persuading Saddam to allow the arms inspectors unrestricted access to Iraqi facilities.

February 3.   A marine corps EA-6B Prowler flying far below the prescribed altitude on a training mission from the air base at Aviano, Italy, severs the cable of a ski resort gondola near Cavalese in the Dolomites, sending 20 civilians hurtling 300 feet to their deaths. The tragedy triggers demonstrations throughout Italy protesting the American presence.

February 12.   **Battleships reinstated.** Pursuant to the Department of Defense authorization bill of January 22, 1996, the battleships *New Jersey* (BB 62) and *Wisconsin* (BB 64) are restored to the Naval Vessel Register. The *Iowa* (BB 61) is to be retained as a source of spare parts.

February 26–April 3.   Joint Task Force Kenya, in which all four armed services are represented, delivers more than 800 tons of food and supplies to the flood-ravaged African nation in Operation Noble Response.

May 4.   The battleship *Missouri* (BB 63), on whose deck Japan signed the instrument of surrender at the end of World War II, is formally transferred to the USS *Mis-*

souri Memorial Association. She is to be preserved on Battleship Row in Pearl Harbor.

June 6.   When a border dispute between Eritrea and Ethiopia turns nasty, elements of the 11th Marine Expeditionary Unit (Special Operations Capable), deployed with the *Tarawa* (LHA 1) Amphibious Ready Group, evacuate 105 American and 67 other foreign nationals from Asmara, Eritrea, in two C-130 Hercules transports (Operation Safe Departure).

June 12.   **Land Attack Destroyer (DD 21).** The navy signs a preliminary agreement with rivals Bath Iron Works and Ingalls Shipbuilding for a new type of a destroyer (DD 21) especially suitable for deployment in joint littoral warfare as well as operations on the high seas. The winning design is to be announced on March 31 2001. The *Zumwalt* class, as it is to be known, will replace the *Perry*-class guided-missile frigates and *Spruance*-class destroyers presently in service. A total of 32 vessels are to be built, with the first delivery to take place in 2010. Among the ship's notable features will be a 155-mm Advanced Gun System (AGS) with a range of 100 nautical miles.

July 25.   The carrier *Harry S. Truman* (CVN 75) is commissioned.

August 7.   **Embassy bombings.** Nearly simultaneous bomb blasts rock the U.S. embassies at Nairobi, Kenya, and Dar-es-Salaam, Tanzania. Altogether, 256 persons, including 12 Americans, are killed and more than 1,100 injured.

August 20.   **Retaliation.** U.S. intelligence quickly links the embassy bombings to a terrorist network directed by a renegade Saudi multimillionaire, Osama bin Laden. On this date, naval vessels launch more than 75 Tomahawk cruise missiles at bin Laden's training camps in eastern Afghanistan and 6 others at a pharmaceutical factory at Khartoum, Sudan, believed to be producing chemical weapons. Approximately 60 terrorists are killed and wounded in the camps, and the factory is heavily damaged. After the attack the Sudanese government protests that the factory produced only pharmaceuticals.

November 14.   The cat-and-mouse game in the Persian Gulf continues when on October 31 Iraqi President Saddam Hussein again violates the terms of the Gulf War ceasefire by suspending all official contact with the U.N. arms inspection teams. The United States and Great Britain respond, as they had at the beginning of the year, by building up military forces in the region. An air strike on Iraq is scheduled for this date. Twenty minutes before it is to begin, Saddam announces a (short-lived) change of heart. Iraq will cooperate with the arms inspectors.

November 16.   Richard Danzig becomes the 71st secretary of the navy.

December 16–19.   **Air strikes on Iraq (Operation Desert Fox).** For more than a year, Saddam Hussein has persistently obstructed the activities of the U.N. arms inspectors. Following a report by Richard Butler, the British head of the inspection teams, detailing Iraqi intransigence, duplicity, and deceit, President Clinton orders "a strong, sustained series of air strikes" against Iraq. They begin about 11:00 P.M. (Gulf time) on the 16th, only hours after the last inspectors have left the country. The first night's attacks are entirely a navy show, and the women sailors in the *Enterprise* (CVN 65) become the first in the U.S. Navy to engage in combat operations as the carrier's aircraft add to the destruction wrought by approximately 250 Tomahawk missiles launched by seven surface vessels and a submarine. Subsequently, air force B-52s launch another 90 missiles. Twelve Royal Air Force GR-1 Tornado fighter-bombers and six reconnaissance planes also participate in the strikes. Targets include barracks, headquarters buildings, command-and-control facilities—particularly those associated with the Republican Guard—and weapons research, development, and storage sites. By the close of the operation, U.S. and British aircraft have flown 650 attack missions and naval vessels have launched more than 325 Tomahawks. No aircraft have been lost, and it is estimated that 70 to 80 percent of the targets have been damaged or destroyed. Successful as Desert Fox has been as a military exercise, however, it fails to convince Saddam Hussein to mend his ways. The arms inspectors are not re-admitted.

December 19.   The marine guard at the U.S. embassy in Damascus, Syria, uses tear gas to disperse a threatening mob that has broken into the embassy compound to protest Operation Desert Fox.

Between waves of air strikes against Iraq during Operation Desert Fox, aviation ordnancemen load a Sidewinder air-to-air missile aboard an F/A-18 Hornet of navy Fighter-Attack Squadron 105 on the flight deck of the *Enterprise*. *Official U.S. Navy photograph (PHAN Jason D. Malcom).*

1999

January 4. The battleship *Iowa* (BB 61) replaces the *New Jersey* (BB 62), whose guns were damaged during her demilitarization in 1995, on the Naval Vessel Register. The latter is to be preserved as a memorial and museum at Camden, New Jersey.

January 24. **Northern Watch action.** A marine corps EA-6B Prowler and two air force F-16CJ Fighting Falcons fire high-speed antiradiation missiles (HARMs) at an Iraqi SAM site near Mosul that has illuminated them with its radar. This is among the earliest incidents in a year in which, after eight years of acquiescence, Iraq aggressively challenges the enforcement of the northern no-fly zone. On more than a hundred occasions Iraqi antiaircraft batteries or SAM sites fire at or illuminate coalition aircraft, which reply with HARMs or laser-guided bombs. In 2000 the number of incidents falls to 30.

February 17. The final flight of Antarctic Development Squadron (VXE) 6 marks the end of the navy's presence in Antarctica. Established in 1955 to support U.S. and New Zealand bases on the coast of the Ross Sea, the squadron logged more than 200,000 flight hours.

March 24–June 10. **NATO air war with Yugoslavia (Operation Allied Force).** The relative peace that settled over the territories of the former Yugoslavian federation with the conclusion of the Dayton Accords late in 1995 did not last long. By the middle of 1998 Serbian regular and paramilitary forces controlled by Slobodan Milosevic, president of Yugoslavia since 1997, are engaged in another ugly conflict, this time in the Serbian province of Kosovo. The Yugoslav constitution of 1974 had granted Kosovo autonomy. Milosevic revoked this autonomy soon after entering office in 1989 and in the following years steadily subordinated the province to the authority of the central government. The resulting resentment among the province's largely ethnic Albanian inhabitants gave rise in 1996 to the Kosovo Liberation Army (KLA), a guerrilla (some say terrorist) organization whose attacks on Serbian government forces are countered by a ruthless program of pacification and "ethnic cleansing." The latter inflames public opinion in the United States and western Europe, already horrified by revelations of atrocities committed during the ethnic cleansing of Bosnia. A NATO show of aerial force (Operation Determined Falcon) on June 14, 1998, obviously an invitation to Milosevic to reflect on the Bosnian bombing

campaign, has no effect. A cease-fire arranged in October has collapsed by January, and a NATO-sponsored attempt to negotiate a settlement at Rambouillet, France, in February proves unsuccessful. Following Milosevic's rejection of a last-minute U.S. peace plan on March 23, NATO authorizes air strikes against Yugoslavia. The Senate approves U.S. participation by a vote of 58 to 41. This will be the first time in its 50-year history that NATO has engaged in hostilities.

The attacks begin at 8:00 P.M. (local time) on this date. Sixty NATO aircraft including U.S. Marine Corps F/A-18 Hornets and navy EA-6B Prowlers fly from Aviano, Istrana, and Gioia del Colle, Italy, to attack airfields, radar sites, command and control centers, army installations, and assorted other targets throughout Yugoslavia. Their efforts are seconded by Tomahawk missiles launched by the Aegis cruiser *Philippine Sea* (CG 58), the guided-missile destroyer *Gonzalez* (DDG 66), the destroyers *Nicholson* (DD 982) and *Thorn* (DD 988), and the submarines *Miami* (SSN 755) and *Norfolk* (SSN 714) in the Adriatic. No carrier is on hand until April 3, when the *Theodore Roosevelt* (CVN 71) reaches the scene. Its air wing will fly 4,270 of a total of 38,000 NATO combat sorties.

In succeeding weeks the target list expands to include troop units, arms and aircraft factories, power plants, oil refineries and storage facilities, bridges, radio and television transmitters, government and party offices, and one of President Milosevic's two Belgrade residences, which is believed to have a command bunker in its basement. During the same period allied air strength increases from the original 400 to 1,050 planes from 14 of NATO's 19 nations. The U.S. contingent—723 aircraft—constitutes 69 percent of the total force, flies 53 percent of all strike sorties and delivers 80 percent of all ordnance. NATO command of the air is virtually absolute. Recurrent antiaircraft fire and an occasional SAM are largely ineffective, and by March 30 more than half of Yugoslavia's 15 MiG-29s have been shot down, 3 on the first night—2 by U.S. Air Force F-15 Strike Eagles and 1 by a Royal Netherlands Air Force F-16 Fighting Falcon. Aside from an unmanned reconnaissance plane, only one NATO aircraft is lost, a USAF F-117A Nighthawk stealth fighter hit by a SAM on March 27, and both airmen are rescued.

Sadly, the effects of NATO's aerial supremacy are slow to influence events in Kosovo. Serbian army units lie low, and the state police and paramilitary forma-

An F-14 Tomcat of navy Fighter Squadron 14 launches from the *Theodore Roosevelt* in the Adriatic on June 9, 1999, the penultimate day of Operation Allied Force. *Official U.S. Navy photograph (PH2 Jonathan Byrd).*

tions accelerate their brutal campaign of ethnic cleansing, a process with which, in the absence of ground controllers, NATO warplanes are only intermittently able to interfere. At the commencement of Operation Allied Force, 45,000 ethnic-Albanian Kosovars had sought refuge in Albania and Macedonia; by its conclusion, 855,000 have done so.

The campaign continues for 78 days. Its duration disconcerts some analysts, who, taking Operation Deliberate Force as a model, had anticipated a quick decision; but in the context of Serb nationalism Kosovo is much more important than Bosnia-Herzegovina. In the end, however, Milosevic is compelled to come to terms. Serb forces evacuate the province, which regains its autonomy and is occupied by 50,000 U.N. (including 7,000 U.S.) peacekeepers constituting Kosovo Force (KFOR); the refugees are urged to return, and a three-mile-wide demilitarized zone is established along the Yugoslav border. The first unit to reach the U.S. occupation zone is Battalion Landing Team 3/8 of the 26th Marine Expeditionary Unit (Special Operations Capable). It is relieved by the army's 1st Infantry Division early in July.

April 19. **Vieques.** Two wayward bombs dropped by a marine F/A-18 Hornet kill a civilian security guard, David Sanes Rodriguez, at the navy's live-firing target range on Vieques, a 52-square-mile island municipality (population 9,400) off the east coast of Puerto Rico. The incident galvanizes all three Puerto Rican political parties to unite in demanding the closure of the fir-

ing range, which has been in use since 1946. The navy counters that the range is vital to its training programs. Exercises are suspended but protests continue as negotiations begin.

May 14. **Osprey.** The marine corps formally accepts the first of four approved, initial-production standard models of the long-awaited MV-22 Osprey tilt-rotor aircraft with which it plans to replace its aging CH-46 Sea Knight and CH-53 Sea Stallion helicopters. The corps is scheduled to acquire a total of 360 Ospreys.

May 17. Navy F/A-18 Hornets and air force A-10 Thunderbolt IIs patrolling the southern no-fly zone respond to Iraqi ground fire by attacking antiaircraft artillery and SAM sites.

June 16. Iraqi antiaircraft fire provokes an attack by navy F/A-18 Hornets and British GR-1 Tornadoes on two radar sites and a SAM site in the southern no-fly zone.

July 1. General James L. Jones, Jr., becomes the 32nd commandant of the marine corps.

July 18. Navy F-14 Tomcats, F/A-18 Hornets and air force F-16 Fighting Falcons respond to Iraqi antiaircraft fire at planes patrolling the southern no-fly zone by attacking a SAM site.

August 10. Iraqi antiaircraft fire and a SAM launch in the southern no-fly zone provoke another retaliatory action, in which Navy F-14 Tomcats, F/A-18 Hornets, and air force F-16 Fighting Falcons strike antiaircraft artillery positions and radar sites.

An E-2C Hawkeye of Carrier Airborne Early Warning Squadron (VAW) 124 receiving the Go signal to launch from the *Theodore Roosevelt* in the Persian Gulf, July 30, 1999. The carrier was deployed in support of Operation Southern Watch. *Official U.S. Navy photograph (PHAN Jeremy Hall).*

An MV-22 Osprey, rotors tilted up, sets down on the landing helicopter dock ship *Essex* during operational trials off the coast of California in February 2000. *Official U.S. Navy photograph (PH 3 Jason A. Pylarinos).*

September 2.   **New Attack Submarine (NSSN).** The keel is laid on the *Virginia* (SSN 774), the first of a new class of Tomahawk-armed nuclear attack submarines designed with a view to littoral as well as blue-water operations. She is to be delivered in 2004. A total of 30 *Virginia*-class boats are scheduled to be built over a period of 18 years, gradually replacing the *Los Angeles* class.

October 7–November 26.   The *Belleau Wood* (LHA 3) Amphibious Ready Group, with the 31st Marine Expeditionary Unit (Special Operations Capable) embarked, is assigned to support International Force Timor, an Australian-led U.N. peacekeeping force. Widespread violence had erupted following a referendum (August 30) in which East Timor voted for independence from Indonesia, when forces opposed to independence sought to terrorize the local populace. On October 26 the *Belleau Wood* group is relieved by the *Peleliu* (LHA 5) Amphibious Ready Group with the 11th Marine Expeditionary Unit (Special Operations Capable) embarked. These and other marine units revisit East Timor the following year to signal continuing U.S. support of the territory's transition to nationhood.

November 17.   A navy F/A-18 Hornet on patrol in the southern no-fly zone launches missiles against an Iraqi radar site that had locked on it.

December 31.   In accordance with the treaty concluded in September 1977, the last U.S. forces withdraw from the Panama Canal Zone.

2000

January 31.   The White House announces that an agreement has been reached with the government of Puerto Rico regarding the navy's Vieques firing range. U.S. forces can use the range until May 2003, but their ordnance must be inert; for its part, Vieques will receive a $40 million aid package and 8,000 acres of the naval reservation. Prior to February 2002 there is to be a referendum (subsequently scheduled for November 6, 2001) in which the residents of Vieques will determine the island's future. A decision to allow the navy to stay and use live ammunition will be rewarded by another $50 million of economic aid.

April 8.   One of the marine corps's new MV-22 Ospreys crashes near Marana, Arizona, with the loss of all 19 persons on board. All Ospreys are grounded pending an investigation, which attributes the loss to a combination of human factors.

May 6.   The destroyer *Stump* (DD 978) becomes the first vessel to use the Vieques firing range since April 1999.

May 25.   The marine corps allows its Ospreys to resume flights, but until more operational experience is acquired they are to carry only aircrew.

July 21.   Admiral Vern Clark becomes the 27th chief of naval operations.

August 8.   The Confederate submarine *H. L. Hunley* is raised from the bottom of Charleston harbor and taken ashore to undergo state-of-the-art conservation. The first submarine to sink an enemy vessel (see February 17, 1864), she had been located in 1995 by the National Underwater and Marine Agency (NUMA), a private organization founded by bestselling author Clive Cussler.

October 4.   Yugoslavian president Slobodan Milosevic, the man most responsible for the wars in Slovenia, Bosnia, and Kosovo, is overthrown in the streets of Belgrade after trying to fudge the results of an election that he clearly lost. His successor, the election's real winner, is Vojislav Kostunica, a politically moderate anticommunist. He assumes office on October 7.

October 12.   **Attack on the Cole.** Two hours after entering port at Aden, Yemen, to take on fuel, the *Arleigh Burke*–class destroyer *Cole* (DDG 67), en route from Norfolk, Virginia, to the Persian Gulf, is struck by a small craft carrying two terrorists and several hundred pounds of high explosives. The blast rips a hole 40-feet square in the *Cole*'s port side amidships. Seventeen sailors are killed and 39 wounded. A magnificent effort by the ship's crew keeps her afloat. On October 29 the crippled destroyer is taken aboard the Norwegian commercial heavy-lift ship *Blue Marlin* to be transported to the United States and rebuilt. No terrorist group claims responsibility for the attack, but American suspicions center on the network headed by Osama bin Laden.

October 30.   **Reputations.** For years interested citizens have advocated the official rehabilitation of three officers whom they believe were made scapegoats at the end of World War II: Admiral Husband E. Kimmel and Lieutenant General Walter C. Short, respectively commander in chief, Pacific Fleet, and commander of the Hawaiian Department at the time of the attack on Pearl Harbor, and Captain

The destroyer *Cole*, the sizeable hole in her port side clearly visible, rests atop the Norwegian heavy-lift ship *Blue Marlin* at Aden on October 30, 2000, at the beginning of her voyage home. *Official U.S. Navy photograph (AESC Pat S. Draham).*

Charles B. McVay III, commanding officer of the heavy cruiser *Indianapolis* (CA 35) when she was sunk by a Japanese submarine (see July 29, 1945). Kimmel and Short were the only World War II commanders not permitted to retire in their highest wartime ranks, and McVay was the only captain court-martialed for the loss of a ship as a result of enemy action. On this date, their supporters' campaign is crowned with success when President Clinton signs the National Defense Authorization Act for Fiscal Year 2001. A "Sense of Congress" resolution included in the bill asserts that Kimmel and Short "were not provided with necessary and critical intelligence" prior to the attack on Pearl Harbor and McVay was not culpable in the sinking of his ship. The resolution proposes that Kimmel and Short be restored to their highest ranks and McVay's personnel record be amended to reflect "that he is exonerated for the loss of the USS *Indianapolis.*"

December 11.   A marine corps MV-22 Osprey crashes after completing night training exercises near Jacksonville, North Carolina, killing all four crewmen. All Ospreys are again grounded pending an investigation. The findings identify specific mechanical problems but no fundamental flaw in tilt-rotor technology.

December 16.   **JSF.** The Lockheed Martin demonstrator of the JSF X-35C, the carrier variant of the Joint Strike Fighter being developed in competition with Boeing for the U.S. and British armed forces, makes its first flight. The X-35C is scheduled to join the fleet, where it will complement the F/A-18E/F, in 2010. A short take-off/vertical landing (STOVL) variant, the JSF X-35B, is intended for the U.S. Marine Corps, the Royal Navy, and the Royal Air Force.

2001

January 13.   The future of the Vieques firing range is cast into doubt when the newly elected governor of Puerto Rico, Sila Maria Calderon of the Popular Democratic Party, repudiates the agreement reached in January 2000 and asks President Clinton to order an immediate end to firing exercises. The issue remains unresolved at the time the administration of President George W. Bush enters office on January 20.

January 26.   Donald W. Rumsfeld becomes the 21st secretary of defense. He had held the same post from 1975 to 1977.

February 9.   **Greeneville incident.** Nine miles south of Oahu, Hawaii, the submarine *Greeneville* (SSN 772) demonstrates a rapid-surfacing maneuver ("emergency blow") to a party of 16 civilians aboard for the day on the navy's Distinguished Visitor Program. Unfortunately, the submarine's officers are unaware that a 190-foot Japanese trawler, the *Ehime Maru,* is entering the area. The *Greeneville*'s rudder smashes through the trawler's stern and the vessel sinks within minutes with the loss of 9 of the 35 persons aboard. At the ensuing court of inquiry, a fire-control technician reveals that he did not inform the submarine's captain, Commander Scott Waddle, that his sonar equipment showed a surface vessel approaching because he did not believe the reading could be correct; but it also becomes clear that some of the safety precautions required before a rapid-surface drill were rushed. On April 23, at an admiral's mast held by Admiral Thomas Fargo, commander-in-chief of the Pacific Fleet, Commander Waddle receives a letter of reprimand and a suspended sentence of a 50 percent reduction in pay for two months. He is to retire by October 1.

February 16.   **Air strike on Iraq.** Twenty-four U.S. and British warplanes, including F/A-18 Hornets from the U.S. carrier *Harry S. Truman* (CVN 75), attack five air-defense sites in southern Iraq. The raid was provoked by recent improvements in the Iraqi radar net, which have increased the danger to Northern and Southern Watch patrols. Four of the sites are above the 33rd parallel, the northern boundary of the southern no-fly zone. This is the first time that positions outside the no-fly zone have been hit since Operation Desert Fox in December 1998.

March 4.   The nuclear carrier *Ronald Reagan* (CVN 76), ninth of the *Nimitz* class, is christened by Mrs. Reagan. This ship is the first naval vessel to be named for a living ex-president.

March 12.   Five U.S. servicemen and a New Zealand army officer are killed and three other Americans seriously injured when an F/A-18C Hornet from the carrier *Harry S. Truman* (CVN 75) accidentally releases three 500-pound bombs prematurely during Operation Desert Spring, a multinational live-fire exercise in northern Kuwait.

April 1.   Former Yugoslav president Slobodan Milosevic, whom the U.N. tribunal at The Hague has indicted for war crimes in Kosovo, is arrested by state police following a 26-hour standoff outside his Belgrade villa. The United States had threatened to suspend

$100 million in economic aid to Yugoslavia unless Milosevic was taken into custody by March 31. On April 2, the Bush administration certifies that Yugoslavia is eligible for continued aid, even though President Kostunica has announced that his government will try Milosevic for corruption and abuse of power rather than surrender him to the War Crimes Tribunal. Secretary of State Colin Powell emphasizes, however, that U.S. support of an international donors conference on aid to Yugoslavia scheduled for June will depend on "continued progress."

April 1. **EP-3 Incident.** At approximately 9:05 A.M. (local time), two Communist Chinese J-8 fighters begin to harass a navy four-engine EP-3E Aries II electronic surveillance plane over the South China Sea some 70 miles southeast of Hainan island. This is nothing unusual; Chinese fighters had intercepted and often harassed American intelligence-gathering flights on 43 previous occasions since December. Today, however, one of the J-8s, overtaking the American aircraft from below and to port, comes too close and the EP-3's outboard propeller chops it in half. The Chinese pilot ejects but is not recovered. None of the U.S. plane's 24 crewmembers are injured, but two of its engines are disabled and it plummets 8,000 feet before the pilot, Lieutenant Shane Osborn, succeeds in regaining control. He then lands at the Lingshui military airfield on Hainan. During the flight and the first 15 minutes on the ground, the crew manages to complete its checklist for the destruction of classified materials and equipment. China interns the aircraft and crew and demands that the United States apologize for the incident and cease flying patrols off its coast. The Chinese claim the EP-3 caused the collision; that it had violated Chinese air space, which China insists extends for 200 miles from its shore (rather than the internationally recognized 12 miles); and that the EP-3 did not have permission to land, despite the fact that the pilot had declared a "Mayday" and sent at least 15 distress signals, any one of which is considered under international law to clear the sender to land on the nearest airfield. Intense negotiations eventuate in a carefully crafted letter of April 9 stating that the United States is "very sorry" the Chinese pilot was lost and the EP-3 landed without clearance. The crew is freed two days later. Although a U.S. technical team determines that the aircraft is repairable, China refuses to allow it to depart under its own power but specifies on May 28 that it may be disassembled and flown off in a Russian transport.

April 4.   The navy disables the last remaining stock of napalm bombs in the United States.

April 12.   The navy informs the Puerto Rican government that it plans to hold training exercises on the Vieques firing range—the first since December 2000—commencing on April 27.

April 24.   Governor Sila Maria Calderon signs a bill just passed by the Puerto Rican legislature restricting permissible environmental noise to a decibel level that would preclude the navy's use of the Vieques firing range. Minutes later, she files suit on behalf of the Puerto Rican government against the U.S. Navy and Department of Defense for allegedly breaking a promise to suspend exercises there until federal health authorities could examine the possibility that the noise levels they produce could be responsible for cardiovascular abnormalities detected in study samples of Vieques children and fishermen. The governor also asks navy and DoD officials to postpone the planned exercise.

April 25.   With the exercise still scheduled to start in two days, Governor Calderon seeks a temporary restraining order from the U.S. district court in Washington, D.C. On April 26, Judge Gladys Kessler denies the request, explaining that the attorneys for Puerto Rico failed to show that Vieques residents would be "irreparably harmed" by the proceedings.

April 27–May 1.   **Vieques protests.** Hundreds of activists from Puerto Rico and the U.S. mainland converge on Vieques to protest firing exercises conducted by the *Enterprise* (CVN 65) carrier battle group and the *Kearsarge* (LHD 3) amphibious ready group. On several occasions the training program is delayed by the need to round up protesters who have made their way into the firing range to act as human shields. Among 183 persons arrested and charged with trespassing are U.S. Representative Luis Gutierrez (D-Ill.); environmental lawyer and activist Robert F. Kennedy Jr.; Puerto Rican Independence Party President Ruben Berrios; and civil rights leader Reverend Al Sharpton.

May 1.   **Missile defense.** Speaking at the National Defense University in Washington, D.C., President Bush declares that the United States should construct a missile defense system to shield it and its allies from small-scale attacks by rogue states (read: North Korea, Iran, and Iraq) and at the same time reduce its offensive nuclear arsenal. The president acknowledges that the deployment of such a system would be incompatible with the terms of the Anti-Ballistic Missile (ABM) Treaty concluded with the Soviet Union in May 1972, but he argues that the treaty has become irrelevant to American security needs: "[It] does not recognize the present or point to the future. It enshrines the past." Administration spokesmen suggest that a partial defense system could become operational by 2004. Critics charge that the development of an effective missile defense is technologically infeasible and would likely incite a new nuclear arms race. After early talks with U.S. emissaries, Russia, China, and NATO register disapproval.

May 7. The United States resumes intelligence flights in international air space off the coast of China. An unarmed, unescorted air force RC-135 from Kadena Air Base on Okinawa completes its mission without encountering Chinese aircraft.

May 24. Gordon R. England becomes the 72nd secretary of the navy.

June 5. At a hearing of the Congressional Hispanic Caucus, a number of protesters arrested on Vieques on April 28, including Representative Gutierrez, testify that they were treated inhumanely by security personnel. Navy spokesmen deny that anyone was mistreated.

June 12. The future of the DD 21 land-attack destroyer is cast into doubt when a panel on military effectiveness appointed by Secretary of Defense Rumsfeld reports that the vessel would not be a substantial improvement over existing platforms.

June 15. Vieques settlement. In a press conference at the Pentagon, Secretary of the Navy England states that the navy will discontinue using the Vieques firing range in May 2003. Accordingly, he will ask Congress to cancel the referendum scheduled for November 2001 and will name a panel of experts to locate another training site. The decision to give up the facility had been announced by President Bush two days earlier, following a meeting in which Secretary England broached the idea to senior White House staff. Those opposed to the use of the range protest that it should be closed forthwith; conservative Republicans protest that it should not be closed at all.

June 18–19. Some 30 persons, among them Mrs. Jackie Jackson, wife of Reverend Jesse Jackson, are arrested for trespassing after cutting their way through the fence or otherwise infiltrating the Vieques bombing range in an attempt to disrupt exercises being conducted by the *Theodore Roosevelt* (CVN 71) carrier battle group.

June 23. An international conference on Yugoslavia is scheduled to convene at Brussels, Belgium, on June 29. Fearful of losing millions of dollars in badly needed economic aid unless it complies with prospective donors' demands to transfer former president Milosevic to the U.N. War Crimes Tribunal at The Hague, the Serbian cabinet drafts a decree authorizing his extradition.

June 28. Serbia surrenders Milosevic. The Yugoslav Constitutional Court, whose members were appointed by Milosevic, suspends the decree allowing him to be extradited until it rules on the measure's legality. The Serbian government responds by flying him to the NATO base at Tuzla, Bosnia, from which he is immediately transported to the War Crimes Tribunal jail at Scheveningen, near The Hague. President Kostunica, who was not consulted, denounces the action as unconstitutional. Milosevic will be the first former head of state tried by the War Crimes Tribunal.

June 29. At Brussels, the United States and other Western nations pledge 1.28 billion dollars in economic aid for Yugoslavia.

July 5. Return of the EP-3. In accordance with an agreement reached with the People's Republic of China, the navy EP-3 forced to land on Hainan island on April 1 has been disassembled and a giant Russian Antonov (AN)-124 transport chartered to carry it to the United States. On this date, the Russian transport flies the EP-3 to Dobbins Air Reserve Base at Marietta, Georgia. The aircraft is to be reassembled by Lockheed Martin and returned to service.

July 12. In conformity with a congressional resolution contained in the 2001 defense authorization act signed by President Clinton on October 30, 2000, Secretary of the Navy England directs that a document be placed in the personnel record of Captain Charles B. McVay III exonerating him for the loss of the heavy cruiser *Indianapolis* (CA 35) in 1945.

July 16. The Navy–National Oceanic and Atmospheric Administration *Monitor* 2001 Expeditions Team raises the 30-ton steam engine of the Civil War ironclad *Monitor,* which had sunk in a storm while under tow off Hatteras Island, North Carolina, on December 31, 1862. On March 30 of that year she had engaged the CSS *Virginia* in the first battle between ironclad warships. Her wreck had been located in 1974. The engine will be conserved and displayed at The Mariners' Museum in Newport News, Virginia.

July 29.   On Vieques, 81 percent of 5,893 voters participate in a nonbinding referendum called by Governor Calderon in advance of the congressionally sanctioned referendum scheduled for November 6 on whether the navy should continue to use the island's firing range. Sixty-eight percent vote that the navy should close the range at once and withdraw from the island; 30 percent vote that the navy should stay and resume using live ordnance; and 1.7 percent vote to uphold the existing arrangement, according to which the range will remain open until May 2003.

August 10.   A significant increase in Iraqi anti-aircraft fire and missile launches at coalition aircraft patrolling the southern no-fly zone provokes what is officially described as a routine strike against communications, radar, and missile sites southeast of Baghdad. Fifty U.S. and British planes, including F-14 Tomcats and F/A-18 Hornets from the *Enterprise* (CVN 65), take part. Altogether, Operation Northern and Southern Watch aircraft have conducted more than 25 strikes in the no-fly zones this year to date.

September 11.   **Attack on America.** The most shocking act of terrorism ever perpetrated is put into execution when, beginning at 8:27 A.M. EDT, 19 Middle Eastern men seize control of four airliners: United Airlines Flight 175, a Boeing 767 en route from Boston to Los Angeles; American Airlines Flight 11, another 767 flying the same route; American Airlines Flight 77, a Boeing 757 en route from Dulles International Airport, Virginia, to Los Angeles; and United Airlines Flight 93, another 757 en route from Newark, New Jersey, to San Francisco. American Flight 11 crashes into the North Tower of New York's World Trade Center at 8:48 A.M. United Flight 175 strikes the South Tower at 9:05. The intense heat produced by the burning aviation fuel wilts the buildings' steel skeletons and the South Tower collapses at 9:50; the North Tower follows at 10:29. Meanwhile, at 9:40, American Flight 77 slams into the side of the Pentagon. United Flight 93 is also believed to have been bound for Washington, but it never reaches there. The passengers, learning of the crashes by in-flight telephone calls, tackle the hijackers and at 10:03 the plane goes down in a field near Shankesville, Pennsylvania, some 80 miles southeast of Pittsburgh. All 266 persons aboard the four aircraft perish. Another 125 die at the Pentagon. The number killed at the World Trade Center, initially estimated at 6,000, is finally set at 2,830—more than in the attack on Pearl Harbor. No group asserts responsibility for the outrage, but suspicion immediately centers on al-Qaeda ("the Base"), an international terrorist organization founded in 1994 by the Saudi militant Osama bin Laden with the aim of eliminating American influence in the Middle East.

September 12.   A U.N. Security Council resolution calls upon all nations to collaborate in apprehending those responsible for the September 11 attacks.

September 12.   In a television address to a stunned nation, President George W. Bush declares war on terrorism.

September 15.   The hospital ship *Comfort* (T-AH 20) docks in Manhattan to assist at the disaster site. She had been activated in Baltimore on the 12th and returns there early in October.

September 16.   **Ultimatum to the Taliban.** Addressing a joint session of Congress, President Bush confirms that Osama bin Laden's al-Qaeda is responsible for the atrocities of 9/11, as well as the bombing of the U.S. embassies in Kenya and Tanzania in 1998 and the attack on the USS *Cole* (DDG 67) in 2000. Al-Qaeda's headquarters and training camps are located in Afghanistan, where bin Laden enjoys a cozy relationship with the Taliban, a Muslim fundamentalist regime that seized power in 1996 from the Northern Alliance (also known as the United Front) during a still-simmering civil war. Declaring that those who shelter or support terrorists are as culpable as the terrorists themselves, the president demands that the Taliban close al-Qaeda's training camps and surrender bin Laden to the United States. The Taliban prevaricates.

September 30.   **QDR.** Although largely completed by September 11, the second Quadrennial Defense Review calls for the "transformation" of the U.S. armed services to enhance their ability to counter "asymmetrical" (terrorist) threats. Friends are to be reassured and potential foes deterred by forward-deployed forces in "critical regions"—Europe, Northeast Asia, the East Asian littoral, and the Middle East/Southwest Asia. Military strength will be maintained at a level sufficient to win two overlapping major conflicts and a limited number of contingency operations. The Navy Department's share of the base force is set at 12 carrier battle groups, 12 amphibious ready groups, 108 (plus 8 reserve) surface combatants, 55 attack submarines, 3 marine divisions, and 3 marine air wings.

October 2.   NATO's secretary general, Lord Robertson, declares that "clear and compelling" evidence presented by the United States has satisfied its 18 NATO allies that al-Qaeda is responsible for the attack on

America. By this date the Bush administration has obtained the approval or active support of virtually every government in the world for its campaign against al-Qaeda in particular and terrorism in general.

October 7. America strikes back (Operation Enduring Freedom). Time runs out for the Taliban at 9:30 P.M. local time (12:30 P.M. EDT), when U.S. and British aircraft and 50 sea-launched Tomahawk cruise missiles attack 31 targets in or around six Afghan cities—Kabul, Kandahar, Jalalabad, Herat, Mazar-e Sharif, and Konduz. The strike force is composed of 15 U.S. long-range bombers—B-1B Lancers and B-52 Stratofortresses flying from Diego Garcia in the Indian Ocean and B-2 Spirits from Whiteman Air Force Base, Missouri—and 25 F-14 Tomcats and F/A-18 Hornets from the carriers *Carl Vinson* (CVN 70) and *Enterprise* (CVN 65). The naval air wings' sorties are the longest ever flown by carrier aircraft and the B-2s' the longest ever flown by any aircraft. The Tomahawks are launched by the Aegis cruiser *Philippine Sea* (CG 58), the Aegis destroyers *John Paul Jones* (DDG 53) and *McFaul* (DDG 74), the destroyer *O'Brien* (DD 975), a *Los Angeles*–class submarine, and a British attack submarine. Targets include airfields, air defense sites, command-and-control centers, troop concentrations, al-Qaeda training camps and facilities, and the Kandahar residential compound of the Taliban's reclusive leader, Mullah Mohammad Omar. Another nighttime strike on 13 targets by a lesser number of aircraft and 15 more Tomahawks follows on October 8, and the first daylight raids take place on the 9th. Thereafter the bombardments become round-the-clock, with the *Enterprise* staging operations after dark. Command of the air is quickly achieved. None of the Taliban's approximately 20 fighters attempts to challenge the attackers and anti-aircraft fire, and some SAMs score no hits. Not a single manned aircraft will be lost to enemy action before the Taliban is toppled. Although USAF F-15E Strike Eagles flying from an "undisclosed location" appear mid-month, carrier aircraft continue to form by far the most numerous element of each day's attacks. By the time the *Carl Vinson* is relieved by the *John C. Stennis* (CVN 74) on December 15, her airwing will have flown 4,200 sorties and dropped two million pounds of bombs.

On the ground, the Taliban commands an estimated 40,000 seasoned fighters. The majority are deployed against its old enemy, the Northern Alliance, which retains control of the northernmost ten percent of the country and has about 15,000 men under arms. The bombing campaign is intended to enable the Northern Alliance to take the offensive. The alliance duly does so, and on October 16 its forces reach the outskirts of Mazar-e Sharif, a sizeable city and strategic road junction in northeastern Afghanistan, but on the 21st they are pushed back. As days and then weeks pass with no new ground action, some analysts begin to worry that tactical bombing will not be effective against the Taliban's technologically unsophisticated, relatively dispersed forces and that if, as a last resort, the United States sends an army into Afghanistan, it will become embroiled in the same sort of guerilla war the Soviet army was unable to extinguish during its decade-long occupation of the country (1979–1989). There are also concerns that to continue bombing during the Muslim holy month of Ramadan, which begins on November 16, will alienate friendly Muslim nations and that, in any event, the onset of the fierce Afghan winter will shut down operations before a decision can be reached.

None of these fears is realized. The war's Muslim supporters raise no serious objection to the prosecution of hostilities during Ramadan; the pace of operations outstrips the advent of winter; and tactical bombing proves extremely effective. The bombing campaign succeeds because it's directed by small numbers of U.S. special forces—at peak strength, no more than 300—serving as forward ground controllers with the Northern Alliance. As recently as the Gulf War, smart bombs accounted for only about 6 percent of those expended; in Afghanistan, they account for more than 90 percent. Even so, accidents happen. On December 5, for example, three U.S. and six Afghan troops are killed and many others wounded when, as a result of human error or mechanical failure, a B-52's satellite-guided 2,000-pound bomb impacts 100 yards from their position. On the whole, however, the accuracy attained is unparalleled in the history of warfare.

October 12. The carrier *Kitty Hawk* (CV 63) arrives in the northern Arabian Sea, minus most of her air wing, to serve as an advanced base for joint special forces.

October 18. Four terrorists found guilty of the 1998 African embassy bombings are sentenced in U.S. district court in New York to life imprisonment without parole.

October 26.　Lockheed Martin is awarded the contract for the systems development and demonstration phase of the F-35 Joint Strike Fighter (JSF). Pratt and Whitney is to provide the engines. The F-35 is intended to remain the world's best strike aircraft through 2040.

October 28–November 4.　**Targeting change.** In the course of this week, the emphasis of the bombing campaign in Afghanistan shifts from Taliban and al-Qaeda fixed assets, virtually all of which have already been hit, to the front-line formations opposing the Northern Alliance. The results are soon apparent.

November 1.　**DD(X) vice DD 21.** The *Zumwalt*-class DD 21 land attack destroyer program is terminated. Work done on the project will be applied to the development of a family of combatants—the DD(X) destroyer, CG(X) cruiser, and a smaller littoral combat ship.

November 5.　**The Northern Alliance takes the offensive.** Just as growing numbers of commentators begin to conclude that the war is not going well, the Northern Alliance renews its advance on Mazar-e Sharif—and, in a week, overruns half of Afghanistan. Mazar-e Sharif is occupied on November 9; four provincial capitals to its west are taken on the 10th; Herat is captured on the 12th; Konduz is encircled that same day; and Kabul, the nation's capital, is entered unopposed on the 13th. No doubt encouraged by these successes, another anti-Taliban grouping, the Eastern Alliance, captures Jalalabad on the 14th and Ghazni a day later. The speed of the Northern Alliance's advance alarms some western policymakers almost as much as it does the Taliban. Afghan politics are divided along tribal lines. The Northern Alliance is largely composed of Tajiks, Uzbeks, and Hazaras, but southern and eastern Afghanistan are inhabited mainly by Pashtuns, and it is feared that an attempt by the alliance to impose an exclusionary government will invite civil war. Fortunately, the alliance proclaims the intention to form an inclusive government, and on November 18 it agrees to send representatives to a U.N.–sponsored conference on the future of Afghanistan.

November 13–27.　**Siege of Konduz.** The last Taliban stronghold in northern Afghanistan is stoutly defended by a force estimated to include 3,000 of the foreign zealots—Arabs, Pakistanis, and Chechens—who offer the stiffest resistance throughout the campaign. Heavy and repeated U.S. air strikes contribute materially to the capture of the city and the surrender of some 6,000 Taliban.

November 13.　President Bush and Russian president Vladimir Putin agree to reduce their countries' strategic nuclear arsenals by two-thirds. This will leave the United States and Russia with 1,700 to 2,200 warheads apiece.

November 14.　**Advance on Kandahar.** In southern Afghanistan two Pashtun tribal forces move against Kandahar, the spiritual center of the Taliban regime—one from the southeast under Gul Agra Shirzai, an erstwhile governor of the city, and the other from the northeast under Hamid Karzai, a relative of the exiled King Mohammad Zahir Shah. Shirzai reaches the international airport, 12 miles south of the city, on December 2 but, despite U.S. air support, is forced to fall back a day later.

November 25.　**Marines ashore.** Some 200 members of the 15th Marine Expeditionary Unit (Special Operations Capable) helicopter from the amphibious assault ship *Peleliu* (LHA 5) to seize a forward operating base in southern Afghanistan. The site is a deserted airfield, soon christened Camp Rhino, 55 miles south of Kandahar. Within a week, more than 1,000 troops from the 15th and 26th Marine Expeditionary Units (Special Operations Capable)—the latter from the *Bataan* (LHD 5) amphibious ready group—are on the scene. Their mission is to interrupt Taliban communications by offensive ground and air patrolling.

November 25–28.　**Prison revolt.** Some 600 foreign Taliban captured at Konduz on the 24th are incarcerated in Qalai Janghi fort, a 19th-century mud work six miles west of Mazar-e Sharif. The next day they rush their

Members of the 15th Marine Expeditionary Unit (Special Operations Capable) survey their camp's perimeter from a light armored vehicle during the advance to Kandahar. *Official U.S. Marine Corps photograph (Sgt. Joseph R. Chenelly).*

guards and seize control of the fort. The uprising is suppressed with the aid of air strikes directed by U.S. and British special forces. Aside from a number who take refuge in underground chambers, virtually all the Taliban are killed. Four U.S. servicemen are wounded and Johnny "Mike" Spann, a CIA officer and former marine captain who had been interrogating the prisoners, becomes the first American to die in combat in Afghanistan. Northern Alliance casualties are 40 dead and 100 wounded.

November 26.   Marine AH-1W Super Cobra helicopters based on Camp Rhino direct an attack by F-14s from the carrier *Carl Vinson* (CVN 70) on a Taliban column of approximately 15 armored vehicles.

December 1.   Eighty-four dispirited Taliban emerge from the bowels of Qalai Janghi. Among them is John Walker Lindh (recently, "Abu Hamid"), a 20-year-old Californian convert to Islamic fundamentalism whom Mike Spann had questioned shortly before the revolt.

December 4.   **Tora Bora.** A new front opens when the Eastern Alliance advances against an estimated 2,000 al-Qaeda Arab fighters literally holed up in Tora Bora, a sophisticated cave complex in the White Mountains 55 miles southwest of Jalalabad. U.S. intelligence believes that Osama bin Laden is in the area, and aircraft have been pounding it for several days. The aerial bombardment is intensified to support the Eastern Alliance offensive.

December 5.   A motorized column, including light armored vehicles, of the 15th Marine Expeditionary Unit (Special Operations Capable) rolls north from Camp Rhino to interdict Taliban road traffic below Kandahar.

December 5.   The United States and Russia state that they have reduced the number of their strategic nuclear weapons to the levels prescribed by the START I Treaty.

December 6.   **New Afghan government.** Representatives of four Afghan factions meeting under U.N. auspices at Koenigswinter, Germany, agree on an interim government headed by the Pashtun leader Hamid Karzai. At the end of six months a *loya jirga* (grand council) is to convene to form a new government that will hold free elections within two years.

December 7.   **Capture of Kandahar.** Negotiations conducted by Hamid Karzai lead to the unopposed occupation of Kandahar. Native Taliban foot soldiers are to surrender their weapons and return to their homes.

Although pockets of resistance remain, the Taliban regime, which many observers were convinced would prove so formidable, has ceased to exist on Day 62 of the war. Unfortunately, its leader, Mullah Mohammad Omar, is among the diehards who escape.

December 7.   The marines operating south of Kandahar destroy a three-vehicle convoy that tries to break through one of their checkpoints. Seven suspected Taliban or al-Qaeda are killed.

December 12.   Multiple malfunctions cause an air force B-1B bomber inbound for Afghanistan to go out of control over the Indian Ocean and the crew ejects 30 miles north of Diego Garcia. A navy P-3 Orion and an air force KC-10 Extender circle the four airmen until they are rescued two hours later by the guided missile destroyer *Russell* (DDG 59).

December 12.   **Vieques settlement (II).** In October the Navy Department postponed the November referendum on the Vieques training range until January 2002. On this date the House and Senate Armed Services Committee passes a resolution, promptly approved by Congress, canceling the referendum and prohibiting the facility from being abandoned until the navy and marine corps can certify that they have identified an equally suitable alternative site.

December 13.   The U.S. government releases a home video discovered in Jalalabad of a recent meeting between Osama bin Laden and a fundamentalist Muslim cleric. During their conversation bin Laden gleefully takes credit for the attack on America.

December 13.   President Bush formally notifies Russia that the United States plans to withdraw from the 1972 Anti-Ballistic Missile (ABM) Treaty.

December 14.   **Marines reach Kandahar.** The column from Camp Rhino, reinforced two days earlier by elements of the 26th Marine Expeditionary Unit (Special Operations Capable), occupies Kandahar International Airport. The next day the marines start to build a temporary prison camp capable of holding 300 al-Qaeda and foreign Taliban detainees. The first inmates enter the facility on December 18.

December 16.   The Eastern Alliance claims victory in Tora Bora. Some 200 Taliban and al-Qaeda have been killed and 11 captured, and as many as 2,000 are believed to be in flight. In succeeding weeks U.S. and British special forces join the Afghans in searching the caves in the area. Numerous bodies and a good deal of military equipment are discovered, but no trace is found of Osama bin Laden.

December 17.   The U.S. mission in Kabul, which had been closed on January 31, 1989, immediately following the Soviet withdrawal from Afghanistan, is reopened.

December 22.   Hamid Karzai officially enters office as interim prime minister of Afghanistan.

December 27.   Secretary of Defense Donald Rumsfeld announces that the al-Qaeda and Taliban in U.S. custody will be transferred to the naval base at Guantánamo, Cuba. A two-and-one-half acre prison cage named Camp X-Ray is quickly extemporized.

December 30.   The Pentagon reports that the 101st Airborne Division will relieve the marines at Kandahar.

2002

January 9.   A KC-130R Hercules of Marine Aerial Refueler/Transport Squadron (VMGR) 352 goes down near Shamsi military airfield in southwestern Pakistan. All seven marines on board are killed.

January 11.   The first 20 of the 371 Taliban and al-Qaeda detainees held by the United States are flown to Guantánamo. By February 12 the number in confinement there has grown to 254.

January 12.   A letter to the commandant of the marine corps alleging that the inquiries into the MV-22 Osprey crash in April 2000 had been mishandled prompts a new investigation of the Osprey program.

January 19.   Marine forces transfer control of Kandahar International Airport to the 101st Airborne Division. Their withdrawal is completed when the last elements of the 26th Marine Expeditionary Unit (Special Operations Capable) return to the *Bataan* (LHD 5) amphibious ready group on February 8.

January 20.   Two marines are killed and five injured when their CH-53E Super Stallion helicopter crashes shortly after takeoff from Bagram air base, Afghanistan.

January 21.   U.S. and British aircraft answer Iraqi fire at Operation Southern Watch patrols by striking an anti-

An F/A-18 Hornet of Marine Fighter-Attack Squadron 314—the "Black Knights"—returns to the *John C. Stennis* after completing a mission in support of Operation Enduring Freedom on February 21, 2002. *Official U.S. Navy photograph (PHAN Michael Arteaga).*

aircraft artillery emplacement at Tallil, 170 miles southeast of Baghdad.

January 29.   In his State of the Union address, President Bush declares that Iran, Iraq, and North Korea constitute an "axis of evil" that the United States "will not permit . . . to threaten us with the world's most destructive weapons."

February 4.   Iraqi fire at Operation Northern Watch patrols provokes an attack by U.S. and British aircraft on air defense sites northeast of Mosul.

February 4.   The Bush administration's budget calls for $379 billion of $2.13 trillion to be allocated to defense—5.6 percent of the total and 14 percent ($48 billion) higher than in 2001. This would represent proportionally the greatest increase in defense spending since the first Reagan administration.

February 28.   For the second time this year, U.S. and British aircraft patrolling the no-fly zone over northern Iraq respond to ground fire by striking air defense installations north of Mosul.

Glossary

Brig A sailing vessel having two square-rigged masts

Caique A type of sailing vessel common to the eastern Mediterranean, characterized by a high bow and rounded stern

Carronade A short-barreled, short-ranged naval gun used in the late eighteenth and early nineteenth centuries, which was extremely destructive at close quarters

Gundalow A barge with single mast; sometimes spelled *gondola*

Felucca A lateen-rigged coasting vessel found principally in the Mediterranean

Frigate In the Age of Sail, a ship having a single enclosed gundeck. (The upper deck would also carry a number of guns, but it was not counted as a gundeck.) These vessels were designed to carry from 28 to 44 guns; resourceful captains often added others.

Lugger A Northern European coasting vessel distinguished by her rig, each mast carrying a single, four-sided sail, called a lug sail, suspended from an oblique spar

Master An obsolete naval rank between midshipman and lieutenant, introduced in 1837 and replaced by that of lieutenant (junior grade) in 1883

Master Commandant Another obsolete naval rank, intermediary to lieutenant and captain, replaced by that of commander in 1838

Naval Cadet The term used in lieu of midshipman from 1882 until 1902

Polacre A three-masted, Mediterranean vessel on which the foremast is lateen-rigged and the main and mizzenmast are square-rigged; sometimes spelled *polacca*

Schooner A sailing vessel with two or more masts rigged fore-and-aft

Ship In strict sailing terminology, a vessel having three or more square-rigged masts and a bowsprit

Ship of the line In the Age of Sail, naval vessels were divided into six "rates" or classes according to the number of guns they carried. The first three classes, vessels considered sufficiently powerful to take their place in the line of battle, were called ships of the line (first, second, or third rate). These vessels had two or three gundecks and carried at least 64, but usually more guns. Frigates were fifth and sixth rates.

Ship sloop A ship-rigged sloop of war

Sloop A small sailing vessel having a single mast rigged fore-and-aft

Sloop of war A generic term used during the Age of Sail to describe any small, cruising vessel, regardless of her rig, carrying fewer guns than a frigate, usually under 20

Spar torpedo A weapon used by small craft, mostly Confederate, during the Civil War. It consisted of a powder charge with a percussion fuse—in effect, a contact mine—mounted on a spar protruding from the bow of its carrier, which aimed to ram it into an enemy ship.

1. The Northern Theater, War of the Revolution and War of 1812 (present political boundaries)

2. The Mississippi Valley (political boundaries as of 1861)

GEORGIA

ATLANTIC OCEAN

St. Mary's

Jacksonville

F L O R I D A

St. Johns R.

Palatka

Ft. King

GULF

OF

MEXICO

Wahoo Swamp

Withlacoochee R.

Big Cypress Swamp

Lake Tohopekaliga

Cape Canaveral (Kennedy)

Ft. Brooke

Egmont Key

Tampa Bay

Manatee R.

St. Lucie R.

Lake Okeechobee

Jupiter Inlet

Charlotte Harbor
Useppa Is.

Caloosahatchee R.

EVERGLADES

Ft. Dallas

Cape Florida

Shark R.

Carysfort Reef

Cape Sable

Tea Table Key

Key West

0   25   50   75
MILES

3. Florida

4. The West Indies

5. Mexico

6. Central America

7. Europe and the Mediterranean (political boundaries as of 1910)

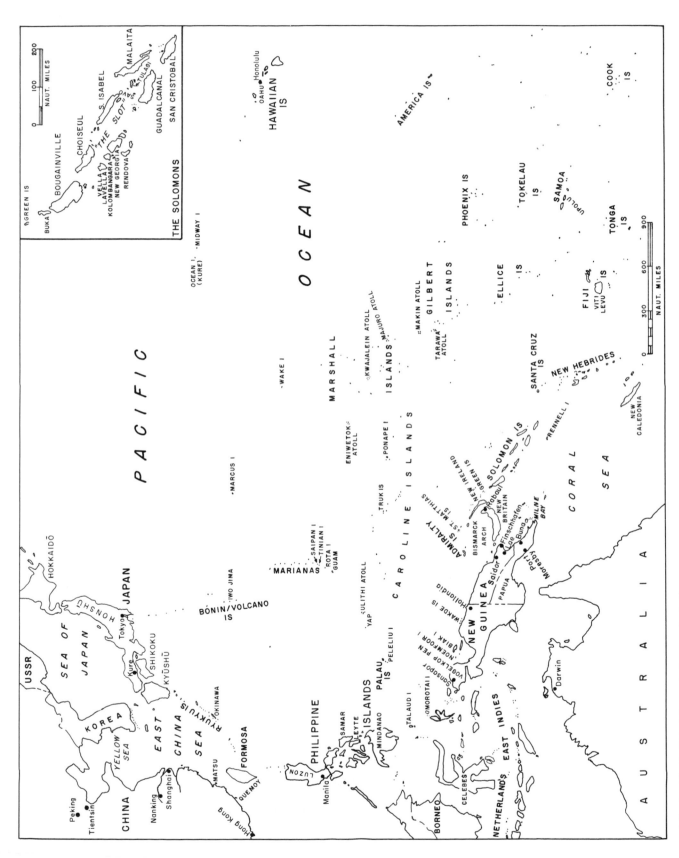

8. The Pacific (political boundaries as of 1941)

9. The Philippines

10. The East Indies (political boundaries as of 1941)

11. Korea

12. Southeast Asia

13. Saudi Arabia and the Persian Gulf

14. Yugoslavia and Successor States

15. Afghanistan and Pakistan

Bibliography

NOTE: The United States Naval Institute *Proceedings* is abbreviated *USNIP*.

Allen, Gardner W. *Our Naval War with France.* Reprint, n.p.: Archon Books, n.d.

———. *Our Navy and the West Indian Pirates.* Salem, Mass.: Essex Institute, 1929.

Anderson, R. C. *Naval Wars in the Levant, 1559–1853.* Princeton, N.J.: Princeton University Press, 1952.

Arkin, William M., and Joshua Handler. *Naval Accidents, 1945–1988.* Washington, D.C.: Greenpeace Neptune Papers, No. 3, 1989.

Bamford, James. "The Walker Espionage Case." *USNIP,* vol. 112, no. 5 (May 1986).

Bartlett, Merrill L., and Jack Sweetman. *The U.S. Marine Corps: An Illustrated History.* Annapolis: Naval Institute Press, 2001.

Bauer, K. Jack. *Surfboats and Horse Marines: U.S. Naval Operations in the Mexican War, 1846–1848.* Annapolis: U.S. Naval Institute, 1969.

Blair, Clay, Jr. *Silent Victory: The U.S. Submarine War against Japan.* Philadelphia: J. B. Lippincott, 1975.

Boatner, Lieutenant Colonel Mark M., III. *The Civil War Dictionary.* New York: David McKay Company, 1959.

Bonds, Ray, ed. *The Vietnam War.* New York: Crown Publishers, 1979.

Bonnel, Ulane. "The French Navy and the Independence of the United States." New York: Service de Presse et de l'Information, Ambassade de France, n.d. [1976].

Braswell, Lieutenant Commander Don, USN. "The Super Hornet Solution." *USNIP,* vol. 127, no. 2 (February 2001).

Breemer, Jan S. *U.S. Naval Developments.* Annapolis: The Nautical & Aviation Publishing Company of America, 1983.

Buell, Thomas B. *Master of Sea Power: A Biography of Fleet Admiral Ernest J. King.* Boston: Little, Brown and Company, 1980.

———. *The Quiet Warrior: A Biography of Admiral Raymond A. Spruance.* Boston: Little, Brown and Company, 1974..

Buker, George E. *Swamp Sailors: Riverine Warfare in the Everglades, 1835–1842.* Gainesville, Florida: The University Presses of Florida, 1975.

Bureau of Aeronautics, Department of the Navy. *A Calendar of Significant Events in the Growth and Development of United States Naval Aviation, 1898–1956.* n.p. [1957].

Cagle, Commander Malcolm W., and Commander Frank A. Manson. *The Sea War in Korea.* Annapolis: U.S. Naval Institute, 1957.

Cagle, Vice Admiral Malcolm W. "Task Force 77 in Action off Vietnam." *USNIP,* vol. 98, no. 831 (May 1972).

Callahan, Edward W., ed. *List of Officers of the Navy of the United States and of the Marine Corps, from 1775 to 1900.* New York: L. R. Hamersly and Company, 1901.

Chapelle, Howard I. *The History of the American Sailing Navy: The Ships and Their Development.* Reprint, New York: Bonanza Books, n.d.

Churchill, Winston S. *The Second World War.* 6 vols. Boston: Houghton Mifflin, 1948–53.

Clowes, William Laird. *The Royal Navy: A History from the Earliest Times to the Present.* 5 vols. London: Sampson, Low, Marston and Company, 1899.

Coletta, Paolo E. *Admiral Bradley A. Fiske and the American Navy.* Lawrence, Kans.: The Regents Press of Kansas, 1979.

———. *The American Naval Heritage in Brief.* Second edition. Washington, D.C.: University Press of America, 1980.

Coletta, Paolo E., K. Jack Bauer, and Robert G. Albion, eds. *American Secretaries of the Navy.* 2 vols. Annapolis: Naval Institute Press, 1980.

Cooney, Commander David M. *A Chronology of the U.S. Navy, 1775–1965.* New York: Franklin Watts, 1965.

Cushman, Lieutenant General John H., USA (Ret.). "Out of Somalia: United Shield." *USNIP*, vol. 121, no. 5 (May 1995).

Deutermann, Captain P. T., USN (Ret.). "The USS *Iowa* Investigation Report." *USNIP*, vol. 116, no. 5 (May 1990).

Diaz, Lieutenant Charley L., USCG. "DOD Plays in the Drug War." *USNIP*, vol. 116, no. 5 (May 1990).

Dull, Paul S. *A Battle History of the Imperial Japanese Navy (1941–1945)*. Annapolis: Naval Institute Press, 1978.

Dupuy, R. Ernest, and Trevor N. Dupuy. *The Encyclopedia of Military History*. Revised ed. New York: Harper & Row, 1977.

Edney, Admiral Leon, USN (Ret.). "Super Hornet Is the Bridge." *USNIP*, vol. 123, no. 9 (September 1997).

Ellsworth, Captain Harry Allanson, USMC. *One Hundred Eighty Landings of United States Marines, 1800 to 1934*. Washington, D.C.: History and Museums Division, Headquarters, U.S. Marine Corps, 1974.

Emmons, Lieutenant George, USN. *The Navy of the United States, from the Commencement, 1775 to 1853 . . .* Washington, D.C.: Gideon and Company, 1853.

Esposito, Colonel Vincent J., chief ed. *The West Point Atlas of American Wars*. 2 vols. New York: Frederick A. Praeger, 1959.

Ferrante, Anne A. "Chronology of the U.S. Marine Corps in . . ." Duplicated chronologies for 1986–1989. Washington, D.C.: History and Museums Division, Headquarters, U.S. Marine Corps, 1987–90.

———. "Current Chronology of the U.S. Marine Corps." From *Fortitudine*, the newsletter of the History and Museums Division, Headquarters U.S. Marine Corps. *1991*, vol. 22, no. 1 (Summer 1992); *1992*, vol. 23, no. 1 (Summer 1993); *1993*, vol. 24, no. 1 (Summer 1994); *1994*, vol. 25, no. 1 (Summer 1995); *1995*, vol. 26, no. 1 (Summer 1996); *1996*, vol. 27, no. 1 (Summer 1997); *1997*, vol. 28, no. 1 (Summer 1999); *1998*, vol. 28, no. 3 (Winter 2000).

Fleming, Peter. *The Siege at Peking*. New York: Harper and Row, [1959].

Fowler, William M., Jr. *Rebels under Sail: The American Navy during the Revolution*. New York: Charles Scribner's Sons, 1976.

Friedman, Norman. "The *Vincennes* Incident." *USNIP*, vol. 115, no. 5 (May 1989).

Frost, John. *The Pictorial Book of the Commodores; Comprising Lives of Distinguished Commanders in the Navy of the United States*. New York: Nafis & Cornish, 1845.

Fuller, Captain Stephen M., USMCR, and Graham A. Cosmas. *Marines in the Dominican Republic, 1916–1924*. Washington, D.C.: History and Museums Division, Headquarters, U.S. Marine Corps, 1974.

Goralski, Robert. *World War II Almanac, 1931–1945*. New York: G. P. Putnam's Sons, 1981.

Gordon, Michael R., and General Bernard E. Trainor. *The Generals' War: The Inside Story of the Conflict in the Gulf.* Boston: Little, Brown, 1995.

Gray, Edwyn. *The Killing Time: The U-Boat War 1914–1918*. New York: Charles Scribner's Sons, 1972.

Griffing, Midshipman D. A. "Vanished Ships of the United States Navy." First Class term paper, U.S. Naval Academy, 1952.

Grossnick, Roy A., et al. *United States Naval Aviation, 1910–1995*. Washington, D.C.: Naval Historical Center, 1997.

Guttridge, Leonard F., and Jay D. Smith. *The Commodores*. New York: Harper and Row, 1969.

Hagan, Kenneth J., ed. *In Peace and War: Interpretations of American Naval History, 1775-1978*. Westport, Conn.: Greenwood Press, 1978.

Heinl, Colonel Robert Debs, USMC. *Soldiers of the Sea: The United States Marine Corps, 1775–1962*. Annapolis: U.S. Naval Institute, 1962.

Hobbs, William Herbert. *Peary*. New York: Macmillan, 1936.

Holmes, W. J. *Double-Edged Secrets: U.S. Naval Intelligence in the Pacific during World War II*. Annapolis: Naval Institute Press, 1979.

Hook, Thom. *Shenandoah Saga*. Annapolis: Air Show Publishers, 1973.

———. *Sky Ship: The Akron Era*. Annapolis: Airshow Publishers, 1976.

James, William. *A Full and Correct Account of the Military Occurrences of the Late War between Great Britain and the United States of America*. 2 vols. London: the author, 1818.

Johnson, Robert Underwood, and Clarence Clough Buel, eds. *Battles and Leaders of the Civil War*. 4 vols. New York: Century Company, 1884, 1887–88.

Knox, Captain Dudley W. *A History of the United States Navy*. New York: G. P. Putnam's Sons, 1936.

Kotz, Nick. "Breaking Point." *The Washingtonian*, vol. 32, no. 3 (December 1996).

Langley, Lester D. *The Banana Wars: An Inner History of the American Empire, 1900–1934*. Lexington, Ken.: The University Press of Kentucky, 1983.

Langston, Captain Bud, USN, and Lieutenant Commander Don Bringle, USN. "Operation Praying Mantis: The Air View." *USNIP*, vol. 115, no. 5 (May 1989).

Long, David F. *Nothing Too Daring: A Biography of Commodore David Porter*. Annapolis: U.S. Naval Institute, 1970.

Love, Robert William Jr., ed. *The Chiefs of Naval Operations*. Annapolis: Naval Institute Press, 1980.

McCrocklin, James H. *Garde d'Haiti, 1915–1934: Twenty Years of Organization and Training by the United States Marine Corps*. Annapolis: U.S. Naval Institute, 1956.

McCullough, David. *The Path between the Seas: The Creation of the Panama Canal, 1870–1914.* New York: Simon and Schuster, 1977.

McDonald, Admiral Wesley L., USN (Ret.). "The Convoy Mission." *USNIP,* vol. 114, no. 5 (May 1988).

McKee, Christopher. *Edward Preble: A Naval Biography, 1761–1807.* Annapolis: Naval Institute Press, 1972.

Mersky, Peter B., and Norman Polmar. *The Naval Air War in Vietnam.* Annapolis: The Nautical & Aviation Publishing Company of America, 1981.

Miller, Nathan. *The U.S. Navy: An Illustrated History.* New York and Annapolis: American Heritage Publishing Co., Inc., and Naval Institute Press, 1977.

Miller, Colonel William M., USMC, Major John H. Johnstone, USMC, and Carolyn A. Tyson. *A Chronology of the United States Marine Corps,* vols. I–II (1775–1946). Washington, D.C.: History and Museums Division, Headquarters, U.S. Marine Corps, 1965.

Millett, Alan R. *Semper Fidelis: The History of the United States Marine Corps.* New York: Macmillan, 1980.

Morison, Samuel Eliot. *History of United States Naval Operations in World War II.* 15 vols. Boston: Little, Brown and Company, 1947–62.

———. *John Paul Jones: A Sailor's Biography.* Boston: Little, Brown and Company, 1959.

———. *"Old Bruin": Commodore Matthew C. Perry, 1794–1858.* Boston: Little, Brown and Company, 1967.

Morison, Samuel Loring. "Changes in U.S. Naval Forces." *USNIP,* vol. 127, no. 5 (May 2001).

———. "U.S. Naval Battle Force Changes." This compendium appears in the *Naval Review* published each May as the fifth number of the Naval Institute *Proceedings,* 1994–2000, vols. 120–27 (May 1994–May 2000). The first installment is titled "Ships' Status Changes."

Moskin, J. Robert. *The U.S. Marine Corps Story.* 3rd revised edition. New York: McGraw-Hill, [1992].

Mukri, Lieutenant Commander Kevin M., USN. "Fiery Vigil: Out from the Ash." *USNIP,* vol. 118, no. 5 (May 1992).

Naval and Maritime Chronology, 1961–1971. Annapolis: Naval Institute Press, 1973.

"Naval and Maritime Events," 1972–1981. This compilation appeared in the annual *Naval Review* issue of the U.S. Naval Institute *Proceedings.* Those for 1972–1976 (*USNIP,* vol. 100, no 855–vol. 103, no. 891, May 1973–May 1977) were written by Commander J. B. Finkelstein; for 1977–1981 (*USNIP,* vol. 104, no. 903–vol. 108, no. 951, May 1978–May 1982), by Captain Brent Baker. In 1983 the feature was replaced by four separate articles on the past year's operations of the U.S. Navy, Marine Corps, Coast Guard, and Merchant Marine.

Naval History Division, Navy Department. *Civil War Chronology, 1861–1865.* 5 vols. Washington, D.C.: Government Printing Office, 1961–65.

———. *Dictionary of American Naval Fighting Ships.* 8 vols. Washington, D.C.: Government Printing Office, 1959–81.

Navy Department. *Official Records of the Union and Confederate Navies in the War of the Rebellion.* Series 1 and 2 (27 + 3 vols.). Washington, D.C.: Government Printing Office, 1894–1927.

———. *Register of the Commissioned and Warrant Officers of the United States, including Officers of the Marine Corps . . .* Washington, D.C.: various printers and editions, 1814–.

Neeser, R. W. *Statistical and Chronological History of the United States Navy, 1775–1907.* 2 vols. Reprint, New York: Burt Franklin, 1970.

Nixon, Richard. *The Memoirs of Richard Nixon.* New York: Grosset and Dunlap, 1978.

O'Rourke, Ronald. "Gulf Operations." *USNIP,* vol. 115, no. 5 (May 1989).

———. "The Tanker Mission." *USNIP,* vol. 114, no. 5 (May 1988).

Palmer, Michael A. "The Navy Did Its Job." *USNIP,* vol. 117, no. 5 (May 1991).

Parker, Lieutenant Colonel T. W., USMC. "Operation Sharp Edge." *USNIP,* vol. 117, no. 5 (May 1991).

Parks, Colonel W. Hays, USMCR. "Crossing the Line." *USNIP,* vol. 112, no. 11 (November 1986).

———. "Tailhook: What Happened, Why, & What's to Be Learned." *USNIP,* vol. 120, no. 9 (September 1994).

Paullin, Charles Oscar. *Paullin's History of Naval Administration, 1775–1911.* Annapolis: U.S. Naval Institute, 1968.

Pawlisch, Hans S. "Operation Praying Mantis: The Revenge of the *Samuel B. Roberts* Incident." *Pull Together: Newsletter of the Naval Historical Foundation and the Naval Historical Center,* vol. 28, no. 1 (spring/summer 1989).

Perkins, Captain J. B., III, USN. "Operation Praying Mantis: The Surface View." *USNIP,* vol. 115, no. 5 (May 1989).

Ponko, Vincent, Jr. *Ships, Seas and Scientists.* Annapolis: Naval Institute Press. 1974.

Potter, E. B. *The Naval Academy Illustrated History of the United States Navy.* New York: Thomas Y. Crowell, 1971.

———. *Nimitz.* Annapolis: Naval Institute Press, 1976.

Potter, E. B., and Fleet Admiral Chester W. Nimitz, eds. *Sea Power: A Naval History.* Englewood Cliffs, N.J.: Prentice-Hall, 1960.

Quick, John. *Dictionary of Weapons and Military Terms.* New York: McGraw-Hill, 1973.

Rappaport, Armin. *A History of American Diplomacy.* New York: Macmillan, 1975.

Reilly, John C., Jr., and Robert L. Scheina. *American Battleships, 1886–1923*. Annapolis: Naval Institute Press, 1980.

Reynolds, Clark G. *Famous American Admirals*. New York: Van Nostrand Reinhold, 1978.

Richards, Lieutenant Colonel T. A., USMC. "Marines in Somalia, 1991." *USNIP*, vol. 119, no. 5 (May 1993).

Roberts, Major Ron, USMC. "Desert Fox: The Third Night." *USNIP*, vol. 125, no. 4 (April 1999).

Robertson, Bruce, ed. *Air Aces of the 1914–1918 War*. 2nd ed. Letchworth, Herts.: Harleyford Publications, Ltd., 1959.

Rohwer, Jürgen, and G. Hummelchen, trs. Derek Masters. *Chronology of the War at Sea, 1939–1945*. 2 vols. London: Ian Allen, 1972–74.

Roscoe, Theodore. *United States Destroyer Operations in World War II*. Annapolis: U.S. Naval Institute, 1953.

———. *United States Submarine Operations in World War II*. Annapolis: U.S. Naval Institute, 1949.

Scharf, J. Thomas. *History of the Confederate States Navy*. Reprint, n.p.: Fairfax Press, 1977.

Schley, Rear Admiral Winfield Scott. *Forty-five Years under the Flag*. New York: D. Appleton, 1904.

Seager, Robert, II. *Alfred Thayer Mahan: The Man and His Letters*. Annapolis: Naval Institute Press, 1977.

Sheehan, Neil. *The Arnheiter Affair*. New York: Dell Publishing Company, 1973.

Simmons, Dr. Dean, Dr. Phillip Gould, Dr. Verena Vomastic, and Lieutenant Colonel Philip Walsh, USMC (Ret.). "Air Operations over Bosnia." *USNIP*, vol. 123, no. 5 (May 1997).

Simmons, Brigadier General Edwin, USMC (Ret.). "Getting the Job Done." *USNIP*, vol. 117, no. 5 (May 1991).

Spears, John R. *The History of Our Navy*. 5 vols. New York: Charles Scribner's Sons, 1899.

Sprague, John T. *The Origin, Progress and Conclusion of the Florida War*. Reprint, Gainesville, Fla.: University of Florida Press, 1964.

Stackpole, Lieutenant General H. C., III, USMC. "Angels from the Sea." *USNIP*, vol. 118, no. 5 (May 1992).

Stevenson, Jonathan. *Losing Mogadishu: Testing U.S. Policy in Somalia*. Annapolis: Naval Institute Press, 1995.

Stumpf, Lieutenant Commander Robert E., USN. "Air War with Libya." *USNIP*, vol. 112, no. 8 (August 1986).

Sweetman, Jack. *The Landing at Veracruz: 1914*. Annapolis: U.S. Naval Institute, 1968.

———. *The U.S. Naval Academy: An Illustrated History*. Annapolis: Naval Institute Press. 1979.

———, ed. *Great American Naval Battles*. Annapolis: Naval Institute Press, 1998.

Symonds, Craig L. *A Battlefield Atlas of the Civil War*. Annapolis: The Nautical and Aviation Publishing Company of America, 1983.

Tolley, Rear Admiral Kemp. *Yangtze Patrol: The U.S. Navy in China*. Annapolis: Naval Institute Press, 1971.

Trevor, Scott. "Tomorrow's Fleet." *USNIP*, vol. 116, no. 7 (July 1990).

Truver, Scott C. "Maritime Terrorism, 1985." *USNIP*, vol. 112, no. 5 (May 1986).

"U.S. Marine Corps in . . .". This is one of the articles that replaced the "Naval and Maritime Events" chronology in the *Naval Review* published each May as the fifth number of the Naval Institute *Proceedings*. That for 1982 (*USNIP*, vol. 109, 1983) was written by Danny J. Crawford and Anne A. Ferrante; those for 1983 and 1984 (*USNIP*, vols. 110–11, 1984–85) by Anne A. Ferrante and Colonel John G. Miller, USMC; those for 1985 and 1986 (*USNIP*, vols. 112–13, 1986–87) by Brigadier General Edwin H. Simmons, USMC (Ret.), and Anne A. Ferrante; those for 1987 through 1990 (*USNIP*, vols. 114–17, 1988–91) by Colonel John C. Scharfen, USMC (Ret.); for 1991 (*USNIP*, vol. 118, 1992) by Colonel John J. Grace, USMC (Ret.); for 1992 (*USNIP*, vol. 119, 1993) by Colonel Mackubin T. Owens, Jr., USMC; for 1993 (*USNIP*, vol. 120, 1994) by Lieutenant Colonel David Evans, USMC (Ret.); and for 1994–2001 (*USNIP*, vols. 121–28, 1995–2002), by Major then Lieutenant Colonel Frank G. Hoffman, USMCR.

"U.S. Naval Operations in . . .". Another of the articles that replaced "Naval and Maritime Events" in the *Naval Review* published each May as the fifth number of the Naval Institute *Proceedings*. Those for 1982 through 1986 (*USNIP*, vols. 109–13, 1983–87) were written by Christopher C. Wright; that for 1987 (*USNIP*, vol. 114) by Frank Elliot; those for 1988–92 (*USNIP*, vols. 115–19, 1989–93) by John F. Morton; and those for 1993–2001 (*USNIP*, vols. 120–28, 1994–2002) by Scott C. Truver.

U.S. Senate, Subcommittee on Veterans' Affairs. *Medal of Honor Recipients, 1863–1963*. Washington, D.C.: Government Printing Office, 1964.

Van Deurs, Rear Admiral George. *Wings for the Fleet*. Annapolis: U.S. Naval Institute, 1966.

Vlahos, Michael. "The *Stark* Report." *USNIP*, vol. 114, no. 5 (May 1988).

Wright, Arthur Reginald. *Contact! Careers of U.S. Naval Aviators Assigned Numbers 1 to 2000*. Washington, D.C.: Naval Aviation Register, 1967.

"The Year in Review . . .". This chronology of U.S. naval aviation appears annually in the July–August issue of *Naval Aviation News*. Those for 1996 and 1997 (vols. 78–79, 1997–98) were written by William T. Baker; those for 1998 and 1999 (vols. 80–81, 1999–2000) by William T. Baker and Mark L. Evans.

Calendar Index

December

Index of American Naval Vessels

Numbers in italics in the following three indexes represent photographs.

This index includes airships, ships of the Continental, Confederate, and state navies, privateers, the U.S. Coast Guard and its precursors, the Naval Overseas Transportation Service (NOTS), the Military Sea Transportation Service (MSTS), and vessels operated by the U.S. Army. Ships for which no other service is cited are U.S. Navy.

In cases of two or more vessels having the same name prior to the introduction of hull numbers, the type of each vessel is specified.

Note on hull numbers: The practice of identifying vessels by hull numbers, prefaced by a letter designator indicating their class, was adopted by the U.S. Navy in 1920. These numbers were assigned, retroactively, to almost every vessel then in inventory, as well as to all subsequent construction. It is possible, as a result of reclassification, for a ship to have more than one hull number in the course of her career. For example, the *Princeton* began life as a simple aircraft carrier, CV 37, in 1945. In 1952 she was redesignated an attack carrier, CVA 37; two years later she was converted into an antisubmarine warfare carrier, becoming CVS 37; and in 1959 she underwent another conversion, this time into an amphibious assault ship, to end her days as LPH 5. The meaning of the letter designator (some obsolete) of every class of ship listed in the index appears below.

DE	Destroyer Escort		PCH	Patrol Craft, Hydrofoil
DER	Radar-picket Destroyer Escort		PG	Patrol Gunboat
DLG	Guided-missile Frigate		PR	River Gunboat
DLGN	Guided-missile Frigate, Nuclear-powered		PT	Motor Torpedo Boat
DM	Destroyer Minelayer		SC	Submarine Chaser
DMS	Destroyer Minesweeper		SP	Motor Patrol Boat
DSV	Deep-submergence Vehicle		SS	Submarine
FF	Frigate		SSBN	Ballistic-missile Submarine, Nuclear-powered
FFG	Guided-missile Frigate		SSG	Guided-missile Submarine
LCSL	Landing Craft, Infantry (Support)		SSN	Submarine, Nuclear-powered
LHA	Amphibious Assault Ship (General Purpose)		T-AGOR	Oceanographic Research Ship, attached to the Military Sea Transportation Service (subsequently Military Sealift Command)
LHD	Amphibious Assault Ship			
LKA	Amphibious Cargo Ship (formerly AKA)			
LPD	Amphibious Transport, Dock		T-AGS	Surveying Ship, attached to the Military Sealift Command
LPH	Amphibious Assault Ship			
LSD	Landing Ship, Dock		T-AH	Hospital Ship, attached to the Military Sealift Command
LST	Landing Ship, Tank			
MSB	Minesweeper, Boat		TB	Torpedo Boat
MSC	Minesweeper, Coastal		YTM	Yard Tug, Medium
PBR	Patrol Boat, River		ZR	Rigid Airship
PCF	Patrol Craft, Inshore		ZRS	Rigid Airship, Scouting

Index of Other Vessels

The following abbreviations are used:

HIJMS	His Imperial Japanese Majesty's Ship	HMNZS	His/Her Majesty's New Zealand Ship
HMS	His/Her Majesty's Ship (Great Britain)	HNMS	Her Netherlands Majesty's Ship
HMAS	His/Her Majesty's Australian Ship	KM	Kriegsmarine (Germany, Third Reich)
		SMS	Seiner Majestät Schiff (Imperial Germany)

General Index

★ *Note:* The following army, coast guard, marine, and navy units are listed in a generally ascending order of magnitude. Changes in the com-
position and titles of forces over the years make the progression approximate.

ABOUT THE AUTHOR

Jack Sweetman taught at the U.S. Naval Academy for twenty years. A graduate of Stetson University, he served as a company commander in the U.S. Army and was later a Ford Fellow at Emory University, where he earned a Ph.D. in 1973. He is the author, editor, or translator of numerous Naval Institute Press books, including *The Landing at Veracruz: 1914; The U.S. Naval Academy: An Illustrated History; The Great Admirals: Command at Sea, 1587–1945; Great American Naval Battles;* and, with Lt. Col. Merrill L. Bartlett, *The U.S. Marine Corps: An Illustrated History.* Since 1984 he has served as series editor for the press's Classics of Naval Literature collection. A recipient of the U.S. Navy League's Alfred Thayer Mahan Award for Literary Achievement, the *Naval History* Author of the Year Award, and the North American Society for Oceanic History's John Lyman Book Award, Dr. Sweetman was recently elected a Fellow of the Royal Historical Society.

Chronology: 1775–2001

Note: A number of events external to the operations of the American sea services have been included in this time line with the aim of providing historical perspective.

	1775	The American Revolution (to 1783)
	76	Declaration of Independence
	79	*Bonhomme Richard* vs. *Serapis*
	1780	
	81	Cornwallis surrenders at Yorktown
	82	Watt develops a practical steam engine
	1785	Liquidation of the Continental Navy
AMERICAN PRESIDENCIES:		
	88	Ratification of the Constitution
GEORGE WASHINGTON	89	The French Revolution (to 1799)
	1790	
	93	French Reign of Terror (to 1794)
	94	Founding of the U.S. Navy
	1795	
JOHN ADAMS	97	
	98	Founding of the U.S. Marine Corps; Quasi-War with France (to 1801)
	1800	
THOMAS JEFFERSON	01	War with Tripoli (to 1805)
	03	Louisiana Purchase
	04	Napoleon crowns himself emperor
	1805	Nelson destroys the Franco-Spanish fleet at the Battle of Trafalgar
	07	Fulton's *Clermont* establishes the first scheduled steamship service
JAMES MADISON	09	
	1810	
	12	War of 1812 (to 1815); Napoleon invades Russia
	14	USS *Fulton* (I), first naval steamer
	1815	Battle of Waterloo
JAMES MONROE	17	
	19	The *Savannah* becomes the first steamship to cross the Atlantic
	1820	
	23	Proclamation of the Monroe Doctrine
JOHN QUINCY ADAMS	**1825**	
	26	First U.S. Navy circumnavigation
ANDREW JACKSON	29	
	1830	First passenger railroads
	1835	The Seminole War (to 1842)

MARTIN VAN BUREN	37	
	38	Wilkes Expedition (to 1842)
	1840	Morse patents the telegraph
WILLIAM H. HARRISON (1841) AND JOHN TYLER	41	*Somers* mutiny
JAMES K. POLK	**1845**	Founding of the U.S. Naval Academy
	46	Mexican War (to 1848)
ZACHARY TAYLOR	49	
MILLARD FILLMORE	**1850**	Abolition of flogging in the U.S. Navy
FRANKLIN PIERCE	53	Perry mission to Japan (to 1854)
	54	Britain, France, and Turkey defeat Russia in the Crimean War (to 1856)
	1855	
JAMES BUCHANAN	57	
	59	John Brown's Raid
	1860	
ABRAHAM LINCOLN	61	The Civil War (to 1865)
	62	First battle between ironclads
	63	Lincoln issues the Emancipation Proclamation
ANDREW JOHNSON	**1865**	Lee surrenders at Appomattox
	66	Successful laying of the Atlantic Cable
ULYSSES S. GRANT	69	Opening of the Suez Canal
	1870	
	71	Unification of Germany
	73	Founding of the U.S. Naval Institute
	1875	
	76	Bell invents the telephone
RUTHERFORD B. HAYES	77	
	79	Edison invents the incandescent electric light
	1880	
JAMES A. GARFIELD (1881) AND CHESTER A. ARTHUR	81	Founding of the Office of Naval Intelligence
	84	Founding of the Naval War College
GROVER CLEVELAND	**1885**	
BENJAMIN HARRISON	89	
	1890	Mahan publishes *The Influence of Sea Power upon History*
GROVER CLEVELAND	93	
	1895	Marconi invents the radio
WILLIAM MCKINLEY	97	
	98	Spanish-American War
	99	Philippine Insurrection (to 1901)

	1900	Boxer Rebellion (to 1901)
WILLIAM MCKINLEY (1901) AND	01	
THEODORE ROOSEVELT		
	03	The Wright brothers make the first powered flight
	1905	
	07	Cruise of the Great White Fleet (to 1909)
WILLIAM HOWARD TAFT	09	Peary reaches the North Pole
	1910	
	12	Sinking of the *Titanic*
WOODROW WILSON	13	
	14	World War I (to 1918)
	1915	Zeppelin raids on England
	16	Battle of Jutland
	17	The Russian Revolution
	18	HMS *Argus*, first aircraft carrier
	19	Rutherford splits the atom
	1920	
WARREN G. HARDING	21	
	22	Mussolini comes to power
CALVIN COOLIDGE	23	
	1925	First practical use of radar
	27	Lindbergh flies across the Atlantic
HERBERT C. HOOVER	29	New York stock market crash ushers in Great Depression
	1930	
	31	Japan invades Manchuria
FRANKLIN D. ROOSEVELT	33	The New Deal; Hitler comes to power
	1935	Italy invades Ethiopia
	36	German troops occupy the Rhineland
	37	Japan invades China
	38	Germany annexes Austria
	39	World War II (to 1945)
	1940	Fall of France and Battle of Britain
	41	Japanese attack on Pearl Harbor
	42	Battle of Midway
	43	The German Sixth Army is destroyed at Stalingrad
	44	First jet aircraft becomes operational

FRANKLIN D. ROOSEVELT (1945) AND HARRY S. TRUMAN	**1945**	First atomic bombs dropped; founding of the United Nations
	47	Truman Doctrine
	48	Communist coup in Czechoslovakia
	49	Communist victory in China
	1950	Korean War (to 1953)
DWIGHT D. EISENHOWER	53	Death of Stalin
	54	The Geneva Accords end France's Vietnam War
	1955	
	57	The Soviet Union launches Sputnik, the first man-made earth satellite
	1960	First Polaris missile launch
JOHN F. KENNEDY	61	Building of the Berlin Wall
	62	Cuban Missile Crisis
LYNDON B. JOHNSON	63	
	64	Tonkin Gulf Incident
	1965	U.S. ground troops are committed to the Vietnam War
	68	Soviet invasion of Czechoslovakia
RICHARD M. NIXON	69	The United States places the first man on the moon
	1970	
	73	The Paris Accords end America's Vietnam War
GERALD R. FORD	74	
	1975	Fall of South Vietnam
JIMMY CARTER	77	Panama Canal Treaty
	79	Soviet occupation of Afghanistan (to 1988)
	1980	The Solidarity labor union is organized in Poland
RONALD REAGAN	81	
	83	U.S. intervention in Grenada
	1985	Gorbachev comes to power
	87	Tanker escort in the Persian Gulf (to 1988)
GEORGE BUSH	89	Fall of the Berlin Wall
	1990	Reunification of Germany
	91	The Gulf War
BILL CLINTON	93	
	94	U.S. withdraws from Somalia
	1995	Dayton Accords
	98	Air strikes on Iraq (Operation Desert Fox)
	99	NATO air war with Yugoslavia
	2000	Attack on the *Cole*
GEORGE W. BUSH	01	